lonely planet

New York City

"All you've got to do is decide to go and the hardest part is over.

So go!"

TONY WHEELER, COFOUNDER – LONELY PLANET

Regis St Louis, Robert Balkovich, Ray Bartlett, Ali Lemer,
Michael Grosberg, Brian Kluepfel

Contents

Plan Your Trip 1

Welcome to New York City 4
New York City's Top 16 .. 6
What's New 17
Need to Know 18
First Time New York City 20
Getting Around 22
Top Itineraries 24
If You Like 26
Month By Month 29
Travel with Children 33
Like a Local 35
For Free 37
Eating 39
Drinking & Nightlife ... 43
Entertainment 46
Shopping 50
Sports & Activities 53
LGBTIQ New York City 56

Explore New York City 58

Lower Manhattan & the Financial District 62
SoHo & Chinatown 86
East Village & the Lower East Side 107
West Village, Chelsea & the Meatpacking District 132
Union Square, the Flatiron District & Gramercy 164
Midtown 175
Upper East Side 211
Upper West Side & Central Park 226
Harlem & Upper Manhattan 245
Brooklyn 260
Queens 301
Day Trips from New York City 319
Sleeping 330

Understand New York City 347

New York City Today 348
History 350
The NYC Table 359
The Arts 363
Architecture 367
Queer City: From Stonewall to Marriage Equality 372
NYC on Screen 375

Survival Guide 379

Transportation 380
Directory A–Z 386
Index 393

New York City Maps 403

400TMAX / GETTY IMAGES ©

PEDRAG VUCKOVIC / GETTY IMAGES ©

(left) **Pretzels p39** Enjoy delicious food from all over the globe.

(above) **Lower Manhattan p62** The business end of the island is filled with must-see sights.

(right) **Taxis p383** New York City's yellow cabs are iconic.

PESKYMONKEY / GETTY IMAGES ©

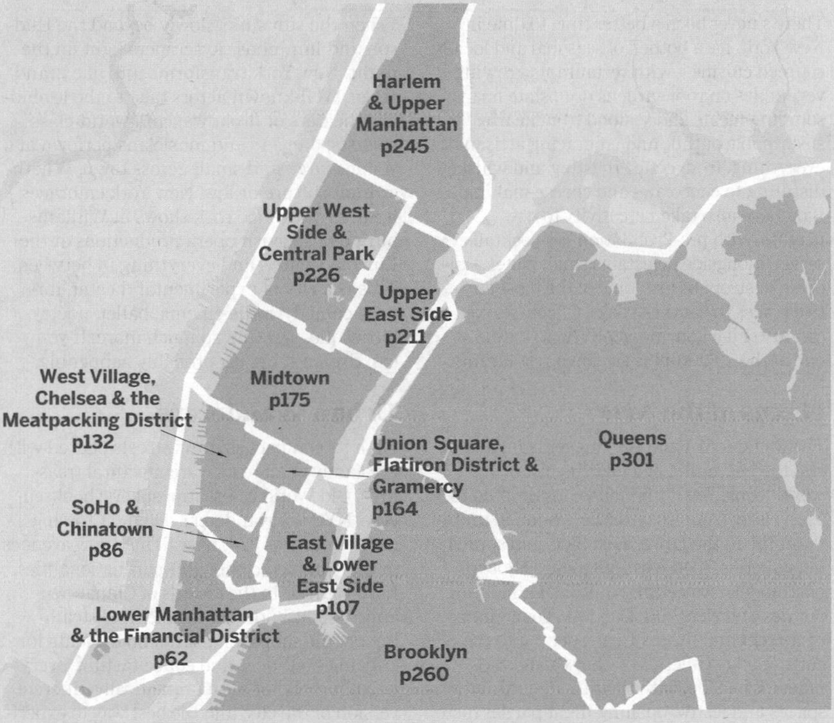

Welcome to New York City

Epicenter of the arts. Dining and shopping capital. Trendsetter. New York City wears many crowns, and spreads an irresistible feast for all.

Culinary Capital

There's never been a better time to dine in New York. It's a hotbed of seasonal and locally sourced cuisine – with restaurants growing vegetables on roof gardens or upstate farms, sourcing meats and seafood from nearby sustainable outfits, and embracing artisanal everything, from coffee roasting and whiskey distilling to chocolate- and cheese-making. Bars have also taken creativity to new heights, with pre-Prohibition-era cocktails served alongside delectable small plates – indeed, gastropubs are some of the most creative places to eat these days. Of course, you can also hit a gourmet food truck or dine at one of the 20,000-plus sit-down restaurants.

Nexus of the Arts

The Met, MoMA and the Guggenheim are just the beginning of a dizzying list of art-world icons. You'll find museums devoted to everything from fin de siècle Vienna to immigrant life in the Lower East Side, and sprawling galleries filled with Japanese sculpture, postmodern American painting, Himalayan textiles and New York City lore. For a glimpse of current and future greats, delve into the cutting-edge galleries of Chelsea and the Lower East Side, with their myriad exhibition spaces and festive opening-night parties (usually Thursday night if you want to join in).

The Night Is Young

When the sun sinks slowly beyond the Hudson and luminous skyscrapers light up the night, New York transforms into one grand stage. Well-known actors take to the legendary theaters of Broadway and world-class soloists, dancers and musicians perform at venues large and small across town. Whether high culture or low, New York embraces it all: in-your-face rock shows at Williamsburg dives, lavish opera productions at the Lincoln Center, and everything in between. This is a city of experimental theater, improv comedy, indie cinema, ballet, poetry, burlesque, jazz and so much more. If you can dream it up, it's probably happening.

Urban Wanderers

With its compact size and streets packed with eye candy of all sorts – architectural treasures, Old World cafes, atmospheric booksellers – NYC is a wanderer's delight. Crossing continents is as easy as walking a few avenues in this jumbled city of 200-plus nationalities. Lose yourself in the crowds of Chinatown amid bright Buddhist temples and steaming noodle shops, then stroll up to Nolita for enticing boutiques and coffee-tasting. Every neighborhood offers a dramatically different version of the city, and the best way to experience it is to walk its streets.

Why I Love New York City

By Regis St Louis, Writer

While there are many reasons to fall for New York, I've always loved the energy here. There's so much creativity, with wildly imaginative works filling the city's galleries and concert halls – not to mention the restaurants, with ever more inventive mash-ups of global cuisines. Despite living for many years in New York, I never tire of exploring the metropolis. With the mere swipe of a MetroCard, you can visit colorful neighborhoods that contain an astonishing variety of cultures and ethnicities. The people, the food, the art: NYC has many virtues, which is why so many can't imagine living anywhere else.

For more about our writers, see p448.

Above: Times Square (p177)

New York City's Top 16

1

GINGERLOCKS / BUDGET TRAVEL ©

Statue of Liberty & Ellis Island *(p64)*

1 Since its unveiling in 1886, Lady Liberty has welcomed millions of immigrants, sailing into New York Harbor in the hope of a better life. It now welcomes millions of tourists, many of whom head up to her crown for one of New York City's finest skyline and water views. Close by lies Ellis Island, the American gateway for over 12 million new arrivals between 1892 and 1954. These days it's home to one of the city's most moving museums, paying tribute to these immigrants and their indelible courage.

Lower Manhattan & the Financial District

Broadway & Times Square *(p177)*

2 Sizzling lights, electrifying energy: this is the America of the world's imagination. Stretching from 40th St to 54th St, between Sixth and Eighth Aves, Broadway is NYC's dream factory – a place where romance, betrayal, murder and triumph come with dazzling costumes and stirring scores. The district's undisputed star is bright, blinding Times Square. More than the meeting point of Broadway and Seventh Ave, this is America in concentrate – an intense, intoxicating rush of Hollywood billboards, shimmering cola signs, and buffed topless cowboys.

Midtown

2

3

SHUTTERSTOCK ©

4

ALEXANDER PROKOPENKO / SHUTTERSTOCK ©

Central Park (p228)

3 London has Hyde Park. Paris has the Bois de Boulogne. And New York City has Central Park. One of the world's most renowned green spaces, it checks in with 843 acres of rolling meadows, boulder-studded outcrops, elm-lined walkways, manicured European-style gardens, a lake and a reservoir – not to mention an outdoor theater, a memorial to John Lennon, an idyllic waterside eatery (the Loeb Boathouse) and one very famous statue of Alice in Wonderland. The big challenge? Figuring out where to begin.

Upper West Side & Central Park

Metropolitan Museum of Art

(p214)

4 With more than two million objects in its collections, the Met is simply dazzling. Its great works span the world, from the chiseled sculptures of ancient Greece to the evocative tribal carvings of Papua New Guinea. The Renaissance galleries are packed with Old World masters, while the relics of ancient Egypt fire the imagination – particularly the Temple of Dendur, complete with its 2000-year-old stone walls covered in hieroglyphics and carvings of papyrus seemingly growing from a pond. After you think you've seen enough, head up to the rooftop for a sweeping view over Central Park.

Upper East Side

The High Line

(p136)

5 A resounding triumph of urban renewal, the High Line is – without a doubt – New York's proudest testament to the continuous effort to transform the scarring vestiges of the city's industrial past into eye-pleasing spaces. Once an unsightly elevated train track that snaked between slaughterhouses and low-end domestic dwellings, the High Line is today an unfurled emerald necklace of park space that encourages calm, crowds, and has – unsurprisingly – acted as a veritable real estate magnet luring world-class architects to the neighborhood to create gorgeous iterations of residential eye candy.

West Village, Chelsea & the Meatpacking District

Music & Nightlife *(p43)*

6 Trendy all-night lounges tucked behind the walls of a Chinese restaurant; taco shops that clandestinely host late-night cabarets; stadium-size clubs that clang to the thump of DJ-ed beats; and after-after-after-parties on the roof as the sun rises. An alternate universe lurks between the cracks of everyday life, and it welcomes savvy visitors just as much as locals in the know. If New York doesn't turn into a pumpkin come midnight, why should you? ROOFTOP BAR AT INK48 (P341)

Drinking & Nightlife

Brooklyn *(p260)*

7 Retro cocktail lounges peddling a Depression-era vibe. Artsy eateries dishing out everything from vegan comfort food to Michelin-starred gastronomy. And enough music halls and rowdy beer gardens to keep the most dedicated night owls up for weeks. Prefer the daylight hours? Brooklyn has gorgeous green spaces (Prospect Park, Brooklyn Bridge Park), stellar art collections (including the hallowed Brooklyn Museum) and kitschy seaside fun along an old-school boardwalk (Coney Island!). Don't tell Manhattan, but you could easily have a stellar NYC experience without ever venturing out of Brooklyn. *THE MONA LISA OF WILLIAMSBURG* ARTWORK BY COLOSSAL MEDIA AND STEVEN PAUL

Brooklyn

6

Food Scene *(p39)*

8 One of New York's greatest assets is the sheer variety of its restaurants. In a single neighborhood you'll find vintage-filled gastropubs, sushi counters, tapas bars, French bistros, barbecue joints, pizza parlors, vegan cafes and good old-fashioned delis, whipping up toasted bagels with lox and cream cheese. And that's just the beginning. There's no wrong way to eat a meal, whether that means ordering from a food truck, nibbling your way through a market or sliding into that soft leather booth for a 4am feast after a night on the town. PIZZA AT ROBERTA'S (P287)

Eating

Empire State Building *(p180)*

9 The striking art-deco skyscraper may no longer be New York's tallest building, but it remains one of its most recognizable icons. The ESB has appeared in dozens of films and still provides one of the best views in town – particularly around sunset when the twinkling lights of the city (and neighboring states) switch on. The beloved landmark hasn't stopped turning heads, especially since the addition of LED lights which create more than 16 million color possibilities. Keep your eye to the sky on big holidays, when dramatic displays light up the night sky.

Midtown

Brooklyn Bridge *(p262)*

10 Completed in 1883, this Gothic Revival masterpiece – crafted entirely from granite – has inspired poetry (Jack Kerouac's 'Brooklyn Bridge Blues'), music (Frank Sinatra's 'Brooklyn Bridge') and plenty of art (Walker Evans' photography). It is also the most scenic way to cross from Manhattan into Brooklyn. Go early in the morning (we're talking sun-up) to have the bridge largely to yourself. Come at sunset for romantic views as the amber skies form a magnificent backdrop to Lower Manhattan. Aside from strolling that plank path, you can also ride a bike across the bridge.

Brooklyn

MoMA *(p182)*

11 Quite possibly the greatest hoarder of modern masterpieces on earth, the Museum of Modern Art (MoMA) is a cultural promised land. It's here that you'll see Van Gogh's *The Starry Night*, Cézanne's *The Bather*, Picasso's *Les Demoiselles d'Avignon*, Pollock's *One: Number 31* and Warhol's *Campbell's Soup Cans*. Just make sure you leave time for Chagall, Dix, Rothko, de Kooning and Haring, a free film screening, a glass of vino in the Sculpture Garden, a little designer retail therapy, and a fine-dining feed at its lauded in-house restaurant, the Modern.

Midtown

EMMA SHAW / LONELY PLANET ©

1000 WORDS / SHUTTERSTOCK ©

One World Observatory *(p71)*

12 New York's tallest and most anticipated skyscraper has arrived – a soaring 104-story landmark that looms like a beacon above Lower Manhattan. Take a high-speed ride in a 'sky pod' to the top for fabulous views over the city and surrounding states. Apart from the jaw-dropping panorama, a visit here gives insight into the workers who helped build the tower, and shows the very bedrock upon which the tower stands. There's also a virtual time-lapse that shows the evolution of the city skyline from the 1600s to the present.

Lower Manhattan & the Financial District

12

13

Neighborhood Rambling

(p144)

13 One of the best ways to see New York is to pick a neighborhood, put on your walking shoes and spend the day exploring. Greenwich Village is a fine place to start, with picturesque cobblestone streets dotted with sunlit shops, narrow sidewalk cafes and quaint restaurants that beckon you inside. For a different take on New York, head over to the bohemian East Village, overload your senses down in Chinatown or take in the local scene in gallery-filled Chelsea. This is a city that invites endless wandering.

West Village, Chelsea & the Meatpacking District

Out on the Water *(p76)*

14 Step off the island of Manhattan onto a ferry and you'll have a new appreciation for those pedestrian-clogged streets as the city skyline rises slowly into view. Governors Island makes a fine destination, with new parkland, art exhibitions and peaceful, car-free lanes to stroll or cycle along. You can also hop across to Brooklyn aboard the East River Ferry. The dock near Brooklyn Bridge Park makes an excellent entry point to the borough. Meanwhile, the free Staten Island ferry provides superb views of the Statue of Liberty.

Lower Manhattan & the Financial District

Shopping *(p50)*

15 Take it from the likes of Holly Golightly and Carrie Bradshaw, New York is a beacon of the material world. Hundreds of creators – both local and international – descend upon the city with alacrity to display their wares. You'll find dozens of ways to empty your coffers, but at the end of the day, shopping in New York isn't about collecting a closet full of items, it's about accessing the city's myriad subcultures through their art and artifacts. MACY'S (P209)

Shopping

WILLBRASIL21 / GETTY IMAGES ©

BRAVOKILOVIDEO / SHUTTERSTOCK ©

National September 11 Memorial & Museum *(p68)*

16 Rising from the ashes of Ground Zero, the National September 11 Memorial & Museum is a beautiful, dignified response to the city's darkest chapter. Where the Twin Towers once soared, two reflecting pools now weep like dark, elegant waterfalls. Framing them are the names of those who lost their lives on September 11, 2001 and in the 1993 World Trade Center bombing. Deep below lies the Memorial Museum, a powerful, poignant exploration of these catastrophic events, the latter of which was the deadliest attack on American soil.

Lower Manhattan & the Financial District

What's New

Stonewall National Monument

In 2016 outgoing President Barack Obama designated 7.7 acres of the West Village as a US National Monument, the first such designation in American history to honor the LGBT civil rights movement. (p139)

NYC by Ferry

New York is once again embracing ferries, with routes linking Manhattan, Brooklyn and Queens. There's even a new route between Lower Manhattan and Rockaway – a scenic sail to the beach for the same price as a subway ride. (p384)

Eating Green

The hunger for vegetarian and vegan dining only continues to grow. You'll find meat-free restaurants all across the city, including hot spots like the Seasoned Vegan (p254) in Harlem and Michelin-starred Nix (p145) in Greenwich Village.

New Met Museum

In 2016, the Met Breuer took over the space of the former Whitney Museum on the Upper East Side. Dedicated to works by modern and contemporary artists, it has earned top reviews from critics. (p218)

Sounds of Harlem

Harlem has become one of the best places to hear eclectic global sounds thanks to several live music spots that have opened in recent years. The Israeli-African–owned Silvana (p256) and Shrine (p257) host a stellar lineup of bands and singers every night of the week.

Uncommons

New York now has its own board-game cafe. Down in the West Village, you can stay up late playing board games while sipping craft brews and munching on mozzarepas. (p151)

Chefs Club

At this new space in Nolita, celebrated chefs from around the globe take over the kitchen for tenures ranging from a few weeks to several months. (p97)

Second Avenue Subway

After 10 years of construction and nearly $4.5 billion in costs, the Second Ave subway line has opened. The new extension of the Q train now has stops at 72nd, 86th and 96th Sts, providing handy access to the Upper East Side.

Food, Glorious Food

The casual dining scene just keeps getting better, with the addition of new food halls around the city. DeKalb Market Hall (p276) has dozens of tempting culinary stalls, and rides on the success of legendary establishments like Chelsea Market (p147).

Cultural Upgrade

The MoMA is undergoing a major redesign that will add 50,000 sq ft of new gallery space. The museum will stay open during construction, which is due for completion in 2019. (p182)

For more recommendations and reviews, see **lonelyplanet.com/new-york-city**

Need to Know

For more information, see Survival Guide (p379)

Currency
US dollar (US$)

Language
English

Visas
The US Visa Waiver Program allows nationals of 38 countries to enter the US without a visa, but you must fill out an ESTA application before departing.

Money
ATMs widely available; credit cards accepted at most hotels, stores and restaurants. Farmers markets, food trucks and some restaurants and bars are cash-only.

Cell Phones
International travelers can use local SIM cards in a smartphone provided it is unlocked. Alternatively, you can buy a cheap US phone and load it up with prepaid minutes.

Time
Eastern Standard Time (GMT/UTC minus five hours)

Tourist Information
There are official NYC Visitor Information Centers throughout the city. The main office is in Midtown (p390).

Daily Costs

Budget: Less than $100
- ➡ Dorm bed: $40–70
- ➡ Slice of pizza: around $4
- ➡ Food-truck taco: from $3
- ➡ Bus or subway ride: $3

Midrange: $100–300
- ➡ Double room in a midrange hotel: from around $200
- ➡ Brunch for two at a midrange restaurant: $70
- ➡ Dinner for two at a midrange eatery: $130
- ➡ Craft cocktail at a lounge: $14–19
- ➡ Discount TKTS ticket to a Broadway show: $80

Top End: More than $300
- ➡ Luxury stay at the NoMad Hotel: $325–850
- ➡ Tasting menu at a top-end restaurant: $90–325
- ➡ A 1½-hour massage at the Great Jones Spa: $200
- ➡ Metropolitan Opera orchestra seats: $100–390

Advance Planning

Two months before Book hotel reservations as soon as possible – prices increase the closer you get to your arrival date. Snag tickets to Broadway shows.

Three weeks before If you haven't done so already, score a table at your top-choice high-end restaurant.

One week before Surf the web and scan blogs and Twitter for the latest restaurant and bar openings, plus upcoming art exhibitions.

Useful Websites

NYC: The Official Guide (www.nycgo.com) New York City's official tourism portal.

Explore Brooklyn (www.explorebk.com) Brooklyn-specific events and listings.

Free Williamsburg (www.freewilliamsburg.com), **Brokelyn** (www.brokelyn.com) and **Brooklyn Based** (www.brooklynbased.com) Keep tabs on the latest borough news and events.

New York Magazine (www.nymag.com) Comprehensive, current listings for bars, restaurants, entertainment and shopping.

New York Times (www.nytimes.com) Excellent local news coverage and theater listings.

Lonely Planet (www.lonelyplanet.com/usa/new-york-city) Destination information, hotel bookings, traveler forum and more.

WHEN TO GO

Summers can be scorching hot, though it also brings a packed lineup of events. Winters are not without their blizzards. Spring or autumn can be the best times to explore.

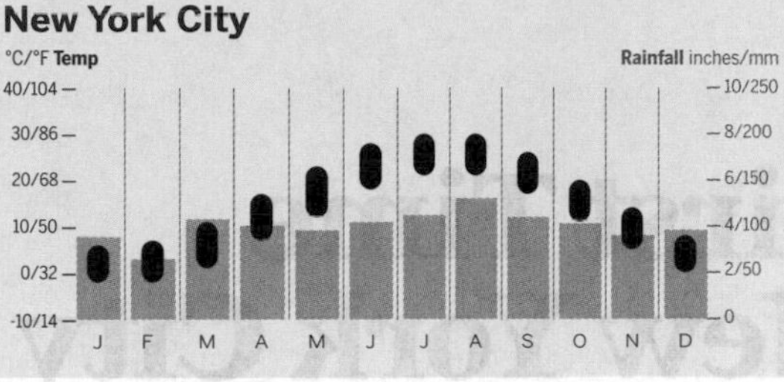

Arriving in New York City

John F Kennedy International Airport The AirTrain ($5) links to the subway ($2.75), which makes the one-hour journey into Manhattan. Express bus to Grand Central or Port Authority costs $18. Taxis cost a flat $52 excluding tolls, tip and rush hour surcharge.

LaGuardia Airport The closest airport to Manhattan but least accessible by public transit: take the Q70 express bus from the airport to the 74th St–Broadway subway station. Express bus to Midtown costs $15. Taxis range from $34 to $53, excluding tolls and tip.

Newark Liberty International Airport Take the AirTrain to Newark Airport train station, and board any train bound for New York's Penn Station ($13). Taxis range from $60 to $80 (plus $15 toll and tip). Allow 45 minutes to one hour of travel time.

For much more on **arrival** see p380

Getting Around

Check the Metropolitan Transportation Authority website (www.mta.info) for public transportation information (buses and subway). Delays have increased as ridership has expanded.

Subway Inexpensive, somewhat efficient and operates around the clock, though can be confusing. Single ride is $2.75 with a MetroCard.

Buses Convenient during off hours – especially when transferring between the city's eastern and western sides. Uses the MetroCard; same price as the subway.

Taxi Meters start at $2.50 and increase roughly $5 for every 20 blocks. See www.nyc.gov/taxi.

Bicycle The city's popular bike share Citi Bike provides excellent access to most parts of Manhattan.

Inter-borough ferries The New York City Ferry (www.ferry.nyc) provides handy transport between waterside stops in Manhattan, Brooklyn and Queens.

For more on **getting around** see p382

Sleeping

In general, expect high prices and small spaces. Room rates waver by availability, not by any high-season or low-season rules. Of course, you'll pay dearly during holidays. Accommodations fill up quickly – especially in summer – and range from boxy cookie-cutter chains to stylish boutiques. No Manhattan neighborhood has a monopoly on one style and you'll find better-value hotels in Brooklyn and Queens. A few B&Bs and hostels are scattered throughout.

Useful Websites

newyorkhotels.com (www.newyorkhotels.com) The self-proclaimed official website for hotels in NYC.

NYC (www.nycgo.com/hotels) Loads of listings from the NYC Official Guide.

Lonely Planet (www.lonelyplanet.com/usa/new-york-city/hotels) Accommodations reviews and online booking service.

For much more on **sleeping** see p330

First Time New York City

For more information, see Survival Guide (p379)

Checklist

➡ Ensure your passport is valid for at least six months past your arrival date.

➡ Check you meet all ESTA visa requirements for travel to the US.

➡ Check airline baggage restrictions.

➡ Arrange for appropriate travel insurance.

➡ Inform your credit-/debit-card company of your travels.

➡ Book popular restaurants, shows and accommodations well in advance.

What to Pack

➡ Good walking shoes – New York City is best seen on foot, so make sure your shoes are super comfy.

➡ Dress shoes and a stylish outfit for smart restaurants and bars.

➡ If traveling with medications, ensure you bring enough for your trip.

➡ US electrical adapter.

Top Tips for Your Trip

➡ MetroCards are valid on subways, buses, ferries and the tramway to Roosevelt Island. If staying a while, buy a 7-Day Unlimited Pass.

➡ Subway lines run both local and express trains.

➡ If the number on a taxi's top light is lit, it's available.

➡ When giving an address, always include the nearest cross street/s (eg 700 Sixth Ave *at* 22nd St).

➡ The TKTS Booth in Times Square (p179) sells half-price, same-day tickets to selected shows and musicals. The South Street Seaport (p63) and Downtown Brooklyn (p47) branches also sell next-day matinee tickets.

What to Wear

If visiting during New York's hot, humid summer, pack light garments. Fashionable shorts, T-shirts, summer dresses and skirts are all acceptable daywear, though higher-end restaurants and bars often call for more stylish attire, so bring at least one evening dress or long-sleeved shirt, pair of pants and dress shoes. Fluctuating temperatures in spring and fall call for layers: long pants, jeans or warmer dresses, mixed with T-shirts, long-sleeve shirts, sweaters, a smart blazer for men and a jacket for women. New York winters can be brutally cold, requiring gloves, scarf, hat, insulated, waterproof jacket and waterproof boots. In the evenings, 'dress to impress' remains the rule at many restaurants, bars and entertainment venues.

Be Forewarned

New York City is one of the safest cities in the USA – in 2017 homicides fell to a record low of fewer than 300 and overall violent crime statistics declined for the 27th straight year. Still, it's best to take a common-sense approach to the city.

➡ Don't walk around alone at night in sparsely populated areas.

➡ Carry your daily walking-around money inside your clothing or in a front pocket rather than in a handbag or a back pocket.

➡ Be aware of pickpockets, particularly in busy areas.

➡ While it's generally safe to ride the subway after midnight, you may want to take a taxi instead, especially if traveling alone.

Money

ATMs widely available; credit cards accepted at most hotels, stores and restaurants. Farmers markets, food trucks and some restaurants and bars are cash-only.

For more information, see p388.

Taxes & Refunds

Restaurants and retailers never include the sales tax – 8.875% – in their prices, so beware of ordering the $4.99 lunch special when you only have $5 to your name. Several categories of so-called luxury items, including rental cars and dry-cleaning, carry an additional city surcharge of 5%, so you wind up paying an extra 13.875% in total for these services. Clothing and footwear purchases under $110 are tax free. Hotel rooms in New York City are subject to a 14.75% tax, plus a flat $3.50 occupancy tax per night. Since the US has no nationwide value-added tax (VAT), there is no opportunity for foreign visitors to make 'tax-free' purchases.

Tipping

Tipping is *not* optional; only withhold tips in cases of outrageously bad service.

Restaurant servers 18–20%, unless a gratuity is already charged on the bill.

Bartenders 15–20% per round, per drink $1 for standard drinks, and $2 per specialty cocktail.

Taxi drivers 10–15%, rounded up to the next dollar.

Airport & hotel porters $2 per bag, minimum per cart $5.

Hotel maids $2–4 per night, left in envelope or under the card provided.

GARY_ATHAM / LONELY PLANET ©

Flatiron Building (p167)

Etiquette

Politeness It's common courtesy to greet nearby staff when entering or leaving a shop, cafe or restaurant.

Greetings Shake hands with men and women when meeting for the first time and when saying goodbye. Female friends are greeted with a single (air) kiss.

Taboo Topics Although Donald Trump is almost universally reviled in NYC, politics and religion are topics best avoided.

Transport Allow passengers to exit the subway car before entering; don't block the doors.

Gratuity Not optional in restaurants or bars; don't forget to tip.

Getting Around

For more information, see Transportation (p380)

Check the Metropolitan Transportation Authority website (www.mta.info) for public transportation information (buses and subway). Delays have increased as ridership has expanded.

Subway Inexpensive, somewhat efficient and operates around the clock, though can be confusing. Single ride is $2.75 with a MetroCard.

Buses Convenient during off hours – especially when transferring between the city's eastern and western sides. Uses the MetroCard; same price as the subway.

Taxi Meters start at $2.50 and increase roughly $5 for every 20 blocks. See www.nyc.gov/taxi.

Bicycle The city's popular bike share Citi Bike provides excellent access to most parts of Manhattan.

Inter-borough ferries The New York City Ferry (www.ferry.nyc) provides handy transport between waterside stops in Manhattan, Brooklyn and Queens.

Key Phrases

Boro Taxi If you're north of 116th St in Manhattan or in the outer boroughs, you can hail these green taxis, which have metered rates identical to yellow cabs.

Car service You can phone a car service (often a black sedan) to pick you up. Useful on return trips to the airport or if needing outer-borough transport (where taxis are in short supply).

Citi Bike The ubiquitous blue bikes that are part of NYC's bike-sharing scheme, with hundreds of quick-hire kiosks around town.

Express train/local train Express subway trains make limited stops, skipping many stations; local trains stop at every station. To switch between the two, often you just have to cross the platform.

LIRR The Long Island Rail Road, useful for speedy transport to JFK airport and for beach getaways.

MetroCard The flimsy yellow-and-blue card, which you load with credit, then swipe through for every ride on the subway or bus.

Uptown/Downtown Uptown means going north (Upper East Side, Harlem etc), downtown means going south (SoHo, Lower Manhattan etc).

Key Routes

Scenic views Take the J, M or Z line over the Williamsburg Bridge or the B, D, N or Q line over the Manhattan Bridge for great views of Manhattan. There's also the Roosevelt Island Tramway (p191).

Uptown bound The 4, 5 and 6 lines go to the Upper East Side, as does the new Second Ave Q line. For the Upper West Side take the B, C, 1, 2 or 3 trains.

How to Hail a Taxi

➡ To hail a yellow cab, look for one with its roof light lit (if it's not lit, the cab is taken).

➡ Stand in a prominent place on the side of the road and stick out your arm.

➡ Once inside the cab, tell them your destination (it's illegal for drivers to refuse you a ride).

➡ Pay your fare at the end, either with cash or credit card (via the touch screen in back). Don't forget to tip 10% to 15%.

TOP TIPS

➡ Pay attention to 'Downtown' vs 'Uptown' subway station entrances. Sometimes there are separate entrances (usually across the street from one another) depending on which direction the train is going.

➡ Plan your route carefully. Sometimes walking a few blocks can get you to a faster or more direct subway line, thereby saving you time in the end.

➡ For short trips, consider hopping on a Citi Bike.

When to Travel

➡ Rush hour is never just an hour! On weekdays, from 8am to 9:30am and 4:30pm to 6:30pm, trains and buses are frustratingly packed.

➡ If it's not possible to avoid traveling at these peak times, allow extra time to get places (particularly to/from the airport).

➡ Hailing a cab can be difficult on weekdays from 4pm to 5pm when many drivers change shifts. And when it's raining, finding an available taxi can seem a monumental challenge.

Etiquette

➡ Have your MetroCard ready before you go through the gate. New Yorkers are skilled at moving through the ticket barriers without breaking stride.

➡ On subway platforms, stand to the side of the train doors and wait for passengers to exit before boarding.

➡ On escalators, stand on the right hand side or use the left if you want to walk down/up.

➡ When walking on the sidewalk, think of yourself as a car on the street: don't stop short, pay attention to the speed limit, and pull off to the side if you need to look at a map or dig through your bag for an umbrella.

Tickets & Passes

➡ The yellow-and-blue MetroCards (www.mta.info/metrocard) are the swipe cards used for all of NYC's public transportation. You can purchase or add value at one of several easy-to-use automated machines at any station. Each ride on the subway or bus (except for express buses) deducts $2.75 from the card.

➡ Purchase the MetroCard itself for $1 at kiosks in subway stations, and load it with credit ($20, which will give you eight rides and change, is a good start). If you plan to ride a lot, buy a 7-Day Unlimited Pass ($32). These cards are handy for travelers – particularly if you're jumping around town to a few different places in one day.

➡ The subway kiosks take credit or ATM cards (larger machines also take cash). When you need to add more credit, just insert your card and follow the prompts (tip: when it asks for your ZIP, input '99999' if you're not from the USA).

➡ Transfers from subway to bus, or bus to subway, are free. Just swipe/insert your card, and no extra charge will be deducted.

For much more on **getting around** see p382

CITI BIKES

To use a Citi Bike, purchase a 24-hour or three-day access pass ($12 or $24 plus tax) at any Citi Bike kiosk. You will then be given a five-digit code to unlock a bike. Return the bike to any station within 30 minutes to avoid incurring extra fees. Reinsert your credit card (you won't be charged) and follow the prompts to check out a bike again. You can make an unlimited number of 30-minute check-outs during those 24 hours or seven days.

Top Itineraries

Day One

Upper West Side & Central Park (p226)

Spend the morning exploring the wonders of **Central Park**, taking in the fortress-like walls of skyscrapers surrounding the green. Start at **Columbus Circle**, then head in the northeast direction passing the **Central Park Zoo**, the **Bethesda Fountain**, the **Conservatory Water** and **Strawberry Fields** on the western side. If you have kids in tow, check out the dinosaur skeletons at the **American Museum of Natural History**, then hit up the **Loeb Boathouse** to rent rowboats.

Lunch Pick up supplies at Zabar's (p242) for a picnic in Central Park.

Midtown (p175)

It's now time to uncover some of the city's architectural wonders: **Grand Central Terminal**, the **Chrysler Building**, the **New York Public Library** and **Rockefeller Center**. Round it off with a visit to the city's museum darling: **MoMA**.

Dinner For Broadway-goers, do an early dinner at ViceVersa (p198).

Midtown (p175)

Spend the evening under the starry lights of **Broadway**, checking out a blockbuster show or something distinctly ahead of the curve at **Playwrights Horizon** or **Signature Theatre**. Soak up the Las Vegas–like atmosphere of **Times Square** from the **TKTS Booth**, swig cocktails at **Rum House**, then head to the **Top of the Rock** to bid the city goodnight.

Day Two

Upper East Side (p211)

Start at the staggering **Metropolitan Museum of Art**. Wander through the Egyptian and Roman collections, take in European masters, then head up to the rooftop (in summer) for a view over Central Park. Afterwards, visit the nearby **Neue Galerie** for a feast of German and Austrian art in a 1914 mansion.

Lunch Lunch on Austrian specialties at elegant Café Sabarsky (p220).

SoHo & Chinatown (p86)

Head down to SoHo for an afternoon of shopping along **Prince** and **Spring Streets** amid crowds of tourists seeking the best brands in the world. Wander over to Chinatown's **Mulberry Street**, which feels worlds away from mainstream consumerism, but is – in reality – only a few blocks over. Stroll by the neighborhood's **Buddhist temples**, stopping for custard tarts and almond ice cream.

Dinner Feast on delectable flavors from southern Europe at Boulud Sud (p236).

Upper West Side & Central Park (p226)

Head to a pre-theater dinner at Boulud Sud, a celebrated Mediterranean restaurant. Then cross the street to **Lincoln Center** for opera at the **Metropolitan Opera House** or a symphony in **Avery Fisher Hall**. Later, head to drinks (book ahead) at the fabulously original **Manhattan Cricket Club**.

Day Three

Brooklyn (p260)

Catch the East River Ferry over to Dumbo, and admire the magnificent view of Manhattan from the lush new **Brooklyn Bridge Park**. Afterwards, stroll through the cobblestone streets of Dumbo, browsing bookshops, boutiques and cafes. Don't miss the vintage **Jane's Carousel** and more great views from the **Empire Fulton Ferry**.

Lunch Fill up on good-value lunch specials at atmospheric AlMar (p277).

Brooklyn (p260)

Travel up to the **Brooklyn Museum** for a look at fascinating works from Africa, the Americas and Ancient Egypt, plus excellent temporary shows. Afterwards take a stroll in **Prospect Park**, pausing for refreshments at the scenic new **Lakeside** complex.

Dinner Partake of Brooklyn's culinary renaissance at Marlow & Sons (p287).

Brooklyn (p260)

Jump in a Boro Taxi up to **Williamsburg**, on the northern side of the borough, for oysters and bespoke cocktails at **Maison Premiere**. Head up to rooftop bar, **The Ides**, for a fabulous view over the city. End the night across the street at the **Brooklyn Bowl**, with a side of bowling and some groovy musical acts.

Day Four

Lower Manhattan & the Financial District (p62)

Catch the **Staten Island Ferry** in the early morning and watch the sun come up over Lower Manhattan. Then head skyward for a marvelous view from the **One World Observatory**. Afterwards, visit the moving **National September 11 Memorial** and **Museum**.

Lunch Munch on gourmet goodies at the food-loving Chelsea Market (p147).

West Village, Chelsea & the Meatpacking District (p132)

Head up to the Meatpacking District and visit the gorgeous new **Whitney Museum of American Art**. Afterwards, take the nearby steps up to the **High Line** for a wander along a once-abandoned rail line. Along the way stop for snacks, coffee breaks and intriguing views over the streetscape.

Dinner Dine on creative Asian fusion at RedFarm (p147).

West Village, Chelsea & the Meatpacking District (p132)

Stroll the lovely, meandering streets of Greenwich Village and delve into its soul-filled roots for an evening of intimate live jazz at **Mezzrow**, **Smalls** or the **Village Vanguard**. Afterwards, stop by for a bit of wine and snacks at buzzing **Buvette**, then head over to **Cielo** for dancing in one of the city's best little clubs.

If You Like...

Museums

Metropolitan Museum of Art The most incredible encyclopedic museum in the Americas comes stocked with its own Egyptian temple. (p214)

MoMA NYC's darling museum has brilliantly curated spaces boasting the best of the world's modern art. (p182)

Guggenheim Museum The exhibits can be uneven, but the architecture is the real star in this Frank Lloyd Wright–designed building. (p213)

Whitney Museum of American Art Celebrated for cutting-edge contemporary and 20th-century works. See future American greats at the Whitney Biennial. (p139)

Frick Collection This Gilded Age mansion has Vermeers, El Grecos and Goyas and a stunning courtyard fountain. (p218)

Cloisters Museum & Gardens Medieval treasures including a beguiling 16th-century tapestry that depicts a unicorn hunt. (p252)

Brooklyn Museum Ancient Egyptian treasures, a stellar collection of American painting and a cutting-edge feminist arts center. (p265)

Lower East Side Tenement Museum Fantastic insight into life as an immigrant during the 19th and early 20th centuries. (p109)

Skyline Views

Empire State Building The iconic building offers sweeping city views from its sky-high observation deck. (p180)

KEEP SMILING PHOTOGRAPHY / SHUTTERSTOCK ©

Coney Island (p275)

Brooklyn Bridge Park Wide-open views of downtown Manhattan and the Brooklyn and Manhattan Bridges. (p263)

Governors Island A lush, car-free space in the harbor with photogenic views of Manhattan and Lady Liberty. (p76)

Top of the Strand Go one better than staring at Midtown's mix of scrapers and swig a drink while you're part of the view. (p202)

The Standard Hotel Check out the downtown views from the rooftop perch of the very hip Le Bain. (p152)

Brooklyn Heights Promenade Staggering view of Manhattan, 24 hours a day. (p267)

Roosevelt Island River and skyscraper views from Louis Kahn's Franklin D Roosevelt Four Freedoms Park. (p189)

Cantor Roof Garden Bar From late April through October, the rooftop garden at the Met offers incredible views. (p215)

East River State Park Take in an inspiring sweep of Midtown from the Williamsburg waterfront. (p274)

Historic Sights

Ellis Island The gateway to freedom and opportunity for so many of America's immigrants. (p66)

Frick Collection A rare mansion from the Gilded Age survives as a museum on the Upper East Side. (p218)

Lower East Side Tenement Museum Get insight into how the early immigrants lived, on an eye-opening tour of a preserved tenement. (p109)

Museum of Chinese in America Learn about a much ignored group who made profound contributions to the country. (p89)

Morgan Library & Museum Browse the exquisite interiors of the former home of industrialist JP Morgan. (p190)

Morris-Jumel Mansion Museum This Georgian-Federal structure is the oldest house in Manhattan. (p252)

Historic Richmond Town A time-stuck village in Staten Island that's home to the country's oldest schoolhouse. (p75)

Gracie Mansion A graceful Federal-style structure now serves as the mayor's home. (p219)

Free Stuff

Central Park New York's quintessential green space. (p228)

High Line Visitors come to stroll, sit and picnic 30ft above the city, enjoying fabulous views of Manhattan's ever-changing urban landscape. (p136)

Staten Island Ferry The journey between Lower Manhattan and the Staten Island neighborhood of St George is one of NYC's finest free adventures. (p384)

National Museum of the American Indian The collections at this Smithsonian affiliate include stunning decorative arts, textiles and ceremonial objects. (p72)

David Zwirner One of the greatest Chelsea galleries. (p149)

Brooklyn Bridge Park A gorgeous park hugging the East River with jaw-dropping views of Lower Manhattan. (p263)

SummerStage A series of outdoor concerts in Central Park held from June till early September. (p233)

American Folk Art Museum A glimpse into an alternative art world, with free music on Friday nights. (p234)

Big Apple Greeter tours Reserve in advance for a free tour of a neighborhood of your choice from a local keen to show off their city. (p385)

National September 11 Memorial A sombre, moving memorial. (p68)

For more top New York spots, see the following:

- ➡ Eating (p39)
- ➡ Drinking & Nightlife (p43)
- ➡ Entertainment (p46)
- ➡ Shopping (p50)
- ➡ Sports & Activities (p53)
- ➡ LGBTIQ New York City (p56)

Old-School New York

Coney Island An amusement center that dates back to the early days of the 20th century; don't forget the hot dogs at Nathan's Famous. (p275)

Barney Greengrass After a century in the business, BG still serves up some of the best smoked fish in the city. (p236)

Russian & Turkish Baths Steam your stress away in this East Village classic, now over 120 years old. (p131)

Katz's Delicatessen Smoked meat that will please even the biggest kvetchers. (p119)

Marie's Crisis Show tunes and singing patrons at this legendary West Village gay bar. (p152)

Zabar's An emporium for all types of Upper West Side food-a-holics since the 1930s. (p242)

McSorley's Old Ale House Abraham Lincoln, Boss Tweed and Woody Guthrie are among the many who've raised a glass or two at this sawdust-on-the-floor pub. (p123)

Green Spaces

Central Park The city's most famous park has more than 800 acres of rolling meadows and boulder-topped hillocks. (p228)

High Line A thin stripe of green with wild plants and surprising vantage points atop a former rail line. (p136)

Prospect Park Brooklyn's favorite outdoor space for picnics, kite-flying, running and ambling amid beautifully landscaped scenery. (p264)

Hudson River Park Manhattan's looking greener than ever thanks to new parkland running up its western side. (p140)

Brooklyn Bridge Park This new park lines the waterfront along Dumbo, all the way to the foot of Atlantic Ave. (p263)

Green-Wood Cemetery A lush oasis with great views and rambling paths that dates back to the 1830s. (p269)

Brooklyn Botanic Garden Three-season beauty with cherry blossoms in spring, vibrant summery blooms, and fiery blazes in autumn. (p273)

Staying Up Late

Smalls Catch 1am 'after hours' shows at this atmospheric West Village jazz spot. (p158)

Silvana Head up to Harlem for nightly world music jams followed by DJ-fueled revelry. (p256)

IFC Center Watch midnight screenings of cult classics in the West Village. (p159)

Chinatown A secreted scatter of late-night lounges tucked behind the unassuming facades of hole-in-the-wall chow spots. (p100)

Rue B This tiny late-night jazz den in the East Village is a great spot to end the night. (p120)

Slipper Room Catch a riotously fun burlesque show at this cheeky den of debauchery on the Lower East Side. (p127)

Employees Only No need to eat sickening fast food after midnight. This West Village gastrobar serves a good menu past 3am. (p150)

Veselka The go-to place when you've just got to have *varenyky* (homemade dumplings) at 4am. (p116)

Ultimate Indulgences

Barneys The fashionista's aspirational closet comes with a hefty price tag. (p208)

Dough Home to some of the best doughnuts on the planet. (p279)

Pegu Club Stylish lounge, with a great ambience and welcome lack of pretension (never mind the $15 cocktails). (p101)

Brandy Library Nurse a glass of rare, amber-hued Armagnac at this refined retreat. (p81)

Bowery Hotel Treat yourself to a luxury stay in this beautifully designed downtown pad. (p335)

Hidden Hangouts

Beauty & Essex Hidden behind a pawnshop facade is an enchanting drinking den. (p126)

Bathtub Gin Slide behind a false wall at the back of a modest coffee shop for Prohibition-chic styling and retro cocktails. (p154)

Mulberry Project An unassuming set of stairs leads to the swank cocktail laboratory of the international owners and their coterie of server-friends. (p101)

Smith & Mills Push the unmarked door to find a kooky industrial interior (think 1900s factory) and smooth libations. (p83)

Freemans Walk down a tiny alley to find quaint cabin-like surrounds and legions of faithful brunchers. (p120)

Little Branch You'd never guess that great cocktails are crafted inside this seemingly abandoned West Village building. (p151)

Apothéke Apothecary turned cocktail lounge hidden deep in Chinatown. (p101)

PDT Secret bar concealed behind a hot-dog eatery; enter through the phone booth. (p123)

Venturing off the Beaten Path

Flushing Go on a foodie safari deep in the heart of Queens and browse New York's biggest and best Chinatown. (p306)

New York Botanical Garden A vast garden in the Bronx is home to 50 acres of forest and a Victorian-style conservatory. (p258)

Inwood Hill Park It's part of Manhattan, but it doesn't feel like it – this park remains wonderfully wild. (p252)

Queens Museum Excellent exhibits without the fanfare and crowds of some of Manhattan's other museum spaces. (p307)

Dyckman Farmhouse Museum Manhattan's last surviving Dutch farmhouse. (p252)

Red Hook Wander old cobblestone streets near the Brooklyn waterfront, stopping for refreshment at dive bars and seafood spots. (p268)

Ditmas Park Spend an afternoon peeking at gorgeous old houses, followed by drinks at a neighborhood bar. (p272)

Month By Month

TOP EVENTS

Tribeca Film Festival, April

Cherry Blossom Festival, April or May

SummerStage, June through August

Independence Day, July

Village Halloween Parade, October

January

The winter doldrums arrive following the build-up of Christmas and New Year's Eve. Despite the long nights, New Yorkers take advantage of the frosty weather, with outdoor ice skating and weekend ski trips to the Catskills.

New Year's Day Swim

What better way to greet the new year than with an icy dip in the Atlantic? Join the Coney Island Polar Bear Club for this annual brrrr fest (www.polarbearclub.org).

No Pants Subway Ride

On the second Sunday in January, some 4000 New Yorkers spice things up with a bit of leg nudity on public transit. Anyone can join in, and there's usually an after-party for the cheeky participants. Check the website for meeting times and details.

Winter Jazzfest

In mid-January, this four-day music fest (www.winterjazzfest.com) brings over 100 acts playing at nearly a dozen venues around the city. Most of the action happens around the West Village.

February

The below-freezing temperatures make February a good time to stay indoors nursing a drink or a warm meal at a cozy bar or bistro.

Lunar (Chinese) New Year Festival

One of the biggest Chinese New Year celebrations in the country, this display of fireworks and dancing dragons draws mobs of thrillseekers into the streets of Chinatown. The date of Chinese New Year typically falls in early February.

Winter Restaurant Week

From late January to early February, celebrate the dreary weather with slash-cut meal deals at some of the city's finest eating establishments during New York's Winter Restaurant Week (www.nycgo.com/restaurant-week), which actually runs for about three weeks. A three-course lunch costs around $26 ($40 for dinner).

March

After months of freezing temperatures and thick winter coats, the odd warm spring day appears and everyone rejoices – though it's usually followed by a week of subzero drear as winter lingers on.

Armory Show

New York's biggest contemporary art fair (www.thearmoryshow.com) sweeps into the city in March, showcasing the works of thousands of artists from around the world on two piers that jut into the Hudson River.

St Patrick's Day Parade

A massive audience, rowdy and wobbly from cups of green beer, lines Fifth Ave on March 17 for this popular parade of bagpipe blowers, floats and clusters of Irish-lovin' politicians. The parade, which was first held here in 1762, is the city's oldest and largest.

April

Spring finally appears: optimistic alfresco joints have a sprinkling of street-side chairs as the city squares overflow with bright tulips and blossom-covered trees.

Tribeca Film Festival

Created in response to the tragic events of September 11, Robert De Niro's downtown film festival (p48) has quickly become a star in the indie movie circuit. You'll have to make some tough choices: over 150 films are screened during the 10-day fest.

May

April showers bring May flowers in the form of brilliant bursts of blossoms adorning the flowering trees all around the city. The weather is warm and mild without the unpleasant humidity of summer.

Cherry Blossom Festival

Known in Japanese as Sakura Matsuri (p273), this annual tradition, held on one weekend in late April or early May, celebrates the magnificent flowering of cherry trees in the Brooklyn Botanic Garden. It's complete with entertainment and activities, plus refreshments and awe-inspiring beauty.

Fleet Week

For one week at the end of May, Manhattan resembles a 1940s movie set as clusters of fresh-faced, uniformed sailors go 'on the town' to look for adventures. Non-swabby visitors can take free tours of ships that have arrived from various corners of the globe.

TD Bank Five Boro Bike Tour

Bike Month features two-wheelin' tours, parties and other events for pedal-pushing New Yorkers. TD Bank Five Boro Bike Tour, the main event, sees thousands of cyclists hit the pavement for a 42-mile ride, much of it on roads closed to traffic or on waterfront paths.

June

Summer's definitely here and locals crawl out of their office cubicles to relax in the city's green spaces. Parades roll down the busiest streets and portable movie screens are strung up in several parks.

Bryant Park Summer Film Festival

June through August, Bryant Park hosts free Monday-night outdoor screenings (p37) of classic Hollywood films, which kick off after sundown. Arrive early (the lawn area opens at 5pm and folks line up by 4pm).

Mermaid Parade

Celebrating sand, sea and summer is this wonderfully quirky afternoon parade (p36). It's a flash of glitter and glamour, as elaborately costumed folks display their fishy finery along the Coney Island boardwalk. Held on the last Saturday of the month; all in costume are welcome.

NYC Pride

Gay Pride Month culminates in a major march down Fifth Ave on the last Sunday of the month. NYC Pride (www.nycpride.org) is a five-hour spectacle of dancers, drag queens, gay police officers, leathermen, lesbian soccer-moms and representatives of every other queer scene under the rainbow.

Puerto Rican Day Parade

The second weekend in June attracts thousands of flag-waving revelers for the annual Puerto Rican Day Parade. Now in its fifth decade, it runs up Fifth Ave from 44th to 86th Sts.

River to River Festival

Performers bring theater, music, dance and film to downtown parks for 12 days in June. Over 100 free events (p37) take place at outdoor spaces in Lower Manhattan and Governors Island.

> **SUMMERSTAGE**
>
> Central Park's SummerStage (p233), which runs from June through August, features an incredible lineup of music and dance throughout summer. Django Django, Femi Kuti, Shuggie Otis and the Martha Graham Dance Company are among recent standouts. Most events are free. There's also a SummerStage Kids program.

(Top) NYC Pride march
(Bottom) Chinese dragon in the Lunar New Year Festival parade (p29)

ANDREI ORLOV / SHUTTERSTOCK ©

MANDRITOIU / SHUTTERSTOCK ©

July

As the city swelters, locals flee to beachside escapes on Long Island. It's a busy month for tourism, however, as holidaying North Americans and Europeans fill the city.

☆ Shakespeare in the Park

The much-loved Shakespeare in the Park (p233) pays tribute to the Bard, with free performances in Central Park. The catch? You'll have to wait hours to score tickets, or win them in the lottery. Tickets are given out at noon; arrive no later than 10am.

July Fourth Fireworks

America's Independence Day is celebrated on the 4th of July with dramatic fireworks over the East River, starting at 9pm. Good viewing spots include the waterfronts of the Lower East Side and Williamsburg, Brooklyn, or any high rooftop or east-facing Manhattan apartment.

September

Labor Day officially marks the end of the Hamptons' share-house season as the blistering heat of summer fades to more tolerable levels. As locals return to work, the cultural calendar ramps up.

☆ BAM's Next Wave Festival

Celebrated for over 30 years, the Brooklyn Academy of Music's Next Wave Festival (p294), which runs through December, showcases world-class avant-garde theater, music and dance.

Electric Zoo

Celebrated over the Labor Day weekend, Electric Zoo (www.electriczoofestival.com) is New York's electronic music festival held in sprawling Randall's Island Park. Past headliners have included Moby, Afrojack, David Guetta, Martin Solveig and The Chemical Brothers.

Feast of San Gennaro

Rowdy, loyal crowds descend on the narrow streets of Little Italy for carnival games and more Italian treats than you can stomach in one evening. Held over 11 days in mid-September, it remains an old-world tradition; 2017 marked San Gennaro Festival's (p92) 90th year.

October

Brilliant bursts of color fill the trees as temperatures cool and alfresco cafes finally shutter their windows. Along with May, October is one of the most pleasant and scenic months to visit NYC.

Blessing of the Animals

In honor of the Feast Day of St Francis, which falls early in the month, pet owners flock to the grand Cathedral Church of St John the Divine for the annual Blessing of the Animals with their sidekicks – poodles, lizards, parrots, llamas, you name it.

Comic Con

Enthusiasts from near and far gather at this annual beacon of nerd-dom (www.newyorkcomiccon.com) to dress up as their favorite characters and cavort with like-minded anime aficionados.

Open House New York

The country's largest architecture and design event, Open House New York (www.ohny.org) features special architect-led tours, plus lectures, design workshops, studio visits and site-specific performances all over the city.

Village Halloween Parade

On Halloween, New Yorkers don their wildest costumes for a night of revelry. See the most outrageous displays at the Village Halloween Parade (p36) that runs up Sixth Ave in the West Village. It's fun to watch, but even better to join in.

November

As the leaves tumble, light jackets are replaced by wool. A headliner marathon is tucked into the final days of prehibernation weather, then families gather to give thanks.

New York City Marathon

Held in the first week of November, this annual 26-mile run (www.nycmarathon.org) draws thousands of athletes from around the world, and many more excited viewers line the streets to cheer the runners on.

New York Comedy Festival

Funny-makers take the city by storm during the New York Comedy Festival (p47) with stand-up sessions, improv nights and big-ticket shows hosted by the likes of Rosie O'Donnell and Ricky Gervais.

Rockefeller Center Christmas Tree Lighting

The flick of a switch ignites the massive Christmas tree in Rockefeller Center, officially ushering in the holiday season. Bedecked with over 25,000 lights, it is NYC's unofficial Yuletide headquarters and a must-see for anyone visiting the city during December.

Thanksgiving Day Parade

Massive helium-filled balloons soar overhead, high-school marching bands rattle their snares and millions of onlookers bundle up with scarves and coats to celebrate Thanksgiving (the fourth Thursday in November) with Macy's famous 2.5-mile-long parade.

December

Winter's definitely here, but there's plenty of holiday cheer to warm the spirit. Fairy lights adorn most buildings and Fifth Ave department stores (as well as Macy's) create elaborate worlds within their storefront windows.

New Year's Eve

The ultimate place to ring in the New Year, Times Square swarms with millions who come to stand squashed together like sardines, swig booze, freeze in subarctic temperatures, witness the annual dropping of the ball and chant the '10…9…8…' countdown in perfect unison.

Travel with Children

New York City has loads of activities for young ones, including imaginative playgrounds and leafy parks where kids can run free, plus lots of kid-friendly museums and sights. Other highs: carousel rides, puppet shows and noshing at markets around town.

Teacup ride in Central Park (p228)

Attractions

For many kids, some of New York City's top attractions are a world of fun.

Wildlife

The city has a number of zoos. The best, by far, is the Bronx Zoo (p258), which is known for its well-designed habitats. (The Congo Gorilla Forest is a stunner.) Otherwise, if you're pressed for time, the zoos in Central Park and Prospect Park are great for short visits.

Statue of Liberty

The boat ride to Lady Liberty (p65) offers the opportunity to chug around New York Harbor and get to know an icon that most kids only know from textbooks.

On Top of the World

A glass-roofed elevator leads to the Top of the Rock (p191), a lookout that offers glittering views of New York.

Coney Island

Hot dogs. Ice cream. Amusement-park rides. Coney Island (p275) is just the ticket if you're in need of some lowbrow entertainment.

Best Museums

The American Museum of Natural History (p234), with its dinosaurs, marine world, planetarium and IMAX films, should not be missed. Nearly every big museum – the Metropolitan Museum of Art (p214), the Museum of Modern Art (p182), Guggenheim Museum (p213), Museum of the City of New York (p219) and Cooper-Hewitt National Design Museum (p218) – all have kids' programs, but many smaller institutions are even more appealing for young visitors. The Lower East Side Tenement Museum (p109) offers an interactive tour where kids can meet an immigrant (costumed interpreter) of centuries past.

Toddler Time

For tots aged one to five, hit the Children's Museum of the Arts (p90) in West SoHo and the Brooklyn Children's Museum (p273) in Crown Heights. Both have story times, art classes, craft hours and painting sessions.

CITY TRAILS

For an insight into New York aimed directly at kids, pick up a copy of Lonely Planet's *City Trails: New York*. Perfect for children aged eight and up, it opens up a world of intriguing stories and fascinating facts about New York's people, places, history and culture.

Five & Over

Bigger kids can clamber on vintage subway cars at the New York Transit Museum (p266) or slide down a pole at the New York City Fire Museum (p90). Out in Astoria, the Museum of the Moving Image (p306) has hands-on exhibits for kids.

Best Parks & Playgrounds

Central Park

More than 800 acres of green space, a lake that can be navigated by rowboat, a carousel, a zoo and a massive statue of Alice in Wonderland. Heckscher playground, near Seventh Ave and Central Park South, is the biggest and best of Central Park's (p228) 21 playgrounds.

Prospect Park

Brooklyn's hilly 585-acre Prospect Park (p264) has abundant amusement for kids, including a zoo, several playgrounds, hands-on playthings at Lefferts Historic House and an ice-skating rink that becomes a roller rink and water splash area in summer. Pedal boats and kayaks for Brooklyn's only lake and a variety of kid-friendly bikes are available at the LeFrank Center at Lakeside in the park.

Brooklyn Bridge Park

Check out the park's fun new playgrounds, then hit the water-filled play area on Pier 6, followed by pizza at waterfront Fornino (p277). Pier 2 has shuffleboard and bocce courts and a roller rink that becomes an ice-skating rink in the winter.

Hudson River Park

Coursing along Manhattan's western side, this park (p140) offers loads of kiddy excitement, including mini-golf near Moore St (Tribeca), a fun playground near West St (West Village), a carousel off W 22nd St, watery fun at W 23rd & Eleventh Ave, and a science-themed play space near W 44th St.

The High Line

NYC's celebrated elevated green space (p136) has food vendors, water features (which kids can splash through) and great views, plus warm-weather family events – story time, science and craft projects, fun with food, and more. Check the website (www.thehighline.org/activities/family_programs) for details.

Riverside Park

Riverside Park (p233) on the Upper West Side has a bicycle trail with views of the Hudson River. Take a break at the River Run Playground (at W 83rd St) or at whimsical Hippo Playground (at W 91st St).

Fun for Kids & Parents

Markets around NYC are great snack spots, particularly Smorgasburg (p285), which has vendors selling everything from popsicles, doughnuts and pickles to tacos and pork sandwiches. The Chelsea Market (p147) also has many temptations – assemble a picnic then head over to the Hudson River Park for a waterside picnic.

Kid-Friendly Theater

Tiny Puppetworks (p296) in Brooklyn's Park Slope has amusing weekend puppet shows throughout the year.

Need to Know

Car Seats Children under seven can ride on an adult's lap in a taxi or you can use your own car seat. Ride-sharing services may have car seats.

Babysitters Contact the Baby Sitters' Guild (www.babysittersguild.com).

Resources Check out Time Out New York Kids (www.timeout.com/new-york-kids) and Mommy Poppins (www.mommypoppins.com).

Subway Children under 44in (110cm) ride free.

Like a Local

New Yorkers have developed winning strategies when it comes to nightlife, dining out and partaking of the city's cultural calendar. From long weekend brunches to leisurely spring days in the park, there are plenty of ways to go local – without having to pay those ridiculous rents.

STUART MONK / SHUTTERSTOCK ©

Wollman Skating Rink (p244)

Dos & Don'ts: On the Street

➡ Hail a cab only if the roof light is on. If it's not lit, the cab is taken, so put your arm down already!

➡ You needn't obey 'walk' signs – simply cross the street when there isn't oncoming traffic.

➡ When negotiating pedestrian traffic on the sidewalk think of yourself as a vehicle – don't stop short, follow the speed of the crowd around you and pull off to the side if you need to take out your map or umbrella. Most New Yorkers are respectful of personal space, but they will bump into you – and not apologize – if you get in the way.

➡ When boarding the subway, wait until the passengers disembark, then be aggressive enough when you hop on so that the doors don't close in front of you.

➡ In New York you wait 'on line' instead of 'in line'; you'll also hear 'quarter of' rather than 'quarter to'.

➡ Oh, and it's How-sten St, not Hugh-sten, got it?

Eating & Drinking

The Culture of Brunch

Brunch in New York is deeply woven into the city's social fabric, much like teatime for British royals. It typically happens between 11am and 4pm on weekends (though some places, especially in Brooklyn, have begun serving brunch every day). The meal provides a perfect setting for friends to catch up on the week's events and the weekend's shenanigans over dishes constructed of breakfast materials and an indiscriminate mix of cocktails or coffee.

Weekends Are for Amateurs

New Yorkers tend to avoid the big clubs, packed bars and certain neighborhoods (East Village, Lower East Side) on the weekends when you find yourself among a high proportion of less sophisticated types. Instead, weeknights can be great for going out – with fewer crowds, fewer of the aforementioned types, and more creative folk who don't work the typical nine-to-five (actors, writers, artists). Plus, you'll be able to score happy-hour and early-in-the-week specials.

Bar Food

Many of New York's best bars blur the boundary between eating and drinking. Slide onto a bar stool, pick up a menu, and you'll often be faced with some surprising dining options. That could be oysters at the bar, small sharing plates (seared scallops, sliders, truffle-oil fries), cheese boards and charcuterie or anything else – roasted beet salads, gourmet sandwiches, braised artichokes, rack of lamb. When planning a meal, don't limit yourself to a sit-down restaurant – you can also eat and drink your way around a neighborhood by stopping in at gastropubs.

Joining In

Truth be told, watching a parade can be a pretty dull affair. It's much more fun to take part. Along those lines, there are many ways you can join in the action. Don an outrageous costume for the **Village Halloween Parade** (www.halloween-nyc.com; Sixth Ave, from Spring St to 16th St; ⌚7-11pm Oct 31) or the summertime **Mermaid Parade** (www.coneyisland.com; ⌚late Jun) in Coney Island. Sign up for an organized race in the city (New York Road Runners stages dozens of annual runs). Take a rock-climbing class at Brooklyn Boulders (p300) or Cliffs (p318) in Queens. Polish up those old poems and take the stage at open-mic night at Nuyorican Poets Café (p127), or if there's music in you, try the open-mic at Sidewalk Café (p128). Meanwhile, Brooklyn Brainery (p300) offers evening and weekend courses in all sorts of topics. Whatever your passion – chess, hip-hop, drawing, architecture, beer-making – you'll find it in NYC, and be surrounded by plenty of like minds.

New York's Twitterati

Check out our favorite members of New York's Twitterati, who are always tweeting about the city's latest musts:

Everything NYC (@EverythingNYC) Hunting down the best things to see, do and eat in the Big Apple.

Pete Wells (@pete_wells) Restaurant critic of the *New York Times*.

New Yorker (@NewYorker) Insightful commentary on politics and culture.

Guest of a Guest (@guestofaguest) In-the-know info on NYC parties, social and fashion scenes.

Gothamist (@gothamist) News and curiosities in NYC.

Hyperallergic (@Hyperallergic) Tweets from NYC's favorite art blogazine.

Colson Whitehead (@colsonwhitehead) Manhattan native, novelist and *New Yorker* contributor.

Paul Goldberger (@paulgoldberger) Pulitzer Prize–winning architecture critic.

Tom Colicchio (@tomcolicchio) Celebrity chef and owner of the popular Craft franchise.

Sam Sifton (@samsifton) Food editor at the *New York Times*.

Seasonal Activities

Winter

Even dreary winter weather brings its delights – namely, ice skating! Beginning in November or December, the city's skating rinks provide ample amusement (and a good prequel to fireside drinks in a toasty bar afterwards). Locals skip tourist-swarmed Rockefeller Center and Bryant Park and instead head to Central Park, Prospect Park or Riverbank State Park for skating.

Spring

The city's blossoming parks are the place to be for spring picnics, sun-drenched strolls and lazy days lounging on the grass. Top spots for flower-gazing: the New York Botanical Garden and the Brooklyn Botanic Garden. The latter hosts a lovely Cherry Blossom Festival, much adored by Brooklynites.

Summer

Summer is the time for free open-air events: film screenings in Bryant Park, street festivals around town, and concerts in Central Park, Hudson River Park, Prospect Park and other green spaces around the city.

Fall

In fall the cultural calendar ramps up again as the city's premier performing arts halls open their seasons (which run from September through May) and galleries kick off their new shows (Thursday night, incidentally, is when the art openings happen).

For Free

The Big Apple isn't exactly the world's cheapest destination. Nevertheless, there are many ways to kick open the NYC treasure chest without spending a dime – free concerts, theater and film screenings, pay-what-you-wish nights at museums, city festivals, plus loads of green space.

KAMIRA / SHUTTERSTOCK ©

HBO Bryant Park Summer Film Festival

Live Music, Theater & Dance

In summer there are scores of free events around town. From June through early September, SummerStage (p233) features over 100 free performances at 17 parks around the city, including Central Park. You'll have to be tenacious to get tickets to Shakespeare in the Park (p233), held also in Central Park, but it's well worth the effort. Top actors like Meryl Streep and Al Pacino have taken the stage in years past. Prospect Park has its own venerable open-air summer concert and events series: Celebrate Brooklyn (p268).

Summertime also brings free film screenings and events to the water's edge during the **River to River Festival** (www.rivertorivernyc.com; ⏲Jun) at Hudson River Park in Manhattan and at **Brooklyn Bridge Park** (www.brooklynbridgepark.org; ⏲May-Oct). Another great option for film lovers is the free **HBO Bryant Park Summer Film Festival** (www.bryantpark.org; ⏲mid-Jun–Aug) screenings on Monday nights.

A few places offer free music throughout the year. BAMcafe (p294) in Brooklyn has free concerts (world music, R&B, jazz, rock) on select Friday and Saturday nights. In Harlem, Marjorie Eliot (p257) opens her home for free jazz jams on Sunday.

Museums

Always Free

- ➡ The High Line (p136)
- ➡ National September 11 Memorial (p68)
- ➡ National Museum of the American Indian (p72)
- ➡ Museum at FIT (p194)
- ➡ Hamilton Grange (p251)
- ➡ American Folk Art Museum (p234)
- ➡ Nicholas Roerich Museum (p234)

Admission by Donation

- ➡ American Museum of Natural History (p234)
- ➡ Brooklyn Museum (p265)
- ➡ Museum of the City of New York (p219)
- ➡ Brooklyn Historical Society (p266)

Free or Pay-What-You-Wish on Certain Days

- ➡ MoMA (p182) – 4–9pm Friday
- ➡ Guggenheim Museum (p213) – 5:45–7:45pm Saturday
- ➡ Whitney Museum of American Art (p139) – 7–10pm Friday
- ➡ Neue Galerie (p218) – 6–8pm first Friday of month
- ➡ Frick Collection (p218) – 2–6pm Wednesday & 6–9pm first Friday of month
- ➡ New Museum of Contemporary Art (p110) – 7–9pm Thursday
- ➡ New-York Historical Society (p233) – 6–8pm Friday
- ➡ Jewish Museum (p218) – 5–8pm Thursday and Saturday
- ➡ Rubin Museum of Art (p141) – 6–10pm Friday
- ➡ Asia Society & Museum (p219) – 6–9pm Friday, September to June
- ➡ Japan Society (p190) – 6–9pm Friday
- ➡ MoMA PS1 (p303) – Free with your MoMA ticket
- ➡ National September 11 Memorial Museum (p68) – 5–8pm Tuesday

Need to Know

Handy websites for tracking down free and discounted events in the city include Club Free Time (www.clubfreetime.com) and the Skint (www.theskint.com). These have daily listings of free tours, concerts, workshops, talks, art openings, book readings and more.

On the Water

The free Staten Island Ferry (p384) provides magical views of the Statue of Liberty, and you can enjoy them with a cold beer (available on the boat). While it's not free, for just $2.75 you can sail from Lower Manhattan across to Brooklyn, Queens or all the way out to Rockaway on the NYC Ferry (www.ferry.nyc) – a great alternative to the subway. From May to October, you can also take a ferry (free on summer weekend mornings, $2 at other times) over to Governors Island (p76), a car-free oasis with priceless views.

For a bit more adventure, take out a free kayak, available in the Hudson River Park, Brooklyn Bridge Park and Red Hook (p300).

TV Tapings

Some of America's top evening shows (p207) are taped right here in New York City. *The Late Show with Stephen Colbert*, *The Daily Show with Trevor Noah* and *The Tonight Show Starring Jimmy Fallon* all give out free tickets to their shows. Go online to reserve seats.

Walking Tours

One of the best ways to experience the city is to have a local show you around. The highly recommended Big Apple Greeter (p385) provides free tours by locals who love showing off their cities.

Wi-Fi

If you're out for the day and need to get online, you'll find free wi-fi in public parks such as the High Line, Bryant Park, Battery Park, Tompkins Square Park and Union Square Park. Most cafes and many restaurants also offer free wi-fi.

ONNES / GETTY IMAGES ©

Gansevoort Market (p142)

Eating

From inspired iterations of world cuisine to quintessentially local nibbles, New York City's dining scene is infinite, all-consuming and a proud testament to its kaleidoscope of citizens. Even if you're not an obsessive foodie hitting ethnic enclaves or the newest cult-chef openings, an outstanding meal is always only a block away.

To Market, to Market

Don't let the concrete streets and buildings fool you – New York City has a thriving greens scene that comes in many shapes and sizes. At the top of your list should be the Chelsea Market (p134), which is packed with gourmet goodies of all kinds – both shops (where you can assemble picnics) and food stands (where you can eat on-site). Many other food halls have opened in recent years, including Gansevoort Market (p142) in the Meatpacking District and a trio of food halls at Brookfield Place (p80), in Lower Manhattan. Across the river, there's the brand-new DeKalb Market Hall (p276) in downtown Brooklyn, plus the small food hall of Berg'n (p284) out in Crown Heights.

Many neighborhoods in NYC have their own Greenmarket. One of the biggest is the Union Square Greenmarket (p172), open four days a week throughout the year. Check Grow NYC (www.grownyc.org/greenmarket) for a list of the other 50-plus markets around the city.

Out in Brooklyn, the best weekend markets for noshers (rather than cook-at-home types) are Smorgasburg (p285), with over 100 craft food vendors, and the Brooklyn Flea Market (p298), which has several dozen stalls.

NEED TO KNOW

Opening Hours

Generally speaking, meal times often bleed together as New Yorkers march to the beat of their own drum: breakfast is served from 7am to noon, lunch from 11:30am to 3pm, and dinner stretches between 5pm and 11pm. The popular weekend brunch lasts from 11am until 4pm.

Price Ranges

The following price ranges refer to a main dish, exclusive of tax and tip:

$ under $15

$$ $15–25

$$$ more than $25

Tipping

New Yorkers tip between 18% and 20% of the final price of the meal. For takeout, it's polite to drop a few dollars in the tip jar.

Reservations

Popular restaurants abide by one of two rules: either they take reservations and you need to plan in advance (weeks or months early for the real treasures) or they only seat patrons on a first-come basis, in which case you should arrive when they open, and eat early. Otherwise, you might be looking at a two-hour wait. Apps like Open Table and Resy can get you a last-minute table.

Websites & Blogs

Yelp (www.yelp.com) Comprehensive user-generated content and reviews.

Open Table (www.opentable.com) Click-and-book reservation service.

Tasting Table (www.tastingtable.com) Sign up for handy news blasts about the latest and greatest.

Eater (https://ny.eater.com) Food news and restaurant round-ups.

Serious Eats (http://newyork.seriouseats.com) Restaurant gossip and articles on the cuisine scene.

Grub Street (www.grubstreet.com) In-the-know articles on NYC dining.

Restaurant Girl (www.restaurantgirl.com) Blogger and restaurant critic eating her way around the city.

Eating My NYC (https://eatingmynyc.com) Native New Yorker food guru.

Also popular are high-end market-cum-grocers like Eataly (p169) and Dean & DeLuca (p103), where fresh produce and ready-made fare are given the five-star treatment. Whole Foods is another big draw, particularly its ecofriendly, locavore-focused Brooklyn outpost (p281).

And, in market gossip, food-show host Anthony Bourdain still plans on opening a massive international market with more than 100 stalls, though the arrival date has been pushed back several times – and the location is yet to be confirmed.

Tours & Courses

There's no better way to engage with the city's infinite dining scene than to link up with a savvy local for a food tour or cooking class. Check out the following winners:

Institute of Culinary Education (p85) America's largest cooking school offers accessible, top-notch cooking courses, as well as foodie tours.

Urban Oyster (www.urbanoyster.com) High-quality, themed foodie tours mostly in Lower Manhattan and Brooklyn.

Scott's Pizza Tours (p278) Offbeat and always fun, Scott promises to unveil all of the secrets of the city's pizza-pie scene.

Nosh Walks (p385) Myra Alperson leads wide-ranging food tours focusing on NYC's rich ethnic cuisine.

Pizza A Casa (www.pizzaacasa.com) Much-loved pie school on the Lower East Side specializing in rolling and decorating dough.

Chopsticks & Marrow (www.chopsticksandmarrow.com) Fantastic Queens food blog by local Joe DiStefano, who also runs food tours.

League of Kitchens (www.leagueofkitchens.com) Cooking classes taught by immigrant women in their own kitchens, in Brooklyn and Queens.

Vegetarians & Vegans

Though the city's herbivore scene has long lagged behind that of West Coast cities, and was for years mocked by serious foodies, many former naysayers are beginning to come around. That's thanks in part to the local-food movement, as well as a slew of new eateries that have enticed skeptics by injecting big doses of cool ambience – and top-notch wine, liquor and dessert options – into the mix. Topping the list is Nix (p145), a brilliantly creative vegetarian restaurant that's earned rave reviews and a Michelin star. Even the most meat-heavy

Eating by Neighborhood

four-star restaurants are figuring out the lure of legume; the market-inspired *le potager* section on the menu at Café Boulud (p221) offers highbrow veggie dishes, while on Monday night Dovetail (p237) hosts a decadent prix-fixe vegetarian feast.

Vegans have much to celebrate with the arrival of excellent eateries serving up guilt-free goodness all around town. Top choices include Modern Love (p285), which serves up comfort fare out in Williamsburg, and elegant Blossom (p149), with locations in Chelsea and elsewhere. Other icons include Candle Cafe (p220), which has several locations around the city, and the soul food gem, Seasoned Vegan (p254), up in Harlem.

Food Trucks & Carts

Skip the bagel- and hot-dog-vending food carts. These days, there's a new mobile crew in town dishing up high-end treats and unique fusion fare. The trucks ply various routes, stopping in designated zones throughout the city – namely around Union Square, Midtown and the Financial District – so if you're looking for a particular grub wagon, it's best to follow them on Twitter. Here are a few of our favorites:

Mad Sq Eats (p169) Sumptuous pop-up food fest on the edge of Madison Square Park.

Kimchi Taco (www.twitter.com/kimchitruck) Mouthwatering combo of Korean beef served in tacos.

Calexico Cart (www.calexico.net/locations) Hearty rich burritos, tacos and quesadillas.

MysttikMasaala (www.facebook.com/MysttikMasaala) Lip-smacking Indian cooking with three roving locations.

King Souvlaki (p311) Worth the trip out to Astoria for the legendary Greek snack food.

Cool Haus (https://cool.haus/foodtrucks) Magnificent ice-cream sandwiches and other treats.

Lonely Planet's Top Choices

Chefs Club (p97) Visiting chefs from around the globe showcase outstanding recipes.

Battersby (p279) Farm-to-table brilliance on Brooklyn's restaurant-lined Smith St.

Gramercy Tavern (p170) Prime produce, culinary finesse and the choice of bustling tavern or fine-dining den.

RedFarm (p147) Savvy Sino-fusion dishes boast bold flavors, but it doesn't take itself too seriously.

Dovetail (p237) Simplicity is key at this stunner – vegetarians unite on Mondays.

Foragers Table (p150) A triumph of farm-to-table cooking with flavorful sustainable recipes in Chelsea.

Best by Budget

$

Chelsea Market (p147) Foods from around the world served up in a sprawling converted factory.

Taïm (p143) Outstanding falafel sandwiches.

Mamoun's (p142) Famous, spicy shawarma sandwiches at rock-bottom prices.

Golden Shopping Mall (p314) All things Asian and edible in Queens.

$$

Upstate (p117) A seafood feast awaits in the East Village.

Babu Ji (p145) A celebration of Indian street food in a cheeky dining room near Union Square.

$$$

Eleven Madison Park (p169) Arresting, cutting-edge cuisine laced with unexpected whimsy.

Blue Hill (p147) A West Village classic using ingredients sourced straight from the upstate farm.

Degustation (p118) A tiny eatery where you can watch the chefs create edible works of art.

Jeffrey's Grocery (p146) Much-loved West Village neighborhood spot.

Best by Cuisine

Asian

Uncle Boons (p96) Zesty, Michelin-starred Thai with a generous serve of fun in Nolita.

Zenkichi (p286) Candlelit culinary temple of exquisite sushi.

Lan Larb (p96) Real-deal northeastern Thai in a cheap, cheery hole-in-the-wall on the edge of Chinatown.

Italian

Il Buco Alimentari & Vineria (p97) Be transported to the old country in this standout.

Rosemary's (p145) A beautifully designed West Village spot with memorable cooking.

Roman's (p280) Changing seasonal menu of Italian invention.

Barbuto (p145) Serves creative modern Italian fare in a buzzing space.

Vegetarian

Nix (p145) Serving some of the best cruelty-free dishes in the city.

Butcher's Daughter (p96) Inventive vegetarian menu.

Modern Love (p285) Comfort-food classics with outstanding vegan plates.

Best Bakeries

Dough (p279) Probably NYC's best doughnut, in Brooklyn.

Four & Twenty Blackbirds (p281) Heavenly slices of homemade pies in Gowanus.

Dominique Ansel Kitchen (p143) Sweet magnificence from NYC's most famous pastry chef in the West Village.

Arcade Bakery (p77) One of the city's finest almond croissants in an unexpected Tribeca setting.

Best Brunch

Estela (p99) Brilliant seasonal plates in a buzzing wine bar.

Rabbithole (p287) Excellent brunch plates served daily till 5pm at this Williamsburg gem.

Cookshop (p149) Great indoor-outdoor dining spot.

Cafe Mogador (p117) An icon of the East Village brunch scene.

ViceVersa (p198) Elegant Italian and first-rate brunch spot in the shadow of the Theater District.

Best Old-School NYC

Barney Greengrass (p236) Perfect plates of smoked salmon and sturgeon for over 100 years.

Russ & Daughters (p131) A celebrated Jewish deli.

Zabar's (p242) Upper West Side store selling gourmet, kosher foods since the 1930s.

Margon (p197) Unfussy, unchanged Cuban lunch counter.

Best Upscale Market Groceries

Eataly (p169) A mecca for lovers of Italian food.

Whole Foods, Brooklyn (p281) Ecofriendly shopping in the reinvented Gowanus neighborhood.

Union Square Greenmarket (p172) Delicious veggies and bakery items from upstate producers.

Le District (p81) A sprawling food emporium packed with Gallic larder essentials.

Radegast Hall & Biergarten (p290)

Drinking & Nightlife

You'll find all species of thirst-quenching venues here, from terminally hip cocktail lounges and historic dive bars to specialty tap rooms and Third Wave coffee shops. Then there's the legendary club scene, spanning everything from celebrity staples to gritty, indie hangouts. Head downtown or to Brooklyn for the parts of the city that, as they say, truly never sleep.

Historic Cocktails, Crafty Beers

Here in the land where the term 'cocktail' was born, mixed drinks are still stirred with the utmost gravitas. From Jillian Vose at Dead Rabbit (p81) to Eben Freeman at Genuine Liquorette (p101), the city's top barkeeps are virtual celebrities, their deft precision creating some of the world's most sophisticated and innovative libations. Often it's a case of history in a glass: New York's obsession with rediscovered recipes and Prohibition-era style continues to drive many a cocktail list.

The city's craft beer culture is equally dynamic, with an ever-expanding bounty of breweries, bars and shops showcasing local artisanal brews. While Brooklyn may no longer be the major beer exporter of yesteryear, craft breweries like Brooklyn Brewery (p275) and Sixpoint (www.sixpoint.com) have put it back on the map. Other boroughs are also making amber waves, with start-ups including SingleCut Beersmiths (www.singlecutbeer.com) and Big Alice Brewery (www.bigalicebrewing.com) in Queens, as well as Bronx Brewery (p258) and Gun Hill Brewing Co (www.gunhillbrewing.com) in the Bronx.

NEED TO KNOW

Websites

New York Magazine (www.nymag.com/nightlife) Brilliantly curated nightlife options by the people who know best.

Thrillist (www.thrillist.com) A roundup of what's hot or coming soon on the NYC bar scene, including interviews with industry peeps.

Urbandaddy (www.urbandaddy.com) More up-to-the-minute info and a handy 'hot right now' list.

Time Out (www.timeout.com/newyork/nightlife) Reviews and on-the-ball listings of where to drink and dance.

partyearth (www.partyearth.com/newyork) Detailed club reviews from some of the city's savviest party kids.

Opening Hours

Opening times vary. While some dive bars open as early as 8am, most drinking establishments get rolling around 5pm. Numerous bars stay open until 4am, while others close around 1am early in the week and 2am from Thursday to Saturday. Clubs generally operate from 10pm to 4am or 5pm.

How Much

Happy hour beers typically start from $4; expect to pay about $7 or $8 for a regular draft, and more for imported bottles. Glasses of wine start at around $9. Specialty cocktails run from $14 to well over $20. Expect to pay between $5 and $30 to get into clubs.

Clubbing

New Yorkers are always looking for the next big thing, so the city's club scene changes faster than a New York minute. Promoters drag revelers around the city for weekly events held at all of the finest addresses, and when there's nothing on, it's time to hit the dancefloor stalwarts.

When clubbing it never hurts to plan ahead; having your name on a guest list can relieve unnecessary frustration and disappointment. If you're an uninitiated partier, dress the part. If you're fed the 'private party' line, try to bluff – chances are high that you've been bounced. Also, don't forget a wad of cash as many nightspots (even the swankiest ones) often refuse credit cards, and in-house ATMs scam a fortune in fees.

The Caffeinated City

A boom in specialty coffee roasters has transformed New York's once-dismal caffeine culture. More locals are cluing-in on single-origin beans and different brewing techniques, with numerous roasters now offering cupping classes for curious drinkers. Many are transplants from A-list coffee cities, among them Portland's Stumptown (p199) and the Bay Area's Blue Bottle (p293). The Australian influence is especially notable, with antipodean mavericks including Little Collins (p199) and Bluestone Lane (p81).

Drinking & Nightlife by Neighborhood

Lower Manhattan & the Financial District (p81) FiDi office slaves loosen their ties in everything from specialist beer and brandy bars to revered cocktail hot spots.

SoHo & Chinatown (p100) Stylish cocktail lounges, a sprinkling of dives and a few speakeasy-style bars.

East Village & the Lower East Side (p120) Proud home of the original-flavor dive bar, the East Village is brimming with options.

West Village, Chelsea & the Meatpacking District (p150) Jet-setters flock here, with wine bars, backdoor lounges and gay hangouts.

Union Square, Flatiron District & Gramercy (p170) Vintage drinking dens, swinging cocktail bars and fun student hangouts – this trio spans all tastes.

Midtown (p199) Rooftop bars with skyline views, historic cocktail salons and rough-n-ready dive bars: welcome to Midtown.

Harlem & Upper Manhattan (p256) A burgeoning mix of fabulous live music spots, speakeasy-style bars and old-school dives.

Brooklyn (p288) Brooklyn offers everything on the nightlife spectrum with Williamsburg as its heart.

Lonely Planet's Top Choices

Silvana (p256) Hidden basement bar in Harlem with great live music every night of the week.

House of Yes (p290) Unrivaled destination for a wild night out at this Bushwick warehouse space.

Apothéke (p101) An atmospheric lounge and former opium den with great cocktails hidden away in Chinatown.

Rue B (p120) An appealing little East Village den with live jazz and a fun crowd.

Maison Premiere (p290) Absinthe, juleps and oysters shine bright at this Big Easy tribute in Williamsburg.

Best Cocktails

Bar Goto (p126) Lower East Side icon under the helm of New York's most famous mixologist.

Dead Rabbit (p81) Meticulously researched cocktails, punches and pop-inns – lightly hopped ales spiked with different flavors – in a snug FiDi den.

Employees Only (p150) Award-winning barkeeps and arresting libations in the timeless West Village.

Lantern's Keep (p202) Classic, elegant libations in a historic Midtown hotel.

Genuine Liquorette (p101) A Cali-style bodega in Little Italy, where innovative drinks meet playful irreverence.

Best Beer

Spuyten Duyvil (p291) A much-loved Williamsburg spot serving unique, high-quality crafts.

Bier International (p257) Some of Europe's finest beers on draft at this Harlem hall.

Astoria Bier & Cheese (p316) Artisanal suds meet gourmet cheeses in Astoria, Queens.

Bohemian Hall & Beer Garden (p316) Czech brews served with thick accents at NYC's favorite beer garden.

Birreria (p171) Unfiltered, unpasteurized Manhattan ales on a Flatiron rooftop.

Best Wine Selection

Terroir Tribeca (p83) An enlightened, encyclopedic wine list in trendy Tribeca.

La Compagnie des Vins Surnaturels (p101) A love letter to Gallic wines steps away from Little Italy.

Buvette (p150) A buzzing, candlelit wine bar on a tree-lined West Village street.

Immigrant (p122) Wonderful wines and service in a skinny East Village setting.

Best Classic Date Bars

Manhattan Cricket Club (p237) Intimate, handsomely designed cocktail spot.

Pegu Club (p101) Made-from-scratch concoctions in a Burma-inspired SoHo hideaway.

Ten Bells (p123) Candlelit beauty with great drinks and tapas in the Lower East Side.

Little Branch (p151) Speakeasy-chic is all the craze, but no one does it quite like this West Village hideout.

Best Coffee

Stumptown Coffee Roasters (p199) Hipster baristas serving Portland's favorite cup o' joe.

Bluestone Lane (p81) Aussie brewing prowess in the shadow of Wall St.

La Colombe (p103) Sucker-punch roasts for the downtown cognoscenti.

Little Collins (p199) A tribute to Melbourne coffee culture in Midtown East.

Kaffe 1668 South (p83) Caffeinated glory (and room to sit) in Tribeca.

Best Dance Clubs & House DJs

Cielo (p152) A thumping, modern classic in the Meatpacking District.

Le Bain (p152) Well-dressed crowds still pack this favorite near the High Line.

Berlin (p120) Yesteryear's free-spirited dance days live on at this concealed East Village bolt-hole.

Bossa Nova Civic Club (p293) A hip little Bushwick haunt for those craving off-the-radar thrills.

Best Dive Bars

Spring Lounge (p101) Soaks, ties and cool kids unite at this veteran Nolita rebel.

Sunny's (p288) Our favorite Red Hook dive, near the Brooklyn waterfront.

Cowgirl SeaHorse (p81) Always a good time at this nautically themed drinkery in Lower Manhattan.

Best Mocktails

North End Grill (p81) Vibrant juices and artisanal flavors at Danny Meyer's downtown bar-and-grill.

NoMad (p340) Sophisticated mocktails in a luxe, Victoriana oasis.

Flatiron Lounge (p171) Fresh, seasonal mocktails and deco design in Flatiron.

HIROYUKI ITO / CONTRIBUTOR / GETTY IMAGES ©

The New York City Ballet performing *Glass Pieces* at the David H Koch Theater (p232)

Entertainment

Actors, musicians, dancers and artists flock to the bright lights of the Big Apple, hoping to finally get that big break. The result? Audiences are spoiled by the continual influx of supremely talented, dedicated, boundary-pushing performers. Like the saying goes: if you can make it here, you can make it anywhere.

Theater

From the legendary hit factories of Broadway to the scruffy black-box theaters that dot countless downtown blocks, NYC boasts the full gamut of theater experiences. The most celebrated scene is, of course, Broadway – nicknamed the Great White Way in 1902 for its bright billboard lights. There's something truly magical about sitting in one of the ornate Broadway theaters and letting the show take you to another world as the lights dim.

The term 'off Broadway' is not a geographical one – it simply refers to theaters that are smaller in size (200 to 500 seats) and usually have less of a glitzy production budget than the big hitters. Off Off Broadway takes place in even smaller theaters, with shows that are often inexpensively produced and experimental in nature.

A few of the best non-Broadway venues are the Public Theater (p104), Performing Garage (home to experimental Wooster Group), St Ann's Warehouse (p294) and the Brooklyn Academy of Music (p294); the latter two are in Brooklyn. Otherwise, the highest concentration is in the East and West Villages.

Traditional theaters aside, another great place to catch a show is at Shakespeare in the

Park (p233). Though the wait for tickets is long, you'll be rewarded with free seats to see star-studded performances in the open air in Central Park.

Live Music

NYC is the country's live music capital, and just about every taste can be catered for here within a variety of wonderful venues spread throughout the boroughs. However, some of the highest-profile opera and classical music is performed at the Lincoln Center; jazz greats and up-and-coming talents play at clubs throughout town, but especially in Harlem, Midtown and the Village. Big name indie rockers earn their stripes downtown, as well as in North Brooklyn. Major acts play in stadiums like Madison Square Garden and the Barclays Center, and summertime brings outdoor music festivals, notably several prominent hip-hop fests. For current listings, check out *New York Magazine* and *Time Out*.

Dance

Dance fans are spoiled for choice in this town, which is home to both the New York City Ballet (p240) and the **American Ballet Theatre** (Map p432; ☎212-477-3030; www.abt.org; David H Koch Theater, Lincoln Center, 64th St, at Columbus Ave; Ⓢ1 to 66th St-Lincoln Center). Another key venue dedicated to dance is the Joyce Theater (p159), which stages acclaimed contemporary productions by dance companies from every corner of the globe. There are also modern dance companies galore, including those of masters Alvin Ailey, Paul Taylor, Merce Cunningham, Martha Graham, Bill T Jones, Mark Morris and a slew of up-and-comers, which often take to the stage downtown and at the Brooklyn Academy of Music (p294).

Note that there are two major dance seasons: first in spring from March to May, then in late fall from October to December. But rest assured that there's always someone putting on the moves.

Comedy

A good laugh is easy to find in the Big Apple, where comedians sharpen their stand-up and improv chops practicing new material or hoping to get scouted by a producer or agent. The best spots for some chuckles are downtown, particularly around Chelsea and Greenwich Village. Several festivals, including **New York Comedy Festival** (www.nycomedyfestival.com; ⌚Nov), draw big names throughout the year.

NEED TO KNOW

Calendars & Reviews

- Playbill (www.playbill.com), the publisher of that happy little yellow-and-white program provided at Broadway plays, also has an online version.
- Talkin' Broadway (www.talkingbroadway.com) has dishy reviews as well as a board for posting extra tickets to buy or sell.
- Traditional publications include the *New York Times*, *New York Magazine* and *Time Out*.

Ticket Agencies

To purchase tickets for shows, you can either head directly to the venue's box office, or use one of several ticket agencies (most of which add a surcharge) to order by phone or online.

Broadway Line (www.broadway.org) Provides descriptions and good prices for shows on the Great White Way.

SmartTix (www.smarttix.com) A great source for practically anything but Broadway, with info on comedy, cabaret, performance art, music, dance and downtown theater.

Telecharge (www.telecharge.com) Sells tickets for Broadway and off-Broadway shows.

Theatermania (www.theatermania.com) For any form of theater; provides listings, reviews and ticketing.

Ticketmaster (www.ticketmaster.com) An old chestnut, Ticketmaster sells tickets for every conceivable form of big-time entertainment.

TKTS Booths Cut-price same-day tickets to Broadway shows, with locations in Midtown (p179), South Street Seaport (p63) and **Downtown Brooklyn** (www.tdf.org; 1 Metrotech Center, cnr Jay St & Myrtle Ave, Promenade, Downtown Brooklyn; ⌚11am-6pm Tue-Sat, often closed 3-3:30pm; ⓈA/C, F, R to Jay St-Metrotech).

Film & TV

Feasting on films in NYC is quite a different experience to the traditional American blockbuster-at-the-multiplex scene. Film-going is a serious venture here, as evidenced by the preponderance of movie houses that show indie, classic, avant-garde, foreign and otherwise nonstandard fare. Frequent film festivals, such as the **Tribeca Film Festival** (212-941-2400; www.tribecafilm.com; Apr), provide additional texture to the movie-going scene.

One of the least-known gems for films is Museum of Modern Art (p182), which has a rich collection of movies spanning all genres and corners of the world. The Film Society of Lincoln Center (p241) stages an incredible array of documentary and art-house films. Also worth checking out is the BAM Rose Cinemas (p294), which does similar fare as well as revivals.

A handful of TV shows (p38) are taped in Midtown Manhattan, including *Saturday Night Live* and *The Late Show with Stephen Colbert*. You can be an audience member by signing up online or trying for standby tickets.

Opera & Classical Music

When thinking about opera, one name rules the roost: the Metropolitan Opera (p240), which stages lavish and exceptional productions. However, many other forms live within the city limits. The laudable company **Amore Opera** (Map p434; 347-948-4588; www.amoreopera.org; Riverside Theatre, 91 Claremont St, btwn 120th & 122nd Sts; tickets from $40; S 1 to 116th St, 1 to 125th St) performs impressive works in its new uptown home of the Riverside Theatre. Other roving companies include **Opera on Tap** (www.operaontap.org/newyork), which stages performances not at grand theaters but bars around Brooklyn. Another creative Brooklyn outfit is **LoftOpera** (347-915-5638; www.loftopera.com; Brooklyn; tickets $30), which, true to name, performs condensed operas in a loft in Gowanus.

The choices for orchestras, chamber music and soloists are abundant, with the more cutting-edge options often stealing center stage. For all things traditional on a grand scale, don't miss Lincoln Center (p232) and the famously stunning Carnegie Hall (p205). For something more cutting edge, check out the eclectic lineup at the Brooklyn Academy of Music.

Richard Rodgers Theatre (p204), the home of *Hamilton*

Entertainment by Neighborhood

Lower Manhattan & the Financial District (p83) Tribeca is home to the Flea Theater and SoHo Rep, two venerable theater companies.

East Village & the Lower East Side (p126) Experimental performance spaces, poetry slams and stand-up comics fill basements with laughter.

West Village, Chelsea & the Meatpacking District (p155) Unofficial HQ of the world's jazz club scene, plus dance troupes galore in Chelsea.

Midtown (p203) Razzle-dazzle extravaganzas, fresh American theater, world-class jazz sessions and stand-up comedy blue bloods.

Upper West Side & Central Park (p240) Lincoln Center supplies an endless amount of high culture, while other venues provide more intimate settings.

Brooklyn (p294) A little bit of everything, from classical offerings to the indie rock bands in Williamsburg.

Lonely Planet's Top Choices

Richard Rodgers Theatre (p204) Home to one of Broadway's greatest hits: *Hamilton*, an American history lesson set to urban rhythms.

Brooklyn Academy of Music (p294) This hallowed theater hosts cutting-edge works, particularly during its celebrated Next Wave Festival.

Eugene O'Neill Theatre (p204) Stages some of Broadways best productions, like the uproarious *Book of Mormon*.

Jazz at Lincoln Center (p205) Glittering evening views of Central Park and world-class musical acts.

Carnegie Hall (p205) Legendary concert hall, blessed with perfect acoustics; hosts everything from opera to jazz.

Brooklyn Bowl (p295) Great lineup of funk, indie rock and global beats, plus beer and bowling!

Best Broadway Shows

Book of Mormon (p204) Brilliantly funny, award-winning show by the creators of *South Park*.

Chicago (p206) One of the most scintillating shows on Broadway.

Kinky Boots (p205) Book well ahead to score seats for this over-the-top musical.

Hamilton (p204) If you can't get tickets, try standing in the cancellation line outside the theater.

Best off-Broadway Theater

Playwrights Horizons (p205) Showcase of powerfully written plays.

Signature Theatre (p205) Stages works by some of the world's top playwrights.

Soho Rep (p84) Some of the city's most powerful and inventive drama.

St Ann's Warehouse (p294) A creative dynamo based in beautiful new space near the Brooklyn waterfront.

Best Opera & Classical Music

Metropolitan Opera House (p240) Enchanting setting for seeing some of the world's best opera.

National Sawdust (p294) Cutting-edge contemporary composers who fuse classical, opera and global sounds.

Brooklyn Academy of Music (p294) Innovative works by Brooklyn's renowned hit-maker.

Bargemusic (p297) String quartets on a barge parked on the East River.

Best For Dance

Joyce Theater (p159) NY's best venue devoted solely to dance.

New York Live Arts (p158) Experimental leanings with performances by troupes from around the globe.

New York City Center (p206) Excellent lineup of dance companies and mini-festivals.

Brooklyn Academy of Music (p294) Catch Mark Morris Dance Group and many others.

Best For Film

Nitehawk Cinema (p295) Nibble great food and sip cocktails while watching first-run and foreign flicks in Williamsburg.

Film Forum (p104) Another downtown film innovator with an excellent indie repertoire.

Museum of Modern Art (p183) A must for film lovers, with a brilliantly curated film calendar.

Film Society of Lincoln Center (p241) Two excellent theaters at the epicenter of NYC creativity.

Best For Jazz

Jazz at Lincoln Center (p205) Innovative fare under the guidance of jazz luminary Wynton Marsalis.

Village Vanguard (p158) Legendary West Village jazz club.

Smalls (p158) Tiny West Village basement joint that evokes the feel of decades past.

Barbès (p294) Obscure but celebratory rhythms from around the globe in Park Slope.

Birdland (p206) Sleek Midtown space that hosts big-band sounds, Afro-Cuban jazz and more.

Best For Rock

Bowery Ballroom (p128) Celebrated downtown concert hall.

Music Hall of Williamsburg (p296) Indie rock galore out in Brooklyn.

Rockwood Music Hall (p127) Music all the time at this Lower East Side spot.

Bell House (p295) South Brooklyn charmer with an innovative lineup of indie and folk sounds.

Best For Laughs

Upright Citizens Brigade Theatre (p203) Hilarious comedy sketches and improv.

Caroline's on Broadway (p206) The go-to spot for seeing famous comics perform.

Creek and the Cave (p317) Offbeat comedy clubhouse in Long Island City.

GORAN BOGICEVIC / SHUTTERSTOCK ©

Brooklyn Flea (p298)

Shopping

Not surprisingly for a capital of commercialism, creativity and fashion, New York City is quite simply one of the best shopping destinations on the planet. Every niche is filled. From indie designer-driven boutiques to landmark department stores, thrift shops to haute couture, record stores to the Apple store, antiques to edible gourmet groceries, it's quite easy to blow one's budget.

Fashion Epicenter

One of the world's fashion capitals, NYC is ever setting trends for the rest of the country to follow. For checking out the latest designs hitting the streets, it's worth browsing some of the best-loved boutiques around town – regardless of whether you intend to spend. A few favorites include Opening Ceremony, Issey Miyake, Marc Jacobs, Steven Alan, Rag & Bone, John Varvatos, By Robert James and Piperlime.

If time is limited, or you simply want to browse a plethora of labels in one go, then head to those heady conglomerations known worldwide as department stores. New York has a special blend of alluring draws – in particular don't miss Barneys (p208), Bergdorf Goodman (p208), Macy's (p209) and Bloomingdale's (p208).

NYC Icons

A few stores have cemented their status as NYC legends. This city just wouldn't quite be the same without them. For label hunters, Century 21 (p84) is a Big Apple institution, with wears by D&G, Prada, Marc Jacobs and many others at low prices. Book lovers of the world unite at the Strand (p160), the city's biggest and best bookseller. Run by Hassidic Jews and employing mechanized whimsy, B&H Photo Video (p209) is a mecca for digital and audio geeks. For secondhand clothing, home furnishings and books, good-hearted Housing Works (p162), with many locations around town, is a perennial favorite.

Flea Markets & Vintage Adventures

As much as New Yorkers gravitate towards all that's shiny and new, it can be infinitely fun to riffle through closets of unwanted wares and threads. The most popular flea market is the Brooklyn Flea (p298), housed in all sorts of spaces throughout the year. Another gem is Artists & Fleas (p299), with scores of vendors. The East Village is the city's de facto neighborhood for secondhand and vintage stores – the uniform of the unwavering legion of hipsters.

Sample Sales

While clothing sales happen year-round – usually when seasons change and old stock must be moved out – sample sales are held frequently, mostly in the huge warehouses in the Fashion District of Midtown or in SoHo. While the original sample sale was a way for designers to get rid of one-of-a-kind prototypes that weren't quite up to snuff, most sample sales these days are for high-end labels to get rid of overstock at wonderfully deep discounts. For the latest sample sales, check out **NY Racked** (http://ny.racked.com/sales). Consignment stores are another fine place to look for top (gently used) fashions at reduced prices; label hunters find the Upper East Side prime territory with standouts like Michael's (p225).

NEED TO KNOW

Websites

Racked (www.ny.racked.com) Informative shopping blog with its finger on the pulse.

New York Magazine (www.nymag.com) Trustworthy opinions on the Big Apple's best places to swipe your plastic.

The Glamourai (www.theglamourai.com) Glossy downtown fashion blog that's packed with cutting-edge style ideas.

Ones to Follow

Women's Wear Daily (twitter.com/wwd) The latest fashion news in NYC and beyond from one of the top insider publications.

Andre Leon Talley (www.twitter.com/OfficialALT) Anna Wintour's top fashion editor in the know at *Vogue*.

New York Times (www.twitter.com/NYTFashion) Everything that's happening in the fashion industry.

Opening Hours

In general, most businesses are open from 10am to around 7pm on weekdays and 11am to around 8pm Saturdays. Sundays can be variable – some stores stay closed while others keep weekday hours. Stores tend to stay open later in the neighborhoods downtown. Small boutiques often have variable hours – many open at noon.

Sales Tax

Clothing and footwear that costs less than $110 is exempt from sales tax. For everything else, you'll pay 8.875% retail sales tax on every purchase.

Shopping by Neighborhood

Lower Manhattan & the Financial District (p84) While not a shopping hot spot per se, Lower Manhattan serves up a trickle of gems.

SoHo & Chinatown (p104) West Broadway is a veritable outdoor mall of encyclopedic proportions. It's like the UN of retail.

East Village & the Lower East Side (p128) Hipster treasure trove of vintage wares and design goods.

West Village, Chelsea & the Meatpacking District (p160) Bleecker St, running off Abingdon Sq, is lined with boutiques, with a handful on nearby W 4th St.

Midtown (p208) Epic department stores, global chains and the odd in-the-know treasure – window shoppers unite!

Upper East Side (p224) The country's most expensive boutiques are found along Madison Ave.

Upper West Side & Central Park (p242) Home to some great bookshops (new and used), along with some little boutiques.

Brooklyn (p297) A healthy mix of independent boutiques and thrift stores.

Lonely Planet's Top Choices

Barneys (p208) Serious fashionistas shop at Barneys, well-known for its spot-on collections of in-the-know labels.

Brooklyn Flea (p298) Plenty of vintage furnishings, retro clothing and bric-a-brac.

ABC Carpet & Home (p172) Spread over six floors like a museum, ABC is packed with treasures large and small.

MoMA Design & Book Store (p209) The perfect one-stop shop for coffee-table tomes, art prints and 'Where-did-you-get-that?' homewares.

Idlewild Books (p161) An inspiring place for travelers and daydreamers with titles spanning the globe.

Fishs Eddy (p174) Beautiful pieces for the home at this eye-catching store near Union Square.

Best Fashion Boutiques

Rag & Bone (p104) Beautifully tailored clothes for men and women, in SoHo and elsewhere.

John Varvatos (p129) Rugged but worldly wearables in a former downtown rock club.

Opening Ceremony (p104) Head-turning, cutting-edge threads and kicks for the fashion avant-garde in SoHo.

Best for Women

Shishi (p242) Get a new wardrobe without breaking the bank at this Upper West Side gem.

Verameat (p128) Exquisite jewelry that treads between beauty and whimsy.

MiN New York (p104) Unique perfumes in an apothecary-like setting.

Best for Men

By Robert James (p130) Rugged menswear by a celebrated new local designer.

Nepenthes New York (p209) Japanese collective selling covetable, in-the-know labels.

Odin (p105) Tiny downtown boutique for one-of-a-kind pieces.

Best for Children

Dinosaur Hill (p129) In the East Village, you'll find fun, creative toys, books and music to inspire young minds.

Mary Arnold Toys (p224) A treasure trove of games, toys and other gift ideas.

Books of Wonder (p174) Great gift ideas for kids, plus in-store readings.

Best Vintage Stores

Beacon's Closet (p160) Get a new outfit without breaking the bank at this great vintage shop.

Screaming Mimi's (p162) Lots of appealing clothes from decades past.

Resurrection (p106) Mint-condition pieces from couture labels.

Best Bookshops

Strand Book Store (p160) Hands-down NYC's best used bookstore.

McNally Jackson (p105) Great SoHo spot for book browsing and author readings.

Housing Works Book Store (p106) Used books and a cafe in an atmospheric setting in Nolita.

192 Books (p163) The perfect neighborhood bookshop in Chelsea.

Best Music Stores

Rough Trade (p293) Vinyl is far from dead at this sprawling new music shop and concert space.

A-1 Records (p129) Endless bins of records in the East Village.

Black Gold Records (p297) Rare vinyl (plus coffee and taxidermy).

Best Homewares Design Stores

Shinola (p84) Unusual accessories from a cutting-edge Detroit design house in Tribeca.

A&G Merch (p299) Clever decorating ideas from this artful shop.

Magpie (p242) Ecofriendly curios to feather your nest.

Best NYC Souvenirs

Lower East Side Tenement Museum (p109) Books, jewelry, bags, scarves and more.

New York Public Library (p191) Stationery, tote bags, library lion bookends and literary-minded graphic T-shirts.

Museum of the City of New York (p219) All manner of quality NYC-themed gifts from the eye-catching museum store.

Best Unique Gifts

De Vera (p105) Beautiful glasswares and art objects.

Brooklyn Superhero Supply Co (p299) A quirky collection of gear for budding superheroes with earnings going to a good cause.

Obscura Antiques (p128) A cabinet of curiosities packed with strange and eerie objects.

Bowne Stationers & Co (p85) From vintage New York posters to city-themed stationery at this heritage printer.

Sports & Activities

Although hailing cabs in New York City can feel like a blood sport, and waiting on subway platforms in summer heat is steamier than a sauna, New Yorkers still love to stay active in their spare time. And considering how limited the green spaces are in the city, it's surprising for some visitors just how active the locals can be.

Spectator Sports

BASEBALL

New York is one of the last remaining corners of the USA where baseball reigns supreme over football and basketball. Tickets start at around $15 – a great deal for seeing the home teams playing in their recently opened stadiums. The two Major League Baseball teams play 162 games during the regular season from April to October, when the playoffs begin.

New York Yankees (p258) The Bronx Bombers are the USA's greatest dynasty, with over two dozen World Series championship titles since 1900.

New York Mets (p317) In the National League since 1962, the Mets remain New York's 'new' baseball team, and won the pennant in 2015.

BASKETBALL

Two NBA (National Basketball Association) teams play in New York City. The blue-and-orange New York Knicks (www.nyknicks.com) are loved by New Yorkers, occasional scandal aside, and play their home games at Madison Square Garden (p206). On the other side of the East River, the Brooklyn Nets, formerly the New Jersey Nets, play at the high-tech Barclays Center (p296). The NBA season lasts from October to May or June. New York Liberty, the professional women's basketball team, have played in the finals four times, but have yet to win a championship. The WBNA season runs from May to October, with home games lighting up Madison Square Garden.

FOOTBALL

Most of New York tunes into its NFL (National Football League) teams: the New York Giants (www.giants.com), one of the NFL's oldest teams, with four Super Bowl victories, most recently in 2011, and the New York Jets (www.newyorkjets.com), whose games are always packed.

Both teams play at **MetLife Stadium** (☎201-559-1500, box office 201-559-1300; www.metlifestadium.com; Meadowlands Sports Complex, East Rutherford, NJ; 🚌351 from Port Authority, 🚆NJ Transit from Penn Station to Meadowlands) in New Jersey (from Manhattan take NJ Transit via Seacaucus Junction, $11 return).

Football season runs from August to January or February. The NFL season has 16 regular-season games (most held on Sunday afternoon), then up to three playoff games before the Super Bowl.

HOCKEY

The NHL (National Hockey League) has three franchises in the greater New York area; each team plays three or four games weekly during the season from September to April.

New York Rangers (www.nyrangers.com) Manhattan's favorite hockey squad plays at Madison Square Garden.

New York Islanders (www.newyorkislanders.com) NYC hasn't given much Islander love since the remarkable four-consecutive-year Stanley Cup streak in the '80s. Their stock is on the rise, however, since their move to Brooklyn's Barclays Center (p296) in 2015.

ROLLER DERBY

NYC's only all-female and skater operated roller derby league, **Gotham Girls Roller Derby** (www.gothamgirlsrollerderby.com; tickets $20-50; ⌚Mar-Aug; 👪), has four borough-inspired home teams: the Bronx Gridlock, Brooklyn Bombshells, Manhattan Mayhem and Queens of Pain. These are some of the highest-level players of the sport you're likely to see: their top

NEED TO KNOW

Websites

NYC Parks (www.nycgovparks.org) Details on park services, including free pools and basketball courts, plus borough biking maps.

New York Road Runners Club (www.nyrr.org) Organizes weekend runs and races citywide.

Central Park (www.centralparknyc.org) Lists myriad activities and events held at NYC's best-loved green space.

NYC (www.nycgo.com/sports) Lists all the major sporting events and activities happening in town.

Buying Tickets

With so many teams and overlapping seasons, a game is rarely a day away. Some teams' hotlines or box offices sell tickets directly (available under 'Tickets' on the relevant websites), but most go via Ticketmaster (www.ticketmaster.com). The other major buy/sell outlet is StubHub (www.stubhub.com).

travel team, the All-Stars, are five-time world champions – including a recent undefeated stretch for four years running.

Games are held monthly from March through August at various locations around the city; they're somewhat raucous but family-friendly events. It's a great chance for young girls to see the pint-sized Gotham Girls Junior Derby skaters kick some ass in exhibition matches at half-time. Games often sell out, so buy your ticket in advance if you don't want to chance it at the door.

Running

Central Park's loop roads are best during traffic-free hours, though you'll be in the company of many cyclists and in-line skaters. The 1.6-mile path surrounding the Jacqueline Kennedy Onassis Reservoir (where Jackie O used to run) is for runners and walkers only; access it between 86th and 96th Sts. Running along the Hudson River is a popular path, best from about 30th St to Battery Park in Lower Manhattan. The Upper East Side has a path that runs along FDR Dr and the East River (from 63rd St to 115th St). Brooklyn's Prospect Park has plenty of paths (and a 3-mile loop), while 1.3-mile-long Brooklyn Bridge Park has incredible views of Manhattan. The New York Road Runners Club organizes weekend runs citywide, including the New York City Marathon.

Cycling

NYC has taken enormous strides in making the city more bike-friendly, adding hundreds of miles of bike lanes in recent years. That said, we recommend that the uninitiated stick to the less hectic trails in the parks and along the waterways.

Citi Bike (www.citibikenyc.com) is handy for quick jaunts, but for longer rides, you'll want a proper rental. Biking tours let you cover a lot of ground and are worth considering. Bike the Big Apple (p385) is recommended.

Water Sports

This is an island, after all, and as such there are plenty of opportunities for getting out on the water. The Downtown Boathouse (p85) offers free 20-minute kayaking (including equipment) in the protected embayment of the Hudson River; it also has a Governors Island location. The Manhattan Community Boathouse (p210), located at the 56th St pier, also has free kayaking, plus lessons.

In Central Park, Loeb Boathouse (p244) rents rowboats for romantic trysts, and even fills Venice-style gondolas in summer. For a sailing adventure, hop aboard the Schooner Adirondack (p163) at Chelsea Piers.

Surfers may be surprised to find a tight group of wave worshippers within city limits, at Queens' Rockaway Beach (p307) at 90th St, which is a 75-minute ride on the A train from Midtown.

Street Sports

With all that concrete around, New York has embraced a number of sports and events played directly on the streets themselves. Those with hoop dreams will find pick-up basketball games all over the city, the most famous courts being the West 4th Street Basketball Courts, known as 'the Cage'. Or try Holcombe Rucker Park up in Harlem – that's where many NBA bigshots cut their teeth. You'll also find pick-up games in Tompkins Square Park and Riverside Park.

Lesser-known handball and stickball are also popular in NYC – you'll find one-wall courts in outdoor parks all over the city. For stickball, link up with the Bronx-based Emperors Stickball League (www.stickball.com) to check out its Sunday games during the warmer months.

Lonely Planet's Top Choices

Central Park (p228) The city's playground has rolling hills, forested paths, open green spaces and a beautiful lake.

Chelsea Piers Complex (p163) Every activity imaginable – from kickboxing to ice hockey – under one gigantic roof.

New York Spa Castle (p318) A bathing behemoth with good prices, inspired by ancient Korean traditions of wellness.

Brooklyn Bridge Park (p263) This beautifully designed waterfront green space is Brooklyn's pride and joy.

Prospect Park (p264) Escape the crowds at Brooklyn's gorgeous park, with trails, hills, a canal, lake and meadows.

Spectator Sports

New York Yankees (p258) One of the country's successful baseball teams.

New York Giants (p53) Football powerhouse that, despite the name, plays in New Jersey.

New York Knicks (p206) See the Knicks sink a few three-pointers at Madison Square Garden.

Brooklyn Nets (p296) The hot new NBA team in town and symbol of Brooklyn's resurgence.

Brooklyn Cyclones (p296) See a Minor League Baseball game near Coney Island's boardwalk.

New York Mets (p317) NYC's other baseball team play their games at Citi Field in Queens.

Best Urban Green Spaces

Governors Island (p76) Car-free island just a quick hop from Lower Manhattan or Brooklyn.

Bryant Park (p193) A small appealing oasis amid the skyscrapers of Midtown.

Madison Square Park (p167) A pretty little park between Midtown and downtown.

Fort Greene Park (p269) Lovely little oasis of greenery in Brooklyn that's perfect for a picnic.

Gantry Plaza State Park (p305) A lovely riverside spot to relax in Long Island City, Queens.

Inwood Hill Park (p252) Serene setting of forest and salt marsh in Upper Manhattan.

Best Indoor Activities

Cliffs (p318) Massive climbing center in Long Island City, Queens.

Brooklyn Boulders (p299) Another great spot for rock climbers – this one's in south Brooklyn.

Jivamukti (p174) Lavish yoga center near Union Square.

Area Yoga & Spa (p300) A great choice for yoga in health-minded Cobble Hill.

24 Hour Fitness (p210) Work out at all hours (and many locations) at this full-service fitness center.

MNDFL (p163) Feel rejuvenated following an enriching meditation class.

Best Spas

New York Spa Castle (p318) An enchanting wonderland of waterfalls and steam rooms far out in Queens.

Russian & Turkish Baths (p131) An East Village icon since 1892.

Great Jones Spa (p106) Book a massage, then enjoy the steam room, hot tub and rock sauna.

Best Bowling

Brooklyn Bowl (p300) A Williamsburg classic that's equal parts hipster hangout, concert space and bowling alley.

Chelsea Piers Complex (p163) Take in a bit of bowling, followed by a stroll along the Hudson.

Lucky Strike (p210) A fun night of bowling in Midtown.

Best Out-of-the-Box Activities

Royal Palms (p289) A mecca for shuffleboard lovers, this place has shuffleboard courts, plus food trucks and microbrews.

New York Trapeze School (p163) Channel your inner circus star at this trapeze school.

Gotham Girls Roller Derby (p53) Watch one of the world's elite teams in a hard-hitting sport blazing through various locations.

Jump into the Light VR (p106) Go on daring, high-jinks adventures at this cutting-edge virtual reality arcade.

Best Gardens

Brooklyn Botanic Garden (p272) Japanese gardens, native flora and photogenic springtime cherry blossoms.

New York Botanical Garden (p258) Fifty acres of old-growth forest up in the Bronx.

Cloisters Museum & Gardens (p252) Pretty gardens next to a medieval-esque building.

High Line (p136) Wild plants and towering weeds steal the show.

☆ LGBTIQ New York City

From hand-locked married couples leaving the City Clerk's office wearing matching Bride & Bride hats to a rainbow-hued Empire State Building at Pride, there's no doubt that New York City is one of the world's great gay cities. Indeed, few places come close to matching the breadth and depth of queer offerings here, from cabarets and clubs to festivals and readings.

School Night Shenanigans

Here in the Big Apple, any night of the week is fair game to paint the town rouge – especially for the gay community, who attack the weekday social scene with gusto. Wednesday and Thursday nights roar with a steady stream of parties, and locals love raging on Sunday (especially in summer). While there's undoubtedly much fun to be had on Friday and Saturday nights, weekend parties tend to be more 'bridge and tunnel' – Manhattanites often use these nonwork days to catch up with friends, check out new restaurants and attend house parties.

Promoters

One of best ways to dial into the party hotline is to follow the various goings-on of your favorite promoter. Here are some of ours:

BoiParty (www.boiparty.com)

The Saint at Large (www.saintatlarge.com)

Daniel Nardicio (www.danielnardicio.com)

Josh Wood (www.joshwoodproductions.com)

Spank (www.spankartmag.com)

LGBT by Neighborhood

East Village & Lower East Side Slightly grittier, sweatier, grungier versions of the west side haunts.

Union Square, Flatiron District & Gramercy Hosts a small spillover of gay venues from the East Village, West Village and Chelsea.

West Village, Chelsea & the Meatpacking District Classic bars and clubs in the Village, with a wilting scene in high-rent Chelsea.

Midtown Hell's Kitchen is the city's 21st-century gay epicenter, with a plethora of gay and gay-friendly eateries, bars, clubs and shops.

Brooklyn Multi-neighborhood borough with gays of every ilk, and diverse watering holes peppered throughout.

LGBT RESOURCES

One of the largest centers of its kind in the world, the LGBT Community Center (p160) provides a ton of regional publications about gay events and nightlife, and hosts frequent special events – dance parties, art exhibits, Broadway-caliber performances, readings and political panels. Plus it's home to the National Archive for Lesbian, Gay, Bisexual & Transgender History (accessible to researchers by appointment); a small exhibition space, the Campbell-Soady Gallery; and a cyber center.

Lonely Planet's Top Choices

NYC Pride (p30) Rainbow-clad pomp and circumstance.

Leslie-Lohman Museum of Gay & Lesbian Art (p90) The world's first LGBT art museum.

Industry (p203) One of the best-loved bar-clubs in kicking Hell's Kitchen.

Marie's Crisis (p152) Sing your heart out at this deliriously fun showtunes bar in the West Village.

Duplex (p159) Camp quips, smooth crooners and a riotously fun piano bar define this Village veteran.

Eagle NYC (p155) Love-it-or-loathe-it debauchery and plenty of leather.

Best Places to Stay

Ink48 (p341) Skyline views and a hop away from Hell's Kitchen bars and clubs.

Standard East Village (p336) Crisp, fresh, boutique chic in the funky East Village.

Chelsea Pines Inn (p336) Hollywood posters, diva-moniker rooms and a Chelsea address.

Hotel Gansevoort (p337) Jet-setter cool and a rooftop pool in the Meatpacking District.

Best Old-School Hangouts

Marie's Crisis (p152) One-time hooker hangout turned Village showtune piano bar.

Stonewall Inn (p154) Scene of rioting drag queens during the Stonewall riots of '69.

Julius Bar (p153) The oldest gay in the Village.

Cock (p123) Tongue-in-cheek sleaze in a former gay-punk hangout.

Best for Women

Ginger's (p290) Happy hour specials, karaoke and Sunday bingo pull the girls at Brooklyn's G-Spot.

Cubbyhole (p153) A no-attitude Village veteran with jukebox tunes and chatty regulars.

Henrietta Hudson (p154) A fun, classic dive packed with super-cool rocker chicks.

Best Daytime Scene

Brunch on Ninth Avenue (p142) Pick a sidewalk table and do your bit for Neighborhood Watch, Hell's Kitchen–style.

Shopping in Chelsea (p160) Style-up at Nasty Pig and other queer-centric Chelsea boutiques.

Pier 45 (p139) Butt-hugging trunks and loved-up couples make this a summertime sunbaking staple.

Fire Island (p322) Mingle with the hot and rich at this sand-dune-swept playground just off of Long Island.

Best for Dancing Queens

Industry (p203) As night deepens, this Hell's Kitchen hit turns from buzzing bar to thumping club.

Monster (p154) Cheeky go-go boys and cheekier drag queens keep the punters purring in the basement.

Therapy (p203) Small fun dancefloor when you need a break from the mega clubs.

Best for Weeknights

Therapy (p203) Evening music, drag and showbiz guests give school nights some much-needed razzle dazzle.

Flaming Saddles (p203) Boot-scootin' barmen pouring liquor down your throat – who said weeknights were boring?

Boxers NYC (p172) This sports bar sees dudes tackling the tighter ends on and off the field.

Best Events

NYC Pride (p30) A monthlong celebration in June, with parties, cultural events and the famous march down Fifth Ave.

NewFest (www.newfest.org) NYC's premier queer film fest, with a weeklong program of flicks in October.

MIX New York Queer Experimental Film Festival (www.facebook.com/mixnyc) Four days of avant-garde and political queer cinema in March.

Explore New York City

Lower Manhattan & the Financial District 62
Top Sights 64
Sights 72
Eating 77
Drinking & Nightlife 81
Entertainment 83
Shopping 84
Sports & Activities 85

SoHo & Chinatown ... 86
Top Sights 88
Sights 90
Eating 93
Drinking & Nightlife 100
Entertainment 103
Shopping 104
Sports & Activities 106

East Village & the Lower East Side 107
Top Sights 109
Sights 114
Eating 115
Drinking & Nightlife 120
Entertainment 126
Shopping 128
Sports & Activities 131

West Village, Chelsea & the Meatpacking District 132
Top Sights 134
Sights 139
Eating 142
Drinking & Nightlife 150
Entertainment 155
Shopping 160
Sports & Activities 163

Union Square, the Flatiron District & Gramercy 164
Top Sights 166
Sights 167
Eating 168
Drinking & Nightlife 170
Entertainment 172
Shopping 172
Sports & Activities 174

Midtown 175
Top Sights 177
Sights 190
Eating 194
Drinking & Nightlife 199
Entertainment 203
Shopping 208
Sports & Activities 210

Upper East Side 211
Top Sights 213
Sights 218
Eating 219
Drinking & Nightlife 221
Entertainment 223
Shopping 224
Sports & Activities 225

Upper West Side & Central Park 226
Top Sights 228
Sights 233
Eating 234
Drinking & Nightlife 237
Entertainment 240
Shopping 242
Sports & Activities 243

Harlem & Upper Manhattan 245
Top Sights 247
Sights 249
Eating 253
Drinking & Nightlife 256
Entertainment 257
Shopping 259
Sports & Activities 259

Brooklyn 260
Top Sights 262
Sights 266
Eating 276
Drinking & Nightlife 288
Entertainment 294
Shopping 297
Sports & Activities 299

Queens 301
Top Sights 303
Sights 305
Eating 308
Drinking & Nightlife 316
Entertainment 317
Shopping 318
Sports & Activities 318

Day Trips from New York City 319

Sleeping 330

WTC Transportation Hub (p69)

PIERRE JEAN DURIEU / SHUTTERSTOCK ©

NEW YORK CITY'S TOP SIGHTS

Statue of Liberty 64
Ellis Island 66
National September 11 Memorial 68
One World Trade Center ... 70
Chinatown 88
Lower East Side Tenement Museum 109
New Museum of Contemporary Art 110
St Marks Place 112
Chelsea Market 134
High Line 136
Washington Square Park 138
Union Square 166
Times Square 177
Empire State Building 180
Museum of Modern Art ... 182
Grand Central Terminal ... 184
Rockefeller Center 186
Chrysler Building 187
Roosevelt Island 189
Guggenheim Museum ... 213
Metropolitan Museum of Art 214
Central Park 228
Lincoln Center 232
Cathedral Church of St John the Divine 247
Brooklyn Bridge 262
Brooklyn Bridge Park 263
Prospect Park 264
Brooklyn Museum 265
MoMA PS1 303

Neighborhoods at a Glance

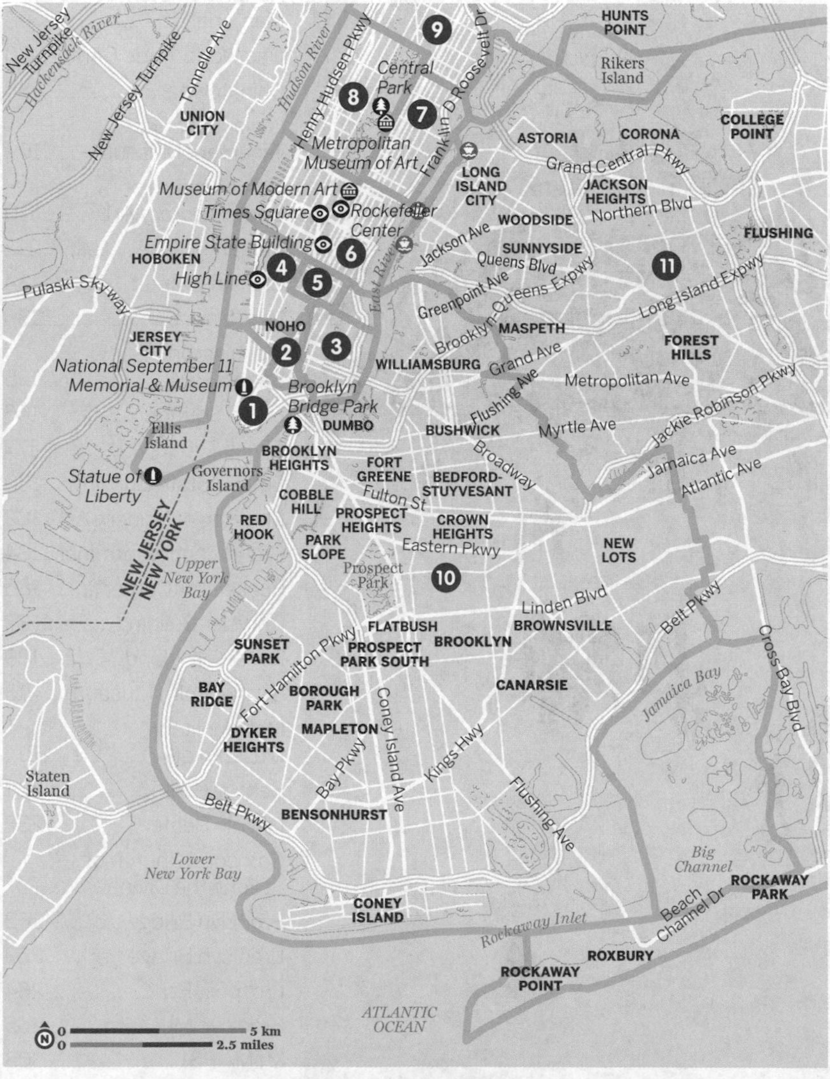

❶ Lower Manhattan & the Financial District p62

Home to icons such as Wall St, the National September 11 Memorial and Museum, and the Statue of Liberty, the southern end of Manhattan pulses with business-like energy during the day before settling into quiet nights. Tribeca, however, continues to hum well after dark with its cache of restaurants and lounges.

❷ SoHo & Chinatown p86

Sacred temples, hawkers peddling bric-a-brac and steam-filled soup-dumpling parlors line the hurried streets of Chinatown, with SoHo next door providing the counterpoint with streamlined thoroughfares and storefronts representing all of the biggest-name brands in the world. Tucked somewhere in between is Little Italy (emphasis on the 'little').

❸ East Village & the Lower East Side p107

Old meets new on every block of this downtown duo – two of the city's hottest 'hoods for nightlife and cheap eats that lure students, bankers and scruffier types alike.

❹ West Village, Chelsea & the Meatpacking District p132

Quaint, twisting streets and well-preserved town houses offer endless options for intimate dining and drinking in the West Village. The Meatpacking District next door has trendy nightlife options galore; further up is Chelsea, home to hundreds of art galleries and a vibrant gay scene.

❺ Union Square, the Flatiron District & Gramercy p164

Though short on sights, there's lots happening on and around Union Square, which bustles with a medley of protesters, buskers and businessfolk. North of there is grassy Madison Square Park, an elegant oasis en route to Midtown. The peaceful streets around Gramercy are mostly residential with a handful of high-end eating and drinking spots.

❻ Midtown p175

This is the home of the NYC found on postcards: Times Square, Empire State Building, Broadway theaters, canyons of skyscrapers, and bustling crowds. The Museum of Modern Art (MoMA), Bryant Park, the grand shops along Fifth Ave and the gay bars of Hell's Kitchen are also here.

❼ Upper East Side p211

High-end boutiques line Madison Ave and mansions run parallel along Fifth Ave, which culminates in an architectural flourish called Museum Mile – one of the most cultured strips in the city, if not the world.

❽ Upper West Side & Central Park p226

New York's antidote to the endless stretches of concrete, Central Park is a verdant escape from honking horns and sunless sidewalks. Lining the park with inspired residential towers, the Upper West Side is home to the Lincoln Center.

❾ Harlem & Upper Manhattan p245

Harlem and Hamilton Heights – a bastion of African American culture – offers global cuisine and a buzzing music scene. Head up to Inwood for leafy park space, or try Morningside Heights to soak up some student life.

❿ Brooklyn p260

These days Brooklyn is shorthand for 'artsy cool' the world over, but there's far more here than hipster stereotypes. This sprawling borough is home to some of NYC's most interesting, historic and culturally diverse neighborhoods, with fantastic dining, drinking, shopping and entertainment options.

⓫ Queens p301

A patchwork of communities, Queens is trailblazer territory for return visitors and locals alike. Gorge at the ethnic delis of Astoria, ogle contemporary art in Long Island City, and ride the surf in Rockaway Beach.

Lower Manhattan & the Financial District

WALL STREET & THE FINANCIAL DISTRICT | NEW YORK HARBOR | BATTERY PARK CITY | EAST RIVER WATERFRONT | CITY HALL & CIVIC CENTER

Neighborhood Top Five

❶ **Statue of Liberty** (p64) Climbing up inside America's most famous statue, peering out from her crown and seeing the world's greatest city spread out before you.

❷ **National September 11 Memorial & Museum** (p68) Reflecting on loss, hope and resilience at New York City's beautifully transformed Ground Zero.

❸ **One World Trade Center** (p70) Zipping up to the top of the Western Hemisphere's tallest building for a knockout panorama of Manhattan and beyond at One World Observatory.

❹ **Staten Island Ferry** (p85) Taking in sunset-blazing skyscrapers while crossing the harbor on one of New York City's fantastic – and free – floating icons.

❺ **Ellis Island** (p66) Exploring the making of modern America at the country's most historically significant, and most personally poignant, point of entry.

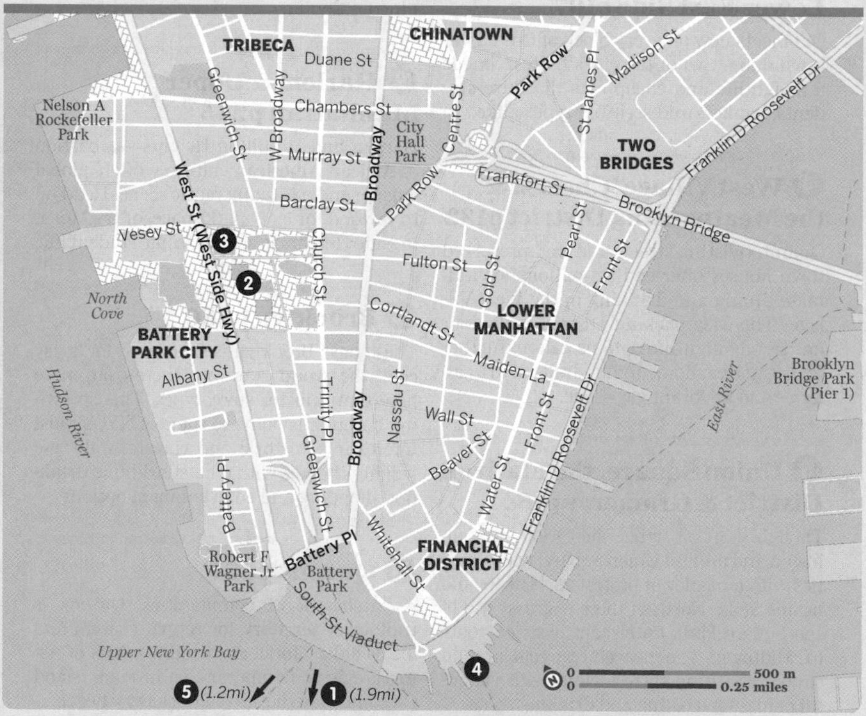

For more detail of this area see Map p406

Explore Lower Manhattan & the Financial District

A little planning will save you a lot of time in Lower Manhattan. Book tickets online to the unmissable Ellis Island (p66) and Statue of Liberty (p64; if you can, catch an early ferry and avoid weekends, especially in summer). You'll need a good four or five hours to explore the two sights properly, and you'll want to bring a picnic lunch (the food on-site is awful). Online ticket purchasing is also highly recommended for both the National September 11 Memorial Museum and the neighboring One World Observatory.

Several museums around the Battery, including the Skyscraper Museum (p76), Museum of Jewish Heritage (p74) and National Museum of the American Indian (p72), can easily fill a half a day. To experience the Financial District's power-broking intensity, go during business hours. But to calmly contemplate the area's Federal homes, Greek Revival temples and early-modern skyscrapers, go after hours.

If the weather is on your side, soak up some rays and river views on Pier 15 at South Street Seaport, or walk across the Brooklyn Bridge for jaw-dropping views of Lower Manhattan. For an evening buzz on any night, head to Tribeca's renowned eateries and drinking dens.

Local Life

➡ **Coffee** Ditch the corporate chains for in-the-know Bluestone Lane (p81) and La Colombe (p83).

➡ **Wine** Swill free vino on Sunday afternoons at Pasanella & Son (p85).

➡ **Shopping** Browse the aisles at Pearl River Mart (p84) for fun gifts with an Asian flair.

➡ **Culture** Catch encore-provoking drama at the Flea Theater (p83).

➡ **Escape** Cycle, relax and eye-up art on the summer oasis that is Governors Island (p76).

Getting There & Away

➡ **Subway** The Financial District is well serviced by subway lines, connecting the area to the rest of Manhattan, Brooklyn, Queens and the Bronx. Fulton St is the main interchange station, connecting the A/C, J/Z, 2/3 and 4/5 lines. The 1 train terminates at South Ferry, from where the Staten Island Ferry departs.

➡ **Bus** From the Staten Island Ferry terminal, useful routes include the M15 (to East Village, Midtown East, Upper East Side and East Harlem) and the M55 and M20 (to Tribeca, West Village, Chelsea and Midtown West).

➡ **Boat** The Staten Island Ferry Terminal (p85) is at the southern end of Whitehall St. Ferries to Governors Island (p76) leave from the adjacent Battery Maritime Building. Services to Liberty and Ellis Islands (p65) depart from nearby Battery Park.

Lonely Planet's Top Tip

Looking for discounted tickets to Broadway shows? Skip the long lines at the TKTS Booth in Times Square for the much quieter **TKTS Booth** (www.tdf.org; cnr Front & John Sts; ⏲11am-6pm Mon-Sat, to 4pm Sun; Ⓢ A/C, 2/3, 4/5, J/Z to Fulton St; R/W to Cortlandt St) at South Street Seaport. Queues usually move a little faster and you can also purchase tickets for next-day matinees (something you can't do at Times Square). The TKTS smartphone app offers real-time listings of what's on sale.

Best Places to Eat

➡ Locanda Verde (p80)

➡ Bâtard (p80)

➡ North End Grill (p81)

➡ Brookfield Place (p80)

➡ Two Hands (p80)

For reviews, see p77.

Best Places to Drink

➡ Dead Rabbit (p81)

➡ Brandy Library (p81)

➡ Smith & Mills (p83)

➡ Bluestone Lane (p81)

For reviews, see p81.

Best Places to Conjure the Past

➡ Ellis Island (p66)

➡ Fraunces Tavern Museum (p72)

➡ South Street Seaport Museum (p76)

➡ African Burial Ground National Monument (p77)

➡ Federal Hall (p73)

For reviews, see p66.

HAYLEON68 / BUDGET TRAVEL ©

TOP SIGHT
STATUE OF LIBERTY

Lady Liberty has been gazing sternly toward 'unenlightened Europe' since 1886. Dubbed the 'Mother of Exiles,' the statue symbolically admonishes the rigid social structures of the old world. 'Give me your tired, your poor, your huddled masses yearning to breathe free, the wretched refuse of your teeming shore,' she declares in Emma Lazarus' famous 1883 poem 'The New Colossus.'

From the Suez to the City

To the surprise of many, France's jumbo-sized gift to America was not originally conceived with the US in mind. Indeed, when sculptor Frédéric-Auguste Bartholdi began planning the piece, his vision was for a colossal sculpture to guard the entrance to the Suez Canal in Egypt, one of France's greatest 19th-century engineering achievements. Bartholdi's ode to Gallic ingenuity would incorporate elements of two of the Seven Wonders of the Ancient World: the Colossus of Rhodes and the lighthouse of Alexandria. Despite its appeal to human vanity, the ambitious monument failed to attract serious funding from either France or Egypt, and Bartholdi's dream seemed destined for the scrap heap. Salvation would come from Bartholdi's friend, Edouard René Lefèbvre de Laboulaye. A French jurist, writer and antislavery activist, de Laboulaye proposed a gift to America as a symbol of the triumph of Republicanism and of the democratic values that underpinned both France and the US. Seeing an opportunity too good to miss, Bartholdi quickly set to work, tweaking his vision and turning his Suez flop into 'Liberty Enlightening the World' – an enviable gift to commemorate America's centennial of the Declaration of Independence.

DID YOU KNOW?

- The Statue of Liberty weighs 225 tons and stretches 305ft and 1in from ground to torch-tip.

PRACTICALITIES

- Map p406, C8
- 212-363-3200, tickets 877-523-9849
- www.nps.gov/stli
- Liberty Island
- adult/child incl Ellis Island $18.50/9, incl crown $21.50/12
- 8:30am-5:30pm, hours vary by season
- to Liberty Island, S 1 to South Ferry or 4/5 to Bowling Green, then

Creating the Lady

The artist spent most of 20 years turning his dream – to create the hollow monument and mount it in the New York Harbor – into reality. Along the way it was hindered by serious financial problems, but was helped in part by the fund-raising efforts of newspaper publisher Joseph Pulitzer. Lending a further hand was poet Emma Lazarus, whose ode to Lady Liberty was part of a fund-raising campaign for the statue's pedestal, designed by American architect Richard Morris Hunt. Bartholdi's work on the statue was also delayed by structural challenges – a problem resolved by the metal framework mastery of railway engineer Gustave Eiffel (yes, of the famous tower). The work of art was finally completed in France in 1884 (a bit off schedule for the centennial). It was shipped to NYC as 350 pieces packed into 214 crates, reassembled over a span of four months and placed on the US-made granite pedestal. Its spectacular October 1886 dedication included New York's first ticker-tape parade and a flotilla of almost 300 vessels. Put under the administration of the National Park Service in 1933, a restoration of the Lady's oxidized copper began in 1984, the same year the monument made it onto the UN's list of World Heritage Sites.

Liberty Today

Folks who reserve their tickets in advance are able to climb the (steep) 393 steps to Lady Liberty's crown, from where the city and harbor views are breathtaking. That said, crown access is extremely limited, and the only way in is to reserve your spot in advance; the further in advance you can do it, the better (a six-month lead time is allowed). Each customer may only reserve a maximum of four crown tickets, and children must be at least 4ft tall to access the crown.

If you miss out on crown tickets, you may have better luck with tickets to the pedestal, which also offers commanding views. Like crown tickets, pedestal tickets are limited and should be reserved in advance, either online or by phone. Only crown and pedestal ticket holders have access to the Statue of Liberty museum in the pedestal.

If you don't have crown or pedestal tickets, don't fret. All ferry tickets to Liberty Island offer basic access to the grounds, including guided ranger tours or self-guided audio tours. The grounds also host a gift shop and cafeteria. (Tip: bring your own nibbles and enjoy them by the water with the Manhattan skyline stretched out before you.)

TOP TIP

If you want to see both the Statue of Liberty and Ellis Island, you'll have to get a **ferry** (Map p406; ☎877-523-9849; www.statuecruises.com; adult/child from $18.50/9; ⏱departures 8:30am-4pm; Ⓢ4/5 to Bowling Green; R/W to Whitehall St; 1 to South Ferry) before 2pm. Security screening at the ferry terminal is airport-style – leave the pocketknives at home – and can take up to 90 minutes in high season.

Advance ticket purchase is strongly recommended: it guarantees you a specific time to visit, plus allows you to skip the insanely long queues of people who didn't plan ahead.

SYMBOLS

The book of law in the statue's left hand is inscribed with July IV MDCCLXXVI (4 July 1776), the date of American Independence. The rays on her crown represent the seven seas and continents; the 25 windows adorning it symbolize gemstones. At her feet, chains and a broken shackle indicate her status as free from oppression and servitude. The torch is a 1986 replacement of the original, which is now housed at the on-site museum.

TOP SIGHT
ELLIS ISLAND

Ellis Island is America's most famous and historically important gateway – where old-world despair met new-world promise. Between 1892 and 1924, over 12 million immigrants passed through this processing station, dreams in tow. An estimated 40% of Americans today have at least one ancestor who was processed here, confirming this tiny harbor island's major role in the making of modern America.

Restoration

After a $160 million restoration, the island's Main Building was reopened to the public as the Ellis Island Immigration Museum in 1990. Now anybody who rides the ferry to the island can experience a cleaned-up, modern version of the historic new-arrival experience, with the museum's interactive exhibits paying homage to the hope, jubilation and sometimes bitter disappointment of the millions who came here in search of a new beginning. Among them were Hungarian Erik Weisz (Harry Houdini), Italian Rodolfo Guglielmi (Rudolph Valentino) and Brit Archibald Alexander Leach (Cary Grant).

Immigration Museum Exhibits

The museum's exhibits are spread over three levels. To get the most out of your visit, opt for the 50-minute self-guided audio tour (free with ferry ticket, available from the museum lobby). Featuring narratives from a number of sources, including historians, architects and the immigrants themselves, the tour brings to life the museum's hefty collection of personal objects, official documents, photographs and film footage. It's an evocative experience to witness personal memories – both good and bad – in the very halls and corridors in which they occurred.

The collection itself is divided into a number of permanent and temporary exhibitions. If you're very short on time, skip *Journeys: The Peopling of America 1550–1890* on the 1st floor and focus on the 2nd floor, where you'll find the two most fascinating exhibitions. *Through America's Gate* examines the step-by-step process faced by the newly arrived (including the chalk-marking of those suspected of illness, a wince-inducing eye examination, and 29 questions) in the beautiful, vaulted Registry Room, while *Peak Immigration Years* explores the motives behind the immigrants' journeys and the challenges they faced once free to begin their new American lives. Particularly interesting is the collection of old photographs, which offers intimate glimpses into the daily lives of these courageous new Americans.

For a history of the rise, fall and resurrection of the building itself, make time for the *Restoring a Landmark* exhibition on the 3rd floor; its tableaux of trashed desks, chairs and other abandoned possessions are strangely haunting. Best of all, the audio tour offers optional, in-depth coverage for those wanting to delve deeper into the collections and the island's history. If you don't feel like opting for the audio tour, you can always pick up one of the phones in each display area and listen to the recorded, affecting memories of real Ellis Island immigrants, taped in the 1980s. Another option is the free, 45-minute guided tour with a park ranger. If booked three weeks in advance by phone, the tour is also available in American Sign Language.

DON'T MISS

- Immigration Museum exhibits
- Main Building architecture
- American Immigrant Wall of Honor & Fort Gibson ruins

PRACTICALITIES

- Map p406, B8
- 212-363-3200, tickets 877-523-9849
- www.nps.gov/elis
- Ellis Island
- ferry incl Statue of Liberty adult/child $18.50/9
- 8:30am-6pm, hours vary by season
- to Ellis Island, S 1 to South Ferry or 4/5 to Bowling Green, then

Main Building Architecture

With the Main Building, architects Edward Lippincott Tilton and William A Boring created a suitably impressive and imposing 'prologue' to America. The designing duo won the contract after the original wooden building burnt down in 1897. Having attended the École des Beaux-Arts in Paris, it's not surprising that they opted for a beaux-arts aesthetic for the project. The building evokes a grand train station, with majestic triple-arched entrances, decorative Flemish bond brickwork, and granite quoins (cornerstones) and belvederes. Inside, it's the 338ft-long Registry Room (also known as the Great Hall) on the 2nd floor that takes the breath away. Under its beautiful vaulted ceiling, the newly arrived lined up to have their documents checked (people such as polygamists, paupers, criminals and anarchists were turned back). The original plaster ceiling was severely damaged by an explosion of munition barges at nearby Black Tom Wharf. It was a blessing in disguise – the rebuilt version was adorned with striking, herringbone-patterned tiles by Rafael Guastavino. The Catalan-born engineer is also behind the beautiful tiled ceiling at the Grand Central Oyster Bar & Restaurant (p197) at Grand Central Terminal.

American Immigrant Wall of Honor & Fort Gibson Ruins

Accessible from the 1st-floor *Journeys: The Peopling of America 1550–1890* exhibit is the outdoor American Immigrant Wall of Honor, inscribed with the names of over 700,000 immigrants. Believed to be the world's longest wall of names, it's a fund-raising project, allowing any American to have an immigrant relative's name recorded for the cost of a donation. Construction of the wall in the 1990s uncovered the remains of the island's original structure, Fort Gibson; you can see the ruins at the southwestern corner of the memorial. Built in 1808, the fortification was part of a harbor-defense system against the British that also included Castle Clinton in Battery Park and Castle Williams on Governors Island. During this time, Ellis Island measured a modest 3.3 acres of sand and slush – between 1892 and 1934, the island expanded dramatically thanks to landfill brought in from the ballast of ships and construction of the city's subway system.

AN IRISH DEBUT

Ellis Island's very first immigrant was 15-year-old Anna 'Annie' Moore. After a 12-day journey in steerage from County Cork, Ireland, Annie arrived on January 1, 1892, accompanied by her brothers Phillip and Anthony; the three were headed to America to join their parents, who had migrated to New York City four years earlier. She later married German immigrant Joseph Augustus Schayer and gave birth to at least 11 children, only five of whom survived. Annie died on December 6, 1924, and was laid to rest at Calvary Cemetery, Queens.

HOSPITAL OF ALL NATIONS

At the turn of the 20th century, the since-defunct hospital on Ellis Island was one of the world's largest. Consisting of 22 buildings and dubbed the 'Hospital of All Nations,' it was America's front line in the fight against 'imported' diseases. The institution's fascinating history is vividly relayed in writer/producer Lorie Conway's documentary and accompanying book *Forgotten Ellis Island.* A guided 'Hard Hat Tour' ($53.50) of the unrestored hospital can be booked when you reserve your ticket online.

YASSILHEM / SHUTTERSTOCK ©

TOP SIGHT
NATIONAL SEPTEMBER 11 MEMORIAL

The National September 11 Memorial and Museum is a dignified tribute to the victims of the worst terrorist attack to occur on American soil. Titled *Reflecting Absence*, the memorial's two massive reflecting pools feature the names of the thousands who lost their lives. Beside them stands the Memorial Museum, a striking, solemn space documenting that fateful fall day in 2001.

DON'T MISS

- Reflecting Pools
- Memorial Museum
- Santiago Calatrava's Oculus

PRACTICALITIES

- www.911memorial.org
- 180 Greenwich St
- admission free
- 7:30am-9pm
- S E to World Trade Center; R/W to Cortlandt St; 2/3 to Park Pl

Reflecting Pools

Surrounded by a plaza planted with more than 400 swamp white oak trees, the 9/11 Memorial's reflecting pools occupy the original footprints of the ill-fated Twin Towers. From their rim, a steady cascade of water pours 30ft down toward a central void. The flow of the water is richly symbolic, beginning as thousands of smaller streams, merging into a massive torrent of collective confusion, and ending with a slow journey toward an abyss. Bronze panels frame the pools, inscribed with the names of those who died in the terrorist attacks of September 11, 2001, and in the World Trade Center car bombing on February 26, 1993. Designed by Michael Arad and Peter Walker, the pools are both striking and deeply poignant.

Memorial Museum

The contemplative energy of the monument is further enhanced by the **National September 11 Memorial Museum** (Map p406; www.911memorial.org/museum; museum adult/child $24/15, 5-8pm Tue free; 9am-8pm Sun-Thu, to 9pm Fri & Sat, last entry 2hr before close). Standing between the reflective pools, the museum's glass entrance pavilion eerily evokes a toppled tower. Inside the entrance, an escalator leads down to the museum's subterranean main lobby. On the descent, visitors stand in the shadow of two steel tridents, originally embedded in the bedrock at the base of the North Tower. Each over 80ft tall and 50 tons in weight, they once provided the structural support that allowed the towers to soar over 1360ft into the sky. They remained standing in the subsequent sea of rubble, becoming immediate symbols of resilience.

The tridents are two of over 10,300 objects in the museum's collection. Among these are the Vesey Street Stairs. Dubbed the 'Survivors Stairs,' they allowed hundreds of workers to flee the WTC site on the morning of 9/11. At the bottom of these stairs is the moving In Memoriam gallery, its walls lined with the photographs and names of those who perished. Interactive touch screens and a central reflection room shed light on the victims' lives. Their humanity is further fleshed out by the numerous personal effects on display. Among these is a dust-covered wallet belonging to Robert Joseph Gschaar, an insurance underwriter working on level 92 of the South Tower. The wallet's contents include a photograph of Gschaar's wife, Myrta, and a $2 bill, given to Myrta by Gschaar as a symbol of their second chance at happiness.

Around the corner from the In Memoriam gallery is the New York City Fire Department's Engine Company 21. One of the largest artifacts on display, its burnt-out cab is testament to the inferno faced by those at the scene. The fire engine stands at the entrance to the museum's main Historical Exhibition. Divided into three sections – *Events of the Day, Before 9/11* and *After 9/11* – its collection of videos, real-time audio recordings, images, objects and testimonies provide a rich, meditative exploration of the tragedy, the events that preceded it (including the WTC bombing of 1993), and the stories of grief, resilience and hope that followed.

The *Historical Exhibition* spills into the monumental Foundation Hall, flanked by a massive section of the original slurry wall, built to hold back the waters of the Hudson River during the towers' construction. It's also home to the last steel column removed during the clean-up, adorned with the messages and mementos of recovery workers, first-responders and loved ones of the victims.

ANGEL OF 9/11

One of the Memorial Museum's most curious (and famous) artifacts is the so-called 'Angel of 9/11,' the eerie outline of a woman's anguished face on a twisted girder believed to originate from the point where American Airlines Flight 11 slammed into the North Tower. (Experts have a more prosaic explanation: natural corrosion and sheer coincidence.)

CALATRAVA ARCHITECTURE

The image of a flying dove allegedly inspired Santiago Calatrava's dramatic white Oculus above the new WTC Transportation Hub. Made from 36,500 tons of steel, the arresting structure streams natural light into the $3.9 billion transit center, which serves 250,000 train commuters daily. A whopping two-and-a-half times bigger than Grand Central Terminal, it also features multiple levels of retail and dining space. Every year on September 11, the central skylight is opened for 102 minutes, the length of time from the first attack to the collapse of the second tower.

KEV LLEWELLYN / SHUTTERSTOCK ©

TOP SIGHT
ONE WORLD TRADE CENTER

Filling what was a sore and glaring gap in the Lower Manhattan skyline, One World Trade Center symbolizes rebirth, determination and resilience. More than just another super-tall skyscraper, it's a richly symbolic giant, well aware of the past yet firmly focused on the future. For lovers of New York, it's also the hot new stop for dizzying, unforgettable urban views.

The Building

Leaping up from the northwest corner of the World Trade Center site, the 104-floor tower is architect David M Childs' redesign of Daniel Libeskind's original 2002 concept. Not only the loftiest building in America, this tapered giant is currently the tallest building in the Western Hemisphere – not to mention the fourth tallest in the world by pinnacle height. The tower soars skywards with chamfered edges, resulting in a series of isosceles triangles that, seen from the building's base, reach to infinity. Crowning the structure is a 408ft cabled-stayed spire. Co-designed by sculptor Kenneth Snelson, it brings the building's total height to 1776ft, a symbolic reference to the year of American independence.

Indeed, symbolism feeds several aspects of the building: the tower's footprint is equal to those of the original Twin Towers, while the observation decks match the heights of those in the old complex. Unlike the original towers, however, One WTC was built with a whole new level of safety in mind, its precautionary features including a 200ft-high blast-resistant base (clad in over 2000 pieces of glimmering prismatic glass) and 39.4in-thick concrete walls encasing all elevators, stairwells, and communication and safety systems. One thing not foreseen by the architects and engineers, though, was the antenna's noisy

DON'T MISS

- A photo from the base looking up
- Sky Pod elevators
- Observatory views

PRACTICALITIES

- One WTC
- Map p406, B4
- cnr West & Vesey Sts
- S E to World Trade Center; 2/3 to Park Pl; A/C, J/Z, 4/5 to Fulton St; R/W to Cortlandt St

disposition: the strong winds that race through its lattice design producing a haunting, howling sound known to keep some locals up at night.

One World Observatory

Not one to downplay its assets, the skyscraper is home to **One World Observatory** (Map p406; ☎844-696-1776; www.oneworldobservatory.com; cnr West & Vesey Sts; adult/child $34/28; ⊙9am-8pm, last ticket sold at 7:15pm; Ⓢ E to World Trade Center; 2/3 to Park Pl; A/C, J/Z, 4/5 to Fulton St; R/W to Cortlandt St), the city's loftiest observation deck. While the observatory spans levels 100 to 102, the experience begins at the ground-floor Global Welcome Center, where an electronic world map highlights the many homelands of the building's visitors (with data relayed from ticket scans). The bitter bickering that plagued much of the project's development is all but forgotten in the adjoining *Voices* exhibition, where architects and construction workers wax lyrically about the tower's formation on 144 video screens.

After a quick rundown of the site's geology, the real thrills begin as you step inside one of five Sky Pod elevators, among the fastest in the world. As the elevators begin their 1250ft skyward journey, LED wall panels kick into action. Suddenly you're in a veritable time machine, watching Manhattan's evolution from forested island to teeming concrete jungle. Forty-seven seconds (and 500 years) later, you're on level 102, where another short presentation ends with a spectacular reveal.

Skip the overpriced eateries on level 101 and continue down to the real highlight: level 100. Waiting for you is an epic, 360-degree panorama guaranteed to keep you busy searching for landmarks, from the Brooklyn and Manhattan Bridges to Lady Liberty and the Woolworth, Empire State and Chrysler buildings. If you need a hand, interactive mobile tablets programmed in eight languages are available for hire ($15). As expected, the view is extraordinary – try to go on a clear day – taking in all five boroughs and three adjoining states. For a close-up view of the Midtown skyscrapers, however, you're better off scaling the Empire State Building or the Rockefeller Center's Top of the Rock.

FAMOUS RESIDENTS

VIP buildings demand VIP clients, and One World Trade Center delivers. Its most famous tenant is Condé Nast Publications, which made the move from 4 Times Square in 2014. The company's portfolio includes high-end magazines like *Vogue*, *Vanity Fair*, *GQ*, *Architectural Digest* and – aptly enough – *The New Yorker*. As to be expected, the company's headquarters are nothing short of fabulous, complete with dramatic spiral staircase and a glamorous cafeteria with gourmet bites and a million-dollar view.

TICKETS & TIPS

Prepurchase your tickets online (www.oneworldobservatory.com/tickets) to avoid the longest queues. Tickets purchased online using a smartphone don't require a printout; simply take a screenshot of your ticket (including the bar code) and scan it on arrival.

When purchasing your ticket, you'll select a specific visiting time; head in by 9:15am for short waiting periods and thin crowds. Sunset is the busiest time.

Whatever the hour, always arrive 15 minutes before your scheduled visiting time to avoid delays at security.

SIGHTS

Wall Street & the Financial District

Most of Lower Manhattan's must-see sights are in the Financial District, among them Colonial-era New York churches and the site of George Washington's first presidential inauguration. Modern history is documented in a string of commendable museums, including the unmissable National September 11 Memorial Museum.

NATIONAL SEPTEMBER 11 MEMORIAL MONUMENT

See p68.

NATIONAL SEPTEMBER 11 MEMORIAL MUSEUM MUSEUM

See p68.

ONE WORLD TRADE CENTER NOTABLE BUILDING

See p70.

ONE WORLD OBSERVATORY VIEWPOINT

See p70.

NATIONAL MUSEUM OF THE AMERICAN INDIAN MUSEUM

Map p406 (212-514-3700; www.nmai.si.edu; 1 Bowling Green; 10am-5pm Fri-Wed, to 8pm Thu; S 4/5 to Bowling Green; R/W to Whitehall St) FREE An affiliate of the Smithsonian Institution, this elegant tribute to Native American culture is set in Cass Gilbert's spectacular 1907 **Custom House**, one of NYC's finest beaux-arts buildings. Beyond a vast elliptical rotunda, sleek galleries play host to changing exhibitions documenting Native American art, culture, life and beliefs. The museum's permanent collection includes stunning decorative arts, textiles and ceremonial objects that document the diverse native cultures across the Americas.

The four giant female sculptures outside the building are the work of **Daniel Chester French**, who would go on to sculpt the seated Abraham Lincoln at Lincoln Memorial in Washington, DC. Representing (from left to right) Asia, North America, Europe and Africa, the figures offer a revealing look at America's worldview at the beginning of the 20th century.

The museum also hosts a range of cultural programs, including dance and music performances, readings for children, craft demonstrations, films and workshops. The museum shop is well-stocked with Native American jewelry, books, CDs and crafts.

FRAUNCES TAVERN MUSEUM MUSEUM

Map p406 (212-425-1778; www.fraunces tavernmuseum.org; 54 Pearl St, btwn Broad St & Coenties Slip; adult/6-18yr/under 6yr $7/4/free; noon-5pm Mon-Fri, 11am-5pm Sat & Sun; S J/Z to Broad St; 4/5 to Bowling Green; R/W to Whitehall St; 1 to South Ferry) Combining five early-18th-century structures, this unique museum/restaurant/bar pays homage to the nation-shaping events of 1783, the momentous year in which the British officially relinquished control of New York following the end of the Revolutionary War, and General George Washington gave a farewell speech to the officers of the Continental Army in the 2nd-floor dining room before returning to his home at Mt Vernon.

The site was originally built in the early 1720s as a tony residence for merchant Stephen De Lancey's family; barkeeper Samuel Fraunces purchased it in 1762 and turned it into a tavern called the Queen's Head. After the war, when New York was the nation's first capital, the space was used by the Departments of War, Treasury and Foreign Affairs. The tavern was closed and fell into disuse in the 19th century, then was damaged during several massive fires that destroyed most colonial buildings and Dutch-built structures in the area. In 1904, a historical society named the Sons of the Revolution bought the building and returned it to an approximation of its colonial-era look – an act believed to be the first major attempt at historical preservation in the USA.

TRINITY CHURCH CHURCH

Map p406 (212-602-0800; www.trinitywall street.org; 75 Broadway, at Wall St; 7am-6pm; S 1, R/W to Rector St; 2/3, 4/5 to Wall St) New York City's tallest building upon completion in 1846, Trinity Church features a 280ft-high bell tower and a richly colored stained-glass window over the altar. Famous residents of its serene cemetery include Founding Father and first Secretary of the Treasury (and Broadway superstar) Alexander Hamilton, while its excellent music series include Concerts at One (1pm Thursdays) and magnificent choir concerts, including an annual December rendition of Handel's *Messiah*.

The original Anglican parish church was founded by King William III in 1697 and once presided over several constituent chapels, including St Paul's Chapel (p73). Its huge landholdings in Lower Manhattan made it the country's wealthiest and most influential church throughout the 18th century. It was destroyed by fire in 1776; its second incarnation was demolished in 1839. The third and current church, designed by English architect Richard Upjohn, helped launch the picturesque neo-Gothic movement in America.

ST PAUL'S CHAPEL CHURCH

Map p406 (☎212-602-0800; www.trinitywallstreet.org; 209 Broadway, at Fulton St; ⏲10am-6pm Mon-Sat, 7am-6pm Sun, churchyard closes 4pm; **S**A/C, J/Z, 2/3, 4/5 to Fulton St; R/W to Cortlandt St; E to Chambers St) After his inauguration in 1789, George Washington worshipped at this classic revival brownstone chapel, which found new fame in the aftermath of September 11. Although the World Trade Center was destroyed just a block away, St Paul's sustained only one broken pane of glass, earning it the nickname, 'The Little Chapel That Stood.' In the days following, it offered round-the-clock refuge, spiritual and emotional support and food service to first responders and rescue workers.

The austere white interior stands in contrast to the gilded 'Glory' altarpiece, which was designed by Pierre L'Enfant, who would later design the master street plan for Washington, DC. Displays along the sides tell the story of St Paul's in NYC history, while the small Chapel of Remembrance at the back displays touching artifacts from September 11, including a cross created from steel debris found in the destruction.

A major renovation was completed in 2016, which also marked the 250th anniversary of the church's life. The cemetery behind the church (which closes at 4pm) is the final resting place for a number of notable Revolutionary-era Americans.

MUSEUM OF AMERICAN FINANCE MUSEUM

Map p406 (☎212-908-4110; www.moaf.org; 48 Wall St, btwn Pearl & William Sts; adult/child $8/free; ⏲10am-4pm Tue-Sat; **S**2/3, 4/5 to Wall St) Money makes this interactive museum go round. It focuses on historic moments in American financial history, and its permanent collections include rare historic currency (including Confederate currency used by America's southern states during the Civil War), stock and bond certificates from the Gilded Age, the oldest known photograph of Wall St and a stock ticker from circa 1875.

Once the headquarters for the Bank of New York, the building itself is a lavish spectacle, with 30ft ceilings, Palladian windows, a majestic staircase to the mezzanine, glass chandeliers, and murals depicting historic scenes of banking and commerce.

FEDERAL RESERVE BANK OF NEW YORK NOTABLE BUILDING

Map p406 (☎212-720-6130; www.newyorkfed.org; 33 Liberty St, at Nassau St, entrance at 44 Maiden Lane; reservation required; ⏲guided tours 1pm & 2pm Mon-Fri; **S**A/C, J/Z, 2/3, 4/5 to Fulton St) FREE The best reason to visit the Federal Reserve Bank is the chance to (briefly) ogle at its high-security vault – more than 10,000 tons of gold reserves reside here, 80ft below ground. You'll only see a small part of that fortune, but signing on to a free tour (the only way down; book several months ahead) is worth the effort.

While you don't need to join a guided tour to browse the bank's interactive museum, which delves into the bank's history and research, you will still need to book a time online. Bring your driver's license or passport.

FEDERAL HALL MUSEUM

Map p406 (☎212-825-6990; www.nps.gov/feha; 26 Wall St; ⏲9am-5pm Mon-Fri year-round, plus 9am-5pm Sat Jul-Oct; **S**J/Z to Broad St; 2/3, 4/5 to Wall St) FREE A Greek Revival masterpiece, Federal Hall houses a museum dedicated to postcolonial New York. Themes include George Washington's inauguration, Alexander Hamilton's relationship with the city, and the struggles of John Peter Zenger, a printer who on this site in 1734 was jailed, tried and eventually acquitted of libel for exposing government corruption in his newspaper. There's also a visitor information hall with city maps and brochures.

Distinguished by a huge statue of George Washington out front, the building itself stands on the site of New York's second City Hall, completed in 1703. The building was remodeled by French engineer Pierre L'Enfant in 1788 and renamed Federal Hall; George Washington took his oath of office as the first US president on its balcony on April 30, 1789. (The museum's artifacts include the very slab of stone on which Washington stood.) After that structure's demolition in 1812, the current building rose in its place between 1834 and 1842, serving as the US Customs House until 1862.

Free 30-minute tours are offered each day at 10am, 1pm, 2pm and 3pm. Call ahead to inquire about tour times and Saturday opening hours, as these are sometimes reduced due to staffing constraints.

ARTISTS SPACE GALLERY

Map p406 (☎212-226-3970; www.artistsspace.org; 55 Walker St, btwn Broadway & Church St, SoHo; ⏲hours vary; Ⓢ A/C/E, N/Q/R, 1 to Canal St) FREE One of the first alternative spaces in New York, Artists Space made its debut in 1972. Its mission was to support contemporary artists working in the visual arts, from video, electronic media and performance, to architecture and design. Now in a new location, more than 40 years on, it remains a solid choice for those seeking crisp, provocative and experimental creativity. Check the website for upcoming exhibitions.

USCGC LILAC SHIP

Map p406 (www.lilacpreservationproject.org; Pier 25, at N Moore St; ⏲4-7pm Thu, 2-7pm Sat & Sun late May-Oct; 👪; Ⓢ 1 to Franklin St; A/C/E to Canal St) FREE Lovers of all things maritime can step aboard the US Coast Guard Cutter *Lilac,* the last existing steam-powered lighthouse tender in the US, which once brought supplies to lighthouses and their keepers before American lighthouses were automated. Launched in 1933, *Lilac* was decommissioned in 1972 and since 2011 has been berthed at Pier 25, undergoing restoration work and serving as an educational and community resource.

BOWLING GREEN PARK

Map p406 (cnr Broadway & State St; Ⓢ 4/5 to Bowling Green; R/W to Whitehall St) New York's oldest – and possibly tiniest – public park is purportedly the spot where Dutch settler Peter Minuit paid Native Americans the equivalent of $24 to purchase Manhattan Island. At its northern edge stands Arturo Di Modica's 7000lb bronze *Charging Bull,* placed here permanently after it mysteriously appeared in front of the New York Stock Exchange in 1989, two years after a market crash.

Attention and controversy returned to the park in March, 2017, when a financial firm installed *Fearless Girl,* a statue posed as if in defiant opposition to the bull. Some cheered it as a potent symbol of feminism or anti-capitalism. Di Modica, however, decried it as a warping and misreading of his artwork and called for Fearless Girl's immediate removal. Public wrangling and negotiations followed and her survival was extended to 2018.

New York Harbor

STATUE OF LIBERTY MONUMENT

See p64.

ELLIS ISLAND LANDMARK

See p66.

Battery Park City

★**MUSEUM OF JEWISH HERITAGE** MUSEUM

Map p406 (☎646-437-4202; www.mjhnyc.org; 36 Battery Pl; adult/child $12/free, 4-8pm Wed free; ⏲10am-6pm Sun-Tue, to 8pm Wed & Thu, to 5pm Fri mid-Mar–mid-Nov, to 3pm Fri rest of year, closed Sat; 👪; Ⓢ 4/5 to Bowling Green; R/W to Whitehall St) An evocative waterfront museum exploring all aspects of modern Jewish identity and culture, from religious traditions to artistic accomplishments. The museum's core exhibition includes a detailed exploration of the Holocaust, with personal artifacts, photographs and documentary films providing a personal, moving experience. Outdoors is the **Garden of Stones** installation. Created by artist Andy Goldsworthy and dedicated to those who lost loved ones in the Holocaust, its 18 boulders form a narrow pathway for contemplating the fragility of life.

The building itself consists of six sides and three tiers to symbolize the Star of David and the six million Jews who perished in WWII. Exhibitions aside, the venue also hosts films, music concerts, ongoing lecture series and special holiday performances. Frequent, free workshops for families with children are also on offer, while the on-site, kosher cafe serves light food, including lox (smoked salmon) in more flavors than you knew existed.

BATTERY PARK PARK

Map p406 (www.nycgovparks.org; Broadway, at Battery Pl; ⏲sunrise-1am; Ⓢ 4/5 to Bowling Green; R/W to Whitehall St; 1 to South Ferry) Skirting the southern edge of Manhattan, this 12-acre oasis lures with public artworks, meandering walkways and perennial gardens. Its memorials include a Holocaust Memorial and the Irish Hunger Memorial. It was on this very part of the island that the Dutch settled in 1623. And it was right here that the first 'battery' of cannons was erected to defend the fledgling settlement of New Amsterdam. You'll also find historic **Castle Clinton** (Map p406; ☎212-344-7220; www.nps.gov/cacl/index.

WORTH A DETOUR

STATEN ISLAND

The land of Shaolin (according to the Wu Tang Clan), of velour sweatsuits, homes of clapboard and aluminum siding and three cast members of MTV's *Jersey Shore*, Staten Island feels a world away from Manhattan. If not for its namesake ferry, which docks in downtown St George, it would be mostly forgotten. Unfashionably suburban, it's not without its drawcards, especially cultural and gustatory ones. In the summer, there are also fun Minor League Baseball games at the waterfront **County Bank Ballpark** (718-720-9265; www.siyanks.com; Richmond County Bank Ballpark, 75 Richmond Tce; tickets $12; ticket office 9am-5pm Mon-Fri; Staten Island).

Snug Harbor Cultural Center & Botanical Garden (718-425-3504; www.snug-harbor.org; 1000 Richmond Tce; galleries & Chinese Scholar's Garden adult/child $8/free, grounds free; grounds dawn-dusk daily, Chinese Scholar's Garden 10am-5pm Wed-Sun, 11am-4pm Fri-Sun Nov-Mar, Newhouse Center for Contemporary Art 10am-5pm Wed-Sun, Noble Maritime Collection 1-5pm Thu-Sun, Staten Island Museum 11am-5pm Tue-Fri, 10am-5pm Sat & Sun; S40 to Snug Harbor), Staten Island's top sight, offers a tranquil sweep of gardens, heritage buildings and gallery spaces. Highlights include the artwork-packed Staten Island Museum, an ancient-style Chinese Scholar's Garden, a Tuscan Garden modeled on Florence's Villa Gamberaia, and a fascinating maritime museum. It's 2 miles west of the ferry terminal; catch bus S40, which stops by the main entrance.

In the center of Staten Island, 100-acre **Historic Richmond Town** (718-351-1611; www.historicrichmondtown.org; 441 Clarke Ave; adult/child $8/5, Fri free; 1-5pm Wed-Sun, from noon Jun-Aug; S74 to Arthur Kill Rd & Clarke Ave) includes famous buildings like the two-story, 300-year-old, redwood Voorlezer's House, the US's oldest schoolhouse. Guides lead tours (included with admission) at 1:30pm on weekdays and at 1:30pm and 3:30pm on weekends. The site is about 40 minutes from the ferry by bus.

Alice Austen was the first woman of note on the American photography scene and her harborside **home** (718-816-4506; www.aliceausten.org; 2 Hylan Blvd, at Edgewater St; suggested donation $3; 11am-5pm Tue-Sun Mar-Dec, by appointment only Jan & Feb; S51 to Hylan Blvd & Bay St) explores both her life and artistic legacy. The house is just north of the Verrazano–Narrows Bridge, about a 15-minute, 2.4-mile bus ride from the ferry.

A short walk from the ferry terminal, **Enoteca Maria** (718-447-2777; www.enotecamaria.com; 27 Hyatt St; mains $16-25; noon-11pm Wed-Fri, from 3pm Sat & Sun; ; Staten Island) is a delightful, warmly lit Italian eatery that serves up exquisite old-world recipes made with care by sweet but deeply knowledgeable *nonne* (Italian grandmothers). Reservations are essential.

For fair-trade coffee, hummus sandwiches, used books and a side of social activism, don't miss **Everything Goes Book Café & Neighborhood Stage** (718-447-8256; www.etgstores.com/bookcafe; 208 Bay St; sandwiches $4-7; noon-9pm Tue-Thu, to 10pm Fri & Sat, noon-5pm Sun; ; Staten Island). From the ferry terminal, walk half a mile south along Bay St to get there.

Visiting **Lakruwana** (347-857-6619; http://lakruwana.com; 668 Bay St, cnr Broad St; mains $12-14; noon-3pm & 5-10pm Tue-Fri, noon-10pm Sat & Sun; Staten Island) is like stepping inside a Hindu temple. The atmospheric eatery serves up mouthwatering curries, saffron-tinged rice and other delicacies from Sri Lanka. Weekends are the best, when a buffet offers a wide array of temptations. Afterwards, don't miss the small downstairs museum with its exquisite ceremonial objects from Sri Lanka. It's about 1.2 miles south of the ferry terminal.

Reason enough to stick around after you arrive by ferry, the **Flagship Brewing Company** (718-448-5284; www.flagshipbrewery.nyc; 40 Minthorne St; 2-10pm Tue & Wed, noon-midnight Thu-Sat, noon-8pm Sun; Staten Island) serves up thirst-quenching craft brews in a sprawling taproom that also hosts live bands throughout the month.

To reach the island, hop aboard the free Staten Island Ferry (p85), which connects Lower Manhattan to St George on the northern tip of Staten Island. Ferry services run around the clock.

WORTH A DETOUR

GOVERNORS ISLAND

Off-limits to the public for 200 years, former military outpost **Governors Island** (☎212-825-3045; www.govisland.com; ⏰10am-6pm Mon-Fri, to 7pm Sat & Sun May-Oct; Ⓢ4/5 to Bowling Green; 1 to South Ferry) FREE is now one of New York's most popular seasonal playgrounds. Each summer, free ferries make the seven-minute trip from Lower Manhattan across to the 172-acre oasis. Thirty acres of island parkland include 6-acre, art-studded **Liggett Terrace**; 10-acre **Hammock Grove** (complete with 50 hammocks); and the 14-acre **Play Lawn**, with natural-turf ball fields for adult softball and Little League baseball.

Things got even better in July, 2016, with the completion of **The Hills**, an ambitious quartet of constructed hills offering spectacular city and harbor views; one of the hills has four slides built-in, including the longest in NYC (57ft). Inspiring views are also on tap along the **Great Promenade**: running for 2.2 miles along the island's perimeter, the path takes in everything from Lower Manhattan and Brooklyn to Staten Island and New Jersey. **Bike rental** is available on the island.

Besides serving as a successful military fort in the Revolutionary War, the Union Army's central recruiting station during the Civil War, and the take-off point for Wilbur Wright's famous 1909 flight around the Statue of Liberty, Governors Island is where the 1988 Reagan/Gorbachev summit signaled the beginning of the end of the Cold War. You can visit the spot where that famous summit took place at the Admiral's House, a grand, colonnaded military residence built in 1843 that's part of the elegant ghost-town area of **Nolan Park**.

Other historic spots include **Fort Jay**, fortified in 1776 for what became a failed attempt to prevent the British from invading Manhattan; **Colonel's Row**, a collection of lovely 19th-century brick officers' quarters; and the creepy **Castle Williams**, a 19th-century fort that was later converted to a military penitentiary. The best way to explore it all is with the **National Park Service** (www.nps.gov/gois), whose rangers conduct guided tours of the historic district (see the website for specific days and times).

For one weekend in June, art is in focus as **Figment** (www.figmentproject.org), an interactive art festival, takes over the island.

To get to the island, take the **ferry** (Map p406; www.govisland.com; Battery Maritime Bldg, 10 South St; round-trip adult/child $2/free, 10-11:30am Sat & Sun free; ⏰departures 10am-4:15pm Mon-Fri, to 5:30pm Sat & Sun May-Oct; Ⓢ1 to South Ferry; R/W to Whitehall St; 4/5 to Bowling Green) from the Battery Maritime Building.

htm; ⏰7:45am-5pm) and the ferry service to Ellis Island and the Statue of Liberty.

Warning! There is an ongoing turf war of hustlers scamming tourists looking to visit the Statue of Liberty. Only one company, Statue Cruises, sells these tickets. If not purchased online, buy them at the ticket office in Castle Clinton. Walk right past the official-looking touts selling fake tickets, or tickets for other boat companies.

SKYSCRAPER MUSEUM — MUSEUM

Map p406 (☎212-968-1961; www.skyscraper.org; 39 Battery Pl; $5; ⏰noon-6pm Wed-Sun; Ⓢ4/5 to Bowling Green; R/W to Whitehall) Fans of phallic architecture will appreciate this compact, high-gloss gallery, examining skyscrapers as objects of design, engineering and urban renewal. Temporary exhibitions dominate the space, with past exhibitions exploring everything from New York's new generation of super-slim residential towers, to the world's new breed of supertalls. Permanent fixtures include information on the design and construction of the Empire State Building and World Trade Center.

⊙ East River Waterfront

SOUTH STREET SEAPORT MUSEUM — MUSEUM

Map p406 (www.southstreetseaportmuseum.org; 12 Fulton St; printing press & shop free; Ⓢ2/3, 4/5, A/C, J/Z to Fulton St) Celebrating its 50th anniversary in 2017, this museum located amid the cobblestone streets of the South Seaport consists of fascinating exhibitions exploring the city's maritime history, an 18th-century printing press and shop (p85), as well as a handful of mighty sailing ships on Pier 16. Among these is the Pioneer (p85), a 19th-century vessel offering two-hour harbor cruises in the warmer months.

City Hall & Civic Center

WOOLWORTH BUILDING NOTABLE BUILDING

Map p406 (203-966-9663; www.woolworthtours.com; 233 Broadway, at Park Pl; 30/60/90min tours $20/30/45; S R/W to City Hall; 2/3 to Park Pl; 4/5/6 to Brooklyn Bridge-City Hall) The world's tallest building upon completion in 1913, Cass Gilbert's 60-story, 792ft-tall Woolworth Building is a neo-Gothic marvel, elegantly clad in masonry and terracotta. (It was surpassed in height by the Chrysler Building in 1930.) The landmarked lobby – a breathtaking spectacle of dazzling, Byzantine-like mosaics – is accessible only on prebooked **guided tours**, which also offer insight into the building's more curious original features, among them a dedicated subway entrance and a secret swimming pool.

At its dedication, the building was described as a 'cathedral of commerce'; though meant as an insult, FW Woolworth, head of the five-and-dime chain-store empire headquartered there, took the comment as a compliment and began throwing the term around himself. Today, it's more like a cathedral of condos, as the top 30 floors have been converted to ultraluxury residences, including a 'Pinnacle Penthouse' that takes up the top *seven* floors.

AFRICAN BURIAL GROUND NATIONAL MONUMENT MEMORIAL

Map p406 (212-637-2019; www.nps.gov/afbg; 290 Broadway, btwn Duane & Reade Sts; memorial 10am-4pm Tue-Sat Apr-Oct, visitor center 10am-4pm Tue-Sat year-round; S J/Z to Chambers St; R/W to City Hall; 4/5/6 to Brooklyn Bridge-City Hall) FREE In 1991, construction workers here uncovered more than 400 stacked wooden caskets, just 16ft to 28ft below street level. The boxes contained the remains of both enslaved and free African Americans from the 17th and 18th centuries (nearby Trinity Church would not allow them to be buried in its graveyard). Today, a poignant **memorial site** and a **visitor center** with educational displays honor the estimated 15,000 men, women and children buried here.

EATING

The Financial District's food scene is enjoying new verve thanks to the myriad upmarket fast-casual options at Brookfield Place, perfect bedfellows to more established winners like North End Grill (p81) and Shake Shack. Further north, Tribeca is no stranger to cool, with a string of celeb-chef hot spots and one of New York's best on-the-go eateries, Arcade Bakery.

ARCADE BAKERY BAKERY $

Map p406 (212-227-7895; www.arcadebakery.com; 220 Church St, btwn Worth & Thomas Sts; pastries from $3, sandwiches $9, pizzas $9-13; 8am-4pm Mon-Fri; S 1 to Franklin St) It's easy to miss this little treasure in the vaulted lobby of a 1920s office building, with a counter trading in beautiful, just-baked goods. Edibles include artful sandwiches and (between noon and 4pm) a small selection of puff-crust pizzas with combos like mushroom, caramelized onion and goat's cheese. Top of the lot is one of the city's finest almond croissants.

SHAKE SHACK FAST FOOD $

Map p406 (646-545-4600; www.shakeshack.com; 215 Murray St, btwn West St & North End Ave; burgers $5.55-9.95; 11am-11pm; ; S A/C, 1/2/3 to Chambers St) Danny Meyer's cult burger chain is fast food at its finest: cotton-soft burgers made with prime, freshly

SOUTH STREET SEAPORT

Before Hurricane Sandy flooded this enclave of cobbled streets, maritime warehouses and tourist-oriented shops in 2012, locals tended to leave this area to the tourists, as its nautical and historic importance was diluted by the manufactured 'Main Street' feel, street performers and poor-quality, often-mobbed restaurants. Revitalization and redevelopment have been slow, but recently momentum has picked up. A glossy, four-story mall on Pier 17, with a massive food court and rooftop entertainment, is scheduled to open by summer 2018; super-tall buildings might also be on the horizon. Like elsewhere in the city, the new and the novel are threatening historic preservation, but a few bars and restaurants have maintained their atmospheric authenticity and are worth a look.

PRICEM / SHUTTERSTOCK ©

TRAVELVIEW / SHUTTERSTOCK ©

A.RUIZ / SHUTTERSTOCK ©

1. Registry Room, Ellis Island (p66)
Approximately 40% of Americans have an ancestor who was processed through Ellis Island.

2. Lower Manhattan & the Financial District (p62)
Lower Manhattan's skyline is dominated by One World Trade Center (p70), the tallest building in New York City.

3. Statue of Liberty (p64)
The 393 steps to the crown make for an arduous climb, but from here there are breathtaking views over the city and harbor.

4. Staten Island Ferry (p85)
Board an orange ferryboat for a charming, and free, cruise between Staten Island and Lower Manhattan.

3

EVE81 / SHUTTERSTOCK ©

ground mince; hormone- and antibiotic-free hot dogs; and seriously good cheesy fries. Drink local with an ale from Brooklyn Brewery or a calorific frozen custard shake that will barely flow through a straw.

EL LUCHADOR MEXICAN **$**

Map p406 (646-398-7499; www.elluchador.nyc; 87 South St, at John St; mains $7.25-9.50; 11am-10pm; ; M15 to Pearl St/Fulton St, 2/3 to Wall St) Look for the giant silver 1960s Airstream trailer and you'll find yourself in the courtyard of this corner joint featuring fresh-made burritos, tacos and quesadillas made with short ribs, carnitas, adobo chicken or roasted portobello mushrooms. It's a welcome, more down-to-earth alternative to the other options available around South Street Seaport.

DA MIKELE PIZZA **$$**

Map p406 (212-925-8800; www.luzzosgroup.com/about-us-damikele; 275 Church St, btwn White & Franklin Sts; pizzas $17-21; noon-10:30pm Sun-Wed, to 11:30pm Thu-Sat; 1 to Franklin St; A/C/E, N/Q/R, J/Z, 6 to Canal St) An Italo-Tribeca hybrid where pressed tin and recycled wood meet retro Vespa, Da Mikele channels the *dolce vita* (sweet life) with its weeknight *aperitivo* (5pm to 7pm), where your drink includes a complimentary spread of lip-smacking bar bites. However, pizzas are the specialty. We're talking light, beautifully charred revelations, simultaneously crisp and chewy, and good enough to make a Neapolitan weep.

BROOKFIELD PLACE FOOD HALL, MARKET **$$**

Map p406 (212-978-1698; www.brookfieldplaceny.com; 230 Vesey St, at West St; ; E to World Trade Center; 2/3 to Park Pl; R/W to Cortlandt St; 4/5 to Fulton St; A/C to Chambers St) This polished, high-end office and retail complex offers two fabulous food halls. Francophile foodies should hit Le District (p81), a charming and polished marketplace with several stand-alone restaurants and counters selling everything from stinky cheese to steak *frites*. One floor above is **Hudson Eats** (Map p406; 212-417-2445; 10am-9pm Mon-Sat, noon-7pm Sun;), a fashionable enclave of upmarket fast bites, from sushi and tacos to salads and burgers.

TWO HANDS AUSTRALIAN **$$**

Map p406 (www.twohandsnyc.com; 251 Church St, btwn Franklin & Leonard Sts; lunch & brunch mains $14-19, dinner $18-29; 8am-10pm; ; 1 to Franklin St; N/Q/R/W, 6 to Canal St) A palette of pale blues and whitewashed brick walls gives this modern cafe-restaurant an appealing, airy feel. Daytime menus offer light dishes from smashed avocado or mushroom toast to its Aussie-style burger (with cheese, fried egg and beet relish), while dinner gets a bit more serious with salmon with herb tahini and broccolini or roast chicken. The coffee's top-notch, too.

GRAND BANKS SEAFOOD **$$**

Map p406 (212-660-6312; www.grandbanks.org; Pier 25, near N Moore St; oysters $3-4, mains $23-27; 3pm-midnight Mon & Tue, from noon Wed-Fri, from 11am Sat & Sun May–mid-Oct; 1 to Franklin St; A/C/E to Canal St) Chef Kerry Heffernan's menu features sustainably harvested seafood at this restaurant on the *Sherman Zwicker*, a 1942 schooner moored on the Hudson, with the spotlight on Atlantic Ocean oysters (alternatively, try the ceviche, lobster rolls or soft-shell crab). It's mobbed with dressy crowds after work and on weekends; come for a late-dinner sundowner and enjoy the stupendous sunset views.

★LOCANDA VERDE ITALIAN **$$$**

Map p406 (212-925-3797; www.locandaverdenyc.com; 377 Greenwich St, at N Moore St; mains lunch $23-34, dinner $25-38; 7am-11pm Mon-Thu, to 11:30pm Fri, 8am-11:30pm Sat, to 11pm Sun; A/C/E to Canal St; 1 to Franklin St) Step through the velvet curtains into a scene of loosened button-downs, black dresses and slick bar staff behind a long, crowded bar. This celebrated brasserie showcases modern, Italo-inspired fare like housemade rigatoni with rabbit *genovese* or grilled swordfish with eggplant caponata. Weekend brunch is no less creative: try scampi and grits or lemon ricotta pancakes with blueberries.

BÂTARD MODERN AMERICAN **$$$**

Map p406 (212-219-2777; www.batardtribeca.com; 239 W Broadway, btwn Walker & White Sts; 2/3/4 courses $58/75/85; 5:30-10:30pm Mon-Sat, plus noon-2:30pm Fri; 1 to Franklin St; A/C/E to Canal St) Austrian chef Markus Glocker heads this warm, Michelin-starred hot spot, where a pared-back interior puts the focus squarely on the food. Glocker's dishes are beautifully balanced and textured, whether it's a crispy *branzino* (sea bass) with cherry tomatoes, basil and asparagus; risotto with rabbit sausage, broccoli spigarello and preserved lemon; or scallop crudo with avocado mousse, lime, radish and black sesame.

NORTH END GRILL AMERICAN $$$

Map p406 (☎646-747-1600; www.northendgrillnyc.com; 104 North End Ave, at Murray St; mains lunch $27-36, dinner $36-48; ⏰11:30am-10pm Mon-Thu, to 10:30pm Fri, 11am-10:30pm Sat, 11am-8pm Sun; 📶; Ⓢ1/2/3, A/C to Chambers St; E to World Trade Center) Handsome, smart and friendly, this is celeb chef Danny Meyer's take on the American grill. Top-tier produce (including herbs and vegetables from the restaurant's own rooftop garden) forms the basis for modern takes on comfort grub, happily devoured by suited silver foxes and a scattering of more casual passersby.

LE DISTRICT FRENCH, FOOD HALL $$$

Map p406 (☎212-981-8588; www.ledistrict.com; Brookfield Place, 225 Liberty St, at West St; market mains $12-30, Beaubourg dinner mains $25-37; ⏰Beaubourg 7:30am-11pm Mon-Fri, from 8am Sat & Sun, other hours vary; 📶; ⓈE to World Trade Center; 2/3 to Park Place; R/W to Cortlandt St; 4/5 to Fulton St; A/C to Chambers St) Paris on the Hudson reigns at this sprawling French food emporium selling everything from high-gloss pastries and pretty *tartines* to stinky cheese and savory steak *frites*. Main restaurant **Beaubourg** has a large bistro menu, but for a quick sit-down feed, head to the **Market District** counter for a burger or the **Cafe District** for a savory crepe.

The **Garden District** offers fresh produce, groceries and a salad bar that's perfect for putting together an impromptu alfresco lunch by the river.

Opening hours vary at each of restaurants and the Market, Cafe and Garden District areas, so check the website for specific times.

DRINKING & NIGHTLIFE

Corporate types don't always bolt for the 'burbs when 5pm hits: many loosen their ties in the wine bars and pubs around Stone St, Wall St and South Street Seaport. Tribeca keeps its cool with artisanal coffee shops and venerated cocktail dens.

★**DEAD RABBIT** COCKTAIL BAR

Map p406 (☎646-422-7906; www.deadrabbitnyc.com; 30 Water St, btwn Broad St & Coenties Slip; ⏰taproom 11am-4am, parlor 5pm-2am Mon-Sat, to midnight Sun; ⓈR/W to Whitehall St; 1 to South Ferry) Named in honor of a dreaded Irish-American gang, this most-wanted rabbit is regularly voted one of the world's best bars. Hit the sawdust-sprinkled Taproom for specialty beers, historic punches and pop-inns (lightly soured ale spiked with different flavors). Come evening, scurry upstairs to the cozy Parlor for meticulously researched cocktails. The Wall St crowd packs the place after work.

★**BLUESTONE LANE** COFFEE

Map p406 (☎646-684-3771; www.bluestonelaneny.com; 30 Broad St, entrance on New St; ⏰7am-5:30pm Mon-Fri, 8am-4:30pm Sat & Sun; ⓈJ/Z to Broad St; 2/3, 4/5 to Wall St) While the NYSE busies itself with stocks, its tiny Aussie neighbor does a roaring trade in killer coffee. Littered with retro Melbourne memorabilia and squeezed into the corner of an art-deco office block, it's never short of smooth suits and homesick antipodeans craving a cup of decent, velvety Joe.

BRANDY LIBRARY COCKTAIL BAR

Map p406 (☎212-226-5545; www.brandylibrary.com; 25 N Moore St, near Varick St; ⏰5pm-1am Sun-Wed, 4pm-2am Thu, 4pm-4am Fri & Sat; Ⓢ1 to Franklin St) When sipping means serious business, settle in at this uber-luxe 'library', its handsome club chairs facing floor-to-ceiling, bottle-lined shelves. Go for top-shelf cognac, malt scotch or vintage brandies, expertly paired with nibbles such as Gruyère-cheese puffs and a wonderful tartare made to order. Saturday nights are generally quieter than weeknights, making it a civilized spot for a weekend tête-à-tête.

COWGIRL SEAHORSE BAR

Map p406 (☎212-608-7873; www.cowgirlseahorse.com; 259 Front St, at Dover St; ⏰11am-11pm Mon-Thu, 11am-late Fri, 10am-late Sat, 10am-11pm Sun; ⓈA/C, J/Z, 2/3, 4/5 to Fulton St) In a sea of very serious bars and restaurants, Cowgirl SeaHorse is a party ship. Its nautical theme and perfect bar fare – giant plates of nachos piled with steaming meat, and frozen margaritas so sweet and tangy you won't be able to say no to a second round – make this dive a can't-miss for those looking to let loose.

TERROIR TRIBECA WINE BAR

Map p406 (☎212-625-9463; www.wineisterroir.com; 24 Harrison St, at Greenwich St; ⏰4pm-midnight Mon & Tue, to 1am Wed-Sat, to 11pm Sun; Ⓢ1 to Franklin St) Award-winning Terroir gratifies oenophiles with its well-versed, well-priced wine list (the offbeat, entertaining menu

Neighborhood Walk
Lower Manhattan Landmarks

START LA COLOMBE
END FEDERAL HALL
LENGTH 2.5 MILES; THREE HOURS

Intimate, circuitous and sometimes confusing side streets, Gothic churches and early-20th-century skyscrapers: Lower Manhattan is an area steeped in history.

Start with coffee at **1 La Colombe**. In the 19th century, its building was a stop on the abolitionist 'underground railway,' a secret network of routes and safe houses allowing enslaved African Americans to reach free states and Canada. A plaque on the Lispenard St wall commemorates the fact.

Further west, the intersection of Varick and N Moore Sts is where you'll find **2 8 Hook & Ladder**, better known as ghost-control headquarters in the 1984 film *Ghostbusters*.

Continue south on Varick St, and turn left into Leonard St. On the southeast corner at the intersection with Church St stands the **3 Textile Building**, built in 1901. Its architect, Henry J Hardenbergh, subsequently designed Midtown's monumental Plaza Hotel.

Further south on Church St, turn left onto Park Pl and right onto Broadway to the neo-Gothic **4 Woolworth Building** (p77).

Continue south on Broadway, cross Vesey St and you'll see **5 St Paul's Chapel** (p73) on your right – it's the only pre–Revolutionary War church left intact in the city.

Directly behind it lies the World Trade Center site, now home to the **6 National September 11 memorial** (p68) and **7 museum** (p68). The museum houses artifacts relating to the 2001 terrorist attacks, while the memorial itself is marked by two giant reflecting pools set in the footprints of the collapsed towers. Soaring above them is the 1776ft One World Trade Center, whose sky-high **8 observatory** (p71) offers jaw-dropping views of the city and beyond.

Further south on Broadway, **9 Trinity Church** (p72) was NYC's tallest building upon completion in 1846. Its cemetery is the final resting place of American Founder (and Broadway star) Alexander Hamilton.

Head east onto Wall St to the **10 New York Stock Exchange** and **11 Federal Hall** (p73).

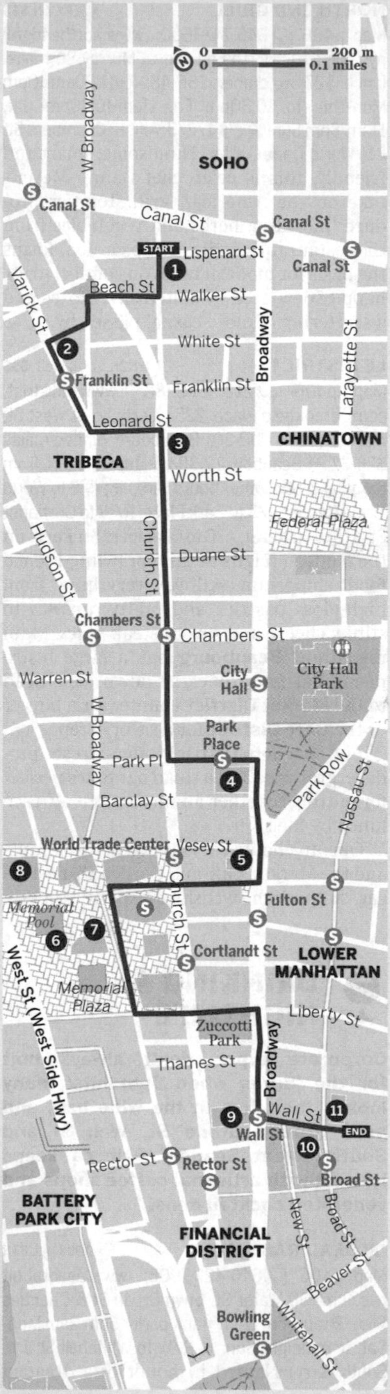

book is a must-read). Drops span the Old World and New, among them natural wines and inspired offerings from smaller producers. A generous selection of wines by the glass makes your global wine tour a whole lot easier. Offers early *and* late happy hours, too.

PIER A HARBOR HOUSE BAR

Map p406 (☎212-785-0153; www.piera.com; 22 Battery Pl, Battery Park; ⏰11am-2am Mon-Wed, to 4am Thu-Sat, to midnight Sun; 📶; Ⓢ4/5 to Bowling Green; R/W to Whitehall St; 1 to South Ferry) Looking dashing after a major restoration, Pier A is a super-spacious, casual eating and drinking house right on New York Harbor. If the weather's fine, try for a seat on the waterside deck – picnic benches, sun umbrellas and an eyeful of New York skyline offer a brilliant spot for sipping craft beers or one of the house cocktails on tap.

LA COLOMBE COFFEE

Map p406 (☎212-343-1515; www.lacolombe.com; 319 Church St, at Lispenard St; ⏰7:30am-6:30pm Mon-Fri, from 8:30am Sat & Sun; ⓈA/C/E to Canal St) Coffee and a few baked treats is all you'll get at this roaster but, man, are they good. Join cool kids and clued-in Continentals for dark, intense espresso and signature offerings like draft latte, a naturally sweet iced caffe latte. Also on tap is La Colombe's cold-pressed Pure Black Coffee, steeped in oxygen-free stainless steel wine tanks for 16 hours.

WEATHER UP COCKTAIL BAR

Map p406 (☎212-766-3202; www.weatherupnyc.com; 159 Duane St, btwn Hudson St & W Broadway; ⏰5pm-1am Mon-Wed, to 2am Thu-Sat, to 10pm Sun; Ⓢ1/2/3 to Chambers St) Simultaneously cool and classy: softly lit subway tiles, amiable and attractive barkeeps and seductive cocktails make for a bewitching trio at Weather Up. Sweet-talk the staff over a Fancy Free (bourbon, maraschino, orange and Angostura Bitters). Failing that, comfort yourself with some satisfying bites like oysters and steak tartare. There's a Brooklyn branch in Prospect Heights (p290).

MACAO TRADING CO COCKTAIL BAR

Map p406 (☎212-431-8642; www.macaonyc.com; 311 Church St, btwn Lispenard & Walker Sts; ⏰bar 5pm-2am Sun-Wed, to 4am Thu-Sat; ⓈA/C/E to Canal St) Though we love the 1940s-style 'gambling parlor' bar/restaurant, it's the downstairs 'opium den' (open Thursday to Saturday) that gets our hearts racing. A Chinese-Portuguese fusion of grub and liquor, both floors are a solid spot for late-night sipping and snacking, especially if you've got a soft spot for sizzle-on-the-tongue libations.

KAFFE 1668 SOUTH COFFEE

Map p406 (☎212-693-3750; www.kaffe1668.com; 275 Greenwich St, btwn Warren & Murray Sts; ⏰6:30am-9pm Mon-Thu, to 8:30pm Fri, 7am-8pm Sat & Sun; 📶; ⓈA/C, 1/2/3 to Chambers St) A coffee-geek mecca, with dual Synesso espresso machines pumping out single-origin magic. There's a large communal table speckled with suits and laptop-tapping creatives, and more seating downstairs.

SMITH & MILLS COCKTAIL BAR

Map p406 (☎212-226-2515; www.smithandmills.com; 71 N Moore St, btwn Hudson & Greenwich Sts; ⏰11am-2am Sun-Wed, to 3am Thu-Sat; Ⓢ1 to Franklin St) Petite Smith & Mills ticks all the cool boxes: unmarked exterior, design conscious industrial interior, and expertly crafted cocktails with a penchant for the classics. Space is limited so head in early if you fancy kicking back on a plush banquette. A seasonal menu spans light snacks to a particularly notable burger pimped with caramelized onions.

☆ ENTERTAINMENT

★FLEA THEATER THEATER

Map p406 (☎tickets 212-226-0051; www.theflea.org; 20 Thomas St, btwn Church St & Broadway; 👪; ⓈA/C, 1/2/3 to Chambers St; R/W to City Hall) One of NYC's top off-off-Broadway companies, Flea is famous for staging innovative and timely new works. A brand-new location offers three performance spaces, including one named for devoted alum Sigourney Weaver. The year-round program also includes music and dance productions, as well as shows for young audiences (aged five and up) and a rollicking late-night competition series of 10-minute plays.

SOHO REP THEATER

Map p406 (Soho Repertory Theatre; ☎212-941-8632; www.sohorep.org; 46 Walker St, btwn Church St & Broadway; ⓈA/C/E, 1 to Canal St) This is one of New York's finest off-Broadway companies, wowing theater fans and critics with its annual trio of sharp, innovative new works. Allison Janney, Ed O'Neill and John C Reilly all made their professional debuts here, and the company's productions have garnered more than a dozen Obie

(Off-Broadway Theater) Awards. Check the website for current or upcoming shows.

CITY VINEYARD LIVE MUSIC

Map p406 (www.citywinery.com; Pier 26, near N Moore St; S1 to Franklin St; A/C/E to Canal St) This waterside bar-restaurant has an intimate, 233-seat cabaret-style theater that features live music nightly. The calendar tends toward emerging singer-songwriters, folk superstars and occasionally indie rock bands; past performers include notables such as Suzanne Vega, Squirrel Nut Zippers, Shawn Colvin, Robyn Hitchcock, Los Lobos, Aimee Mann, Billy Bragg and Yo La Tengo.

SHOPPING

While the Financial District is not a shopping destination per se, bargain-hunters flock here for cut-price fashion mecca Century 21. Further north in Tribeca, hit the lower end of Hudson St and surrounding streets for high-end interior design, antiques and a handful of niche shops peddling everything from local threads to handmade axes.

★PHILIP WILLIAMS POSTERS VINTAGE

Map p406 (212-513-0313; www.postermuseum.com; 122 Chambers St, btwn Church St & W Broadway; 10am-7pm Mon-Sat; SA/C, 1/2/3 to Chambers St) You'll find nearly half a million posters in this cavernous treasure trove, from oversized French advertisements for perfume and cognac to Eastern European film posters and retro-fab promos for TWA. Prices range from $15 for small reproductions to thousands of dollars for rare, showpiece originals like an AM Cassandre. There's a second entrance at 52 Warren St.

★CENTURY 21 FASHION & ACCESSORIES

Map p406 (212-227-9092; www.c21stores.com; 22 Cortlandt St, btwn Church St & Broadway; 7:45am-9pm Mon-Wed, to 9:30pm Thu & Fri, 10am-9pm Sat, 11am-8pm Sun; SA/C, J/Z, 2/3, 4/5 to Fulton St; R/W to Cortlandt St) For penny-pinching fashionistas, this giant cut-price department store is dangerously addictive. Physically dangerous as well, considering the elbows you might have to throw to ward off the competition beelining for the same rack. Not everything is a knockout or a bargain, but persistence pays off. You'll also find accessories, shoes, cosmetics, homewares and toys.

★PEARL RIVER MART DEPARTMENT STORE

Map p406 (212-431-4770; www.pearlriver.com; 395 Broadway, at Walker St; 10am-7:20pm; SN/Q/R/W, J/M/Z, 6 to Canal St) Pearl River has been a downtown shopping staple for 40 years, chock-full of a dizzying array of Asian gifts, housewares, clothing and accessories: silk men's pajamas, cheongsam dresses, blue-and-white Japanese ceramic tableware, clever kitchen gadgets, paper lanterns, origami and calligraphy kits, bamboo plants and more lucky-cat figurines than you can wave a paw at. A great place for gifts.

BEST MADE COMPANY FASHION & ACCESSORIES

Map p406 (646-478-7092; www.bestmadeco.com; 36 White St, at Church St; noon-7pm Mon-Sat, 11am-7pm Sat, 11am-6pm Sun; SA/C/E to Canal St; 1 to Franklin St) Give your next camping trip a Manhattan makeover at this store/design-studio hybrid. Pick up cool handcrafted axes, leather duffel bags, sunglasses, enamel camping mugs and even designer dartboards and first-aid kits, many emblazoned with their signature 'X' logo. A small, smart collection of men's threads includes designer flannel shirts and pullovers, sweatshirts and rugged knitwear from Portland's Dehen Knitting Mills.

SHINOLA FASHION & ACCESSORIES

Map p406 (917-728-3000; www.shinola.com; 177 Franklin St, btwn Greenwich & Hudson Sts; 11am-7pm Mon-Sat, noon-6pm Sun; S1 to Franklin St) Well known for its coveted wristwatches, Detroit-based Shinola branches out with a super-cool selection of Made-in-USA life props. Bag anything from leather iPad cases and journal covers to grooming products, jewelry and limited-edition bicycles with customized bags. Added bonuses include complimentary monogramming of leather goods and stationery, and an in-house espresso bar, **Smile Newstand** (Map p406; 917-728-3023; www.thesmilenyc.com; 7am-7pm Mon-Fri, 8am-7pm Sat, 8am-6pm Sun;).

PASANELLA & SON WINE

Map p406 (212-233-8383; www.pasanellaandson.com; 115 South St, btwn Peck Slip & Beekman St; 10am-9pm Mon-Sat, noon-7pm Sun; SA/C, J/Z, 2/3, 4/5 to Fulton St; R/W to Cortlandt St) Oenophiles adore this savvy wine peddler, with its 400-plus drops both inspired and affordable. The focus is on small producers, with a number of biodynamic and organic winemakers in the mix. It offers an impressive choice of American whiskeys, free wine-tastings of the week's new arrivals on Sundays, and themed wine-and-cheese tastings throughout the year.

BOWNE STATIONERS & CO GIFTS & SOUVENIRS

Map p406 (☎646-628-2707; 211 Water St, btwn Beekman & Fulton Sts; ⏰11am-7pm; Ⓢ2/3, 4/5, A/C, J/Z to Fulton St) Suitably set in cobbled South Street Seaport and affiliated with the attached South Street Seaport Museum (p76), this 18th-century veteran stocks reproduction vintage New York posters and NYC-themed notepads, pencil cases, cards, stamps and even wrapping paper. At the **printing workshop** you can order customized business cards or hone your printing skills in monthly classes (see the museum website's Events page).

STEVEN ALAN FASHION & ACCESSORIES

Map p406 (☎212-343-0692; www.stevenalan.com; 103 Franklin St, btwn Church St & W Broadway; ⏰11am-7pm Mon-Sat, noon-6pm Sun; ⓈA/C/E to Canal St; 1 to Franklin St) New York designer Steven Alan mixes his hip, heritage-inspired threads for men and women with a beautiful edit of clothes from indie-chic labels like France's Arpenteur and Scandinavia's Acne and Norse Projects. Accessories include hard-to-find fragrances, bags, jewelry and a selection of shoes by cognoscenti brands such as Common Projects and Isabel Marant Étoile.

CITYSTORE GIFTS & SOUVENIRS

Map p406 (☎212-386-0007; www.nyc.gov/citystore; North Plaza, Municipal Bldg, 1 Centre St, at Chambers St; ⏰10am-5pm Mon-Fri; Ⓢ4/5/6 to Brooklyn Bridge-City Hall; R/W to City Hall; J/Z to Chambers St) Score all manner of officially produced New York City memorabilia here, from authentic-looking taxi medallions, sewerhole-cover coasters and borough-themed T-shirts to NYPD baseball caps, subway station signs and books about NYC. (Curious, though less relevant for the average visitor, are the municipal building codes and other regulatory guides for sale.)

SPORTS & ACTIVITIES

★STATEN ISLAND FERRY CRUISE

Map p406 (www.siferry.com; Whitehall Terminal, 4 South St, at Whitehall St; ⏰24hr; Ⓢ1 to South Ferry; R/W to Whitehall St; 4/5 to Bowling Green) FREE Staten Islanders know these hulking, orange ferryboats as commuter vehicles, while Manhattanites like to think of them as their secret, romantic vessels for a spring-day escape. Yet many tourists (at last count, two million a year) are clued into the charms of the Staten Island Ferry, whose 25-minute, 5.2-mile journey across the harbor between Lower Manhattan and the Staten Island neighborhood of St George is one of NYC's finest free adventures.

INSTITUTE OF CULINARY EDUCATION COOKING, WINE

Map p406 (ICE; ☎212-847-0700; http://recreational.ice.edu; Brookfield Place, 225 Liberty St; courses $90-250; ⓈE to World Trade Center; 4/5 to Fulton St; R/W to Cortlandt St) Release your inner Jean-Jacques with a cooking course at the Institute of Culinary Education, which runs the country's largest program of cooking, baking and wine-appreciation courses, from 90-minute classes to multiday sessions. Courses range from Tuscan cooking and American comfort food to knife skills and classic cocktails. Restless foodies can choose from numerous culinary tours of the city (from $50).

PIONEER BOATING

Map p406 (☎212-748-8600; www.southstreetseaportmuseum.org; box office 12 Fulton St; adult/child $32/28; ⏰varies; Ⓢ2/3, 4/5, A/C to Fulton St) In the warmer months, break free with a salty sail aboard one of the South Street Seaport's historic schooners, the *Pioneer*. Tickets can be purchased via the South Street Seaport Museum website, or at the museum box office.

DOWNTOWN BOATHOUSE KAYAKING

Map p406 (www.downtownboathouse.org; Pier 26, near N Moore St; ⏰9am-5pm Sat & Sun mid-May–mid-Oct, plus 5-7:30pm Tue-Thu mid-Jun–mid-Sep; Ⓢ1 to Houston St) FREE New York's most active public boathouse offers free, walk-up, 20-minute kayaking sessions (including equipment) in a protected embayment in the Hudson River on weekends and some weekday evenings. For more activities – kayaking trips, stand up paddle boarding and classes – check out www.hudsonriverpark.org for the four other kayaking locations on the Hudson River. There's also a summer-only kayaking location on Governors Island (p76).

SoHo & Chinatown

SOHO, NOHO & NOLITA | CHINATOWN & LITTLE ITALY

Neighborhood Top Five

❶ Shopping (p104) Maxing out the credit cards on SoHo's big-name fashion streets, followed by cool-hunting and lesser-known labels on the cognoscenti sidewalks of nearby Nolita and NoHo.

❷ **Chinatown** (p88) Slurping soup dumplings and haggling for designer wares of ambiguous authenticity amid the sizzling lights of Chinatown.

❸ **Little Italy** (p92) Getting your fix of rich sugo or a delicate tiramisu, while listening in on grandfathers sipping grappa and speaking in the mother tongue.

❹ **Merchant's House Museum** (p91) Snooping around this time-jarred, possibly haunted museum, imagining NYC life in the wild and dusty 1800s.

❺ **Peking Duck House** (p100) Sharing a tender, succulent Peking duck in the quintessential spot to have it if you're not in Beijing.

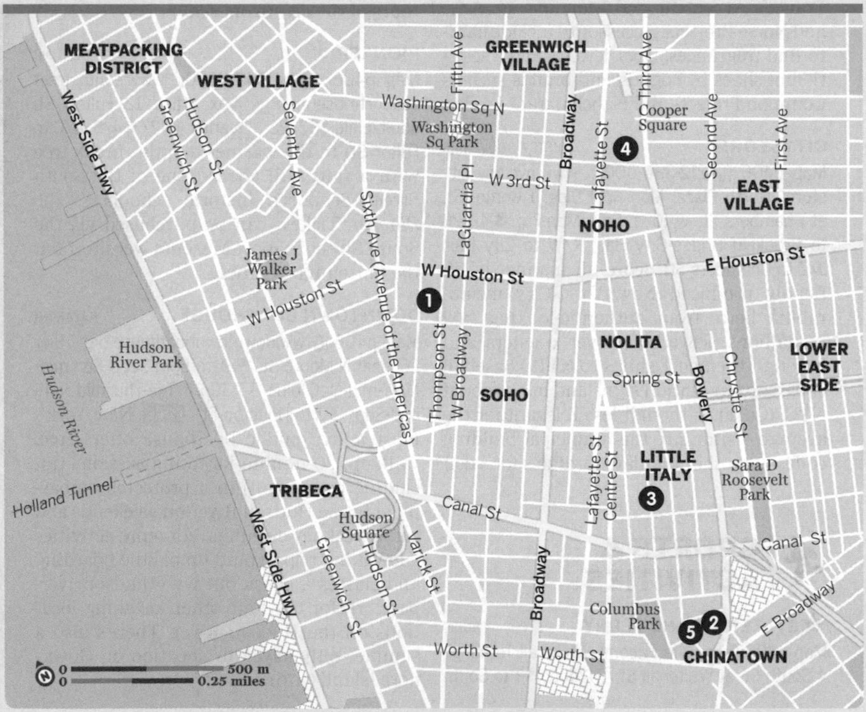

For more detail of this area see Map p408 and p411

Explore SoHo & Chinatown

Like a colorful quilt of subneighborhoods sewn together in mismatched patches, the areas orbiting SoHo (SOuth of HOuston) feel like a string of mini republics. Style mavens boutique-hop in booming Nolita (NOrth of LIttle ITAly), Italo-Americans channel Napoli in ever-shrinking Little Italy, and Chinese extended families gossip over *xiao long bao* (soup dumplings) in hyperactive Chinatown.

Lower-rise buildings inject these streets with a cozy, village-like vibe (main drags Broadway and Canal St excepted). Celebrities, cast-iron lofts and A-list boutiques stud SoHo's cobbled side streets, while humbler 19th-century tenements and quirkier one-off boutiques flavor Nolita.

In Chinatown, an 'anything goes' spirit wafts up like stall smoke, with frenzied crowds and hawkers mingling and haggling under faded billboards. The best way to weave your way around here is on foot. And don't bother planning your route of attack. It's all about letting your senses guide you. Whether you're following your nose down an alleyway for freshly baked pork buns, or your ears to a prayer gong in a heady Buddhist temple, unexpected surprises are always at the ready.

Local Life

➡ **Family style** Hit Chinatown's bustling dining dens with a handful of friends and eat 'family style' (order a ton of dishes and sample spoonfuls of each). You'll think the waiter left a zero off the bill.

➡ **Side streets** The stretch of Broadway cutting through SoHo is reserved for the legions of tourists – you'll find New Yorkers scouring the one-of-a-kind boutiques on the side streets for idiosyncratic buys and slashed prices.

➡ **Cultural breaks** It's not all retail therapy in SoHo. Take time to explore the area's artistic legacy at spaces such as Drawing Center (p90) and the Leslie-Lohman Museum of Gay & Lesbian Art (p90), or just marvel at 280,000lb of dirt at the New York Earth Room (p91).

Getting There & Away

➡ **Subway** The subway lines dump off along various points of Canal St (J/Z, N/Q/R/W and 6). Once you arrive, it's best to explore on foot. The neighborhood's downtown location makes it easy to access from Midtown and Brooklyn.

➡ **Bus & Taxi** Avoid taking cabs or buses – especially in Chinatown, as the traffic is full-on. For SoHo, have your taxi let you off along Broadway if you aren't fussed about your final destination. Don't take cabs south of Canal St if you're simply planning to wander around Chinatown. The area is so small that you'll make much better time on foot than waiting for lights to change.

Lonely Planet's Top Tip

Serious shopaholics should consult the city's in-the-know retail blogs (p51) before hitting SoHo and surrounds – there's always some sort of 'sample sale' or offer going on, not to mention the opening of yet another boutique stocking fresh, emerging design talent.

Best Places to Eat

- Uncle Boons (p96)
- Dutch (p97)
- Il Buco Alimentari & Vineria (p97)
- Prince Street Pizza (p93)
- Chefs Club (p97)

For reviews, see p93.

Best Places to Drink

- Pegu Club (p101)
- Spring Lounge (p101)
- Genuine Liquorette (p101)
- Joe's Pub (p103)
- Apothéke (p101)

For reviews, see p100.

Best Shopping

- MoMA Design Store (p102)
- Rag & Bone (p104)
- MiN New York (p104)
- Evolution Nature Store (p106)
- Saturdays (p104)

For reviews, see p104.

RYAN DEBERARDINIS / SHUTTERSTOCK ©

TOP SIGHT
CHINATOWN

Catch the whiff of fresh fish and ripe persimmons, hear the clacking of mah-jongg tiles on makeshift tables, drool over dangling duck roasts swinging in store windows, and shop for everything imaginable, from rice-paper lanterns and 'faux-lex' watches to tire irons and a pound of pressed nutmeg. America's biggest Chinatown is your oyster!

DON'T MISS

- A family-style meal at a bustling, back-alley dive
- Museum of Chinese in America
- Canal St vendors and street life
- Mahayana Temple
- Peking Duck House
- Apothéke

PRACTICALITIES

- Map p411, B3
- www.explorechinatown.com
- south of Broome St & east of Broadway
- (S)N/Q/R/W, J/Z, 6 to Canal St; B/D to Grand St; F to East Broadway

Canal Street

Walking down Canal St is like a game of Frogger played on the streets of Shanghai. This is Chinatown's spine, where you'll dodge oncoming human traffic as you scurry into side streets to scout treasures from the Far East. You'll pass stinky seafood stalls hawking slippery fish; mysterious herb shops peddling a witch's cauldron's worth of roots and potions; storefront bakeries with steamy windows and the tastiest 80¢ pork buns you've ever had; restaurants with whole, roasted ducks and pigs hanging by their skinny necks in the windows; produce markets piled high with fresh lychee, bok choy and Asian pears; and street vendors selling every iteration of knock-off, from Gucci sunglasses to Prada bags.

Buddhist Temples

Chinatown is home to Buddhist temples large and small, public and obscure. They are easily stumbled upon during a full-on stroll of the neighborhood, and at least two such temples are considered landmarks. The **Eastern States Buddhist Temple** (Map p411; ☎212-966-6229; 64 Mott St, btwn Bayard & Canal Sts, Chinatown; ⊙8:30am-6pm; (S)N/Q/R/W, J/Z, 6 to Canal St) is filled with hundreds of Buddhas, while the **Mahayana Temple** (Map p411; ☎212-925-8787; http://

en.mahayana.us; 133 Canal St, at Manhattan Bridge Plaza, Chinatown; 8:30am-6pm; S B/D to Grand St; J/Z to Bowery; 6 to Canal St) holds one golden, 16ft-high Buddha, sitting on a lotus and edged with offerings of fresh oranges, apples and flowers. Mahayana is the largest Buddhist temple in Chinatown, and its entrance, which overlooks the frenzied vehicle entrance to the Manhattan Bridge, is guarded by two proud and handsome golden lions. Step inside and you'll find a simple interior of wooden floor and red paper lanterns, dramatically upstaged by the temple's magnificent Buddha, thought to be the largest in the city.

Food Glorious Food

The most rewarding experience for Chinatown neophytes is to access this wild and wonderful world through their taste buds. More than any other area of Manhattan, Chinatown's menus sport wonderfully low prices, uninflated by ambience, hype or reputation. But more than cheap eats, the neighborhood is rife with family recipes passed across generations and continents. Food displays and preparation remain unchanged and untempered by American norms; it's not unusual to walk by storefronts sporting a tangled array of lacquered animals – chickens, rabbit and duck, in particular – ready to be chopped up and served at a family banquet. Steaming street stalls clang down the sidewalk serving pork buns and other finger-friendly food. Don't forget to wander down the back alleys for a Technicolor assortment of spices and herbs to perfect your own Eastern dishes.

Museum of Chinese in America

In a space designed by architect Maya Lin (designer of the famed Vietnam Memorial in Washington, DC), the **Museum of Chinese in America** (MOCA; Map p411; 212-619-4785; www.mocanyc.org; 215 Centre St, btwn Grand & Howard Sts, Chinatown; adult/child $10/5, first Thu of month free; 11am-6pm Tue, Wed & Fri-Sun, to 9pm Thu; S N/Q/R/W, J/Z, 6 to Canal St) is a multifaceted space whose engaging permanent and temporary exhibitions shed light on Chinese American life, both past and present. Browse through interactive multimedia exhibits, maps, timelines, photos, letters, films and artifacts.The museum's anchor exhibit, *With a Single Step: Stories in the Making of America*, provides an often intimate glimpse into topics including immigration, cultural identity and racial stereotyping.

HISTORY OF CHINESE IMMIGRANTS

The history of Chinese immigrants in New York City is a long and tumultuous one. The first Chinese people to arrive in America came to work under difficult conditions on the Central Pacific Railroad; others were lured to the West Coast in search of gold. When prospects dried up, many moved east to NYC to work in factory assembly lines and in the laundry houses of New Jersey.

THE CHINESE EXCLUSION ACT

A rising racist sentiment led to the 1882 passage of the Chinese Exclusion Act, which made naturalization an impossibility and largely squashed the opportunity for mainland Chinese to find work in the US for a span of just over 60 years. When the ban was finally lifted in 1943, the number of Chinese who were able to enter the country was still extremely limited by the quota stipulated under the Magnuson Act, which was enforced until 1965. Today it's estimated that over 150,000 citizens fill the bursting, tenement-like structures orbiting Mott St.

SIGHTS

SoHo, NoHo & Nolita

INTERNATIONAL CENTER OF PHOTOGRAPHY — GALLERY

Map p408 (ICP; ☎212-857-0003; www.icp.org; 250 Bowery, btwn Houston & Prince, Nolita; adult/child $14/free, by donation Thu 6-9pm; ⏰10am-6pm Tue-Sun, until 9pm Thu; Ⓢ F to 2nd Ave; J/Z to Bowery) ICP is New York's paramount platform for photography, with a strong emphasis on photojournalism and changing exhibitions on a wide range of themes. Past shows have included work by Sebastião Salgado, Henri Cartier-Bresson, Man Ray and Robert Capa. Its 11,000-sq-ft home on the Bowery, which opened in 2016 (formerly, it was in Midtown), places it close to the epicenter of the downtown art scene.

The center is also a school, offering coursework (for credit) and a public lecture series. Stop by the excellent gallery shop, great for instant cameras and photography tomes, cool little gifts and NYC souvenirs.

DRAWING CENTER — GALLERY

Map p408 (☎212-219-2166; www.drawingcenter.org; 35 Wooster St, btwn Grand & Broome Sts, SoHo; adult/child $5/free; ⏰noon-6pm Wed & Fri-Sun, to 8pm Thu; Ⓢ A/C/E, 1, N/Q/R to Canal St) America's only nonprofit institute focused solely on drawings, the Drawing Center uses work by masters as well as unknowns to juxtapose the medium's various styles. Historical exhibitions have included work by Michelangelo, James Ensor and Marcel Duchamp, while contemporary shows have showcased heavyweights such as Richard Serra, Ellsworth Kelly and Richard Tuttle. As to the themes themselves, expect anything from the whimsical to the politically controversial.

Artist lectures and performance-art programs are hot tickets here; check the website for upcoming events.

NEW YORK CITY FIRE MUSEUM — MUSEUM

Map p408 (☎212-691-1303; www.nycfiremuseum.org; 278 Spring St, btwn Varick & Hudson Sts, SoHo; adult/child $8/5; ⏰10am-5pm; Ⓢ C/E to Spring St) In a grand old firehouse dating from 1904, this ode to firefighters includes a fantastic collection of historic equipment and artifacts. Eye up everything from horse-drawn firefighting carriages and early stovepipe firefighter hats to Chief, a four-legged firefighting hero from Brooklyn. Exhibits trace the development of the NYC firefighting system, and the museum's heavy equipment and friendly staff make this a great spot for kids.

The New York Fire Department (FDNY) lost half of its members in the collapse of the World Trade Center on September 11, 2001, and memorials and exhibits have become a permanent part of the collection. Fans can stock up on books about firefighting history and official FDNY clothing and patches in the gift shop.

CHILDREN'S MUSEUM OF THE ARTS — MUSEUM

Map p408 (☎212-274-0986; www.cmany.org; 103 Charlton St, btwn Greenwich & Hudson Sts, SoHo; admission $12, 4-6pm Thu by donation; ⏰noon-5pm Mon, noon-6pm Thu & Fri, 10am-5pm Sat & Sun; 👪; Ⓢ 1 to Houston St; C/E to Spring St) This small but worthy stop encourages kids aged 10 months to 15 years to view, make and share art. Rotating exhibitions aside, the center offers a vast program of daily activities for fledgling artists, from sculpture and collaborative mural painting, to songwriting and children's book design. It also runs movie nights and other special treats. See the website for upcoming offerings.

LESLIE-LOHMAN MUSEUM OF GAY & LESBIAN ART — MUSEUM

Map p408 (☎212-431-2609; www.leslielohman.org; 26 Wooster St, btwn Grand & Canal Sts, Little Italy; suggested donation $8; ⏰noon-6pm Wed & Fri-Sun, to 8pm Thu; Ⓢ A/C/E, N/Q/R, 1 to Canal St) FREE Newly expanded in 2017, the world's first museum dedicated to LGBT themes stages six to eight annual exhibitions of both homegrown and international art. Offerings have included solo-artist retrospectives as well as themed shows exploring the likes of art and sex along the New York waterfront. Much of the work on display is from the museum's own collection, which consists of over 24,000 works. The space also hosts queer-centric lectures, readings, film screenings and performances; check the website for updates.

DONALD JUDD HOME STUDIO — GALLERY

Map p408 (☎212-219-2747; http://juddfoundation.org; 101 Spring St, at Mercer St, SoHo; guided tour adult $25, free guided tour 1-5pm Thu-Sat; ⏰by prebooked guided tour Tue-Sat; Ⓢ N/R to Prince St; 6 to Spring St) The former home and studio of the late American artist Donald Judd offers a fascinating glimpse into the life and artistic practices of the minimalist maverick. Guided tours of the space run for approximately 90 minutes and must be booked online (tours often sell out a month in advance). The home studio also hosts drawing classes and art talks; see the website for details.

NEW YORK EARTH ROOM GALLERY

Map p408 (☎212-989-5566; www.earthroom.org; 141 Wooster St, btwn Prince & W Houston Sts, SoHo; ⊙noon-3pm & 3:30-6pm Wed-Sun, closed mid-Jun–mid-Sep; **S**N/R to Prince St) **FREE** Since 1980 the oddity of the New York Earth Room, the work of artist Walter De Maria, has been wooing the curious with something not easily found in the city: dirt (250 cu yd, or 280,000lb, of it, to be exact). Walking into the small space is a heady experience, as the scent will make you feel like you've entered a wet forest; the sight of such beautiful, pure earth in the midst of this crazy city is surprisingly moving.

BROKEN KILOMETER GALLERY

Map p408 (☎212-989-5566; www.diaart.org; 393 W Broadway, btwn Spring & Broome Sts, SoHo; ⊙noon-3pm & 3:30-6pm Wed-Sun, closed mid-Jun–mid-Sep; **S**N/R to Prince St, C/E to Spring St) **FREE** Occupying a cavernous ground-floor space in SoHo is this 1979 installation by the late American artist Walter De Maria. The work consists of 500 solid brass rods, positioned in five parallel rows, with the space between the rods increasing by 5mm with each consecutive space, from front to back. The result: a playful subversion of spacial perception. The rods appear to be identically spaced, even though at the back they're as much as 2ft apart. No photos allowed.

BASILICA OF ST PATRICK'S OLD CATHEDRAL CHURCH

Map p408 (☎212-226-8075; www.oldcathedral.org; 263 Mulberry St, entrance on Mott St, Nolita; ⊙6am-9pm; **S**N/R to Prince St; B/D/F/M to Broadway-Lafayette St; 6 to Bleecker St) Though St Patrick's Cathedral is now famously located on Fifth Ave in Midtown, its first congregation was housed here, in this restored Gothic Revival church. Designed by Joseph-François Mangin and constructed between 1809 and 1815, the church was once the seat of religious life for the Archdiocese of New York, as well as an important community center for new immigrants, mainly from Ireland.

TOP SIGHT
MERCHANT'S HOUSE MUSEUM

Built in 1832 and purchased by merchant magnate Seabury Tredwell three years later, this red-brick mansion remains the most authentic Federal house (of which there are about 300) in town. It's an antiquarian's dream, as much about the city's mercantile past as it is a showcase of 19th-century high-end domestic furnishings. Everything in the house is testament to what money could buy, from the mahogany pocket doors, bronze gasoliers and marble mantelpieces, to the elegant parlor chairs, attributed to noted furniture designer Duncan Phyfe. Even the elaborate system of multilevel call bells for the servants works to this day.

Many believe that the ghost of Gertrude Tredwell – Seabury's youngest child and the building's last resident – haunts the old mansion, making cameo appearances late in evenings and sometimes at public events. At a Valentine's Day concert a few years back several attendees witnessed the shadow of a woman walk up to the performers and take a seat in the parlor chairs. Appropriately, the museum offers ghost tours after dark (usually in late October), as well as lectures, special events and historical walking tours of NoHo. Check the website.

DON'T MISS

- Chairs attributed to Duncan Phyfe
- Maids' quarters

PRACTICALITIES

- Map p408, G2
- ☎212-777-1089
- www.merchantshouse.org
- 29 E 4th St, btwn Lafayette St & Bowery
- adult/child $15/free
- ⊙noon-5pm Fri-Mon, to 8pm Thu, guided tours 2pm Thu-Mon & 6:30pm Thu
- **S**6 to Bleecker St; B/D/F/M to Broadway-Lafayette St

When the church was built, the city hadn't yet spread this far north and the building's calculated isolation was a welcome relief from the hostility of New York's Protestant majority. Anti-Catholic sentiments also led to the construction of the church grounds' brick wall, an attempt to hinder stone-throwers.

The church and its beautiful graveyard feature in Martin Scorsese's celluloid classic *Mean Streets* (1973). It's a spot well-known to the Italian-American auteur, who grew up in nearby Elizabeth St.

Chinatown & Little Italy

CHINATOWN AREA

See p88.

MULBERRY STREET STREET

Map p411 (Little Italy; SN/Q/R, J/Z, 6 to Canal St; B/D to Grand St) Named for the mulberry farms that once stood here, Mulberry St is now better known as the meat in Little Italy's sauce. It's an animated strip, packed with smooth-talking restaurant hawkers (especially between Hester and Grand Sts), wisecracking baristas and a healthy dose of kitschy souvenirs.

Despite the neighborhood's many changes over the years, history looms large. It was inside restaurant **Da Gennaro** (Map p411; 212-431-3934; www.dagennarorestaurant.com; 129 Mulberry St, at Hester St, Little Italy; pizzas $19-23, mains $17-42; 10am-midnight Sun-Thu, to 1am Fri & Sat; SN/Q/R, J/Z, 6 to Canal St; B/D to Grand St), formerly Umberto's Clam House, that 'Crazy Joe' Gallo was gunned down on April 2, 1972, an unexpected birthday surprise for the Brooklyn-born mobster. One block further north stands fourth-generation **Alleva** (Map p411; 212-226-7990; www.allevadairy.com; 188 Grand St, at Mulberry St, Little Italy; 9:30am-7pm Mon-Sun; SJ/Z, N/Q/R, 6 to Canal St; B/D to Grand St), one of the city's original cheese shops and famed for its mozzarella. Across the street on Grand lies another veteran, Ferrara Cafe & Bakery (p100), celebrated for its classic Italian pastries and gelati. Back on Mulberry, old-time Mulberry Street Bar (p101) was a favorite haunt of the late Frank Sinatra; its own TV cameos include *Law & Order* and *The Sopranos*.

TOP SIGHT
LITTLE ITALY

In the last 50 years, New York's Little Italy has shrunk from a big, brash boot to an ultra-slim sandal. A mid-century exodus to the suburbs of Brooklyn and beyond has see this once-strong Italian neighborhood turn into a micro pastiche of its former self. Indeed, Little Italy is little more than Mulberry Street these days, an endearingly kitsch strip of gingham-tablecloths, mandolin muzak and nostalgia for the old country.

Come late September, the street turns into a raucous, 11-day block party for the **San Gennaro Festival** (www.sangennaro.org), a celebration honoring the patron saint of Naples. It's a loud, convivial affair, with food and carnival stalls, free entertainment, and more big hair than Jersey Shore.

It's also on Mulberry St that you'll find the tiny **Italian American Museum** (Map p411; 212-965-9000; www.italianamericanmuseum.org; 155 Mulberry St, at Grand St, Little Italy; suggested donation $7; noon-6pm Fri-Sun; SJ/Z, N/Q/R/W, 6 to Canal St; B/D to Grand St), a random mishmash of historical objects documenting early Italian life in NYC, from Sicilian marionettes to old Italian comics starring New York's famous mafia-busting cop, Giuseppe 'Joe' Petrosino.

DON'T MISS

- Mulberry St
- San Gennaro Festival in September
- Pizza by the slice
- Great tiramisu

PRACTICALITIES

- Map p411, B2
- SN/Q/R/W, J/Z, 6 to Canal St; B/D to Grand St

Alcohol was openly traded on the corner of Mulberry and Kenmare Sts during Prohibition, leading to its nickname, the 'Curb Exchange.' That police headquarters at the time were only a block away at 240 Centre St is testament to the power of good old-fashioned bribes. From this point north, the old-school delis and restaurants of Little Italy give way to the new-school boutiques, galleries and restaurants of Nolita. Take a gander at what was once the **Ravenite Social Club** (Map p408; 247 Mulberry St, Nolita; S 6 to Spring St; N/R to Prince St) to see how things have really changed around here. Now a designer shoe store, it was once a mobster hangout (originally known as the Alto Knights Social Club). Indeed, it was right here that big hitters such as Lucky Luciano and John Gotti (as well as the FBI, which kept a watchful eye from the building across the street) logged time. Only the shop's tile floor remains from the day, the shop windows once an intimidating brick wall.

COLUMBUS PARK PARK

Map p411 (Mulberry & Bayard Sts, Chinatown; S J/Z, N/Q/R, 6 to Canal St) Mah-jongg meisters, slow-motion tai-chi practitioners and old aunties gossiping over homemade dumplings: it might feel like Shanghai, but this leafy oasis is core to NYC history. In the 19th century, this was part of the infamous Five Points neighborhood, the city's first tenement slums and the inspiration for Martin Scorsese's *Gangs of New York*.

The 'five points' were the five streets that used to converge here; now you'll find the intersection of only Mosco, Worth and Baxter Sts. Aside from serving up an intriguing slice of multicultural life, the park's other perk these days is its public bathroom, making it the perfect place for a pit stop.

CHURCH OF THE TRANSFIGURATION CHURCH

Map p411 (212-962-5157; www.transfigurationnyc.org; 29 Mott St, btwn Bayard & Mosco Sts, Chinatown; donations welcome; English-language services 12:10pm daily, 6pm Sat, 11:30am Sun; S J/Z, N/Q/R, 6 to Canal St) It's been serving New York's immigrant communities since 1801, and the Church of the Transfiguration doesn't stop adapting. First it was the Irish, then Italians and now Chinese. Indeed, the sermons here are delivered in Cantonese, Mandarin and English. This small landmark is not far from Pell and Doyers Sts, two winding paths worth exploring.

EATING

SoHo, NoHo & Nolita

In the land of acronyms, there are only three letters you need to know: Y.U.M. The thrifty are spoiled for choice in metastasizing Chinatown, where heaping portions are served up for pennies on the dollar. Seafood of every variety, including items you'll never find in your local grocery store, chill on ice in markets spilling onto the street. SoHo is still the land of louche Euro brasseries, but hip, closet-sized eateries featuring every manner of cuisine, cult-status delis and Michelin-starred New American restaurants are no longer only the domain of the East and West Villages just beyond.

★PRINCE STREET PIZZA PIZZA $

Map p408 (212-966-4100; 27 Prince St, btwn Mott & Elizabeth Sts, Nolita; pizza slices from $2.95; 11:45am-11pm Sun-Thu, to 2am Fri & Sat; S N/R to Prince St; 6 to Spring St) It's a miracle the oven door hasn't come off its hinges at this classic slice joint, its brick walls hung with shots of B-list celebrity fans. Ditch the average cheese slice for the exceptional square varieties (the pepperoni will blow your socks off, Tony). The sauces, mozzarella and ricotta are made in-house and while the queues can get long, they usually move fast.

TWO HANDS CAFE $

Map p411 (www.twohandsnyc.com; 164 Mott St, btwn Broome & Grand Sts, Nolita; dishes $9-15; 8am-5pm; ; S B/D to Grand St; J/Z to Bowery) Named after the crime-com film starring Heath Ledger, Two Hands encapsulates Australia's relaxed, sophisticated cafe culture. Dream of Byron Bay over small-batch specialty coffee and out-of-the-box grub, such as sweet-corn fritters ($14) with spinach, avocado, sour cream, pickled beets and chili, or a healthier-than-thou açaí bowl ($12).

RUBY'S CAFE $

Map p408 (212-925-5755; www.rubyscafe.com; 219 Mulberry St, btwn Spring & Prince Sts, Nolita; mains $10-15; 9am-11pm Mon-Thu, to midnight Fri & Sat; S 6 to Spring St; N/R to Prince St) Almost always packed, this minute, cash-only cafe has all the bases covered: 'brekkie' friendly avo toast (mashed avocado on ciabatta or eight-grain toast), buttermilk pancakes, competent pastas and salads, and (above all else) lusty burgers named after Australian surf beaches.

PAUL DE GREGORIO / GETTY IMAGES ©

1. Cannoli in Little Italy (p99)
Indulge in Italian cuisine in the city.

2. Mahayana Temple (p88)
The temple entrance is guarded by two proud golden lions.

3. SoHo (p102)
Wander around SoHo's cobbled streets and towering apartment blocks.

4. Chinatown street stall (p89)
The best way to experience Chinatown is through its delicious food.

3

Flat white coffees and Aussie beers complete your Down Under dining adventure.

GREY DOG AMERICAN $

Map p408 (☎212-966-1060; www.thegreydog.com; 244 Mulberry St, Nolita; mains $9-14; ⏰7:30am-10pm Mon-Fri, 8:15am-10pm Sat & Sun; SF/M/D/B train to Broadway-Lafayette) Whether you're looking to share a plate of cheese with your friends or indulge in a proper New York brunch, the Grey Dog won't disappoint. It does scrumptious takes on American classics that have full-on flavor without overdoing it. The order-at-the-counter system keeps this place bustling all day long. It stays open after the kitchen closes for desserts and cocktails.

LAN LARB THAI $

Map p411 (☎646-895-9264; www.lanlarb.com; 227 Centre St, at Grand St, SoHo; dishes $9-21; ⏰11:30am-10:15pm; SN/Q/R/W, J/Z, 6 to Canal St) Food fiends flock to Lan Larb for cheap, flavor-packed Thai. It specializes in *larb,* a spicy, minced-meat salad from Thailand's northeast Isan region (try the duck version; $12). Other top choices include sucker-punch *som tam* (green papaya salad; $11) and a delicate *kui teiw nam tok nuer* (dark noodle soup with beef, morning glory, scallion, cilantro and bean sprouts; $11).

TACOMBI FONDA NOLITA MEXICAN $

Map p408 (☎917-727-0179; www.tacombi.com; 267 Elizabeth St, btwn E Houston & Prince Sts, Nolita; tacos $4-7; ⏰11am-midnight Mon-Wed, to 1am Thu-Sat; SF to 2nd Ave; 6 to Bleecker St) Festively strung lights, foldaway chairs and Mexican men flipping tacos in an old VW Kombi: if you can't make it to the Yucatan shore, here's your Plan B. Casual, convivial and ever-popular, Tacombi serves up fine, fresh tacos, including a *barbacoa* (roasted black Angus beef). Wash down the goodness with a pitcher of sangria and start plotting that south-of-the-border getaway.

LOVELY DAY THAI $

Map p408 (☎212-925-3310; www.lovelydaynyc.com; 196 Elizabeth St, btwn Spring & Prince Sts, Nolita; mains $9-18; ⏰11am-10:45pm Sun-Thu, to midnight Fri & Sat; SJ/Z to Bowery; 6 to Spring St) With a look best described as doll-house-meets-hipster-diner, super-cute Lovely Day seems like an incongruous setting for cheap, Thai-influenced deliciousness. But life is full of surprises, and you'll find a steady stream of fans chowing down competent pad thai ($10.50) and fusion dishes, such as ginger fried chicken with spicy aioli ($8.50). Cash or Amex only.

CAFÉ GITANE MEDITERRANEAN $

Map p408 (☎212-334-9552; www.cafegitanenyc.com; 242 Mott St, at Prince St, Nolita; salads $9.50-16, mains $14-17; ⏰8:30am-midnight Sun-Thu, to 12:30am Fri & Sat; 🖉; SN/R to Prince St; 6 to Spring St) Clear the Gauloise smoke from your eyes and blink twice if you think you're in Paris: bistroesque Gitane has that kind of louche vibe. This is a classic see-and-be-seen haunt, popular with salad-picking models and the odd Hollywood regular. Join them for a nibble on the likes of blueberry and almond friands (small French cakes), heart-of-palm salad or Moroccan couscous with organic chicken. Cash only.

MARCHÉ MAMAN BISTRO $

Map p411 (☎212-226-0700; www.mamannyc.com; 239 Centre St, Nolita; mains $12-16, ice cream $4; ⏰8am-4pm Mon-Fri, from 9am Sat & Sun, ice cream noon-6pm Mon-Fri) Offering a fresh French take on all that Little Italy has to offer, this clean cafe and 'secret garden' feels like it's been picked up and placed here from Provence. Enjoy fantastic avocado tartinettes with lox ($10) or other items from the rotating menu. Its 'Milkmade Ice Cream' is tops – the 'blue corn waffle cone' is a mouthwatering best seller.

The owner is the creator of the Yellow Table blog (www.theyellowtable.com) and does cooking workshops here as well.

★UNCLE BOONS THAI $$

Map p408 (☎646-370-6650; www.uncleboons.com; 7 Spring St, btwn Elizabeth St & Bowery, Nolita; small plates $12-16, large plates $21-29; ⏰5:30-11pm Mon-Thu, to midnight Fri & Sat, to 10pm Sun; 📶; SJ/Z to Bowery; 6 to Spring St) Michelin-star Thai served up in a fun, tongue-in-cheek combo of retro wood-paneled dining room with Thai film posters and old family snaps. Spanning the old and the new, zesty, tangy dishes include fantastically crunchy *mieng kum* (betel-leaf wrap with ginger, lime, toasted coconut, dried shrimp, peanuts and chili; $12), *kao pat puu* (crab fried rice; $26) and banana blossom salad ($15).

BUTCHER'S DAUGHTER VEGETARIAN $$

Map p408 (☎212-219-3434; www.thebutchersdaughter.com; 19 Kenmare St, at Elizabeth St, Nolita; salads & sandwiches $12-14, dinner mains $16-19; ⏰8am-11pm; 🖉; SJ to Bowery; 6 to Spring

St) The butcher's daughter certainly has rebelled, peddling nothing but fresh herbivorous fare in her whitewashed cafe. While healthy it is, boring it's not: everything from the soaked organic muesli to the spicy kale Caesar salad with almond Parmesan or the dinnertime Butcher's burger (vegetable and black-bean patty with cashew cheddar cheese) is devilishly delish.

SIGGI'S CAFE **$$**

Map p408 (212-226-5775; www.siggysgoodfood.com; 292 Elizabeth St, btwn E Houston & Bleecker Sts, NoHo; dishes $13-25; 11am-10:30pm Mon-Sat; ; S 6 to Bleecker St; B/D/F/M to Broadway-Lafayette St) Organic deliciousness awaits at this casual, art-slung cafe (bonus points for the wintertime fireplace). All bases are covered, from soups and salads, to made-from-scratch burgers, sandwiches, even vegetarian lasagna. Virtuous libations include smoothies and freshly squeezed juices, with optional health-boosting supplements. Vegan and gluten-free diners won't go hungry either.

LA ESQUINA MEXICAN **$$**

Map p408 (646-613-7100; www.esquinanyc.com; 114 Kenmare St, at Petrosino Sq, Nolita; tacos from $3.25, mains cafe $15-25, brasserie $18-34; taqueria 11am-1:45am daily, cafe noon-midnight Mon-Fri, from 11am Sat & Sun, brasserie 6pm-2am daily; S 6 to Spring St) This mega-popular and quirky little spot combines three places really: a stand-while-you-eat taco window, a casual Mexican cafe (entrance on Lafayette St) and a dim, slinky, cavernous brasserie downstairs requiring reservations. Standouts include the *elotes callejeros* (grilled corn with queso Cotija cheese, mayo and chili powder), pulled pork tacos and mango-jicama salad.

★CHEFS CLUB FUSION **$$$**

Map p408 (212-941-1100; www.chefsclub.com; 275 Mulberry St, Nolita; mains $19-68; 6-10:30pm Mon-Thu, to 11:30pm Fri & Sat) In a building used in part for the show *Will & Grace*, Chefs Club sounds more like a discount warehouse than the spectacular dining spot it really is: visiting chefs prepare a menu for anywhere from three weeks to three months, offering their finest selections in menus that span the flavors of the globe.

★DUTCH MODERN AMERICAN **$$$**

Map p408 (212-677-6200; www.thedutchnyc.com; 131 Sullivan St, at Prince St, SoHo; mains lunch $18-37, dinner $28-66; 11:30am-11pm Mon-Thu, from 10am Sun, to 11:30pm Fri & Sat; S C/E to Spring St; R/W to Prince St; 1 to Houston St) Whether perched at the bar or dining snugly in the back room, you can always expect smart, farm-to-table comfort grub at this see-and-be-seen stalwart. Flavors traverse the globe, from crispy fish tacos with wasabi and yuzu ($18) to veal schnitzel ($35). Reservations are recommended, especially for dinner and all day on weekends. Cocktails delight – try the Macadamia Maitai ($16).

★IL BUCO ALIMENTARI & VINERIA ITALIAN **$$$**

Map p408 (212-837-2622; www.ilbucovineria.com; 53 Great Jones St, btwn Bowery & Lafayette St, NoHo; mains lunch $16-34, dinner $34-65; 8am-11pm Mon-Thu, 9am-midnight Fri-Sun; ; S 6 to Bleecker St; B/D/F/M to Broadway-Lafayette St) Whether it's espresso at the front bar, something from the deli or long-and-lazy Italian feasting in the sunken dining room, Il Buco's trendier spin-off delivers the goods. Brickwork and giant industrial lamps set a hip-n-rustic tone, echoed in the menu. Great for just dessert and coffee, too. Its olive-oil cake with rhubarb and strawberries is divine ($11).

BISTRO LES AMIS FRENCH **$$$**

Map p408 (212-226-8645; www.bistrolesamis.com; 180 Spring St, SoHo; prix-fixe lunch/dinner $14/36, dinner mains $27-40; 11:30am-11:30pm Sun-Thu, to 12:30am Fri & Sat; S C/E to Spring St) Lovely little spot with alfresco dining that has inexpensive prix-fixe options both for lunch and dinner. Inside it's a romantic wood and white-tablecloth decor, outside the tables line the corner of Spring and Thompson Sts. French onion soup is a great choice for a chilly afternoon. Bon appetit!

CHERCHE MIDI AMERICAN, FRENCH **$$$**

Map p408 (212-226-3055; www.cherchemidiny.com; 282 Bowery, at E Houston St, Nolita; lunch 2-course prix fixe $25, dinner mains $19-39; noon-3:30pm Mon-Fri, from 11am Sat & Sun, 6-10pm Sun-Mon, to 11pm Tue-Thu, to midnight Fri & Sat; ; S F to 2nd Ave) Chipped subway tiles, red banquettes and a nostalgic amber glow: Montparnasse meets Manhattan at this studiously vintage spot. Stay pure with lunchtime salade Niçoise or tartine, or salute Franco-American fraternity with the all-day prime-rib burger, pimped with cognac-spiked bacon marmalade, aged Gruyère and perfect fries. If it's on the dinner menu, make sure someone orders the lobster ravioli in ginger *beurre blanc*.

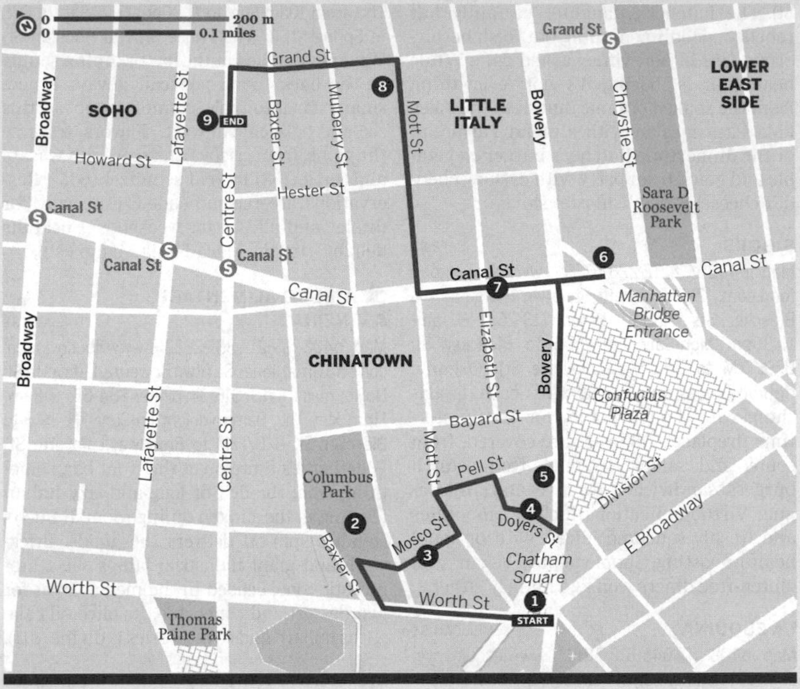

Neighborhood Walk Inside Chinatown

START CHATHAM SQ
END MUSEUM OF CHINESE IN AMERICA
LENGTH 0.9 MILES; 1½ HOURS

Begin exploring at **1 Chatham Square**, home to the Kim Lau Memorial Arch, erected in 1962 to honor the Chinese Americans who have fallen in battle. There's also a statue of Lin Ze Xu, a Qing-dynasty scholar whose anti-drug trafficking stance largely led to the First Opium War in 1839.

From Chatham Sq head northwest on Worth St until you hit **2 Columbus Park** (p93), Chinatown's unofficial living room. In the 19th century, this was NYC's notorious Five Points slum, famous for its debauchery. To the east, slip into **3 Mosco Street**, known in the 19th century as Bandits Roost, a menacing hangout for Irish gangs. Turn left into Mott St, right into Pell St, then right into **4 Doyers Street**, a crooked lane dubbed 'Barbers Row' for its bounty of hair snippers. The lane's popularity with feuding tongs (secret societies) early last century earned it the nickname Bloody Angle. American composer and lyricist Irving Berlin practiced upstairs at number 10, while at number 12 stands the neighborhood's oldest Chinese restaurant, wokking since 1920.

Turn left into Bowery and head north. At the southwest corner of Pell St and Bowery stands **5 Edward Mooney House**, NYC's oldest town house, built in 1785 by butcher Edward Mooney. This Georgian-Federal–style veteran has housed a store, hotel, billiards parlor and Chinese social club; it's now a bank. Continue north on Bowery to Canal St, where you'll see Manhattan Bridge and, just beyond that, the **6 Mahayana Buddhist Temple** (p88). See the massive golden Buddha inside, then dive into **7 Canal Street**, Chinatown's hyperactive spine and NYC's one-time Jewish Diamond District. Make a right on Mott St for superlative steamed *bao* (Chinese steamed bun, usually served as dim sum) at **8 Golden Steamer** (p100). Turn left into Grand St and left again at Centre St, delving into the Chinese-American experience at the **9 Museum of Chinese in America** (p89).

ESTELA MODERN AMERICAN $$$

Map p408 (212-219-7693; www.estelanyc.com; 47 E Houston St, btwn Mulberry & Mott Sts, Nolita; lunch mains $13-30, dinner mains $17-39; 5:30-11pm Sun-Thu, to 11:30pm Fri & Sat; S B/D/F/M to Broadway-Lafayette St; 6 to Bleecker St) Estela is on many of NYC's top spots to eat list, but it may be resting on its laurels just a bit. The food is tasty, no question, with quirky flavor combos that will keep you guessing, but tables are so tightly packed it's tough to have a conversation without meeting those sitting next to you, and portions are tiny.

That said, if you're prepared to wait, happy to dine in close proximity to others and don't need to be taking anything home in a doggie bag, it's delicious, and choices like fluke and sea urchin pâté ($23) or parsnip ice cream ($12) will tantalize the epicurious. Brunch on Friday to Sunday is extremely popular.

Chinatown & Little Italy

BAZ BAGELS JEWISH $

Map p411 (212-335-0609; www.bazbagel.com; 181 Grand St, btwn Baxter & Mulberry Sts, Little Italy; bagels $12-16; 7am-3pm Mon-Fri, 8am-4pm Sat & Sun; S J/Z, N/Q/R, 6 to Canal St; B/D to Grand St) A shamelessly flamboyant combo of pink, palm prints and portraits of Dolly and Barbra, New York's campest diner keeps things fabulous with its hand-rolled, kettle-boiled bagels. Star of the show is the Mooch ($16), an epic concoction that's half Scottish salmon, half cold-smoked sable and utterly scrumptious. Bagels aside, other standouts include blintzes and latkes, the latter made to the owner's grandmother's recipe.

DI PALO DELI $

Map p411 (212-226-1033; www.dipaloselects.com; 200 Grand St, at Mott St, Little Italy; sandwiches $7-10; 9am-7pm Mon-Sat, to 5pm Sun; S B/D to Grand St; N/Q/R, J/Z, 6 to Canal St) The *porchetta* sandwich from this fifth-generation family-run business is the only sandwich option; a crusty baguette stuffed with melt-in-your-mouth roast pork seasoned with garlic, fennel and herbs. Not only is it sinfully good, it's huge, so opt for just one slice of *porchetta* when asked. Available from 1:30pm (though this can vary), it sells out in 20 minutes.

DELUXE GREEN BO CHINESE $

Map p411 (Nice Green Bow; 212-625-2359; www.deluxegreenbo.com; 66 Bayard St, btwn Elizabeth & Mott Sts, Chinatown; mains $5.95-19.95; 11am-midnight; S N/Q/R, J/Z, 6 to Canal St; B/D to Grand St) It's all about the food at this no-frills Chinese spot: gorgeous *xiao long bao* served in steaming drums, heaping portions of noodles and gleaming plates of salubrious, sautéed spinach. Cash only.

NOM WAH TEA PARLOR CHINESE $

Map p411 (212-962-6047; www.nomwah.com; 13 Doyers St, Chinatown; dim sum from $3.75; 10:30am-9pm Sun-Thu, to 10pm Fri & Sat; S J/Z to Chambers St; 4/5/6 to Brooklyn Bridge-City Hall) Hidden down a narrow lane, Nom Wah Tea Parlor might look like an old-school American diner, but it's actually the oldest dim-sum place in town. Grab a table or seat at one of the red banquettes or counter stools and point at the mouthwatering (and often greasy) delicacies pushed around on carts.

XI'AN FAMOUS FOODS CHINESE $

Map p411 (www.xianfoods.com; 45 Bayard St, btwn Elizabeth St & Bowery, Chinatown; dishes $3-12; 11:30am-9pm Sun-Thu, to 9:30pm Fri & Sat; S N/Q/R/W, J/Z, 6 to Canal St, B/D to Grand St) Food bloggers hyperventilate at the mere mention of this small chain's hand-pulled noodles. Another star menu item is the spicy cumin lamb burger – tender lamb sautéed with ground cumin, toasted chili seeds, peppers, red onions and scallions.

BÁNH MÌ SAIGON BAKERY VIETNAMESE $

Map p411 (212-941-1541; www.banhmisaigonnyc.com; 198 Grand St, btwn Mulberry & Mott Sts, Little Italy; sandwiches $3.50-6; 8am-6pm; S N/Q/R, J/Z, 6 to Canal St) This no-frills storefront doles out some of the best banh mi in town – we're talking crisp, toasted baguettes generously stuffed with hot peppers, pickled carrots, daikon, cucumber, cilantro and your choice of meat. Top billing goes to the classic BBQ pork version. Tip: head in by 3pm as the banh mi sometimes sell out, upon which the place closes early. Cash only.

AUGUST GATHERINGS CHINESE $

Map p411 (212-274-1535; www.augustgatheringsny.com; 266 Canal St, btwn Lafayette St & Cortland Alley, Chinatown; mains $14-35; 10am-11pm; S 6, N/R/Q, J/Z to Canal St) It's a good sign when other local restaurant staff can be found at this spruced-up, well-managed place chowing down on outstanding roast meats, especially duck and other far-above-average Cantonese fare. Symbolic perhaps of the evolution of the neighborhood,

August Gatherings sits next to a McDonald's on always-bustling Canal St, and also offers plenty of Americanized Chinese dishes.

BUDDHA BODAI CHINESE $

Map p411 (212-566-8388; www.chinatownvegetarian.com; 5 Mott St, Chinatown; mains $9-22; 10am-10pm; ; J/Z to Chambers St; 4/5/6 to Brooklyn Bridge-City Hall) Serves exquisite vegetarian cuisine with Cantonese flavors like a vegan duck casserole, spinach rice rolls and vegetarian 'roast pork' buns. Since another restaurant with the same name and similar menu opened a few blocks away in 2015, this restaurant (which opened in 2004) is referred to as the 'Original Buddha Bodai'.

GOLDEN STEAMER CHINESE $

Map p411 (212-226-1886; 143a Mott St, btwn Grand & Hester Sts, Chinatown; buns $0.80-1.50; 7am-7:30pm; B/D to Grand St; N/Q/R, 6 to Canal St; J/Z to Bowery) Squeeze into this hole-in-the-wall for some of the fluffiest, tastiest *bao* (steamed buns) in Chinatown. Made on-site by bellowing Chinese cooks, fillings include succulent roast pork, Chinese sausage, salted egg and the crowd favorite – pumpkin. For something a little sweeter, try the egg custard tart.

FERRARA CAFE & BAKERY BAKERY, CAFE $$

Map p411 (212-226-6150; www.ferraranyc.com; 195 Grand St, btwn Mulberry & Mott Sts, Little Italy; pastries $7-9; 8am-midnight, to 1am Fri & Sat; J/Z, N/Q/R, 6 to Canal St; B/D to Grand St) Here since 1882, just a half block from Mulberry, is the legendary Ferrara Cafe & Bakery, brimming with classic Italian pastries and old-school ambience. The tiramisu, layers of espresso-dipped ladyfingers and rich marscarpone cheese with a lovely hint of vanilla, is heavenly.

NYONYA MALAYSIAN $$

Map p411 (212-334-3669; www.ilovenyonya.com; 199 Grand St, btwn Mott & Mulberry Sts, Little Italy; mains $8-26; 11am-11pm Sun-Thu, to midnight Fri & Sat; N/Q/R/W, J/Z, 6 to Canal St; B/D to Grand St) Take your palate to steamy Melaka at this bustling temple to Chinese-Malay cuisine. Savor the sweet, the sour and the spicy in classics such as tangy Assam fish-head casserole ($20), rich beef *rendang* (spicy dry curry; $14.50) and refreshing *rojak* (savory fruit salad tossed in a piquant tamarind dressing; $6.25). Vegetarians, be warned: there's not much on the menu for you. Cash only.

AMAZING 66 CHINESE $$

Map p411 (212-334-0099; www.amazing66.com; 66 Mott St, btwn Canal & Bayard Sts, Chinatown; mains $11-29; 11am-11pm; N/Q/R/W, J/Z, 6 to Canal St) One of the best places to chomp on Cantonese cuisine, bright, bustling Amazing 66 draws waves of local Chinese immigrants pining for a taste of home. Join them for standout dishes such as barbecued honey spare ribs, shrimp with black-bean sauce and salt-and-pepper chicken wings. Lunch specials start at $7.

★PEKING DUCK HOUSE CHINESE $$$

Map p411 (212-227-1810; www.pekingduckhousenyc.com; 28a Mott St, Chinatown; Peking duck per person $45; 11:30am-10:30pm Sun-Thu, 11:45am-11pm Fri & Sat; J/Z to Chambers St, 6 to Canal St) Offering arguably the best Peking duck in the region, the eponymous restaurant has a variety of set menus that include the house specialty. The space is fancier than some Chinatown spots, making it great to come with someone special. Do have the duck: perfectly crispy skin and moist meat make the slices ideal for a pancake, scallion strips and sauce.

DRINKING & NIGHTLIFE

From reformed speakeasies to secretive cocktail dens, an air of history and mystique surrounds many of this neighborhood's drinking holes.

★GHOST DONKEY BAR

Map p408 (212-254-0350; www.ghostdonkey.com; 4 Bleecker St, NoHo; 5pm-2am; 6 to Bleecker St; B/D/F/M to Broadway-Lafayette St) Laid-back meets trippy meets craft at this one-of-a-kind, classy mezcal house that gives vibes of Mexico, the Middle East and the Wild West. If the moon had a saloon, this place would fit right in. Dark, dim, yet pink, with low-cushioned couches encircling lower coffee tables, this bar also serves excellent craft cocktails. (Try the frozen house margarita! Tasty, right?)

★GENUINE LIQUORETTE COCKTAIL BAR

Map p411 (212-726-4633; www.genuineliquorette.com; 191 Grand St, at Mulberry St, Little Italy; 6pm-midnight Sun, Tue & Wed, to 2am Thu-Sat, from 5pm Fri; J/Z, N/Q/R/W, 6 to Canal St; B/D to Grand St) What's not to love about a jamming basement bar with canned cocktails and a Farrah Fawcett–themed restroom? You're even free to grab bottles and mixers and make your own drinks. At the helm is Ashlee, the beverage director, who regularly invites New York's finest barkeeps to create cocktails using less-celebrated hooch.

★APOTHÉKE COCKTAIL BAR

Map p411 (212-406-0400; www.apothekenyc.com; 9 Doyers St, Chinatown; 6:30pm-2am Mon-Sat, from 8pm Sun; S J/Z to Chambers St; 4/5/6 to Brooklyn Bridge-City Hall) It takes a little effort to track down this former opium-den-turned-apothecary bar on Doyers St. Inside, skilled barkeeps work like careful chemists, using local, seasonal produce from Greenmarkets to produce intense, flavorful 'prescriptions.' Their cocktail ingredient ratio is always on point, such as the pineapple-cilantro blend in the Sitting Buddha, one of the best drinks on the menu.

SPRING LOUNGE BAR

Map p408 (212-965-1774; www.thespringlounge.com; 48 Spring St, at Mulberry St, Nolita; 8am-4am Mon-Fri, from noon Sat & Sun; S 6 to Spring St; R/W to Prince St) This neon-red rebel has never let anything get in the way of a good time. In Prohibition days, it peddled buckets of beer. In the '60s its basement was a gambling den. These days, it's best known for its kooky stuffed sharks, early-start regulars and come-one, come-all late-night revelry. Perfect last stop on a bar-hopping tour of the neighborhood.

PEGU CLUB COCKTAIL BAR

Map p408 (212-473-7348; www.peguclub.com; 77 W Houston St, btwn W Broadway & Wooster St, SoHo; 5pm-2am Sun-Wed, to 4am Thu-Sat; S B/D/F/M to Broadway-Lafayette St; C/E to Spring St) Dark, elegant Pegu Club (named after a legendary gentleman's club in colonial-era Rangoon) is an obligatory stop for cocktail connoisseurs. Sink into a velvet lounge and savor seamless libations such as the silky-smooth Earl Grey MarTEAni (tea-infused gin, lemon juice and raw egg white). Grazing options are suitably Asianesque, among them duck wontons and Mandalay coconut shrimp.

LA COMPAGNIE DES VINS SURNATURELS WINE BAR

Map p411 (212-343-3660; www.compagnienyc.com; 249 Centre St, btwn Broome & Grand Sts, Nolita; wines by the glass $11-22; 5pm-1am Mon-Wed, to 2am Thu & Fri, 3pm-2am Sat, to 1am Sun; S 6 to Spring St; R/W to Prince St) A snug melange of Gallic-themed wallpaper, svelte armchairs and tea lights, La Compagnie des Vins Surnaturels is an offshoot of a Paris bar by the same name. Head sommelier Theo Lieberman steers an impressive, French-heavy wine list, with some 600 drops and no shortage of arresting labels by the glass. A short, sophisticated menu includes house-made charcuterie and chicken rillettes.

MULBERRY PROJECT COCKTAIL BAR

Map p411 (646-448-4536; www.mulberryproject.com; 149 Mulberry St, btwn Hester & Grand Sts, Little Italy; 6pm-2am Sun-Thu, to 4am Fri & Sat; S N/Q/R, J/Z, 6 to Canal St) Lurking behind an unmarked door is this intimate, cavernous cocktail den, with its festive, 'garden-party' backyard – one of the best spots to chill in the 'hood. Bespoke, made-to-order cocktails are the specialty, so disclose your preferences and let the barkeep do the rest. If you're peckish, choose from a competent list of bites that might include peach salad with pecorino cheese.

FANELLI'S CAFE BAR

Map p408 (212-226-9412; 94 Prince St, at Mercer St, SoHo; 10am-1am Mon-Thu, to 2am Fri & Sat, to midnight Sun; S N/R to Prince St) Cozy, convivial Fanelli's is the consummate soak, pouring drinks on this corner since 1847. And while SoHo may have changed over the years, Fanelli's remains true to its earthy roots – tinted mirrors, hanging pugilists and all. Skip the average food; you're here to swill and reminisce among friends, new and old.

JIMMY COCKTAIL BAR

Map p408 (212-201-9118; www.jimmysoho.com; James New York, 15 Thompson St, at Grand St, SoHo; 5pm-1am Mon-Wed, to 2am Thu-Fri, 3pm-2am Sat, 3pm-1am Sun; S A/C/E, 1 to Canal St) Lofted atop the James New York hotel in SoHo, Jimmy is a sky-high hangout with sweeping views of the city below. The summer months teem with tipsy patrons who spill out onto the open deck; in cooler weather, drinks are slung indoors from the centrally anchored bar guarded by floor-to-ceiling windows. An outdoor pool adds to the fun.

MULBERRY STREET BAR BAR

Map p411 (212-226-9345; www.mulberrystreetbar.com; 176 Mulberry St, at Broome St, Little Italy; 11am-3am Sun-Thu, to 4am Fri & Sat; S B/D to Grand St; J/Z to Bowery) Frank Sinatra liked this 100-year-old Little Italy hang, which

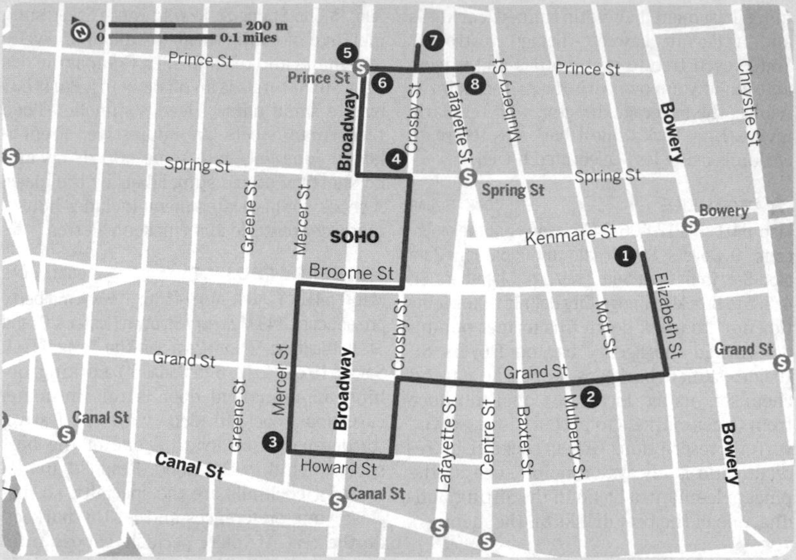

Local Life
An Artisanal Afternoon in SoHo

Shopaholics across the world lust for SoHo and its sharp, trendy whirlwind of flagship stores, coveted labels and strutting fashionistas. Look beyond the giant global brands, however, and you'll discover a whole other retail scene, one where talented artisans and independent, one-off enterprises keep things local, unique and utterly inspiring. Welcome to SoHo at its homegrown best.

❶ A Shop with Single Origin
Charge up with a cup of single-origin coffee from **Café Integral** (Map p408; ☎646-801-5747; www.cafeintegral.com; 149 Elizabeth St, btwn Broome & Kenmare Sts, Nolita; ⏰7am-6pm Mon-Fri, from 8am Sat & Sun; Ⓢ N/Q/R, J/Z, 6 to Canal St), an airy spot on Elizabeth St. Add a great pastry or croissant and you're ready to take yourself outside.

❷ Top-notch Tiramisu
Ferrara Cafe & Bakery (p100) has a huge selection of goodies but don't pass up the chance to indulge in a world-class tiramisu. Best to eat on the spot or you can get it to go.

❸ Perfect Jeans
3x1 (Map p408; ☎212-391-6969; www.3x1.us; 15 Mercer St, btwn Howard & Grand Sts, SoHo; ⏰11am-7pm Mon-Sat, noon-6pm Sun; Ⓢ N/Q/R/W, J/Z, 6 to Canal St) lets you design your perfect pair of jeans. Choose hems for ready-to-wear pairs (women's from $250, men's from $265), customize fabric and detailing on existing cuts ($625 to $850), or create your most flattering pair from scratch ($1500).

❹ Modern Art
This branch of the hugely popular **MoMA Design Store** (Map p408; ☎646-613-1367; http://store.moma.org; 81 Spring St, at Crosby St, SoHo; ⏰10am-8pm Mon-Sat, 11am-7pm Sun; Ⓢ N/R to Prince St; 6 to Spring St) has stylish, unique gifts, souvenirs and clothing. Trash cans, skateboards, even art-inspired flatware can all be yours.

❺ Curbside Culture
The sidewalk engraving on the northwest corner of Prince St and Broadway is the work of Japanese-born sculptor Ken Hiratsuka, who has carved almost 40 sidewalks since moving to NYC in 1982. While this took about five hours of actual work, its completion took two years (1983–84), as Hiratsuka's illegal nighttime chiseling was often disrupted by pesky police patrols.

Dean & DeLuca

❻ A Gourmet Nibble

NYC loves its luxe grocers and **Dean & DeLuca** (Map p408; ☎212-226-6800; www.deananddeluca.com; 560 Broadway, at Prince St, SoHo; pastries from $3, sandwiches $11; ⏰7am-9pm Mon-Fri, 8am-9pm Sat & Sun; Ⓢ N/R to Prince St; 6 to Spring St) is one of the biggest names around town. If you're feeling peckish, ready-to-eat delectables include freshly baked cheese sticks, gourmet quesadillas and almond croissants.

❼ Fragrance Flights

Drop into library-like apothecary MiN New York (p104) and request a free 'fragrance flight,' a guided exploration of the store's extraordinary collection of tantalizing 'stories' told in scent. The staff are welcoming and you may go home smelling like a rose, a spa, the surf or the sea.

❽ Books & Conversation

If MiN ignites a passion for fragrance, scan the shelves at McNally Jackson (p105) for a title on the subject. This is one of the city's best-loved independent bookstores, stocked with cognoscenti magazines and books, and an in-house cafe for quality downtime and conversation. In short, a pleasing downtown epilogue.

was also used as a backdrop for scenes in *The Sopranos, Godfather III* and *Donnie Brasco*. And you'll like it for hanging around, even as Little Italy slowly disappears. The gruff, old-school bartenders add to the charm, as does the odd mix of wide-eyed tourists, crusty regulars and overflow of hipsters.

RANDOLPH CAFE, COCKTAIL BAR

Map p411 (☎646-383-3623; www.randolphnyc.com; 349 Broome St, btwn Bowery & Elizabeth St, Nolita; ⏰5pm-2am Mon-Wed, 5pm-4am Thu & Fri, 1pm-4am Sat, 1pm-midnight Sun; 📶; Ⓢ J/Z to Bowery) Randolph serves diverse, creative cocktails in an expansive, dark-wood spot that seems perfect for crowds. Afternoons are quiet, almost contemplative, the kind of place where writers might come with a laptop or an Underwood and write that perfect draft… while drinking draft. Apropos, it offers its own Randolph beer on tap, currently a sessions IPA. Happy hour runs daily to 8pm.

LA COLOMBE COFFEE

Map p408 (☎212-625-1717; www.lacolombe.com; 270 Lafayette St, btwn Prince & Jersey Sts, Nolita; ⏰7:30am-6:30pm Mon-Fri, from 8:30am Sat & Sun; Ⓢ N/R to Prince St; 6 to Spring St) Spent SoHo shoppers reboot at this pocket-sized espresso bar. The brews are strong, full-bodied and worthy of any bar in Italy (note the cool Rome wall mural). If you're feeling nibbly, a small selection of edibles includes cookies and croissants. You'll find a bigger branch in nearby **NoHo** (Map p408; ☎212-677-5834; 400 Lafayette St, at 4th St; Ⓢ 6 to Bleecker St; B/D/F/M to Broadway-Lafayette St), with more seating but longer queues.

☆ ENTERTAINMENT

JOE'S PUB LIVE MUSIC

Map p408 (☎212-539-8778, tickets 212-967-7555; www.joespub.com; Public Theater, 425 Lafayette St, btwn Astor Pl & 4th St, NoHo; Ⓢ 6 to Astor Pl; R/W to 8th St-NYU) Part bar, part cabaret and performance venue, intimate Joe's serves up both emerging acts and top-shelf performers. Past entertainers have included Patti LuPone, Amy Schumer, the late Leonard Cohen and British songstress Adele (in fact, it was right here that Adele gave her very first American performance, back in 2008).

FILM FORUM CINEMA

Map p408 (☎212-727-8110; www.filmforum.com; 209 W Houston St, btwn Varick St & Sixth Ave, SoHo;

noon-midnight; 1 to Houston St) Plans are in the works to expand to four screens, but for now Film Forum is still a three-screen nonprofit cinema with an astounding array of independent films, revivals and career retrospectives from greats such as Orson Welles. Theaters are small, so get there early for a good viewing spot. Showings often include director talks or other film-themed discussions for hardcore cinephiles.

PUBLIC THEATER LIVE PERFORMANCE

Map p408 (212-539-8500; www.publictheater.org; 425 Lafayette St, btwn Astor Pl & 4th St, NoHo; 6 to Astor Pl; R/W to 8th St-NYU) This legendary theater was founded as the Shakespeare Workshop back in 1954 and has launched some of New York's big hits, including *Hamilton* back in 2015. Today, you'll find a lineup of innovative programming as well as reimagined classics from the past, with Shakespeare in heavy rotation. Speaking of the bard, the Public also stages star-studded Shakespeare in the Park performances during the summer.

SHOPPING

SoHo bursts at its fashionable seams with stores big and small. Hit Broadway for Main St chains, shoe shops and jean outlets, or the streets to the west for higher-end fashion and accessories. Over on Lafayette, shops cater to the DJ and skate crowds with indie labels and vintage thrown into the mix. If indie-chic is your thing, continue east to Nolita, home of tiny jewel-box boutiques selling unique threads, kicks and accessories. Mott St is best for browsing, followed by Mulberry and Elizabeth. For medicinal herbs, exotic Eastern fruits, woks and Chinese teapots, scour the frenetic streets of Chinatown.

★MIN NEW YORK COSMETICS

Map p408 (212-206-6366; www.min.com; 117 Crosby St, btwn Jersey & Prince Sts, SoHo; 11am-7pm Tue-Sat, noon-6pm Mon & Sun; B/D/F/M to Broadway-Lafayette St; N/R to Prince St) This super-friendly, chic, library-like fragrance apothecary has exclusive perfumes, bath and grooming products, and scented candles. Look out for artisanal fragrance 'stories' from MiN's own line. Prices span affordable to astronomical, and the scents are divine. Unlike many places, here there's no pressure to buy.

★SATURDAYS FASHION & ACCESSORIES

Map p408 (212-966-7875; www.saturdaysnyc.com; 31 Crosby St, btwn Broome & Grand Sts, SoHo; store 10am-7pm, coffee bar 8am-7pm Mon-Fri, 10am-7pm Sat & Sun; ; N/Q/R/W, J/Z to Canal St; 6 to Spring St) SoHo's version of a surf shop sees boards and wax paired up with designer grooming products, graphic art and surf tomes, and Saturdays' own line of high-quality, fashion-literate threads for dudes. Styled-up, grab a coffee from the in-house espresso bar, hang in the back garden and fish for some crazy, shark-dodging tales. There's a second branch in the West Village (p161).

RAG & BONE FASHION & ACCESSORIES

Map p408 (212-219-2204; www.rag-bone.com; 117-119 Mercer St, btwn Prince & Spring Sts, SoHo; 11am-9pm Mon-Sat, 11am-7pm Sun; N/R to Prince St) Downtown label Rag & Bone is a hit with many of New York's coolest, sharpest dressers – both men and women. Detail-oriented pieces range from clean-cut shirts and blazers and graphic tees to monochromatic sweaters, feather-light strappy dresses, leather goods and Rag & Bone's highly prized jeans. The tailoring is generally impeccable, with accessories including shoes, hats, bags and wallets.

OPENING CEREMONY FASHION & ACCESSORIES, SHOES

Map p408 (212-219-2688; www.openingceremony.com; 35 Howard St, btwn Broadway & Lafayette St, SoHo; 11am-8pm Mon-Sat, noon-7pm Sun; N/Q/R/W, J/Z, 6 to Canal St) Unisex Opening Ceremony is famed for its never-boring edit of A-list indie labels. It showcases a changing roster of names from across the globe, both established and emerging; complementing them are Opening Ceremony's own avant-garde creations. No matter who's hanging on the racks, you can always expect showstopping, 'where-did-you-get-that?!' threads that are street smart, bold and refreshingly unexpected.

DE VERA ANTIQUES

Map p408 (212-625-0838; www.deveraobjects.com; 1 Crosby St, at Howard St, SoHo; 11am-7pm Tue-Sat; N/Q/R/W, J/Z, 6 to Canal St) Federico de Vera travels the globe in search of rare and exquisite jewelry, carvings, lacquerware and other *objets d'art* for this jewel-box of a store. Illuminated vitrines display works such as 200-year-old Buddhas, Venetian glassware and gilded, inlaid boxes from the Meiji period, while oil paintings and carvings along the walls complete the museum-like experience.

ODIN FASHION & ACCESSORIES

Map p411 (212-966-0026; www.odinnewyork.com; 161 Grand St, btwn Lafayette & Centre Sts, Nolita; 11am-8pm Mon-Sat, noon-7pm Sun; S 6 to Spring St; N/R to Prince St) Odin's flagship men's boutique carries hip downtown labels, and a select edit of imports, among them Nordic labels Acne. Other in-store tempters include fragrances, jewelry from Brooklyn creatives such as Naval Yard and Uhuru, and street-smart footwear from cult labels like Common Projects. You'll find another branch in the West Village (p160).

MCNALLY JACKSON BOOKS

Map p408 (212-274-1160; www.mcnallyjackson.com; 52 Prince St, btwn Lafayette & Mulberry Sts, Nolita; store 10am-10pm Mon-Fri, to 9pm Sun, cafe 9am-9pm Mon-Fri, from 10am Sat, 10am-8pm Sun; S N/R to Prince St; 6 to Spring St) Bustling indie MJ stocks an excellent selection of magazines and books, covering contemporary fiction, food writing, architecture and design, art and history. If you can score a seat, the in-store cafe is a fine spot to settle in with some reading material or to catch one of the frequent readings and book signings held here.

For anyone who aspires to be a (self) published author, you can print out your own tome on the bookstore's Espresso print-on-demand book machine.

INA WOMEN VINTAGE

Map p408 (212-334-9048; www.inanyc.com; 21 Prince St, btwn Mott & Elizabeth Sts, Nolita; noon-8pm Mon-Sat, to 7pm Sun; S 6 to Spring St; N/R to Prince St) Pre-loved, high-end fashion, shoes and accessories for female fashionistas.

JOE'S JEANS FASHION & ACCESSORIES

Map p408 (212-925-5727; www.joesjeans.com; 77 Mercer St, btwn Spring & Broome Sts, SoHo; 11am-7pm Mon-Sat, noon-6pm Sun; S N/R to Prince St; 6 to Spring St) Sex up your pins with a pair of jeans from this cult LA label. Options include 'Flawless' denim, which has stretch fabric to flatter your form, as well as skinny jeans designed to fit more shapes than just 'supermodel.' Mix and match with super-comfy shirts, hoodies, sweaters and the ever-popular denim jacket.

INA MEN VINTAGE

Map p408 (212-334-2210; www.inanyc.com; 19 Prince St, at Elizabeth St, Nolita; noon-8pm Mon-Sat, to 7pm Sun; S 6 to Spring St; N/R to Prince St) Male style-meisters love INA for pre-loved, luxury clothes, shoes and accessories. Edits are high quality across the board, with sought-after items, including the likes of Rag & Bone jeans, Alexander McQueen wool pants, Burberry shirts and Church's brogues.

RUDY'S MUSIC MUSIC

Map p408 (212-625-2557; http://rudysmusic.com; 461 Broome St, btwn Greene & Mercer Sts, SoHo; 10:30am-7pm Mon-Sat; S 6 to Spring St; N/R to Prince St) Some of the world's biggest names in music shop here – not surprising given that the store stocks one of the world's finest collections of D'Angelico guitars. A repair service is also offered. Rock on!

UNIQLO FASHION & ACCESSORIES

Map p408 (877-486-4756; www.uniqlo.com; 546 Broadway, btwn Prince & Spring Sts, SoHo; 10am-9pm Mon-Sat, 11am-8pm Sun; S R/W to Prince St; 6 to Spring St) This enormous, three-story Japanese emporium, the company's first location in the US, owes its popularity to good-looking, good-quality apparel at discount prices. You'll find Japanese denim, Mongolian cashmere, graphic T-shirts, svelte skirts, high-tech thermals and endless racks of colorful ready-to-wear items – with most things falling below the $100 mark.

ADIDAS FLAGSHIP STORE SHOES

Map p408 (212-966-0954; www.adidas.com; 115 Spring St, btwn Greene & Mercer Sts, SoHo; 10am-8pm Mon-Sat, 11am-7pm Sun; S N/R to Prince St) Iconic triple-striped sneakers at the Adidas flagship store. Kicks aside, pimp your look with hoodies, track wear, T-shirts and accessories, including eye wear, watches and retro-funky bags.

For an alternate big-box retail experience, head to the 29,500-sq-ft **Adidas sneaker emporium** (Map p408; 212-529-0081; 610 Broadway, at Houston St, SoHo; 10am-9pm Mon-Sat, 11am-8pm Sun; S B/D/F/M to Broadway-Lafayette St; N/R to Prince St) a few blocks north.

RESURRECTION VINTAGE

Map p408 (212-625-1374; www.resurrectionvintage.com; 45 Great Jones Rd, btwn Lafayette & Bowery Sts, NoHo; 11am-7pm Mon-Sat; S 6 to

Spring St; N/R to Prince St) Resurrection gives new life to cutting-edge designs from past decades. Striking, mint-condition pieces cover the eras of mod, glam-rock and new-wave design, and design deities such as Marc Jacobs have dropped by for inspiration. Top picks include Halston dresses and Courrèges coats and jackets.

FJÄLLRÄVEN SPORTS & OUTDOORS

Map p408 (☎646-682-9253; www.fjallraven.us; 38 Greene St, SoHo; ⌚10am-8pm Mon-Sat, to 7pm Sun; SN/Q/R/W to Canal St, B/D/F/M to Broadway-Lafayette St) Once known only to Swedes and Danes and a few lucky tourists, this uber-popular backpack with the unmistakable fox logo and impossible-to-pronounce name is now ubiquitous in big cities around the world, and you'll see plenty as you walk around. Buy a rainbow of colors here, in small or large, as well as other outdoorsy-type goods.

PURL SOHO ARTS & CRAFTS

Map p408 (☎212-420-8796; www.purlsoho.com; 459 Broome St, btwn Greene & Mercer Sts, SoHo; ⌚noon-7pm Mon-Fri, to 6pm Sat & Sun; S6 to Spring St; N/R to Prince St) The brainchild of a former *Martha Stewart Living* editor, Purl is a colorful library of fabric and yarn that feels like an in-person Etsy boutique, with inspiration for DIY crafts galore and a scatter of finished products that make unique stocking stuffers.

NEW KAM MAN HOMEWARES

Map p411 (☎212-571-0330; www.newkamman.com; 200 Canal St, btwn Mulberry & Mott Sts, Chinatown; ⌚9:30am-7:30pm; SN/Q/R, J/Z, 6 to Canal St) Head past hanging ducks to the basement of this classic Canal St food store for cheap Chinese and Japanese tea sets, plus kitchen products like chopsticks, bowls, stir-frying utensils and rice cookers. Upstairs is a wide selection of Asian foods.

HOUSING WORKS BOOKSTORE BOOKS

Map p408 (☎212-334-3324; www.housingworks.org/locations/bookstore-cafe; 126 Crosby St, btwn E Houston & Prince Sts, SoHo; ⌚9am-9pm Mon-Fri, 10am-5pm Sat & Sun; SB/D/F/M to Broadway-Lafayette St; N/R to Prince St) Relaxed, earthy and featuring a great selection of secondhand books, vinyl, CDs and DVDs you can buy for a good cause (proceeds go to the city's HIV-positive and AIDS-infected homeless population), this creaky hideaway is a very local place to while away a few quiet afternoon hours browsing or sitting in the on-site cafe.

Check the website for regular events, which include highly entertaining Moth StorySLAM (www.themoth.org) competitions.

EVOLUTION NATURE STORE GIFTS & SOUVENIRS

Map p416 (☎212-343-1114; www.theevolutionstore.com; 687 Broadway, btwn W 3rd & W 4th Sts; ⌚11am-8pm; SR/W to 8th Ave-NYU; 6 to Astor Pl) In the market for a shrunken head? Perhaps a dried scarab beetle? This SoHo favorite has display cases full of strange finds from all over the world. The store is cavernous and often busy, especially on weekends when people doing the SoHo boutique crawl wander in to ogle the oddities.

AJI ICHIBAN FOOD

Map p411 (☎212-233-7650; 37 Mott St, btwn Bayard & Mosco Sts, Chinatown; ⌚10am-7pm Mon-Fri, to 8pm Sat & Sun; SN/Q/R, J/Z, 6 to Canal St) This Hong Kong chain is a dream come true for anyone with a sweet tooth, whether from Asia or not. Defy your dentist with sesame-flavored marshmallows, milk candy jellies, honey candy, and preserved plum and rose. Savory fans can snack Asian-style on the likes of dried spicy squid or anchovy, crab chips and ubiquitous wasabi peas.

SPORTS & ACTIVITIES

GREAT JONES SPA SPA

Map p408 (☎212-505-3185; www.gjspa.com; 29 Great Jones St, btwn Lafayette St & Bowery, NoHo; ⌚9am-10pm; S6 to Bleecker St; B/D/F/M to Broadway-Lafayette St) Don't skimp on the services at this downtown feng shui–designed place, whose offerings include blood-orange salt scrubs and stem-cell facials. If you spend over $100 per person (not difficult: hour-long massages/facials start at $145/135), you get access to the water lounge with thermal hot tub, sauna, steam room and cold plunge pool (swimwear required).

TOP SIGHT
NEW MUSEUM OF CONTEMPORARY ART

The New Museum of Contemporary Art's Lower East Side avatar, designed by renowned Japanese architecture firm SANAA, is proof that it's not just what's inside a museum that makes it noteworthy. The street view of the museum alone manages to punctuate the neighborhood with something unique, and its cache of artistic work will dazzle just as much as its facade.

A Museum with a Mission

Founded in 1977 by Marcia Tucker and housed in five different locations over the years, the museum's mission statement is simple: 'New art, new ideas.' The institution gave gallery space to artists Keith Haring, Jeff Koons, Joan Jonas, Mary Kelly and Andres Serrano at the beginning of their careers, and continues to show contemporary heavy-hitters. The city's sole museum dedicated to contemporary art has brought a steady menu of edgy works in new forms, such as seemingly random, discarded materials fused together and displayed in the middle of a vast room.

The museum also houses the New Museum Cafe, a great spot for sampling the gourmet goodies of NYC purveyors, including baked goods by Cafe Grumpy, teas by McNulty, coffee by Intelligentsia and sandwiches by Duck's Eatery.

In Orbit

It's now been several years since the New Museum has taken hold, inspiring nearby structures to adopt similarly ethereal designs. Perhaps most interestingly, the museum has become somewhat of a magnetic force attracting a clutch of small workshops and creative spaces (p114) to its orbit.

DON'T MISS

- The facade from across the street
- New Museum Cafe
- New Museum Store

PRACTICALITIES

- Map p414, A3
- ☎212-219-1222
- www.newmuseum.org
- 235 Bowery, btwn Stanton & Rivington Sts, Lower East Side
- adult/child $18/free, 7-9pm Thu by donation
- ⏱11am-6pm Tue, Wed & Fri-Sun, to 9pm Thu
- Ⓢ R/W to Prince St; F to 2nd Ave; J/Z to Bowery; 6 to Spring St

East Village & the Lower East Side

EAST VILLAGE | LOWER EAST SIDE

Neighborhood Top Five

❶ **New Museum of Contemporary Art** (p110) Admiring the off-white webbing of the boxy facade of this museum, then wandering in to appreciate mind-bending iterations of art across myriad media.

❷ **Lower East Side Tenement Museum** (p109) Witnessing the shockingly cramped conditions of early immigrants at this brilliantly curated museum.

❸ **St Marks Place** (p112) Passing knickknack shops and sake bars on St Marks Place, then heading to the neighboring streets for a quieter round of nibbling and boutique-ing.

❹ **Alphabet City** (p108) Hitting up pubs and cocktail lounges, stopping for a bite to eat along the way.

❺ **Vanessa's Dumpling House** (p119) Sampling some of the best, and most affordable, dumplings in the city.

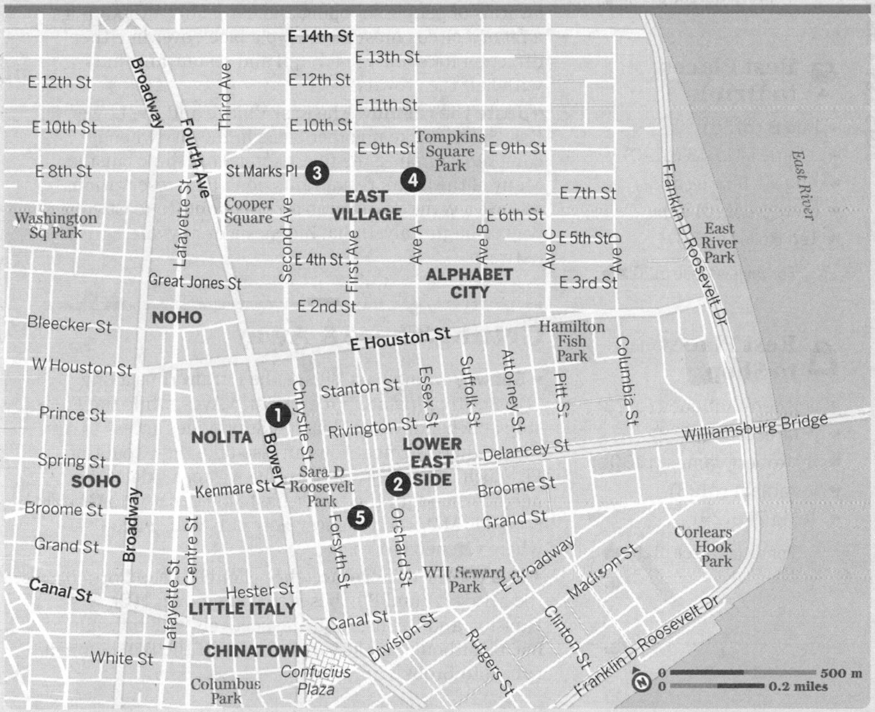

For more detail of this area see Map p412 and p414➡

Lonely Planet's Top Tip

A lot of the restaurants in this neck of the woods don't take reservations, so stop by the restaurant of your choosing in the early afternoon (2pm should do the trick) and place your name on the roster for the evening meal – chances are high that they'll take your name and you'll get seated right away when you return for dinner later on.

Best Places to Eat

- Upstate (p117)
- Degustation (p118)
- Momofuku Noodle Bar (p116)
- Mamoun's (p115)
- Veselka (p116)

For reviews, see p115.

Best Places to Drink

- Rue B (p120)
- Jimmy's No 43 (p120)
- Angel's Share (p122)
- Immigrant (p122)
- Ten Bells (p123)

For reviews, see p120.

Best Places to Shop

- Obscura Antiques (p128)
- A-1 Records (p129)
- By Robert James (p130)
- Verameat (p128)
- Tokio 7 (p129)

For reviews, see p128.

Explore East Village & the Lower East Side

If you've been dreaming of those quintessential New York City moments – graffiti on crimson brick, skyscrapers rising overhead, punks, grannies and financial-industry types walking side by side, cute cafes with rickety tables spilling out onto the sidewalks – then the East Village is your Holy Grail. Stick to the area around Tompkins Square Park (p113), and the lettered avenues (known as Alphabet City) to its east, for interesting little nooks in which to eat and drink – as well as a collection of great community gardens that provide leafy respite and the occasional live performance. The streets below Houston St and east of the Bowery are packed with cool boutiques and inventive restaurants, with the odd divey, grungy punk bar still surviving amid the trendy speakeasys. During the day, the vibe is relaxed, whereas at night, when the drinks are flowing, the hormones are pulsing and the crowds descend, it's a very different place. It's a mixed bag, indeed, and perhaps one of the most emblematic of today's city.

Local Life

- **One block over** Famed St Marks Place (p112) draws swarms of people shopping and carousing – though it's a bit of a circus most days. Hop a block over in either direction for some great retail and restaurant finds with half the crowds.
- **Taste the rainbow** The East Village and the Lower East Side are like no other place in the city when it comes to sampling the finest spread of ethnic cuisine. Many of the area's restaurants don't take reservations, so have a wander and grab an open table to feast your way through Italy, India, Indonesia or anywhere in-between.

Getting There & Away

- **Subway** In the East Village the L train runs along 14th St, stopping at First and Third Aves, while the F stop at Second Ave at Houston St provides access to the southern stretch. You can also take the 6 to Astor Pl, which lets you off right on the western side of the neighborhood. In the Lower East Side the B/D to Grand St and F, M/J/Z to Delancey-Essex Sts will get you where you need to go.
- **Bus** For the eastern stretches of either neighborhood, the M14, M21 and B39 buses that run down 14th, Houston and Delancey Sts, respectively, will be your friend (although make sure to jump off the B39 before it runs into Brooklyn).

TOP SIGHT
LOWER EAST SIDE TENEMENT MUSEUM

There's no museum in New York that humanizes the city's colorful past quite like the Lower East Side Tenement Museum, which puts the neighborhood's heartbreaking but inspiring heritage on full display in several re-creations of former tenements. Always evolving, it has a variety of tours and talks beyond the museum's walls – a must for anyone interested in old New York.

DON'T MISS

- Themed walks around the neighborhood
- A peek into the 1870s and the 1930s on the Hard Times tour
- A prix-fixe meal called Tasting at the Tenement (Thursdays at 6:30pm)
- The free 30-minute film shown in the visitor center

PRACTICALITIES

- Map p414, B3
- 877-975-3786
- www.tenement.org
- 103 Orchard St, btwn Broome & Delancey Sts, Lower East Side
- tours adult/student & senior $25/20
- 10am-6:30pm Fri-Wed, to 8:30pm Thu
- S B/D to Grand St; J/M/Z to Essex St; F to Delancey St

Inside the Tenement

A wide range of tenement tours lead visitors into the building where hundreds of immigrants lived and worked over the years. Hard Times, one of the most popular tours, visits apartments from two different time periods – the 1870s and the 1930s. There you'll see the squalid conditions tenants faced – in the early days there was a wretched communal outhouse and no electricity or running water – and what life was like for the families who lived there. Other tours focus on Irish immigrants and the harsh discrimination they faced, sweatshop workers and 'shop life' (with a tour through a re-created 1870s German beer hall).

Neighborhood Tours

A great way to understand the immigrant experience is on a walking tour around the neighborhood. These tours, ranging from 75 minutes to two hours, explore a variety of topics. Foods of the Lower East Side looks at the ways traditional foods have shaped American cuisine; Then & Now explores how the neighborhood has changed over the decades; Outside the Home looks at life beyond the apartment – where immigrants stored (and lost) their life savings, the churches and synagogues so integral to community life, and the meeting halls where poorly paid workers gathered to fight for better conditions.

Meet Victoria

Travel back to 1916 and meet Victoria Confino, a 14-year-old girl from a Greek Sephardic family. Played by a costumed interpreter, Victoria interacts with visitors and answers questions about what her life was like in those days. It's especially recommended for kids, as visitors are free to handle household objects. This one-hour tour is held on weekends year-round, and daily during the summer.

103 Orchard Street

The visitor center at 103 Orchard St has a museum shop and a small screening room that plays an original film about the history and influence of immigrants on the Lower East Side. Several evenings a month, the museum hosts talks here, often relating to the present immigrant experience in America. The building itself was, naturally, a tenement too – ask the staff about the interesting families of East European and Italian descent that once dwelled here.

SANAA's Vision

While exhibits rotate through the museum, regularly changing the character of the space within, the shell – an inspired architectural gesture – remains a constant, acting as a unique structural element in the diverse cityscape, while also simultaneously fading into the background and allowing the exhibits to shine.

The building's structure is the brainchild of the hot Japanese firm SANAA – a partnership between two great minds, Kazuyo Sejima and Ryue Nishizawa. In 2010 SANAA won the coveted Pritzker Prize (think the Oscars of architecture) for its contributions to the world of design. Its trademark vanishing facades are known worldwide for abiding by a strict adherence to a form-follows-function design aesthetic, sometimes taking the land plot's footprint into the overall shape of the structure. The box-atop-box scheme provides a striking counterpoint to the clusters of crimson brick and iron fire escapes outside, while alluding to the geometric exhibition chasms within.

MUSEUM SHOP

If you aren't so keen on the current exhibits, it's still worth stopping by the museum's store to peruse some of the excellent coffee-table books – sometimes the take-homes include savvy collaborations with showcased artists. The shop has the same hours of operation as the museum.

To save cash, stop by on Thursday evening between 7pm and 9pm, when admission is pay what you wish. Depending on the show, the crowds can be sizable. We recommend lining up by 6:45pm.

FIRST SATURDAYS FOR FAMILIES

On the first Saturday of the month, the New Museum hosts special events for budding artists, with hands-on crafts and activities for kids aged four to 15. Free museum admission is included for adults (it's always free for kids).

OSUGI / SHUTTERSTOCK ©

TOP SIGHT
ST MARKS PLACE

In New York every street tells a story, from the action unfurling before your eyes to the dense history hidden behind colorful facades. St Marks Place is one of the best strips of pavement for storytelling, as almost every building lining these blocks is rife with tales from a time when the East Village embodied a far more lawless spirit.

Astor Place

To the west of St Marks Place is **Astor Place** (Map p412; 8th St, btwn Third & Fourth Aves; S N/R to 8th St-NYU, 6 to Astor Pl), a crowded crisscrossing of streets anchored by a curious square sculpture that's affectionately (and appropriately) known by locals as *The Cube*. A favorite meeting spot for neighborhood dwellers, this work of art – actually named *Alamo* – weighs over 1800lb and is made entirely of Cor-Tensteel.

Originally Astor Place was the home of the Astor Opera House (now gone), which attracted the city's wealthy elite for regular performances in the mid-1800s. The square was also the site of the notorious Astor Place riots, in which the city's protesting Irish population caused such a stir about their homeland potato famine that the police fired shots into the masses, injuring hundreds and killing at least 18 people.

Today the square is largely known as the former home of the *Village Voice* and the **Cooper Union** (Foundation Building, Great Hall; Map p412; www.cooper.edu; 7 E 7th St, btwn Third & Fourth Aves, East Village; S 6 to Astor Pl, N/R to 8th St-NYU) design institute.

DON'T MISS

- The *Physical Graffiti* buildings made famous by Led Zeppelin (numbers 96 and 98)
- Brunch at one of the tasty cafes
- Tompkins Square Park at the end of the street
- Sake bombs at one of the basement Japanese bars
- Shopping for knick-knacks and odd souvenirs

PRACTICALITIES

- Map p412, C2
- St Marks Pl, Ave A to Third Ave, East Village
- S N/R/W to 8th St-NYU; 6 to Astor Pl

Third Avenue to Avenue A

Easily one of NYC's most famous streets, St Marks Place is also one of the city's smallest, occupying only three blocks between Astor Pl and Tompkins Square Park. The road, however, is jam-packed with historical tidbits that would delight any trivia buff. Until recently, 2 St Marks Place was known as the St Mark's Ale House (the St Mark's Hotel still stands), but for a time it was the famous Five-Spot, where jazz fiend Thelonious Monk got his start in the 1950s. A cast of colorful characters have left their mark at 4 St Marks Place: Alexander Hamilton's son built the structure, James Fenimore Cooper lived here in the 1830s and Yoko Ono's Fluxus artists descended upon the building in the 1960s. The buildings at 96 and 98 St Marks Place are immortalized on the cover of Led Zepellin's *Physical Graffiti* album. Though it closed in the 1990s, 122 St Marks Place was the location of a popular cafe called Sin-é, where Jeff Buckley and David Gray often performed.

Tompkins Square Park

St Marks Place terminates at a welcome clearing of green deep in the heart of the East Village. The 10.5-acre **Tompkins Square Park** (Map p412; www.nycgovparks.org; E 7th & 10th Sts, btwn Aves A & B; ⏲6am-midnight; S6 to Astor Pl) honors Daniel Tompkins, who served as governor of New York from 1807 to 1817 (and as the nation's vice president after that, under James Monroe). It's like a friendly town square for locals, who gather for chess at concrete tables, picnics on the lawn on warm days and spontaneous guitar or drum jams on various grassy knolls. It's also the site of basketball courts, a fun-to-watch dog run (a fenced-in area where humans can unleash their canines), frequent summer concerts and an always-lively kids' playground. The park, which recently underwent a facelift, wasn't always a place for such clean fun, however. In the 1980s it was a dirty, needle-strewn homeless encampment, unusable for folks wanting a place to stroll or picnic. A contentious turning point came when police razed the band shell and evicted more than 100 squatters living in a tent city in the park in 1988 (and again in 1991). That first eviction turned violent; the Tompkins Square Riot, as it came to be known, ushered in the first wave of yuppies in the dog run, fashionistas lolling on the grass and undercover narcotics agents trying to pass as druggie punk kids. These days there's not much drama, outside of the occasional music and arts festival that attempts to briefly reclaim the park's bohemian glory days.

PUNK ROCK SHOPS

The East Village was once the home base for emerging punk rock acts – many would frequent the clothing shops along St Marks to assemble their trademark looks. Although most joints have gone the way of the dodo in favor of more tourist-friendly wares, there are still a few spots that remain.

TOP BRUNCH SPOTS

In addition to all of its quirky and historical landmarks, St Marks has some wonderful places to stop for a bite. Weekend brunches in the East Village are a great bet, as the local restaurants are typically less expensive (and less scene-y) than the hot spots in neighboring 'hoods. Try Cafe Mogador (p117), which fuses American favorites with an assortment of Middle Eastern plates.

SIGHTS

East Village

ST MARKS PLACE STREET

See p112.

TOMPKINS SQUARE PARK MUSEUM

See p113.

ST MARK'S IN THE BOWERY CHURCH

Map p412 (212-674-6377; www.stmarksbowery.org; 131 E 10th St, at Second Ave, East Village; 10am-6pm Mon-Fri; S L to 3rd Ave; 6 to Astor Pl) Though it's most popular with East Village locals for its cultural offerings – such as poetry readings hosted by the Poetry Project or cutting-edge dance performances from Danspace and the Ontological Hysteric Theater – St Mark's is also a historic site. This Episcopal church stands on the site of the farm *(bouwerij)* owned by Dutch Governor Peter Stuyvesant, whose crypt lies under the grounds.

In addition to the cultural offerings, the church hosts many events and talks on current political issues. Its website has a schedule of upcoming dates.

EAST RIVER PARK PARK

Map p412 (www.nycgovparks.org/parks/east-river-park; FDR Dr & E Houston St; sunrise-1am; S F to Delancey-Essex Sts) In addition to the great ballparks, running and biking paths, 5000-seat amphitheater that hosts concerts and expansive patches of green, this park has cool, natural breezes and fine views of the Williamsburg, Manhattan and Brooklyn Bridges.

Although flanked by a looming housing project and the clogged FDR Dr on one side and the less-than-pure East River on the other, it's a fine spot for a stroll or a morning run.

Lower East Side

LOWER EAST SIDE TENEMENT MUSEUM MUSEUM

See p109.

LOWER EAST SIDE GALLERIES

Though Chelsea may be the heavy hitter when it comes to the New York gallery scene, the Lower East Side has dozens of quality showplaces. One of the early pioneers, the **Sperone Westwater gallery** (Map p414; 212-999-7337; www.speronewestwater.com; 257 Bowery, btwn E Houston & Stanton Sts, Lower East Side; 10am-6pm Tue-Sat; S F to 2nd Ave), which opened in 1975, represents art-world darlings, such as William Wegman and Richard Long, and its new home was designed by the famed Norman Foster, who's already made a splash in NYC with his Hearst Building and Avery Fisher Hall designs. Nearby, the avant-garde **Salon 94** has two Lower East Side outposts: one secreted away on **Freeman Alley** (Map p414; www.salon94.com; 1 Freeman Alley, off Rivington, Lower East Side; S F to 2nd Ave; J/Z/M to Bowery) and another on **Bowery** (Map p414; 212-979-0001; www.salon94.com; 243 Bowery, cnr Stanton St, Lower East Side; 11am-6pm Tue-Sat; S F to 2nd Ave; J/Z/M to Bowery) near the New Museum of Contemporary Art. The latter has a 20ft LCD video wall that broadcasts video art out into the street. A few blocks north is the 4000-sq-ft **Hole** (Map p412; 212-466-1100; www.theholenyc.com; 312 Bowery, at Bleecker, East Village; noon-7pm Wed-Sun; S 6 to Bleeker St; B/D/F/M to Broadway-Lafayette St) – known as much for its art as for its rowdy openings that gather both scenesters of the downtown art circuit and well-known faces, such as Courtney Love and Salman Rushdie.

Broome St between Chrystie and Bowery is quickly becoming the nexus of the Lower East Side art scene, with galleries such as **White Box**, **Canada** and **Jack Hanley** right next door to one another. Another buzzing strip of galleries runs down Orchard St between Rivington and Canal Sts.

Other popular, contemporary spaces include **Lehmann Maupin** (Map p414; 212-254-0054; www.lehmannmaupin.com; 201 Chrystie St, btwn Stanton & Rivington Sts, Lower East Side; 10am-6pm Tue-Sat; S F to Delancey-Essex Sts), **Mesler/Feuer** (Map p414; www.meslerfeuer.com; 319 Grand St, 2nd fl, btwn Allen & Orchard Sts, Lower East Side; 11am-6pm Wed-Sun; S J/M/Z/F to Delancey/Essex St; B/D to Grand St) and **Lesley Heller** (Map p414; 212-410-6120; www.lesleyheller.com; 54 Orchard St, btwn Grand & Hester, Lower East Side; 11am-6pm Wed-Sat, from noon Sun; S B/D to Grand St; F to East Broadway).

NEW MUSEUM OF CONTEMPORARY ART MUSEUM

See p110.

ANASTASIA PHOTO GALLERY

Map p414 (www.anastasia-photo.com; 143 Ludlow St, btwn Stanton & Rivington Sts, Lower East Side; ⏲11am-7pm Tue-Sun; SF to Delancey St; J/M/Z to Essex St) This small gallery specializes in documentary photography and photojournalism. Expect evocative, thought-provoking works covering subjects such as poverty in rural America, the ravages of war and disappearing cultures in Africa. Works are beautifully shot, and the staff member on hand can give a meaningful context to the images.

MUSEUM AT ELDRIDGE STREET SYNAGOGUE MUSEUM

Map p414 (☎212-219-0302; www.eldridgestreet.org; 12 Eldridge St, btwn Canal & Division Sts, Lower East Side; adult/child $14/8, Mon by suggested donation; ⏲10am-5pm Sun-Thu, to 3pm Fri; SF to East Broadway) This landmark house of worship, built in 1887, was once a center of Jewish life before falling into squalor in the 1920s. Left to rot, the synagogue was restored following a 20-year-long, $20-million restoration that was completed in 2007, and it now shines with original splendor. Museum admission includes a **guided tour** of the synagogue, which departs hourly, with the last one starting at 4pm.

KEHILA KEDOSHA JANINA SYNAGOGUE & MUSEUM SYNAGOGUE

Map p414 (☎212-431-1619; www.kkjsm.org; 280 Broome St, at Allen St, Lower East Side; ⏲11am-4pm Sun, service 9am Sat; SF, J/M/Z to Delancey-Essex Sts) This small synagogue is home to an obscure branch of Judaism, the Romaniotes, whose ancestors were slaves sent to Rome by ship but rerouted to Greece by a storm. This is their only synagogue in the Western Hemisphere, and includes a small museum bearing artifacts, such as hand-painted birth certificates, an art gallery, a Holocaust memorial for Greek Jews and costumes from Janina, the Romaniote capital of Greece.

SARA D ROOSEVELT PARK PARK

Map p414 (Houston St, at Chrystie St, Lower East Side; SF to Delancey-Essex Sts) Spiffed up in recent years, this three-block-long park is a hive of activity on weekends, with basketball courts, a small soccer pitch (with synthetic turf) and a well-loved playground (just north of Hester St). Tai chi practitioners, vegetable sellers (on the nearby cross streets) and strollers of all ages and ethnic backgrounds add to the ever-evolving scene.

EATING

Here lies the epitome of what is beautiful in New York's dining scene: mind-blowing variety – which can cover the full spectrum of continents and budgets – in just a single city block. You'll find every type of taste-bud tantalizer from hole-in-the-wall Italian trattorias, Sichuan hot pot spots, innovative sandwich shops, Ukrainian *pierogi* (dumpling) palaces, dozens of sushi and ramen joints, pizza parlors and falafel huts. E 6th St between First and Second Aves, sometimes known as 'Curry Row,' is no longer chock-a-block with cheap Bangladeshi-owned Indian restaurants, but still has a few holdouts.

East Village

ESPERANTO BRAZILIAN $

Map p412 (www.esperantony.com; 145 Ave C, at E 9th St, East Village; mains $18-24; ⏲10am-11pm Sun-Thu, to midnight Fri & Sat; SL to 1st Ave) Esperanto's vibrant green facade and large patio call to mind the glory days of Alphabet City, before the neighborhood began to trend toward gray and glass condos and sleek cocktail bars. Here you can sit outside all night sipping caipirinhas or enjoying strips of brilliantly bloody steak with chimichurri sauce. It's also a great place to get *feijoada* (traditional Brazilian meat stew).

MAMOUN'S MIDDLE EASTERN $

Map p412 (☎646-870-5785; http://mamouns.com; 30 St Marks Pl, btwn Second & Third Aves, East Village; sandwiches $4-7, plates $7-12; ⏲11am-2am Mon-Wed, to 3am Thu, to 5am Fri & Sat, to 1am Sun; S6 to Astor Pl; L to 3rd Ave) This former grab-and-go outpost of the beloved NYC falafel chain has expanded its iconic St Marks storefront with more seating inside and out. Come late on a weekend to find a line of inebriated bar hoppers ending the night with a juicy shawarma covered in Mamoun's famous hot sauce.

BAIT & HOOK SEAFOOD $

Map p412 (☎212-260-8015; www.baitandhooknyc.com; 231 Second Ave, at E 14th St, East Village; specials start at $5, mains $12-18; ⊙noon-11pm Sun-Wed, noon-midnight Thu-Sat; Ⓢ L train to 1st Ave) This Manhattan bar has happy hour specials worth celebrating and theme days that can't be missed. There's a good time any day of the week, be it Mussel Monday or Taco Tuesday. The interior is bright, airy and tastefully decorated with nautical kitsch.

ARTICHOKE BASILLE'S PIZZA PIZZA $

Map p412 (☎212-228-2004; www.artichokepizza.com; 328 E 14th St, btwn First & Second Aves, East Village; artichoke slice $5; ⊙10am-5am; Ⓢ L to 1st Ave) This mini-chain run by two Italian guys from Staten Island is legendary among New Yorkers who like their pizza full of toppings. The signature pie is a rich, cheesy treat with artichokes and spinach; the plain Sicilian is thinner, with emphasis solely on the crisp crust and savory sauce. Lines usually form fast.

MIKEY LIKES IT ICE CREAM $

Map p412 (www.mikeylikesiticecream.com; 199 Ave A, btwn E 12th & E 13th Sts, East Village; single scoop $4; ⊙noon-midnight Sun-Thu, to 2am Fri & Sat; Ⓢ L to 1st Ave) There's more than meets the eye at this tiny blue-and-white ice-cream shop. The homemade flavors are delicious and come in wild combinations: balsamic macerated strawberries with black pepper or banana ice cream with chocolate-covered peanuts. Founder and owner Mike Cole's inspirational story makes the hip-hop-inspired ice cream all the sweeter.

MIGHTY QUINN'S BARBECUE $

Map p412 (☎212-677-3733; www.mightyquinnsbbq.com; 103 Second Ave, at 6th St, East Village; single serving of meat $8-10; ⊙11:30am-11pm Sun-Thu, to midnight Fri & Sat; Ⓢ 6 to Astor Pl; F to 2nd Ave) Grab yourself a tray and join hordes of barbecue lovers at this buzzing, very popular meat eatery. Tender brisket, smoky spare ribs, juicy piles of pulled pork and ample portions of sides (coleslaw, sweet potato casserole, baked beans) add up to a decadent carnivorous feast.

MUD CAFE $

Map p412 (☎212-529-8766; www.onmud.com; 307 E 9th St, btwn Second & First Aves, East Village; mains $6-13, brunch $18.50; ⊙7:30am-midnight Mon-Fri, from 8am Sat & Sun; Ⓢ L to 3rd Ave; L to 1st Ave; 4/6 to Astor Pl) This 9th St nook is a favorite among East Villagers looking for a quick caffeine fix, a hearty breakfast after a long night out or a friendly place to chat with old friends (there's no wi-fi). The everyday brunch (coffee, craft beer or mimosa and any main course) is a deal at $18.50. Head out back for a surprisingly large garden.

RAI RAI KEN RAMEN $

Map p412 (☎212-477-7030; 218 E 10th St, btwn First & Second Aves, East Village; ramen $10-13; ⊙11:30am-11:45pm; Ⓢ L to 1st Ave; 6 to Astor Pl) Rai Rai Ken's storefront may only be the size of its door, but it's pretty hard to miss since there's usually a small congregation of hungry locals lurking out the front. Inside, low-slung wooden stools are arranged around the noodle bar, where the cooks busily churn out piping-hot portions of tasty pork-infused broth.

VESELKA EASTERN EUROPEAN $

Map p412 (☎212-228-9682; www.veselka.com; 144 Second Ave, at 9th St, East Village; mains $10-19; ⊙24hr; Ⓢ L to 3rd Ave; 6 to Astor Pl) A bustling tribute to the area's Ukrainian past, Veselka dishes out *pierogi* (handmade dumplings) and veal goulash amid the usual suspects of greasy comfort food. The cluttered spread of tables is available to loungers and carbo-loaders all night long, though it's a favorite any time of day, and a regular haunt for writers, actors and East Village characters.

★MOMOFUKU NOODLE BAR NOODLES $$

Map p412 (☎212-777-7773; www.noodlebar-ny.momofuku.com; 171 First Ave, btwn E 10th & 11th Sts, East Village; mains $16; ⊙noon-11pm Sun-Thu, to 1am Fri & Sat; Ⓢ L to 1st Ave; 6 to Astor Pl) With just 30 stools and a no-reservations policy, you'll always have to wait to cram into this bustling phenomenon. Queue for the namesake special: homemade ramen noodles in broth, served with poached egg and pork belly or some interesting combos. The menu changes daily and includes buns (such as brisket and horseradish), snacks (smoked chicken wings) and desserts.

UPSTATE SEAFOOD $$

Map p412 (☎212-460-5293; www.upstatenyc.com; 95 First Ave, btwn E 5th & 6th Sts, East Village; mains $15-30; ⊙5-11pm; Ⓢ F to 2nd Ave) Upstate serves outstanding seafood dishes and craft beers. The small, always-changing menu

COMMUNITY GARDENS

After a stretch of arboreal abstinence in New York City, the community gardens of Alphabet City are breathtaking. A network of gardens was carved out of abandoned lots to provide low-income neighborhoods with a communal backyard. Trees and flowers were planted, sandboxes were built, found-art sculptures erected and domino games played – all within green spaces wedged between buildings or even claiming entire blocks. And while some were destroyed – in the face of much protest – to make way for the projects of developers, plenty of green spots have held their ground. You can visit most on weekends, when the gardens tend to be open to the public; many gardeners are activists within the community and are a good source of information about local politics.

Le Petit Versailles (Map p412; www.alliedproductions.org; 346 E Houston St, at Ave C, East Village; ⌚2-7pm Thu-Sun; Ⓢ F to Delancey St; J/M/Z to Essex St) is a unique marriage of a verdant oasis and an electrifying arts organization, offering a range of quirky performances and screenings to the public. The **6th & B Garden** (Map p412; www.6bgarden.org; E 6th St & Ave B, East Village; ⌚1-6pm Sat & Sun Apr-Oct; Ⓢ 6 to Astor Pl; L to 1st Ave) is a well-organized space that hosts free music events, workshops and yoga sessions; check the website for details. Three dramatic weeping willows, an odd sight in the city, grace the twin plots of **La Plaza Cultural** (Map p412; www.laplazacultural.com; E 9th St, at Ave C, East Village; ⌚10am-7pm Sat & Sun Apr-Oct; Ⓢ F to 2nd Ave; L to 1st Ave). Also check out the **All People's Garden** (Map p412; 293 E 3rd St, btwn Aves C & D, East Village; ⌚1-5pm Sat & Sun Apr-Oct; Ⓢ F to 2nd Ave) and **Brisas del Caribe** (Map p412; 237 E 3rd St, East Village; ⌚1-5pm Sat & Sun Apr-Oct; Ⓢ F to 2nd Ave).

features the likes of beer-steamed mussels, seafood stew, scallops over mushroom risotto, softshell crab and wondrous oyster selections. There's no freezer – seafood comes from the market daily, so you know you'll be getting only the freshest ingredients. Lines can be long, so go early.

LUZZO'S — PIZZA $$

Map p412 (☎212-473-7447; www.luzzosgroup.com; 211 First Ave, btwn E 12th & 13th Sts, East Village; pizzas $18-25; ⌚noon-11pm Sun-Thu, to midnight Fri & Sat; Ⓢ L to 1st Ave) Fan-favorite Luzzo's occupies a thin, rustically designed sliver of real estate in the East Village, which is stuffed to the gills each evening as discerning diners feast on thin-crust pizzas, kissed with ripe tomatoes and cooked in a coal-fired stove. Cash only.

LAVAGNA — ITALIAN $$

Map p412 (☎212-979-1005; www.lavagnanyc.com; 545 E 5th St, btwn Aves A & B, East Village; mains $19-34; ⌚6-11pm Mon-Thu, to midnight Fri, noon-3:30pm & 5pm-midnight Sat, to 11pm Sun; 🍷👪; Ⓢ F to 2nd Ave) Dark wood, flickering candles and a fiery glow from a somewhat open kitchen help make homey Lavagna a late-night hideaway for lovers. But it's laid-back enough to make it appropriate for children, at least in the early hours before the smallish space fills up. Delicious pastas, thin-crust pizzas and hearty mains, such as baby rack of lamb, are standard fare.

CAFE MOGADOR — MOROCCAN $$

Map p412 (☎212-677-2226; www.cafemogador.com; 101 St Marks Pl, btwn 1st St & Ave A, East Village; mains lunch $9-18, dinner $16-22; ⌚9am-midnight Sun-Thu, until 1am Fri & Sat; Ⓢ 6 to Astor Pl) Family-run Mogador is a long-running NYC classic, serving fluffy piles of couscous, chargrilled lamb and *merguez* (a spicy lamb or beef sausage) over basmati rice, as well as satisfying mixed platters of hummus and baba ganoush. The standouts, however, are the tagines – traditionally spiced, long-simmered chicken or lamb dishes served up five different ways.

A garrulous young crowd packs the space, spilling out onto the small cafe tables on warm days. Brunch (served weekends from 9am to 4pm) is excellent.

WESTVILLE EAST — MODERN AMERICAN $$

Map p412 (☎212-677-2033; www.westvillenyc.com; 173 Ave A, btwn E 10th & E 11th Sts, East Village; mains $13-23; ⌚10am-11pm; Ⓢ L to 1st Ave; 6 to Astor Pl) Market-fresh veggies and mouthwatering mains are the name of the game at Westville, and it doesn't hurt that the cottage-chic surrounds are undeniably charming. It's a favorite among New Yorkers at lunchtime when they take a break from their jobs to scarf down kale salads or hot dogs.

IPPUDO NY NOODLES **$$**

Map p412 (☎212-388-0088; www.ippudo.com/ny; 65 Fourth Ave, btwn 9th & 10th Sts, East Village; ramen $15; ⊙11am-3:30pm & 5-11:30pm Mon-Thu, to 12:30am Fri, 11am-11:30pm Sat, to 10:30pm Sun; Ⓢ R/W to 8th St-NYU; 4/5/6, N/Q/R/W, L to 14th St-Union Sq; 6 to Astor Pl) The good folks from Ippudo have kicked things up a notch here – they've taken their mouthwatering ramen recipe (truly, it's delicious) and spiced it up with sleek surrounds (hello shiny black surfaces and streamers of cherry red) and blasts of rock and roll on the overhead speakers.

DEGUSTATION MODERN EUROPEAN **$$$**

Map p412 (☎212-979-1012; www.degustation-nyc.com; 239 E 5th St, btwn Second & Third Aves, East Village; small plates $12-22, tasting menu $85; ⊙6-11:30pm Tue-Sat; Ⓢ 6 to Astor Pl) Blending Iberian, French and new-world recipes, Degustation does a beautiful array of tapas-style plates at this narrow, 19-seat eatery. It's an intimate setting, with guests seated around a long wooden counter while chef Oscar Islas Díaz and his team are center stage, firing up mole octopus and oyster tacos, among other inventive dishes.

PRUNE AMERICAN **$$$**

Map p412 (☎212-677-6221; www.prunerestaurant.com; 54 E 1st St, btwn First & Second Aves, East Village; dinner $24-33, mains brunch $14-24; ⊙5:30-11pm, also 10am-3:30pm Sat & Sun; Ⓢ F to 2nd Ave) Expect lines around the block on the weekend, when the hungover show up to cure their ills with Prune's brunches and excellent Bloody Marys (in 11 varieties). The small room is always busy as diners pour in for grilled trout with mint and almond salsa, seared duck breast and rich sweetbreads. Reservations available for dinner only.

HEARTH ITALIAN **$$$**

Map p412 (☎646-602-1300; www.restauranthearth.com; 403 E 12th St, at First Ave, East Village; single dishes $14-29, tasting menu per person $78; ⊙6-10pm Mon-Thu, to 11pm Fri, 11am-2pm & 6-11pm Sat, 11am-3:30pm & 6-10pm Sun; Ⓢ L to 1st Ave; L, N/Q/R/W, 4/5/6 to 14th St-Union Sq) A staple for finicky, deep-pocketed diners, Hearth boasts a warm, brick-walled interior. The menu changes seasonally, but you can usually count on roasted meats and well-seasoned sautéed veggies with a few standbys, such as liver pâté or sage butter gnocchi.

Lower East Side

AN CHOI VIETNAMESE **$**

Map p414 (☎212-226-3700; http://anchoinyc.com; 85 Orchard St, btwn Broome & Grand Sts, Lower East Side; banh mi from $10, mains from $13; ⊙6pm-midnight Mon, from noon Tue-Thu, noon-2am Fri & Sat, noon-midnight Sun; Ⓢ B/D to Grand St; F to Delancey St; J/M/Z to Essex St) With faded communist party posters on the wall and a bar that looks like it was lifted out of the '70s, An Choi has cultivated a throwback style that denizens of the East Village love. It doesn't hurt that the food, simple Vietnamese dishes like pho (noodle soup) and *banh mi* (baguette) sandwiches, is tasty and not too expensive given the hipster credentials.

KUMA INN ASIAN **$**

Map p414 (☎212-353-8866; www.kumainn.com; 113 Ludlow St, btwn Delancey & Rivington Sts, Lower East Side; small dishes $9-15; ⊙6-11pm Sun-Thu, to midnight Fri & Sat; Ⓢ F, J/M/Z to Delancey-Essex Sts) Reservations are a must at this popular spot in a secretive 2nd-floor location (look for a small red door with 'Kuma Inn' painted on the concrete side). The Filipino- and Thai-inspired tapas runs the gamut from vegetarian summer rolls (with peanut plum sauce) to spicy drunken shrimp, and pan-roasted scallops with bacon and sake.

Bring your own beer, wine or sake (corkage fee applies).

SPAGHETTI INCIDENT ITALIAN **$**

Map p414 (☎646-896-1446; www.spaghettiincidentnyc.com; 231 Eldridge St, btwn Stanton & E Houston Sts, Lower East Side; mains $11-14; ⊙noon-10:30pm Sun & Mon, to 11:30pm Tue-Sat; Ⓢ F to 2nd Ave) Grab a seat at the marble-topped bar or one of the side tables and watch the cooks whip up tasty dishes of spaghetti beautifully topped with fresh ingredients, such as kale pesto, chopped salmon and asparagus in a light cream sauce, or Italian sausage and broccoli rabe. The flavors (and prices!) are quite good. Salads, arancini and affordable wines round out the menu.

MEATBALL SHOP ITALIAN $

Map p414 (212-982-8895; www.themeatballshop.com; 84 Stanton St, btwn Allen & Orchard Sts, Lower East Side; sandwiches $13; 11:30am-2am Sun-Thu, to 4am Fri & Sat; S 2nd Ave; F to Delancey St; J/M/Z to Essex St) Elevating the humble meatball to high art, the Meatball Shop serves up five varieties of juiciness (including a lentil vegetarian option and a mac 'n' cheese special). Order those balls on a hero (a long roll), add mozzarella and spicy tomato sauce, and voila, you have a tasty, if happily downmarket, meal. This branch boasts a rock-and-roll vibe, with tattooed waitstaff and prominent beats.

There are six other branches in NYC. Check the website for details.

VANESSA'S DUMPLING HOUSE CHINESE $

Map p414 (212-625-8008; www.vanessas.com; 118a Eldridge St, btwn Grand & Broome Sts, Lower East Side; dumplings $1.50-6; 10:30am-10:30pm Mon-Sat, to 10pm Sun; S B/D to Grand St; J to Bowery; F to Delancey St) Tasty dumplings – served steamed, fried or in soup – are whipped together in iron skillets at light speed and tossed into hungry mouths at unbeatable prices.

★CLINTON STREET BAKING COMPANY AMERICAN $$

Map p414 (646-602-6263; www.clintonstreetbaking.com; 4 Clinton St, btwn Stanton & Houston Sts, Lower East Side; mains $12-20; 8am-4pm & 5:30-11pm Mon-Sat, 9am-5pm Sun; S J/M/Z to Essex St; F to Delancey St; F to 2nd Ave) Mom-and-pop shop extraordinaire, Clinton Street Baking Company gets the blue ribbon in so many categories – best pancakes (blueberry!), best muffins, best po'boys (Southern-style sandwiches), best biscuits etc – that you're pretty much guaranteed a stellar meal no matter what time you stop by. In the evenings, you can opt for 'breakfast for dinner' (pancakes, eggs Benedict), fish tacos or the excellent buttermilk fried chicken.

RUSS & DAUGHTERS CAFE EASTERN EUROPEAN $$

Map p414 (212-475-4881; www.russanddaughterscafe.com; 127 Orchard St, btwn Delancey & Rivington Sts, Lower East Side; mains $13-20; 9am-10pm Mon-Fri, from 8am Sat & Sun; S F to Delancey St; J/M/Z to Essex St) Sit down and feast on bagels and lox in the comfort of an old-school diner. Aside from rich slices of smoked fish, you can nibble on potato latkes, warm up over a bowl of borscht or feast on eggs Benny.

KATZ'S DELICATESSEN DELI $$

Map p414 (212-254-2246; www.katzsdelicatessen.com; 205 E Houston St, at Ludlow St, Lower East Side; sandwiches $15-22; 8am-10:45pm Mon-Wed & Sun, to 2:45am Thu, from 8am Fri, 24hr Sat; S F to 2nd Ave) Though visitors won't find many remnants of the classic, old-world Jewish LES dining scene, there are a few stellar holdouts, among them Katz's Delicatessen, where Meg Ryan faked her famous orgasm in the 1989 movie *When Harry Met Sally*. If you love classic deli grub like pastrami and salami on rye, it just might have the same effect on you.

These days the lines are breathtakingly long, and the prices are high (Katz's signature hot pastrami sandwich costs a hefty $21.45). However, for all but the gluttonous, most sandwiches can easily feed two. Go very early or late to avoid the worst of the crowds.

DIMES CAFE $$

Map p414 (212-925-1300; www.dimesnyc.com; 49 Canal St, btwn Orchard & Ludlow Sts, Lower East Side; mains breakfast $8-13, dinner $15-24; 8am-10pm Mon-Fri, 9am-8pm Sat & Sun; ; S F to East Broadwy, B/D to Grand St) This tiny, sun-drenched eatery has a strong local following for its friendly service and healthy, good-value dishes. A design-minded group crowds in for breakfast tacos (served until 4pm), bowls of granola with açaí berries, creative salads (with sunchokes, anchovies, goat cheese) and heartier dishes for dinner (striped bass with green curry, pulled pork with jasmine rice).

FAT RADISH MODERN BRITISH $$$

Map p414 (212-300-4053; www.thefatradishnyc.com; 17 Orchard St, btwn Hester & Canal Sts, Lower East Side; mains $23-28; 5:30pm-midnight Mon-Sat, to 10pm Sun, also 11am-3:30pm Sat & Sun; S F to East Broadway; B/D to Grand St) The young and fashionable pack into this dimly lit dining room with exposed white brick and industrial touches. There's a loud buzz and people checking each other out but the mains, typical of the local, seasonal, haute-pub-food fad, are worth your attention. Start with big briny oysters before moving on to heritage pork chop with glazed squash or brook trout with seaweed aioli.

FREEMANS AMERICAN $$$

Map p414 (☎212-420-0012; www.freemansrestaurant.com; end of Freeman Alley, Lower East Side; mains lunch $14-18, dinner $26-33; ⏲11am-11:30pm Tue-Fri, from 10am Sat, 10am-11pm Sun, from 11am Mon; SF to 2nd Ave) Tucked down a back alley, the charmingly located Freemans draws a mostly hipster crowd who let their chunky jewelry clang on the wooden tables as they lean over to sip overflowing cocktails. Potted plants and antlers lend an endearing hunting-cabin vibe – a charming escape from the bustle (when there isn't a crowd inside).

DRINKING & NIGHTLIFE

The Lower East Side still clings to its status as the coolest 'hood in Manhattan. While some bars are favored by the 'bridge and tunnel' gang (and tourists, ahem), locals adore newfound clubs staging Manhattan's next indie-rock kings. There's something for everyone here – just walk up and down the tiny blocks and peek in. In the East Village, the further east you go, the looser things get. You'll find dirty dive bars stuffed to the gills with NYC students, and secret swanky lounges tucked behind the Japanese restaurant right next door. Things are positively packed come the weekend.

East Village

RUE B BAR

Map p412 (☎212-358-1700; www.ruebnyc188.com; 188 Ave B, btwn E 11th & 12th Sts, East Village; ⏲5pm-4am; SL to 1st Ave) There's live jazz (and the odd rockabilly group) every night from 9pm to midnight at this tiny, amber-lit drinking den on a bar-dappled stretch of Ave B. A young, celebratory crowd packs the small space – so mind the tight corners, lest the trombonist end up in your lap. B&W photos of jazz greats and other NYC icons enhance the ambience.

BERLIN CLUB

Map p412 (☎646-827-3689; 25 Ave A, btwn First & Second Aves, East Village; ⏲8pm-4am; SF to 2nd Ave) Like a secret bunker hidden beneath the ever-gentrifying streets of the East Village, Berlin is a throwback to the neighborhood's more riotous days of wildness and dancing. Once you find the unmarked entrance, head downstairs to the grotto-like space with vaulted brick ceilings, a long bar and tiny dancefloor, with funk and rare grooves spilling all around.

It draws a fun, bohemian crowd: a mix of class and trash, with little pretension. It's small and can get crowded, so brace yourself.

WAYLAND BAR

Map p412 (☎212-777-7022; www.thewaylandnyc.com; 700 E 9th St, cnr Ave C, East Village; ⏲5pm-4am; SL to 1st Ave) Whitewashed walls, weathered floorboards and salvaged lamps give this urban outpost a Mississippi flair, which goes well with the live music (bluegrass, jazz, folk) featured Monday to Wednesday nights. The drinks, though, are the real draw – try the 'I Hear Banjos-Encore,' made of apple-pie moonshine, rye whiskey and applewood smoke, which tastes like a campfire (but slightly less burning).

Decent drink specials and $1 oysters from 4pm to 7pm on weekdays.

JIMMY'S NO 43 BAR

Map p412 (☎212-982-3006; www.jimmysno43.com; 43 E 7th St, btwn Second & Third Aves, East Village; ⏲4pm-1am Mon & Tue, to 2pm Wed & Thu, to 4am Fri, 1pm-4am Sat, to 1am Sun; SR/W to 8th St-NYU; F to 2nd Ave; 6 to Astor Pl) Barrels and stag antlers line the walls up to the ceiling of this cozy basement beer hall as locals chug their drinks. Select from more than 50 imported favorites (a dozen on draft) to go with a round of delectable, locally sourced bar nibbles.

ANGEL'S SHARE BAR

Map p412 (☎212-777-5415; 8 Stuyvesant St, 2nd fl, near Third Ave & E 9th St; ⏲6pm-1:30am Sun-Wed, to 2am Thu, to 2:30am Fri & Sat; S6 to Astor Pl) Show up early and snag a seat at this hidden gem, behind a Japanese restaurant on the same floor. It's quiet and elegant, with seriously talented mixologists serving up creative cocktails, plus a top flight collection of whiskeys. You can't stay if you don't have a table or a seat at the bar, and they tend to go fast.

Views of Stuyvesant Pl and Third Ave are a bonus – it feels like you're kicking back in a friend's apartment.

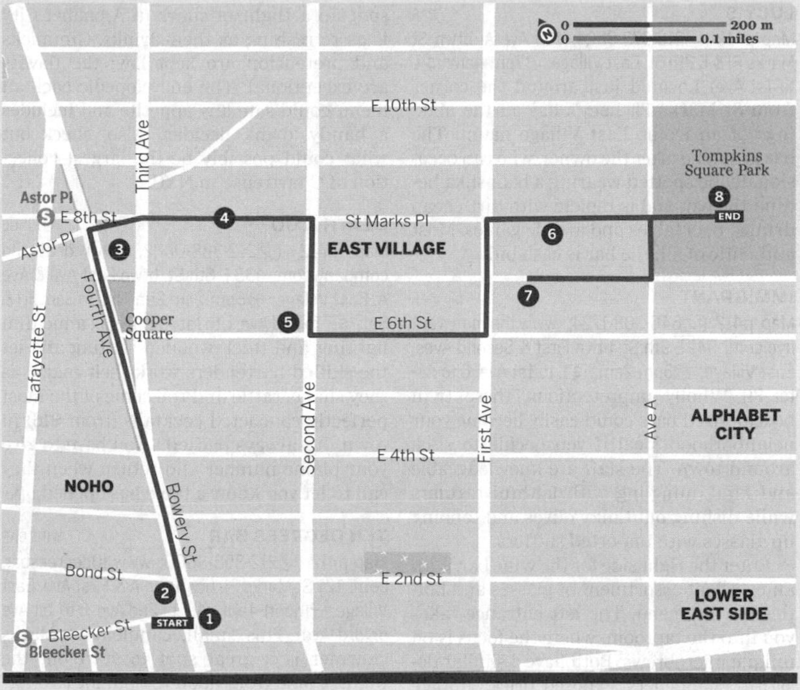

Neighborhood Walk
East Village Nostalgia

START JOHN VARVATOS
END TOMPKINS SQUARE PARK
LENGTH 1.5 MILES; 1½ HOURS

From Bleecker St subway station, head east along the leafy like-named street for a few blocks until you reach the ❶ **John Varvatos boutique** (p128), which once housed legendary music venue CBGB. Other than the fading posters and graffitied walls, little remains of the concert hall, but it's still a pilgrimage for music enthusiasts. The corner just north of here marks the block-long ❷ **Joey Ramone Place**, named after the late Ramones singer.

Head north on the Bowery to Astor Pl. Turn right and head east through the square to reach ❸ **Cooper Union** (p112), where in 1860 presidential hopeful Abraham Lincoln rocked a skeptical New York crowd with a rousing anti-slavery speech.

Continue east on ❹ **St Marks Place**, a block full of tattoo parlors and cheap eateries. Rising rents have pushed out many of the establishments that made this street famous, but you can still get a feeling for what this stretch was like in its heyday.

Head south down Second Ave to E 6th St and you'll see an bank, where the long-defunct ❺ **Fillmore East**, a 2000-seat live-music venue run by promoter Bill Graham from 1968 to 1971, once operated. In the '80s the space was transformed into the Saint – the legendary club that kicked off a joyous, drug-laden, gay disco culture.

Cross Second Ave at E 6th St and head down the block-long strip of Indian restaurants. At First Ave, turn left, rejoin St Marks Pl and turn right. The row of tenements is the site of Led Zeppelin's ❻ **Physical Graffiti cover** (96–98 St Marks Pl), where Mick and Keith sat in 1981 in the Stones' hilarious video for 'Waiting on a Friend.' Then head down to E 7th between First Ave and Ave A and pop into ❼ **Trash & Vaudeville** (p129), a St Marks stalwart that recently relocated.

End your stroll at infamous ❽ **Tompkins Square Park** (p113); here, drag queens started the Wigstock summer festival at the bandshell where Jimi Hendrix played in the 1960s.

LUCY'S BAR

Map p412 (212-673-3824; 135 Ave A, btwn St Marks Pl & E 9th St, East Village; 7pm-4am; S L to 1st Ave) Located just around the corner from St Marks Pl, Lucy's has all the makings of an iconic East Village haunt. The bar is named after the owner, who can occasionally be spotted wearing a babushka behind the bar, and is replete with dirt-cheap drinks, pool tables and arcade games. Most authentic of all: the bar is cash only.

IMMIGRANT BAR

Map p412 (646-308-1724; www.theimmigrantnyc.com; 341 E 9th St, btwn First & Second Aves, East Village; 5pm-2am; S L to 1st Ave; 6 to Astor Pl) Wholly unpretentious, these twin boxcar-sized bars could easily become your neighborhood local if you decide to stick around town. The staff are knowledgeable and kind, mingling with faithful regulars while dishing out tangy olives and topping up glasses with imported snifters.

Enter the right side for the wine bar, with an excellent assortment of glasses and bottles on the menu. The left entrance takes you into the taproom, where the focus is on unique microbrews. Both have a similar design – chandeliers, exposed brick, vintage charm.

POURING RIBBONS COCKTAIL BAR

Map p412 (917-656-6788; www.pouringribbons.com; 225 Ave B, 2nd fl, btwn E 13th & 14th Sts, East Village; 6pm-2am; S L to 1st Ave) Finding such a well-groomed and classy spot up a flight of stairs in Alphabet City is as refreshing as their drinks. Gimmicks and pretension are kept low; the flavors are exceptional. The encyclopedic cocktail menu could sate any appetite and includes a handy 'drink decider.' Also, check out what could possibly be the largest collection of Chartreuse in NYC.

ANOTHER SIDE OF GAY NYC

If Chelsea is a muscly, overachieving jock, then the Lower East Side is his wayward, punk younger brother. Amid the frat dives and cocktail lounges you'll find many gay bars catering to guys who prefer flannels and scruff to tank tops and six-pack abs. **Nowhere** (Map p412; 212-477-4744; www.nowherebarnyc.com; 322 E 14th St, btwn First & Second Aves, East Village; 3pm-4am; S L to 1st Ave) and **Phoenix** (Map p412; 212-477-9979; www.phoenixbarnyc.com; 447 East 13th St, btwn First Ave & Ave A, East Village; 3pm-4am; S L to 1st Ave) are great places to meet some new friendly faces, while the Cock caters to a friskier crowd. The drinks are also typically much cheaper.

DEATH & CO LOUNGE

Map p412 (212-388-0882; www.deathandcompany.com; 433 E 6th St, btwn First Ave & Ave A, East Village; 6pm-2am Sun-Thu, to 3am Fri & Sat; S F to 2nd Ave; L to 1st Ave) Relax amid dim lighting and thick wooden slatting and let the skilled bartenders work their magic as they shake, rattle and roll some of the most perfectly concocted cocktails (from $16) in town. It's always packed – you have to give your phone number and return when they call to let you know a table has opened up.

TEN DEGREES BAR WINE BAR

Map p412 (212-358-8600; www.10degreesbar.com; 121 St Marks Pl, btwn Ave A & First Ave, East Village; noon-4am; S F to 2nd Ave; L to 1st Ave or 3rd Ave) This small, candlelit St Marks charmer is a great spot to start out the night. Come from noon to 8pm for two-for-one drink specials (otherwise, it's $12 to $15 for cocktails). Go for the couches up front or grab a tiny table in the back nook.

PROLETARIAT BAR

Map p412 (www.proletariatny.com; 102 St Marks Pl, btwn Ave A & First Ave, East Village; 5pm-2am; S L to 1st Ave) The cognoscenti of NYC's beer world pack this tiny, 10-stool bar just west of Tompkins Square Park. Promising 'rare, new and unusual beers,' Proletariat delivers the goods with a changing lineup of brews you won't find elsewhere. Recent hits have included Brooklyn and New Jersey drafts from artisanal brewers.

CROCODILE LOUNGE LOUNGE

Map p412 (212-477-7747; www.crocodileloungenyc.com; 325 E 14th St, btwn First & Second Aves, East Village; 3pm-4am; S L to 1st Ave) Hankering for Williamsburg but too lazy to cross the river? Dive into Crocodile Lounge, the outpost of Brooklyn success story Alligator Lounge. The lure of cheap drinks and signature free pizza with every drink (yes, really) makes this hideout a hit with East Village 20-somethings seeking budget-friendly fun. There's a Skee-Ball league (Tuesday), trivia (Wednesday and Sunday) and bingo (Thursday).

WEBSTER HALL CLUB

Map p412 (☎212-353-1600; www.websterhall.com; 125 E 11th St, near Third Ave, East Village; ⏰10pm-4am Thu-Sat; **S** L, N/Q/R/W, 4/5/6 to 14th St-Union Sq) The granddaddy of dance halls, Webster Hall has been around so long (performances have been under way since 1886) that it was granted landmark status in 2008. Following the old 'if it ain't broke, don't fix it' adage, what you'll get here is cheap drinks, pool tables, and enough room on the dance floor to work up a good sweat.

THREE SEAT ESPRESSO & BARBER CAFE

Map p412 (www.threeseatespresso.com; 137 Ave A, btwn St Marks Pl & E 9th St; ⏰7am-8pm Mon-Fri, from 8am Sat, 8am-7pm Sun; **S** L to 1st Ave) New Yorkers are all about efficiency, which Three Seat Espresso & Barber excels at. Frothy lattes and cappuccinos are served in the front of the shop, while in the back is a barber shop (men's haircut from $30) for those who want to combine their morning coffee with a touch up to their coif.

ABC BEER CO BAR

Map p412 (☎646-422-7103; www.abcbeer.co; 96 Ave C, btwn 6th & 7th Sts, East Village; ⏰noon-midnight Sun-Thu, to 2am Fri & Sat; **S** F to 2nd Ave; L to 1st Ave) At first glance, ABC looks like a dimly lit beer shop (indeed bottles are available for purchase); but venture deeper inside and you'll find a small indie rock-playing gastropub in back, with a long communal table, a few plush leather sofas and chairs set against the brick walls.

MCSORLEY'S OLD ALE HOUSE BAR

Map p412 (☎212-473-9148; www.facebook.com/McSorleysOldAleHouse; 15 E 7th St, btwn Second & Third Aves, East Village; ⏰noon-12:30am; **S** 6 to Astor Pl) Around since 1854, McSorley's feels far removed from the East Village veneer of cool: you're more likely to drink with frat boys, tourists and the odd fireman. It's hard to beat the cobwebs, sawdust floors and flip waiters who slap down two mugs of the house's ale for every one ordered.

PDT BAR

Map p412 (☎212-614-0386; www.pdtnyc.com; 113 St Marks Pl, btwn Ave A & First Ave, East Village; ⏰6pm-2am Sun-Thu, to 4am Fri & Sat; **S** L to 1st Ave) PDT, which stands for 'Please Don't Tell,' scores high on novelty. You enter through the phone booth at the hotdog snack shop (Crif Dogs) next door. Once you're given the OK (reservations are recommended to avoid being turned away), you'll step into an intimate low-lit bar with the odd animal head on the wall.

COCK GAY

Map p412 (www.thecockbar.com; 93 Second Ave, btwn E 5th & 6th Sts, East Village; ⏰11pm-4am; **S** F/M to 2nd Ave) A dark, dank spot that's proud of its sleazy-chic reputation, this is the place to join lanky hipster boys and rage until you're kicked out at 4am. Varying theme nights present popular parties with live performers, DJs, drag-queen hostesses, nearly naked go-go boys and porn videos on constant loops. It's wild and friendly.

🍷 Lower East Side

TEN BELLS BAR

Map p414 (☎212-228-4450; www.tenbellsnyc.com; 247 Broome St, btwn Ludlow & Orchard Sts, Lower East Side; ⏰5pm-2am Mon-Fri, from 3pm Sat & Sun; **S** F to Delancey St; J/M/Z to Essex St) This charmingly tucked-away tapas bar has a grotto-like design, with flickering candles, dark tin ceilings, brick walls and a U-shaped bar that's an ideal setting for a conversation with a new friend.

The chalkboard menu hangs on both walls and features excellent wines by the glass, which go nicely with *boquerones* (marinated anchovies), *txipirones en su tinta* (squid in ink sauce) and regional cheeses. Come for happy hour when oysters are $1 each and a carafe of wine costs $15. The unsigned entrance is easy to miss; it's right next to the shop Top Hat.

BAR GOTO BAR

Map p414 (☎212-475-4411; www.bargoto.com; 245 Eldridge St, btwn E Houston & Stanton Sts, Lower East Side; ⏰5pm-midnight Tue-Thu & Sun, to 2am Fri & Sat; **S** F to 2nd Ave) Maverick mixologist Kenta Goto has cocktail connoisseurs spellbound at his eponymous hot spot. Expect meticulous, elegant drinks that revel in Koto's Japanese heritage (the sake-spiked Sakura Martini is utterly smashing), paired with authentic, Japanese comfort bites, such as *okonomiyaki* (savory pancakes).

JADIS WINE BAR

Map p414 (☎212-254-1675; www.jadisnyc.com; 42 Rivington St, btwn Eldridge & Forsyth Sts, Lower East Side; ⏰5pm-2am; **S** F to 2nd Ave; J/Z to Bowery) French for 'in olden days,' Jadis

1. Katz's Delicatessen (p119)
One of the last holdouts of the old-world Jewish LES dining scene.

2. McSorley's Old Ale House (p123)
Abraham Lincoln enjoyed a drink at this bar, which has been around since 1854.

3. St Marks Place (p112)
Buildings lining St Marks Place are filled with enough history to delight trivia buffs.

2

JAN HALASKA / ALAMY ©

3

STEVE TULLEY / ALAMY ©

channels a bit of European nostalgia with its worn brick walls, antique fixtures and warmly lit interior. You'll find around two dozen or so wines by the glass, with French labels taking pride of place. Snacks include escargots, salads, pressed sandwiches, homemade quiches and rich cheeses.

ATTABOY COCKTAIL BAR

Map p414 (134 Eldridge St, btwn Delancey & Broome Sts, Lower East Side; ⏲6pm-4am; S B/D to Grand St) One of those no-door-sign, speakeasy-vibe bars that are two-a-penny these days, this one is a notch above, serving knockout artisanal cocktails – that will set you back $17 each. There is no menu, so let the expert bartenders guide you.

BARRIO CHINO COCKTAIL BAR

Map p414 (☎212-228-6710; 253 Broome St, btwn Ludlow & Orchard Sts, Lower East Side; ⏲11:30am-4:30pm & 5:30pm-1am; S F, J/M/Z to Delancey-Essex Sts) An eatery that spills easily into a party scene, with an airy Havana-meets-Beijing vibe and a focus on fine sipping tequilas. Or stick with fresh blood-orange or black-plum margaritas, guacamole and chicken tacos.

BEAUTY & ESSEX BAR

Map p414 (☎212-614-0146; www.beautyandessex.com; 146 Essex St, btwn Stanton & Rivington Sts, Lower East Side; ⏲5pm-midnight Mon-Wed, to 1am Thu & Fri, 11:30am-3pm & 5pm-1am Sat, 11:30am-midnight Sun; S F to Delancey St; J/M/Z to Essex St) Venture behind a tawdry pawnshop front–space for a world of glamour. Beyond lies 10,000 sq ft of sleek lounge space, complete with leather sofas and banquettes, dramatic amber-tinged lighting and a curved staircase that leads to yet another lounge and bar area. The exuberance, high prices and pretentious crowd give the place a Gatsby-esque vibe.

Ladies in need of a drink might want to bypass the bar and pay a visit to the powder room, where there's complimentary champagne (sorry, fellas).

ROUND K CAFE

Map p414 (www.roundk.com; 99 Allen St, btwn Delancey & Broome Sts, Lower East Side; ⏲8am-10pm Mon-Wed, to midnight Thu & Fri, 9am-midnight Sat, to 10pm Sun; S B/D to Grand St; F to Delancey St; J/M/Z to Essex St) There's something special about this charmingly hidden Korean-run cafe. Step inside and smell the coffee roasting, admire some antique-looking machinery, then order a perfectly made latte – and perhaps some Mom's Toast (a waffle with bourbon-infused bananas) – take your delicate porcelain and pull back the curtain to reveal a quiet seating area lit with Tiffany-style glass lamps.

☆ ENTERTAINMENT

METROGRAPH CINEMA

Map p414 (☎212-660-0312; www.metrograph.com; 7 Ludlow St, btwn Canal & Hester Sts, Lower East Side; tickets $15; S F to East Broadwy, B/D to Grand St) The newest movie mecca for downtown cinephiles, this two-screen theater with red velvet seats shows curated art-house flicks. Most you'll never find at any multiplex, though the odd mainstream pic like *Magic Mike* is occasionally screened. In addition to movie geeks browsing the bookstore, you'll find a stylish and glamorous set at the bar or in the upstairs restaurant.

PERFORMANCE SPACE NEW YORK THEATER

Map p412 (☎212-477-5829; https://performancespacenewyork.org; 150 First Ave, at E 9th St, East Village; S L to 1st Ave; 6 to Astor Pl) Formerly PS 122, this cutting-edge theater reopened in January 2018 with an entirely new facade, state-of-the-art performance spaces, artist studios, a new lobby and roof deck. The bones of the former schoolhouse remain, as does its experimental theater bonafides: Eric Bogosian, Meredith Monk, the late Spalding Gray and Elevator Repair Service have all performed here.

SLIPPER ROOM LIVE PERFORMANCE

Map p414 (☎212-253-7246; www.slipperroom.com; 167 Orchard St, entrance on Stanton St, Lower East Side; admission $10-20; S F to 2nd Ave) This two-story club hosts a wide range of performances, including Seth Herzog's popular variety show *Sweet* at 9pm on Tuesday (admission $10) and several weekly burlesque shows, which feature a mash-up of acrobatics, sexiness, comedy and absurdity – generally well worth the entry price. Full event calendar and tickets available online.

ROCKWOOD MUSIC HALL LIVE MUSIC

Map p414 (☎212-477-4155; www.rockwoodmusichall.com; 196 Allen St, btwn Houston & Stanton Sts, Lower East Side; ⏲5:30pm-2am Mon-Fri, from

3pm Sat & Sun; S F to 2nd Ave) Opened by indie rocker Ken Rockwood, this breadbox-sized concert space has three stages and a rapid-fire flow of bands and singer/songwriters. If cash is tight, try stage 1, which has free shows, with a maximum of one hour per band (die-hards can see five or more performances a night). Music kicks off at 3pm on weekends and 6pm on weeknights.

All shows have a one-drink minimum for standing room and two drinks for those sitting.

PIANOS LIVE MUSIC

Map p414 (212-505-3733; www.pianosnyc.com; 158 Ludlow St, at Stanton St, Lower East Side; cover $8-12; 2pm-4am; S F to 2nd Ave) Nobody's bothered to change the sign at the door, a leftover from the location's previous incarnation as a piano shop. Now it's dedicated to a mix of musical genres and styles, leaning more toward pop, punk and new wave, but throwing in some hip-hop and indie for good measure. Sometimes you get a double feature – one act upstairs and another below.

NEW YORK THEATRE WORKSHOP THEATER

Map p412 (212-460-5475; www.nytw.org; 79 E 4th St, btwn Second & Third Aves, East Village; S F to 2nd Ave) For more than 30 years this innovative production house has been a treasure trove for those seeking cutting-edge, contemporary plays with purpose. It was the originator of two big Broadway hits, *Rent* and *Urinetown* – plus it's where the musical *Once* had its off-Broadway premiere – and offers a constant supply of high-quality drama.

STONE LIVE MUSIC

Map p412 (www.thestonenyc.com; Ave C, at E 2nd St, Lower East Side; admission $20; from 8:30pm Tue-Sun; S F to 2nd Ave) Created by renowned downtown jazz cat John Zorn, the Stone is about the music and nothing but the music, in all its experimental and avant-garde forms. There's no bar or frills of any kind – just folding chairs in a dark space on a concrete floor.

ANTHOLOGY FILM ARCHIVES CINEMA

Map p412 (212-505-5181; www.anthologyfilmarchives.org; 32 Second Ave, at 2nd St, East Village; S F to 2nd Ave) Opened in 1970, this theater is dedicated to the idea of film as an art form. It screens indie works by new filmmakers and revives classics and obscure oldies, from the surrealist works of Spanish director Luis Buñuel to Ken Brown's psychedelia.

ABRONS ARTS CENTER ARTS CENTER

Map p414 (212-598-0400; www.abronsartscenter.org; 466 Grand St, cnr Pitt St, Lower East Side; ; S F, J, M, Z to Delancey St-Essex St) This venerable cultural hub has three theaters, the largest being the Playhouse Theater (a national landmark), with its own lobby, fixed seats on a rise, a large, deep stage and good visibility. A mainstay of the downtown Fringe Festival, Abrons Art Center is also your best bet to catch experimental and community productions, as well as art exhibits.

Not afraid of difficult subjects, Abrons sponsors plays, dance and photography exhibits that don't get much play elsewhere.

LA MAMA ETC THEATER

Map p412 (212-352-3101; www.lamama.org; 74a E 4th St, btwn Bowery & Second Ave, East Village; tickets from $20; S F to 2nd Ave) A long-standing home for onstage experimentation (the ETC stands for Experimental Theater Club), La MaMa is now a three-theater complex with a cafe, an art gallery, and a separate studio building that features cutting-edge dramas, sketch comedy and readings of all kinds. There are $10 tickets available for each show. Book early to score a deal!

NUYORICAN POETS CAFÉ LIVE PERFORMANCE

Map p412 (212-780-9386; www.nuyorican.org; 236 E 3rd St, btwn Aves B & C, East Village; tickets $8-25; S F to 2nd Ave) Still going strong after 40-plus years, the legendary Nuyorican is home to poetry slams, hip-hop performances, plays, and film and video events. It's a piece of East Village history, but also a vibrant and still-relevant nonprofit arts organization. Check the website for the events calendar and buy tickets online for the more popular weekend shows.

MERCURY LOUNGE LIVE MUSIC

Map p414 (212-260-4700; www.mercuryloungenyc.com; 217 E Houston St, btwn Essex & Ludlow Sts, Lower East Side; cover charge $10-15; 6pm-3am; S F/V to Lower East Side-2nd Ave) The Mercury dependably pulls in a cool new or comeback band everyone downtown wants to see – such as Dengue Fever or the Slits. The sound is good, with an intimate seating area and dance space.

BOWERY BALLROOM LIVE MUSIC

Map p414 (☎212-533-2111, 800-745-3000; www.boweryballroom.com; 6 Delancey St, at Bowery St, Lower East Side; ⓈJ/Z to Bowery; B/D to Grand St) This terrific, medium-sized venue has the perfect sound and feel for well-known indie-rock acts such as The Shins, Stephen Malkmus and Patti Smith.

SIDEWALK CAFÉ LIVE MUSIC

Map p412 (☎212-473-7373; www.sidewalkny.com; 94 Ave A, at 6th St, East Village; ⏲11am-4am; ⓈF to 2nd Ave) Anti-folk forever! Never mind the Sidewalk's burger-bar appearance outside – inside is the home of New York's 'anti-folk' scene, where the Moldy Peaches carved out their legacy before Juno got knocked up. The open-mic 'anti-hootenanny' is Monday night. Other nights host a wide range of sounds: garage rock, indie pop, bluesy piano and all things anti-folk.

SHOPPING

Whether it be clothing, furniture or food, these neighborhoods cater to the strange, obscure and cutting edge. Secondhand stores like Tokio 7 trade in unique looks from worldwide names as well as Japanese designers, while Obscura Antiques (p128) has you covered for skulls, Victorian-era medical equipment and any creepy paraphernalia you might need. The encroaching chain stores have zapped a little of the edginess, but many of the iconic old stores are still around (Trash & Vaudeville) and plenty of the newer shops cater to those looking for the LES and East Village vibe (John Varvatos).

East Village

OBSCURA ANTIQUES ANTIQUES

Map p412 (☎212-505-9251; www.obscuraantiques.com; 207 Ave A, btwn E 12th & 13th Sts, East Village; ⏲noon-8pm Mon-Sat, to 7pm Sun; ⓈL to 1st Ave) This small cabinet of curiosities pleases both lovers of the macabre and inveterate antique hunters. Here you'll find taxidermied animal heads, tiny rodent skulls and skeletons, butterfly displays in glass boxes, Victorian-era post-mortem photography, disturbing little (dental?) instruments, German landmine flags (stackable so tanks could see them), old poison bottles and glass eyes.

Dig deeper to find cane-toad purses (sure to please the Aussie crowd), Zippos from Vietnam soldiers, anatomical drawings, a two-headed calf, a stuffed hyena and other items not currently available at the local department store.

STILL HOUSE HOMEWARES

Map p412 (☎212-539-0200; www.stillhousenyc.com; 117 E 7th St, btwn First Ave & Ave A, East Village; ⏲noon-8pm; Ⓢ6 to Astor Pl) Step into this petite, peaceful boutique to browse sculptural glassware and pottery: hand-blown vases, geometric tabletop objects, ceramic bowls and cups, and other finery for the home. You'll also find minimalistic jewelry, delicately bound notebooks and small framed artworks for the wall.

Still House has lots of great gift ideas, and the objects are small enough to bring home. They are quite delicate, though, so make sure they're well wrapped.

VERAMEAT JEWELRY

Map p412 (☎212-388-9045; www.verameat.com; 315 E 9th St, btwn First & Second Aves, East Village; ⏲10am-8pm; Ⓢ6 to Astor Pl; F/M to 2nd Ave) Designer Vera Balyura creates exquisite little pieces with a dark sense of humor in this delightful small shop on 9th St. Tiny, artfully wrought pendants, rings, earrings and bracelets appear almost too precious... until a closer inspection reveals zombies, Godzilla robots, animal heads, dinosaurs and encircling claws – bringing a whole new level of miniaturized complexity to the realm of jewelry.

You'll also find a delightfully specific collection of pins and key chains inspired by classic TV and movies. There's also a location in Williamsburg.

JOHN VARVATOS FASHION & ACCESSORIES

Map p412 (☎212-358-0315; www.johnvarvatos.com; 315 Bowery, btwn E 1st & 2nd Sts, East Village; ⏲noon-8pm Mon-Fri, from 8pm Sat, noon-6pm Sun; ⓈF/M to 2nd Ave; 6 to Bleecker St) Set in the hallowed halls of former punk club CBGBs, this John Varvatos store goes to great lengths to tie fashion to rock and roll, with records, '70s audio equipment and even electric guitars for sale alongside JV's denim, leather boots, belts and graphic tees. Sales associates dressed in Varvatos' downtown cool seem far removed from the Bowery's gritty past.

JOHN DERIAN COMPANY HOMEWARES
Map p412 (212-677-3917; www.johnderian.com; 6 E 2nd St, btwn Bowery & Second Ave, East Village; 11am-7pm Tue-Sun; S F/M to 2nd Ave) John Derian is famed for its decoupage: pieces from original botanical and animal prints stamped under glass. The result is a beautiful collection of one-of-a-kind plates, paperweights, coasters, lamps, bowls and vases.

There are adjoining stores, **John Derian Dry Goods** and **John Derian Furniture**, next door.

TOKIO 7 FASHION & ACCESSORIES
Map p412 (212-353-8443; www.tokio7.net; 83 E 7th St, near First Ave, East Village; noon-8pm; S 6 to Astor Pl) This revered, hip consignment shop, on a shady stretch of E 7th St, has good-condition designer labels for men and women at some fairly hefty prices. The Japanese-owned store often features lovely pieces by Issey Miyake and Yohji Yamamoto, as well as a well-curated selection of Dolce & Gabbana, Prada, Chanel and other top labels.

Watch out for the giant alien-Predator-like thing out front (made of repurposed machine parts).

A-1 RECORDS MUSIC
Map p412 (212-473-2870; www.a1recordshop.com; 439 E 6th St, btwn First Ave & Ave A, East Village; 1-9pm; S F/M to 2nd Ave) One of the last of the many record stores that once graced the East Village, A-1 has been around for over two decades. The cramped aisles, filled with a large selection of jazz, funk and soul, draw vinyl fans and DJs from far and wide.

DINOSAUR HILL TOYS
Map p412 (212-473-5850; www.dinosaurhill.com; 306 E 9th St, btwn First & Second Aves, East Village; 11am-7pm; S 6 to Astor Pl) A small, old-fashioned toy store that's inspired more by imagination than Disney movies, this shop has loads of great gift ideas: Czech marionettes, shadow puppets, micro building blocks, calligraphy sets, toy pianos, art and science kits, kids' music CDs from around the globe, and wooden blocks in half-a-dozen different languages, plus natural-fiber clothing for infants.

LODGE FASHION & ACCESSORIES
Map p412 (212-777-0350; https://lodgegoods.com; 220 E 10th St, btwn First & Second Aves, East Village; noon-8pm Mon, Fri & Sat, to 9pm Tue-Thu, to 7pm Sun; S L to 1st Ave) Leather wallets from Coronado and Baxter shaving kits line the flannel- and wood-covered shelves of this men's clothing and accessories boutique. You won't find anything for cheap, but if you're in the market for an indestructible backpack or beard oil, it's worth checking out. Don't be surprised if you are offered a bourbon while you're browsing.

NO RELATION VINTAGE VINTAGE
Map p412 (L Train Vintage; 212-228-5201; www.norelationvintage.com; 204 First Ave, btwn E 12th & 13th Sts, East Village; noon-8pm Mon-Thu & Sun, to 9pm Fri & Sat; S L to 1st Ave) Among the many vintage shops of the East Village, No Relation is a winner for its wide-ranging collections that run the gamut from designer denim and leather jackets to vintage flannels, funky sneakers, plaid shirts, irreverent branded T-shirts, varsity jackets, clutches and more. Sharpen your elbows: hipster crowds flock here on weekends.

TRASH & VAUDEVILLE CLOTHING
Map p412 (212-982-3590; www.trashandvaudeville.com; 96 East 7th St, btwn First Ave & Ave A, East Village; noon-8pm Mon-Thu, 11:30am-8:30pm Sat, 1-7:30pm Sun; S 6 to Astor Pl) The two-story capital of punk-rock Trash & Vaudeville is the veritable costume closet for singing celebs like Debbie Harry, who found their groove in the East Village when it played host to a much grittier scene. On any day of the week you'll find everyone from drag queens to themed partygoers scouting out the most ridiculous shoes, shirts and hair dye.

Lower East Side

TICTAIL MARKET FASHION & ACCESSORIES
Map p414 (917-388-1556; https://tictail.com; 90 Orchard St, at Broome St, Lower East Side; noon-9pm Mon-Sat, to 6pm Sun; S B/D to Grand St; F to Delancey St; J/M/Z to Essex St) Tictail Market is located on a corner on the Lower East Side, but it specializes in clothing, accessories, trinkets and art from around the world. All products are sourced directly from the designers and artists so you can be sure you're supporting a small business with each purchase. The collection is eclectic, but tends to lean toward a cool, minimalist aesthetic.

BY ROBERT JAMES FASHION & ACCESSORIES

Map p414 (☎212-253-2121; www.byrobertjames.com; 74 Orchard St, btwn Broome & Grand Sts, Lower East Side; ⊙noon-8pm Mon-Sat, to 6pm Sun; S F to Delancey St; J/M/Z to Essex St) Rugged, beautifully tailored menswear is the mantra of Robert James, who sources and manufactures right in NYC (the design studio is just upstairs). The racks are lined with slim-fitting denim, handsome button-downs and classic-looking sports coats. Lola, James' black lab, sometimes roams the store. He also has a store in Williamsburg.

YUMI KIM CLOTHING

Map p414 (☎212-420-5919; www.yumikim.com; 105 Stanton St, btwn Ludlow & Essex Sts, Lower East Side; ⊙noon-7:30pm; S F to Delancey St; J/M/Z to Essex St; F/M to 2nd Ave) To add a burst of color to your wardrobe, head to Yumi Kim, a delightful little boutique selling fun dresses, blouses, skirts, jumpsuits and accessories all adorned with bright floral and tropical prints. The cuts are quite flattering, and most are made of 100% silk – making them good lightweight options for travel.

EDITH MACHINIST VINTAGE

Map p414 (☎212-979-9992; www.edithmachinist.com; 104 Rivington St, btwn Ludlow & Essex Sts, Lower East Side; ⊙noon-7pm Tue-Thu, to 6pm Sun, Mon & Fri; S F to Delancey St; J/M/Z to Essex St) To properly strut about the Lower East Side, you've got to dress the part. Edith Machinist can help you achieve that rumpled but stylish look in a hurry – a bit of vintage glam via knee-high soft suede boots, 1930s silk dresses and ballet-style flats.

ASSEMBLY FASHION & ACCESSORIES

Map p414 (☎212-253-5393; www.assemblynewyork.com; 170 Ludlow St, btwn Stanton & Houston Sts, Lower East Side; ⊙11am-7pm; S F/M to 2nd Ave) Whitewashed floorboards and an air of stylish whimsy define this dapper men's and women's shop in the Lower East Side. There's lots of covet-worthy wares on display, showcasing obscure designers from East and West. Look for canvas high tops by Shoes Like Pottery, satchels by Le Bas, chunky jewelry by Open House and outerwear by the shop's in-house label Assembly.

REFORMATION CLOTHING

Map p414 (☎646-448-4925; www.thereformation.com; 156 Ludlow St, btwn Rivington & Stanton Sts, Lower East Side; ⊙noon-8pm Mon-Sat, to 7pm Sun; S F to Delancey St or 2nd Ave; J/M/Z to Essex St) This stylish boutique sells beautifully designed garments with minimal environmental impact. Aside from its green credentials, it sells unique tops, blouses, sweaters and dresses, with fair prices in comparison to other Lower East Side boutiques.

Clothes are manufactured in California using renewable energy and shipped in 100% recycled packaging. Plus it ticks other progressive boxes: fair-labor practices, support for volunteer organizations and other policies unusual for a clothing company.

TOP HAT GIFTS & SOUVENIRS

Map p414 (☎212-677-4240; www.tophatnyc.com; 245 Broome St, btwn Ludlow & Orchard Sts, Lower East Side; ⊙noon-8pm; S B/D to Grand St) Sporting curios from around the globe, this whimsical little shop is packed with intrigue: from vintage Italian pencils and handsomely miniaturized leather journals to beautifully carved wooden bird whistles. Looking for an endless rain album, a toy clarinet, Japanese fabrics, a crumpled map of the night sky or geometric Spanish cups and saucers? You'll find all these and more here.

MOO SHOES SHOES

Map p414 (☎212-254-6512; www.mooshoes.com; 78 Orchard St, btwn Broome & Grand Sts, Lower East Side; ⊙11:30am-7:30pm Mon-Sat, noon-6pm Sun; S F to Delancey St; J/M/Z to Essex St) This cruelty-free, earth-friendly boutique sells surprisingly stylish microfiber (faux leather) shoes, handbags and wallets. Look for fashionable pumps from Olsenhaus, rugged men's Oxfords by Novacos and sleek Matt & Nat wallets.

A recently opened Moo Shoes grocer, basically a small cafe and sandwich shop, is attached.

ECONOMY CANDY FOOD

Map p414 (☎212-254-1531; www.economycandy.com; 108 Rivington St, at Essex St, Lower East Side; ⊙9am-6pm Sun & Tue-Fri, 10am-6pm Sat & Mon; S F, J/M/Z to Delancey St-Essex St) Bringing sweetness to the 'hood since 1937, this candy shop is stocked with floor-to-ceiling goods in package and bulk, and is home to some beautiful antique gum machines. You'll find everything from childhood favorites like jelly beans, lollipops, gum balls,

Cadbury imports, gummy worms and rock candy, to more grown-up delicacies such as halvah, green tea bonbons, hand-dipped chocolates, dried ginger and papaya.

There's also an eye-catching assortment of collectible Pez dispensers.

BLUESTOCKINGS BOOKS

Map p414 (212-777-6028; www.bluestockings.com; 172 Allen St, btwn Stanton & Rivington Sts, Lower East Side; 11am-11pm; F/M to Lower East Side-2nd Ave) This independent bookstore is the place to expand your horizons on feminism, queer and trans issues, globalism and African American studies, among other topics. It's also the site of an organic, fair-trade cafe with vegan treats, as well as myriad readings and speaking events.

RUSS & DAUGHTERS FOOD

Map p414 (212-475-4800; www.russanddaughters.com; 179 E Houston St, btwn Orchard & Allen Sts, Lower East Side; 8am-7pm Mon-Wed, to 7pm Thu, to 6pm Fri-Sun; F to 2nd Ave) In business since 1914, this landmark establishment serves up Eastern European Jewish delicacies, such as caviar, herring and lox, and, of course, smear by the pound. It's a great place to load up for a picnic or stock your fridge with breakfast goodies.

A Russ & Daughters Cafe (p119) with sit-down service is a few blocks away.

SPORTS & ACTIVITIES

JUMP INTO THE LIGHT VR AMUSEMENT PARK

Map p414 (646-590-1172; https://jumpintothelight.com; 180 Orchard St, East Village; $29; 1pm-midnight Mon-Wed, 11am-2am Thu-Sat, to midnight Sun; F to Delancy) Ready to jump off a skyscraper, climb a mountain, parachute from a plane and kill a whole bunch of zombies? Then head to this incredible, first-of-its-kind virtual reality arcade, where you can explore all the different activities and, best of all, start to understand how cool VR is going to be. Interactive artwork and other futuristic tech is also on display.

RUSSIAN & TURKISH BATHS BATHHOUSE

Map p412 (212-674-9250; www.russianturkishbaths.com; 268 E 10th St, btwn First Ave & Ave A, East Village; per visit $45; noon-10pm Mon-Tue & Thu-Fri, from 10am Wed, from 9am Sat, from 8am Sun; L to 1st Ave; 6 to Astor Pl) Since 1892, this cramped and grungy downtown spa has been drawing a polyglot and eclectic mix: actors, students, frisky couples, singles-on-the-make, Russian regulars and old-school locals, who strip down to their skivvies (or the roomy cotton shorts provided) and rotate between steam baths, an ice-cold plunge pool, a sauna and the sundeck.

Most hours are coed (clothing required), but there are several blocks of men-/women-only hours (clothing optional). There are also massages, scrubs and Russian oak-leaf treatments available. The on-site cafe serves specials like Polish sausage and blinis; you can don one of the house-provided robes while eating.

A long-running and fairly operatic feud between the two co-owners means days are split evenly between them. Passes and gift cards purchased from one manager can only be used during his hours. Check the website for more info on operating hours and the manager calendar.

West Village, Chelsea & the Meatpacking District

WEST VILLAGE & THE MEATPACKING DISTRICT | CHELSEA

Neighborhood Top Five

❶ **High Line** (p136) Packing a picnic lunch from Chelsea Market and having a uniquely pastoral moment on the thin strand of green along the High Line as it soars above the gridiron.

❷ **Chelsea Galleries** (p148) Checking out the city's brightest art stars at top galleries, such as Pace Gallery.

❸ **Washington Square Park** (p138) Walking through the park, pausing under the signature arch, then loitering at the fountain to eavesdrop on gossiping NYU kids.

❹ **Rubin Museum of Art** (p141) Exploring fascinating exhibitions from the Himalayas and beyond.

❺ **Stonewall National Monument** (p139) Taking a few moments to reflect on the night that sparked the LGBTQ rights movement at one of the country's newest national parks.

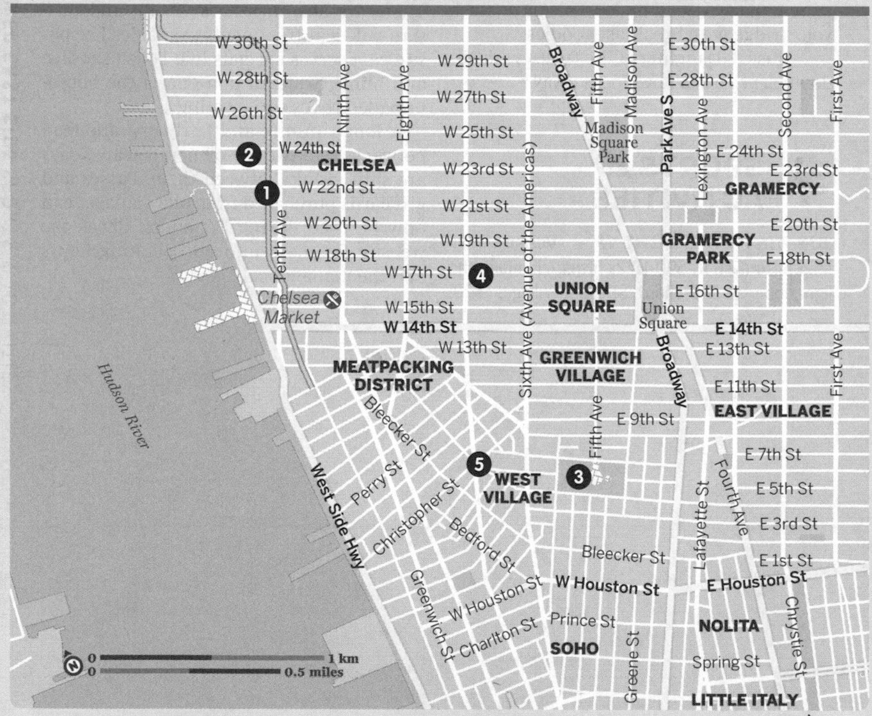

For more detail of this area see Map p416 and p420

Explore West Village, Chelsea & the Meatpacking District

There's a good reason why this area is known as the Village: it actually looks like one! Quiet lanes carve their way between brown-brick town houses offering endless strolling for locals appreciating good weather or tourists coming to see what the fuss is about. The Village is indeed picturesque, and the best way to uncover its treasures is to simply have a wander. When your feet grow tired of negotiating the cobbled streets you'll find that you're never too far from a cafe serving up a frothy cappuccino or a glass of wine.

A stroll through the Meatpacking District, once filled with slaughterhouses, takes you past sleek boutiques and roaring nightclubs. Chelsea, which is just to the north, sits right in the middle of the West Village and Midtown, and carries a bit of flavor from each. It's the de facto neighborhood for the city's sociable gay community, and its broad avenues are lined with breezy cafes, themed bars and sweaty clubs. The neighborhood's massive gallery scene can be found in the West 20s.

Local Life

- **Eighth Avenue Brunch** If you're a dude looking to meet (or at least look at) other dudes, but the cruisey bar scene isn't your style, then opt for the weekend brunch scene along Eighth Ave. You'll spot piles of friendly Chelsea boys drinking their hangovers off in tight jeans and even tighter T-shirts.
- **West Village Cafes** The quizzes and surveys can't be wrong – the West Village is the most desirable residential neighborhood in Manhattan, so do as the locals do and make the most of this quaint district stacked to the brim with cute cafes. Grab a book and a latte and hunker down for a blissful afternoon of people-watching.
- **Gallery Hopping** Join the fashionable, art-minded crowds at the latest gallery shows in Chelsea. Thursday night, when some galleries have openings (and free wine), is a good time to roam.

Getting There & Away

- **Subway** Sixth Ave, Seventh Ave and Eighth Ave are graced with convenient subway stations, but public transportation slims further west. Take the A/C/E or 1/2/3 lines to reach this colorful clump of neighborhoods – disembark at 14th St (along either service) if you're looking for a good place to make tracks, or W 4th St-Washington Sq to be taken right to the heart of the Village.
- **Bus** Try M14, or the M8 if you're traveling across town and want to access the westernmost areas of Chelsea and the West Village by public transportation.

Lonely Planet's Top Tip

It's perfectly acceptable to arm yourself with a map (or rely on your smartphone) to get around the West Village's charming-but-challenging side streets. Even some locals have a tricky time finding their way! Just remember that 4th St makes a diagonal turn north – breaking away from usual east–west street grid – and you'll quickly become a Village pro.

Best Places to Eat

- Jeffrey's Grocery (p146)
- RedFarm (p147)
- Chelsea Market (p147)
- Blue Hill (p147)
- Barbuto (p145)

For reviews, see p142.

Best Places to Drink

- Employees Only (p150)
- Buvette (p150)
- Pier 66 Maritime (p154)
- Smalls (p158)
- Duplex (p159)

For reviews, see p150.

Best Bookstores

- Printed Matter (p163)
- Strand Book Store (p160)
- Three Lives & Company (p161)
- 192 Books (p163)

For reviews, see p160.

TOP SIGHT
CHELSEA MARKET

In a shining example of redevelopment and preservation, the Chelsea Market has transformed a former factory into a shopping concourse that caters to foodies and fashionistas.

Browsing & Business Spaces

Browse the various nonfood offerings at Imports from Marrakesh, which specializes in Moroccan art and design; check out the latest literary hits at Posman Books; search for a new outfit or home accessory at Anthropologie; or pick up a bottle at the expert-staffed Chelsea Wine Vault.

The market only takes up the lower part of a larger, million-sq-ft space, occupying a full city block, which is the current home of TV channels the Food Network, Oxygen Network and NY1, the local news channel. Cellists and bluegrass players fill the main walkway with music, and the High Line passes right by the rear of the building.

Foodie Hub

More than two dozen food vendors ply their temptations, including Mokbar (ramen with Korean accents), Takumi Taco (mixing Japanese and Mexican ingredients), **Tuck Shop** (Map p420; www.tuckshopnyc.com; Chelsea Market, 75 Ninth Ave, btwn W 15th & W 16th Sts, Chelsea; pies $6; ⌚11am-9pm Mon-Sat, to 7pm Sun; Ⓢ A/C/E, L to 8th Ave-14th St) (Aussie-style savory pies), Bar Suzette (crepes), Num Pang (Cambodian sandwiches), Ninth St Espresso (perfect lattes), Doughnuttery (piping hot mini-doughnuts) and L'Arte de Gelato (rich ice cream).

If you're after something more indulgent, linger over a meal at the Green Table, which serves farm-fresh organic ingredients; sample the first-rate seafood and raw bar at Cull & Pistol; or stop by Friedman's Lunch for upscale American comfort food.

DON'T MISS

- Takumi
- Lobster Place
- Chelsea Thai Wholesale
- Artists and Fleas

PRACTICALITIES

- Map p420, D5
- ☎212-652-2121
- www.chelseamarket.com
- 75 Ninth Ave, at W 15th St, Chelsea
- ⌚7am-9pm Mon-Sat, 8am-8pm Sun
- Ⓢ A/C/E, L to 8th Ave-14th St

Also worth visiting are two of the market's longtime tenants, Chelsea Thai Wholesale (unpretentious, tasty Thai food) and the Lobster Place (overstuffed lobster rolls and killer sushi).

Discount Fashion Bonanza

Those looking for a bargain on high-end fashions should head to the event space near the Ninth Ave entrance. There are frequent pop-up shops and sample sales featuring racks of discounted men and women's clothing.

At the other end of the market near the Tenth Ave entrance is Artists and Fleas, a permanent market for local designers and craftspeople to sell their wares. It's the place to stop for a quirky new wallet, trendy pair of sunglasses or a piece of statement jewelry.

There's also a large Anthropologie at the Ninth Ave entrance. The clothing is located on the basement level, where you'll also find an impressively large discount rack.

NATIONAL BISCUIT COMPANY

The long brick edifice occupied by Chelsea Market was built in the 1890s to house a massive bakery complex that became the headquarters of the National Biscuit Company (better known as Nabisco, makers of Saltines, Fig Newtons and Oreos). The market, which opened in the 1990s, is now a base camp for gourmet outlets and apparel boutiques.

Get your food to go – seating is limited at most of the eateries, but there is general seating throughout the market.

TOP SIGHT
HIGH LINE

It's hard to believe that the High Line – a shining example of urban renewal – was once a dingy rail line that anchored an unsavory district of slaughterhouses. Today, this eye-catching attraction is one of New York's best-loved green spaces, drawing visitors who come to stroll, sit and picnic 30ft above the city, while enjoying fabulous views of Manhattan's ever-changing skyline.

Industrial Past

Long before the High Line was a beacon for New Yorkers looking for a respite from the grind of the city, eager tourists and playful families, it was a dodgy elevated train that ran through neighborhoods of thugs and slaughterhouses. The tracks that would one day become the High Line were commissioned in the 1930s when the municipal government decided to raise the street-level tracks after years of accidents that gave Tenth Ave the nickname 'Death Avenue.' The project drained over $150 million in funds (equivalent to around $2 billion by today's dime) and took roughly five years to complete. After two decades of effective use, a rise in truck transportation led to the eventual decrease in usage, and finally, in the 1980s, the rails became obsolete. Petitions were signed by local residents to remove the eyesores, but in 1999 a committee called the Friends of the High Line – founded by Joshua David and Robert Hammond – was formed to save the rusting iron and transform the tracks into a unique elevated green space.

DON'T MISS

- The amphitheater-style viewing platforms at 17th and 26th Sts
- The Chelsea Market Passage between 15th and 16th Sts where you'll find art installations and food vendors in the warmer months

PRACTICALITIES

- Map p416, A2
- 212-500-6035
- www.thehighline.org
- Gansevoort St, Meatpacking District
- 7am-11pm Jun-Sep, to 10pm Apr, May, Oct & Nov, to 7pm Dec-Mar
- M11 to Washington St; M11, M14 to 9th Ave; M23, M34 to 10th Ave, S A/C/E, L to 8th Ave-14th St; 1, C/E to 23rd St

A Green Future

On a warm spring day in 2009, the High Line – full of blooming flowers and broad-leaved trees – opened to the public, the first of three phases that today link the Meatpacking District and Midtown. Section 1 starts at Gansevoort St and runs parallel to Tenth Ave up to W 20th St. Full of sitting space in various forms – from giant chaises longues to bleacher-like benching – the first part quickly became the setting for various public works and activities, many geared toward the neighborhood's growing population of families. Two years later, Section 2 opened, adding another 10 blocks of green-ified tracks. The final section opened in 2014. Here the High Line meanders from 30th up to 34th St, going up to and around the West Side Rail Yards in a U-like fashion. As it veers west toward twelfth Ave, the path widens, and you have open views of the Hudson, with the rusting, weed-filled railroad tracks running alongside the walkway (the designers wanted to evoke the same sense of overgrown wilderness in the heart of the metropolis that greeted visitors who stumbled upon the tracks prior to the park's creation). This section also features a dedicated children's play area – a jungle gym made up of exposed beams covered in a soft play surface.

To reach the High Line, there are numerous stairways along the park, including Gansevoort, 14th, 16th, 18th, 20th, 23rd, 26th, 28th, 30th and 34th Sts. There are also strategically placed elevators at Gansevoort, 14th, 16th, 23rd, 30th and 34th Sts.

More Than Just a Public Space

In the early 1900s, the western area around the Meatpacking District and Chelsea was the largest industrial section of Manhattan, and a set of elevated rail tracks were created to move freight off the cluttered streets below. As NYC evolved, the rails eventually became obsolete, and in 1999 a plan was made to convert the scarring strands of metal into a public green space. On June 9, 2009, phase one of the city's most beloved urban renewal project opened with much ado, and it's been one of New York's star attractions ever since.

The High Line's civic influence extends far beyond being the trendsetter in the island's re-greenification. As the West Village and Chelsea continue to embrace their new-found residential nature, the High Line is making a dedicated move toward becoming more than just a public place but an inspired meeting point for families and friends. As you walk along the High Line you'll find staffers wearing shirts with the signature double-H logo who can point you in the right direction or offer you additional information about the converted rails. There are also myriad staffers behind the scenes organizing public art exhibitions and activity sessions. Special tours and events explore a variety of topics: history, horticulture, design, art and food. Check the event schedule on www.thehighline.org for the latest details.

FRIENDS OF THE HIGH LINE

If you're interested in helping support the High Line through financial donations, you can become a member of the Friends of the High Line association through the website. 'Spike'-level members receive a discount at stores in the area, from Diane von Furstenberg's boutique to **Amy's Bread** (Map p420; ☎212-462-4338; www.amysbread.com; Chelsea Market, 75 Ninth Ave, btwn W 15th & W 16th Sts, Chelsea; ⏰7am-8pm Mon-Fri, 8am-8pm Sat, until 7pm Sun; Ⓢ A/C/E, L to 8th Ave-14th St).

The High Line invites various gastronomic establishments from around the city to set up vending carts and stalls so that strollers can enjoy to-go items on the green. Expect a showing of the finest coffee and ice-cream establishments during the warmer months.

PUBLIC ART

In addition to being a haven of hovering green, the High Line is also an informal art space featuring a variety of installations, both site-specific and stand-alone. For detailed information about the public art on display at the time of your visit, check out art.thehighline.org.

TOP SIGHT
WASHINGTON SQUARE PARK

What was once a potter's field and a square for public executions is now the unofficial town square of the Village. Encased in perfectly manicured brownstones and gorgeous twists of modern architecture, Washington Square Park is a striking garden space in the city – especially as you're welcomed by the iconic Stanford White Arch on the north side of the green.

History

Although now quite ravishing, Washington Square Park had a long and sordid history before finally blossoming into the paradigm of public space we see today (thanks largely to a $30 million renovation completed in 2014).

When the Dutch settled Manhattan to run the Dutch East India Company, they gave what is now the park to their freed black slaves. The land was squarely between the Dutch and Native American settlements, so, in a way, the area acted as a buffer between enemies. Though somewhat marshy, it was arable land and farming took place for around 60 years.

At the turn of the 19th century, the municipality of New York purchased the land for use as a burial ground straddling the city's limit. At first the cemetery was mainly for indigent workers, but the space quickly reached capacity during an outbreak of yellow fever. Over 20,000 bodies remain buried under the park today.

By 1830 the grounds were used for military parades, and then quickly transformed into a park for the wealthy elite who were constructing lavish town houses along the surrounding streets.

DON'T MISS

- Stanford White Arch
- Central fountain
- Greek Revival houses surrounding the park
- The birdman, often found on a bench near the southwest entrance with dozens of pigeons roosting on him

PRACTICALITIES

- Map p416, F4
- Fifth Ave at Washington Sq N, West Village
-
- S A/C/E, B/D/F/M to W 4th St-Washington Sq; R/W to 8th St-NYU

Stanford White Arch

The iconic Stanford White Arch, colloquially known as the Washington Square Arch, dominates the park with its 72ft of beaming white Dover marble. Originally designed in wood to celebrate the centennial of George Washington's inauguration in 1889, the arch proved so popular that it was replaced with stone six years later and adorned with statues of the general in war and peace. In 1916 artist Marcel Duchamp famously climbed to the top of the arch by its internal stairway and declared the park the 'Free and Independent Republic of Washington Square.'

A Political Stage

Washington Square Park has long provided a stage for political activity, from local protests against proposed changes to the shape and usage of the park, to issues of national importance such as the 1912 protests for better working conditions.

In 2007 Democratic Party candidate Barack Obama led a rally here to drum up support for his successful presidential bid. Turnout was, unsurprisingly, overwhelming.

SIGHTS

If you're an art-lover, this trio of neighborhoods is not to be missed. The Whitney Museum of American Art (in the Meatpacking District) should feature prominently in any itinerary, followed by an exploration of Chelsea's galleries (in the West 20s) – the epicenter of NYC's art world. Other major sights include the High Line, a former rail line turned green space, the nearby Hudson River Park, which provides a tranquil setting for relaxing along the waterfront, as well as the newly christened Stonewall National Monument right in the center of the West Village and across the street from the eponymous bar.

West Village & the Meatpacking District

HIGH LINE — PARK

See p136.

WASHINGTON SQUARE PARK — PARK

See p138.

★WHITNEY MUSEUM OF AMERICAN ART — MUSEUM

Map p416 (☎212-570-3600; www.whitney.org; 99 Gansevoort St, at Washington St, West Village; adult/child $25/free, pay-what-you-wish 7-10pm Fri; ⏲10:30am-6pm Mon, Wed, Thu & Sun, to 10pm Fri & Sat; Ⓢ A/C/E, L to 8th Ave-14th St) After years of construction, the Whitney's new downtown location opened to much fanfare in 2015. Perched near the foot of the High Line (p136), this architecturally stunning building – designed by Renzo Piano – makes a suitable introduction to the museum's superb collection. Inside the spacious, light-filled galleries, you'll find works by all the great American artists, including Edward Hopper, Jasper Johns, Georgia O'Keeffe and Mark Rothko.

In addition to rotating exhibits, the **Whitney Biennial** is held on even-numbered years; it's an ambitious survey of contemporary art that rarely fails to generate controversy.

STONEWALL NATIONAL MONUMENT — NATIONAL PARK

Map p416 (www.nps.gov/ston/index.htm; W 4th St, btwn Christopher & Grove Sts, West Village; ⏲9am-dusk; Ⓢ 1 to Christopher St-Sheridan Sq; A/C/E, B/D/F/M to W 4th St-Washington Sq) In 2016 President Barack Obama declared Christopher Park, a small fenced-in square with benches and some greenery, a national park and on it the first national monument dedicated to LGBTQ history. The park is small, but it's well worth stopping here to reflect on the Stonewall uprising of 1969, when LGBTQ citizens fought back against discriminatory policing of their communities. Many cite these events as the crucible of the modern LGBTQ rights movement in the US.

SALMAGUNDI CLUB — GALLERY

Map p416 (☎212-255-7740; www.salmagundi.org; 47 Fifth Ave, btwn W 11th & 12th Sts, West Village; ⏲1-6pm Mon-Fri, to 5pm Sat & Sun; Ⓢ 4/5/6, L, N/Q/R/W to 14th St-Union Sq) Far removed from the flashy Chelsea gallery scene, the Salmagundi Club features several gallery spaces focusing on representational American art set in a stunning historic brownstone on Fifth Ave below Union Sq. The club is one of the oldest art clubs in the US (founded in 1871) and still offers classes and exhibitions for its members.

GRACE CHURCH — CHURCH

Map p416 (☎212-254-2000; www.gracechurch-nyc.org; 802 Broadway, at 10th St, West Village; ⏲noon-5pm, services daily; Ⓢ R/W to 8th St-NYU; 6 to Astor Pl) This Gothic Revival Episcopal church, designed in 1843 by James Renwick Jr, was made of marble quarried by prisoners at 'Sing Sing,' the state penitentiary in the town of Ossining, 30 miles up the Hudson River (which, legend has it, is the origin of the expression 'being sent upriver'). After years of neglect, Grace Church has been beautifully restored.

It's now a National Landmark, whose elaborate carvings, towering spire and verdant, groomed yard are sure to stop you in your tracks as you make your way down this otherwise ordinary stretch of the Village. The stained-glass windows inside are stunning, and the soaring interior makes a perfect setting for the frequent musical programming (recently there was a series of 'Bach at Noon' organ concerts). Free guided tours are offered at 1pm on Sundays.

PIER 45 — PARK

Map p416 (W 10th St, at Hudson River, West Village; Ⓢ 1 to Christopher St-Sheridan Sq) Still known to many as the Christopher St Pier, this is an 850ft-long finger of concrete, spiffily renovated with a grass lawn, flowerbeds, a comfort station, an outdoor cafe, tented shade shelters and a stop for the New York Water Taxi.

Now part of the Hudson River Park, it's a magnet for downtowners of all stripes, from local families with toddlers in daylight to mobs of young gay kids who flock here at night from all over the city (and beyond) thanks to the pier's long-established history as a gay cruising hangout. The spot offers sweeping views of the Hudson and cool, relieving breezes in the thick of summer.

ABINGDON SQUARE SQUARE

Map p416 (Hudson St, at 12th St, West Village; ⓈA/C/E, L to 8th Ave-14th St) This historical dot on the landscape (just a quarter-acre) is a lovely little patch of green, home to grassy knolls, beds of perennial flowers and winding bluestone paths, as well as a popular Saturday Greenmarket. It's a great place to enjoy a midday picnic or rest after an afternoon of wandering the winding West Village streets.

After getting horizontal, look up at the southern end of the park and you'll see the *Abingdon Doughboy,* a bronze statue dedicated to servicemen from the neighborhood who gave their lives in WWI (when soldiers were commonly known as 'doughboys').

NEW YORK UNIVERSITY UNIVERSITY

Map p416 (NYU; ☎212-998-4550; www.nyu.edu; Welcome Center, 50 W 4th St, West Village; ⓈA/C/E, B/D/F/M to W 4th St-Washington Sq; N/R to 8th St-NYU) In 1831 Albert Gallatin, formerly Secretary of the Treasury under President Thomas Jefferson, founded an intimate center of higher learning open to all students, regardless of race or class background. He'd scarcely recognize the place today, as it's swelled to a student population of around 50,000, with more than 16,000 employees, and schools and colleges at six Manhattan locations.

It just keeps growing, too – to the dismay of landmark activists and business owners, who have seen buildings rapidly bought out by the academic giant (or destroyed through careless planning, such as with the historic Provincetown Playhouse) and replaced with ugly dormitories or administrative offices. Still, some of its crevices are charming, such as the leafy courtyard at its School of Law, or impressively modern, like

TOP SIGHT
HUDSON RIVER PARK

The High Line may be all the rage these days, but one block away stretches a 5-mile-long ribbon of green that has transformed the city over the past 10 years.

Covering 550 acres, and running from Battery Park at Manhattan's southern tip to 59th St in Midtown, the Hudson River Park is Manhattan's wondrous backyard. The long riverside path is a great spot for running and cycling, and the **Waterfront Bicycle Shop** (Map p416; ☎212-414-2453; www.bikeshopny.com; 391 West St, btwn W 10th & Christopher Sts; rental per 1hr/all day $12.50/35; ⏲10am-7pm) is a convenient place to rent bikes. Several **boathouses** (p85) offer kayak hire and longer excursions for the more experienced. There's also beach volleyball, basketball courts, a skate park and tennis courts. Families with kids have loads of options, including four sparkling-new playgrounds, a carousel and mini golf.

Those who simply need a break from the city come here to loll on the grass for a bout of people-watching and river contemplation, while those seeking something less sedate can join the sangria- and sun-loving crowds at the dockside Frying Pan (p154). The park also offers great sunset views and is the ideal place to catch July 4 Fireworks (arrive early to get a spot).

DON'T MISS

- Kayaking on the river
- Sunset strolls
- Summertime drinks at *Frying Pan*

PRACTICALITIES

- Map p416, C7
- www.hudsonriverpark.org
- West Village
- 👪
- 🚌M11 to Washington St; M11, M14 to 9th Ave; M23, M34 to 10th Ave, Ⓢ1 to Hudson Ave; A/C/E, L to 8th Ave-14th St; 1, C/E to 23rd St

the Skirball Center for the Performing Arts, where top-notch dance, theater, music, spoken-word and other performances wow audiences at the 850-seat theater.

NYU's academic offerings are highly regarded and wide-ranging, especially its film, theater, writing, medical and law programs. For a unique experience that will put you on the fast track to meeting locals, sign up for a weekend or one-day class – from American history to photography – offered by the School of Professional Studies and Continuing Education, and open to all.

SHERIDAN SQUARE SQUARE

Map p416 (btwn Washington Pl & W 4th St, West Village; S1 to Christopher St-Sheridan Sq) The shape of a triangle, Sheridan Sq isn't much more than a few park benches and some trees surrounded by an old-fashioned wrought-iron gate. But its location (in the heart of gay Greenwich Village) has meant that it has witnessed every rally, demonstration and uprising that has contributed to New York's gay rights movement.

Chelsea

CHELSEA MARKET MARKET

See p134.

★RUBIN MUSEUM OF ART GALLERY

Map p420 (212-620-5000; www.rmanyc.org; 150 W 17th St, btwn Sixth & Seventh Aves, Chelsea; adult/child $15/free, 6-10pm Fri free; 11am-5pm Mon & Thu, to 9pm Wed, to 10pm Fri, to 6pm Sat & Sun; S1 to 18th St) The Rubin is the first museum in the Western world to dedicate itself to the art of the Himalayas and surrounding regions. Its impressive collections include embroidered textiles from China, metal sculptures from Tibet, Pakistani stone sculptures and intricate Bhutanese paintings, as well as ritual objects and dance masks from various Tibetan regions, spanning from the 2nd to the 19th centuries.

Rotating exhibitions have included the enlightening 'Red Book of CJ Jung' and 'Victorious Ones,' which comprised sculptures and paintings of Jinas, the founding teachers of Jainism. The Cafe Serai serves traditional Himalayan foods and features live music on Wednesday nights, from 6pm onward. Later in the week, the cafe transforms into the K2 Lounge, where you can sip wine and martinis after visiting the galleries on free Friday evenings.

GENERAL THEOLOGICAL SEMINARY GARDENS

Map p420 (212-243-5150; www.gts.edu; 440 W 21st St, btwn Ninth & Tenth Aves, Chelsea; 10am-5:30pm Mon-Fri; S1, C/E to 23rd St) FREE Founded in 1817, this is the oldest seminary of the Episcopal Church in America. The school, which sits in the midst of the beautiful Chelsea historic district, has been working hard lately to make sure it can preserve its best asset – the garden-like campus snuggled in the middle of its full block of buildings – even as Chelsea development sprouts up all around it.

This peaceful haven is the perfect spot for finding respite, either before or after your neighborhood gallery crawl. To visit, ring the buzzer at the garden gate, located halfway down 21st St between Ninth and Tenth Aves.

CHELSEA HOTEL HISTORIC BUILDING

Map p420 (222 W 23rd St, btwn Seventh & Eighth Aves, Chelsea; S1, C/E to 23rd St) This red-brick hotel, built in the 1880s and featuring ornate iron balconies and no fewer than seven plaques declaring its literary landmark status, has played a major role in pop-culture history. It's where the likes of Mark Twain, Thomas Wolfe, Dylan Thomas and Arthur Miller hung out; Jack Kerouac allegedly crafted *On the Road* during one marathon session here; and it's where Arthur C Clarke wrote *2001: A Space Odyssey*.

Dylan Thomas died of alcohol poisoning while staying at the Chelsea Hotel in 1953, and Nancy Spungen died here after being stabbed by her Sex Pistols boyfriend Sid Vicious in 1978. Among the many celebs who have logged time living at the Chelsea are Joni Mitchell, Patti Smith, Robert Mapplethorpe, Stanley Kubrick, Dennis Hopper, Edith Piaf, Bob Dylan and Leonard Cohen, whose song 'Chelsea Hotel' recalls a romp with Janis Joplin (who spent time here, too).

Sadly, the hotel's days of artistry and intrigue are long gone and the building's ultimate destiny is in limbo after a development deal to convert it into condos fell through.

GAGOSIAN GALLERY

Map p420 (212-741-1111; www.gagosian.com; 555 W 24th St, btwn Tenth & Eleventh Aves, Chelsea; 10am-6pm Mon-Sat; S1, C/E to 23rd St) International works dot the walls at the Gagosian in Chelsea. The ever-revolving exhibits feature greats such as Julian Schnabel, Willem de Kooning, Andy Warhol and

Basquiat. Gagosian offers a different vibe than most of the one-off galleries, as it's part of a constellation of showrooms that spreads well across the globe.

Also check out the 522 W 21st St location, which easily rivals some of the city's museums with its large-scale installations.

CHEIM & READ GALLERY

Map p420 (☎212-242-7727; www.cheimread.com; 547 W 25th St, btwn Tenth & Eleventh Aves, Chelsea; ⏲10am-6pm Tue-Sat; Ⓢ1, C/E to 23rd St) With its stock of artists including Bill Jensen, Jannis Kounellis, Jenny Holzer and Tal R, Cheim & Read showcases everything from giant canvases to bombastic sculptures. If the timing is right, you might catch William Eggleston's evocative photographs hanging on the wall.

EATING

While the West Village is known for its classy, cozy and intimate spots, the adjacent Meatpacking District's dining scene is a bit more ostentatious, complete with nightclub-like queues behind velvet ropes, bold decor and swarms of trend-obsessed patrons. Chelsea strikes a balance between the two with a brash assortment of *très* gay eateries along the uber-popular Eighth Ave (a must for see-and-be-seen brunch), and more cafes lining Ninth Ave further west. In the warmer months expect windows and doors to fling open and plenty of alfresco seating to spill out onto the streets.

West Village & the Meatpacking District

P.S. BURGERS BURGERS $

Map p416 (☎646-998-4685; www.psburgers.com; 35 Carmine St; burgers from $10; ⏲11am-10pm Mon-Fri, noon-10pm Sat & Sun; ⓈA/C/E, B/D/F/M to W 4th St-Washington Sq) P.S. Burgers is an unassuming takeout favorite in the West Village that offers inexpensive specialty burgers inspired by locations around the world. Take a trip to Rio de Janeiro (plantains and a fried egg) or Canada (Canadian bacon and mapled goat cheese). Every burger is cooked to order and there are plenty of classic sides.

RED BAMBOO VEGAN $

Map p416 (☎212-260-7049; www.redbamboo-nyc.com; 140 W 4th St, btwn Sixth Ave & MacDougal St; mains $8-13; ⏲12:30-11pm Mon-Thu, to 11:30pm Fri, noon-11:30pm Sat, to 11pm Sun; ⓈA/C/E, B/D/F/M to W 4th St-Washington Sq) Flaky, hot bites of popcorn shrimp, gooey chicken Parmesan, chocolate cake so rich you can barely finish – Red Bamboo offers all of that and more soul and Asian food options. The catch? Everything on its menu is vegan (some dishes do offer the option of real cheese). This is a must try for vegans, vegetarians or anyone looking to try something new.

MAMOUN'S MIDDLE EASTERN $

Map p416 (www.mamouns.com; 119 MacDougal St, btwn W 3rd St & Minetta Ln, West Village; sandwiches from $3, plates from $6; ⏲11am-5am; ⓈA/C/E, B/D/F/M to W 4th St-Washington Sq) This falafel and shawarma restaurant in lower Manhattan specializes in big, dripping platters and wraps that are served up quick and don't cost much. A NYC favorite, Mamoun's even has its own branded hot sauce. Be warned: it's not for anyone with a sensitive tongue. The West Village location is tiny, but there is some limited seating.

GANSEVOORT MARKET MARKET $

Map p416 (www.gansmarket.com; 353 W 14th St, at Ninth Ave, Meatpacking District; mains $5-20; ⏲8am-8pm; ⓈA/C/E, L to 8th Ave-14th St) Inside a brick building in the heart of the Meatpacking District, this sprawling market is the latest and greatest food emporium to land in NYC. A raw, industrial space lit by skylights, it features several dozen gourmet vendors slinging tapas, arepas, tacos, pizzas, meat pies, ice cream, pastries and more.

TWO BOOTS PIZZA PIZZA $

Map p416 (☎212-633-9096; http://twoboots.com; 201 W 11th St, at Greenwich Ave, West Village; ⏲11am-midnight Sun-Wed, to 1am Thu, to 2am Fri & Sat; ⓈA/C/E, L to 8th Ave-14th St) This ultra-popular mini-chain serves a range of authentic New York–style slices with an eclectic array of toppings. It specializes in tasty vegan alternatives for all of its pizza, as well as the option to order any pizza with a gluten-free crust.

MAH ZE DAHR BAKERY $

Map p416 (☎212-498-9810; https://mahzedahrbakery.com; 28 Greenwich Ave, btwn W 10th & Charles Sts, West Village; pastries from $3; ⏲7am-6pm Mon-Fri, 8am-5pm Sat & Sun;

(S A/C/E, L to 8th Ave-14th St) Tangy, creamy cheesecakes and spongy brioche doughnuts are on offer at this bakery opened by former financial advisor Umber Ahmad, who was discovered when she baked for one of her clients, celebrity chef Tom Colicchio. When you try one of the crumbly scones or rich brownies you'll understand why Colicchio suggested the change of career.

DOMINIQUE ANSEL KITCHEN BAKERY $

Map p416 (212-242-5111; www.dominiqueanselkitchen.com; 137 Seventh Ave, btwn Charles & W 10th Sts, West Village; pastries $4-8; 8am-7pm Mon-Sat, 9am-7pm Sun; S 1 to Christopher St-Sheridan Sq) The famed creator of the cronut owns this small sun-lit bakery in the West Village where you can nibble on perfectly flaky croissants, raspberry passion-fruit pavlova, blueberry shortcake and many other heavenly treats (but no cronuts). There's also light savory fare, such as turkey pot pie with foie gras gravy and edamame avocado toast.

UMAMI BURGERS $

Map p416 (212-677-8626; www.umamiburger.com; 432 Sixth Ave, btwn 9th & 10th Sts, West Village; burgers $10-15; 11:30am-11pm Sun-Thu, to midnight Fri & Sat; S 1 to Christopher St-Sheridan Sq; F/M, L to 6th Ave-14th St) That mysterious fifth taste sensation will be more than satisfied at this stylish burger bar. Combos such as the Truffle (truffled aioli and house-made truffle cheese) and the bacon-topped Manly are first-rate as is the veg-friendly Black Bean. The menu is rounded out with creative cocktails, microbrews on draft and tasty sides (including tempura onion rings).

COTENNA ITALIAN $

Map p416 (www.cotenna.nyc; 21 Bedford St, btwn Downing & W Houston Sts, West Village; mains $12-14; noon-midnight Sun-Thu, to 1am Fri & Sat; S 1 to Houston St) Tucked away on a picturesque corner of the Village, this intimate, attractively designed eatery is a favorite on date night. It has a small menu of affordable pastas (from $12), bruschetta and grilled dishes, though you can also come for wine or cocktails and sharing plates, including *salumi* (cured meat) and cheese boards.

MOUSTACHE MIDDLE EASTERN $

Map p416 (212-229-2220; www.moustachepitzawest.com; 90 Bedford St, btwn Grove & Barrow Sts, West Village; pizzas $11-15; noon-11pm Sun-Thu, to midnight Fri & Sat; S 1 to Christopher St-Sheridan Sq) In its warm, earthy space, small and delightful Moustache serves up rich, flavorful sandwiches (leg of lamb, *merguez* sausage, falafel), thin-crust pizzas, tangy salads and hearty specialties, such as *ouzi* (phyllo stuffed with chicken, rice and spices) and moussaka. The best start to a meal: a platter of hummus or baba ghanoush served with fluffy, piping-hot pita bread.

SAIGON SHACK VIETNAMESE $

Map p416 (212-228-0588; www.saigonshacknyc.com; 114 MacDougal St, btwn Bleecker & 3rd Sts, West Village; mains $7-10; 11am-11pm Sun-Thu, to 1am Fri & Sat; S A/CE, B/D/F/M to W 4th St-Washington Sq) Steaming bowls of pho (noodle soup), tangy *banh mi* (baguette) sandwiches and crunchy spring rolls await at this bustling wood-lined eatery just a few strides from Washington Square Park. The prices are fair and the food arrives in a hurry; the only downside: you might have to wait for a table, as it's a popular draw for the NYU crowd.

CORNER BISTRO BISTRO $

Map p416 (212-242-9502; www.cornerbistrony.com; 331 W 4th St, btwn Jane & 12th Sts, West Village; burgers $10-12; 11:30am-2am Mon-Thu, to 3am Fri & Sat, noon-2am Sun; S A/C/E, L to 8th Ave-14th St) An old-school dive bar with cheap beers on tap – it all sounds pretty standard until you take a mouthwatering bite out of the bacon- and cheese-covered Corner Bistro burger. Nothing beats this juicy meat sandwich with a side scatter of fries.

TAÏM ISRAELI $

Map p416 (212-691-1287; www.taimfalafel.com; 222 Waverly Pl, btwn Perry & W 11th Sts, West Village; sandwiches $7-8; 11am-10pm; S 1/2/3, A/C/E to 14th St; L to 6th Ave-14th St) This tiny joint whips up some of the best falafel in the city. You can order it Green (traditional style), Harissa (with Tunisian spices) or Red (with roasted peppers) – whichever you choose, you'll get it stuffed into pita bread with creamy tahini sauce and a generous dose of Israeli salad.

There are also mixed platters, zesty salads and delicious smoothies (try the date, lime and banana).

VILLAGE NATURAL VEGETARIAN $

Map p416 (212-727-0968; http://villagenatural.net; 46 Greenwich Ave, btwn Charles & Perry Sts, West Village; mains $12-18; 11:30am-10:30pm Mon-Thu, to 11am Fri, 11am-11pm Sat, to 10pm Sun; S A/C/E, L to 8th Ave-14th St)

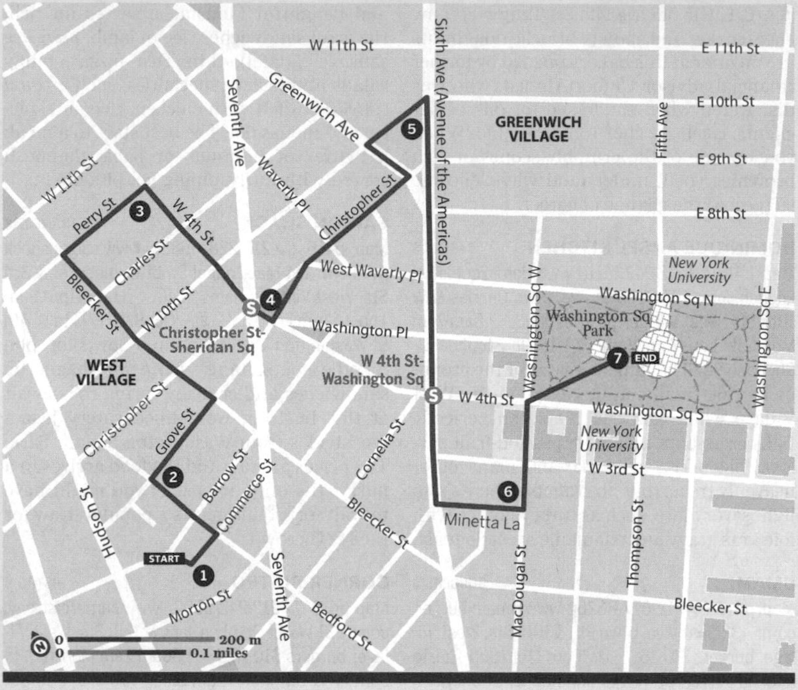

Neighborhood Walk
It Takes a Village

START COMMERCE STREET
END WASHINGTON SQUARE PARK
LENGTH 1.2 MILES; ONE HOUR

Of all the neighborhoods in New York City, Greenwich Village is the most pedestrian-friendly, with its cobbled corners that stray from the signature gridiron that unfurls across the rest of the island. Start your walkabout at the **1 Cherry Lane Theater** (p158). Established in 1924, the small theater is the city's longest continuously running off-Broadway establishment.

Make a left on Bedford and you'll find **2 90 Bedford** on the right-hand side at the corner of Grove St. You might recognize the apartment block as the fictitious home of the cast of *Friends* (sadly, Central Perk was just a figment of the writers' imaginations).

For another iconic TV landmark, wander up Bleecker St and make a right on Perry St, stopping at **3 66 Perry Street**, which was used as the facade and stoop of the city's turn-of-the-21st-century 'It Girl,' Carrie Bradshaw, in *Sex and the City*.

Make a right on W 4th St until you reach Christopher Park, home to the newly designated **4 Stonewall National Monument** (p139). On the north side of the green space is the legendary Stonewall Inn, where a clutch of fed-up LGBTQ men and women rioted for their civil rights in 1969, signaling the start of what would become a civil rights revolution.

Follow Christopher St to Sixth Ave to find the **5 Jefferson Market Library** straddling a triangular plot of land. The 'Ruskinian Gothic' spire was once a fire lookout tower. In the 1870s the building was used as a courthouse but today it houses a branch of the public library.

Stroll down Sixth Ave taking in the flurry of passersby, then make a left on Minetta Lane to swing by **6 Cafe Wha?**, the notorious institution where many young musicians and comedians – such as Bob Dylan and Richard Pryor – got their start.

End your wandering further along MacDougal St in **7 Washington Square Park** (p138), the Village's unofficial town square, which plays host to NYU students, buskers and the not-infrequent political protest.

Vegetarians, vegans and those who dine with them have been flocking to this unpretentious West Village restaurant for ages. The menu is anchored by large portions of stir-fry and pasta, as well as big, hearty salads and veggie burgers.

PEACEFOOD VEGAN $

Map p416 (☎212-979-2288; www.peacefoodcafe.com; 41 E 11th St, btwn University Pl & Broadway, West Village; mains $12-18; ⏰10am-10pm; 🌱; Ⓢ4/5/6, L, N/Q/R to 14th St-Union Sq) Peacefood is a vegan and vegetarian diner's best friend with its tasty pizzas, roasted vegetable dishes, pan-seared dumplings and other delicacies. It gets crowded during the lunch and dinner rush, so prepare to eat in cramped quarters.

★BARBUTO MODERN ITALIAN $$

Map p416 (☎212-924-9700; www.barbutonyc.com; 775 Washington St, at W 12th St, West Village; mains $22-28; ⏰noon-3:30pm & 5:30-11pm Mon-Thu, until midnight Fri & Sat, until 10pm Sun; ⓈA/C/E, L to 8th Ave-14th St; 1 to Christopher St-Sheridan Sq) Occupying a cavernous garage space with sweeping see-through doors that roll up and into the ceiling during the warmer months, Barbuto slaps together a delightful assortment of nouveau Italian dishes, such as duck breast with plum and crème fraîche, and calamari drizzled with squid ink and chili aioli.

NIX VEGETARIAN $$

Map p416 (☎212-498-9393; www.nixny.com; 72 University Pl, btwn 10th & 11th Sts, West Village; mains $20-28; ⏰11:30am-2:30pm & 5:30-11pm Mon-Fri, from 10:30am Sat & Sun; Ⓢ4/5/6, N/Q/R/W, L to 14th St-Union Sq) At this understated Michelin-starred eatery, head chefs Nicolas Farias and John Fraser transform vegetables into high art in beautifully executed dishes that delight the senses. Start off with tandoor bread and creative dips like spiced eggplant with pine nuts before moving on to richly complex plates of cauliflower tempura with steamed buns, or spicy tofu with chanterelle mushrooms, kale and Szechuan pepper.

ROSEMARY'S ITALIAN $$

Map p416 (☎212-647-1818; www.rosemarysnyc.com; 18 Greenwich Ave, at W 10th St, West Village; mains $14-40; ⏰8am-4pm & 5-11pm Mon-Thu, until midnight Fri, from 10am Sat & Sun, until 11pm Sun; Ⓢ1 to Christopher St-Sheridan Sq) One of the West Village's hottest restaurants, Rosemary's serves high-end Italian fare that more than lives up to the hype. In a vaguely farmhouse-like setting, diners tuck into generous portions of housemade pastas, rich salads, and cheese and *salumi* (cured meat) boards. Everything, from the simple walnut herb pesto to the succulent smoked lamb shoulder, is incredible.

MERMAID OYSTER BAR SEAFOOD $$

Map p416 (☎212-260-0100; www.themermaidnyc.com; 79 MacDougal St, btwn Bleecker & W Houston Sts, West Village; small plates $12-15, mains $25-29; ⏰5-10pm Mon, to 10:30pm Tue-Fri, 4-10:30pm Sat, to 10pm Sun; ⓈA/C/E, B/D/F/M to W 4th St-Washington Sq) If you're craving a plate of oysters and don't mind a crowd, head to this West Village favorite. Happy hour is until 7pm daily (all night Monday) when you'll find young professionals crammed into the small restaurant unwinding over $7 glasses of champagne and $1 chef's-choice's oysters. Squeeze yourself into a spot at the bar and enjoy.

BABU JI INDIAN $$

Map p416 (☎212-951-1082; www.babujinyc.com; 22 E 13th St, btwn University Pl & Fifth Ave, West Village; mains $16-26; ⏰5-10:30pm Sun-Thu, to 11:30pm Fri & Sat, also 10:30am-3pm Sat & Sun; Ⓢ4/5/6, N/Q/R/W, L to 14th St-Union Sq) A playful spirit marks this excellent Australian-run Indian restaurant, which recently relocated to Union Sq. You can assemble a meal from street food–style dishes such as *papadi chaat* (chickpeas, pomegranate and yogurt chutney) and potato croquettes stuffed with lobster, or feast on heartier dishes like tandoori lamb chops or scallop coconut curry. A $62 tasting menu is also on offer.

DOMINIQUE BISTRO FRENCH $$

Map p416 (☎646-756-4145; www.dominiquebistro.nyc; 14 Christopher St, at Gay St, West Village; mains $21-41; ⏰9am-midnight Sun-Thu, to 1am Fri & Sat; Ⓢ1 to Christopher St-Sheridan Sq) On one of the prettiest corners in the West Village you'll find this airy space with soaring ceilings, oversized oil canvases and big windows for watching the city stroll past. Chef Dominick Pepe serves classic French bistro fare: start off with pâté or escargots with parsley butter, before moving on to bouillabaisse, duck cassoulet or vegetarian-friendly ratatouille.

You can dine to live music downstairs in the cozy Piano Room. Check the website for the schedule.

MALAPARTE ITALIAN $$

Map p416 (☎212-255-2122; www.malapartenyc.com; 753 Washington St, at Bethune St, West Village; mains $18-27; ⏰10:30am-11pm Mon-Fri, from 11am Sat & Sun; Ⓢ A/C/E, L to 8th Ave-14th St) Tucked away on a peaceful stretch of the West Village, Malaparte is a charming neighborhood trattoria serving simple, beautifully executed Italian dishes – spaghetti with porcini mushrooms, chewy crust pizzas, fennel and arugula salads, grilled *branzino* (sea bass), and tiramisu (of course) for dessert. The focaccia bread basket, which arrives after you sit down, is a nice touch. Cash only.

DOMA NA ROHU EUROPEAN $$

Map p416 (☎347-916-9382; www.doma.nyc; 27½ Morton St, at Seventh Ave, West Village; mains $15-24; ⏰8am-11pm Mon-Thu, to midnight Fri, 9am-midnight Sat, 9am-10:30pm Sun; Ⓢ 1 to Houston St) In a charming tavern setting just off busy Seventh Ave, Doma serves up German and Czech comfort fare with a smile. Come for bratwurst, beef goulash and house-made *spaetzle* (dumplings) with seasonal vegetables, or stop in during happy hour for $3 glasses of beer and snack specials. *Palačinky* (Czech-style crepes) draw the weekend brunch crowd.

MORANDI ITALIAN $$

Map p416 (☎212-627-7575; www.morandiny.com; 211 Waverly Pl, btwn Seventh Ave & Charles St, West Village; mains $18-38; ⏰8am-4pm & 5:30-11pm Mon-Wed, to midnight Thu & Fri, 10am-4:30pm & 5:30pm-midnight Sat, to 11pm Sun; Ⓢ 1 to Christopher St-Sheridan Sq) Run by celebrated restaurateur Keith McNally, Morandi is a warmly lit space that spills onto the sidewalk in summer. The hubbub of garrulous diners resounds amid brick walls, wide plank floors and rustic chandeliers. Squeeze into a table for the full-meal experience – hand-rolled spaghetti with lemon and Parmesan, meatballs with pine nuts and raisins, and grilled whole sea bream.

CAFÉ CLUNY BISTRO $$

Map p416 (☎212-255-6900; www.cafecluny.com; 284 W 12th St, cnr W 12th & W 4th Sts, West Village; mains lunch $12-28, dinner $22-34; ⏰8am-10pm Mon, 8am-11pm Tue-Fri, 9am-11pm Sat, 9am-10pm Sun; Ⓢ A/C/E, L 8th Ave-14th St) Café Cluny brings the charm of Paris to the West Village, with woven bistro-style bar chairs, light wooden upholstery and a selection of *joie-de-vivre*-inducing platters. Service operates in three sections: brunch morning to afternoon, brasserie in the early evening and dinner at night. No matter the hour, the dishes are tasty and well prepared.

SNACK TAVERNA GREEK $$

Map p416 (☎212-929-3499; www.snacktaverna.com; 63 Bedford St, btwn Morton & Commerce Sts, West Village; small plates $14-19, large plates $27-29; ⏰11am-4:30pm & 5:30-11pm Mon-Sat, to 10pm Sun; Ⓢ A/C/E, B/D/F/M to W 4 St-Washington Sq; 1 to Christopher St-Sheridan Sq) So much more than your usual Greek restaurant, Snack Taverna eschews gyros for a seasonal selection of scrumptious small plates to accompany the flavorful selection of market mains. The regional wines are worth a miss, but the Med beers are surprisingly refreshing.

ALTA TAPAS $$

Map p416 (☎212-505-7777; www.altarestaurant.com; 64 W 10th St, btwn Fifth & Sixth Aves, West Village; small plates $11-23; ⏰5:30-11pm Mon-Thu, 5-11:30pm Fri & Sat, 5:30-10:30pm Sun; Ⓢ A/C/E, B/D/F/M to W 4th St-Washington Sq) This gorgeous town house highlights the neighborhood's quaintness, with plenty of exposed brick, wood beams, flickering candles, massive mirrors and romantic fireplace glows. A small-plates menu of encyclopedic proportions cures indecision with the likes of succulent lamb meatballs, roasted scallops with sunchoke puree, Japanese eggplant with feta, fried goat cheese and braised short rib. The wine list is outstanding, too.

URBAN VEGAN KITCHEN VEGAN $$

Map p416 (☎646-438-9939; www.urbanvegankitchen.com; 41 Carmine St, btwn Bleecker & Bedford Sts, West Village; mains brunch $15-22, dinner $17-22; ⏰11am-11pm Mon-Wed, to 11:30pm Thu & Fri, 10am-11:30pm Sat, to 10:30pm Sun; 🖉; Ⓢ A/C/E, B/D/F/M to W 4th St-Washington Sq) Formerly the Blossom Cafe, this spot has a new name but still services killer vegan cuisine in a moody, fun environment. Stop by for brunch and feast on un-chicken and waffles with garlic kale and maple mustard aioli, or come for dinner and grab some double-decker seitan tacos.

★JEFFREY'S GROCERY MODERN AMERICAN $$$

Map p416 (☎646-398-7630; www.jeffreysgrocery.com; 172 Waverly Pl, at Christopher St, West Village; mains $23-30; ⏰8am-11pm Mon-Wed, to 1am Thu-Fri, 9:30am-1am Sat, to 11pm Sun; Ⓢ 1 to Christopher St-Sheridan Sq) This West Village classic is a lively eating and drinking spot that hits all the right notes. Seafood is the focus: there's an oyster bar and beautifully executed selections, such as mussels with crème fraîche, tuna steak tartine, and sharing platters. Meat dishes include hanger steak with roasted veggies in a *romesco* (nut and red pepper) sauce.

★REDFARM FUSION **$$$**

Map p416 (☎212-792-9700; www.redfarmnyc.com; 529 Hudson St, btwn W 10th & Charles Sts, West Village; mains $19-57, dumplings $14-20; ⏲5-11:45pm, plus 11am-2:30pm Sat & Sun, closes 11pm Sun; **S**A/C/E, B/D/F/M to W 4th St-Washington Sq; 1 to Christopher St-Sheridan Sq) RedFarm transforms Chinese cooking into pure, delectable artistry at this small, buzzing space on Hudson St. Fresh crab and eggplant bruschetta, juicy rib steak (marinated overnight in papaya, ginger and soy) and pastrami egg rolls are among the many creative dishes that brilliantly blend cuisines. Other hits include spicy crispy beef, pan-fried lamb dumplings and grilled jumbo-shrimp red curry.

★BLUE HILL AMERICAN **$$$**

Map p416 (☎212-539-1776; www.bluehillfarm.com; 75 Washington Pl, btwn Sixth Ave & Washington Sq W, West Village; prix-fixe menu $95-108; ⏲5-11pm Mon-Sat, to 10pm Sun; **S**A/C/E, B/D/F/M to W 4th St-Washington Sq) A place for slow-food junkies with deep pockets, Blue Hill was an early crusader in the 'Local is Better' movement. Gifted chef Dan Barber, who hails from a farm family in the Berkshires, MA, uses harvests from that land and from farms in upstate New York to create his widely praised fare.

FIFTY AMERICAN **$$$**

Map p416 (☎212-524-4104; www.fiftyrestaurantnyc.com; 50 Commerce St; mains $29-33, cocktails $15; ⏲5:30-10pm Mon-Wed, 5:30-11pm Thu & Fri, 11am-4pm & 5-11pm Sat, 11am-4pm, 5-10pm Sun; **S**A/C/E, B/D/F/M train to W 4th St-Washington Sq) Fifty is located on a perfectly picturesque side street in Manhattan's West Village. The specialty cocktails and delectable new American cuisine make it a worthy match for its legendary location. Everything from the soft lighting to the plush chairs and exquisite glassware makes the whole experience special.

CHUMLEY'S MODERN AMERICAN **$$$**

Map p416 (☎212-675-2081; http://chumleysnewyork.com; 86 Bedford St, btwn Grove & Barrow Sts, West Village; mains $18-34; ⏲5:30-10.15pm Mon-Thu, to 10:30pm Fri & Sat; **S**1 to Christopher St-Sheridan Sq) Occupying the same space as the legendary West Village speakeasy, this new incarnation maintains its historic air while upgrading everything else. The ambitious, seasonal menu includes aged rib-eye and arctic char, but the highlight might be the burger – constructed from two 4oz patties. Walls are lined with portraits and book jackets of Prohibition-era writers, many of whom were once bar patrons.

MINETTA TAVERN BISTRO **$$$**

Map p416 (☎212-475-3850; www.minettatavernny.com; 113 MacDougal St, at Minetta Ln, West Village; mains $25-39; ⏲noon-3pm & 5:30pm-midnight Wed, to 1am Thu & Fri, 11am-3pm & 5:30pm-1am Sat, to midnight Sun, 5:30pm-midnight Mon & Tue; **S**A/C/E, B/D/F/M to W 4th St-Washington Sq) Book in advance, or come early to snag a table on a weeknight, because Minetta Tavern is often packed to the rafters. The snug red-leather banquettes, dark-paneled walls with B&W photos and glowing yellow bistro lamps will lure you in. The flavor-filled bistro fare – pan-seared marrow bones, roasted free-range chicken and briny mussels – will have you wishing you lived upstairs.

Chelsea

★CHELSEA MARKET MARKET **$**

Map p420 (www.chelseamarket.com; 75 Ninth Ave, btwn 15th & 16th Sts, Chelsea; ⏲7am-9pm Mon-Sat, 8am-8pm Sun; **S**A/C/E, L to 8th Ave-14th St) In a shining example of redevelopment and preservation, the Chelsea Market has taken a factory formerly owned by cookie giant Nabisco (creator of Oreo) and turned it into an 800ft-long shopping concourse that caters to foodies. Taking the place of the old factory ovens that churned out massive numbers of biscuits are eclectic eateries that fill the renovated hallways of this food haven.

CHELSEA SQUARE DINER DINER **$**

Map p420 (☎212-691-5400; www.chelseasquareny.com; 368 W 23rd St, at Ninth Ave, Chelsea; mains breakfast $8-16, lunch & dinner $9-33; ⏲24hr; **S**1, C/E to 23rd St) This is one of the biggest and best of the old-school NYC diners. The food is tasty and its location in the heart of the Chelsea bar scene couldn't be better. During the day, you'll find old neighborhood regulars catching up over turkey

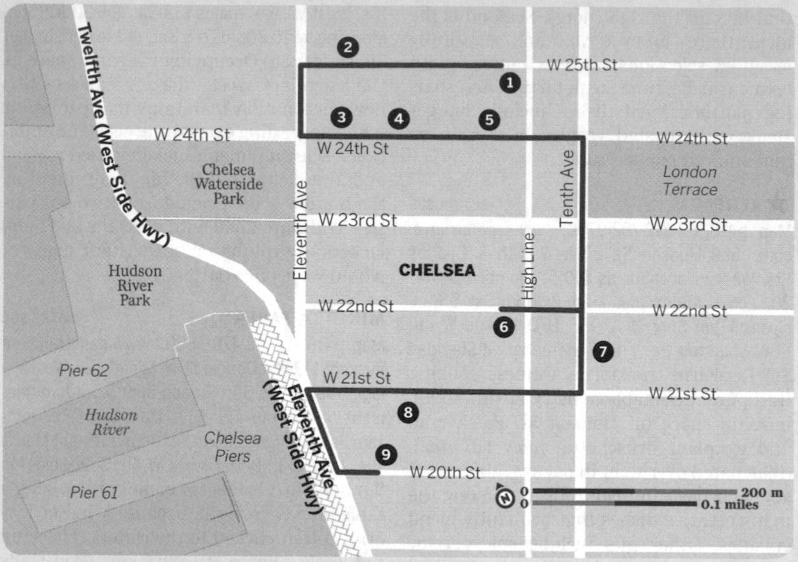

Local Life
Chelsea Galleries

Chelsea is home to the highest concentration of art galleries in NYC. Most lie in the 20s, on the blocks between Tenth and Eleventh Aves, and openings are typically held on Thursday evenings. Most galleries are open Tuesday through Sunday, but double-check opening hours. Pick up Art Info's Gallery Guide (with map) for free at most galleries, or visit www.westchelseaarts.com.

1 Pace Gallery

In a dramatically transformed garage, the **Pace Gallery** (Map p420; ☎212-255-4044; www.pacegallery.com; 510 W 25th St, btwn Tenth & Eleventh Aves; ⏰10am-6pm Tue-Sat; S 1, C/E to 23rd St) has worked with some of the leading artists of recent years, including Sol LeWitt, David Hockney, Chuck Close and Robert Rauschenberg. It has three locations on W 25th St, and one in Midtown.

2 Cheim & Read

Sculptures of every shape, size and material abound at Cheim & Read (p140) and monthly rotations keep the exhibits fresh – expect blazing light installations and inspired photography displays.

3 Gagosian

Gagosian (p139) offers a different vibe to most of the one-off galleries, as it's part of a constellation of showrooms that spreads well across the globe.

4 Mary Boone Gallery

Make an appointment to check out **Mary Boone Gallery** (Map p420; ☎212-752-2929; www.maryboonegallery.com; 541 W 24th St, btwn Tenth & Eleventh Aves; ⏰10am-6pm Tue-Sat), whose owner found fame in the '80s with her eye for Jean-Michel Basquiat and Julian Schnabel. It's considered one of the main 'blue-chip' galleries in the area.

5 Barbara Gladstone Gallery

The curator of the eponymous **Barbara Gladstone Gallery** (Map p420; ☎212-206-9300; www.gladstonegallery.com; 515 W 24th St, btwn Tenth & Eleventh Aves; ⏰10am-6pm Mon-Fri) has learned a thing or two in her 30 years in the Manhattan art world. Ms Gladstone consistently puts together the most talked-about and well-critiqued displays around.

6 Matthew Marks Gallery

Famous for exhibiting big names such as Jasper Johns and Ellsworth Kelly, **Matthew**

ANDERSPHOTO / SHUTTERSTOCK ©

Chelsea

Marks (Map p420; ☎212-243-0200; www.matthewmarks.com; 522 W 22nd St, btwn Tenth & Eleventh Aves; ⏲10am-6pm Tue-Sat) is a true Chelsea pioneer.

❼ 192 Books

This bookstore (p163) makes a fine reprieve from the big gallery experience. Inside, you'll find an edifying selection of literary works covering many genres, plus artist monographs and children's books.

❽ Paula Cooper Gallery

An icon of the art world, **Paula** (Map p420; ☎212-255-1105; www.paulacoopergallery.com; 534 W 21st St, btwn Tenth & Eleventh Aves; ⏲10am-6pm Mon-Fri) was one of the first to move from SoHo to Chelsea. She continues to push boundaries, as she did for her 2011 exhibition *The Clock* when the gallery stayed open 24 hours a day on weekends.

❾ David Zwirner

One of the major players in the art world, **David Zwirner** (Map p420; ☎212-517-8677; www.davidzwirner.com; 537 W 20th St, btwn Tenth & Eleventh Aves; ⏲10am-6pm Tue-Sat) opened a five-story, LEED-certified gallery with 30,000 sq ft of exhibition space in 2013.

clubs and Chelsea boys working on omelets after a long night out.

JUN-MEN RAMEN **$$**

Map p420 (☎646-852-6787; www.junmenramen.com; 249 Ninth Ave, btwn 25th & 26th Sts, Chelsea; ramen $16-19; ⏲11:30am-3pm & 5-10pm Mon-Thu, to 11pm Fri & Sat; Ⓢ1, C/E to 23rd St) This tiny, ultra-modern ramen joint whips up delectably flavored noodle bowls, in variants of pork shoulder, spicy miso or uni mushroom (with sea urchin). Don't skip the appetizers: the yellowtail ceviche and barbecue pork buns are outstanding. Service is speedy, and it's fun to watch the adroit prep team in action in the tiny kitchen at center stage.

BLOSSOM VEGAN **$$**

Map p420 (☎212-627-1144; www.blossomnyc.com; 187 Ninth Ave, btwn 21st & 22nd Sts, Chelsea; mains lunch $15-20, dinner $22-24; ⏲noon-2:45pm daily & 5-9:30pm Mon-Thu, to 10pm Sat & Sun, to 9pm Sun; 🌿; Ⓢ1, C/E to 23rd St) This Chelsea veg oasis – with a sinful wine and chocolate bar attached – is a peaceful, romantic dining room that offers imaginative tofu, seitan and vegetable creations, some raw, all kosher. In addition to its main menus, it also features an 'In Bloom' section on the dinner menu that focuses on fresh, seasonal veggies.

HEATH BRITISH **$$**

Map p420 (☎212-564-1622; www.mckittrickhotel.com/the-heath; 542 W 27th St, btwn Tenth & Eleventh Aves, Chelsea; mains $23-39; ⏲hours vary; Ⓢ1, C/E to 23rd St) The creators of hit interactive theater piece *Sleep No More* operate this atmospheric restaurant next door to their warehouse venue. Like the fictional McKittrick Hotel in the drama, the Heath is set in another place and time (vaguely Britain, 1920s), with suspenders-wearing barkeeps, period furnishings and (fake) smoke wafting over the dining room, as a jazz band performs on stage.

COOKSHOP MODERN AMERICAN **$$**

Map p420 (☎212-924-4440; www.cookshopny.com; 156 Tenth Ave, btwn W 19th & 20th Sts, Chelsea; mains brunch $15-22, lunch $17-21, dinner $22-48; ⏲8am-11pm Mon-Fri, from 10am Sat, 10am-10pm Sun; Ⓢ1, C/E to 23rd St) A brilliant brunching pit stop before (or after) tackling the verdant High Line across the street, Cookshop is a lively place that knows its niche and does it oh so well. Excellent service, eye-opening cocktails (good morning, bacon-infused BLT Mary!), a perfectly baked-bread basket and a selection of inventive egg mains make this a Chelsea favorite on a Sunday afternoon.

LE GRAINNE FRENCH **$$**

Map p420 (☎646-486-3000; www.legrainnecafe.com; 183 Ninth Ave, btwn 21st & 22nd Sts, Chelsea; mains $11-30; ⏲8am-11:30pm; Ⓢ1, C/E to 23rd St) Tap the top of your French onion soup as you dream of ingénue Amélie cracking open her crème brulée; Le Grainne transports the senses from the busy blocks of Chelsea to the backstreets of Paris. The tin-topped eatery excels at lunchtime, when baguette sandwiches and savory crepes are scarfed down amid cramped quarters.

The service is a bit disorganized, but the staff is friendly and the food is worth the wait.

★**FORAGERS TABLE** MODERN AMERICAN **$$$**

Map p420 (☎212-243-8888; www.foragersmarket.com/restaurant; 300 W 22nd St, at Eighth Ave, Chelsea; mains $17-32; ⏲8am-4pm & 5:30-10pm Mon-Fri, 10am-2pm & 5:30-10pm Sat, to 9:30pm Sun; ✎; Ⓢ1, C/E to 23rd St) Owners of this outstanding restaurant run a 28-acre farm in the Hudson Valley, from which much of their seasonal menu is sourced. It changes frequently, but recent temptations include Long Island duck breast with roasted acorn squash, apples, chanterelle mushrooms and figs, grilled skate with red quinoa, creamed kale and *cippolini* onion and deviled farm eggs with Dijon mustard.

DRINKING & NIGHTLIFE

West Village & the Meatpacking District

The key word in the West Village is 'west' – the further toward the Hudson you go, the more likely you are to sidestep the frat party scene found around the NYU campus; generally the going gets good around the crooked lanes west of Sixth Ave.

Just to the north, the Meatpacking District is strictly contemporary in vibe, with sprawling, modern spaces boasting long cocktail lists, velvet-roped entrances and sound systems that'll rattle your brain.

Chelsea is still very much the territory for gay men, but there's a handful of options for all tastes, from speakeasy-chic digs to well-worn dive bars.

HAPPIEST HOUR COCKTAIL BAR

Map p416 (☎212-243-2827; www.happiesthournyc.com; 121 W 10th St, btwn Greenwich St & Sixth Ave, West Village; ⏲5pm-late Mon-Fri, from 2pm Sat & Sun; ⓈA/C/E, B/D/F/M to W 4th St-Washington Sq; 1 to Christopher St-Sheridan Sq) A super-cool, tiki-licious cocktail bar splashed with palm prints, '60s pop and playful mixed drinks that provide a chic take on the fruity beach cocktail. The crowd tends to be button-down after-work types and online daters. Beneath sits its serious sibling, **Slowly Shirley**, an art-deco-style subterranean temple to beautifully crafted, thoroughly researched libations.

BUVETTE WINE BAR

Map p416 (☎212-255-3590; www.ilovebuvette.com; 42 Grove St, btwn Bedford & Bleecker Sts, West Village; ⏲7am-2am Mon-Fri, from 8am Sat & Sun; Ⓢ1 to Christopher St-Sheridan Sq; A/C/E, B/D/F/M to W 4th St-Washington Sq) The rustic-chic decor here (think delicate tin tiles and a swooshing marble counter) makes it the perfect place for a glass of wine – no matter the time of day. For the full experience at this self-proclaimed *gastrothèque,* grab a seat at one of the surrounding tables and nibble on small plates while enjoying old-world wines (mostly from France and Italy).

EMPLOYEES ONLY BAR

Map p416 (☎212-242-3021; www.employeesonlynyc.com; 510 Hudson St, btwn W 10th & Christopher Sts, West Village; ⏲6pm-4am; Ⓢ1 to Christopher St-Sheridan Sq) Duck behind the neon 'Psychic' sign to find this hidden hangout. Bartenders are ace mixologists, fizzing up crazy, addictive libations like the Ginger Smash and an upscale Bellini. Great for late-night drinking and eating, courtesy of the on-site restaurant that serves till 3:30am – housemade chicken soup is ladled out to stragglers. The bar gets busier as the night wears on.

BELL BOOK & CANDLE BAR

Map p416 (☎212-414-2355; www.bbandcnyc.com; 141 W 10th St, btwn Waverly Pl & Greenwich Ave, West Village; ⏲5:30pm-2am Sun-Wed, to 4am Thu-Sat, also 11:30am-3:30pm Sat; ⓈA/C/E, B/D/F/M to W 4th St-Washington Sq; 1 to Christopher St-Sheridan Sq) Step down into this candlelit gastropub for strong, inventive libations with infused spirits and smoky mezcals and hearty late-night pub grub. A twenty-something crowd gathers around the small, packed bar (for $1 oysters and happy-hour drink specials early in the night), though there's a lot more seating in the back, with big booths ideal for larger groups.

UNCOMMONS CAFE

Map p416 (☎646-543-9215; http://uncommonsnyc.com; 230 Thompson St, btwn W 3rd & Bleecker Sts, West Village; board game cover $10; ⏰8:30am-midnight Mon-Thu, to 1am Fri & Sat, to 11pm Sun; 📶; Ⓢ A/C/E, B/D/F/M to W 4th St-Washington-Sq) If you can't get enough board games, make sure to duck into this coffee shop where a small fee ($10) gives you access to an enormous collection of both popular and rare table-top games for as long as you like. The atmosphere is jovial and there is ample space to play, although it can get crowded during peak hours.

ARIA WINE BAR

Map p416 (☎212-242-4233; www.ariawinebar.com; 117 Perry St, btwn Greenwich & Hudson Sts, West Village; ⏰11:30am-10pm Sun-Thu, 11am-11pm Fri & Sat; Ⓢ1 to Christopher St-Sheridan Sq) In the western reaches of the Village, Aria is an inviting music-filled space, with a mix of brick and tile walls and rustic wood tables. There's a good selection of wines by the glass, particularly organic labels, with prices starting around $8 a (small) glass. Recommended *cicchetti* (bite-sized plates, good for sharing) include Gorgonzola-stuffed dates, crab cakes and stewed calamari.

VIN SUR VINGT WINE BAR

Map p416 (☎212-924-4442; www.vinsur20nyc.com; 201 W 11th St, btwn Seventh Ave & Waverly Pl, West Village; ⏰4pm-1am Mon-Fri, to 2am Sat & Sun; Ⓢ A/C/E, L to 8th Ave-14th St) A cozy spot just off Seventh Ave's bustle, Vin Sur Vingt is a slender wine bar with a strip of bar seating and a quaint row of two-seat tables, perfect for a first date. Warning: if you come for a pre-dinner drink, you'll inevitably be charmed into staying through dinner as you munch on the excellent selection of bar bites.

124 OLD RABBIT CLUB BAR

Map p416 (☎212-254-0575; 124 MacDougal St, at Minetta Ln, West Village; ⏰6pm-2am Mon-Wed, to 4am Thu-Sat, to midnight Sun; Ⓢ A/C/E, B/D/F/M to W 4th St-Washington Sq; 1 to Houston St) You'll wanna pat yourself on the back when you find this well-concealed bar (hint: look for the tiny word 'Rabbit' over the door). Once you're inside the narrow, cavern-like space with its low-key vibe, grab a seat at the dimly lit bar and reward yourself with a quenching stout or one of the dozens of imported brews.

LITTLE BRANCH COCKTAIL BAR

Map p416 (☎212-929-4360; 20 Seventh Ave S, at Leroy St, West Village; ⏰7pm-3am Mon-Sat, to 2am Sun; Ⓢ1 to Houston St; A/C/E, B/D/F/M to W 4th St-Washington Sq) If it weren't for lines later in the evening, you'd never guess that a charming drinking den lurked beyond the plain metal door positioned at this triangular intersection – walk downstairs to find a basement bar that feels like a kickback to Prohibition times. Locals clink glasses and sip inventive, artfully prepared cocktails, with live jazz performances Sunday through Thursday nights.

KETTLE OF FISH BAR

Map p416 (☎212-414-2278; www.kettleoffishnyc.com; 59 Christopher St, near Seventh Ave, West Village; ⏰3pm-4am Mon-Fri, from 2pm Sat & Sun; Ⓢ1 to Christopher St-Sheridan Sq; A/C/E, B/D/F/M to W 4th St-Washington Sq) Step into this former Jack Kerouac hangout, full of couches and plump chairs, and prepare to stay for a while because the crowd is simply beguiling. It's a dive bar, a sports bar and a gay bar in one, and everyone mixes happily.

ART BAR BAR

Map p416 (☎212-727-0244; www.artbar.com; 52 Eighth Ave, near Horatio St, Meatpacking District; ⏰4pm-4am; Ⓢ A/C/E, L to 8th Ave-14th St) A decidedly bohemian crowd favors Art Bar, which doesn't look like much up front (booths are crowded too close to the wooden bar), but it has a bit more going on in the back. Grab your beer or a house special (usually martinis) and head for the couches, placed under a huge *Last Supper*-esque mural featuring Jimmy Dean and Marilyn Monroe, among others.

TROY LIQUOR BAR LOUNGE

Map p416 (☎212-699-2410; www.troyliquorbar.com; 675 Hudson St, at W 13th St (entrance on W 13th St), Meatpacking District; ⏰6pm-midnight Wed, to 2am Tue, to 4am Fri & Sat; Ⓢ A/C/E, L to 8th Ave-14th St) Tucked under Bill's Bar & Burger in the Meatpacking District is this indie-rock–loving, graffiti-scrawled hangout. Come for a game of foosball or hide away with your retro cocktail in one of the cave-like nooks.

FAT CAT BAR

Map p416 (☎212-675-6056; www.fatcatmusic.org; 75 Christopher St, btwn 7th Ave & Bleecker St, West Village; cover $3; ⏲2pm-5am Mon-Thu, from noon Fri-Sun; Ⓢ1 to Christopher St-Sheridan Sq; A/C/E, B/D/F/M to W 4th St-Washington Sq) If $16 cocktails and fancy-schmancy Village boutiquery are getting you down, maybe it's time to pay a visit to this run-down little ping-pong hall. Fat Cat is a basement dive that draws a young, unpretentious crowd who want to hang out, shoot some pool, play a little shuffleboard and maybe even get a ping-pong game going.

VOL DE NUIT PUB

Map p416 (☎212-982-3388; www.voldenuitbar.com; 148 W 4th St, btwn Sixth Ave & MacDougal St; ⏲4pm-1am Sun-Thu, to 3am Fri & Sat; ⓈA/C/E, B/D/F/M to W 4th St-Washington Sq) Even all the NYU students can't ruin this: a cozy Belgian beer bar with Delirium Tremens on tap and a few dozen bottle options, including Duvel and Lindemans Framboise (raspberry beer!). You can order *moules* (mussels) and *frites* (fries) to share at the front patio seats, the lounge, the communal wood tables or under the dangling red lights at the bar.

STANDARD BAR

Map p416 (☎877-550-4646, 212-645-4646; www.standardhotels.com; 848 Washington St, btwn 13th & Little W 12th Sts, Meatpacking District; ⓈA/C/E, L to 8th Ave-14th St) Rising on concrete stilts over the High Line, the Standard attracts an A-list crowd, with a chichi lounge and nightclub on the upper floors – the **Top of the Standard** (Map p416; ☎212-645-7600; www.standardhotels.com/high-line; ⏲4pm-midnight Mon-Fri, from 2pm Sat & Sun) and Le Bain. There's also a grill, an eating-and-drinking plaza (that becomes a skating rink in winter), and an open-air beer garden with a classic German menu and frothy drafts.

STANDARD BIERGARTEN BEER GARDEN

Map p416 (☎212-645-4100; www.standardhotels.com; 848 Washington St, btwn 13th & Little W 12th Sts, Meatpacking District; ⏲noon-1am Sun-Thu, to 2am Fri & Sat; ⓈA/C/E, L to 8th Ave-14th St) Come see what the new generation of lawyers, stockbrokers and PR professionals look like with their hair down. The Standard Biergarten is a rowdy good time and on Friday and Saturday nights the crowd is thick with the young elite of Manhattan draining pints of Hefeweizen and challenging each other to ping-pong matches.

BRASS MONKEY BAR

Map p416 (☎212-675-6686; www.brassmonkeynyc.com; 55 Little W 12th St, at Washington St, Meatpacking District; ⏲11:30am-4am; ⓈA/C/E, L to 8th Ave-14th St) While most Meatpacking District bars tend toward the chic, the Monkey is more for beer lovers than those worrying about what shoes to wear. The multifloor Monkey is at ease and down-to-earth, with squeaking wood floors and a nice long list of beers and Scotch. The roof deck is a fine destination in warm weather.

MARIE'S CRISIS BAR

Map p416 (☎212-243-9323; 59 Grove St, btwn Seventh Ave & Bleecker St, West Village; ⏲4pm-3am Mon-Thu, to 4am Fri & Sat, to midnight Sun; Ⓢ1 to Christopher St-Sheridan Sq; A/C/E, B/D/F/M to W 4th St-Washington Sq) Aging Broadway queens, wide-eyed out-of-town gay boys, giggly tourists and various other fans of musical theater assemble around the piano here and take turns belting out campy show tunes, often joined by the entire crowd – and the occasional celebrity. It's old-school fun, no matter how jaded you might be when you go in.

CIELO CLUB

Map p416 (☎212-645-5700; www.cieloclub.com; 18 Little W 12th St, btwn Ninth Ave & Washington St, Meatpacking District; cover $15-25; ⓈA/C/E, L to 8th Ave-14th St) This long-running club boasts a largely attitude-free crowd and an excellent sound system. Join dance lovers on TOCA Tuesdays, when DJ Tony Touch spins classic hip-hop, soul and funk. Other nights feature various DJs from Europe, who mix entrancing, seductive sounds that pull everyone to their feet.

LE BAIN CLUB

Map p416 (☎212-645-7600; www.standardhotels.com; 444 W 13th St, btwn Washington St & Tenth Ave, Meatpacking District; ⏲4pm-3am Mon, to 4am Tue-Thu, 2pm-4am Fri & Sat, to 3am Sun; ⓈA/C/E, L to 8th Ave-14th St) The sweeping rooftop venue at the tragically hip Standard Hotel, Le Bain sees a garish parade of party promoters who do their thing on any day of the week. Brace yourself for skyline views, a dance floor with a giant Jacuzzi built right into it and an eclectic crowd getting wasted on pricey snifters.

COFFEE CULTURE

New York is no longer a second-string city when it comes to great coffee. Celebrated brewmasters, bringing technical wizardry and high-quality single-source coffee beans, have reinvented the simple cup of joe. For a mix of both classic and cutting-edge cafes, the West Village is a great place to start.

Blue Bottle (Map p420; https://bluebottlecoffee.com; 450 W 15th St, btwn 9th & 10th Aves, Chelsea; ⌚7am-6pm Mon-Fri, from 8am Sat & Sun; Ⓢ A/C/E, L to 8th Ave-14th St) Blue Bottle may have originated in Oakland, but New Yorkers have happily embraced this high-quality third-wave roaster. Blue Bottle's small outpost across from the Chelsea Market uses scales and thermometers to make sure your pour over or espresso is perfect. Grab one of the few window seats, or head to one of the mezzanine tables above the baristas.

Stumptown Coffee Roasters (Map p416; ☎855-711-3385; www.stumptowncoffee.com; 30 W 8th St, at MacDougal St, West Village; ⌚7am-8pm; Ⓢ A/C/E, B/D/F/M to W 4th St-Washington Sq) This renowned Portland roaster is helping to reinvent the NYC coffee scene with its exquisitely made brews. It has an elegant interior with coffered ceiling and walnut bar, though its few tables are often overtaken by the laptop-toting crowd.

Joe the Art of Coffee (Map p416; ☎212-924-6750; www.joeheartofcoffee.com; 141 Waverly Pl, at Gay St, West Village; ⌚7am-8pm Mon-Fri, from 8am Sat & Sun; Ⓢ A/C/E, B/D/F/M to W 4th St-Washington Sq) Superb coffee is served at this always-bustling joint sitting squarely on bucolic Waverly Pl in the heart of the Village. Some say this is the best cup of joe in town.

11th St Cafe (Map p416; ☎646-692-4455; www.11thstreetcafe.com; 327 W 11th St, btwn Washington & Columbia Sts, West Village; ⌚7am-6:30pm Mon-Fri, from 7:30am Sat & Sun; wi-fi; Ⓢ 1 to Christopher St-Sheridan Sq) Although the 11th St Cafe looks small, its out-of-the-way location and friendly atmosphere make it the perfect place to bring a laptop or book. It has well-brewed coffee and an impressive selection of affordable breakfast and lunch options, as well as free wi-fi.

When hunger strikes, you can hit up the rooftop crepe stand, which is open all night.

MATCHA BAR — CAFE

Map p416 (www.matchabarnyc.com; 256 W 15th St, btwn Seventh & Eighth Aves, Chelsea; drinks from $6; ⌚8am-7pm Mon-Fri, from 10am Sat & Sun; Ⓢ A/C/E, L to 8th Ave-14th St) When you need a pick-me-up and want a break from espresso, head to this purveyor of powdered green tea, which froths up delicious *matcha* lattes, as well as iced variants (with flavors like Fuji apple ginger or vanilla almond). Other *matcha* treats include macaroons and doughnuts.

CUBBYHOLE — GAY & LESBIAN

Map p416 (☎212-243-9041; www.cubbyholebar.com; 281 W 12th St, at W 4th St, West Village; ⌚4pm-4am Mon-Fri, from 2pm Sat & Sun; Ⓢ A/C/E, L to 8th Ave-14th St) This West Village dive bills itself as 'lesbian, gay and straight friendly since 1994.' While the crowd is mostly ladies, as its motto suggests it's a welcoming place for anyone looking for a cheap drink. It's got a great jukebox, friendly bartenders and plenty of regulars who prefer to hang and chat rather than hook up and leave.

BOOTS AND SADDLE — GAY & LESBIAN

Map p416 (www.bootsandsaddlenyc.com; 100a 7th Ave S, btwn Barrow & Grove Sts, West Village; ⌚2pm-2am Sun-Thu, to 4am Fri & Sat; Ⓢ 1 to Christopher St-Sheridan Sq; A/C/E, B/D/F/M to W 4th St-Washington Sq) Boots and Saddle is affectionately known as one of the scrappiest gay bars in the West Village. Once housed in a tiny street-level space, it's recently moved into a large basement with plenty of room for the drag shows and karaoke nights that have made it a neighborhood favorite. The drinks are cheap and audience participation is expected.

JULIUS BAR — GAY

Map p416 (☎212-243-1928; www.juliusbarny.com; 159 W 10th St, at Waverly Pl, West Village; ⌚11am-4am Mon-Sat, to 3am Sun; Ⓢ A/C/E, B/D/F/M to W 4th St-Washington Sq; 1 to Christopher St-Sheridan Sq) One of the infamous originals

– in fact, it's the oldest operating gay bar in NYC – Julius is a refreshingly unpretentious dive bar through and through. The clientele is a mix of the old queer vanguard and scruffy younger upstarts.

Decent bar food is served in the bar. It recently added a breakfast menu (from 11am to 1pm Saturday and noon to 2pm Sunday).

HENRIETTA HUDSON LESBIAN

Map p416 (212-924-3347; www.henriettahudson.com; 438 Hudson St; 4pm-4am; S1 to Houston St) All sorts of young women, many from neighboring New Jersey and Long Island, storm this sleek lounge, where varying theme nights bring in spirited DJs, who stick to particular genres (hip-hop, house, rock). The owner, Brooklyn native Lisa Canistraci, is a favorite promoter in the world of lesbian nightlife, and is often on hand to mix it up with her fans.

STONEWALL INN GAY

Map p416 (212-488-2705; www.thestonewallinnnyc.com; 53 Christopher St; 2pm-4am; S1 to Christopher St-Sheridan Sq) Site of the Stonewall riots in 1969, this bar, considered almost a pilgrimage site because of its historic significance, pulls in varied crowds for nightly parties catering to everyone under the LGBT rainbow. It's far from trendy and more a welcoming, ordinary watering hole that otherwise might be overlooked.

MONSTER GAY

Map p416 (212-924-3558; www.monsterbarnyc.com; 80 Grove St, at Sheridan Sq, West Village; 4pm-4am Mon-Fri, from 2pm Sat & Sun; S1 to Christopher St-Sheridan Sq; A/C/E, B/D/F/M W 4th St-Washington Sq) It's old-school gayman heaven in here, with a small dance floor downstairs as well as a piano bar and cabaret space. Spirited theme nights range from Latino parties to drag-queen-hosted soirees.

TY'S GAY & LESBIAN

Map p416 (212-741-9641; www.tys.nyc; 114 Christopher St, btwn Bedford & Bleecker Sts, West Village; 2am-2pm Mon-Wed, to 3am Thu, to 4am Fri & Sat, 1pm-4am Sun; S1 to Christopher St-Sheridan Sq; A/C/E, B/D/F/M to W 4th St-Washington Sq) New York's gay bar scene has a reputation for catering to young, model types, but in the West Village you'll find many bars with a more welcoming atmosphere. Ty's has been an established presence in the neighborhood since the '70s. It caters to an older crowd and has a friendly, dive-bar vibe and dirt-cheap drinks.

Chelsea

GALLOW GREEN BAR

Map p420 (212-564-1662; www.mckittrickhotel.com/gallow-green; 542 W 27th St, btwn Tenth & Eleventh Aves, Chelsea; 5pm-midnight Mon-Fri, from noon Sat & Sun; S1, C/E to 23rd St; 1 to 28th St) Run by the creative team behind Sleep No More theater (p155), Gallow Green is a rooftop bar festooned with vines, potted plants and fairy lights. It's a great add-on before or after experiencing the show, with waitstaff in period costume, a live band most nights and tasty rum-filled cocktails. You'll want to make a reservation.

When the cold weather arrives, Gallow Green sets up 'the Lodge,' a cozy chalet, with various astonishingly filled rooms, complete with books, bunk beds, fur rugs, a rocking chair and a fireplace. For a woodsy escape without leaving Midtown, this is it.

PIER 66 MARITIME BAR

Map p420 (212-989-6363; www.pier66maritime.com; Pier 66, at W 26th St, Chelsea; noon-midnight May-Oct; S1, C/E to 23rd St) Salvaged from the bottom of the sea (or at least the Chesapeake Bay), the lightship *Frying Pan* and the two-tiered dockside bar where it's moored are fine go-to spots for a sundowner. On warm days, the rustic open-air space brings in the crowds, who laze on deck chairs and drink ice-cold beers ($7/25 for a microbrew/pitcher).

BATHTUB GIN COCKTAIL BAR

Map p420 (646-559-1671; www.bathtubginnyc.com; 132 Ninth Ave, btwn W 18th & 19th Sts, Chelsea; 5pm-2am Mon-Wed, to 4am Thu & Fri, 11:30am-3:30pm & 5pm-4am Sat, to 2am Sun; SA/C/E, L to 8th Ave-14th St; 1, C/E to 23rd St; 1 to 18th St) Amid New York City's obsession with speakeasy-styled hangouts, Bathtub Gin manages to poke its head above the crowd with its super-secret front door hidden on the wall of the Stone Street Coffee Shop (look for the woman in the bathtub). Once inside, chill seating, soft background beats and kindly staff make it a great place to sling back bespoke cocktails with friends.

PETER MCMANUS TAVERN BAR

Map p420 (212-929-9691; www.petermcmanuscafe.com; 152 Seventh Ave, at 19th St, Chelsea;

⌚10am-4am Mon-Sat, from noon Sun; ⓢ1 to 18th St; 1, C/E to 23rd St) Pouring drafts since the 1930s, this family-run dive is something of a museum to the world of the McManuses: photos of yesteryear, an old telephone booth and Tiffany glass. There's also greasy bar food to eat at the comfy green booths.

GYM SPORTSBAR GAY

Map p420 (☎212-337-2439; www.gymsportsbar.com/nyhome.html; 167 8th Ave # A; drinks from $7; ⌚4pm-2am Mon-Fri, 2pm-2am Sat & Sun; ⓢA/C/E, L to 8th Ave 14th St) In the midst of Chelsea's famous gay nightlife scene, Gym Sportsbar offers a low-key vibe for LGBTQ patrons. There are friendly bartenders, cheap drinks, a pool table in the back, a smoking patio out front and TVs throughout the bar playing whatever sport is in season. Weekday happy hour offers two-for-one drinks.

EAGLE NYC GAY

Map p420 (☎646-473-1866; www.eaglenyc.com; 554 W 28th St, btwn Tenth & Eleventh Aves, Chelsea; ⌚10pm-4am Mon-Sat, from 5pm Sun; ⓢ1, C/E to 23rd St) A bi-level club full of hot men in leather, the Eagle is the choice for out-and-proud fetishists. Its two levels, plus roof deck, offer plenty of room for dancing and drinking, which are done with abandon. There are frequent theme nights, so make sure to check the website lest you arrive without the appropriate attire (which may be nothing).

☆ ENTERTAINMENT

SLEEP NO MORE THEATER

Map p420 (☎866-811-4111; www.sleepnomorenyc.com; 530 W 27th St, btwn Tenth & Eleventh Aves, Chelsea; tickets from $105; ⌚7pm-midnight Mon-Sat; ⓢ1, C/E to 23rd St) One of the most immersive theater experiences ever conceived, *Sleep No More* is a loosely based retelling of *Macbeth* set inside a series of Chelsea warehouses that have been redesigned to look like the 1930s-era McKittrick Hotel and its hopping jazz bar.

It's a choose-your-own-adventure kind of experience, where audience members are free to wander the elaborate rooms (ballroom, graveyard, taxidermy shop, lunatic asylum) and follow or interact with the actors, who perform a variety of scenes that can run from the bizarre to the risqué. Be prepared: you must check in *everything* when you arrive (jackets, bag, cell phone), and you must wear a mask, à la *Eyes Wide Shut*.

LE POISSON ROUGE LIVE MUSIC

Map p416 (☎212-505-3474; www.lepoissonrouge.com; 158 Bleecker St, btwn Sullivan & Thompson Sts, West Village; ⓢA/C/E, B/D/F/M to W 4th St-Washington Sq) This high-concept art space hosts a highly eclectic lineup of live music, with the likes of Deerhunter, Marc Ribot and Yo La Tengo performing in past years. There's a lot of experimentation and cross-genre pollination between classical, folk music, opera and more.

55 BAR LIVE MUSIC

Map p416 (☎212-929-9883; www.55bar.com; 55 Christopher St, at Seventh Ave, West Village; cover $10; ⌚1pm-4am; ⓢ1 to Christopher St-Sheridan Sq) Dating back to the Prohibition era, this friendly basement dive is great for low-key shows without high covers or dressing up. There are regular performances twice nightly by quality artists-in-residence, some blues bands and Miles Davis' super '80s guitarist Mike Stern. There's a two-drink minimum.

CORNELIA STREET CAFÉ LIVE MUSIC

Map p416 (☎212-989-9319; www.corneliastreetcafe.com; 29 Cornelia St, btwn Bleecker & W 4th Sts, West Village; ⌚early show doors open 5:45pm; ⓢA/C/E, B/D/F/M to W 4th St-Washington Sq) This small cafe is known for its intimate music performances with innovative jazz trios, genre-bending vocalists and other musical and visual arts combos. Cornelia Street also has a literary component with monthly storytelling gatherings and open-mic poetry nights and readings.

BAR NEXT DOOR LIVE MUSIC

Map p416 (☎212-529-5945; www.lalanternacaffe.com; 129 MacDougal St, btwn W 3rd & 4th Sts, West Village; cover $12-15; ⌚6pm-2am Sun-Thu, to 3am Fri & Sat; ⓢA/C/E, B/D/F/M to W 4th St-Washington Sq) One of the loveliest hangouts in the neighborhood, the basement of this restored town house is all low ceilings, exposed brick and romantic lighting. You'll find mellow, live jazz nightly, as well as the tasty Italian menu of the restaurant next door, La Lanterna di Vittorio.

Admission is free for the emerging artist sets, held from 6:30pm to 7:45pm Monday through Thursday.

MIZOULA / GETTY IMAGES ©

1. Washington Square Park (p138)
The unofficial town square of Greenwich Village has long provided a stage for political activity.

2. High Line (p136)
Once a dingy rail line, the High Line has become one of New York City's favorite green spaces.

3. Gagosian (p141)
The Gagosian art gallery has ever-changing exhibits featuring international and local artists.

2

MATT MUNRO / LONELY PLANET ©

IRISH REPERTORY THEATRE THEATER

Map p420 (212-727-2737; www.irishrep.org; 132 W 22nd St, btwn Sixth & Seventh Aves, Chelsea; S1, F/M to 23 St; 1 to 18th St) This repertory troupe, based in a Chelsea warehouse, showcases the finest contributions to the theater world from the Irish and Irish-American community.

BARROW STREET THEATER THEATER

Map p416 (212-243-6262; www.barrowstreettheatre.com; 27 Barrow St, btwn Seventh Ave & W 4th St, West Village; S1 to Christopher St-Sheridan Sq or Houston St; A/C/E, B/D/F/M to W 4th St-Washington Sq) A fantastic off-Broadway space in the heart of the West Village showcasing a variety of local and international theater.

ATLANTIC THEATER COMPANY THEATER

Map p420 (212-691-5919; www.atlantictheater.org; 336 W 20th St, btwn Eighth & Ninth Aves, Chelsea; S1, C/E to 23rd St; 1 to 18th St) Founded by David Mamet and William H Macy in 1985, the Atlantic Theater is a pivotal anchor for the off-Broadway community, hosting many Tony Award and Drama Desk winners over the last three decades.

NEW YORK LIVE ARTS DANCE

Map p420 (212-924-0077; www.newyorklivearts.org; 219 W 19th St, btwn Seventh & Eighth Aves, Chelsea; S1 to 18th St) You'll find a program of more than 100 experimental, contemporary performances annually at this sleek dance center, led by artistic director Bill T Jones. International troupes from Serbia, South Africa, Korea and beyond bring fresh works to the stage, with shows that will often include pre- or post-show discussions with choreographers or dancers.

CHERRY LANE THEATER THEATER

Map p416 (212-989-2020; www.cherrylanetheater.org; 38 Commerce St, off Bedford St,

ALL THAT JAZZ

The West Village remains the epicenter of NYC's jazz scene, with memorable performances at basement clubs and polished music halls alike.

Village Vanguard (Map p416; 212-255-4037; www.villagevanguard.com; 178 Seventh Ave S, at W 11th St, West Village; cover around $33; 7:30pm-12:30am; SA/C/E, L to 8th Ave-14th St; 1/2/3 to 14th St) Possibly the city's most prestigious jazz club, the Vanguard has hosted literally every major star of the past 50 years. It started as a home to spoken-word performances and occasionally returns to its roots, but most of the time it's just big, bold jazz all night long. Mind your step on the steep stairs, and close your eyes to the signs of wear and tear – acoustically, you're in one of the greatest venues in the world. There's a one-drink minimum.

Smalls (Map p416; 646-476-4346; www.smallslive.com; 183 W 10th St, btwn W 4th St & Seventh Ave S, West Village; cover $20; 7:05pm-3:30am Mon-Fri, from 4pm Sat & Sun; S1 to Christopher St-Sheridan Sq; A/C/E, B/D/F/M W 4th St-Washington Sq) Living up to its name, this cramped but appealing basement jazz den offers a grab-bag collection of jazz acts who take the stage nightly. Admission includes a come-and-go policy if you need to duck out for a bite. There is an afternoon jam session on Saturday and Sunday that's not to be missed.

Blue Note (Map p416; 212-475-8592; www.bluenote.net; 131 W 3rd St, btwn Sixth Ave & MacDougal St, West Village; SA/C/E, B/D/F/M to W 4th St-Washington Sq) This is by far the most famous (and expensive) of the city's jazz clubs. Most shows are $15 to $30 at the bar or $25 to $45 at a table, but can rise for the biggest stars. There's also jazz brunch on Sundays at 11:30am. Go on an off night, and don't talk – all attention is on the stage!

Mezzrow (Map p416; 646-476-4346; www.mezzrow.com; 163 W 10th St, at Seventh Ave, West Village; 7:30pm-1:30am Sun-Thu, to 2am Fri & Sat; S1 to Christopher St-Sheridan Sq) Locals and tourists alike are still celebrating the arrival of this intimate basement jazz club, which opened its doors in 2014. It's run by the same folks behind nearby Smalls, and admission (generally $20) gets you same-night entry to Smalls.

It's all about the music here (boisterous chattering is not tolerated), with quality acts playing throughout the week. Book upcoming gigs online.

West Village; S1 to Christopher St-Sheridan Sq) A theater with a distinctive charm hidden in the West Village, Cherry Lane has a long and distinguished history. Started by poet Edna St Vincent Millay, it has given a voice to numerous playwrights and actors over the years, remaining true to its mission of creating 'live' theater that's accessible to the public. Readings, plays and spoken-word performances rotate frequently.

DUPLEX CABARET

Map p416 (212-255-5438; www.theduplex.com; 61 Christopher St, at Seventh Ave S, West Village; cover $10-25; 4pm-4am; S1 to Christopher St-Sheridan Sq; A/C/E, B/D/F/M to W 4th St-Washington Sq) Cabaret, karaoke and campy dance moves are par for the course at the legendary Duplex. Pictures of Joan Rivers line the walls, and the performers like to mimic her sassy form of self-deprecation while getting in a few jokes about audience members as well. It's a fun and unpretentious place, and certainly not for the bashful.

At the downstairs piano bar (from 9pm onward), you can sing a tune, or simply watch some extremely talented regulars (including Broadway performers) and staff belt out the hits. There's a two-drink minimum.

JOYCE THEATER DANCE

Map p420 (212-691-9740; www.joyce.org; 175 Eighth Ave, at W 19th St, Chelsea; S1 to 18th St; 1, C/E to 23rd St; A/C/E, L to 8th Ave-14th St) A favorite among dance junkies thanks to its excellent sight lines and offbeat offerings, this is an intimate venue, seating 472 in a renovated cinema. Its focus is on traditional modern companies, such as Martha Graham, Stephen Petronio Company and Parsons Dance, as well as global stars, such as Dance Brazil, Ballet Hispanico and Mal-Paso Dance Company.

KITCHEN THEATER, DANCE

Map p420 (212-255-5793; www.thekitchen.org; 512 W 19th St, btwn Tenth & Eleventh Aves, Chelsea; SA/C/E, L to 8th Ave-14th St) A loft-like experimental space in west Chelsea that also produces edgy theater, readings and music performances; Kitchen is where you'll find new, progressive pieces and works in progress from local movers and shakers.

GOTHAM COMEDY CLUB COMEDY

Map p420 (212-367-9000; www.gothamcomedyclub.com; 208 W 23rd St, btwn Seventh & Eighth Aves, Chelsea; S1, C/E to 23rd St) Fancying itself as a NYC comedy hall of fame, and backing it up with regular big names and Gotham All-Stars shows, this expanded club provides space for comedians who've cut their teeth on HBO, *The Tonight Show with Jimmy Fallon* and *The Late Show with Stephen Colbert.*

COMEDY CELLAR COMEDY

Map p416 (212-254-3480; www.comedycellar.com; 117 MacDougal St, btwn W 3rd St & Minetta Ln, West Village; cover $8-24; SA/C/E, B/D/F/M to W 4th St-Washington Sq) This long-established basement comedy club in Greenwich Village features mainstream material and a good list of regulars (Colin Quinn, Judah Friedlander, Wanda Sykes), plus occasional high-profile drop-ins like Dave Chappelle, Jerry Seinfeld and Amy Schumer. Its success continues: Comedy Cellar now boasts another location at the Village Underground around the corner on W 3rd St.

In addition to the cover there is a two-item (food or drinks) minimum per show.

IFC CENTER CINEMA

Map p416 (212-924-7771; www.ifccenter.com; 323 Sixth Ave, at W 3rd St, West Village; tickets $15; ; SA/C/E, B/D/F/M to W 4th St-Washington Sq) This art-house cinema in NYU-land has a solidly curated lineup of new indies, cult classics and foreign films. Catch shorts, documentaries, '80s revivals, director-focused series, weekend classics and frequent special series, such as cult favorites *(The Shining, Taxi Driver, Aliens)* at midnight.

CINÉPOLIS CHELSEA CINEMA

Map p420 (212-691-5519; www.cinepolisusa.com; 260 W 23rd St, btwn Seventh & Eighth Aves, Chelsea; S1, C/E to 23rd St) After being closed for a while, this beloved neighborhood movie theater has reopened under a new name. In addition to showing first-run films there are weekend midnight showings of *The Rocky Horror Picture Show,* as well as events hosted by local drag star Hedda Lettuce.

ANGELIKA FILM CENTER CINEMA

Map p416 (212-995-2570; www.angelikafilmcenter.com; 18 W Houston St, at Mercer St, West Village; tickets $15; ; SB/D/F/M to Broadway-Lafayette St) Angelika specializes in foreign and independent films and has some quirky charms (the rumble of the subway, long lines and occasionally bad sound). But its roomy cafe is a great place to meet and the beauty of its Stanford White–designed, beaux-arts building is undeniable.

LGBT COMMUNITY CENTER ARTS CENTER

Map p416 (☎212-620-7310; www.gaycenter.org; 208 W 13th St, btwn Seventh & Greenwich Aves, West Village; suggested donation $5; ⊙9am-10pm Mon-Sat, to 9pm Sun; ⓈA/C/E, L to 8th Ave-14th St; 1/2/3 to 14th St) For more than 25 years, this has been the nexus of LGBT culture in the Village. That's because it provides a surrogate home for queer folks who may not feel so comfortable in their actual one. It's host to endless groups who meet here, and you can relax with a coffee and a pastry at the community-oriented cafe run by Think Coffee.

It also provides a ton of regional publications about gay events and nightlife, and hosts frequent special events – dance parties, art exhibits, Broadway-caliber performances, readings and political panels. Plus it's home to the National Archive for Lesbian, Gay, Bisexual & Transgender History (which can be used by researchers by appointment), as well as the small Campbell-Soady Gallery (which holds frequent exhibitions) and a cyber center.

SHOPPING

The West Village is home to some lovely boutiques and other stores overloaded with charm. High-end shoppers stick to top-label stores along Bleecker St between Bank and W 10th Sts. Chelsea has a decent selection of antiques, discount fashion, chain stores and kitsch, along with a hidden bookstore and well-edited thrift shop. The neighborhood standout is the beloved Chelsea Market, a huge concourse packed with top-shelf food, wine, fashion and home goods. The Meatpacking District is all about that sleek, high-ceilinged industrial-chic vibe, with ultra-modern designers reigning at expansive boutiques that are among the most fashionable haunts in town.

West Village & the Meatpacking District

★STRAND BOOK STORE BOOKS

Map p416 (☎212-473-1452; www.strandbooks.com; 828 Broadway, at E 12th St, West Village; ⊙9:30am-10:30pm Mon-Sat, from 11am Sun; ⓈL, N/Q/R/W, 4/5/6 to 14th St-Union Sq) Beloved and legendary, the iconic Strand embodies downtown NYC's intellectual *bona fides* – a bibliophile's Oz, where generations of book lovers carrying the store's trademark tote bags happily lose themselves for hours. In operation since 1927, the Strand sells new, used and rare titles, spreading an incredible 18 miles of books (over 2.5 million of them) among three labyrinthine floors.

TRINA TURK CLOTHING

Map p416 (☎212-206-7383; www.trinaturk.com; 67 Gansevoort St, btwn Greenwich & Washington Sts, West Village; ⊙11am-7pm Mon-Sat, noon-6pm Sun; ⓈA/C/E, L to 8th Ave-14th St) Anyone with a yen for '70s-inspired prints should take themselves to the Trina Turk boutique. The wife and husband team behind the unisex brand have cultivated a range that harkens back to the vibrant heyday of California cool with shift dresses, floral blazers, statement pants, and swimsuits that range from board shorts to ultra-skimpy briefs.

BEACON'S CLOSET VINTAGE

Map p416 (☎917-261-4863; www.beaconscloset.com; 10 W 13th St, btwn Fifth & Sixth Aves, West Village; ⊙11am-8pm; ⓈL, N/Q/R/W, 4/5/6 to 14th St-Union Sq) You'll find a good selection of gently used clothing (which is of a decidedly downtown/Brooklyn hipster aesthetic) at only slightly higher prices than Beacon's sister store in Williamsburg. Thrift shops are thin on the ground in this area, which makes Beacon's even more of a draw. Come midweek or be prepared to brave the crowds.

ODIN CLOTHING

Map p416 (☎212-243-4724; www.odinnewyork.com; 106 Greenwich Ave, near Jane St, West Village; ⊙noon-8pm Mon-Sat, to 7pm Sun; ⓈA/C/E, L to 8th Ave-14th St; 1/2/3 to 14th St) Named after the mighty Norse god, Odin offers a bit of magic for men seeking a new look. The large boutique carries stylish downtown labels, such as Phillip Lim, Band of Outsiders and Edward, and is the place to browse for up-and-coming designers. Other eye candy at the minimalist store includes Comme des Garçons wallets, sleek sunglasses, Sharps grooming products and Taschen coffee-table books.

IDLEWILD BOOKS BOOKS

Map p416 (☎212-414-8888; www.idlewildbooks.com; 170 Seventh Ave S, at Perry St, West Village; ⊙noon-8pm Mon-Thu, to 6pm Fri-Sun; Ⓢ1 to Christopher St-Sheridan Sq; 1/2/3 to 14th St; A/C/E, L to 8th Ave-14th St) Named after JFK airport's original moniker, this indie travel bookshop gets feet seriously itchy. Books are divided by region and cover guidebooks as well as fiction, travelogues, history, cookbooks and other stimulating fare for delving into different corners of the world. The store also runs popular language classes in French, Italian, Spanish and German; see the website for details.

PERSONNEL OF NEW YORK FASHION & ACCESSORIES

Map p416 (☎212-924-0604; www.personnelofnewyork.com; 9 Greenwich Ave, btwn Christopher & W 10th Sts, West Village; ⊙noon-7:30pm Mon-Sat, to 6pm Sun; SA/C/E, B/D/F/M to W 4th St-Washington Sq; 1 to Christopher St-Sheridan Sq) This small, delightful indie shop sells women's designer clothing from unique labels from the East and West Coasts and beyond. Look for easy-to-wear Sunja Link dresses, soft pullover sweaters by Ali Golden, statement-making jewelry by Marisa Mason, comfy canvas sneakers by Shoes Like Pottery and couture pieces by Rodebjer.

THREE LIVES & COMPANY BOOKS

Map p416 (☎212-741-2069; www.threelives.com; 154 W 10th St, btwn Seventh Ave & Waverly Pl, West Village; ⊙10am-8:30pm Mon-Sat, noon-7pm Sun; S1 to Christopher St-Sheridan Sq; A/C/E, B/D/F/M to W 4th St-Washington Sq) Your neighborhood bookstore extraordinaire, Three Lives & Company is a wondrous spot that's tended by a coterie of exceptionally well-read individuals. A trip here is not just a pleasure, it's an adventure into the magical world of words.

GREENWICH LETTERPRESS GIFTS & SOUVENIRS

Map p416 (☎212-989-7464; www.greenwichletterpress.com; 15 Christopher St, at Gay St, West Village; ⊙noon-6pm Sat-Mon, 11am-7pm Tue-Fri; S1 to Christopher St-Sheridan Sq; A/C/E, B/D/F/M to W 4th St; 1/2/3 to 14th St) Founded by two sisters, this cute card shop specializes in wedding announcements and other specially made letterpress endeavors, so skip the stock postcards of the Empire State Building and send your loved ones a bespoke greeting card from this stalwart stationer.

FORBIDDEN PLANET BOOKS

Map p416 (☎212-473-1576; www.fpnyc.com; 832 Broadway, btwn E 12th & 13th Sts, West Village; ⊙9am-10pm Mon-Tue, 8am-midnight Wed, from 9am Thu-Sat, 10am-10pm Mon; SL, N/Q/R/W, 4/5/6 to 14th St Union Sq) Indulge your inner sci-fi and fantasy nerd with heaps of comics, manga, graphic novels, posters and toys. The products represent everything from *Star Wars* and *Doctor Who* to the latest indie sensations. Stop in, or check the website for upcoming book signings and other events.

FLIGHT 001 FASHION & ACCESSORIES

Map p416 (☎212-989-0001; www.flight001.com; 96 Greenwich Ave, btwn Jane St & W 12th St; ⊙11am-7pm Mon-Sat, noon-6pm Sun; SA/C/E, L to 8th Ave-14th St) Check out Flight 001's range of luggage and smaller bags by brands ranging from Bree to Rimowa, kitschy 'shemergency' kits (breath freshener, lip balm, stain remover etc), pin-up–girl flasks, brightly colored passport holders and leather luggage tags, travel guidebooks, toiletry cases, and a range of mini toothpastes, eye masks, pillboxes and the like.

SATURDAYS FASHION & ACCESSORIES

Map p416 (☎347-246-5830; www.saturdaysnyc.com; 17 Perry St, at Waverly St, West Village; ⊙10am-7pm; SA/C/E, L to 8th Ave-14th St; 1/2/3 to 14th St) For a strange sight in the West Village, stop by this eye-catching surf shop, complete with pricey boards by Tudor, Fowler and Haydenshapes. Of course, shopping here is more about buying into the surfing lifestyle – with stylish shades, board shorts, colorful tees and grooming products – for both you and your surfboard.

There's also an on-site cafe that opens at 8am on weekdays.

MCNULTY'S TEA & COFFEE CO, INC FOOD & DRINKS

Map p416 (☎212-242-5351; www.mcnultys.com; 109 Christopher St, btwn Bleecker & Hudson Sts, West Village; ⊙10am-9pm Mon-Sat, 1-7pm Sun; S1 to Christopher St-Sheridan Sq) McNulty's is a sweet addition to the otherwise bawdy Christopher St. Its worn wooden floorboards, fragrant sacks of coffee beans and large glass jars of tea harken back to a different era of Greenwich Village. It's been selling gourmet teas and coffees here since 1895.

YOYA CHILDREN'S CLOTHING

Map p416 (☎646-336-6844; www.yoyanyc.com; 605 Hudson St, btwn Bethune & W 12th Sts, West Village; ⊙11am-7pm Mon-Sat, noon-5pm Sun;

S A/C/E, L to 8th Ave-14th St) For well-made kiddy clothes and accessories visit Yoya, which stocks high-end brands, such as Bobo Choses and 1+ in the family.

MURRAY'S CHEESE FOOD & DRINKS

Map p416 (212-243-3289; www.murrayscheese.com; 254 Bleecker St, btwn Morton & Leroy Sts, West Village; 8am-9pm Mon-Sat, 9am-8pm Sun; S 1 to Christopher St-Sheridan Sq; A/C/E, B/D/F/M to W 4th St-Washington Sq) Founded in 1914, this is one of New York's best cheese shops. Owner Rob Kaufelt is known for his talent for sniffing out devastatingly delicious varieties from around the world. You'll find (and be able to taste) all manner of *fromage,* be it stinky, sweet or nutty, from European nations and small farms in Vermont and upstate New York.

CO BIGELOW CHEMISTS COSMETICS

Map p416 (212-533-2700; 414 Sixth Ave, btwn 8th & 9th Sts, West Village; 7:30am-9pm Mon-Fri, 8:30am-7pm Sat, 8:30am-5:30pm Sun; S 1 to Christopher St-Sheridan Sq; A/C/E, B/D/F/M to W 4th St-Washington Sq) The 'oldest apothecary in America' is a favorite among New Yorkers and a convenient spot to grab upscale lotions and face masks, organic soaps and bath bombs, and basic toiletries. It's a fun place to test high-end products before you grab a tube of toothpaste.

AEDES DE VENUSTAS COSMETICS

Map p416 (212-206-8674; www.aedes.com; 7 Greenwich Ave, at Christopher St, West Village; noon-8pm Mon-Sat, 1-7pm Sun; S A/C/E, B/D/F/M to W 4th St-Washington Sq; 1 to Christopher St-Sheridan Sq) Plush and inviting, Aedes de Venustas ('Temple of Beauty' in Latin) provides more than 40 brands of luxury European perfumes, including Hierbas de Ibiza, Mark Birley for Men, Costes, Odin and Shalini. It also stocks skincare products created by Susanne Kaufmann and Acqua di Rose, and everyone's favorite scented candles from Diptyque.

MASK BAR COSMETICS

Map p416 (www.themaskbar.com; 259 Bleecker St, btwn Cornelia & Jones Sts, West Village; noon-8pm; S A/C/E, B/D/F/M to W 4th St-Washington Sq) The Mask Bar has capitalized on the current sheet mask craze by offering a boutique of treatments for all skin types. Most of the packaging lacks English translation, but the store has placards with information and the attendants are very helpful.

Chelsea

HOUSING WORKS THRIFT SHOP VINTAGE

Map p420 (718-838-5050; www.housingworks.org; 143 W 17th St, btwn Sixth & Seventh Aves, Chelsea; 10am-7pm Mon-Sat, 11am-5pm Sun; S 1 to 18th St) With its swank window displays, this shop looks more boutique than thrift, but its selections of clothes, accessories, furniture, books and records are great value. It's the place to go to find discarded designer clothes for a bargain. All proceeds benefit the charity serving the city's HIV-positive and AIDS homeless communities. There are 13 other branches around town.

SCREAMING MIMI'S VINTAGE

Map p416 (212-677-6464; www.screamingmimis.com; 240 W 14th St, btwn Seventh & Eighth Aves, Chelsea; noon-8pm Mon-Sat, 1-7pm Sun; S A/C/E, L to 8th Ave-14th St) If you dig vintage threads, you may just scream, too. This fun-tastic shop carries an excellent selection of yesteryear pieces, organized – ingeniously – by decade, from the '50s to the '90s. (Ask to see the small, stashed-away collection of clothing from the 1920s through '40s.)

STORY GIFTS & SOUVENIRS

Map p420 (www.thisisstory.com; 144 Tenth Ave, btwn W 18th & 19th Sts, Chelsea; 11am-8pm Mon-Wed, Fri & Sat, to 9pm Thu, to 7pm Sun; S 1, C/E to 23rd St; 1 to 18th St) This high-concept shop near the High Line functions like a gallery, showcasing new themes and products every month or two. The 2000-sq-ft space covers all the bases, from crafty jewelry and eye-catching accessories to lovely stationery, imagination-inspiring toys for kids, thick coffee-table books, environmentally friendly soaps and whimsical souvenirs.

PRINTED MATTER BOOKS

Map p420 (212-925-0325; www.printedmatter.org; 231 Eleventh Ave, btwn 25th & 26th Sts, Chelsea; 11am-7pm Sat & Mon-Wed, to 8pm Thu & Fri, to 6pm Sun; S 7 to 34th St-Hudson Yards; 1 to 28th St) Printed Matter is a wondrous little shop dedicated to limited-edition artist monographs and strange little zines. Here you will find nothing carried by mainstream bookstores; instead, trim shelves hide call-to-arms manifestos, critical essays about comic books, flip books that reveal Jesus' face through barcodes and how-to guides written by prisoners.

192 BOOKS
BOOKS

Map p420 (212-255-4022; www.192books.com; 192 Tenth Ave, btwn W 21st & 22nd Sts, Chelsea; 11am-7pm; S 1, C/E to 23rd St) Located right in the gallery district is this small indie bookstore, with sections on fiction, history, travel, art and criticism. Its rotating art exhibits are a special treat, during which the owners organize special displays of books that relate thematically to the featured show or artist. Weekly book readings feature acclaimed (often NYC-based) authors.

NASTY PIG
CLOTHING

Map p420 (212-691-6067; www.store.nastypig.com; 265 W 19th St, btwn Seventh & Eighth Aves, Chelsea; noon-8pm Mon-Sat, from 1pm Sun; S A/C/E, L to 8th Ave-14th St; 1 to 18th St) T-shirts, socks and underwear bearing the store's namesake, along with a bit of rubber and leather fetish wear, make this an ideal stop for Chelsea boys and their admirers.

SPORTS & ACTIVITIES

MNDFL
MEDITATION

Map p416 (212-477-0487; www.mndflmeditation.com; 10 E 8th St, btwn Fifth Ave & University Pl, West Village; A/C/E, B/D/F/V to W 4th St-Washington Sq; 30/45/60min class $18/25/30; S A/C/E, B/D, F/M to W 4th St-Washington Sq) The benefits of meditation are well-documented – and much needed by many of New York's harried residents. Stop and take time out to clear your head with rejuvenating classes at this peaceful West Village outpost. Your first class is just $10.

CHELSEA PIERS COMPLEX
HEALTH & FITNESS

Map p420 (212-336-6666; www.chelseapiers.com; Pier 62, at W 23rd St, Chelsea; 5:30am-11pm Mon-Fri, 5:30am-9pm Sat & Sun; M23 to Chelsea Piers, S 1, C/E to 23rd St) This massive waterfront sports center caters to the athlete in everyone. You can hit a bucket of golf balls at the four-level driving range, skate on an indoor ice rink or rack up strikes in a jazzy bowling alley. There's basketball at Hoop City, a sailing school for kids, batting cages, a huge gym and covered swimming pool and indoor rock climbing.

A passport, which provides a day pass to the gym and pool, as well as discounts on several other activities, can be purchased for $60. A few snack bars serve sandwiches and pizzas so you can carb-load after your workout. Though the complex is somewhat cut off by the busy West Side Hwy (Eleventh Ave), the wide array of attractions here brings in the crowds; the M23 crosstown bus, which stops right at the main entrance, saves you the long, four-avenue trek from the subway. There is also a taxi stand outside, although during nonpeak hours the line of cabs is fairly short.

NEW YORK TRAPEZE SCHOOL
ADVENTURE SPORTS

Map p416 (212-242-8769; www.newyork.trapezeschool.com; Pier 40, at West Side Hwy, West Village; per class $50-70; Apr-Oct, check online for class schedule; S 1 to Houston St) Fulfill your circus dreams flying from trapeze to trapeze in this open-air tent by the river. It's open from April to October and located on top of Pier 40. The school also has an indoor facility in South Williamsburg, Brooklyn, that's open year-round. Call or check the website for daily class times. There's a one-time $22 registration fee.

SCHOONER ADIRONDACK
CRUISE

Map p420 (212-627-1825; www.sail-nyc.com; Chelsea Piers Complex, Pier 62 at W 22nd St, Chelsea; tours $52-86; S 1, C/E to 23rd St) The two-masted *'Dack* hits the New York Harbor with four two-hour sails daily from May to October. The 1920s-style, 80ft *Manhattan* and 100ft *Manhattan II* yachts offer tours throughout the week. Call or check the website for the latest times.

WEST 4TH STREET BASKETBALL COURTS
BASKETBALL

Map p416 (Sixth Ave, btwn 3rd & 4th Sts, West Village; S A/C/E, B/D/F/M to W 4th St-Washington Sq) Also known as 'the Cage,' this small basketball court enclosed within chain-link fencing is home to some of the best streetball in the country.

Union Square, the Flatiron District & Gramercy

Neighborhood Top Five

❶ **ABC Carpet & Home** (p172) Mentally configuring your fantasy loft while perusing floor after floor of wildly priced but uber-gorgeous home goods.

❷ **Union Square Greenmarket** (p172) Prodding fresh produce and sampling artisanal treats at this greenmarket, which transforms into a delightful Christmas market.

❸ **Flatiron Lounge** (p171) Slurping on flawless happy-hour cocktails at this dark and deco-licious bar.

❹ **Gramercy Park** (p168) Walking around this elegant park, enjoying one of the city's most intimate urban moments.

❺ **Shake Shack** (p167) Snacking on coveted burgers while taking in art installations and the iconic Flatiron Building at Madison Square Park.

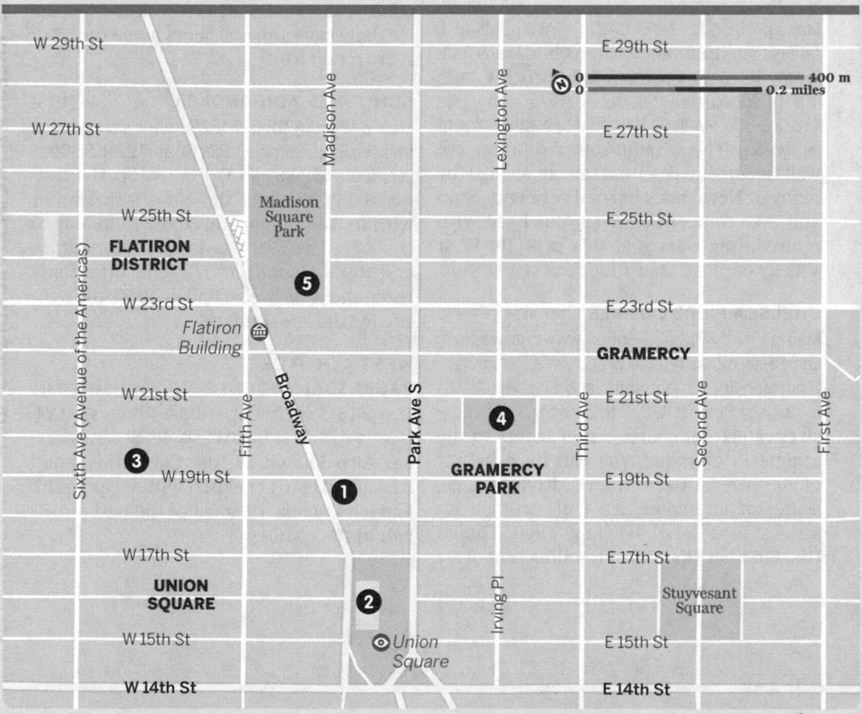

For more detail of this area see Map p422

Explore Union Square, the Flatiron District & Gramercy

There's not a lot of ground to cover, so the best plan of attack is to use the two major public spaces – Union Square (p166) and Madison Square Park (p167) – as your anchors. From Union Square you'll feel the Village and university vibe (NYU is just south and the New School just to the west) spilling over with good cafes, sign-bearing protesters and buskers in the square itself. Walking east or west along 14th St takes you to the East or West Village respectively.

Up toward 23rd St you'll find the namesake Flatiron Building (p167) looming over the commercial quarter, replete with crowded lunch spots and after-work watering holes. East of both public spaces is Gramercy, its distinctly residential vibe tempered with notable, buzzing restaurants.

In Madison Square Park you'll find young PR mavens chatting over lattes, harried lawyers getting away from the office for a moment of peace and in the warmer months foodies flocking to the Mad Sq Eats market located in the northeastern section of the park.

Local Life

➡ **Mad Sq Eats** Each spring and fall, foodies flock to tiny General Worth Sq – wedged between Fifth Ave and Broadway, opposite Madison Square Park – for Mad Sq Eats (p169), a month-long culinary pop-up market. Its 30 or so vendors include some of the city's hottest eateries, cooking up anything from proper pizza to brisket tacos using top local produce.

➡ **Gourmet groceries** Eataly (p169) has made a name for itself as the place to go for Italophile food buffs, but locals do much more of their everyday shopping at health-conscious supermarket Whole Foods.

Getting There & Away

➡ **Subway** A slew of subway lines converge below Union Square, shuttling passengers up Manhattan's East Side on the 4/5/6 lines, straight to Williamsburg on the L, or to Queens on the N/Q/R lines. The L also travels to the West Side, although when there's no traffic it costs about the same to take a cab (for two or more people). Take the Q for an express link to Herald Square and Times Square.

➡ **Bus** The M14A and M14D provide cross-town services along 14th St, while the M23 runs cross-town along 23rd St. Choose the bus over the subway if you're traveling between two eastern points in Manhattan – it's not worth traveling to Union Square to walk back to First Ave.

Lonely Planet's Top Tip

Human traffic can be overwhelming in Union Square, especially along 14th St. If you're in a rush, or trying to hoof it on foot, switch over to 13th St and you'll cover a lot more ground in much less time.

Best Places to Eat

➡ Eleven Madison Park (p169)

➡ Gramercy Tavern (p170)

➡ Maialino (p169)

➡ Clocktower (p170)

➡ Cosme (p170)

For reviews, see p168. ➡

Best Places to Drink

➡ Flatiron Lounge (p171)

➡ Raines Law Room (p171)

➡ Birreria (p171)

➡ Old Town Bar & Restaurant (p171)

➡ Lillie's Victorian Establishment (p171)

For reviews, see p170. ➡

Best Places to Instagram

➡ Gramercy Park (p168)

➡ Flatiron Building (p167)

➡ Madison Square Park (p167)

➡ Union Square (p166)

For reviews, see p166. ➡

TOP SIGHT
UNION SQUARE

Union Square is like the Noah's Ark of New York, rescuing at least two of every kind from the curling seas of concrete. Amid the stone steps and fenced-in foliage you'll see denizens of every ilk: suited businessfolk gulping fresh air during their lunch breaks, dreadlocked loiterers tapping beats on tablas and skateboarders flipping tricks on the southeastern stairs.

Riches & Rags

Opened in 1831, Union Square quickly became the central gathering place for those who lived in the mansions nearby. Concert halls and artist societies further enhanced the cultured atmosphere, and high-end shopping quickly proliferated along Broadway, which was dubbed 'Ladies' Mile.'

When the Civil War broke out, the vast public space (large by New York standards, of course) was center stage for protesters of all sorts, from union workers to political activists. By the height of WWI, the area had fallen largely into disuse, allowing politically and socially driven organizations like the American Civil Liberties Union, the Communist and Socialist Parties, and the Ladies' Garment Workers Union to move in. Many decades later, the square remains a popular site for political and social protests.

For an unforgettable, sweeping view of Union Square and the Empire State Building beyond, hit DSW (p174), a 3rd-floor discount shoe store at the southern end of the square.

DON'T MISS

- Union Square Greenmarket (p172)
- *Metronome* art installation
- The view from DSW shoe store
- Eclectics, sit-ins and buskers

PRACTICALITIES

- Map p422, D4
- www.unionsquarenyc.org
- 17th St, btwn Broadway & Park Ave S, Union Square
- S 4/5/6, N/Q/R, L to 14th St-Union Sq

The Factory

After over a century of the continuous push-and-pull between dapper-dom and political protest, a third – artistic, if not thoroughly hippie-ish – ingredient was tossed into the mix when Andy Warhol moved his Factory to the 6th floor of the Decker Building at 33 Union Sq West. It was here, on June 3,1968, that disgruntled writer Valerie Solanas shot Warhol three times, seriously wounding him. The ground floor of the building is now occupied by a candy-store chain – very Warholian.

Metronome

A walk around Union Square will reveal a string of whimsical, temporary sculptures. Of the permanent offerings is an imposing equestrian statue of George Washington (one of the first public pieces of art in New York City) and a statue of peacemaker Mahatma Gandhi. Trumping both on the southeastern side of the square is a massive art installation that either earns confused stares or simply gets overlooked by passersby. A symbolic representation of the passage of time, *Metronome* has two parts: a digital clock with a puzzling display of numbers, and a wand-like apparatus with smoke puffing out of concentric rings. We'll let you ponder the latter while we give you the skinny on what exactly the winking orange digits denote: the 14 numbers must be split into two groups of seven: the seven from the left tell the current time (hour, minute, second, tenth-of-a-second) and the seven from the right are meant to be read in reverse order; they represent the remaining amount of time in the day.

SIGHTS

Though short on sights per se, there's lots happening on and around Union Square, which bustles with buskers, suits and appetite-piquing produce stalls. To the northwest are the dignified streets of Gramercy, while to the north is Madison Square Garden, where dogs and squirrels meet art installations, readings and a famous little burger shack.

UNION SQUARE — SQUARE

See p166.

MADISON SQUARE PARK — PARK

Map p422 (212-520-7600; www.madisonsquarepark.org; E 23rd to 26th Sts, btwn Fifth & Madison Aves, Flatiron District; 6am-11pm; ; S R/W, F/M, 6 to 23rd St) This park defined the northern reaches of Manhattan until the island's population exploded after the Civil War. These days it's a much-welcome oasis from Manhattan's relentless pace, with a popular children's playground, dog-run area and the **Shake Shack** (Map p422; 646-889-6600; www.shakeshack.com; burgers $4.20-9.50; 7:30am-11pm Mon-Fri, from 8:30am Sat & Sun) burger joint. It's also one of the city's most cultured parks, with specially commissioned art installations and (in the warmer months) activities ranging from literary discussions to live-music gigs. See the website for more information.

THEODORE ROOSEVELT BIRTHPLACE — HISTORIC SITE

Map p422 (212-260-1616; www.nps.gov/thrb; 28 E 20th St, btwn Broadway & Park Ave S, Flatiron District; 40min guided tours 10am, 11am, 1pm, 2pm, 3pm & 4pm Tue-Sat; S R/W, 6 to 23rd St) FREE This National Historic Site is a bit of a cheat, since the physical house where the 26th president was actually born was demolished in his own lifetime. But this building is a worthy reconstruction by his relatives, who took painstaking steps to bring together original furniture from the residence with true-to-the-period restorations.

NATIONAL ARTS CLUB — CULTURAL CENTER

Map p422 (212-475-3424; www.nationalartsclub.org; 15 Gramercy Park S, Gramercy; drawing classes $15-25; S N/R, 6 to 23rd St) Founded in 1898 to promote public interest in the arts, the National Arts Club holds art exhibitions, usually open to the public from 10am to 5pm Monday to Friday (check the website for upcoming

TOP SIGHT
FLATIRON BUILDING

Designed by Daniel Burnham and built in 1902, the 20-story Flatiron Building has a uniquely narrow triangular footprint that resembles the prow of a massive ship. It also features a traditional beaux-arts limestone and terra-cotta facade that gets more complex and beautiful the longer you stare at it. Until 1909 it was the world's tallest building.

Publisher Frank Munsey was one of the building's first tenants. From his 18th-floor offices he published *Munsey's Magazine*, which featured the work of short-story writer O Henry. His musings (in popular stories such as 'The Gift of the Magi'), the paintings of John Sloan and photographs of Alfred Stieglitz best immortalized the Flatiron back in the day. Actress Katharine Hepburn once quipped that she'd like to be admired as much as the grand old building.

While there are plans to transform the Flatiron into a luxurious five-star hotel, progress is on hold until the final business tenants willingly vacate the premises. In the meantime, the ground floor of the building's 'prow' has been transformed into a glassed-in art space. Past installations have included a life-size 3-D-cutout replica of Edward Hopper's 1942 painting *Nighthawks*, its angular diner remarkably similar to the Flatiron's shape.

DON'T MISS

- The view of the facade from Madison Square Park
- Getting up close to appreciate the fine exterior detail
- Flatiron Prow art space

PRACTICALITIES

- Map p422, C2
- Broadway, cnr Fifth Ave & 23rd St, Flatiron District
- S N/R, F/M, 6 to 23rd St

TOP SIGHT
GRAMERCY PARK

Manhattan's early Dutch settlers named the area now known as Gramercy 'Krom Moerasje' (Little Crooked Swamp). The swamp would meet its end in 1831, when lawyer and public official Samuel Ruggles purchased the land. He had the swamp drained and the land carved into 108 lots. Forty-two of these were set aside for an English-style private park, to be held in perpetuity by the residents of its surrounding 66 lots.

Almost two centuries later, Gramercy Park remains a private oasis. Only once has it been made accessible to nonresidents, when Union soldiers were permitted during the Draft Riots of 1863.

Many of the original town houses facing the park were replaced by high-rise apartment buildings through the 1920s. Along the park sits the National Arts Club (p167); its elegance attests to the district's desirable pedigree. Indeed, Gramercy Park has had its fair share of illustrious residents. The town house at 4 Gramercy Park W was home to American publisher James Harper from 1847 to 1869. Mayor of New York City from 1844 to 1845, Harper's flouncy 'mayor's lights' still grace the front of the building. Another famous local was Stanford White, eponymous designer of the triumphal arch in Washington Square.

DON'T MISS

- A slow walk around the park to admire the stunning architecture of the surrounding buildings
- Taking in a gallery show at the National Arts Club

PRACTICALITIES

- Map p422, D3
- E 20th St, btwn Park & Third Aves, Gramercy
- S N/R, 6 to 23rd St

shows). Calvert Vaux – one of the creators of Central Park – designed the building itself, its picture-lined front parlor adorned with a beautiful, vaulted stained-glass ceiling. The place was once home to Samuel J Tilden, a former New York governor, and failed presidential candidate in 1876.

TIBET HOUSE CULTURAL CENTER
Map p422 (☎212-807-0563; www.tibethouse.us; 22 W 15th St, btwn Fifth & Sixth Aves, Union Square; suggested donation $5; ⏰11am-6pm Mon-Fri; S F/M to 14th St, L to 6th Ave) With the Dalai Lama as the patron of its board, this nonprofit cultural space is dedicated to presenting Tibet's ancient traditions through art exhibits, a research library and various publications. Programs on offer include educational workshops, open meditations, retreat weekends, and docent-led tours to Tibet, Nepal and Bhutan.

METROPOLITAN LIFE TOWER HISTORIC BUILDING
Map p422 (1 Madison Ave, btwn E 23rd & E 24th Sts, Flatiron District; S N/R, F/M, 6 to 23rd St) Completed in 1909, this 700ft-high clock tower soaring above Madison Square Park's southeastern corner is the work of Napoleon LeBrun, a Philadelphia-born architect of French stock. Italophiles may feel a certain déjà vu gazing at the tower. After all, LeBrun's inspiration was Venice's world-famous *campanile* (bell tower) in Piazza San Marco. Ironically, LeBrun's New World version is now older than its muse: the original Venetian tower collapsed in 1902, with its replacement not completed until 1912.

EATING

TACOMBI CAFÉ EL PRESIDENTE MEXICAN $
Map p422 (☎212-242-3491; www.tacombi.com; 30 W 24th St, btwn Fifth & Sixth Aves, Flatiron District; tacos $4-5.50, quesadillas $6-9; ⏰11am-midnight Mon-Sat, to 10:30pm Sun; S F/M, R/W to 23rd St) Channeling the cafes of Mexico City, pink-and-green Tacombi covers numerous bases, from juice and liquor bar to taco joint. Score a table, order a margarita and hop your way around a menu of Mexican street-food deliciousness. Top choices include *esquites* (grilled corn with *cotija* cheese and chipotle mayonnaise, served in

a paper cup) and succulent *carnitas michoacan* (beer-marinated pork) tacos.

MAD SQ EATS MARKET $

Map p422 (www.madisonsquarepark.org/mad-sq-food/mad-sq-eats; General Worth Sq, Flatiron District; ⏲spring & fall 11am-9pm; Ⓢ R/W, F/M, 6 to 23rd St) A biannual, pop-up culinary market with stalls run by some of the city's coolest eateries and hottest chefs. Bites span a range of street foods, from arancini and empanadas to lobster rolls and ice-cream sandwiches. See the website for dates and vendors.

BIG DADDY'S DINER $

Map p422 (☎212-477-1500; www.bigdaddysnyc.com; 239 Park Ave S, btwn E 19th & E 20th Sts, Gramercy; mains $13-16; ⏲8am-midnight Mon-Thu, to 5am Fri & Sat, to 11pm Sun; Ⓢ 6 to 23rd St; 4/5/6, L, N/Q/R/W to 14th St-Union Sq) Giant, fluffy omelettes, hearty burgers and heaps of tater tots (regular or sweet potato) have made Big Daddy's a top choice for both breakfast and late-night treats. The interior is all Americana kitsch, but unlike some theme restaurants the food doesn't break the bank and actually satisfies. Don't think about leaving without trying one of its gargantuan shakes.

EISENBERG'S SANDWICH SHOP SANDWICHES $

Map p422 (☎212-675-5096; www.eisenbergsnyc.com; 174 Fifth Ave, btwn W 22nd & 23rd St, Flatiron District; sandwiches $4-13; ⏲6:30am-8pm Mon-Fri, 9am-6pm Sat, to 5pm Sun; Ⓢ R/W to 23rd St) This old-school diner – an anomaly on this mostly upscale stretch of real estate – is filled from morning to close with regulars in for traditional Jewish-diner fare like chopped liver, pastrami and whitefish salad. Grab a stool at the long bar and rub elbows with an eclectic mix of customers who know meatloaf isn't a joke dish.

REPUBLIC ASIAN $

Map p422 (☎212-627-7172; www.thinknoodles.com; 37 Union Sq W, btwn E 16th & E 17th Sts, Union Square; mains $13-16; ⏲11:30am-10:30pm; Ⓢ 4/5/6, N/Q/R, L to 14th St-Union Sq) Eat-and-go Republic feeds the masses with fresh 'n' tasty Asian staples. Slurp away on warming broth noodles, chomp on juicy pad Thai or keep it light with a green papaya and mango salad. Located right on Union Square, it's a handy spot for a cheap, uncomplicated, walk-in bite. It's always crowded, but the service is quick.

BOQUERIA FLATIRON TAPAS $$

Map p422 (☎212-255-4160; www.boquerianyc.com; 53 W 19th St, btwn Fifth & Sixth Aves, Flatiron District; tapas $6-18; ⏲11-10:30pm Sun-Thu, to 11:30pm Fri & Sat; 📶; Ⓢ 1 to 18th St, F/M, R/W to 23rd St) A holy union between Spanish-style tapas and market-fresh fare, Boqueria woos the after-work crowd with a brilliant lineup of small plates and larger *raciones*. Lick lips and fingers over the likes of garlicky shrimp with brandy and *guindilla* pepper, or bacon-wrapped dates stuffed with almonds and Valdeón blue cheese. A smooth selection of Spanish wines tops it all off. *¡Buen provecho!*

EATALY FOOD HALL $$

Map p422 (☎212-229-2560; www.eataly.com; 200 Fifth Ave, at W 23rd St, Flatiron District; ⏲7am-11pm; 🖉; Ⓢ R/W, F/M, 6 to 23rd St) Mario Batali's sleek, sprawling temple to Italian gastronomy is a veritable wonderland. Feast on everything from vibrant *crudo* (raw fish) and *fritto misto* (tempura-style vegetables) to steamy pasta and pizza at the emporium's string of sit-down eateries. Alternatively, guzzle espresso at the bar and scour the countless counters and shelves for a DIY picnic hamper *nonna* would approve of.

★MAIALINO ITALIAN $$$

Map p422 (☎212-777-2410; www.maialinonyc.com; Gramercy Park Hotel, 2 Lexington Ave, at 21st St; mains lunch $24-34, dinner $27-44; ⏲7:30-10am, noon-2pm & 5:30-10pm Mon-Wed, to 10:30pm Thu, 10am-2pm & 5:30-10:30pm Fri, to 10pm Sat; Ⓢ 6, R/W to 23rd St) Fans reserve tables up to four weeks in advance at this Danny Meyer classic, but the best seats in the house are at the walk-in bar, manned by sociable, knowledgeable staffers. Wherever you're plonked, take your taste buds on a Roman holiday. Maialino's lip-smacking, rustic Italian fare is created using produce from the nearby Union Square Greenmarket.

★ELEVEN MADISON PARK MODERN AMERICAN $$$

Map p422 (☎212-889-0905; www.elevenmadisonpark.com; 11 Madison Ave, btwn 24th & 25th Sts, Flatiron District; tasting menu $295; ⏲5:30-10pm Mon-Wed, to 10:30pm Thu-Sun, also noon-1pm Fri-Sun; Ⓢ R/W, 6 to 23rd St) Fine-dining Eleven Madison Park came in at number one in the 2017 San Pellegrino World's 50 Best Restaurants list. Frankly, we're not surprised: this revamped poster child of modern, sustainable American cooking is also one of only six NYC restaurants with three Michelin stars.

★GRAMERCY TAVERN MODERN AMERICAN $$$
Map p422 (☎212-477-0777; www.gramercytavern.com; 42 E 20th St, btwn Broadway & Park Ave S, Flatiron District; tavern mains $29-36, dining room 3-course menu $125, tasting menus $149-179; ⊙tavern noon-11pm Sun-Thu, to midnight Fri & Sat, dining room noon-2pm & 5:30-10pm Mon-Thu, to 11pm Fri, noon-1:30pm & 5:30-11pm Sat, 5:30-10pm Sun; ; SR/W, 6 to 23rd St) Seasonal, local ingredients drive this perennial favorite, a vibrant, country-chic institution aglow with copper sconces, murals and dramatic floral arrangements. Choose from two spaces: the walk-in-only tavern and its à la carte menu, or the swankier dining room and its fancier prix-fixe and degustation feasts. Tavern highlights include a showstopping duck meatloaf with mushrooms, chestnuts and brussels sprouts.

★CRAFT MODERN AMERICAN $$$
Map p422 (☎212-780-0880; www.craftrestaurant.com; 43 E 19th St, btwn Broadway & Park Ave S, Union Square; lunch $29-36, dinner mains $24-55; ⊙noon-2:30pm & 5:30-10pm Mon-Thu, to 11pm Fri, 5:30-11pm Sat, to 9pm Sun; ; S4/5/6, N/Q/R/W, L to 14th St-Union Sq) Humming, high-end Craft flies the flag for small, family-owned farms and food producers, their bounty transformed into pure, polished dishes. Whether nibbling on flawlessly charred braised octopus, pillowy scallops or pumpkin mezzaluna pasta with sage, brown butter and Parmesan, expect every ingredient to sing with flavor. Book ahead Wednesday to Saturday or head in by 6pm or after 9:30pm.

ABC KITCHEN MODERN AMERICAN $$$
Map p422 (☎212-475-5829; www.abckitchennyc.com; 35 E 18th St, at Broadway, Union Square; pizzas $18-22, dinner mains $24-40; ⊙noon-3pm & 5:30-10:30pm Mon-Wed, to 11pm Thu, to 11:30pm Fri, 11am-3pm & 5:30-11:30pm Sat, 11am-3pm & 5:30-10pm Sun; ; S4/5/6, N/Q/R, L to 14th St-Union Sq) Looking part gallery, part rustic farmhouse, sustainable, produce-focused ABC Kitchen is the culinary avatar of the chichi home-goods department store ABC Carpet & Home (p172). Organic gets haute in dishes like Skuna Bay salmon with spring onion-rhubarb compote and lime, or crispy pork confit with smoked-bacon marmalade and braised turnips. For a more casual bite, try the scrumptious whole-wheat pizzas.

CLOCKTOWER MODERN BRITISH $$$
Map p422 (☎212-413-4300; http://theclocktowernyc.com; 5 Madison Ave, btwn 23rd & 24th Sts, Gramercy; dinner mains $25-65; ⊙6:30-10am, 11:30am-3pm & 5:30-10pm Mon & Tue, to 11pm Wed-Fri, dinner 5-11pm Sat, to 10pm Sun; ; SF/M, R/W, 6 to 23rd St) Brits do it best at Jason Atherton's clubby, new A-lister, hidden away inside the landmark Metropolitan Life Tower. This is the latest venture for the Michelin-starred British chef, its wood-and-stucco dining rooms setting a handsome scene for high-end comfort grub like a rack of Colorado lamb with crispy quinoa and a locally sourced duck with a sweet peach salad.

TRATTORIA IL MULINO ITALIAN $$$
Map p422 (☎212-777-8448; www.trattoriailmulino.com; 36 E 20th St, btwn Broadway & Park Ave, Flatiron District; mains $35-52; ⊙11:30am-10pm Mon-Wed, to 11pm Thu & Fri, 4:30-11pm Sat, to 10pm Sun; SR/W, 6 to 23rd St) That head chef Michele Mazza looks uncannily like Italian film star Marcello Mastroianni seems apt – his beautifully prepared dishes personify Italian dolce vita. The pasta dishes and wood-fired pizzas are particularly memorable, while cross-regional influences meet in the zingy, classic-with-a-twist limoncello tiramisu. Attentive service and a chic yet amiable vibe make this spot *perfetto* for a special feed.

COSME MEXICAN $$$
Map p422 (☎212-913-9659; http://cosmenyc.com; 35 E 21st St, btwn Broadway & Park Ave S, Flatiron District; dinner dishes $19-29; ⊙noon-2:30pm & 5:30-11pm Mon-Thu, to midnight Fri, 11:30-2:30 & 5:30-11pm Sat, to 11pm Sun; ; SR/W, 6 to 23rd St) Mexican gets haute at this slinky, charcoal-hued restaurant, home to chef Enrique Olvera and his innovative takes on south-of-the-border flavors. Subvert culinary stereotypes with the likes of delicate, invigorating scallops with avocado and jicama, a fresh bean salad with a charred cucumber vinaigrette, herb guacamole or Cosme's cult-status duck carnitas. Book ahead or try your luck at the walk-in bar.

DRINKING & NIGHTLIFE

Perfectly made classic cocktails and robust wine lists are typical of the bars and lounges in Union Square, Flatiron District and Gramercy. It's a great area for those who like to get gussied up before they go out for a night on the town: you'll find many fellow imbibers

dressed to impress in modern cocktail-hour attire. If you need a regular-guy Irish drinking hole, look on Third Ave north of 14th St.

★FLATIRON LOUNGE COCKTAIL BAR

Map p422 (☎212-727-7741; www.flatironlounge.com; 37 W 19th St, btwn Fifth & Sixth Aves, Flatiron District; ⏰4pm-2am Mon-Wed, to 3am Thu, to 4am Fri, 5pm-4am Sat; 📶; Ⓢ F/M, R/W, 6 to 23rd St) Head through a dramatic archway and into a dark, swinging, art deco–inspired fantasy of lipstick-red booths, racy jazz tunes and sassy grown-ups downing seasonal drinks. Cocktails run $14 a pop, but happy-hour cocktails are only $10 (4pm to 6pm weekdays).

RAINES LAW ROOM COCKTAIL BAR

Map p422 (www.raineslawroom.com; 48 W 17th St, btwn Fifth & Sixth Aves, Flatiron District; ⏰5pm-2am Mon-Wed, to 3am Thu-Sat, 7pm-1am Sun; Ⓢ F/M to 14th St, L to 6th Ave, 1 to 18th St) A sea of velvet drapes and overstuffed leather lounge chairs, the perfect amount of exposed brick, expertly crafted cocktails using meticulously aged spirits – these folks are as serious as a mortgage payment when it comes to amplified atmosphere. Reservations (recommended) are only accepted Sunday to Tuesday. Whatever the night, style up for a taste of a far more sumptuous era.

BIRRERIA BEER HALL

Map p422 (☎212-937-8910; www.eataly.com; 200 Fifth Ave, at W 23rd St, Flatiron District; ⏰11:30am-11pm; Ⓢ F/M, R/W, 6 to 23rd St) The crown jewel of Italian food emporium Eataly (p169) is this rooftop beer garden tucked betwixt the Flatiron's corporate towers. An encyclopedic beer menu offers drinkers some of the best suds on the planet. If you're hungry, the signature beer-braised pork shoulder will pair nicely, or check out the seasonally changing menu of the on-site pop-up restaurant (mains $17 to $37).

The sneaky access elevator is near the checkouts on the 23rd St side of the store.

OLD TOWN BAR & RESTAURANT BAR

Map p422 (☎212-529-6732; www.oldtownbar.com; 45 E 18th St, btwn Broadway & Park Ave S, Union Square; ⏰11:30am-11:30pm Mon-Fri, noon-11:30pm Sat, to 10pm Sun; Ⓢ 4/5/6, N/Q/R/W, L to 14th St-Union Sq) It still looks like 1892 in here, with the mahogany bar, original tile floors and tin ceilings – the Old Town is an old-world drinking-man's classic (and -woman's: Madonna lit up at the bar here – when lighting up in bars was still legal – in her 'Bad Girl' video). There are cocktails around, but most come for beers and a burger (from $11.50).

LILLIE'S VICTORIAN ESTABLISHMENT BAR

Map p422 (☎212-337-1970; www.lilliesnyc.com; 13 E 17th St, btwn Broadway & Fifth Ave, Union Square; ⏰11am-4am; Ⓢ 4/5/6, L, N/Q/R/W to 14th St-Union Sq) This is one of those places where the name says it all. Step in and be taken to the era of petticoats and watch fobs with high, stamped-tin ceilings, red-velvet love seats and walls covered in vintage photographs in extravagant gilded frames. The food and cocktail list is decidedly modern, but the ambience is enough to fulfill the fantasy.

FLATIRON ROOM COCKTAIL BAR

Map p422 (☎212-725-3860; www.theflatironroom.com; 37 W 26th St, btwn Sixth Ave & Broadway, Flatiron District; ⏰4pm-2am Mon-Fri, 5pm-2am Sat, to midnight Sun; Ⓢ R/W to 28th St, F/M to 23rd St) Vintage wallpaper, a glittering chandelier and hand-painted coffered ceilings make for a suitably elegant scene at this grown-up drinking den, its artfully lit cabinets graced with rare whiskeys. Fine cocktails pair nicely with high-end sharing plates, from citrus-marinated olive tapenade to flatbread with *guanciale* (cured pork jowl) and fig. Most nights also feature live music, including bluegrass and jazz. Reservations are highly recommended.

71 IRVING PLACE CAFE

Map p422 (Irving Farm Coffee Company; ☎212-995-5252; www.irvingfarm.com; 71 Irving Pl, btwn 18th & 19th Sts, Gramercy; ⏰7am-8pm Mon-Fri, from 8am Sat & Sun; Ⓢ 4/5/6, N/Q/R/W, L to 14th St-Union Sq) From keyboard-tapping scribes to gossiping friends and academics, this bustling cafe is never short of a crowd. Hand-picked beans are lovingly roasted on a farm in the Hudson Valley (about 90 miles from NYC), and served alongside tasty edibles like Balthazar-baked croissants, granola, egg dishes, bagels and pressed sandwiches.

BEAUTY BAR BAR

Map p412 (☎212-539-1389; www.thebeautybar.com/home-new-york; 231 E 14th St, btwn Second & Third Aves, Union Square; ⏰5pm-4am Mon-Fri, from 2pm Sat & Sun; Ⓢ L to 3rd Ave) A kitschy favorite since the mid-'90s, this homage to old-fashioned beauty parlors pulls in a cool local crowd with its retro soundtrack, nostalgic vibe and $10 manicures (with a free

Blue Rinse margarita thrown in) from 6pm to 11pm on weekdays, and 3pm to 11pm on weekends. Nightly events range from comedy to burlesque.

PETE'S TAVERN BAR

Map p422 (212-473-7676; www.petestavern.com; 129 E 18th St, at Irving Pl, Gramercy; 11am-2:30am Sun-Wed, to 3am Thu, to 4am Fri & Sat; S 4/5/6, N/Q/R/W, L to 14th St-Union Sq) With its original 19th-century mirrors, pressed-tin ceiling and rosewood bar, this dark, atmospheric watering hole has all the earmarks of a New York classic. You can get a respectable prime-rib burger here and choose from 17 draft beers, joined by everyone from posttheater couples and Irish expats to no-nonsense NYU students and the odd celebrity (see photos by the restrooms).

TOBY'S ESTATE CAFE

Map p422 (646-559-0161; www.tobysestate.com; 160 Fifth Ave, btwn 20th & 21st Sts, Flatiron District; 7am-9pm Mon-Fri, 8am-8pm Sat & Sun; S R/W, F/M, 6 to 23rd St) Sydney-born, Williamsburg-roasting Toby's Estate is part of Manhattan's evolving artisanal-coffee culture. Loaded with a custom-made Strada espresso machine, it's tucked away in the Club Monaco store. Join coffee geeks for thick, rich brews, among them a geo-specific Flatiron Espresso Blend. Nibbles include pastries and sandwiches from local bakeries.

BOXERS NYC GAY

Map p422 (212-255-5082; www.boxersnyc.com; 37 W 20th St, btwn Fifth & Sixth Aves, Flatiron District; 4pm-2am Mon-Thu, to 4am Fri, 1pm-4am Sat, 1pm-2am Sun; S F/M, R/W, 6 to 23rd St) The beers and potential new buds are plentiful at this gay sports bar in the heart of the Flatiron District. There's football on TV, buffalo wings at the bar, and topless wait staff keeping the pool cues polished. And in case you think Boxers is all brawn, think again: Tuesday's popular Trivia Night gives brains a good, hard workout.

☆ ENTERTAINMENT

PEOPLES IMPROV THEATER COMEDY

Map p422 (PIT; 212-563-7488; www.thepit-nyc.com; 123 E 24th St, btwn Lexington & Park Aves, Gramercy; ; S F/M, N/R, 6 to 23rd St) Aglow in red neon, this bustling comedy club serves up top-notch laughs at dirt-cheap prices. The string of nightly acts ranges from stand-up to sketch and musical comedy, playing in either the main stage theater or the basement lounge. PIT also runs courses, including three-hour, drop-in improv workshops at its Midtown venue, **Simple Studios** (Map p428; 212-273-9696; http://simplestudiosnyc.com; 134 W 29th St, btwn Sixth & Seventh Aves, Midtown West; 9am-11pm Mon-Fri, to 10pm Sat & Sun; S 1, N/R to 28th St). See the website for all classes and schedules.

IRVING PLAZA LIVE MUSIC

Map p422 (212-777-6817; www.irvingplaza.com; 17 Irving Pl, at 15th St, Union Square; S 4/5/6, N/Q/R, L to 14th St-Union Sq) Rocking since 1978, Irving Plaza has seen them all: the Ramones, Bob Dylan, U2, Pearl Jam, you name it. These days it's a great in-between stage for quirkier rock and pop acts, from indie chicks Sleater-Kinney to hard rockers Disturbed. There's a cozy floor around the stage, and good views from the mezzanine.

SHOPPING

UNION SQUARE GREENMARKET MARKET

Map p422 (www.grownyc.org; Union Square, 17th St btwn Broadway & Park Ave S, Union Square; 8am-6pm Mon, Wed, Fri & Sat; S 4/5/6, N/Q/R, L to 14th St-Union Sq) Don't be surprised if you spot some of New York's top chefs prodding the produce here: Union Square's greenmarket is arguably the city's most famous. Whet your appetite trawling the stalls, which peddle anything and everything from upstate fruit and vegetables to artisanal breads, cheeses and cider.

ABC CARPET & HOME HOMEWARES

Map p422 (212-473-3000; www.abchome.com; 888 Broadway, at E 19th St; 10am-7pm Mon-Wed, Fri & Sat, to 8pm Thu, 11am-6:30pm Sun; S 4/5/6, N/Q/R/W, L to 14th St-Union Sq) A mecca for home designers and decorators brainstorming ideas, this beautifully curated, seven-level temple to good taste heaves with all sorts of furnishings, small and large. Shop for easy-to-pack knickknacks, textiles and jewelry, as well as statement furniture, designer lighting, ceramics and antique carpets. Come Christmas season the shop is a joy to behold.

DSW SHOES

Map p422 (212-674-2146; www.dsw.com; 40 E 14th St, btwn University Pl & Broadway, Union Square; 9am-9:30pm Mon-Sat, from 10am

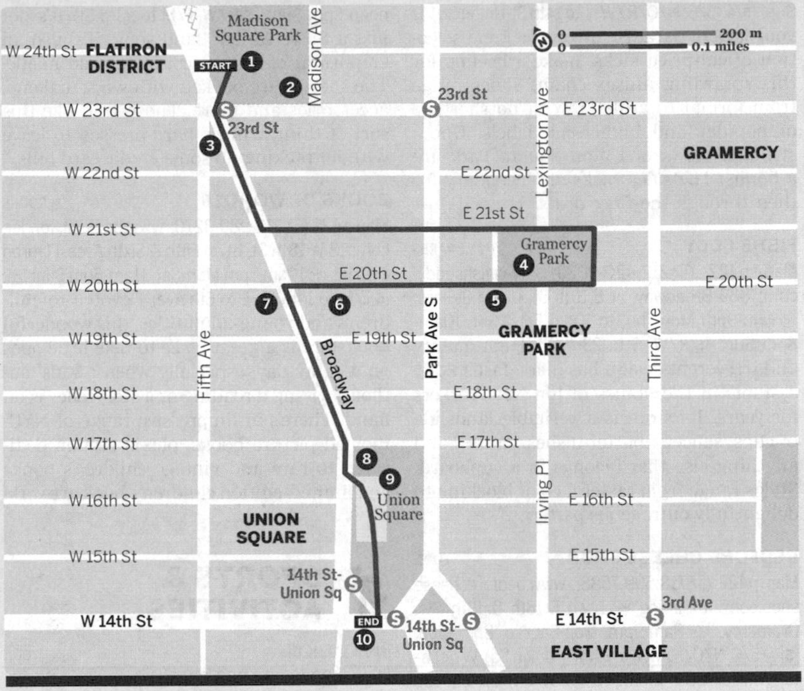

Neighborhood Walk
Be There, Be Square

START MADISON SQUARE PARK
END DSW
LENGTH 2 MILES; TWO HOURS

Start off in leafy ❶ **Madison Square Park** (p167), dotted with historic statues and contemporary installations. If you're hungry, hit up ❷ **Shake Shack** (p167) for a gourmet burger and fries. Before exiting the park, stand at its southwestern corner and take in the arresting ❸ **Flatiron Building** (p167), Chicago architect Daniel Burnham's clever response to the awkward space where Fifth Ave and Broadway meet.

Follow Broadway south to 21st St and go left. Past Park Ave S you'll find yourself alongside ❹ **Gramercy Park** (p168), a private garden reminiscent of those found in Britain. Legendary 19th-century actor Edwin Booth spent his final years living at 16 Gramercy Park S, while actor Margaret Hamilton (best known as the Wicked Witch of the West in the MGM classic *The Wizard of Oz*) was a long-term resident of 34 Gramercy Park E. At 15 Gramercy Park S stands the ❺ **National Arts Club** (p167); its film cameos include Martin Scorsese's *The Age of Innocence* and Woody Allen's *Manhattan Murder Mystery*.

Head back west along 20th St and stop at the reconstructed version of ❻ **Theodore Roosevelt's Birthplace** (p167), which offers hourly tours. On the southwestern corner of Broadway and E 20th St stands the old ❼ **Lord & Taylor Building**, former home of the famous Midtown department store.

Continue south on Broadway and you'll find yourself at the northwestern corner of ❽ **Union Square** (p166). Check out the produce, baked goods and flowers of the ❾ **Greenmarket**, seek out Gandhi near the southwest corner, or grab some food at one of the surrounding eateries for a picnic in the park. If you have any residual energy, cross Union Sq South (14th St) and dive into ❿ **DSW**, a massive warehouse dedicated to heavily discounted designer shoes and accessories. You can also catch some great views of the park and city from the store's windows while trying on your new kicks.

Sun; S 4/5/6, N/Q/R/W, L to 14th St-Union Sq) If your idea of paradise involves a great selection of cut-price kicks, make a beeline for this sprawling unisex chain. Shoes range from formal to athletic, with no shortage of popular and higher-end labels. Unobstructed views of Union Square Park are a bonus. The sales racks are legendary for their through-the-floor deals.

FISHS EDDY HOMEWARES

Map p422 (☎212-420-9020; www.fishseddy.com; 889 Broadway, at E 19th St, Union Square; ⏰9am-9pm Mon-Thu, to 10pm Fri & Sat, 10am-8pm Sun; S R/W, 6 to 23rd St) High-quality and irreverent design has made Fishs Eddy a staple in the homes of hip New Yorkers for years. Its store is a veritable landslide of cups, saucers, butter dishes, carafes and anything else that belongs in a cupboard. Styles range from tasteful color blocking to delightfully outrageous patterns.

BEDFORD CHEESE SHOP FOOD

Map p422 (☎718-599-7588; www.bedfordcheeseshop.com; 67 Irving Pl, btwn E 18th & 19th Sts, Gramercy; ⏰8am-9pm Mon-Sat, to 8pm Sun; S 4/5/6, N/Q/R/W, L to 14th St-Union Sq) Whether you're after local, raw cow's-milk cheese washed in absinthe or garlic-infused goat's-milk cheese from Australia, chances are you'll find it among the 200-strong selection at this outpost of Brooklyn's most celebrated cheese vendor. Pair the cheesy goodness with artisanal charcuterie, deli treats and ready-to-eat sandwiches ($8 to $11), as well as a proud array of Made-in-Brooklyn edibles.

RENT THE RUNWAY CLOTHING

Map p422 (www.renttherunway.com; 30 W 15th St, btwn Fifth & Sixth Aves; ⏰9am-9pm Mon-Fri, to 8pm Sat, to 7pm Sun; S L, F/M to 14th St-6th Ave; 4/5/6, L, N/Q/R/W to 14th St-Union Sq) At the flagship store of this popular fashion rental service anyone can pop in for an affordable fashion consultation ($30) for both planned and last-minute events. It's full of looks by high-end designers (Narciso Rodriguez, Badgley Mischka, Nicole Miller) available to rent. Perfect for those who pack light, but want to make a splash.

ABRACADABRA FASHION & ACCESSORIES

Map p422 (☎212-627-5194; www.abracadabrasuperstore.com; 19 W 21st St, btwn Fifth & Sixth Aves, Flatiron District; ⏰11am-7pm Mon-Sat, noon-5pm Sun; S R/W, F/M to 23rd St) It's not just a Steve Miller Band song, it's also an emporium of horror, costumes and magic. The shelves are packed with wigs, makeup, accessories and more. Those who like this sort of thing will be hard-pressed to leave without racking up some credit-card bills.

BOOKS OF WONDER BOOKS

Map p422 (☎212-989-3270; www.booksofwonder.com; 18 W 18th St, btwn Fifth & Sixth Aves, Flatiron District; ⏰10am-7pm Mon-Sat, 11am-6pm Sun; 👪; S F/M to 14th St, L to 6th Ave) Devoted to children's and young-adult titles, this wonderful bookstore is a great place to take little ones on a rainy day, especially when a kids' author is giving a reading or a storyteller is on hand. There's an impressive range of NYC-themed picture books, plus a section dedicated to rare and vintage children's books and limited-edition children's-book artwork.

SPORTS & ACTIVITIES

JIVAMUKTI YOGA

Map p422 (☎212-353-0214; www.jivamuktiyoga.com; 841 Broadway, 2nd fl, btwn E 13th & 14th Sts, Union Square; classes $15-22; ⏰classes 7am-8:30pm Mon-Fri, 7:45am-8pm Sat & Sun; S 4/5/6, N/Q/R/W, L to 14th St-Union Sq) Considered *the* yoga spot in Manhattan, Jivamukti – in a 12,000-sq-ft locale on Union Sq – is a posh place for Vinyasa, Hatha and Ashtanga classes. The center's 'open' classes are suitable for both rookies and experienced practitioners, and there's an organic, **vegan cafe** on-site too. Gratuitous celebrity tidbit: Uma's little bro Dechen Thurman teaches classes here.

SOUL CYCLE CYCLING

Map p422 (☎212-208-1300; www.soul-cycle.com; 12 E 18th St, btwn Fifth Ave & Broadway, Union Square; classes $34; ⏰classes 7am-7:30pm Mon, 6am-7:30pm Tue-Thu, to 6pm Fri, 8:30am-4pm Sat, to 6pm Sun; S 4/5/6, N/Q/R, L to 14th St-Union Sq) Soul Cycle's wellness recipe (one part spinning class, one part dance party, one part therapy session) makes exercise an easy pill to swallow. There are no membership fees, so locals and tourists alike are welcome. You may even spot a celeb – Jake Gyllenhaal is known to take a class from time to time.

Midtown

MIDTOWN EAST | FIFTH AVENUE | MIDTOWN WEST & TIMES SQUARE

Neighborhood Top Five

❶ **Rockefeller Center** (p186) Playing spot the landmark at the jaw-dropping Top of the Rock observation deck, or sipping cocktails at grown-ups-only SixtyFive five floors down.

❷ **Museum of Modern Art** (p182) Hanging out with Picasso, Warhol and Rothko, or grabbing a spectacular bite to eat or a fine cocktail at this blockbuster museum.

❸ **Argosy** (p208) Perusing the racks for fine art prints, fascinating old used books, or just inhaling the ever-more-rare smell of an actual bookstore.

❹ **Jazz at Lincoln Center** (p205) Slurping martinis, gazing at the spectacular skyline and dabbling in a little hot evening…sax.

❺ Broadway (p178) Adding a little sparkle to life with a toe-tapping, soul-lifting Broadway show.

For more detail of this area see Map p424 and p428

Lonely Planet's Top Tip

Savoring Midtown's A-list restaurants without mortgaging the house is possible if you go for the prix-fixe lunch menu where available. Participants include Michelin-starred Le Bernardin (p198), which offers dishes featured in its evening menus. How far ahead you should book depends on the restaurant. It can sometimes be a one-month wait at Le Bernardin, which offers online reservations.

Best Places to Eat

- Le Bernardin (p198)
- O-ya (p196)
- Modern (p198)
- Totto Ramen (p197)
- Smith (p196)

For reviews, see p194.

Best Places to Drink

- Bar SixtyFive (p202)
- Rum House (p202)
- Jimmy's Corner (p203)
- Flaming Saddles (p203)
- Middle Branch (p202)
- The Campbell (p199)

For reviews, see p199.

Best Places for a Skyline View

- Top of the Rock (p191)
- Bar SixtyFive (p202)
- Empire State Building (p180)
- Robert (p199)
- Franklin D Roosevelt Four Freedoms Park (p190)

For reviews, see p180.

Explore Midtown

Midtown is big, brazen and best seen on foot, so slice it up and enjoy it bit by bit. The top end of Fifth Ave (around the 50s) makes for a fabled introduction, home to Tiffany & Co (p209), the Plaza Hotel (p341), the Museum of Modern Art (MoMA) (p182) and the Rockefeller Center's Top of the Rock (p191) observation decks. A day in Midtown East could easily incorporate rare manuscripts at the Morgan Library & Museum (p190), beaux-arts architecture at Grand Central Terminal (p184), the art-deco lobby of the Chrysler Building (p187) and a tour of the United Nations (p190). If it's a rainy day, explore the gilded New York Public Library (p191).

In Midtown West, design and fashion buffs head to the Museum of Arts & Design (p194) and the Museum at FIT (p194). Between the two is blinding Times Square (p177), most spectacular at night. Its residents include a TKTS Booth (p179) selling cut-price Broadway tickets. The queues are usually shortest after 5:30pm, though the clever buy their tickets at the less crowded South Street Seaport branch. Further west is Hell's Kitchen, packed with great eateries and gay venues.

Local Life

- **Dive bars** Stiff drinks, loosened ties and the whiff of nostalgia await at no-bull bars such as Jimmy's Corner (p203) and Rudy's Bar & Grill (p203).
- **Theater** Look beyond the glitz and kitsch of Broadway for innovative drama at Playwrights Horizons (p205) and Second Stage Theatre (p206).
- **Food** Join all walks of life at time-warped Cuban diner Margon (p197).

Getting There & Away

- **Subway** Times Sq-42nd St, Grand Central-42nd St and 34th St-Herald Sq are Midtown's main interchange stations. A/C/E and 1/2/3 lines run north–south through Midtown West. The 4/5/6 lines run north–south through Midtown East. The central B/D/F/M lines run up Sixth Ave, while N/Q/R/W lines follow Broadway. The 7, E and M lines offer some crosstown service.
- **Bus** Useful for the western and eastern extremes of Midtown. Routes include the M11 (north on Tenth Ave and south on Ninth Ave), the M101, M102 and M103 (north on Third Ave and south on Lexington Ave) and the M15 (north on First Ave and south on Second Ave). Crosstown buses run along 34th and 42nd Sts.
- **Train** Long-distance Amtrak and Long Island Rail Road (LIRR) trains terminate at Penn Station (p382). Jersey's PATH trains stop at 33rd St, while Metro-North commuter trains terminate at Grand Central Terminal (p184).

LUCIANO MORTULA / SHUTTERSTOCK ©

TOP SIGHT

TIMES SQUARE

Love it or hate it, the intersection of Broadway and Seventh Ave – better known as Times Square – is New York City's heart. It's a restless, hypnotic torrent of glittering lights, giant billboards and raw urban energy that doesn't seem to have an off switch: it's nearly as busy in the wee hours as it is in the afternoon.

Hyperactive Heart

This is the New York of collective fantasies – the place where Al Jolson 'makes it' in the 1927 film *The Jazz Singer,* where photojournalist Alfred Eisenstaedt famously captured a lip-locked sailor and nurse on V-J Day in 1945, and where Alicia Keys and Jay-Z waxed lyrically about the concrete jungle.

But for several decades, the dream here was a sordid one. The economic crash of the early 1970s led to a mass exodus of corporations from Times Square. Billboard niches went dark, stores shut and once-grand hotels were converted into SRO (single-room occupancy) dives. While the adjoining Theater District survived, its respectable playhouses shared the streets with porn cinemas and strip clubs. That all changed with tough-talking former mayor Rudolph Giuliani who, in the 1990s, boosted police numbers and lured in a wave of 'respectable' retail chains, restaurants and attractions. By the new millennium, Times Square had gone from X-rated to G-rated, drawing almost 40 million visitors annually.

DON'T MISS

- Taking in Times Square from the TKTS Booth steps
- Seeing a Broadway show
- Sipping a drink at R Lounge
- Staring in awe at the sheer dazzle of it all

PRACTICALITIES

- Map p428, E5
- www.timessquarenyc.org
- Broadway, at Seventh Ave
- Ⓢ N/Q/R/W, S, 1/2/3, 7 to Times Sq-42nd St

How the New York Times Made New Year's Eve

At the turn of the 20th century, Times Square was an unremarkable intersection known as Longacre Sq. This would change with a deal made between subway pioneer August Belmont and *New York Times* publisher Adolph Ochs. Heading construction of the city's

BRILL BUILDING

Standing at the northwest corner of Broadway and 49th St, the **Brill Building** (Map p428; 1619 Broadway, at W 49th St; S N/R/W to 49th St; 1, C/E to 50th St) is widely considered the most important generator of popular songs in the Western world. By 1962, over 160 music businesses were based here, from songwriters and managers to record companies and promoters. It was a one-stop shop for artists, who could craft a song, hire musicians, cut a demo and convince a producer without leaving the building. Among the legends who recorded here were Carol King, Bob Dylan, and Joni Mitchell. When they did leave the building, no doubt many would have headed to W 48th St, a street so packed with music stores it was famously dubbed Music Row.

KISS-IN

Alfred Eisenstaedt's famous 1945 photograph of a smooching US sailor and nurse is the inspiration behind the Times Square Kiss-In. Conducted every five years on the anniversary of the end of World War II, it sees hundreds of couples fill the square to re-create the scene famously captured on the cover of *LIFE* magazine.

first subway line (from Lower Manhattan to Harlem), Belmont astutely realized that a Midtown business hub would encourage use of the line (and maximize profit). Belmont approached Ochs, arguing that moving to Broadway and 42nd St would be a win-win for the broadsheet: an in-house subway station would mean faster distribution of the newspaper, but also more sales to the influx of commuters – and convinced mayor George B McClellan Jr to rename the square in honor of the broadsheet. In the winter of 1904–05, both the subway station and the *Times'* new headquarters at One Times Square made their debut.

In honor of the move, the *Times* hosted a New Year's Eve party in 1904, setting off fireworks from its skyscraper rooftop. By 1907, the square had become so built-up that fireworks were deemed a safety hazard, forcing the newspaper to come up with an alternative crowd-puller. It came in the form of a 700lb, wood-and-iron ball, lowered from the roof of One Times Square to herald the arrival of 1908.

Around one million people still gather in Times Square every New Year's Eve to watch a Waterford crystal ball descend from the building at midnight. Looking up, it's easy to forget that behind the current armor of billboards, the One Times Square building still exists. To see what it looked like in the days of Adolph Ochs, pay a visit to the beautiful DeWitt Wallace Periodical Room at the New York Public Library (p191), whose paintings by muralist Richard Haas include Times Square in the time of streetcars.

How Theater Came to Times Square

By the 1920s, Belmont's dream for Times Square had kicked into overdrive. Not only was it the heart of a growing commercial district, but it had overtaken Union Sq as New York's theater hub. The neighborhood's first playhouse was the long-gone Empire, opened in 1893 and located on Broadway between 40th and 41st Sts. Two years later, cigar manufacturer and part-time comedy scribe Oscar Hammerstein opened the Olympia, also on Broadway, before opening the Republic, now children's theater **New Victory** (Map p428; ☎646-223-3010; www.newvictory.org; 209 W 42nd St, btwn Seventh & Eighth Aves; ; S N/Q/R/W, S, 1/2/3, 7 to Times Sq-42nd St; A/C/E to 42nd St-Port Authority Bus Terminal), in 1900. This led to a string of new venues, among them the still-beating **New Amsterdam Theatre** (Aladdin; Map p428; ☎844-483-9008; www.new-amsterdam-theatre.com; 214 W 42nd St, btwn Seventh & Eighth Aves; ; S N/Q/R/W, S, 1/2/3, 7 to Times Sq-42nd St; A/C/E to 42nd St-Port Authority Bus

Terminal) and **Lyceum Theatre** (Map p428; www.shubert.nyc/theatres/lyceum; 149 W 45th St, btwn Sixth & Seventh Aves; Ⓢ N/R/W to 49th St).

The Broadway of the 1920s was well-known for its lighthearted musicals, commonly fusing vaudeville and music-hall traditions, and producing classic tunes like Cole Porter's 'Let's Misbehave.' At the same time, Midtown's theater district was evolving as a platform for new American dramatists. One of the greatest was Eugene O'Neill. Born in Times Square at the long-gone Barrett Hotel (1500 Broadway) in 1888, the playwright debuted many of his works here, including Pulitzer Prize winners *Beyond the Horizon* and *Anna Christie*. O'Neill's success on Broadway paved the way for other American greats like Tennessee Williams, Arthur Miller and Edward Albee – a surge of serious talent that led to the establishment of the annual Tony Awards in 1947.

Brilliant Broadway

The dozens of Broadway and off-Broadway theaters near Times Square run everything from blockbuster musicals to new and classic drama. Unless there's a specific show you're after, the best – and cheapest – way to score tickets in the area is at the **TKTS Booth** (Map p428; www.tdf.org/tkts; Broadway, at W 47th St; ⏲3-8pm Mon & Fri, 2-8pm Tue, 10am-2pm & 3-8pm Wed & Sat, 10am-2pm Thu, 11am-7pm Sun; Ⓢ N/Q/R/W, S, 1/2/3, 7 to Times Sq-42nd St), where you can line up and get same-day discounted tickets for top Broadway and off-Broadway shows. Smartphone users can download the free TKTS app, which offers rundowns of both Broadway and off-Broadway shows, as well as real-time updates of what's available on that day. Always have a back-up choice in case your first preference sells out, and never buy from scalpers on the street.

The TKTS Booth is an attraction in its own right, with its illuminated roof of 27 ruby-red steps rising a panoramic 16ft 1in above the 47th St sidewalk.

Today's Times Square

The iconic hourglass-shaped plaza is an unmissable homage to the hustle and bustle of big-city life. Nearly as bright at 2am as it is at noon, and always jammed with people, Times Square proves that New York truly is the city that never sleeps. If you don't stroll along this short section of Broadway and feel at least the tiniest twinge of awe, check your pulse. The massive billboards stretch half a skyscraper tall, and LED signs are lit for shows and performances. A mishmash of characters on the square (from the cute, like Elmo, to the noble, like the Statue of Liberty, to the popular, like Marvel action heroes, to the just plain bizarre, like Naked Cowboy) mix with the jumble of humanity from every corner of the globe. Walk around and in minutes you'll hear more languages being spoken than you even knew existed. It's the world's most famous spot to celebrate New Year's Eve to boot. If you have only five minutes to spend in all of New York City, you'll want to spend them here.

TOP SIGHT
EMPIRE STATE BUILDING

BENOIT DAOUST / SHUTTERSTOCK ©

The Chrysler Building may be prettier, and One World Trade Center may be taller, but the queen bee of the New York skyline remains the Empire State Building. NYC's tallest star has enjoyed close-ups in around 100 films, from *King Kong* to *Independence Day*. Heading up to the top is as quintessential as pastrami, rye and pickles at a delicatessen.

By the Numbers

The statistics are astounding: 10 million bricks, 60,000 tons of steel, 6400 windows and 328,000 sq ft of marble. Built on the original site of the Waldorf-Astoria, construction took a record-setting 410 days, using seven million hours of labor and costing a mere $41 million. It might sound like a lot, but it fell well below its $50 million budget (just as well, given it went up during the Great Depression). Coming in at 102 stories and 1472ft from top to bottom, the limestone phallus opened for business on May 1, 1931. Generations later, Deborah Kerr's words to Cary Grant in *An Affair to Remember* still ring true: 'It's the nearest thing to heaven we have in New York.'

Observation Decks

Unless you're Ann Darrow (the unfortunate woman caught in King Kong's grip), heading to the top of the Empire State Building should leave you beaming. There are two observation decks. The open-air 86th-floor deck offers an alfresco experience, with coin-operated telescopes for close-up glimpses of the metropolis in action. Further up, the enclosed 102nd-floor deck is New York's second-highest observation deck, trumped only by the observation deck at One World Trade Center. Needless to say, the views over the city's

DON'T MISS

- ➡ Observation decks at sunset
- ➡ Live jazz Thursday to Saturday nights

PRACTICALITIES

- ➡ Map p424, B7
- ➡ www.esbnyc.com
- ➡ 350 Fifth Ave, at W 34th St
- ➡ 86th-fl observation deck adult/child $34/27, incl 102nd-fl observation deck $54/47
- ➡ ⌚8am-2am, last elevators up 1:15am
- ➡ Ⓢ4, 6 to 33rd; Blue and Orange PATH to 33rd St; B/D/F/M, N/Q/R/W to 34th St-Herald Sq

five boroughs (and five neighboring states, weather permitting) are quite simply exquisite. The views from both decks are especially spectacular at sunset, when the city dons its nighttime cloak in dusk's afterglow. Alas, the passage to heaven will involve a trip through purgatory: the queues to the top are notorious.

An Ambitious Antenna

A locked, unmarked door on the 102nd-floor observation deck leads to one of New York's most outrageous pie-in-the-sky projects to date: a narrow terrace intended to dock zeppelins. Spearheading the dream was Alfred E Smith, who went from failed presidential candidate in 1928 to head honcho of the Empire State Building project. When architect William Van Alen revealed the secret spire of his competing Chrysler Building, Smith went one better, declaring that the top of the Empire State Building would sport an even taller mooring mast for transatlantic airships. While the plan looked good on paper, there were two (major) oversights: dirigibles require anchoring at both ends (not just at the nose as planned) and passengers (traveling in the zeppelin's gondola) cannot exit the craft through the giant helium-filled balloon. Regardless, it didn't stop them from trying. In September 1931, the *New York Evening Journal* threw sanity to the wind, managing to moor a zeppelin and deliver a pile of newspapers fresh out of Lower Manhattan. Years later, an aircraft met up with the building with tragic consequences: a B-25 bomber crashed into the 79th floor on a foggy day in 1945, killing 14 people.

LANGUAGE OF LIGHT

Since 1976, the building's top 30 floors have been floodlit in a spectrum of colors each night, reflecting seasonal and holiday hues. Famous combos include orange, white and green for St Patrick's Day; blue and white for Chanukah; white, red and green for Christmas; and the rainbow colors for Gay Pride weekend in June. For a full rundown of the color schemes, check the website.

SIBLING COMPARISONS

The Empire State Building was designed by the prolific architectural firm Shreve, Lamb and Harmon. According to legend, the skyscraper's conception began with a meeting between William Lamb and building co-financier John Jakob Raskob, during which Raskob propped up a No 2 pencil and asked, 'Bill, how high can you make it so that it won't fall down?' Shreve, Lamb and Harmon's other projects include the skyscraper at 500 Fifth Ave. To compare the soaring siblings, head to the northeast corner of Fifth Ave and 40th St.

DOSFOTOS / GETTY IMAGES ©

TOP SIGHT
MUSEUM OF MODERN ART

MoMA boasts more A-listers than an Oscars after-party: Van Gogh, Matisse, Picasso, Warhol, Rothko, Pollock and Bourgeois. Since its founding in 1929, the museum has amassed almost 200,000 artworks, documenting the creativity of the late 19th century through to today. For art buffs, it's Valhalla. For the uninitiated, it's a crash course in all that is addictive about art.

Collection Highlights

MoMA's permanent collection spans four levels. From time to time major temporary exhibitions may alter the order slightly, but prints, illustrated books and the unmissable Contemporary Galleries are usually on level two; architecture, design, drawings and photography are on level three; and painting and sculpture are on levels four and five. Many of the big hitters are on these last two levels, so tackle the museum from the top down before fatigue sets in. Must-sees include Van Gogh's *Starry Night,* Cézanne's *The Bather,* Picasso's *Les Demoiselles d'Avignon* and Henri Rousseau's *The Sleeping Gypsy,* not to mention iconic American works like Warhol's *Campbell's Soup Cans* and *Gold Marilyn Monroe,* Lichtenstein's equally poptastic *Girl with Ball* and Hopper's haunting *House by the Railroad.* Generally speaking, Mondays and Tuesdays are the best (ie least-crowded) days to visit, except on public holidays. Friday evenings and weekends can be incredibly crowded and frustrating.

DON'T MISS

- Van Gogh's *Starry Night*
- Edward Hopper's *House by the Railroad*
- Andy Warhol's *Gold Marilyn Monroe*
- Dining at Modern

PRACTICALITIES

- MoMA
- Map p428, G2
- ☎212-708-9400
- www.moma.org
- 11 W 53rd St, btwn Fifth & Sixth Aves
- adult/child 16yr & under $25/free, 4-9pm Fri free
- 10:30am-5:30pm Sat-Thu, to 9pm Fri
-
- S E/M to 5th Ave-53rd St; F to 57th; E/B/D to 7th Ave-57th St

Abstract Expressionism

One of the greatest strengths of MoMA's collections is abstract expressionism, a radical movement that emerged in New York in the 1940s and boomed a decade later. Defined by its penchant for irreverent individualism and monumentally scaled works, this so-called New York School helped turn the metropolis into *the* epicenter of Western contemporary art. Among the stars are Rothko's *Magenta, Black, Green on Orange,* Pollock's *One (Number 31, 1950)* and de Kooning's *Painting.*

Abby Aldrich Rockefeller Sculpture Garden

With architect Yoshio Taniguchi's acclaimed reconstruction of the museum in 2004 came the restoration of the Sculpture Garden to the original, larger vision of Philip Johnson's 1953 design. Johnson described the space as a 'sort of outdoor room,' and on warm, sunny days, it's hard not to think of it as a soothing alfresco lounge. One resident that can't seem to get enough of it is Aristide Maillol's *The River,* a larger-than-life female sculpture that featured in Johnson's original garden. She's in fine company too, with fellow works from greats including Matisse, Miró and Picasso. Sitting sneakily above the garden's eastern end is *Water Tower,* a translucent resin installation by British artist Rachel Whiteread. The Sculpture Garden is open free of charge from 9:30am to 10:15am daily, except in inclement weather and during maintenance.

Film Screenings

Not only a palace of visual art, **MoMA** (Map p428) screens an incredibly well-rounded selection of celluloid gems from its collection of over 22,000 films, including the works of the Maysles Brothers and every Pixar animation film ever produced. Expect anything from Academy Award–nominated documentary shorts and Hollywood classics to experimental works and international retrospectives. Best of all, your museum ticket will get you in for free.

Gallery Conversations

To delve a little deeper into MoMA's collection, join one of the museum's lunchtime talks and readings, which offer thought-provoking insight into specific works and exhibitions on view. The talks take place daily at 11:30am and 1:30pm. To check upcoming topics, visit the MoMA website and search for 'Gallery Sessions.'

TOP TIP

To maximize your time and create a plan of attack, download the museum's free smartphone app from the website beforehand. It's available in a number of different languages.

TAKE A BREAK

For communal tables and a casual vibe, nosh on Italian-inspired fare at **Cafe 2** (Map p428; 212-333-1299; www.momacafes.com; Museum of Modern Art, 11 W 53rd St, btwn Fifth & Sixth Aves, 2nd fl; sandwiches & salads $8-14, mains $12-18; 11am-5pm, to 7:30pm Fri; ; S E, M to 5th Ave-53rd St). For table service, opt for **Terrace Five** (Map p428; 212-333-1288; www.moma.org; Museum of Modern Art, 11 W 53rd St, btwn Fifth & Sixth Aves; mains $12-19; 11am-5pm Sat-Thu, to 7:30pm Fri; ; S E, M to 5th Ave-53rd St), which features an outdoor terrace overlooking the Sculpture Garden. If you're after high-end dining, book a table at the Michelin-starred Modern (p198).

FERRAN TRAITE SOLER / GETTY IMAGES ©

TOP SIGHT
GRAND CENTRAL TERMINAL

Threatened by the opening of the original Penn Station, transport magnate Cornelius Vanderbilt transformed his 19th-century Grand Central Depot into a 20th-century showpiece. Grand Central Terminal is New York's most breathtaking beaux-arts building. Grand Central's chandeliers, marble and historic bars and restaurants are a porthole into an era where train travel and romance were not mutually exclusive.

42nd Street Facade

Clad in Connecticut Stony Creek granite at its base and Indiana limestone on top, Grand Central's showpiece facade is crowned by America's greatest monumental sculpture, *The Glory of Commerce.* Designed by the French sculptor Jules-Félix Coutan, the piece was executed in Long Island City by local carvers Donnelly and Ricci. Once completed, it was hoisted up, piece by piece, in 1914. Its protagonist is a wing-capped Mercury, the Roman god of travel and commerce. To the left is Hercules in an unusually placid stance, while looking down on the mayhem of 42nd St is Minerva, the ancient guardian of cities. The clock beneath Mercury's foot contains the largest example of Tiffany glass in the world.

Main Concourse

Grand Central's trump card is more akin to a glorious ballroom than a thoroughfare. The marble floors are Tennessee pink, while the vintage ticket counters are Italian Bottocino marble. The vaulted ceiling is (quite literally) heavenly, its turquoise and gold-leaf mural depicting eight constellations...backwards. A mistake? Apparently not. Its French designer, painter Paul César

DON'T MISS

- Main beaux-arts facade
- Paul César Helleu's celestial mural
- Oysters under Rafael Guastavino's vaulted ceiling
- Cocktails at The Campbell
- A foodie trawl of Grand Central Market

PRACTICALITIES

- Map p424, C5
- www.grandcentralterminal.com
- 89 E 42nd St, at Park Ave
- 5:30am-2am
- S, 4/5/6, 7 to Grand Central-42nd St

Helleu, wished to depict the stars from God's point of view – from the out, looking in. The original, frescoed execution of Helleu's design was by New York-based artists J Monroe Hewlett and Charles Basing. Moisture damage saw it faithfully repainted (alas, not in fresco form) by Charles Gulbrandsen in 1944. By the 1990s, however, the mural was in ruins again. Enter renovation architects Beyer Blinder Belle, who restored the work, but left a tiny patch of soot (in the northwest corner) as testament to just what a fine job they did.

Whispering Gallery, Oyster Bar & Restaurant, & The Campbell

The vaulted landing directly below the bridge linking the Main Concourse and Vanderbilt Hall harbors one of Grand Central's quirkier features, the so-called Whispering Gallery. If you're in company, stand facing the walls diagonally opposite each other and whisper something. If your partner proposes (it happens a lot), chilled champagne is just through the door at the Grand Central Oyster Bar & Restaurant (p197). It's hugely atmospheric (with a vaulted tiled ceiling by Catalan-born engineer Rafael Guastavino), and you're best to stick to what it does exceptionally well: oysters. An elevator beside the restaurant leads up to another historic gem: the deliciously snooty bar The Campbell (p199).

Grand Central Market

Mouthwatering morsels await at the **Grand Central Market** (Map p424; www.grandcentralterminal.com/market; Lexington Ave, at 42nd St, Midtown East; ⏲7am-9pm Mon-Fri, 10am-7pm Sat, 11am-6pm Sun), a 240ft corridor lined with fresh produce and artisan treats. Stock up on anything from crusty bread and fruit tarts to artisanal cheese, chicken pot pies, Spanish quince paste, fruit and vegetables, and roasted coffee beans.

GUIDED TOURS

The **Municipal Art Society** (Map p424; ☎212-935-3960; www.mas.org; tours adult/child from $25/20) runs 75-minute walking tours through Grand Central daily at 12:30pm. Tours start at the information booth in the Main Concourse. The Grand Central Partnership (p210) leads free, 90-minute tours of the terminal and the surrounding neighborhood on Fridays at 12:30pm. Tours commence on the southwest corner of E 42nd St and Park Ave.

THE PRESIDENT'S SECRET

Hidden away under the Waldorf-Astoria hotel is Grand Central's little-known Platform 61. One person who did know it well was President Franklin D Roosevelt. Determined to hide his polio affliction from public view, Roosevelt made good use of the platform's freight elevator. Upon arrival at the station, the president would be driven straight out of his train carriage, along the platform and into the elevator...his public none the wiser.

TOP SIGHT
ROCKEFELLER CENTER

This 22-acre 'city within a city' debuted at the height of the Great Depression. Taking nine years to build, it was America's first multiuse retail, entertainment and office space – a modernist sprawl of buildings (14 of which are the original art-deco structures), outdoor plazas and big-name tenants. Highlights include the Top of the Rock observation deck and NBC Studio Tours.

Top of the Rock

There are views, and then there's *the* view from the Top of the Rock (p191). Crowning the GE Building, 70 stories above Midtown, its blockbuster vista includes one icon that you won't see from atop the Empire State Building – *the* Empire State Building. If possible, head up just before sunset to see the city transform from day to glittering night (if you're already in the area and the queues aren't long, purchase your tickets in advance to avoid the late-afternoon rush). Alternatively, if you don't have under-21s in tow, ditch Top of the Rock for the 65th-floor cocktail bar (p202), where the same spectacular views come with well-mixed drinks…at a cheaper price than the Top of the Rock admission.

Public Artworks

Rockefeller Center features the work of 30 great artists, commissioned around the theme 'Man at the Crossroads Looks Uncertainly but Hopefully at the Future.' Paul Manship contributed *Prometheus,* overlooking the sunken plaza, and *Atlas,* in front of the International Building (630 Fifth Ave). Isamu Noguchi's *News* sits above the entrance to the Associated Press Building (50 Rockefeller Plaza), while José Maria Sert's oil *American Progress* awaits in the lobby of the GE Building. The latter work replaced Mexican artist Diego Rivera's original painting, rejected by the Rockefellers for containing 'communist imagery.'

DON'T MISS

- Sky-high views from the observation deck
- Sunset cocktails at SixtyFive
- José Maria Sert's *American Progress* mural
- *Saturday Night Live* set (NBC Studio Tour)
- Skating at the Rink at Rockefeller Center

PRACTICALITIES

- Map p424, B3
- ☎212-332-6868
- www.rockefellercenter.com
- Fifth to Sixth Aves, btwn W 48th & 51st Sts
- S B/D/F/M to 47th-50th Sts-Rockefeller Center

NBC Studio Tour

TV comedy *30 Rock* gets its name from the GE Building, and the tower is the real-life home of NBC TV. One-hour NBC Studio Tours (p210) – enter from 1250 Sixth Ave – usually include a visit to Studio 8H, home of the iconic *Saturday Night Live* set. Tours have a strict 'no bathrooms policy' (empty your bladder beforehand!) and advance online reservations are strongly recommended. Across 49th St, opposite the plaza, is the glass-enclosed *NBC Today* show studio, broadcasting live from 7am to 11am on weekdays. If you fancy some screen time, head in by 6am to be at the front of the crowd.

Rockefeller Plaza

Come the festive season, Rockefeller Plaza is where you'll find New York's most famous Christmas tree. Ceremoniously lit just after Thanksgiving, it's a tradition that dates back to the 1930s, when construction workers set up a small tree on the site. In its shadow, **Rink at Rockefeller Center** (Map p424; ☎212-332-7654; www.therinkatrockcenter.com; Rockefeller Center, Fifth Ave, btwn W 49th & 50th Sts; adult $25-32, child $15, skate rental $12; ⏲8:30am-midnight mid-Oct–Apr; 👪; S B/D/F/M to 47th-50th Sts-Rockefeller Center) is the city's most famous ice-skating rink. Incomparably magical, it's also undeniably small and crowded. Opt for the first skating period (8:30am) to avoid a long wait. Come summer, the rink becomes a cafe.

TRAVELVIEW / SHUTTERSTOCK ©

TOP SIGHT

CHRYSLER BUILDING

The 77-floor Chrysler Building makes most other skyscrapers look like uptight geeks. Designed by William Van Alen in 1930, it's a dramatic fusion of art deco and Gothic aesthetics, adorned with stern steel eagles and topped by a spire that screams *Bride of Frankenstein*. Constructed as the headquarters for Walter P Chrysler and his automobile empire, the ambitious $15 million building remains one of New York's most poignant symbols.

The Lobby

Although the Chrysler Building has no restaurant or observation deck, its lobby is a lavish consolation prize. Bathed in an amber glow, its Jazz Age vintage is echoed in its architecture – dark, exotic African wood and marble, contrasted against the brash, man-made steel of industrial America. The elaborately veneered elevators are especially beautiful, their Egyptian lotus motifs made of inlaid Japanese ash, Oriental walnut and Cuban plum-pudding wood. When the doors open, you almost expect Bette Davis to strut on out. Above you is painter Edward Trumbull's ceiling mural *Transport and Human Endeavor*. Purportedly the world's largest mural at 97ft by 100ft, its depiction of buildings, airplanes and industrious workers on Chrysler assembly lines shows the golden promise of industry and modernity.

The Spire

Composed of seven radiating steel arches, the Chrysler Building's 185ft spire was as much a feat of vengeance as it was of modern engineering. Secretly constructed in the stairwell, the 200ft creation

DON'T MISS

- *Transport and Human Endeavor* lobby ceiling mural
- William Van Alen's spire
- Facade ornamentation
- View from Third Ave-44th St and the Empire State Building
- René Chambellan and Jacques Delamarre's reliefs, Chanin Building

PRACTICALITIES

- Map p424, C5
- 405 Lexington Ave, at E 42nd St
- lobby 8am-6pm Mon-Fri
- S S, 4/5/6, 7 to Grand Central-42nd St

(dubbed 'the vertex') was raised through a false roof and anchored into place in an impressive 1½ hours. The novel reveal shocked and outraged architect H Craig Severance, who had hoped that his Manhattan Company skyscraper on Wall St would become the world's tallest building. The fait accompli was especially humiliating given that Severance had personally fallen out with architect William Van Alen, a former colleague. Karmic retribution may have been served with the 1931 debut of the even-taller Empire State Building, but Van Alen's crowning glory endures as a showstopping symbol of 20th-century daring.

The Gargoyles

If the spire is the building's diva, the gargoyles are its supporting cast. Pairs of gleaming steel American eagles look ready to leap from the corners of the 61st floor, giving the building a brooding, Gothic edge. Further down on the 31st floor, giant winged hubcaps echo the Chrysler radiator caps of the late 1920s. For a dramatic view of the gargoyles from street level, head to the corner of Lexington Ave and 43rd St and look up.

Chanin Building: A Neighboring Gem

Across the street from the Chrysler Building, on the southwest corner of Lexington Ave and 42nd St, stands another art-deco gem: the **Chanin Building** (Map p424; 122 E 42nd St, at Lexington Ave, Midtown East; S S, 4/5/6, 7 to Grand Central-42nd St). Completed in 1929, the 56-story brick and terra-cotta tower is the work of unlicensed architect Irwin S Chanin, who teamed up with the legally recognized firm Sloan & Robertson to achieve his dream. Yet the star attraction here is the work of René Chambellan and Jacques Delamarre, creators of the exquisite bands of relief at the building's base. While birds and fish create a sense of whimsy in the lower band, the upper band of terra-cotta steals the show with its rich botanical carvings.

CREMASTER 3

The Chrysler Building's lobby and crown feature in *Cremaster 3* (2002), an avant-garde film by award-winning visual artist and filmmaker Matthew Barney. The third installment of an epic five-part film project, it delivers a surreal take on the skyscraper's construction, fusing Irish mythology with genre elements from both zombie and gangster films. To read more about the project, check out www.cremaster.net.

THE CLOUD CLUB

Nestled at the top of the Chrysler Building between 1930 and 1979 was the famed Cloud Club. Its regulars included tycoon John D Rockefeller, publishing magnate Condé Montrose and boxing legend Gene Tunney. The art deco-meets-Hunting Lodge hangout from floors 66 to 68 featured a lounge and dining rooms (including a private room for Walter Chrysler), as well as kitchens, a barber shop and a locker room with sneak cabinets for hiding booze during Prohibition. Chrysler merrily boasted about having the highest toilet in town.

TOP SIGHT
ROOSEVELT ISLAND

Roosevelt Island, a 2-mile sliver of land in the East River between Manhattan and Queens, has an uninteresting residential center and has long been ignored by visitors and locals alike – except for quick trips on its aerial tram for the views. But the stunning Franklin D Roosevelt Four Freedoms Park (p190) at the island's southern tip now offers a good reason to go.

DON'T MISS

- Franklin D Roosevelt Four Freedoms Park
- Viewing platform
- Aerial tram ride
- Renwick Smallpox Hospital ruins

PRACTICALITIES

- Map p424, G1
- S F to Roosevelt Island, from Roosevelt Island Tramway Station, 2nd Ave cnr E 60th St

Early Days

The Canarsee Native Americans called this tiny spit of land 'Minnahanonck' (Nice Island), which they sold as part of a larger parcel to the Dutch in 1633; from then it was used for livestock farming, and called 'Varckens Eylandt' (Hog Island). When the British took control of the area, the island was granted to the Sheriff of New York, John Manning. After his death ownership transferred to his stepdaughter, Mrs Blackwell, and the island was called Blackwell's Island from the 1680s onward. In 1828 it was purchased by the city government, which used it to house various 'undesirables' by building a prison and medical facilities, including a mental health hospital – the **Octagon** tower at its north end still stands as part of a residential complex – and the **Renwick Smallpox Hospital**, whose ruined, eerie-looking facade still stands in the island's southern half. By the mid-20th century most of the institutions on the now-called Welfare Island had been closed down or abandoned. In the 1970s, the city began redeveloping the island by renaming it in honor of President Franklin D Roosevelt and building a series of cookie-cutter brutalist apartment buildings along the island's only road. For years, the only thing Roosevelt Island really had to offer visitors were the views of Manhattan and the picturesque ruins of the old smallpox hospital.

Remembering a President

The island finally hit the architectural map in 2012, when a 4-acre memorial park to President Franklin D Roosevelt opened on its southern tip. Designed by architect Louis Kahn in 1972, its construction stalled later in the decade when Kahn died and New York City almost went into bankruptcy. Despite the long delay, the park was built just as Kahn had originally envisioned, with only minor tweaks. A tapered, V-shaped lawn lined with linden trees leads down to the island's tip, where visitors arrive at a small, open viewing platform with huge slabs of North Carolina granite to either side. At the entrance is a giant bronze bust of President Roosevelt, with his famous 'Four Freedoms' speech carved into the slab of granite behind him. It's a peaceful and sober monument, with many subtle hidden details.

A High-Tech Future

In 2017, a fresh future for the island began with the opening of the first phase of a new advanced engineering school called Cornell Tech, a joint venture between Ivy League school Cornell University and the Technion – Israel Institute of Technology in Haifa. The $2 billion, high-tech campus, which is being built with some of the most energy-efficient technology in the world, is planned for completion via two further stages by 2037. It will eventually span 12 acres and is promised to create 28,000 new jobs and billions of dollars in economic benefits for the city.

SIGHTS

Midtown East

Midtown dazzles with several big-name sights, among them the mega-screens and razzle of Times Square, the modern-art temple MoMA, the observation decks of the Empire State Building and Rockefeller Center, and tours of the diplomatic United Nations. In their shadow lurk a number of lesser-known cultural options, from the marvelous manuscripts and interiors of the Morgan Library and Museum, to no-fee, fashion-focused Museum at FIT and neo-Gothic comeback kid, St Patrick's Cathedral.

GRAND CENTRAL TERMINAL HISTORIC BUILDING
See p184.

CHRYSLER BUILDING HISTORIC BUILDING
See p187.

ROOSEVELT ISLAND AREA
See p189.

★MORGAN LIBRARY & MUSEUM MUSEUM
Map p424 (212-685-0008; www.themorgan.org; 225 Madison, at E 36th St, Midtown East; adult/child $20/free; 10:30am-5pm Tue-Thu, to 9pm Fri, 10am-6pm Sat, 11am-6pm Sun; S 6 to 33rd St) Incorporating the mansion once owned by steel magnate JP Morgan, this sumptuous cultural center houses a phenomenal array of manuscripts, tapestries and books (with no fewer than three Gutenberg Bibles). Adorned with Italian and Dutch Renaissance artworks, Morgan's personal study is only trumped by his personal library (East Room), an extraordinary, vaulted space adorned with walnut bookcases, a 16th-century Dutch tapestry and zodiac-themed ceiling. The center's rotating exhibitions are often superb, as are its regular cultural events.

UNITED NATIONS HISTORIC BUILDING
Map p424 (212-963-4475; http://visit.un.org; visitors gate First Ave at 46th St, Midtown East; guided tour adult/child $20/13, children under 5yr not admitted, grounds access Sat & Sun free; tours 9am-4:45pm Mon-Fri, visitor center also open 10am-4:45pm Sat & Sun; S S, 4/5/6, 7 to Grand Central-42nd St) Welcome to the headquarters of the UN, a worldwide organization overseeing international law, international security and human rights. While the Le Corbusier-designed Secretariat building is off-limits, one-hour guided tours do cover the restored General Assembly Hall, Security Council Chamber, Trusteeship Council Chamber and Economic and Social Council (ECOSOC) Chamber, as well as exhibitions about the UN's work and artworks given by member states. Weekday tours must be booked online and photo ID is required to enter the site.

Free walk-in access to the visitor center only is permitted on weekends (enter at 43rd Street). To the north of the UN complex, which technically stands on international territory, is a serene park featuring Henry Moore's *Reclining Figure,* as well as several other peace-themed sculptures.

MUSEUM OF SEX MUSEUM
Map p424 (212-689-6337; www.museumofsex.com; 233 Fifth Ave, at 27th St; adult $17.50, $20.50 Sat & Sun; 10am-9pm Sun-Thu, 11am-11pm Fri & Sat; S N/R to 23rd St) Get the lowdown on anything from online fetishes to homosexual necrophilia in the mallard duck at this slick ode to all things hot and sweaty. The rotating program of temporary exhibitions has included explorations of cyber sex and retrospectives of controversial artists, while the permanent collection showcases the likes of erotic lithographs and awkward anti-onanism devices.

JAPAN SOCIETY CULTURAL CENTER
Map p424 (www.japansociety.org; 333 E 47th St, btwn First & Second Aves, Midtown East; adult/child $15/free, 6-9pm Fri free; noon-7pm Tue-Thu, to 9pm Fri, 11am-5pm Sat & Sun; S S, 4/5/6, 7 to Grand Central-42nd St) Elegant exhibitions of both traditional and contemporary Japanese art, textiles and design are the main draw at this calming cultural center, complete with indoor gardens and water features. Its theater hosts a range of films and dance and theatrical performances, while those wanting to dig deeper can browse through 14,000 volumes in the research library or attend one of its myriad lectures or workshops.

FRANKLIN D ROOSEVELT FOUR FREEDOMS PARK MEMORIAL
Map p424 (212-204-8831; www.fdrfourfreedomspark.org; Roosevelt Island; 9am-7pm Wed-Mon Apr-Sep, to 5pm Wed-Mon Oct-Mar; S F to Roosevelt Island, Roosevelt Island) FREE Dramatic design, presidential inspiration and a refreshing perspective on the New York skyline make for an arresting trio at the Franklin D Roosevelt Four Freedoms

Park. Clinging to the southern tip of sinuous Roosevelt Island on the East River, this remarkable monument honors America's 32nd president and his State of the Union speech of 1941. In it, Franklin D Roosevelt addressed his desire for a world based upon four essential human freedoms: freedom of speech, freedom of worship, freedom from want and freedom from fear. Designed by renowned architect Louis Kahn in 1973, the monument would only reach completion in 2012, 38 years after Kahn's death.

The wait was worth it. Kahn's luminous granite vision is breathtakingly cinematic in its scale and effect. A sweep of grand, stark steps lead up to a sloping triangular lawn. Fringed by linden trees, the lawn gently spills down to a bronze bust of Roosevelt by American sculptor Jo Davidson. Framing the sculpture is a granite wall, hand engraved with Roosevelt's rousing speech. The wall also serves to separate the bust from 'The Room,' a contemplative granite terrace clinging to the very tip of the island. The combination of lapping waves and hovering skyline are utterly mesmerizing.

Although the F subway line will get you to Roosevelt Island, it's much more fun catching the aerial **tramway car** (☎212-832-4583; http://rioc.ny.gov/tramtransportation.htm; 60th St, at Second Ave; 1-way fare $2.50; ⏲every 15 min 6am-2am Sun-Thu, to 3am Fri & Sat; Ⓢ N/Q/R, 4/5/6 to Lexington Ave-59th St), which glides above the East River. The monument is a 15-minute walk south of both the Roosevelt Island tramway car and subway stations.

SOUTHPOINT PARK PARK, RUINS

Map p424 (☎212-832-4540; East Rd, Roosevelt Island; ⏲6am-10pm; Ⓢ F to Roosevelt Island, 🚊Roosevelt Island) At the southernmost point on Roosevelt Island – which sits in the East River just off midtown Manhattan – is a grassy preserve with breathtaking views and a unique piece of New York history: the crumbling walls and turrets of the **Renwick Smallpox Hospital Ruin**, said to be the most haunted location in the city. It's a must-see for history buffs.

Fifth Avenue

EMPIRE STATE BUILDING HISTORIC BUILDING

See p180.

ROCKEFELLER CENTER HISTORIC BUILDING

See p186.

TOP OF THE ROCK VIEWPOINT

Map p424 (☎212-698-2000, toll free 877-692-7625; www.topoftherocknyc.com; 30 Rockefeller Plaza, entrance on W 50th St, btwn Fifth & Sixth Aves; adult/child $37/31, sunrise/sunset combo $54/43; ⏲8am-midnight, last elevator at 11pm; Ⓢ B/D/F/M to 47th-50th Sts-Rockefeller Center) Designed in homage to ocean liners and opened in 1933, this 70th-floor open-air observation deck sits atop the **GE Building**, the tallest skyscraper at the Rockefeller Center. Top of the Rock beats the Empire State Building (p180) on several levels: it's less crowded, has wider observation decks (both outdoor and indoor) and offers a view of the Empire State Building itself.

NEW YORK PUBLIC LIBRARY HISTORIC BUILDING

Map p424 (Stephen A Schwarzman Building; ☎212-340-0863; www.nypl.org; Fifth Ave, at W 42nd St; ⏲8am-8pm Mon & Thu, 8am-9pm Tue & Wed, 8am-6pm Fri, 10am-6pm Sat, 10am-5pm Sun, guided tours 11am & 2pm Mon-Sat, 2pm Sun; Ⓢ B/D/F/M to 42nd St-Bryant Park, 7 to 5th Ave) FREE Loyally guarded by 'Patience' and 'Fortitude' (the marble lions overlooking Fifth Ave), this beaux-arts show-off is one of NYC's best free attractions. When dedicated in 1911, New York's flagship library ranked as the largest marble structure ever built in the US, and to this day its recently restored **Rose Main Reading Room** steals the breath away with its lavish coffered ceiling. It's only one of several glories inside, among them the **DeWitt Wallace Periodical Room**.

This extraordinary building is home to precious manuscripts by just about every author of note in the English language, including an original copy of the Declaration of Independence and a Gutenberg Bible. The Map Division is equally astounding, with a collection that holds some 431,000 maps, 16,000 atlases and books on cartography, dating from the 16th century to the present. To properly explore this mini-universe of books, art and architectural flourishes, join a **free guided tour** (departing from Astor Hall) or grab a free audioguide from the information desk (also in Astor Hall).

Across its branches, the NYPL keeps brains lubricated with its string of lectures, seminars and workshops, with topics ranging from contemporary art to the writings of Jane Austen. You'll find some of the best at the main branch on 42nd St. You can search all happenings at the library's website.

SKYSCRAPERS IN MIDTOWN

Midtown's skyline is more than just the Empire State and Chrysler Buildings, with enough modernist and postmodernist beauties to satisfy the wildest of high-rise dreams. Here are six of Midtown's finest.

Seagram Building (1956–58; 514ft) A textbook regular, the 38-floor **Seagram Building** (Map p424; 100 E 53rd St, at Park Ave, Midtown East; S 6 to 51st St; E, M to Fifth Ave-53rd St) is one of the world's finest examples of the international style. Its lead architect, Ludwig Mies van der Rohe, was recommended for the project by Arthur Drexler, then-curator of architecture at MoMA. With its low podium, colonnade-like pillars and bronze cladding, Mies cleverly references classical Greek influences.

Lever House (1950–52; 306ft) Upon its debut in 1952, 21-story **Lever House** (Map p424; 390 Park Ave, btwn 53rd & 54th Sts, Midtown East; S E, M to 5th Ave-53rd St) was at the height of the cutting-edge. The UN Secretariat Building was the only other skyscraper to feature a glass skin, an innovation that would redefine urban architecture. The building's form was equally bold: two counter-posed rectangular shapes consisting of a slender tower atop a low-rise base. The open courtyard features marble benches envisioned by Japanese American sculptor Isamu Noguchi, while the lobby exhibits contemporary art especially commissioned for the space.

Citigroup Center (1974–77; 915ft) With its striking triangular roof and candy-like striped facade, Hugh Stubbins' 59-story **Citigroup Center** (Map p424; 139 E 53rd St, at Lexington Ave, Midtown East; S 6 to 51st St; E, M to Lexington Ave-53rd St) signaled a shift from the flat-roof sobriety of the international style. Even more dramatic is the building's base, which is cut away at the four corners, leaving the tower to perch dramatically on a cross-shaped footing. This unusual configuration allowed for the construction of St Peter's Lutheran Church on the site's northwest corner, which replaced the original neo-Gothic church demolished during the skyscraper's construction.

Hearst Tower (2003–06; 597ft) This 46-floor **tower** (Map p428; 949 Eighth Ave, btwn 56th & 57th Sts, Midtown West; S A/C, B/D, 1 to 59th St-Columbus Circle) is one of NYC's most creative works of contemporary architecture, not to mention one of its greenest; around 90% of its structural steel is from recycled sources. Designed by Foster & Partners, its diagonal grid of trusses evokes a jagged glass-and-steel honeycomb. The tower rises above the hollowed-out core of John Urban's 1928 cast-stone Hearst Magazine Building and the lobby is home to Richard Long's *Riverlines*, a 70ft mural made using mud from New York's Hudson River and England's River Avon.

Bank of America Tower (2004–09; 1200ft) Designed by Cook & Fox Architects, the 58-floor **Bank of America Tower** (One Bryant Park; Map p428; Sixth Ave, btwn W 42nd & 43rd Sts; S B/D/F/M to 42nd St-Bryant Park) is famed for its striking crystal shape, piercing 255ft spire, and enviable green credentials. The stats are impressive: a clean-burning, on-site cogeneration plant providing around 65% of the tower's annual electricity requirements; CO_2-detecting air filters that channel oxygenated air where needed; and even destination-dispatch elevators designed to avoid empty-car trips. The role-model skyscraper, the sixth tallest in North America, was awarded 'Best Tall Building in America' at the Council on Tall Buildings & Urban Habitat awards in 2010.

432 Park Avenue (2011–15; 1396ft) It's a case of 'thin is in' with the arrival of 1396ft-tall, $1.3 billion **432 Park Avenue** (Map p424; 432 Park Ave, btwn 56th & 57th Sts, Midtown East; S N/Q/R to Lexington Ave-59th St), a residential tower by Uruguayan architect Rafael Viñoly. Its clean, white, cubic facade inspired by a 1905 trash can by Austrian designer Josef Hoffman, the tower rises above the Midtown skyline like an impossibly slim square tube. It's currently the city's second-tallest building, upstaged only by One World Trade Center. Measured to actual roof height, however, it's actually 28ft taller than its spire-crowned downtown rival.

BRYANT PARK PARK

Map p424 (☎212-768-4242; www.bryantpark.org; 42nd St, btwn Fifth & Sixth Aves; ⊙7am-midnight Mon-Fri, to 11pm Sat & Sun Jun-Sep, shorter hrs rest of yr; Ⓢ B/D/F/M to 42nd St-Bryant Park; 7 to 5th Ave) European coffee kiosks, alfresco chess games, summer film screenings and winter ice skating: it's hard to believe that this leafy oasis was dubbed 'Needle Park' in the '80s. Nestled behind the beaux arts New York Public Library building, it's a whimsical spot for a little time-out from the Midtown madness. Fancy taking a beginner Italian language, yoga or juggling class, joining a trivia contest or signing up for a birding tour? The park offers a daily smorgasbord of quirky activities.

Among the park's attractions is the French-inspired, Brooklyn-made **Le Carrousel** (Map p424; W 40th St, at Sixth Ave; ride $3; ⊙11am-9pm Jan, to 8pm Jun-Oct, reduced hr rest of yr), offering rides. Frequent special events include the Bryant Park Summer Film Festival, popular with post-work crowds lugging cheese-and-wine picnics. Come Christmastime, the place becomes a winter wonderland, with holiday gift vendors lining the park's edge and a popular ice-skating rink sprouting in its middle. Lovely **Bryant Park Grill** (Map p424; ☎212-840-6500; www.arkrestaurants.com/bryant_park; mains $19-47; ⊙11:30am-3:30pm & 5-11pm) is the site of many a New York wedding come springtime, and when it's not closed for a private event, the patio bar is a perfect spot for a twilight cocktail. Next door you'll find its more casual alfresco sibling **Bryant Park Café** (Map p424; ☎212-840-6500; www.arkrestaurants.com/bryant_park; mains $15-45; ⊙7am-10pm mid-Apr–Nov), a much-loved spot for after-five catch-ups.

ST PATRICK'S CATHEDRAL CATHEDRAL

Map p424 (☎212-753-2261; www.saintpatrickscathedral.org; Fifth Ave, btwn E 50th & 51st Sts; ⊙6:30am-8:45pm; Ⓢ B/D/F/M to 47th-50th Sts-Rockefeller Center, E/M to 5th Ave-53rd St) Still shining after a $200 million restoration in 2015, America's largest Catholic cathedral graces Fifth Ave with Gothic Revival splendor. Built at a cost of nearly $2 million during the Civil War, the building did not originally include the two front spires; those were added in 1888. Step inside to appreciate the Louis Tiffany–designed **altar** and Charles Connick's stunning **Rose Window**, the latter gleaming above a 7000-pipe church organ. Walk-in **guided tours** are available several days a week; check the website for details.

A **basement crypt** behind the altar contains the coffins of every New York cardinal and the remains of Pierre Touissant, a champion of the poor and the first African American up for sainthood.

PALEY CENTER FOR MEDIA CULTURAL CENTER

Map p424 (☎212-621-6800; www.paleycenter.org; 25 W 52nd St, btwn Fifth & Sixth Aves; suggested donation adult/child $10/5; ⊙noon-6pm Wed & Fri-Sun, to 8pm Thu; Ⓢ E, M to 5th Ave-53rd St) This pop culture repository offers more than 160,000 TV and radio programs from around the world on its computer catalog. Reliving your favorite TV shows on one of the center's consoles is sheer bliss on a rainy day, as are the excellent, regular screenings, festivals, speakers and performers.

Midtown West & Times Square

TIMES SQUARE AREA

See p177.

MUSEUM OF MODERN ART MUSEUM

See p182.

RADIO CITY MUSIC HALL HISTORIC BUILDING

Map p428 (www.radiocity.com; 1260 Sixth Ave, at W 51st St; tours adult/child $27/20; ⊙tours 9:30am-5pm; 👪; Ⓢ B/D/F/M to 47th-50th Sts-Rockefeller Center) This spectacular Moderne movie palace was the brainchild of vaudeville producer Samuel Lionel 'Roxy' Rothafel. Never one for understatement, Roxy launched his venue on December 23, 1932 with an over-the-top extravaganza that included camp dance troupe the Roxyettes (mercifully renamed the Rockettes). **Guided tours** (75 minutes) of the sumptuous interiors include the glorious auditorium, Witold Gordon's classically inspired mural *History of Cosmetics* in the Women's Downstairs Lounge, and the *très* exclusive VIP Roxy Suite.

As far as catching a show here goes, be warned: the vibe doesn't quite match the theater's glamour these days. That said, there are often some fabulous talents in the lineup, with past performers including Lauryn Hill, Rufus Wainwright, Aretha Franklin and Dolly Parton. And while the word 'Rockettes' provokes eye rolling from most self-consciously cynical New Yorkers, fans of glitz and kitsch might just get a thrill from the troupe's annual **Christmas Spectacular**.

Same-day tickets are available at the candy store beside the Sixth Ave entrance, though it's worth considering paying the extra $5.50 to book your ticket online given that tours can sell out quickly, particularly on rainy days.

MUSEUM OF ARTS & DESIGN MUSEUM

Map p428 (MAD; ☎212-299-7777; www.madmuseum.org; 2 Columbus Circle, btwn Eighth Ave & Broadway; adult/18yr & under $16/free, by donation 6-9pm Thu; ⊙10am-6pm Tue-Sun, to 9pm Thu; ♿; Ⓢ A/C, B/D, 1 to 59th St-Columbus Circle) MAD offers four floors of superlative design and handicrafts, from blown glass and carved wood to elaborate metal jewelry. Its temporary exhibitions are top-notch and innovative: one past show explored the art of scent. Usually on the first Sunday of the month, professional artists lead family-friendly explorations of the galleries, followed by hands-on workshops inspired by the current exhibitions. The museum gift shop sells some fantastic contemporary jewelry, while the 9th-floor restaurant/bar Robert (p199) is perfect for panoramic cocktails.

INTREPID SEA, AIR & SPACE MUSEUM MUSEUM

Map p428 (☎877-957-7447; www.intrepidmuseum.org; Pier 86, Twelfth Ave at W 46th St; adult/child $33/21, discounted for NYC residents; ⊙10am-5pm Mon-Fri, to 6pm Sat & Sun Apr-Oct, 10am-5pm Mon-Sun Nov-Mar; ♿; 🚌westbound M42, M50 to 12th Ave, Ⓢ A/C/E to 42nd St-Port Authority Bus Terminal) In WWII, the USS *Intrepid* survived both a bomb and kamikaze attacks. Thankfully, this hulking aircraft carrier is now a lot less stressed, playing host to a multimillion-dollar interactive military museum that tells its tale through videos, historical artifacts and frozen-in-time living quarters. The flight deck features fighter planes and military helicopters, which might inspire you to try the museum's high-tech flight simulators. Topical rotating exhibits are also part of the fun.

The rides include the G Force Encounter, allowing you to experience the thrill of flying a supersonic jet plane, and the Transporter FX, a flight simulator promising six full minutes of a 'complete sensory overload.' The museum is also home to the guided-missile submarine *Growler* (not for the claustrophobic), a decommissioned Concorde plane, and the former NASA space shuttle *Enterprise*.

MUSEUM AT FIT MUSEUM

Map p428 (☎212-217-4558; www.fitnyc.edu/museum; 227 W 27th St, at Seventh Ave, Midtown West; ⊙noon-8pm Tue-Fri, 10am-5pm Sat; Ⓢ 1 to 28th St) FREE The Fashion Institute of Technology (FIT) lays claim to one of the world's richest collections of garments, textiles and accessories. At last count, there were more than 50,000 items spanning the 18th century to the present day. The school's museum features innovative, rotating exhibitions showcasing both permanent-collection items and on-loan curiosities. Exhibitions aside, the museum also hosts film screenings and talks, including with prolific fashion designers and critics.

HERALD SQUARE SQUARE

Map p428 (cnr Broadway, Sixth Ave & 34th St; Ⓢ B/D/F/M, N/Q/R to 34th St-Herald Sq) This crowded convergence of Broadway, Sixth Ave and 34th St is best known as the home of mammoth department store Macy's (p209), where you can still ride some of the original wooden elevators. As part of the city's 'traffic-free Times Square' plan, you can also (try to) relax in a lawn chair outside the store, slap-bang in the middle of traffic-clogged Broadway. And Koreatown's restaurants are only a block to the east.

EATING

Despite the mediocre chains and tourist-trap restaurants – mostly around Times Square and the Theater District – Midtown is no culinary slouch, with almost 20 Michelin-starred greats. You can tuck into wallet-friendly *chingudi jhola* (spicy prawn curry) in the 'Curry Hill' district (Lexington Ave, roughly between 28th and 33rd Sts) or cult-status ramen on W 52nd St. Perhaps you're more in the mood for cheeseburgers at a speakeasy burger joint, or Cubano sandwiches at a retro diner? Then there are Ninth and Tenth Aves in Hell's Kitchen, constantly evolving, see-and-be-seen, sip-and-sup strips frequented by locals. Ready, set, chomp!

Midtown East & Fifth Avenue

ESS-A-BAGEL DELI $

Map p424 (☎212-980-1010; www.ess-a-bagel.com; 831 Third Ave, at 51st St, Midtown East; bagels sandwiches $3-4.55; ⊙6am-9pm Mon-Fri, to 5pm Sat &

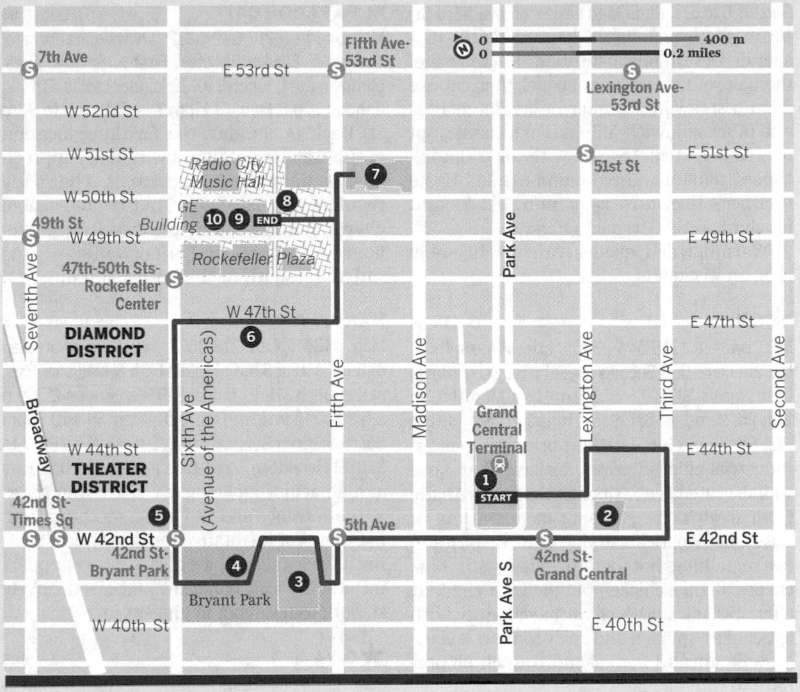

Neighborhood Walk
Iconic Architecture

START GRAND CENTRAL TERMINAL
FINISH ROCKEFELLER CENTER
LENGTH 1.8 MILES; 3½ HOURS

Start your Midtown saunter at beaux-arts marvel ❶ **Grand Central Terminal** (p184). Stargaze at the Main Concourse ceiling and pick up a gourmet treat at the Grand Central Market.

Exit onto Lexington Ave and walk one block east along 44th St to Third Ave for a view of the ❷ **Chrysler Building** (p187). Walk down Third Ave to 42nd St, turn right and slip into the Chrysler Building's sumptuous art-deco lobby, lavished with exotic inlaid wood, marble and purportedly the world's largest ceiling mural.

At the corner of 42nd St and Fifth Ave stands the stately ❸ **New York Public Library** (p191). Step inside the library to peek at its spectacular Rose Reading Room, then nibble on your market treat in neighboring ❹ **Bryant Park** (p193).

On the northwest corner of 42nd St and Sixth Ave soars the ❺ **Bank of America Tower** (p192), NYC's fourth-tallest building and one of its most ecofriendly.

Head north along Sixth Ave to 47th St. Here, between Sixth and Fifth Aves, is the ❻ **Diamond District**, home to more than 2600 independent businesses selling diamonds, gold, pearls, gemstones and watches.

Walk toward Fifth Ave, taking in its swirl of Jewish traders. Turn left into Fifth Ave and admire the splendor of ❼ **St Patrick's Cathedral** (p193), its impressive rose window the work of American artist Charles Connick.

Your last stop is ❽ **Rockefeller Center** (p186), a magnificent complex of art-deco skyscrapers and sculptures. Enter between 49th and 50th Sts to the main plaza and its golden statue of Prometheus. After paying your respects, consider two options: either head to the 70th floor of the GE Building for an unforgettable vista at the ❾ **Top of the Rock** (p191) observation deck (book your tickets online to avoid the longest queues) or, if it's after 5pm, head straight up to cocktail bar ❿ **SixtyFive** (p202), where you can toast while scanning the skyline.

Sun; S 6 to 51st St; E/M to Lexington Ave-53rd St) Fresh, toothsome bagels have made this kosher deli a veritable institution. Tell the bagel monger your preference of bagel, then choose from a sprawling counter of cream cheeses and other sandwich fillings. For a classic, opt for scallion cream cheese with lox (salmon), capers, tomato and red onion ($4.55). If the weather's fine, turn right into 51st St and lunch in pretty Greenacre Park.

Warning: deli queues can get insanely long on weekends.

★SMITH
AMERICAN $$

Map p424 (212-644-2700; http://thesmithrestaurant.com; 956 Second Ave, at 51st St, Midtown East; mains $17-32; 7:30am-11pm Mon-Thu, to 1am Fri, 9am-1am Sat, 9am-11pm Sun; ; S 6 to 51st St) This chic, bustling brasserie has an industrial-chic interior, sociable bar and well-executed grub. Much of the food is made from scratch, the seasonal menus a mix of nostalgic American and Italian inspiration (we're talking hot potato chips with blue cheese fondue, chicken pot pie with cheddar chive biscuit, and Sicilian baked eggs with artichokes, spinach and spicy tomato sauce).

Book ahead for weekend brunch or prepare to wait.

DHABA
INDIAN $$

Map p424 (212-679-1284; www.dhabanyc.com; 108 Lexington Ave, btwn 27th & 28th Sts; mains $13-24; noon-midnight Mon-Thu, noon-1am Fri & Sat, noon-10:30pm Sun; ; S 6 to 28th St) Murray Hill (aka Curry Hill) has no shortage of subcontinental bites, but funky Dhaba packs one serious flavor punch. Mouth-watering standouts include the crunchy, tangy *lasoni gobi* (fried cauliflower with tomato and spices) and the insanely flavorful *murgh bharta* (minced chicken cooked with smoked eggplant).

> **KOREATOWN (KOREA WAY)**
>
> Centered on W 32nd St between Fifth Ave and the intersection of Sixth Ave and Broadway, this Seoul-ful jumble of Korean-owned restaurants, shops, salons and spas will satiate any kimchi pangs. Businesses are dense on the ground and often occupy second floors, some migrating east of Fifth Ave and to 31st and 33rd Sts. Bars and karaoke spots are plentiful and the block stays lively late into the night.

EL PARADOR CAFE
MEXICAN $$

Map p424 (212-679-6812; www.elparadorcafe.com; 325 E 34th St, btwn First & Second Aves, Midtown East; lunch $10-22, dinner mains $18-32; noon-10pm Mon, to 11pm Tue-Sat; S 6 to 33rd St) Back in the day, the far-flung location of this Mexican stalwart was much appreciated by philandering husbands. The shady regulars may have gone, but the old-school charm remains, from the beveled candleholders and dapper Latino waiters to the satisfying south-of-the-border standbys.

HANGAWI
KOREAN, VEGAN $$

Map p424 (212-213-0077; www.hangawirestaurant.com; 12 E 32nd St, btwn Fifth & Madison Aves; mains lunch $11-30, dinner $19-30; noon-2:30pm & 5:30-10:15pm Mon-Thu, to 10:30pm Fri, 1-10:30pm Sat, 5-9:30pm Sun; ; S B/D/F/M, N/Q/R/W to 34th St-Herald Sq) Meat-free Korean is the draw at high-achieving Hangawi. Leave your shoes at the entrance and slip into a soothing, Zen-like space of meditative music, soft low seating and clean, complex dishes. Showstoppers include the leek pancakes and a seductively smooth tofu claypot in ginger sauce.

★O-YA
SUSHI $$$

Map p424 (212-204-0200; https://o-ya.restaurant/o-ya-nyc; 120 E 28th St; nigiri $16-38; 11am-10pm Mon-Sat; S 4/6 to 28th St) With the cheapest nigiri pairs at close to $20 each, this is not a spot you'll come to every day. But if you're looking for a special night out and sushi's in the game plan, come here for exquisite flavors, fish so tender it melts like butter on the tongue, and preparations so artful you almost apologize for eating them.

CANNIBAL BEER & BUTCHER
AMERICAN $$$

Map p424 (212-686-5480; www.cannibalnyc.com; 113 E 29th St, btwn Park Ave S & Lexington Ave, Midtown East; small plates $11-18, mains $42-150; 11am-11:30pm; S 6 to 28th St) The stuff of red-blooded dreams, this hip, eatery/bar/butcher peddles over 200 craft beers and a sharp, seasonal menu of mostly carnivorous sharing plates. Graze on competent, housemade charcuterie and sausages ($14), creative pâtés (think chicken liver with beer, shallot jam and cocoa nibs), all tempered by beautifully textured sides like smoky kale salad with walnuts, Armenian string cheese and bacon.

GRAND CENTRAL OYSTER BAR & RESTAURANT
SEAFOOD $$$

Map p424 (212-490-6650; www.oysterbarny.com; Grand Central Terminal, 42nd St, at Park Ave;

mains $15-39; ⊙11:30am-9:30pm Mon-Sat; S S, 4/5/6, 7 to Grand Central-42nd St) This buzzing bar and restaurant within Grand Central is hugely atmospheric, with a vaulted tiled ceiling by Catalan-born engineer Rafael Guastavino. While the extensive menu covers everything from clam chowder and seafood stews to pan-fried soft-shell crab, the real reason to head here is for the two-dozen oyster varieties. Get slurping.

Midtown West & Times Square

★TOTTO RAMEN JAPANESE $

Map p428 (☎212-582-0052; www.tottoramen.com; 366 W 52nd St, btwn Eighth & Ninth Aves; ramen $11-18; ⊙noon-4:30pm & 5:30pm-midnight Mon-Sat, 4-11pm Sun; S C/E to 50th St) There might be another two branches in Midtown, but purists know that neither beats the tiny 20-seat original. Write your name and number of guests on the clipboard and wait your turn. Your reward: extraordinary ramen. Go for the pork, which sings in dishes like miso ramen (with fermented soybean paste, egg, scallion, bean sprouts, onion and homemade chili paste).

BURGER JOINT BURGERS $

Map p428 (☎212-708-7414; www.burgerjointny.com; Le Parker Meridien, 119 W 56th St, btwn Sixth & Seventh Aves; burgers $9-16; ⊙11am-11:30pm Sun-Thu, to midnight Fri & Sat; S F to 57th St) With only a small neon burger as your clue, this speakeasy-style burger hut lurks behind the lobby curtain in the Le Parker Meridien hotel. Though it might not be as 'hip' or as 'secret' as it once was, it still delivers the same winning formula of graffiti-strewn walls, retro booths and attitude-loaded staff slapping up beef 'n' patty brilliance.

FUKU+ BARBECUE $

Map p428 (☎212-757-5878; http://fukuplus.momofuku.com; 15 W 56th St; mains $8-16; ⊙11am-3pm & 5-10pm Mon-Wed, to 11pm Thu-Fri, noon-9pm Sat & Sun; S E or F to 57th St, N/Q/R to Fifth Ave-59th St) With a Tokyo-stand-up-salaryman-bar type vibe, Fuku+ gets high marks for its chicken and pulled pork, done to perfection. The menu is constantly evolving, but at last check only one item, the pork-bacon burger, was above $15 (and only by a dollar!). Great for those on a budget who still want a very nice meal. There's a full bar too. It's inside **Chambers hotel** (Map p424; ☎212-974-5656; www.chambershotel.com; r from $457; ❄📶🐾).

BENGAL TIGER INDIAN $

Map p428 (☎212-266-2703; www.bengaltigerindianfood.com; 58 W 56th St, btwn Fifth & Sixth Aves; lunch from $10, dinner mains $14-17; ⊙11:30am-3pm, 5-10pm Mon-Fri, to 10:30pm Sat & Sun; S F to 57th St) While it lacks the pomp and circumstance of other Indian restaurants in New York City, the food at Bengal Tiger doesn't need bells and whistles to excite. The lunch deal – two meat or veggie selections, naan, and rice – is affordable and well proportioned, and the same savory delights are served for dinner and catering as well.

LARB UBOL THAI $

Map p428 (☎212-564-1822; www.larbubol.com; 480 Ninth Ave, at 37th St, Midtown West; dishes $11-24; ⊙11:30am-10pm Sun-Thu, to 11pm Fri & Sat; S A/C/E to 34th St-Penn Station) Petite parasols are among the few design concessions at this low-frills joint. But you're here for the fresh, jumping flavors of northeastern Thailand. Drool over *larb* (spicy ground-meat salad), brilliant *nam tok nuer* (grilled beef with lime, fish sauce and palm sugar), and unexpected concoctions like *pla dook pad ped* (stir-fried catfish with Thai eggplant, peppercorn, basil, ginger and spicy curry paste).

MARGON CUBAN $

Map p428 (☎212-354-5013; 136 W 46th St, btwn Sixth & Seventh Aves; sandwiches $11-12, mains from $11; ⊙6am-5pm Mon-Fri, from 7am Sat; S B/D/F/M to 47th-50th Sts-Rockefeller Center) It's still 1973 at this ever-packed Cuban lunch counter, where orange Laminex and greasy goodness never went out of style. Go for gold with its legendary *cubano* sandwich (a pressed panino jammed with rich roast pork, salami, cheese, pickles, *mojo* sauce and mayo). It's obscenely good.

FIKA CAFE $

Map p428 (☎646-490-7650; www.fikanyc.com; 824 Tenth Ave, btwn W 54th & 55th Sts; lunch from $9, coffee from $3; ⊙7am-7pm Mon-Fri, 9am-7pm Sat & Sun; S A/C, B/D, 1 to 59th St-Columbus Circle) There are many coffee chains in New York City, but few match the quality of FIKA. Those looking for a bit of space in normally cramped Manhattan will find the large, airy atmosphere a great respite. The Swedish-inspired pastry and food options are neither too sweet nor too savory, and the coffee is rich and strong.

WHOLE FOODS SUPERMARKET $

Map p428 (212-823-9600; www.wholefoodsmarket.com; Time Warner Center, 10 Columbus Circle; 7am-11pm; S A/C, B/D, 1 to 59th St-Columbus Circle) Load up on freshly baked bread, cheeses, sushi, rotisserie chicken or items off the sprawling buffet counters, then stroll across the road for a memorable picnic in the park.

SOUVLAKI GR GREEK $

Map p428 (212-974-7482; www.souvlakigr.com; 162 W 56th St, btwn Sixth & Seventh Aves; souvlaki $6-9, mains $12-22; 11am-11pm Sun-Thu, to midnight Fri & Sat; S N/Q/R/W to 57th St-7th Ave) Step out of Manhattan and into the Mediterranean – Souvlaki GR is a Greek restaurant in Midtown that offers a truly immersive dining experience. The interior is all cool blues and whites, with stone floors and trellis detailing over the bar. Of course, as the name suggests, you'll find impeccable souvlaki and other Greek specialties here.

DANJI KOREAN $$

Map p428 (212-586-2880; www.danjinyc.com; 346 W 52nd St, btwn Eighth & Ninth Aves, Midtown West; dishes $13-36; noon-2:30pm & 5pm-midnight Mon-Thu, noon-2:30pm & 5pm-1am Fri & Sat, 5-11pm Sun; S C/E to 50th St) Young-gun Hooni Kim woos palates with his Korean creations, served in a snug, slinky, whitewashed space. The simpler lunch menu includes *bibimbap* (a traditional Korean rice dish), while the more expansive dinner list offers small, medium and large plates. Thankfully, both lunch and dinner menus offer Danji's cult-status *bulgogi* beef sliders, made with heavenly, butter-grilled buns. Head in early or queue.

DON ANTONIO PIZZA $$

Map p428 (646-719-1043; www.donantoniopizza.com; 309 W 50th St, btwn Eighth & Ninth Aves, Midtown West; pizzas $10-26; 11:30am-3pm & 4:30-11pm Mon-Thu, 11:30am-11pm Fri-Sat, 11:30am-10:30pm Sun; S C/E, 1 to 50th St) A top spot for authentic Neapolitan-style pizza, this hopping eatery is the offspring of Naples' historic pizzeria Starita. While New York concessions include a cocktail-shaking, solo-diner-friendly bar, the pies here are pure Napoli: chewy, thin-crust wonders with charred edges and sweet, ripe *sugo* (tomato sauce). All pizzas can be made using a wholewheat base, and there's a plethora of gluten-free pizzas too.

★LE BERNARDIN SEAFOOD $$$

Map p428 (212-554-1515; www.le-bernardin.com; 155 W 51st St, btwn Sixth & Seventh Aves; prix-fixe lunch/dinner $88/157, tasting menus $185-225; noon-2:30pm & 5:15-10:30pm Mon-Thu, to 11pm Fri, 5:15-11pm Sat; S 1 to 50th St; B/D, E to 7th Ave) The interiors may have been subtly sexed-up for a 'younger clientele' (the stunning storm-themed triptych is by Brooklyn artist Ran Ortner), but triple-Michelin-starred Le Bernardin remains a luxe, fine-dining holy grail. At the helm is French-born celebrity chef Éric Ripert, whose deceptively simple-looking seafood often borders on the transcendental. Life is short, and you only live (er, eat!) once.

★VICEVERSA ITALIAN $$$

Map p428 (212-399-9291; www.viceversanyc.com; 325 W 51st St, btwn Eighth & Ninth Aves; 3-course lunch $29, dinner mains $24-33; noon-2:30pm & 5-11pm Mon-Fri, 4:30-11pm Sat, 11:30am-3pm & 5-10pm Sun; S C/E to 50th St) ViceVersa is quintessential Italian: suave and sophisticated, affable and scrumptious. The menu features refined, cross-regional dishes like arancini with black truffle and fontina cheese. For a celebrated classic, order the *casoncelli alla bergamasca* (ravioli-like pasta filled with minced veal, raisins and amaretto cookies and seasoned with sage, butter, pancetta and Grana Padano), a nod to chef Stefano Terzi's Lombard heritage.

★MODERN FRENCH $$$

Map p428 (212-333-1220; www.themodernnyc.com; 9 W 53rd St, btwn Fifth & Sixth Aves; 3-/6-course lunch $138/178, 4-/8-course dinner $168/228; restaurant noon-2pm & 5-10:30pm Mon-Sat, bar 11:30am-10:30pm Mon-Sat, to 9:30pm Sun; S E, M to 5th Ave-53rd St) Shining two (Michelin) stars bright, the Modern delivers confident creations like foie gras tart. Fans of *Sex and the City* may know that it was here that Carrie announced her impending marriage to Mr Big. (Hint: If you're on a writer's wage, you can opt for cheaper grub in the adjacent Bar Room.) Cocktails are as tasty as the meals.

NOMAD MODERN AMERICAN $$$

Map p428 (212-796-1500; www.thenomadhotel.com; NoMad Hotel, 1170 Broadway, at 28th St; mains $29-42; noon-2pm & 5:30-10:30pm Mon-Thu, to 11pm Fri, 11am-2:30pm & 5:30-11pm Sat, 11am-2:30pm & 5:30-10pm Sun; S N/R, 6 to 28th St; F/M to 23rd St) Sharing the same name as the 'it kid' hotel it inhabits, and run by the perfectionist restaurateurs behind Michelin-starred Eleven Madison Park (p169), NoMad has become one of Manhattan's culinary highlights. Carved up into a series of distinctly different spaces – including an elegant 'parlor' and a snacks-only 'library' – the restaurant serves delicacies like roasted quail with plums, kale and chanterelle.

TABOON MEDITERRANEAN **$$$**

Map p428 (212-713-0271; www.taboononline.com; 773 Tenth Ave, at 52nd St, Midtown West; meze dishes $18-36, mains $26-39; 5-11pm Mon-Fri, to 11:30pm Sat, 11am-3:30pm & 5-10pm Sun; S C/E to 50th St) Taboon is Arabic for stone oven, and it's the first thing you'll see when stepping through the curtain into this warm, casually chic hot spot. Join urbane theater-goers and Hell's Kitchen muscle boys for Med-inspired dishes like sizzling shrimp with garlic and lemon or truffle-oil-drizzled egg *burek* (soft-poached egg in crispy phyllo dough). Reservations highly recommended…as are the oven-fresh breads.

DRINKING & NIGHTLIFE

Midtown East & Fifth Avenue

★THE CAMPBELL COCKTAIL BAR

Map p424 (212-297-1781; www.thecampbellnyc.com; Grand Central Terminal; noon-2am) As swanky as swank can be, the only thing missing at the Campbell is elevation – you don't get the sweeping skyline view that some NYC bars have. Instead, you can sip top-shelf signature cocktails beneath a stunning hand-painted ceiling, restored along with the room with touches that make it seem Rockefeller or Carnegie might just join you.

WAYLON BAR

Map p428 (212-265-0010; www.thewaylon.com; 736 Tenth Ave, at W 50th St; 4pm-4am Sun-Thu, noon-4am Fri & Sat; S C/E to 50th St) Slip on your spurs, partner, there's a honky-tonk in Hell's! Celebrate Dixie at this saloon-style watering hole, where the jukebox keeps good folks dancing to Tim McGraw's broken heart, where the barkeeps pour American whiskeys and tequila, and where the grub includes Texan-style Frito pie and pulled pork sandwiches. For live country-and-western sounds, stop by some Thursdays between 8pm and 11pm.

Check the website for its live music schedule.

LITTLE COLLINS COFFEE

Map p424 (212-308-1969; http://littlecollinsnyc.com; 667 Lexington Ave, btwn 55th & 56th Sts, Midtown East; 7am-5pm Mon-Fri, 8am-4pm Sat & Sun; S E, M to 53rd St; 4/5/6 to 59th St) Co-owned by Aussie expat Leon Unglik, Little Collins emulates the celebrated cafes of his hometown Melbourne: understatedly cool, welcoming spaces serving superlative coffee and equally tasty grub. The cafe is home to NYC's very first Modbar: high-tech, under-the-counter brewers that look like sleek chrome taps. Don't miss the avocado 'Smash' ($8.95).

ROBERT COCKTAIL BAR

Map p428 (212-299-7730; www.robertnyc.com; Museum of Arts & Design, 2 Columbus Circle, btwn Eighth Ave & Broadway; 11:30am-10pm Mon-Fri, from 10:30am Sat & Sun; S A/C, B/D, 1 to 59th St-Columbus Circle) Perched on the 9th floor of the Museum of Arts & Design (p194), '60s-inspired Robert is technically a high-end, Modern American restaurant. While the food is satisfactory, we say visit late afternoon or post-dinner, find a sofa and gaze out over Central Park with a MAD Manhattan (bourbon, blood orange vermouth and liquored cherries). Check the website for live jazz sessions.

STUMPTOWN COFFEE ROASTERS COFFEE

Map p424 (855-711-3385; www.stumptowncoffee.com; 18 W 29th St, btwn Broadway & Fifth Ave; 6am-8pm Mon-Fri, from 7am Sat & Sun; S N/R to 28th St) Hipster baristas in fedora hats brewing killer coffee? No, you're not in Williamsburg, you're at the Manhattan outpost of Portland's cult-status coffee roaster. The queue is a small price to pay for proper espresso, so count your blessings. It's standing-room only, though weary punters might find a seat in the adjacent Ace Hotel lobby (p340).

MIDDLE BRANCH COCKTAIL BAR

Map p424 (212-213-1350; 154 E 33rd St, btwn Lexington & Third Aves, Midtown East; 5pm-2am; S 6 to 33rd St) Brainchild of the late cocktail deity Sasha Petraske, bi-level Middle Branch injects some much-needed drinking cred in beer-and-margarita-centric Murray Hill. Eye-candy bartenders whip up some of Midtown's sharpest libations, from faithful classics to playful reinterpretations like the Fade Into You ($14).

1

2

3

1. Chrysler Building (p187)
The skyscraper is one of New York's most recognizable buildings.

2. Times Square (p177)
The intersection of Broadway and Seventh Ave is the heart of New York City, attracting almost 40 million tourists each year.

3. Radio City Music Hall (p193)
The sumptuous interiors of Radio City Music Hall can be seen during guided tours.

HELL'S KITCHEN

For years, the far west side of Midtown was a working-class jumble of tenements and food warehouses known as Hell's Kitchen – supposedly its name was muttered by a cop in reaction to a riot in the neighborhood in 1881. A 1990s economic boom seriously altered its character and the area is now best known for its plethora of eateries (especially along Ninth and Tenth Aves between about 37th and 55th Sts) and its heaving gay bars and clubs. The neighborhood, also known as Clinton or Midtown West, has been experiencing rapid development and gentrification, with high-end condo conversions sprouting as fast as inexpensive Thai restaurants on Ninth Ave. Just to the south is the gargantuan Hudson Yards development and the Jacob K Javits Convention Center.

TOP OF THE STRAND COCKTAIL BAR

Map p424 (☎646-368-6426; www.topofthestrand.com; Marriott Vacation Club Pulse, 33 W 37th St, btwn Fifth & Sixth Aves, Midtown East; ⊙5pm-midnight Mon & Sun, to 1am Tue-Sat; Ⓢ B/D/F/M, N/Q/R to 34th St) For that 'Oh my God, I'm in New York' feeling, head to the Marriott Vacation Club Pulse (formerly the Strand Hotel) hotel's rooftop bar, order a martini (extra dirty) and drop your jaw (discreetly). Sporting comfy cabana-style seating, a refreshingly mixed-age crowd and a sliding glass roof, its view of the Empire State Building is simply unforgettable.

Midtown West & Times Square

★**BAR SIXTYFIVE** COCKTAIL BAR

Map p424 (☎212-632-5000; www.rainbowroom.com/bar-sixty-five; 30 Rockefeller Plaza, entrance on W 49th St; ⊙5pm-midnight Mon-Fri, 4-9pm Sun; Ⓢ B/D/F/M to 47th-50th Sts-Rockefeller Center) Not to be missed, sophisticated SixtyFive sits on level 65 of the GE Building at Rockefeller Center (p186). Dress well (no sportswear or guests under 21) and arrive by 5pm for a seat with a multi-million-dollar view. Even if you don't score a table on the balcony or by the window, head outside to soak up that sweeping New York panorama.

RUM HOUSE COCKTAIL BAR

Map p428 (☎646-490-6924; www.therumhousenyc.com; 228 W 47th St, btwn Broadway & Eighth Ave; ⊙noon-4am; Ⓢ N/R/W to 49th St) This sultry slice of old New York is revered for its rums and whiskeys. Savor them straight up or mixed in impeccable cocktails like 'The Escape,' a potent piña-colada for adults. Adding to the magic is nightly live music, spanning solo piano tunes to jaunty jazz trios and sentimental divas. Bartenders here are careful with their craft; don't expect them to rush.

LANTERN'S KEEP COCKTAIL BAR

Map p428 (☎212-453-4287; www.iroquoisny.com; Iroquois Hotel, 49 W 44th St, btwn Fifth & Sixth Aves; ⊙5-11pm Mon, to midnight Tue-Fri, 7pm-1am Sat; Ⓢ B/D/F/M to 42nd St-Bryant Park) Cross the lobby of the **Iroquois Hotel** (Map p428; ☎212-840-3080; r $608; ❄📶) to slip into this dark, intimate cocktail salon. Its specialty is classic drinks, shaken and stirred by passionate, personable mixologists. If you're feeling spicy, request a Gordon's Breakfast (not on the menu!), a fiery melange of gin, Worcestershire sauce, hot sauce, muddled lime and cucumber, salt and pepper. Reservations are recommended.

BAR CENTRALE BAR

Map p428 (☎212-581-3130; www.barcentralenyc.com; 324 W 46th St, btwn Eighth & Ninth Aves, Midtown West; ⊙5pm-midnight; Ⓢ A/C/E to 42nd St-Port Authority) Set in an old brownstone, this unmarked bar is a favorite of Broadway stars, often seen here post-curtain debriefing and unwinding to sultry jazz. It's an intimate spot with a no-standing policy, so consider calling ahead (reservations are taken up to a week in advance). If you're having trouble finding it, it's just up the stairs to the left of Joe Allen's.

JIMMY'S CORNER BAR

Map p428 (☎212-221-9510; 140 W 44th St, btwn Sixth & Seventh Aves; ⊙11:30am-2:30am Mon-Thu, to 4am Fri, 12:30pm-4am Sat, 3pm-2:30am Sun; Ⓢ N/Q/R/W, 1/2/3, 7 to 42nd St-Times Sq; B/D/F/M to 42nd St-Bryant Park) This welcoming, unpretentious dive is run by an old boxing trainer – as if you wouldn't guess by all the framed photos of boxing greats (and lesser-known fighters too). The jukebox, which covers Stax to Miles Davis, is kept low enough for post-work gangs to chat away. Long and narrow, the place looks like it would fit in a traincar.

RUDY'S BAR & GRILL BAR

Map p428 (646-707-0890; www.rudysbarnyc.com; 627 Ninth Ave, at 44th St, Midtown West; 8am-4am Mon-Sat, noon-4am Sun; A/C/E to 42nd St-Port Authority Bus Terminal) The big pantless pig in a red jacket out front marks Hell's Kitchen's best divey hangout, with cheap pitchers of Rudy's two beers, half-circle booths covered in red duct tape, and free hot dogs. A mix of folks come to flirt or watch muted Knicks games as classic rock plays.

FLAMING SADDLES GAY

Map p428 (212-713-0481; www.flamingsaddles.com/nyc; 793 Ninth Ave, btwn 52nd & 53rd Sts, Midtown West; 3pm-4am Mon-Fri, noon-4am Sat & Sun; C/E to 50th St) A country-and-western gay bar in Midtown! *Coyote Ugly* meets *Calamity Jane* at this Hell's Kitchen hangout, complete with studly bar-dancing barmen in skintight jeans, aspiring urban cowboys and a rough 'n' ready vibe. Slip on them Wranglers or chaps and hit the Saddle: you're in for a fun and boozy ride. There's Tex Mex bar food if you get hungry.

INDUSTRY GAY

Map p428 (646-476-2747; www.industry-bar.com; 355 W 52nd St, btwn Eighth & Ninth Aves; 5pm-4am; C/E, 1 to 50th St) What was once a parking garage is now one of the hottest gay bars in Hell's Kitchen – a slick, 4000-sq-ft watering hole with handsome lounge areas, a pool table and a stage for top-notch drag divas. Head in between 4pm and 9pm for the two-for-one drinks special or squeeze in later to party with the eye-candy party hordes. Cash only.

THERAPY GAY

Map p428 (212-397-1700; www.therapy-nyc.com; 348 W 52nd St, btwn Eighth & Ninth Aves, Midtown West; 5pm-2am Sun-Thu, to 4am Fri & Sat; C/E, 1 to 50th St) Multilevel Therapy was the first gay men's lounge/club to draw throngs to Hell's Kitchen, and it still pulls a crowd with its nightly shows (from live music to interviews with Broadway stars) and decent grub served Sunday to Friday (the quesadillas are especially popular). Drink monikers match the theme: 'oral fixation' and 'size queen', to name a few.

BARRAGE GAY

Map p428 (212-586-9390; 401 W 47th St, Hell's Kitchen; 5pm-2am Sun-Thu, to 4am Fri & Sat; C/E to 50th St) Gay bars in the Hell's Kitchen neighborhood of Manhattan are known for being big, fun and loud. While Barrage is certainly a good time, it is decidedly more laid-back than its neighbors. It has a pleasantly dim interior with comfortable lounge seating and unexpected surprises like bar snacks. Most important of all, the drinks are affordable and strong.

☆ ENTERTAINMENT

Hands go raw with applause in Midtown, the city's entertainment nerve center. Whatever you might be hankering for, this neighborhood has you covered: multi-million-dollar musicals and award-winning drama, stadium rock and sports, big-name jazz and blues, world-class chamber music, movies, lectures and more. Much more.

☆ Midtown East & Fifth Avenue

★UPRIGHT CITIZENS BRIGADE THEATRE COMEDY

Map p428 (UCB; 212-366-9176; www.ucbtheatre.com; 555 W 42nd St, btwn Tenth & Eleventh Aves, Hell's Kitchen; free-$10; 7pm-midnight; A/C/E to 42nd St-Port Authority) Comedy sketch shows and improv reign at the new location of the legendary venue, which receives drop-ins from casting directors and often features well-known figures from TV. Entry is cheap, and so are the beer and wine. You'll find quality shows happening nightly, from about 7:30pm, though the Sunday-night Asssscat Improv session is always a riot.

It's free on Sundays after 9:30pm and on Mondays after 11pm, featuring up-and-coming comics. There's also an Upright Citizens Brigade outpost in the East Village. Check the website for popular classes on sketch and improv.

JAZZ STANDARD JAZZ

Map p424 (212-576-2232; www.jazzstandard.com; 116 E 27th St, btwn Lexington & Park Aves; cover $25-40; 6 to 28th St) Jazz luminaries like Ravi Coltrane, Roy Haynes and Ron Carter have played at this sophisticated club. The service is impeccable and the food is great. There's no minimum and it's programmed by Seth Abramson, a guy who really knows his jazz. A popular jazz brunch ($35) is also an option from 11:30am to 2:30pm on Saturday.

BROADWAY BARGAINS

Unless booked many months in advance, must-see Broadway musicals can be prohibitively expensive. Discount ticket agent TKTS (www.tdf.org/nyc/7/TKTS) offers great deals daily, though rarely to the most in-demand shows. For these, your best bet for last-minute discounts is at the theater box office itself.

Many of the hottest shows – including *Hamilton, Kinky Boots* and *Book of Mormon* – run ticket lotteries, usually online via their website, sometimes at the theater itself. If your name is drawn, the show is yours for a steal. The bad news: tickets are limited and in such high demand that you need to be lucky to get them.

Other shows offer a limited number of general rush tickets, available each morning when the box office opens. Again, tickets are limited and in high demand, translating into early-morning queues and long waits.

Several shows also offer Standing Room Only (SRO) tickets, allowing patrons to stand through the performance in numbered spaces the width of a standard seat, usually at the back of the orchestra. Commonly between $27 and $40, SRO tickets can be especially tricky to land, as they are generally only available if the show is sold out. While there's no foolproof way to predict a sold-out show in advance, shows that sell out often include *Hamilton, Book of Mormon* and *Kinky Boots*. Policies can change, so always check the specific show's website before hitting the theater, toes and fingers crossed.

☆ Midtown West & Times Square

★RICHARD RODGERS THEATRE — THEATER

Map p428 (Hamilton; ☎tickets 877-250-2929; www.hamiltonmusical.com; 226 W 46th St, btwn Seventh & Eighth Aves; Ⓢ N/R/W to 49th St) This theater opened in 1926 and is unique for several reasons. One, it was the first to allow all patrons to enter through the same set of doors (there were separate entrances for the less expensive ticket-holders, aka riff-raff, to come through). It also has the honor of being the venue for the highest number of Best Play and Best Musical Tony Awards.

Broadway's hottest ticket, Lin-Manuel Miranda's acclaimed musical *Hamilton,* uses contemporary hip-hop beats to recount the story of America's first secretary of the treasury, Alexander Hamilton. Inspired by Ron Chernow's Hamilton biography, the show has won a flock of awards, with 11 Tony Awards (including Best Musical), a Grammy for its triple-platinum cast album and the Pulitzer Prize for Drama. Book tickets at least six months in advance. Alternatively, head to the online ticket lottery. Winners are able to purchase one or two $10 front-row tickets. *Hamilton* for 10 bucks? Yes, please!

★EUGENE O'NEILL THEATRE — THEATER

Map p428 (Book of Mormon; ☎tickets 212-239-6200; www.bookofmormonbroadway.com; 230 W 49th St, btwn Broadway & Eighth Ave; Ⓢ N/R/W to 49th St, 1 to 50th St, C/E to 50th St) The Eugene O'Neill Theatre's shows have ranged from family-friendly *Annie* all the way to uproarious *The Best Little Whorehouse in Texas,* with nearly as wild an ownership ride as well – bought and sold numerous times over its nearly a century lifetime. It was originally the Forrest Theatre, then the Coronet Theatre, and was finally christened the Eugene O'Neill Theatre in 1959. Among the factoids, playwright Neil Simon owned it before selling in 1982 to its current owners.

Subversive, obscene and ridiculously hilarious, *The Book of Mormon,* a cutting musical satire, is the work of *South Park* creators Trey Parker and Matt Stone and *Avenue Q* composer Robert Lopez. Winner of nine Tony Awards, it tells the story of two naive Mormons on a mission to 'save' a Ugandan village. Book at least three months ahead for the best choice of prices and seats, or pay a premium at shorter notice. Alternatively, head to the theater 2½ hours before the show to enter the lottery. Winners – announced two hours before curtain – get in for a bargain $32. Once the winners are called, a limited number of standing-room tickets are sold at $27 (subject to availability).

★AL HIRSCHFELD THEATRE — THEATER

Map p428 (☎tickets 877-250-2929; www.kinkybootsthemusical.com; 302 W 45th St, btwn Eighth & Ninth Aves; ⊙box office 10am-8pm Mon-Sat, noon-6pm Sun; Ⓢ A/C/E to 42nd St-Port Authority Bus Terminal) Originally the Martin Beck Theatre, this spectacular building was renamed in

2003 when it was purchased from the Beck family. When it opened in 1924 to great acclaim, it proceeded to be the venue for some of Broadway's best-loved shows for decades, including *Pirates of Penzance, Romeo and Juliet, The Crucible, Guys and Dolls, Hair* and many more. Vast and opulent, it has seating over 1400 for performances, with as many as 200 dressing rooms for actors backstage.

If booking last minute, consider attending a weekday or matinee for cheaper tickets. If you're feeling particularly lucky, the show's website runs a daily ticket lottery, which offers $40 tickets for that day's performance. Winners are notified via email three hours before showtime. A limited number of standing-room tickets ($30) may also be offered at the box office (subject to availability, usually only for sold-out shows).

The current production, *Kinky Boots,* was adapted from a 2005 British indie film, and is Harvey Fierstein and Cyndi Lauper's smash hit. It tells the story of a doomed English shoe factory unexpectedly saved by Lola, a business-savvy drag queen. Its solid characters and electrifying energy have not been lost on critics: the musical won six Tony Awards, including Best Musical, in 2013.

★CARNEGIE HALL — LIVE MUSIC

Map p428 (☎212-247-7800; www.carnegiehall.org; 881 Seventh Ave, at W 57th St; ⌚tours 11:30am, 12:30pm, 2pm & 3pm Mon-Fri, 11:30am & 12:30pm Sat Oct-Jun; ⓈN/R/W to 57th St-7th Ave) Few venues are as famous as Carnegie Hall. This legendary music hall may not be the world's biggest, nor its grandest, but it's definitely one of the most acoustically blessed venues around. Opera, jazz and folk greats feature in the Isaac Stern Auditorium, with edgier jazz, pop, classical and world music in the popular Zankel Hall. The intimate Weill Recital Hall hosts chamber-music concerts, debut performances and panel discussions.

From October to June, Carnegie Hall runs one-hour **guided tours** (adult/child $17/12) of the building, shedding light on the venue's storied history (these are subject to performance and rehearsal schedules, so check the website before heading in).

★JAZZ AT LINCOLN CENTER — JAZZ

Map p428 (☎tickets to Dizzy's Club Coca-Cola 212-258-9595, tickets to Rose Theater & Appel Room 212-721-6500; www.jazz.org; Time Warner Center, 10 Columbus Circle, Broadway at W 59th St; ⓈA/C, B/D, 1 to 59th St-Columbus Circle) Perched atop the Time Warner Center, Jazz at Lincoln Center consists of three state-of-the-art venues: the mid-sized **Rose Theater**; the panoramic, glass-backed **Appel Room**; and the intimate, atmospheric **Dizzy's Club Coca-Cola**. It's the last of these that you're most likely to visit, given its nightly shows. The talent is often exceptional, as are the dazzling Central Park views.

SHUBERT THEATRE — THEATER

Map p428 (☎tickets 212-239-6200; http://shubert.nyc; 225 W 44th St, btwn Seventh & Eighth Aves, Midtown West; ⌚box office 10am-8:30pm Mon-Sat, noon-6pm Sun; ♿; ⓈN/Q/R, S, 1/2/3, 7 to Times Sq-42nd St; A/C/E to 42nd St-Port Authority Bus Terminal) The venerable Shubert Theatre is best known for holding the longest-running-show-on-Broadway award: *A Chorus Line* performed 6137 times before ceding its place to other shows like *Crazy for You* and the much-loved *Spamalot*. Like many Broadway theaters, it has New York City landmark designation, and its murals and interior were restored in 1996.

PLAYWRIGHTS HORIZONS — THEATER

Map p428 (☎212-564-1235; www.playwrightshorizons.org; 416 W 42nd St, btwn Ninth & Tenth Aves, Midtown West; ⓈA/C/E to 42nd St-Port Authority Bus Terminal) An excellent place to catch what could be the next big thing, this veteran 'writers' theater' is dedicated to fostering contemporary American works. Notable past productions include Kenneth Lonergan's *Lobby Hero,* Bruce Norris' Tony Award–winning *Clybourne Park,* as well as Doug Wright's *I Am My Own Wife* and *Grey Gardens.*

SIGNATURE THEATRE — THEATER

Map p428 (☎tickets 212-244-7529; www.signaturetheatre.org; 480 W 42nd St, btwn Ninth & Tenth Aves, Midtown West; ⓈA/C/E to 42nd St-Port Authority Bus Terminal) Looking good in its Frank Gehry–designed home – complete with three theaters, bookshop and cafe – Signature Theatre is devoted to the work of its playwrights-in-residence, both past and present. To date, featured dramatists have included Tony Kushner, Edward Albee, Athol Fugard and Kenneth Lonergan. Shows aside, the theater also runs talks with playwrights, directors, designers and actors. Aim to book performances one month in advance.

SECOND STAGE THEATRE — THEATER

Map p428 (Tony Kiser Theatre; ☎tickets 212-246-4422; www.2st.com; 305 W 43rd St, at Eighth Ave, Midtown West; ⌚box office noon-6pm Sun-Fri, to 7pm Sat; S A/C/E to 42nd St-Port Authority Bus Terminal) This is the main venue run by Second Stage Theatre, a nonprofit theater company famed for debuting the work of talented emerging writers as well as that of the country's more established names. If you're after well-crafted contemporary American theater, this is a good place to find it.

MAGNET THEATER COMEDY

Map p428 (tickets 212-244-8824; www.magnettheater.com; 254 W 29th St, btwn Seventh & Eighth Aves, Midtown West; S 1/2 to 28th St; A/C/E to 23rd St; 1/2/3 to 34th St-Penn Station) Tons of comedy in several incarnations (mostly improv) lures the crowds at this theater-cum-training-ground for comics. Performances vary weekly, though regular favorites include Megawitt (featuring the theater's resident ensembles) and the Friday Night Sh*w, the latter using the audience's written rants and confessions to drive the evening's shenanigans.

BIRDLAND JAZZ, CABARET

Map p428 (212-581-3080; www.birdlandjazz.com; 315 W 44th St, btwn Eighth & Ninth Aves; cover $30-50; 5pm-1am; ; S A/C/E to 42nd St-Port Authority Bus Terminal) This bird's got a slick look, not to mention the legend – its name dates from bebop legend Charlie Parker (aka 'Bird'), who headlined at the previous location on 52nd St, along with Miles, Monk and just about everyone else (you can see their photos on the walls). Covers run from $25 to $50 and the lineup is always stellar.

AMBASSADOR THEATRE THEATER

Map p428 (Chicago; tickets 212-239-6200; www.chicagothemusical.com; 219 W 49th St, btwn Broadway & Eighth Ave; S N/R/W to 49th St; 1, C/E to 50th St) A New York landmark, the Ambassador Theatre, constructed in the 1920s, is curiously built kitty-corner on the lot, enabling the small space to have more seating. Like many of its peers it was sold in the '30s by the owners, the Schuberts, and became a mixed-use property for TV and movies, but was eventually repurchased by the family in 1956. Since then it has remained a theater, and currently is the venue for *Chicago*, one of Broadway's most popular shows.

It's a little easier to score tickets to *Chicago* than some of the newer musicals. This Bob Fosse/Kander & Ebb classic tells the story of showgirl Velma Kelly, wannabe Roxie Hart, lawyer Billy Flynn and the fabulously sordid goings-on of the Chicago underworld. Revived by director Walter Bobbie, its sassy, infectious energy more than makes up for the tight-squeeze seating.

NEW YORK CITY CENTER DANCE

Map p428 (212-581-1212; www.nycitycenter.org; 131 W 55th St, btwn Sixth & Seventh Aves, Midtown West; S N/Q/R to 57th St-7th Ave) This Moorish, red-domed landmark hosts dance troupes (including the Alvin Ailey American Dance Theater), theater productions, the New York Flamenco Festival in February or March, and the popular Fall for Dance Festival in September or October.

CAROLINE'S ON BROADWAY COMEDY

Map p428 (212-757-4100; www.carolines.com; 1626 Broadway, at 50th St, Midtown West; S N/Q/R to 49th St; 1, C/E to 50th St) You may recognize this big, bright, mainstream classic from comedy specials filmed here on location. It's a top spot to catch US comedy big guns and sitcom stars.

DON'T TELL MAMA CABARET

Map p428 (212-757-0788; www.donttellmamanyc.com; 343 W 46th St, btwn Eighth & Ninth Aves, Midtown West; 4pm-2:30am Sun-Thu, to 3:30am Fri & Sat; S N/Q/R, S, 1/2/3, 7 to Times Sq-42nd St) Piano bar and cabaret venue extraordinaire, Don't Tell Mama is an unpretentious little spot that's been around for more than 30 years and has the talent to prove it. Its regular roster of performers aren't big names, but true lovers of cabaret who give each show their all, and singing waitstaff add to the fun.

AMC EMPIRE 25 CINEMA

Map p428 (212-398-2957; www.amctheatres.com; 234 W 42nd St, at Eighth Ave, Midtown West; S N/Q/R, S, 1/2/3, 7 to 42nd St-Times Sq) It's pretty cool to gaze out over illuminated 42nd St at this massive cinema complex, and even more thrilling to settle into the stadium-style seating. While it's not the best place to catch mainstream Hollywood flicks (crowds can be massive and rowdy), it's the perfect off-the-radar spot for indies, which screen frequently to civilized numbers.

MADISON SQUARE GARDEN SPECTATOR SPORTS, CONCERT VENUE

Map p428 (MSG, 'the Garden'; www.thegarden.com; 4 Pennsylvania Plaza, Seventh Ave, btwn 31st & 33rd Sts; S A/C/E, 1/2/3 to 34th St-Penn Station) NYC's major performance venue – part of the massive complex housing Penn Station (p382) – hosts big-arena performers, from Kanye West to Madonna. It's also a sports arena, with

New York Knicks (www.nba.com/knicks.com) and **New York Liberty** (www.liberty.wnba.com) basketball games and **New York Rangers** (www.nhl.com/rangers) hockey games, as well as boxing and events like the Annual Westminster Kennel Club Dog Show.

MINSKOFF THEATRE THEATER

(The Lion King; 212-869-0550, tickets 866-870-2717; www.lionking.com; 200 W 45th St, at Seventh Ave, Midtown West; ; S N/Q/R, S, 1/2/3, 7 to Times Sq-42nd St) The expansive Minskoff Theatre has been hosting shows, pageants and events since 1973. It currently is the home to Disney's *The Lion King*.

GERSHWIN THEATRE THEATER

(Wicked; 212-586-6510, tickets 877-250-2929; www.wickedthemusical.com; 222 W 51st St, btwn Broadway & Eighth Ave, Midtown West; ; S C/E,

TV TAPINGS

Wanna be part of a live studio audience for the taping of one of your favorite shows? NYC is the place to do it. Follow the instructions here to gain access to some of TV's big-ticket tapings.

Saturday Night Live (www.nbc.com/saturday-night-live) One of the most popular NYC-based shows, and known for being difficult to get into. That said, you can try your luck by getting your name into the mix in the fall, when seats are assigned by lottery. Simply send an email to snltickets@nbcuni.com in August, or line up by 7am the day of the show on the 48th St side of Rockefeller Plaza for standby lottery tickets. You can choose a stand-by ticket for either the 8pm dress rehearsal or the 11:30pm live broadcast. The tickets are limited to one per person and are issued on a first-come, first-served basis. You will need to bring valid photo ID when the ticket is issued, as well as to the show later that day. Audience members must be 16 or over.

The Late Show with Stephen Colbert (Map p428; www.showclix.com/event/thelateshowwithstephencolbert; 1697 Broadway, btwn 53rd & 54th Sts) Tickets for this hugely popular late-night show are available online, but they commonly sell out on the day of their release. Check *The Late Show*'s official Twitter account (@colbertlateshow) and Facebook page for release date announcements, usually made one to two months in advance. If you do manage to reserve tickets, you will need to line up outside the Ed Sullivan Theater no later than 3:15pm on the day of taping. Given that the show is intentionally overbooked to ensure capacity, consider arriving by 2:30pm to increase your chance of actually getting in. *The Late Show* tapes Monday through Friday at 5pm. Audience members must be 18 or over.

The Daily Show with Trevor Noah (Map p428; www.showclix.com/event/thedailyshowwithtrevornoah; 733 Eleventh Ave, btwn W 51st & W 52nd Sts) Sign up online to catch this popular news parody show. Reservations for shows are released on a gradual basis a few weeks before, so it pays to keep visiting the website. Tapings take place at 6pm and around 7:15pm Monday through Thursday. Check-in begins at 2:30pm, at which time the actual tickets are distributed. Consider arriving early as there is no guarantee of entry. Upon collecting your tickets at the venue you will be given a time to return (usually around 4:30pm). Audience members must be aged 18 or over.

Last Week Tonight with John Oliver (Map p428; www.lastweektickets.com; 528 W 57th St, btwn Tenth & Eleventh Aves) Tickets to this biting British comedian's news recap show are available at www.lastweektickets.com up to two and a half weeks in advance of taping dates. The show is taped at 6:15pm on Sundays at the CBS Broadcast Center (528 W 57th St, between Tenth and Eleventh Aves) and audience members are requested to arrive at least 40 minutes in advance. Minimum age of admission is 18.

Full Frontal with Samantha Bee (http://samanthabee.com) More biting than John Oliver, Samantha Bee offers incisive and utterly hilarious commentary on the politicos and scandal makers hogging the current news headlines. Her late-night shows are taped at 5:45pm on Wednesdays. Go online to get tickets.

For more show ticket details, visit the websites of individual TV stations, or check out www.nycgo.com/articles/tv-show-tapings.

1 to 50th St) Originally known as the Uris Theatre and one of the newest and largest kids on the Broadway block (it seats nearly 2000!), this venue is notable for being the site of one of Broadway's biggest failures: *Via Galactica* (a musical by the same composer who did *Hair*), which closed after only seven shows and lost more than a million dollars. *Singin' in the Rain, Oklahoma!* and the current show *Wicked* are just a few of its many successes.

SHOPPING

Midtown East & Fifth Avenue

BLOOMINGDALE'S DEPARTMENT STORE

Map p424 (212-705-2000; www.bloomingdales.com; 1000 Third Ave, at E 59th St; 10am-8:30pm Mon-Sat, 11am-7pm Sun; ; 4/5/6 to 59th St; N/R/W to Lexington Ave-59th St) Blockbuster Bloomie's is something like the Metropolitan Museum of Art of the shopping world – historic, sprawling, overwhelming and packed with bodies, but you'd be sorry to miss it. Raid the racks for clothes and shoes from a who's who of US and global designers, including many 'new-blood' collections. Refueling pit stops include a branch of cupcake heaven **Magnolia Bakery**.

BERGDORF GOODMAN DEPARTMENT STORE

Map p424 (888-774-2424, 212-753-7300; www.bergdorfgoodman.com; 754 Fifth Ave, btwn W 57th & 58th Sts; 10am-8pm Mon-Sat, 11am-7pm Sun; N/Q/R/W to 5th Ave-59th St, F to 57th St) Not merely loved for its Christmas windows (the city's best), plush BG, at this location since 1928, leads the fashion race, let by its industry-leading fashion director Linda Fargo. A mainstay of ladies who lunch, its drawcards include exclusive collections of Tom Ford and Chanel shoes and a coveted women's shoe department. The men's store is across the street.

BARNEYS DEPARTMENT STORE

Map p424 (212-826-8900; www.barneys.com; 660 Madison Ave, at E 61st St; 10am-8pm Mon-Fri, to 7pm Sat, 11am-7pm Sun; N/R/W to 5th Ave-59th St) Serious fashionistas swipe their plastic at Barneys, respected for its collections of top-tier labels like Isabel Marant Étoile, Mr & Mrs Italy and Lanvin. For (slightly) less expensive deals geared to a younger market, shop street-chic brands on the 8th floor. Other highlights include a basement cosmetics department and Genes, a futuristic cafe with touch-screen communal tables for online shopping.

You'll find other branches on the **Upper West Side** (Map p432; 646-335-0978; 2151 Broadway, btwn 75th & 76th Sts; 10am-7pm Mon-Sat, 11am-6pm Sun; 1/2/3 to 72nd St) in Manhattan and on Atlantic Ave in Brooklyn.

DYLAN'S CANDY BAR FOOD

Map p424 (646-735-0078; www.dylanscandybar.com; 1011 Third Ave, at 60th St, Midtown East; 10am-9pm Mon-Thu, to 11pm Fri & Sat, 11am-9pm Sun; N/Q/R to Lexington Ave-59th St; 4/5 to 59th St) Willy Wonka has nothing on this dental nightmare of giant swirly lollipops, crunchy candy bars, glowing jars of jelly beans, softball-sized cupcakes, sugar-free and kosher treats, not to mention a luminescent staircase embedded with scrumptious, unattainable sweets. There's even a cafe on the 3nd floor if you need an instant sugar rush.

ARGOSY BOOKS, MAPS

Map p424 (212-753-4455; www.argosybooks.com; 116 E 59th St, btwn Park & Lexington Aves, Midtown East; 10am-6pm Mon-Fri, to 5pm Sat Sep–late-May; 4/5/6 to 59th St; N/Q/R to Lexington Ave-59th St) Bookstores like this are becoming as rare as the books they contain, but since 1925 this landmark has stocked fine antiquarian items such as books, old maps, art monographs and more. There's also an interesting booty of Hollywood memorabilia, from personal letters and signed books, to contracts and autographed publicity stills. Prices range from costly to clearance.

TIFFANY & CO JEWELRY, HOMEWARES

Map p424 (212-755-8000; www.tiffany.com; 727 Fifth Ave, at E 57th St; 10am-7pm Mon-Sat, noon-6pm Sun; F to 57th St; N/R/W to 5th Ave-59th St) Ever since Audrey Hepburn gazed longingly through its windows, Tiffany & Co has won countless hearts with its glittering diamond rings, watches, silver Elsa Peretti heart necklaces, crystal vases and glassware. But wait, there's more, including handbags and travel-friendly gifts like letter openers. Swoon, drool, but whatever you do, don't harass the elevator attendants with tired 'Where's the breakfast?' jokes.

UNIQLO FASHION & ACCESSORIES

Map p424 (☎877-486-4756; www.uniqlo.com; 666 Fifth Ave, at E 53rd St; ⊙10am-9pm Mon-Sat, 11am-8pm Sun; Ⓢ E, M to 5th Ave-53rd St) Uniqlo is Japan's answer to H&M and this is its showstopping 89,000-sq-ft flagship megastore. Grab a mesh bag at the entrance and let the elevators whoosh you up to the 3rd floor to begin your retail odyssey. The forte here is affordable, fashionable, quality basics, from T-shirts and undergarments to Japanese denim, cashmere sweaters and super-light, high-tech parkas.

Midtown West & Times Square

★MOMA DESIGN & BOOK STORE GIFTS, BOOKS

Map p428 (☎212-708-9700; www.momastore.org; 11 W 53rd St, btwn Fifth & Sixth Aves; ⊙9:30am-6:30pm Sat-Thu, to 9pm Fri; Ⓢ E, M to 5th Ave-53rd St) The flagship store at the Museum of Modern Art (p182) is a fab spot for souvenir shopping. Besides gorgeous books (from art and architecture tomes to pop-culture readers and kids' picture books), you'll find art prints and posters and one-of-a-kind knickknacks. For furniture, lighting, homewares, jewelry, bags and MUJI merchandise, head to the **MoMA Design Store** across the street.

HELL'S KITCHEN FLEA MARKET MARKET

Map p428 (☎212-220-0239; www.annexmarkets.com/hells-kitchen-foundation; W 39th St, btwn Ninth & Tenth Aves; ⊙9am-5pm Sat & Sun; Ⓢ A/C/E to 42nd St-Port Authority Bus Terminal) This weekend flea market lures both collectors and the common curious with its wonderful booty of vintage furnishings, accessories, clothing and unidentifiable objects from past eras.

NEPENTHES NEW YORK FASHION & ACCESSORIES

Map p428 (☎212-643-9540; www.nepenthesny.com; 307 W 38th St, btwn Eighth & Ninth Aves; ⊙noon-7pm Mon-Sat, to 5pm Sun; Ⓢ A/C/E to 42nd St-Port Authority Bus Terminal) Occupying an old sewing machine shop in the **Garment District**, this cult Japanese collective stocks edgy menswear from the likes of Engineered Garments and Needles, known for their quirky detailing and artisanal production value, with a vintage-inspired Americana workwear type feel. Accessories include bags and satchels, gloves, eyewear and footwear.

MACY'S DEPARTMENT STORE

Map p428 (☎212-695-4400; www.macys.com; 151 W 34th St, at Broadway; ⊙10am-10pm Mon-Sat, 11am-9pm Sun; Ⓢ B/D/F/M, N/Q/R/W to 34th St-Herald Sq; A/C/E to Penn Station) Occupying most of an entire city block, the country's largest department store covers most bases, with fashion, furnishings, kitchenware, sheets, cafes, hair salons and even a branch of the Metropolitan Museum of Art gift store – more 'mid-priced' than 'exclusive,' with mainstream labels and big-name cosmetics. The store also houses a NYC Information Center (p390) with information desk and free city maps.

Macy's offers a 10% discount for tourists with valid ID.

B&H PHOTO VIDEO ELECTRONICS

Map p428 (☎212-444-6600; www.bhphotovideo.com; 420 Ninth Ave, btwn W 33rd & 34th Sts; ⊙9am-7pm Mon-Thu, to 1pm Fri, 10am-6pm Sun, closed Sat; Ⓢ A/C/E to 34th St-Penn Station) Visiting NYC's most popular camera shop is an experience in itself – it's massive and crowded, and bustling with black-clad (and tech-savvy) Hasidic Jewish salesmen. Your chosen item is dropped into a bucket, which then moves up and across the ceiling to the purchase area (which requires waiting in another line).

DRAMA BOOK SHOP BOOKS

Map p428 (☎212-944-0595; www.dramabookshop.com; 250 W 40th St, btwn Seventh & Eighth Aves, Midtown West; ⊙10am-7pm Mon-Wed & Fri, to 8pm Thu, noon-6pm Sun; Ⓢ A/C/E to 42nd St-Port Authority Bus Terminal) Nirvana for Broadway fans, this expansive bookstore has taken its theater (both plays and musicals) seriously since 1917. Staffers are good at recommending worthy selections, which also include books on costume, stage design and other elements of performance, as well as industry journals and magazines. Check the store's website and Facebook page for regular in-store events.

TIME WARNER CENTER MALL

Map p428 (☎212-823-6300; www.theshopsatcolumbuscircle.com; 10 Columbus Circle; ⊙10am-9pm Mon-Sat, 11am-7pm Sun; Ⓢ A/C, B/D, 1 to 59th St-Columbus Circle) A great add-on to an adventure in Central Park, the swank

Time Warner Center has a fine lineup of largely upscale vendors including Coach, Eileen Fisher, Williams-Sonoma, Sephora and J Crew. For salubrious picnic fare, visit the enormous Whole Foods (p198) in the basement.

SPORTS & ACTIVITIES

NBC STUDIO TOURS WALKING

Map p424 (☎212-664-3700; www.thetouratnbcstudios.com; 30 Rockefeller Plaza, entrance at 1250 Sixth Ave; tours adult/child $33/29, children under 6yr not admitted; ⏰8:20am-2pm Mon-Fri, to 5pm Sat & Sun; Ⓢ B/D/F/M to 47th-50th Sts-Rockefeller Center) Peppered with interesting anecdotes, this revamped, one-hour tour takes TV fans through parts of the NBC Studios, home to iconic TV shows *Saturday Night Live* and *The Tonight Show Starring Jimmy Fallon.* Stops usually include the beautifully restored art deco rotunda, two studios and the NBC Broadcast Operations Center. Things get interactive in the Tour Studio, where you can 'star' or 'produce' your own talk show segment. Book online to avoid the queues.

CENTRAL PARK BIKE TOURS CYCLING

Map p428 (☎212-541-8759; www.centralparkbiketours.com; 203 W 58th St, at Seventh Ave; rentals per 2hr/day $20/40, 2hr tours $49; ⏰8am-8pm, tours 9am-4pm; Ⓢ A/C, B/D, 1 to 59th St-Columbus Circle) This place rents out good bikes (helmets, locks and bike map included) and leads two-hour guided tours of Central Park and the Brooklyn Bridge area. See the website for tour times.

MANHATTAN COMMUNITY BOATHOUSE KAYAKING

Map p428 (www.manhattancommunityboathouse.org; Pier 96, at 56th St, Hudson River Park; ⏰10am-6pm Sat & Sun Jun-early Oct, plus 5:30-7:30pm Mon-Wed Jun-Aug; 👪; 🚌M12 to 12th Ave/56th St, Ⓢ A/C, B/D, 1 to 59th St-Columbus Circle) FREE Fancy a quick glide on the mighty Hudson? This volunteer-run boathouse offers free kayaking on summer weekends. No reservations: it's first-come, first-served. It also offers free classes in kayaking technique and safety.

Expect to get wet while paddling – there are changing rooms and lockers at the pier. If you want more than a 20-minute paddle, check out the Downtown Boathouse (p85), off N Moore St, which offers weekend trips out on the Hudson.

GRAND CENTRAL PARTNERSHIP WALKING

Map p424 (☎212-883-2420; www.grandcentralpartnership.nyc) FREE The Grand Central Partnership leads free, 90-minute tours of both the Grand Central Terminal and the surrounding neighborhood on Fridays at 12:30pm. Tours depart from the southwest corner of E 42nd St and Park Ave. It also has a variety of other activities throughout the year.

CIRCLE LINE BOAT TOURS CRUISE

Map p428 (☎212-563-3200; www.circleline42.com; Pier 83, W 42nd St at Twelfth Ave; cruises from adult/child $30/25; 🚌westbound M42 or M50 to 12th Ave, Ⓢ A/C/E to 42nd St-Port Authority) The classic Circle Line guides you through all the big sights from the safe distance of a boat. Options include a 2½-hour full-island cruise, a shorter (90-minute) 'semi-circle' journey and a two-hour evening cruise. From May to October, the outfit also operates adrenaline-fueled cruises aboard the high-speed *Beast.* See the website for schedules.

LUCKY STRIKE BOWLING

Map p428 (☎646-829-0170; www.bowlluckystrike.com; 624-660 W 42nd St, btwn Eleventh & Twelfth Aves, Midtown West; individual games from $10, shoe rental $6; ⏰noon-midnight Sun-Wed, to 1am Thu, to 2am Fri & Sat; Ⓢ A/C/E to 42nd St-Port Authority Bus Terminal) One of the world's few bowling alleys with a dress code, Lucky Strike has pricey drinks, plush lounge fittings and a fashion-conscious crowd – which makes the whole experience more akin to a nightclub than a bowling alley. Book ahead.

24 HOUR FITNESS GYM

Map p424 (☎212-401-0660; www.24hourfitness.com; 153 E 53rd St, btwn Lexington & Third Aves, Midtown East; day/week pass $30/100; ⏰gym 24hr, pool 5am-11pm; Ⓢ E, M to Lexington Ave-53rd St; 6 to 51st) Work up a sweat at this smart, well-equipped chain, which includes top-of-the-range cardio equipment, weights, classes (including BodyPump, BodyCombat and Pilates), a sauna, steam-room and whirlpool. This branch also has a lap pool. Check the website for information on all three Manhattan branches.

Upper East Side

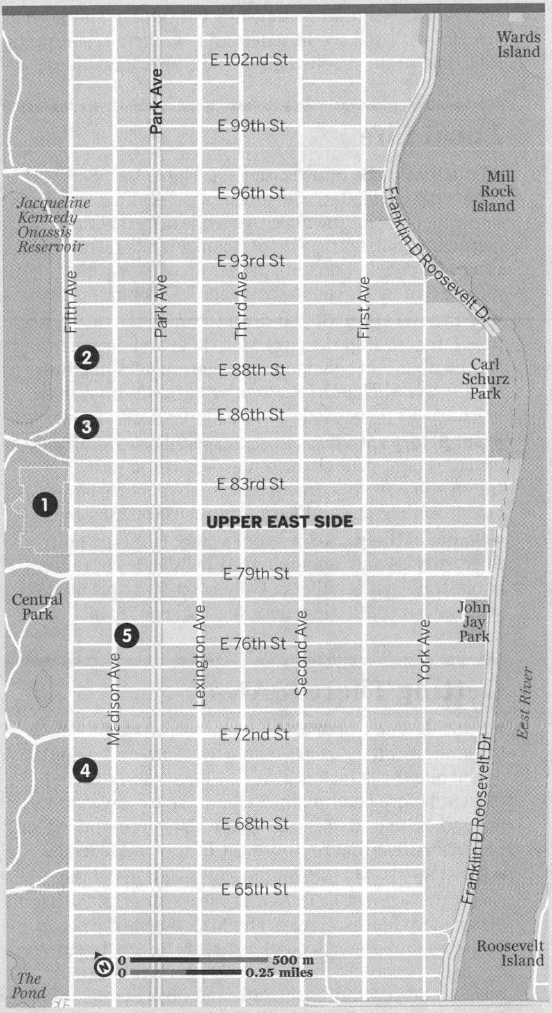

For more detail of this area see Map p430

Neighborhood Top Five

❶ **Metropolitan Museum of Art** (p214) Spending a few hours (or weeks) wandering amid the priceless treasures, from mesmerizing Egyptian artifacts to Renaissance masterpieces.

❷ **Guggenheim Museum** (p213) Walking the spiral ramp of Frank Lloyd Wright's iconic architectural design on the trail of its latest installation of modern art.

❸ **Neue Galerie** (p218) Gazing at the lush, gilded paintings of Gustav Klimt, followed up by a leisurely lunch of Viennese specialties at the museum's elegant cafe.

❹ **Frick Collection Concerts** (p224) Listening to classical music on a Sunday evening, in a beaux-arts mansion surrounded by priceless paintings and sculptures.

❺ **Bemelmans Bar** (p221) Sipping an early evening cocktail at this elegant, mural-lined bar that hearkens back to the city's glorious Jazz Age.

Lonely Planet's Top Tip

The Upper East Side is the epitome of old-school opulence, especially the area that covers the blocks from 60th to 86th Sts between Park and Fifth Aves. If you're looking for eating and drinking spots that are easier on the wallet, head east of Lexington Ave. First, Second and Third Aves are lined with less pricey neighborhood venues.

Best Places to Eat

- Tanoshi (p220)
- Café Boulud (p221)
- Boqueria (p221)
- Café Sabarsky (p220)
- Two Boots (p219)
- Papaya King (p219)

For reviews, see p219.

Best Places to Drink

- Bemelmans Bar (p221)
- Seamstress (p223)
- Drunken Munkey (p223)
- Auction House (p223)
- Caledonia (p221)
- Uva (p223)

For reviews, see p221.

Best Places to Shop

- Encore (p225)
- Flying Tiger Copenhagen (p224)
- Mary Arnold Toys (p224)
- Ricky's NYC (p224)

For reviews, see p224.

Explore Upper East Side

There are infinite ways to tackle this large, well-heeled neighborhood. Start early if you can – visiting the Metropolitan Museum of Art alone can easily take up an entire morning (or more). Pop into Central Park just south of the 79th St Tranverse and join the hordes picnicking or lying about Cedar Hill (also called Cat Hill for its sculpture of a large cat on the hunt); in wintertime you'll see local children sledding down it. Stroll south to the sculpture of *Alice in Wonderland* and then take a break on a bench to gaze at the model boats plying the waters of the Conservatory Water pond.

At 72nd St, scoot east to Madison Ave and head south, where you can then enjoy the sight of some of the country's most extravagant flagship boutiques. The path is strewn with old-world cafes and opulent restaurants. Welcome to the rarefied air of the Upper East Side.

Local Life

- **Lunch with the upper crust** The Upper East Side is famed for its 'ladies who lunch,' a well-coiffed breed known for dispensing air kisses while armed with designer handbags the size of steamer trunks. The best places for people-watching this strain of New Yorker include Sant Ambroeus (p223) and Café Boulud (p221).
- **(Window) shop 'til you drop** Champagne taste on a beer budget? Skip the ritzy Madison Ave boutiques and hit the high-end consignment shops: places like Encore (p225) and Michael's (p225) offer bargains on mildly worn frocks dispensed with by high-society types.
- **Get jittery with it** An upscale neighborhood drinks upscale coffee – single-origin espresso abounds. Indulge in a freshly drawn macchiato at cafes like Via Quadronno (p221) and Sant Ambroeus (p223).
- **Picnic in the park** Save your wallet from the hoity-toity eateries and assemble your own little charcuterie at old-time deli Schaller & Weber (p219), or hit up their sausage bar (p219) next door for a takeout meal.

Getting There & Away

- **Subway** The Upper East Side is served mainly by two lines: the 4/5/6 trains travel north–south on Lexington Ave, while the Q makes a stop at Lexington Ave and 63rd St before heading up Second Ave to new stations at 72nd, 86th and 96th Sts. The F also stops at 63rd and Lex before heading to Roosevelt Island and Queens.
- **Bus** The M1, M2, M3 and M4 buses all make the scenic drive down Fifth Ave alongside Central Park (and also run up Madison Ave). The M15, which travels up First Ave and down Second, is handy for getting around the neighborhood's most easterly parts. Crosstown buses at 66th, 72nd, 79th, 86th and 96th Sts take you through Central Park and to the Upper West Side.

TOP SIGHT
GUGGENHEIM MUSEUM

A sculpture in its own right, this building by architect Frank Lloyd Wright almost overshadows the collection of 20th-century art inside. Even before it opened, the inverted ziggurat structure was derided by some critics but hailed by others, who welcomed it as a beloved architectural icon. Since its opening, this unusual structure has appeared in countless postcards, TV programs and films.

Abstract Roots
The Guggenheim came out of the collection of Solomon R Guggenheim, a New York mining magnate who began acquiring abstract art in his 60s at the behest of his art adviser, an eccentric German baroness named Hilla Rebay. In 1939, with Rebay serving as director, Guggenheim opened a temporary museum on 54th St titled the Museum of Non-Objective Painting. (Incredibly, it had grey velour walls, piped-in classical music and burning incense.) Four years later, the pair commissioned Wright to construct a permanent home for the collection.

Bring on the Critics
When the Guggenheim opened its doors in October 1959, the ticket price was 50¢ and the works on view included pieces by Wassily Kandinsky, Alexander Calder and abstract expressionists Franz Kline and Willem de Kooning.

The structure was savaged by the *New York Times*, but others quickly celebrated it as one of the country's most beautiful buildings. Whether Wright intended to or not, he had given the city one of its most recognizable landmarks.

To the Present
A renovation in the early 1990s added an eight-story tower to the east, which provided an extra 50,000 sq ft of exhibition space. These galleries feature rotating exhibitions from the permanent collection, while the ramps of the Rotunda are occupied by temporary exhibits.

The museum's holdings include works by Kandinsky, Picasso and Jackson Pollock. Over time, other key additions have included paintings by Monet, Van Gogh and Degas, sculpture by Constantin Brancusi, photographs by Robert Mapplethorpe, and key surrealist works donated by Guggenheim's niece Peggy.

Visiting the Museum
The museum's ascending ramp displays rotating exhibitions of modern and contemporary art. Though Wright intended visitors to go to the top and wind their way down, the cramped single elevator doesn't allow for this. Exhibitions, therefore, are installed from bottom to top. Fans of art and design should stop into the on-site **Guggenheim Store** to browse their excellent collection of books, posters, gifts and homewares.

Years in the Making
Like most developments in New York City, the project took forever to come to fruition. Construction was delayed for almost 13 years due to budget constraints, the outbreak of WWII and outraged neighbors who weren't all that excited to see a giant concrete spaceship land in their midst. Construction was finally completed in 1959 – after both Wright and Guggenheim had passed away.

DON'T MISS
- Temporary Rotunda exhibitions (with unusual viewpoints)
- Permanent collection
- Museum shop

PRACTICALITIES
- Map p430, A3
- ☎212-423-3500
- www.guggenheim.org
- 1071 Fifth Ave, cnr E 89th St
- adult/child $25/free, pay-what-you-wish 5:45-7:45pm Sat
- ⌚10am-5:45pm Sun-Wed & Fri, to 7:45pm Sat, closed Thu
- 👪
- Ⓢ4/5/6 to 86th St

HEATHER SHIMMIN / SHUTTERSTOCK ©

TOP SIGHT
METROPOLITAN MUSEUM OF ART

This sprawling, encyclopedic museum, founded in 1870, houses one of the world's largest art collections, with more than two million individual objects, from Egyptian temples to American paintings. 'The Met' attracts over six million visitors a year to its 17 acres of galleries, making it the largest single-site attraction in NYC. In other words: plan on spending some time here.

Egyptian Art

The museum has an unrivaled collection of ancient Egyptian art, some of which dates back to the Paleolithic era. Located to the north of the Great Hall, the 39 Egyptian galleries open dramatically with one of the Met's prized pieces: the Mastaba Tomb of Perneb (c 2300 BC), an Old Kingdom burial chamber crafted from limestone. From here, a web of rooms is cluttered with funerary stelae, carved reliefs and fragments of pyramids. (Don't miss the intriguing models of Meketre, clay figurines meant to help in the afterlife, in Gallery 105.) These eventually lead to the Temple of Dendur (Gallery 131), a sandstone temple to the goddess Isis that resides in a sunny atrium gallery with a reflecting pool – a must-see for the first-time visitor.

Greek & Roman Art

The 27 galleries devoted to classical antiquity are another Met doozy. From the Great Hall, a passageway takes you through a barrel-vaulted room flanked by the chiseled torsos of Greek figures. This spills right into one of the Met's loveliest spaces: the airy Greek and Roman sculpture court (Gallery 162), full of marble carvings of gods and historical

DON'T MISS

- Temple of Dendur
- Paintings by Caravaggio, El Greco, Vermeer and other old masters
- Damascus Room in the Islamic Art galleries
- Cantor Roof Garden Bar

PRACTICALITIES

- Map p430, A5
- ☎212-535-7710
- www.metmuseum.org
- 1000 Fifth Ave, cnr E 82nd St
- 3-day pass adult/senior/child $25/$17/free, residents of New York State & students from Connecticut, New York or New Jersey free
- 10am-5:30pm Sun-Thu, to 9pm Fri & Sat
- (family-friendly)
- S 4/5/6, Q to 86th St

figures. The statue of a bearded Hercules from AD 68–98, with a lion's skin draped about him, is particularly awe-inspiring.

European Paintings

Want Renaissance? The Met's got it. On the museum's 2nd floor, the European Paintings galleries display a stunning collection of masterworks. This includes more than 1700 canvases from the roughly 500-year-period starting in the 13th century, with works by every important painter from Duccio to Rembrandt. In fact, everything here is, literally, a masterpiece. In Gallery 621 are several Caravaggios, including the expertly painted *The Denial of St Peter.* Gallery 611, to the west, is packed with Spanish treasures, including El Greco's famed *View of Toledo.* Continue south to Gallery 632 to see various Vermeers, including *Young Woman with a Water Pitcher.* To the south, in Galleries 634 and 637, you can gaze at several Rembrandts, including a 1660 *Self-Portrait.* And that's just the beginning – you could spend hours exploring these many powerful works.

Art of the Arab Lands

In the southeastern corner of the 2nd floor you'll find the Islamic galleries, with 15 incredible rooms showcasing the museum's extensive collection of art from the Middle East, and Central and South Asia. In addition to garments, secular decorative objects and manuscripts, you'll find gilded and enameled glassware (Gallery 452) and a magnificent 14th-century mihrab (prayer niche) lined with elaborately patterned polychrome tile work (Gallery 455). There's also a superb array of Ottoman textiles (Gallery 459), a medieval-style Moroccan court (Gallery 456) and the 18th-century Damascus Room (Gallery 461).

American Wing

In the northwestern corner, the two-floor American Wing showcases a wide variety of decorative and fine art from throughout US history. These include everything from colonial portraiture to Hudson River School masterpieces to John Singer Sargent's elegantly sexy Madame X (Gallery 771) – not to mention Emanuel Leutze's massive canvas of Washington Crossing the Delaware (Gallery 760).

THE ROOF GARDEN

One of the best spots in the entire museum is the roof garden, which features rotating sculpture installations by contemporary and 20th-century artists. (Jeff Koons, Andy Goldsworthy and Imran Qureshi have all shown here.) Best of all are the views it offers of the city and Central Park. It's also home to the **Cantor Roof Garden Bar** (Map p430; ☎212-570-3711; ⏲11am-4:30pm Sun-Thu, to 8:15pm Fri & Sat mid-Apr–Oct), an ideal spot for a drink – especially at sunset. It's open from April to October.

The most popular galleries with children are generally the Egyptian, African and Oceania galleries (check out the Asmat body masks), and the collection of medieval arms and armor. The Met hosts plenty of youth-centric events (see the website) and distributes a museum brochure and map made specially for kids.

Metropolitan Museum of Art

PLAN OF ATTACK

From the Great Hall, just inside the main entrance, walk through the Egyptian galleries to the ❶ **Temple of Dendur**, dramatically set in a glass-walled gallery.

Stroll through the Charles Engelhard Court, a soaring sunlit atrium packed with American sculptures, to the Arms and Armor galleries. Examine the meticulous craftsmanship of the 16th-century ❷ **Armor of Henry II of France**. The next room (Gallery 371) has four fully armored, mounted horsemen.

Head back into the American Wing and up to the 2nd floor to see the massive ❸ **Washington Crossing the Delaware**. Continue on to the jaw-dropping collection of European masters. Don't miss the Caravaggios in Gallery 621, especially ❹ **The Denial of Saint Peter**.

Cut through the Photography section to 19th- and Early 20th-Century European Paintings and Sculpture for works by Monet, Renoir, Van Gogh and Gauguin. In Gallery 822 is Van Gogh's ❺ **Wheat Field with Cypresses**, which he painted shortly after his famous *Starry Night* (on display at the Museum of Modern Art).

Nearby are the Islamic Art galleries, where you'll find an elaborate ❻ **Mihrab** (prayer niche) next to a medieval-style Moroccan court with gurgling fountain (Gallery 456).

Walk downstairs to the Met's trove of ancient Greek and Roman works. In the largest gallery is the intricate marble sarcophagus ❼ **Triumph of Dionysos and the Seasons**. In the Oceania halls next door is vivid tribal art from New Guinea, including the three ❽ **Asmat Body Masks**; overhead is a painted ceiling from a Kwoma ceremonial house.

Continue to the Modern and Contemporary Art galleries for paintings by O'Keeffe, Dalí, Miró, Hopper and more; Picasso's high cubist ❾ **Still Life with a Bottle of Rum** is in Gallery 905. For a well-earned break, take the nearby elevators to the summertime Cantor Roof Garden Bar or try the stylish Petrie Court Café around the corner.

The Denial of Saint Peter Gallery 621
Painted in the final months of Caravaggio's short, tempestuous life, this magnificent work is a masterpiece of storytelling.

Wheat Field with Cypresses Gallery 822
Van Gogh painted this during a fevered period of production in the summer of 1889, while staying voluntarily at a mental asylum near Arles, France.

Mihrab Gallery 455
One of the world's finest religious architectural decorations, this 8th-century prayer niche from Iran was created by joining cut glazed tiles into a richly ornate mosaic.

Still Life with a Bottle of Rum Gallery 905
Picasso painted this in 1911, during the period when he and Georges Braque developed their new style of cubism together.

Asmat Body Masks Gallery 354
A New Guinea costume like this was worn to represent the spirit of someone who recently died, and featured in ritual dances of the Asmat people.

Triumph of Dionysos and the Seasons Gallery 162
On this marble sarcophagus, you'll see the god Dionysos seated on a panther, joined by four figures representing (from left to right) winter, spring, summer and fall.

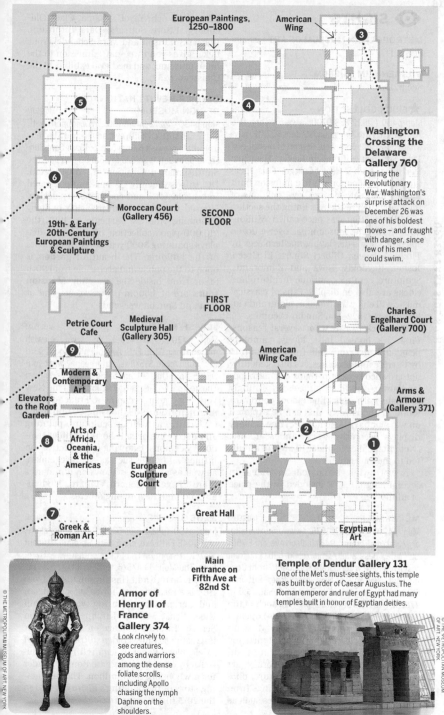

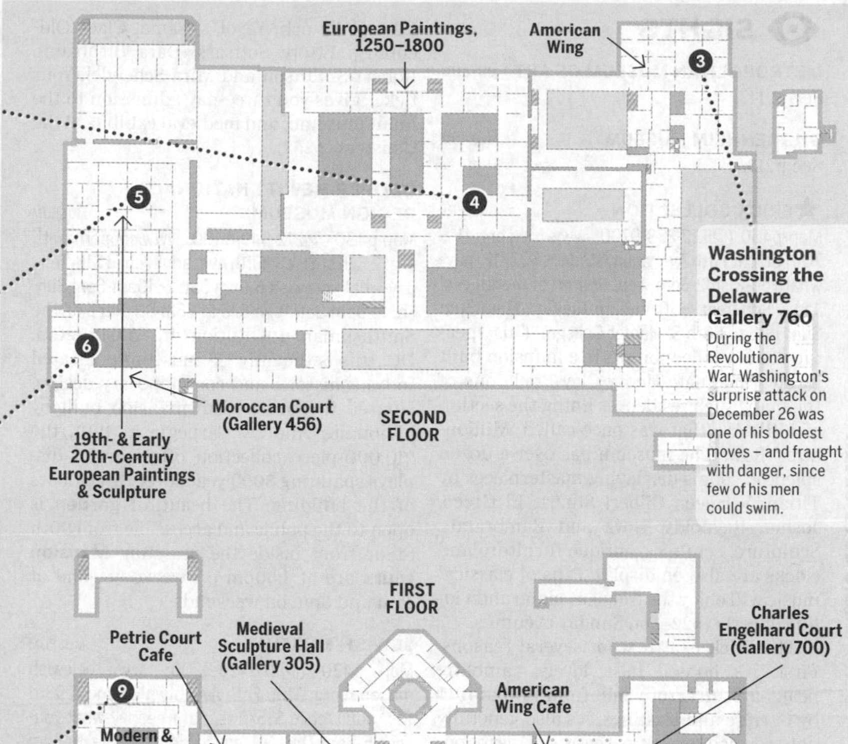

Washington Crossing the Delaware Gallery 760
During the Revolutionary War, Washington's surprise attack on December 26 was one of his boldest moves – and fraught with danger, since few of his men could swim.

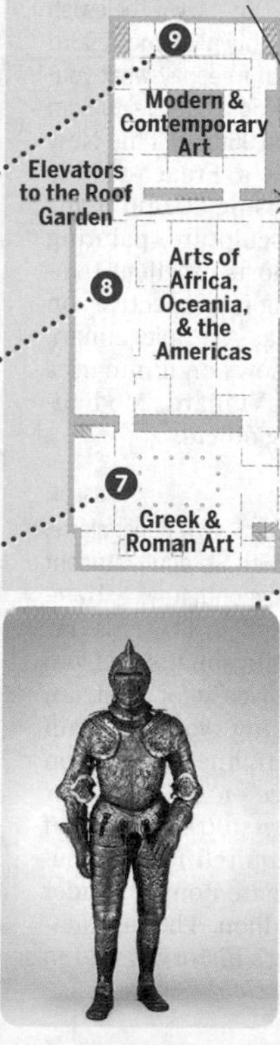

Armor of Henry II of France Gallery 374
Look closely to see creatures, gods and warriors among the dense foliate scrolls, including Apollo chasing the nymph Daphne on the shoulders.

Temple of Dendur Gallery 131
One of the Met's must-see sights, this temple was built by order of Caesar Augustus. The Roman emperor and ruler of Egypt had many temples built in honor of Egyptian deities.

SIGHTS

METROPOLITAN MUSEUM OF ART — MUSEUM

See p214.

GUGGENHEIM MUSEUM — MUSEUM

See p213.

★FRICK COLLECTION — GALLERY

Map p430 (212-288-0700; www.frick.org; 1 E 70th St, cnr Fifth Ave; adult/student $22/12, pay-what-you-wish 2-6pm Wed, first Fri of month excl Jan & Sep free; 10am-6pm Tue-Sat, 11am-5pm Sun; S 6 to 68th St-Hunter College) This spectacular art collection sits in a mansion built by steel magnate Henry Clay Frick, one of the many such residences lining the section of Fifth Ave that was once called 'Millionaires' Row.' The museum has over a dozen splendid rooms displaying masterpieces by Titian, Vermeer, Gilbert Stuart, El Greco, Joshua Reynolds, Goya and Rembrandt. Sculpture, ceramics, antique furniture and clocks are also on display. Fans of classical music will enjoy the frequent piano and violin concerts (p224) on Sunday evenings.

The Frick is a treat for several reasons. First, it's housed in a lovely, rambling beaux-arts structure built from 1913 to 1914 by Carrère and Hastings; it's also generally not crowded (except perhaps during popular shows). And finally, it feels refreshingly intimate, with a trickling indoor courtyard fountain and gardens that can be explored on warmer days. A demure **Portico Gallery** displays decorative works and sculpture. (Note that children under 10 are not admitted to the museum.)

A worthwhile audio tour (available in several languages) is included in the price of admission.

MET BREUER — MUSEUM

Map p430 (212-731-1675; www.metmuseum.org/visit/met-breuer; 945 Madison Ave, cnr E 75th St; 3-day pass adult/senior/child $25/$17/free, residents of New York State & students from Connecticut, New York or New Jersey free; 10am–5:30pm Tue-Thu & Sun, to 9pm Fri & Sat; S 6 to 77th St; Q to 72nd St) The newest branch of the Metropolitan Museum of Art (p214) opened in the landmark former Whitney Museum (p139) building (originally designed by Marcel Breuer) in 2016. Exhibits are dedicated to modern and contemporary art across various media, with sculpture, photographs, video, design and paintings from American and international figures such as Edvard Munch, Yayoi Kusama, Claes Oldenburg, Ettore Sottsass, Dara Birnbaum, Robert Smithson and Mira Schendel. Your ticket gives you three-day admission to the main museum, and medieval exhibits at the Cloisters (p252).

COOPER-HEWITT NATIONAL DESIGN MUSEUM — MUSEUM

Map p430 (212-849-8400; www.cooperhewitt.org; 2 E 91st St, cnr Fifth Ave; adult/child $18/free, pay-what-you-wish 6-9pm Sat; 10am-6pm Sun-Fri, to 9pm Sat; S 4/5/6 to 86th St) Part of the Smithsonian Institution in Washington, DC, this is the only US museum dedicated to both historic and contemporary design. Housed in the 64-room mansion built by billionaire Andrew Carnegie in 1901, the 210,000-piece collection offers artful displays spanning 3000 years over three floors of the building. The beautiful **garden** is open to the public and accessible from 90th St or from inside the museum. **Mansion tours** are at 1:30pm on weekdays, and at 1pm and 3pm on weekends.

JEWISH MUSEUM — MUSEUM

Map p430 (212-423-3200; www.thejewishmuseum.org; 1109 Fifth Ave, btwn E 92nd & 93rd Sts; adult/child $15/free, Sat free, pay-what-you-wish 5-8pm Thu; 11am-5:45pm Sat-Tue, to 8pm Thu, to 4pm Fri; S 6, Q to 96th St) This New York City gem occupies a French-Gothic mansion from 1908, housing 30,000 items of Judaica, as well as sculpture, painting and decorative arts. It hosts excellent temporary exhibits, featuring retrospectives on influential figures such as Art Spiegelman, as well as world-class shows on luminaries Marc Chagall, Édouard Vuillard, Modigliani and Man Ray, among others.

NEUE GALERIE — MUSEUM

Map p430 (212-628-6200; www.neuegalerie.org; 1048 Fifth Ave, cnr E 86th St; adult/student $20/10, 6-8pm 1st Fri of the month free; 11am-6pm Thu-Mon; S 4/5/6 to 86th St) This restored Carrère and Hastings mansion from 1914 is a resplendent showcase for Austrian and German art, featuring works by Paul Klee, Ernst Ludwig Kirchner and Egon Schiele. In pride of place on the 2nd floor is Gustav Klimt's golden 1907 portrait of Adele Bloch-Bauer – acquired for the museum by cosmetics magnate Ronald Lauder for a whopping $135 million. The fascinating story of the painting's history is told in the 2015 film *Woman in Gold*.

GRACIE MANSION HISTORIC BUILDING

Map p430 (www.nyc.gov/gracie; East End Ave, cnr E 88th St; ⏲tours 10am, 11am, 2pm & 3pm Tue; ⓈQ to 86th St) FREE This Federal-style home served as the country residence of merchant Archibald Gracie in 1799. Since 1942, it's been the residence of New York's mayors and their families (with the exception of Michael Bloomberg, who preferred his own plush Upper East Side apartment). The house has been added to and renovated over the years. To visit, you'll have to reserve a spot online for one of the 45-minute house tours held once a week (less frequently during the holiday season).

ASIA SOCIETY & MUSEUM MUSEUM

Map p430 (☎212-288-6400; www.asiasociety.org; 725 Park Ave, cnr E 70th St; adult/child $12/free, 6-9pm Fri Sep-Jun free; ⏲11am-6pm Tue-Sun, to 9pm Fri Sep-Jun; Ⓢ6 to 68th St-Hunter College; Q to 72nd St) Founded in 1956 by John D Rockefeller (an avid collector of Asian art), this cultural center hosts fascinating exhibits (Buddhist art of Myanmar, retrospectives of leading Chinese artists, contemporary Southeast Asian art), as well as Jain sculptures and Nepalese Buddhist paintings. Daily **tours** (free with admission) are offered at 2pm Tuesday through Sunday year-round and at 6:30pm Friday (excluding summer months).

TEMPLE EMANU-EL SYNAGOGUE

Map p430 (☎212-744-1400; www.emanuelnyc.org; 1 E 65th St, cnr Fifth Ave; ⏲10am-4pm Sun-Thu; Ⓢ6 to 68th St-Hunter College) FREE Founded in 1845 as the first Reform synagogue in New York, this temple, completed in 1929, is now one of the largest Jewish houses of worship in the world. An imposing Romanesque structure, it is more than 175ft long and 100ft tall, with a brilliant, hand-painted ceiling featuring gold details.

MUSEUM OF THE CITY OF NEW YORK MUSEUM

Map p430 (☎212-534-1672; www.mcny.org; 1220 Fifth Ave, btwn E 103rd & 104th Sts; suggested admission adult/child $18/free; ⏲10am-6pm; Ⓢ6 to 103rd St) Situated in a Georgian Colonial Revival–style building at the top end of Museum Mile, this local museum focuses solely on New York City's past, present and future. Don't miss the 28-minute film *Timescapes* (on the 2nd floor), which charts NYC's growth from a tiny trading post for Native Americans to burgeoning metropolis.

EATING

★TWO BOOTS PIZZA $

Map p430 (☎212-734-0317; www.twoboots.com; 1617 Second Ave, cnr E 84th St; pizza slices $3.50-4.25; ⏲11:30am-11pm Sun-Tue, to midnight Wed, to 2am Thu, to 4am Fri & Sat; 🌶; ⓈQ, 4/5/6 to 86th St) With the two 'boots' of Italy and Louisiana as inspiration, this quirky, pioneering NYC chain has over 40 original, eclectic pizza flavors in all (with plenty of vegetarian and vegan options) – all named after comedians, scientists, musicians, local sports teams and even fictional characters. Our favorite? The Tony Clifton (shiitake mushrooms, Vidalia onions, mozzarella and red-pepper pesto).

★PAPAYA KING HOT DOGS $

Map p430 (☎212-369-0648; www.papayaking.com; 179 E 86th St, cnr Third Ave; hot dogs $2.50-4.50; ⏲8am-midnight Sun-Thu, to 1am Fri & Sat; Ⓢ4/5/6, Q to 86th St) The *original* hot-dog-and-papaya-juice shop, from 1932, over 40 years before crosstown rival Gray's Papaya (p236) opened, Papaya King has lured many a New Yorker to its neon-lit corner for a cheap and tasty snack of hot dogs and fresh-squeezed papaya juice. (Why papaya? The informative wall signs will explain all.) Try the Homerun, with sauerkraut and New York onion relish.

SCHALLER & WEBER MARKET $

Map p430 (☎212-879-3047; www.schallerweber.com; 1654 Second Ave, cnr E 86th St; sausages from $8 per 12oz; ⏲10am-7pm Mon-Sat; ⓈQ, 4/5/6 to 86th St) This award-winning charcuterie and delicatessen is a holdover from when the Yorkville neighborhood was a largely German enclave. It sells over 15 varieties of sausage made at its factory in Queens – such German classics as *bauernwurst* and *weisswurst*, chicken bratwurst, cheddar-stuffed brat', Irish bangers, Polish kielbasa and more – alongside imported European goodies: cheese, pickles, condiments, chocolate, wine and beer.

Next door is its small 'sausage bar', **Schaller's Stube** (Map p430; ☎646-726-4355; www.schallerstube.com; 1652 Second Ave, cnr E 86th St; sausages $7-14; ⏲11am-11pm Mon-Sat, noon-6pm Sun; ⓈQ, 4/5/6 to 86th St), which sells the wares served on brioche buns with a variety of toppings.

LA ESQUINA TAQUERÍA MEXICAN $

Map p430 (The Corner; ☎646-861-3356; www.esquinanyc.com; 1420 Second Ave, cnr E 73rd

St; tacos $3.75-4.25, tortas $8.50-9.75; ⏲11am-10pm Sun-Thu, to 11pm Fri & Sat; 🖉; Ⓢ Q to 72nd St) This chain of hip new taquerías has acutely designed retro decor – its locations all look like 1950s diners that got stuck in time – but the Mexican menu is full of modern, yet authentic, takes on chicken quesadillas, *barbacoa* lamb-shoulder tacos, *elote callejero* (grilled corn with mayo, cheese and chili powder) and tortilla soup. Crowd-*and* wallet-pleasing.

EARL'S BEER & CHEESE AMERICAN **$**

Map p430 (☎212-289-1581; www.earlsny.com; 1259 Park Ave, btwn E 97th & 98th Sts; grilled cheese $8; ⏲11am-midnight Sun-Thu, to 2am Fri & Sat; Ⓢ 6 to 96th St) This sibling-run, tiny comfort-food outpost channels a hipster hunting vibe, complete with a giant deer-in-the-woods mural and a mounted buck's head. Basic grilled cheese is a paradigm shifter, served with pork belly, fried egg and kimchi. There is also mac 'n' cheese (with goat's cheese and crispy rosemary) and tacos (featuring braised pork shoulder and *queso fresco*).

Earl's has great craft beers and a fine brunch menu (eggs Benedict, yogurt and housemade granola) too.

EL AGUILA MEXICAN **$**

Map p430 (☎212-426-2221; www.elaguilanewyorkrestaurant.com; 1634 Lexington Ave, at 103rd St; tacos from $3, burritos $8; ⏲10am-11pm; Ⓢ 6 to 103rd St) Dig into cheap and cheerful chicken, tongue and *bistec* (grilled steak) tacos at this no-frills, tile-clad taqueria. Tasty alternatives include tamales, tostadas, tortas and veggie burritos, all served with a side of blaring Mexican tunes. If you're heading in for breakfast, dig into the *pan dulce* (a sweet Mexican bun).

★CAFÉ SABARSKY AUSTRIAN **$$**

Map p430 (☎212-288-0665; www.neuegalerie.org/cafes/sabarsky; 1048 Fifth Ave, cnr E 86th St; mains $18-30; ⏲9am-6pm Mon & Wed, to 9pm Thu-Sun; 🖉; Ⓢ 4/5/6 to 86th St) The lines can get long at this popular cafe evoking an opulent, turn-of-the-century Vienna coffeehouse. But the well-rendered Austrian specialties make it worth the wait. Expect crepes with smoked trout, goulash soup and roasted bratwurst. There's also a mouthwatering list of specialty sweets, including a divine Sacher torte (dark chocolate cake with apricot confiture).

UP THAI THAI **$$**

Map p430 (☎212-256-1199; www.upthainyc.com; 1411 Second Ave, btwn E 73rd & 74th Sts; mains $12-28; ⏲11:30am-10:30pm Mon-Thu, to 11:30pm Fri, noon-11:30pm Sat, to 10:30pm Sun; 🖉; Ⓢ Q to 72nd St; 6 to 77th St) The Upper East Side's best Thai place, this narrow but artfully designed restaurant serves a mix of traditional and innovative recipes in an industrial-style fit-out under exposed ceiling beams. Standouts include creamy, rich *tom kha* soup (with coconut broth and vegetables), steamed chive dumplings and crispy duck breast with eggplant and tamarind sauce. (Note: it close from 4pm to 5pm daily.)

BEYOGLU TURKISH **$$**

Map p430 (☎212-650-0850; 1431 Third Ave, cnr E 81st St; mains $15-22, sharing plates $6-12; ⏲noon-10:30pm Sun-Thu, to 11pm Fri & Sat; 🖉; Ⓢ 6 to 77th St; 4/5/6, Q to 86th St) A long-time favorite of Mediterranean-craving Upper East Siders, Beyoglu whips up meze (appetizer) platters that are ideal for sharing, including creamy-rich hummus, juicy lamb kebabs, tender grape leaves and lemon-scented chargrilled octopus. It has an airy, comfy interior, though on sunny days you can sit at a sidewalk table out front. Great wine selection.

CANDLE CAFE VEGAN **$$**

Map p430 (☎212-472-0970; www.candlecafe.com; 1307 Third Ave, btwn E 74th & 75th Sts; mains $15-22; ⏲11:30am-10:30pm Mon-Sat, to 9:30pm Sun; 🖉; Ⓢ Q to 72nd St-2nd Ave) The moneyed yoga set piles into this attractive vegan cafe serving a long list of sandwiches, salads, comfort food and market-driven specials. The specialty here is the housemade seitan. There is a juice bar and a gluten-free menu.

For a more upscale take on the subject, check out its sister restaurant, **Candle 79** (Map p430; ☎212-537-7179; www.candle79.com; 154 E 79th St, cnr Lexington Ave; mains $20-25; ⏲noon-3:30pm & 5:30-10:30pm Mon-Sat, to 4pm & 10pm Sun; 🖉; Ⓢ 6 to 77th St), four blocks away.

★TANOSHI SUSHI **$$$**

Map p430 (☎917-265-8254; www.tanoshisushinyc.com; 1372 York Ave, btwn E 73rd & 74th Sts; chef's sushi selection $80-100; ⏲seatings 6pm, 7:30pm & 9pm Mon-Sat; Ⓢ Q to 72nd St) It's not easy to snag one of the 20 stools at Tanoshi, a wildly popular, pocket-sized sushi spot. The setting may be humble, but the flavors are simply magnificent. Only sushi is on offer and only *omakase* (chef's selection)

– which might include Hokkaido scallops, king salmon or mouthwatering *uni* (sea urchin). BYO beer, sake or whatnot. Reserve well in advance.

BOQUERIA SPANISH **$$$**

Map p430 (☎212-343-2227; www.boquerianyc.com; 1460 Second Ave, btwn E 76th & 77th Sts; tapas $6-18, paella for 2 $48-69; ⏰noon-10:30pm Sun-Thu, 11am-11:30pm Fri & Sat; ✍; Ⓢ6 to 77th St; Q to 72nd St) This lively, much-loved tapas place brings a bit of downtown cool to the Upper East Side, with nicely spiced *patatas bravas* (fried potatoes in tomato sauce), tender slices of *jamon ibérico* (cured ham) and rich *pulpo a la plancha* (grilled octopus). Head chef Marc Vidal also creates an exquisite seafood paella. Wash it down with a pitcher of excellent sangria.

CAFÉ BOULUD FRENCH **$$$**

Map p430 (☎212-772-2600; www.cafeboulud.com/nyc; 20 E 76th St, btwn Fifth & Madison Aves; mains around $45; ⏰7am-10:30am, noon-2:30pm & 5:45-10:30pm Mon-Fri, from 8am Sat & Sun; ✍; Ⓢ6 to 77th St) This Michelin-starred bistro – part of Daniel Boulud's gastronomic empire – attracts a rather staid crowd with its globe-trotting French cuisine. Seasonal menus include classic dish coq au vin, as well as more inventive fare such as scallop *crudo* (raw) with white miso. Foodies on a budget will be interested in the three-course prix-fixe lunch ($45; two courses for $39).

The adjacent 40-seat **Bar Pleiades** (Map p430; ☎212-772-2600; www.barpleiades.com; 20 E 76th St, btwn Fifth & Madison Aves; ⏰noon-midnight; Ⓢ6 to 77th St) serves seasonal cocktails, along with a full bar menu (think oysters, and fennel-and-duck sausages), plus live jazz on Friday nights (9pm to midnight).

VIA QUADRONNO CAFE **$$$**

Map p430 (☎212-650-9880; www.viaquadronno.com; 25 E 73rd St, btwn Madison & Fifth Aves; sandwiches $8-15, mains $23-40; ⏰8am-11pm Mon-Fri, from 9am Sat, 10am-9pm Sun; ✍; Ⓢ6 to 77th St) A little slice of Italy that looks like it's been airlifted into New York, this cozy cafe-bistro has exquisite coffee, as well as a mind-boggling selection of sandwiches – piled high with delectable ingredients, such as prosciutto and Camembert. There are soups, pastas and a very popular daily lasagna. For a splurge, try the cheese or beef fondue set for two.

Quick coffees and snacks are also available at the granite counter.

DRINKING & NIGHTLIFE

Drinking options on the Upper East Side have traditionally been either pricey, luxe lounges or frat-house sports bars ('Beer pong, anyone?'). Times are changing, however, with downtown-cool cocktail lounges and classy gastropubs opening up in recent years.

CALEDONIA BAR

Map p430 (☎212-734-4300; www.caledoniabar.com; 1609 Second Ave, btwn E 83rd & 84th Sts; ⓈQ, 4/5/6 to 86th St) The name of this dimly lit, dark-wood bar is a dead giveaway: it's devoted to Scottish whisky, with over a hundred single-malts to choose from (be they Highlands, Islands, Islay, Lowlands or Speyside), as well as some blends and even a few from the US, Ireland and Japan. The bartenders know their stuff and will be happy to make recommendations.

ETHYL'S ALCOHOL & FOOD BAR

Map p430 (☎212-300-4132; www.ethylsnyc.com; 1629 2nd Ave, btwn E 84th & 85th Sts; ⏰4pm-4am Mon-Fri, from noon Sat & Sun) This funky, divey 1970s-themed bar harks back to the gritty, artsy NYC of yore, before famed punk club CBGBs became a fashion boutique. (The $14 cocktails make it decidedly modern.) There's '60s/'70s music nightly from bands or DJs, plus go-go dancers and occasional burlesque shows. The booze flows till 4am every night, which is rare for this part of town.

BEMELMANS BAR LOUNGE

Map p430 (☎212-744-1600; www.thecarlyle.com; Carlyle Hotel, 35 E 76th St, cnr Madison Ave; ⏰noon-1am; Ⓢ6 to 77th St) Sink into a chocolate-leather banquette and take in the glorious, old-school elegance of this fabled bar – the sort of place where the waiters wear white jackets, a pianist tinkles away on a baby grand and the ceiling is 24-carat gold leaf. The walls are covered in charming murals by the bar's namesake Ludwig Bemelman, famed creator of the *Madeline* books.

Show up before 9pm if you don't want to pay a cover charge (per person $15 to $35).

SEAMSTRESS BAR

Map p430 (☎212-288-8033; www.seamstressny.com; 339 E 75th St, btwn First & Second Aves; ⏰5:30pm-midnight Sun-Thu, to 2am Fri & Sat; ⓈQ to 72nd St; 6 to 77th St) This rare uptown gem serves craft cocktails and seasonal pub

Neighborhood Walk
Memorable Manhattan Movies

START BLOOMINGDALE'S
END METROPOLITAN MUSEUM OF ART
LENGTH 1.5 MILES; TWO HOURS

An exploration of Manhattan's most storied film sites takes you past movie locations big and small.

Start outside **1 Bloomingdale's** (p208), where Darryl Hannah and Tom Hanks shattered televisions in *Splash* (1984) and Dustin Hoffman hailed a cab in *Tootsie* (1982). West of here, 10 E 60th St is the site of the now-defunct **2 Copacabana**, a nightclub (now an upscale restaurant) that hosted Ray Liotta and Lorraine Bracco in *Goodfellas* (1990) and a coked-up lawyer played by Sean Penn in *Carlito's Way* (1993).

Continue west to **3 Central Park** (p228), which has appeared in *The Royal Tenenbaums* (2001), *Ghostbusters* (1983), *The Muppets Take Manhattan* (1983), *Barefoot in the Park* (1967) and the cult classic *The Warriors* (1979). From here, head east to Park Ave. At 620 Park Ave (at 65th St) is the building that housed **4 John Malkovich's apartment** in Charlie Kaufman's *Being John Malkovich* (1999). Seven blocks to the north, 114 E 72nd St is the **5 highrise** where Sylvia Miles lured Jon Voight in *Midnight Cowboy* (1969).

One block to the east and south is 171 E 71st St, a town house featured in one of the most famous movies ever filmed in New York: this was **6 Holly Golightly's apartment** in *Breakfast at Tiffany's* (1961). Continuing east to Third Ave, you'll find **7 JG Melon** at the corner of 74th St; besides being a good spot for a beer and a burger, it was also the site of a meeting between Dustin Hoffman and Meryl Streep in *Kramer vs Kramer* (1979).

Head west to Madison Ave; the posh **8 Carlyle Hotel**, at the corner of 76th St, is where Woody Allen and Dianne Wiest had a date from hell in *Hannah and Her Sisters* (1986). From the Carlyle, it's a short walk north and west to the **9 Metropolitan Museum of Art** (p214) at 82nd St and Fifth Ave, where Angie Dickinson had a fatal encounter in *Dressed to Kill* (1980) and Billy Crystal chatted up Meg Ryan in *When Harry Met Sally* (1989).

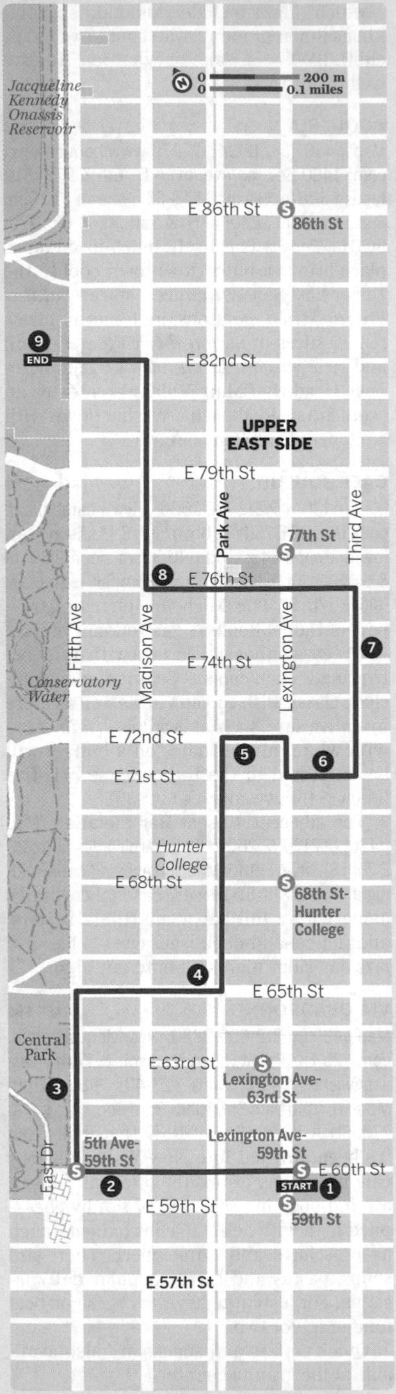

fare in a screen-free environment that feels much more downtown. Sit at the bar or arrive early and sink into a dark leather banquette. Nibble on oysters, raw field greens or a mutton burger, while sipping complex libations made of rye whiskey, pomegranate liqueur and other unusual spirits.

UVA WINE BAR

Map p430 (☎212-472-4552; www.uvanyc.com; 1486 Second Ave, btwn E 77th & 78th Sts; ⏰4pm-2am Mon-Fri, from 11am Sat, 11am-1am Sun; Ⓢ6 to 77th St) Rustic brick walls, low-lit chandeliers and worn floorboards give this lively eating and drinking spot the feel of an old European tavern. There are dozens of wines by the glass (from $9) plus wine flights (before 7pm), allowing you to sample a range of varietals (particularly Italian). In summer, head for the lovely patio out back.

DAISY BAR

Map p430 (☎646-964-5756; www.thedaisynyc.com; 1641 Second Ave, cnr E 85th St; ⏰4pm-2am Mon-Fri, 11am-4am Sat & Sun; ⓈQ, 4/5/6 to 86th St) Swish gastropub Daisy serves up craft cocktails and creative, seasonal bar plates like duck-fat fingerlings and steak tartare. Unlike most other Upper East Side bars, there are no TVs or packs of loud partygoers here – it's a laid-back, low-lit spot, with art deco touches, good grooves, skilled bartenders and a friendly crowd.

DRUNKEN MUNKEY LOUNGE

Map p430 (☎646-998-4600; www.drunkenmunkeynyc.com; 338 E 92nd St, btwn First & Second Aves; ⏰4:30pm-2am Mon-Thu, to 3am Fri, 11am-3am Sat, to 2am Sun; ⓈQ, 6 to 96th St) This playful lounge channels colonial-era Bombay with vintage wallpaper, cricket-ball door handles and jauntily attired waitstaff. The monkey chandeliers may be pure whimsy, but the craft cocktails and tasty curries (small, meant for sharing) are serious business. Gin, not surprisingly, is the drink of choice. Try the Bramble: Bombay gin, blackberry liqueur and fresh lemon juice and blackberries.

AUCTION HOUSE BAR

Map p430 (☎212-427-4458; www.theauctionhousenyc.com; 300 E 89th St, at Second Ave; ⏰7:30pm-2am Sun-Thu, to 4am Fri & Sat; ⓈQ to 86th St) Dark maroon doors lead into a candlelit hangout that's perfect for a relaxing drink. Victorian-style couches and fat, overstuffed easy chairs are strewn about the wood-floored rooms. Take your well-mixed cocktail to a seat by the fireplace and admire the scene reflected in the gilt-edged mirrors propped up on the walls.

IRVING FARM ROASTERS COFFEE

Map p430 (☎646-861-2949; www.irvingfarm.com; 1424 Third Ave, cnr E 81st St; ⏰10am-8pm Mon-Fri, from 11am Sat & Sun; Ⓢ6 to 77th St; 4/5 to 86th St) This pioneering New York artisanal coffeehouse – it roasts its own beans in a tiny town 98 miles upstate – serves up full-bodied espressos and single-origin pour-overs, along with a small yet tasty cafe menu. This is the largest of its nine Manhattan locations, with a roomy seating area at the back. Its policy is 'no wi-fi' – bring a book.

SANT AMBROEUS COFFEE

Map p430 (☎212-339-4051; www.santambroeus.com; entrance on E 61st St, 540 Park Ave, Loews Regency Hotel; ⏰7am-8pm Mon-Fri, from 8am Sat & Sun; ⓈF, Q to Lexington Ave-63rd St; 4/5/6 to 59th St) Sidle up to the rust-colored marble counters and enjoy your espresso standing in the Italian manner. This coffee-bar outpost of the Milan-inspired **restaurant** (Map p430; ☎212-570-2211; www.santambroeus.com; 1000 Madison Ave, btwn E 77th & 78th Sts; panini $14-19, mains $26-69; ⏰7am-11pm Mon-Fri, from 8am Sat & Sun; 🖉; Ⓢ6 to 77th St) of the same name offers a range of desserts and pastries, plus some of its signature panini. Though located in the Loews Regency Hotel, the entrance is around the corner on 61st.

OSLO COFFEE ROASTERS COFFEE

Map p430 (www.oslocoffee.com; 422 E 75th St, btwn York & First Aves; coffee from $3; ⏰7am-7pm Mon-Fri, from 8am Sat & Sun; ⓈQ to 72nd St; 6 to 77th St) A somewhat-remote outpost of the Williamsburg-based roasters, Oslo whips up magnificent brews, espressos and lattes – all fair trade and organic, of course. A minus: the small shop has little seating, though there are some benches out front.

☆ ENTERTAINMENT

92ND STREET Y CULTURAL CENTER

Map p430 (☎212-415-5500; www.92y.org; 1395 Lexington Ave, cnr E 92nd St; 👪; ⓈQ, 6 to 96th St) In addition to its wide spectrum of concerts, dance performances, literary readings and family-friendly events, this nonprofit cultural center hosts an excellent lecture and conversation series. Playwright Edward Albee, cellist Yo-Yo Ma, comedian Steve Martin and novelist Salman Rushdie have all taken the stage here.

FRICK COLLECTION CONCERTS CLASSICAL MUSIC

Map p430 (212-288-0700; www.frick.org; 1 E 70th St, cnr Fifth Ave; $45; 5pm Sun; S 6 to 68th St-Hunter College; Q to 72nd St) Once a month this opulent mansion-museum (p218) hosts a Sunday 5pm concert that brings in world-renowned performers, such as cellist Yehuda Hanani and violinist Thomas Zehetmair.

CAFÉ CARLYLE JAZZ

Map p430 (212-744-1600; www.thecarlyle.com; Carlyle Hotel, 35 E 76th St, cnr Madison Ave; cover $95-215, food & drink min $25-75; shows at 8:45pm & 10:45pm; S 6 to 77th St) This swanky spot at the Carlyle Hotel draws top-shelf talent. Woody Allen plays his clarinet here with the Eddy Davis New Orleans Jazz Band on Mondays at 8:45pm (September through May). Bring mucho bucks: the cover charge doesn't include food or drinks, and there's a minimum spend. The dress code is 'chic' – gentlemen, wear a jacket.

COMIC STRIP LIVE COMEDY

Map p430 (212-861-9386; www.comicstriplive.com; 1568 Second Ave, btwn E 81st & 82nd Sts; cover charge $15-20, plus 2-item min; shows 8pm Mon-Sun, plus 10:30pm Fri & Sat; S Q, 4/5/6 to 86th St) Big names Chris Rock, Sarah Silverman, Aziz Ansari, Jerry Seinfeld and Ellen DeGeneres have all performed at this club. Not recently, maybe, but you're sure to find somebody cribbing their acts here most nights. With high prices for food and drinks you may not be laughing when you see the bill. Reservations required.

SHOPPING

Madison Ave isn't for amateurs. Some of the globe's glitziest shops line the stretch from 60th St to 72nd St, with flagship boutiques from the world's top designers, including Gucci, Prada and Cartier. A handful of consignment stores offer preloved designer deals. Further east, a range of more general – though still upmarket – stores line Lexington, Third and Second Aves, with everything from cosmetics and fashion to books and quirky gifts.

FLYING TIGER COPENHAGEN GIFTS & SOUVENIRS

Map p430 (917-388-2812; www.flyingtiger.com; 1282 Third Ave, cnr E 74th St; 10am-8pm Mon-Sat, 11am-6pm Sun; S Q to 72nd St; 6 to 77th St) This eclectic Danish design store is an emporium of quirky-yet-useful items. Almost everything is priced under $5 and festooned with bright colors and fun patterns: housewares, art supplies, writing journals, toys and games, accessories etc. It's great for low-priced gifts or emergency travel spares (eg USB cables, mini umbrellas). Ever wanted a Doodling Robot? You'll find it here.

MARY ARNOLD TOYS TOYS

Map p430 (212-744-8510; www.maryarnoldtoys.com; 1178 Lexington Ave, btwn E 80th & 81st Sts; 9am-6pm Mon-Fri, from 10am Sat, 10am-5pm Sun; ; S 4/5/6 to 86th St) Several generations of Upper East Siders have spent large chunks of their childhood browsing the stuffed shelves of this personable local toy store, opened in 1931. Its range is extensive – stuffed animals, action figures, science kits, board games, arts and crafts, educational toys, you name it. Check the website for free monthly events, such as scavenger hunts or Lego-making sessions.

RICKY'S NYC COSMETICS

Map p430 (212-988-2291; www.rickysnyc.com; 1425 Second Ave, cnr E 74th St; 9am-9pm Mon-Sat, 10am-8pm Sun; S Q to 72nd St) One of the many branches of this classic New York beauty shop, Ricky's carries a huge variety of makeup, skincare and hair products from around the world (brands include NYX, Klorane, OPI), plus salon-quality accessories and appliances. It also has a range of fun and quirky gifts, and at Halloween time it's a go-to shop for costumes and theatrical makeup.

DIPTYQUE PERFUME

Map p430 (212-879-3330; www.diptyqueparis.com; 971 Madison Ave, cnr E 76th St; 10am-7pm Mon-Sat, noon-6pm Sun; S 6 to 77th St) Come out smelling like a rose – or wisteria, jasmine, cypress or sandalwood – at this olfactory oasis. Parisian company Diptyque has been creating signature scents since 1961, using innovative combinations of plants, woods and flowers. Besides perfumes and other personal fragrances (our favorite is the woodsy Tam Dao), it also has a large range of candles, lotions and soaps.

JACADI CHILDREN'S CLOTHING

Map p430 (212-717-9292; www.jacadi.us; 1260 3rd Ave, btwn E 72nd & 73rd Sts; 10am-6pm Mon-Sat, 11:30am-5:30pm Sun; ; S Q to 72nd St; 6 to 68th St-Hunter College) Fashionistas aren't born: they're made. And where better to start than with some on-trend duds from this Parisian purveyor of effortlessly chic kids' clothes and shoes? With a range of seasonal choices for girls and boys (newborns to tweens) – scalloped-collar cardigans, shearling-cuff boots – your kids will be the best-dressed in their class.

ENCORE CLOTHING

Map p430 (212-879-2850; www.encoreresale.com; 1132 Madison Ave, btwn E 84th & 85th Sts, 2nd fl; 10am-6:30pm Mon-Sat, noon-6pm Sun; S 4/5/6 to 86th St) Upper East Side fashionistas have been emptying out their closets at this pioneering consignment and resale shop since 1954. (Even Jacqueline Kennedy Onassis used to sell her clothes here.) Expect to find a gently worn selection of name brands such as Louboutin, Fendi and Dior. Prices are high, but infinitely better than retail.

MICHAEL'S CLOTHING

Map p430 (212-737-7273; www.michaelsconsignment.com; 1041 Madison Ave, btwn E 79th & 80th Sts, 2nd fl; 10am-6pm Mon-Sat, to 8pm Thu; S 6 to 77th St) In operation since the 1950s, this vaunted Upper East Side resale store features high-end labels, including Chanel, Gucci and Prada – and an entire shelf dedicated to Jimmy Choo heels. Almost everything on display is less than two years old. It's pricey but cheaper than shopping the flagship boutiques on Madison Ave.

SHAKESPEARE & CO BOOKS

Map p430 (212-772-3400; www.shakeandco.com; 939 Lexington Ave, cnr E 69th St; 7:30am-8pm Mon-Fri, 8am-7pm Sat, 9am-6pm Sun; ; S 6 to 68th St) No relation to the Paris seller, this popular bookstore is one of NYC's great indie options. There's a wide array of contemporary fiction and nonfiction, art and local history books, plus a small but unique collection of periodicals, while an Espresso book machine churns out print-on-demand titles. The small cafe up front serves coffee, tea and light meals.

SPORTS & ACTIVITIES

ART FARM IN THE CITY PLAYGROUND

Map p430 (212-410-3117; www.theartfarms.org/afic; 419 E 91st St, btwn First & York Aves; per child Open Play/Fun Friday $20/45; Open Play 12:30-3:30pm Mon-Thu, Fun Fridays 9:30-11:30am Fri; ; S Q to 96th St) If your little ones have museum fatigue, let them recharge at this kids' activity center. Open Play Time (for kids six months to eight years old) features arts and crafts, and cuddling with the resident animals, while Fun Friday session (18 months to eight years) adds in baking time and musical sing-alongs. All children must be accompanied by an adult.

Upper West Side & Central Park

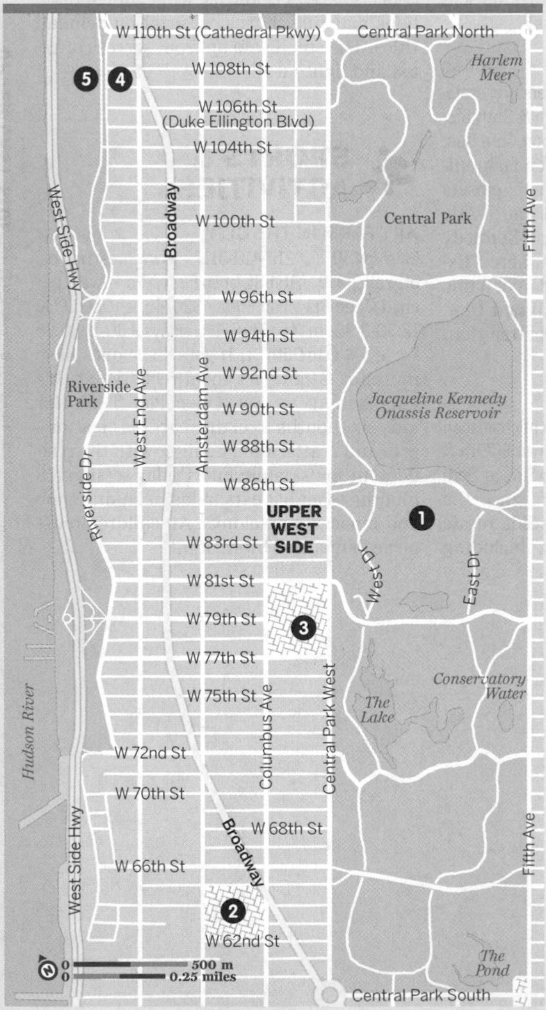

For more detail of this area see Map p432

Neighborhood Top Five

❶ **Central Park** (p228) Escaping the city's frantic urban madness with a day spent picnicking on Sheep Meadow, row-boating on the lake and strolling the grand Literary Walk.

❷ **Lincoln Center** (p232) Plunging into the sheer depth of artistic choices at this world-class arts center with some of the world's best opera, ballet, classical music, film and theatre.

❸ **American Museum of Natural History** (p234) Walking among some of the world's largest dinosaurs and running your hand along the pitted surface of the largest meteorite in the US.

❹ **Nicholas Roerich Museum** (p234) Taking a pilgrimage to Tibet through the mind of a remarkable man, all inside a beautiful 19th-century town house.

❺ **Riverside Park** (p233) Jogging, cycling or even just strolling along the Hudson waterfront as the sun goes down over the river's far shore.

Explore Upper West Side & Central Park

The central western section of Manhattan offers a lot of ground to cover, so the best plan of attack will depend on what you want to see. Traveling with tykes? Dazzle their budding brains with a visit to the American Museum of Natural History (p234), followed by a journey through the sprawling wonderland that is Central Park (p228). (The street running parallel to the park, Central Park West, is lined with stately apartment buildings that are lovely to admire if you can deal with the real-estate envy.) If the arts are high on your list, head to Lincoln Center (p232), where the Metropolitan Opera, the New York Philharmonic and the New York City Ballet offer vibrant doses of culture. But if your idea of a good time is just ambling around a neighborhood, then take in the sights on and around Broadway in the 70s, an area packed with bustling shops and fine architecture. To experience a quieter green space, head to Riverside Park (p233), along the far western edge of Manhattan, for a nice long stroll with views of the Hudson River – particularly lovely at sunset.

Local Life

➡ **Go fishing** Wood-smoked lox. Briny pickled herring. Meaty sturgeon. It doesn't get more Upper West Side than examining the seafood treats at Zabar's (p242) and Barney Greengrass (p236).

➡ **Central chill** You can pick out the tourists in Central Park (p228) because they're rushing between sights. Make like a local by picking out a patch of green with good views and letting the world pass by.

➡ **Catch a flick** Manhattan's die-hard film buffs can be found taking in quality cinema courtesy of the Film Society of Lincoln Center (p241).

➡ **Late-night munchies** Nothing is more New York than soaking up the evening's liquor damage with a 2am hot dog from Gray's Papaya (p236).

Getting There & Away

➡ **Subway** The 1, 2 and 3 lines are good for destinations between Broadway and the river, while the B and C trains are best for museums and Central Park (which can be accessed from every side). The A/C, B/D and 1 stop at Columbus Circle and 59th St, at Central Park's southwestern corner, and go north from there; the N/R/W line goes to the southeast. The 2 or 3 stops at the northern gate in Harlem.

➡ **Bus** The M104 runs along Broadway; the M10 along the park's scenic western edge. Crosstown routes at 66th, 72nd, 79th, 86th and 96th Sts go through the park to the Upper East Side, stopping at Central Park West and Fifth Ave – not inside the park.

Lonely Planet's Top Tip

The best way to cover all 840 acres of Central Park is to rent a bicycle; Bike & Roll (p243), Toga Bike Shop (p244) and Champion Bicycles (p244) all offer rentals. A full ride of the Central Park loop is 6.2 miles long, and takes in both hilly and flat terrain (the northern half is generally hillier than the south). You can see more information and a map of the park's paths at the Central Park Conservancy website (www.centralparknyc.org).

Best Places to Eat

➡ Jacob's Pickles (p236)
➡ Burke & Wills (p237)
➡ Peacefood Cafe (p235)
➡ Kefi (p236)
➡ Dovetail (p237)

For reviews, see p234. ➡

Best Places to Drink

➡ Manhattan Cricket Club (p237)
➡ Dead Poet (p240)
➡ West End Hall (p240)
➡ West 79th Street Boat Basin Café (p235)

For reviews, see p237. ➡

Best Live Music Spots

➡ Metropolitan Opera House (p240)
➡ SummerStage (p233)
➡ Smoke (p241)
➡ Cleopatra's Needle (p242)
➡ Beacon Theatre (p241)

For reviews, see p240. ➡

GABRIELPEVIDE / GETTY IMAGES ©

TOP SIGHT
CENTRAL PARK

With more than 800 acres of picturesque meadows, ponds and woods, Central Park might seem to be Manhattan in its raw state. But the park, designed by Frederick Law Olmsted and Calvert Vaux, is the result of serious engineering: thousands of workers shifted 10 million cartloads of soil to transform swamp and rocky outcroppings into the 'people's park' of today.

Birth of a Park
In the 1850s, this area of Manhattan was occupied by pig farms, a garbage dump, a bone-boiling operation and an African American village. It took 20,000 laborers two decades to transform this terrain into a park. Today, Central Park has more than 24,000 trees, 136 acres of woodland, 21 playgrounds and seven bodies of water – and more than 38 million visitors a year.

Bethesda Terrace & the Mall
The arched walkways of **Bethesda Terrace** (Map p432; 66th to 72nd St; SB, C to 72nd St), crowned by the magnificent **Bethesda Fountain** (Map p432; SB, C to 72nd St), have long been a gathering area for New Yorkers. To the south is the Mall (featured in countless movies), a promenade shrouded in mature North American elms. The southern stretch, known as **Literary Walk** (Map p432; btwn 67th & 72nd Sts; SN/R/W to 5th Ave-59th St), is flanked by statues of famous authors.

Central Park Zoo
Officially known as Central Park Wildlife Center (but no one calls it that), this small **zoo** (Map p432; 212-439-6500; www.centralparkzoo.com; 64th St, at Fifth Ave; adult/child $12/7; 10am-5pm Mon-Fri, to 5:30 Sat & Sun; ; SN/Q/R to 5th Ave-59th St) is home to penguins, snow

DON'T MISS
- The Mall
- The Reservoir
- Bethesda Fountain
- Conservatory Garden

PRACTICALITIES
- Map p432, D5
- www.centralparknyc.org
- 59th to 110th Sts, btwn Central Park West & Fifth Ave
- 6am-1am
-

leopards, poison dart frogs and red pandas. Feeding times in the sea-lion and penguin tanks make for a rowdy spectacle. The attached **Tisch Children's Zoo** (Map p432; 212-439-6500; www.centralparkzoo.com; at W 65th & Fifth Ave; adult/child $12/7; 10am-5pm Mon-Fri, to 5:30pm Sat & Sun; ; S N/Q/R to 5th Ave-59th St), a petting zoo, has alpacas and mini-Nubian goats and is perfect for small children.

Conservatory Water & Alice in Wonderland

North of the zoo (at 74th St) is Conservatory Water, where model sailboats drift lazily and kids scramble about on a toadstool-studded statue of Alice in Wonderland. There are Saturday story hours (www.hcastorycenter.org) at 11am from June to September at the Hans Christian Andersen statue, to the west of the water.

Great Lawn & the Ramble

The **Great Lawn** (Map p432; btwn 79th & 86th Sts; mid-Apr–mid-Nov; S B, C to 86th St) is a massive emerald carpet at the center of the park, surrounded by ball fields and London plane trees. (It's where Simon & Garfunkel played their famous 1981 concert.) Immediately to the southeast is **Delacorte Theater** (Map p432; www.publictheater.org; enter at W 81st St; S B, C to 81st St), home to an annual Shakespeare in the Park festival, as well as Belvedere Castle (p244), a bird-watching lookout. Further south is the leafy **Ramble** (Map p432; midpark from 73rd to 79th Sts; S B,C to 81st St), a popular birding destination. On the southeastern end is the Loeb Boathouse (p244), home to a waterside restaurant that offers rowboat rentals and gondola rides.

Jacqueline Kennedy Onassis Reservoir

The reservoir (at 90th St) takes up almost the entire width of the park and serves as a gorgeous reflecting pool for the city skyline. It is surrounded by a 1.58-mile track that draws legions of joggers in the warmer months. Nearby, at Fifth Ave and 90th St, is a statue of New York City Marathon founder Fred Lebow, peering at his watch.

Strawberry Fields

This tear-shaped **garden** (Map p432; at 72nd St on the west side; S A/C, B to 72nd St) serves as a memorial to former Beatle John Lennon, who lived directly across the street in the **Dakota apartment building** (Map p432; 1 W 72nd St; S B, C to 72nd St). The garden, which was underwritten by his widow Yoko Ono, is composed of a grove of stately elms and a tiled mosaic that reads, simply, 'Imagine.'

CONSERVATORY GARDEN

If you want a little peace and quiet (as in, no runners, cyclists or buskers), the 6-acre **Conservatory Garden** (Map p432; Fifth Ave at 105th St; 8am-5pm Nov-Feb, to 6pm Mar & Oct, to 7pm Apr & Sep, to 7:30pm or 8pm Aug, to 8pm May-Jul; S 6 to 103rd St) serves as one of the park's official quiet zones. And it's beautiful, to boot: bursting with crabapple trees, meandering boxwood and, in the spring, lots of flowers.

NORTH WOODS & BLOCKHOUSE

The North Woods, on the west side between 106th and 110th Sts, is home to the park's oldest structure, the **Blockhouse** (Map p432; www.centralparknyc.org; Central Park, near 108th St & Central Park West), a military fortification from the War of 1812.

VISITING THE PARK

Guided walking tours (some free) are available via the **Central Park Conservancy** (Map p424; 212-310-6600; www.centralparknyc.org/tours; 14 E 60th St, btwn Madison & Fifth Aves; S N/R/W to 5th Ave-59th St), a nonprofit organization that supports park maintenance. It can also design custom tours.

Central Park

THE LUNGS OF NEW YORK

The rectangular patch of green that occupies Manhattan's heart began life in the mid-19th century as a swampy piece of land that was carefully bulldozed into the idyllic nature-scape you see today. Since officially becoming Central Park, it has brought New Yorkers of all stripes together in interesting and unexpected ways. The park has served as a place for the rich to show off their fancy carriages (1860s), for the poor to enjoy free Sunday concerts (1880s) and for activists to hold be-ins against the Vietnam War (1960s).

Since then, legions of locals – not to mention travelers from all kinds of faraway places – have poured in to stroll, picnic, sunbathe, play ball and catch free concerts and performances of works by Shakespeare.

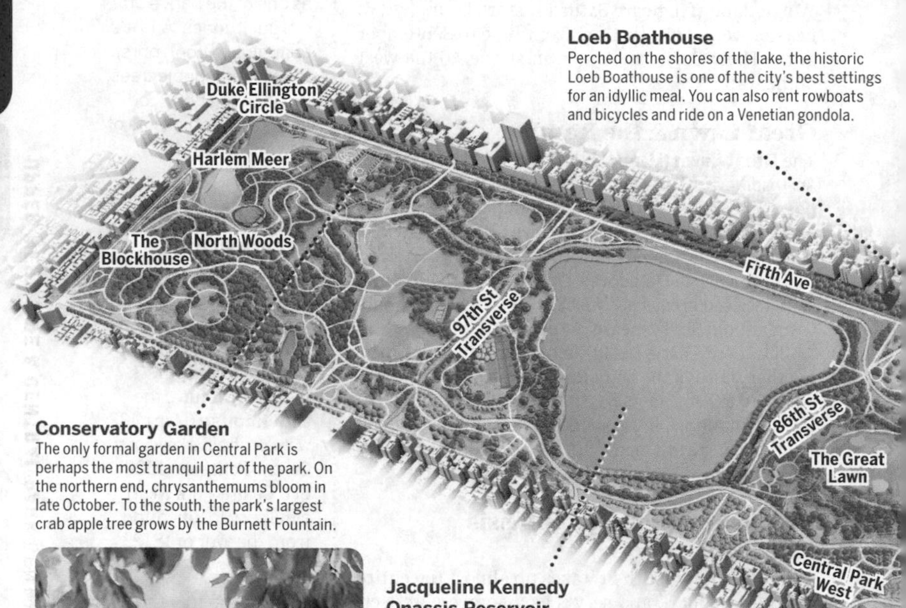

Loeb Boathouse
Perched on the shores of the lake, the historic Loeb Boathouse is one of the city's best settings for an idyllic meal. You can also rent rowboats and bicycles and ride on a Venetian gondola.

Conservatory Garden
The only formal garden in Central Park is perhaps the most tranquil part of the park. On the northern end, chrysanthemums bloom in late October. To the south, the park's largest crab apple tree grows by the Burnett Fountain.

STUDIOLASKA/SHUTTERSTOCK ©

Jacqueline Kennedy Onassis Reservoir
This 106-acre body of water covers roughly an eighth of the park's territory. Its original purpose was to provide clean water for the city. Now it's a good spot to catch a glimpse of water birds.

LULU AND ISABELLE/SHUTTERSTOCK ©

Belvedere Castle
A so-called 'Victorian folly,' this Gothic-Romanesque castle serves no other purpose than to be a very dramatic lookout point. It was built by Central Park co-designer Calvert Vaux in 1869.

The park's varied terrain offers a wonderland of experiences. There are quiet, woodsy knolls in the north. To the south is the reservoir, crowded with joggers. There are European gardens, a zoo and various bodies of water. For maximum flamboyance, hit the Sheep Meadow on a sunny day, when all of New York shows up to lounge.

Central Park is more than just a green space. It is New York City's backyard.

FAST FACTS

- ➡ The landscape architects were Frederick Law Olmsted and Calvert Vaux.
- ➡ Construction commenced in 1858.
- ➡ The park covers 843 acres.
- ➡ Hundreds of movies have been shot on location, from Depression-era blockbuster *Gold Diggers* (1933) to monster-attack flick *Cloverfield* (2008).

Conservatory Water
This pond is popular in the warmer months, when children sail their model boats across its surface. Conservatory Water was inspired by 19th-century Parisian model-boat ponds and figured prominently in EB White's classic book, *Stuart Little*.

CHRISTOPHER PENLER/SHUTTERSTOCK ©

KRIDSADA KAMSOMEAT/SHUTTERSTOCK ©

Bethesda Fountain
This neoclassical fountain is one of New York's largest. It's capped by the *Angel of the Waters*, which is supported by four cherubim. The fountain was created by bohemian-feminist sculptor Emma Stebbins in 1868.

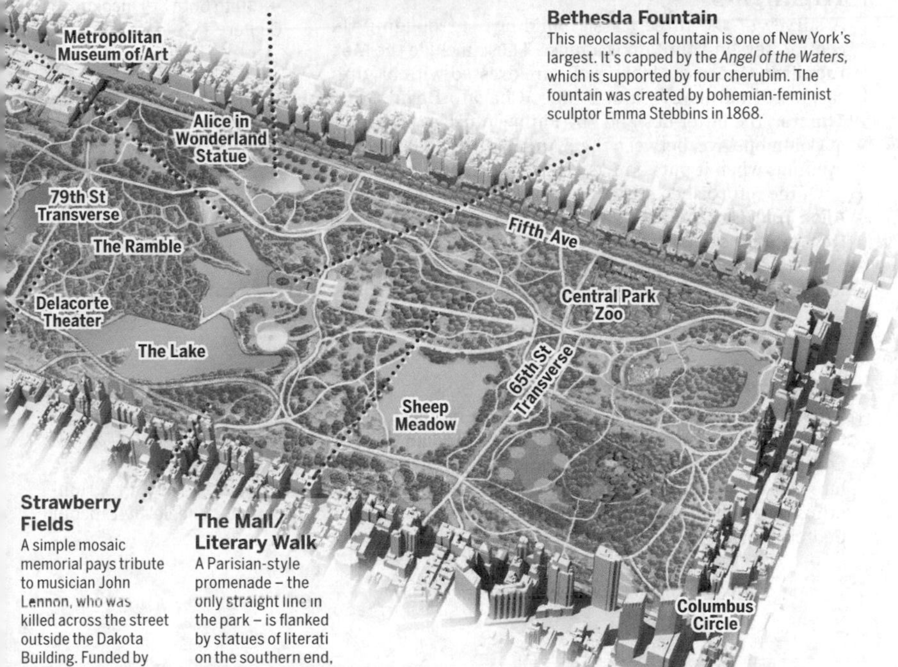

Strawberry Fields
A simple mosaic memorial pays tribute to musician John Lennon, who was killed across the street outside the Dakota Building. Funded by Yoko Ono, its name is inspired by the Beatles song 'Strawberry Fields Forever.'

The Mall/ Literary Walk
A Parisian-style promenade – the only straight line in the park – is flanked by statues of literati on the southern end, including Robert Burns and Shakespeare. It is lined with rare North American elms.

TOP SIGHT
LINCOLN CENTER

This stark arrangement of gleaming modernist temples contains some of Manhattan's most important performance spaces, home to the finest opera, ballet and symphony orchestra in New York City. Various other venues are tucked in and around the 16-acre campus, including two theaters, two film-screening centers and the world-renowned Julliard School.

A History of Building & Rebuilding

Built in the 1960s, this imposing arts campus replaced a neighborhood of tenements called San Juan Hill (gleefully bulldozed by urban planner Robert Moses), a predominantly African American neighborhood where the exterior shots for the movie *West Side Story* were filmed. In addition to being a controversial urban-planning move, Lincoln Center wasn't exactly well-received at an architectural level – it was relentlessly criticized for its conservative design, fortresslike aspect and poor acoustics. For the center's 50th anniversary (2009–10), Diller Scofidio + Renfro and other architects gave the complex a much-needed and critically acclaimed freshening up.

Highlights

A survey of the three classic buildings surrounding the central Revson Fountain is a must. These include the **Metropolitan Opera** (its lobby walls are dressed with brightly saturated murals by painter Marc Chagall) **David Geffen Hall** and the **David H Koch Theater**, the latter designed by Philip Johnson. (These are all located on the main plaza at Columbus Ave, between 62nd and 65th Sts.) The **Revson Fountain** is spectacular in the evenings when it puts on Las Vegas–like light shows.

Of the refurbished structures, there are a number that are worth examining, including **Alice Tully Hall**, now displaying a very contemporary translucent, angled facade, and the **David Rubenstein Atrium** (Map p432; ☎212-721-6500; http://atrium.lincolncenter.org; 61 W 62nd St, at Broadway; ⌚atrium 8am-10pm Mon-Fri, 9am-10pm Sat & Sun, ticket box office noon-7pm Tue-Sat, to 5pm Sun), a public space offering a lounge area (with free wi-fi), a cafe, an information desk and a ticket vendor selling discounted same-day tickets to Lincoln Center performances. Free events are held here on Thursday evenings.

Performances & Screenings

On any given night, there are at least 10 performances happening throughout Lincoln Center – and even more in summer, when **Lincoln Center Out of Doors** (a series of dance and music concerts) and **Midsummer Night Swing** (ballroom dancing under the stars) lure those who love their culture alfresco. For details on seasons, tickets and programming – which runs the gamut from opera to dance to theater to ballet – check the Lincoln Center website.

DON'T MISS

- Revson Fountain
- Marc Chagall murals
- Attending a performance

PRACTICALITIES

- Map p432, B7
- ☎212-875-5456, tours 212-875-5350
- www.lincolncenter.org
- Columbus Ave, btwn W 62nd & 66th Sts
- tours adult/student $25/20
- ⌚tours 11:30am & 1:30pm Mon-Sat, 3pm Sun
- 👪
- S 1 to 66th St-Lincoln Center

SIGHTS

CENTRAL PARK
PARK

See p228.

LINCOLN CENTER
ARTS CENTER

See p232.

STRAUS PARK
PARK

Map p432 (www.nycgovparks.org; Broadway btwn 106th & 107th Sts; S 1 to 103rd or 110th Sts) This leafy little triangle is dedicated to the memory of Ida and Isidor Straus, a wealthy couple (Isidor owned Macy's) who died together in 1912 on the *Titanic,* when Ida insisted on staying with her husband instead of boarding a lifeboat. A curving granite exedra bears a fitting biblical quote: 'Lovely and pleasant were they in their lives and in their death they were not divided.' Its many shaded benches make it a popular neighborhood spot on a warm day.

NEW-YORK HISTORICAL SOCIETY
MUSEUM

Map p432 (212-873-3400; www.nyhistory.org; 170 Central Park West, at W 77th St; adult/child $20/6, by donation 6-8pm Fri, library free; 10am-6pm Tue-Thu & Sat, to 8pm Fri, 11am-5pm Sun; ; S B, C to 81st St-Museum of Natural History) As the antiquated hyphenated name implies, the Historical Society is the city's oldest museum, founded in 1804 to preserve the city's historical and cultural artifacts. Its collection of more than 60,000 objects is quirky and fascinating and includes everything from George Washington's inauguration chair to a 19th-century Tiffany ice-cream dish (gilded, of course), plus a remarkable collection of Hudson River School paintings. However, it's far from stodgy, having moved into the 21st century with renewed vigor and purpose.

Redesigned with a sleek and modern aesthetic and an emphasis on interactive technology, the building houses several museums in one. The 4th floor is now occupied by the immersive Center for Women's History, the only one of its kind in a major American museum, part of the revamped Henry Luce III Center. Plus, there's a children's museum, lectures and other educational activities.

A few other notable treasures of the permanent collection include a leg brace worn by President Franklin D Roosevelt, a 19th-century mechanical bank in which a political figure slips coins into his pocket and photographer Jack Stewart's graffiti-covered door from the 1970s (featuring tags by known graffiti writers such as Tracy 168). In the lobby, be sure to look up: the ceiling mural from Keith Haring's 1986 'Pop Shop' hangs above the admissions desk.

RIVERSIDE PARK
PARK

Map p432 (212-870-3070; www.riversideparknyc.org; Riverside Dr, btwn 68th & 155th Sts; 6am-1am; ; S 1/2/3 to any stop btwn 66th & 157th Sts) A classic beauty designed by Central Park creators Frederick Law Olmsted and Calvert Vaux, this waterside spot, running north on the Upper West Side and banked by the Hudson River from 59th to 155th Sts, is lusciously leafy. Plenty of bike paths, playgrounds and dog runs make it a family favorite. Views from the park make the Jersey side of the Hudson look quite pretty.

From late March through October (weather permitting), lively waterside restaurant West 79th Street Boat Basin Café (p235) serves a light menu at the level of

SUMMER HAPPENINGS IN CENTRAL PARK

During the warm months, Central Park is home to countless cultural events, many of which are free. The two most popular are **Shakespeare in the Park** (www.publictheater.org), which is managed by the Public Theater, and **SummerStage** (www.cityparksfoundation.org/summerstage; Rumsey Playfield, Central Park, access via Fifth Ave & 69th St; Jun-Sep; ; S 6 to 68th St-Hunter College), a series of free concerts.

Tickets for Shakespeare in the Park are given out at 1pm on the day of the performance, but if you want to be sure of getting a seat, line up by 8am and make sure you have something to sit on, and your entire group with you. Tickets are free and there's only one per person; no latecomers are allowed in line.

SummerStage concert venues are generally opened to the public 1½ hours prior to the start of the show. But if it's a popular act, start queuing up early or you won't get in.

TOP SIGHT AMERICAN MUSEUM OF NATURAL HISTORY

Founded in 1869, this classic museum contains a veritable wonderland of some 30 million artifacts, plus a cutting-edge planetarium. From October through May, it's home to the Butterfly Conservatory, featuring 500-plus butterflies from around the globe. But perhaps best known are its Fossil Halls containing nearly 600 specimens, including the skeletons of a massive mammoth and a fearsome *Tyrannosaurus rex*.

There are plentiful animal exhibits, galleries devoted to gems and an IMAX theater. The Hall of Ocean Life contains dioramas devoted to ecology and conservation, as well as a beloved 94ft replica of a blue whale suspended from the ceiling. At the 77th St Grand Gallery, visitors are greeted by a 63ft, 19th-century canoe, carved by the Haida people of British Columbia.

For the space set, the Rose Center for Earth & Space is the star of the show. Its mesmerizing glass-box facade – home to space-show theaters and the planetarium – is an otherworldly setting. *Dark Universe*, narrated by Neil deGrasse Tyson, explores the mysteries and wonders of the cosmos; it screens every half hour for most of the day.

DON'T MISS

- *Tyrannosaurus rex*
- Hall of Ocean Life
- Hayden Big Bang Theater

PRACTICALITIES

- Map p432, C5
- 212-769-5100
- www.amnh.org
- Central Park West, at W 79th St
- suggested admission adult/child $23/13
- 10am-5:45pm
- S B, C to 81st St-Museum of Natural History; 1 to 79th St

79th St. Pier i Café (p236), an outdoor cafe nine blocks south on the waterfront, is another option.

NICHOLAS ROERICH MUSEUM MUSEUM
Map p432 (212-864-7752; www.roerich.org; 319 W 107th St, btwn Riverside Dr & Broadway; noon-5pm Tue-Fri, 2-5pm Sat & Sun; S 1 to Cathedral Pkwy-110th St) FREE This compelling little museum, housed in a three-story town house from 1898, is one of Manhattan's best-kept secrets. It displays 150 paintings by the prolific Nicholas Konstantinovich Roerich (1874–1947), a Russian-born poet, philosopher and painter. His most remarkable works are his stunning depictions of the Himalayas, where he and his family settled in 1928. Indeed, his mountainscapes are truly a wonder to behold: icy Tibetan peaks in shades of blue, white, green and purple, channeling a Georgia O'Keeffe/Rockwell Kent vibe.

AMERICAN FOLK ART MUSEUM MUSEUM
Map p432 (212-595-9533; www.folkartmuseum.org; 2 Lincoln Sq, Columbus Ave, btwn 65th & 66th Sts; 11:30am-7pm Tue-Thu & Sat, noon-7:30pm Fri, noon-6pm Sun; S 1 to 66th St-Lincoln Center) FREE This tiny institution offers rotating exhibitions that fill its three small galleries. Past exhibits have included quilts made from military fabrics by 19th-century soldiers, fashion in folk art, and American posthumous portraiture. The gift shop is a trove of unique, artsy items: books, jewelry, accessories, scarves, home decor etc. There's free music on Wednesdays (at 2pm) and Fridays (5:30pm).

During the months of November and December, the museum opens on Mondays from 11:30am to 7pm.

EATING

Though not particularly a dining destination, this huge swath of Manhattan nonetheless manages to serve up everything from old-style bagels to fancy French cassoulet to the latest in New American cooking. It's also an optimal area for off-the-hook picnic fixings: head to Zabar's (p242) or Whole Foods (p198) in the basement of Time Warner Center to pick up delicacies for an alfresco meal in nearby Central Park.

CAFE LALO DESSERTS $

Map p432 (☎212-496-6031; www.cafelalo.com; 201 W 83rd St, btwn Amsterdam & Columbus Ave; desserts around $10; ⊙9am-1am Sun-Thu, to 3am Fri & Sat; Ⓢ1 to 79th St; B, C to 81st St-Museum of Natural History) The vintage French posters and the marble-topped tables make this longtime Upper West Side date spot feel like a Parisian cafe. But forget decor – you're here for the mind-blowing array of desserts: choose (if you can) from 27 different cakes, 23 flavors of cheesecake, nine types of pie, a dozen kinds of fruit tart, cookies, pastries, zabaglione, chocolate mousse and more.

In a DIY mood? Get the chocolate fondue with fresh and dried fruit (for two). How about something sweet and buzzy? The affogato is a serving of rich vanilla ice cream 'drowned' (their word) with espresso and cognac. Don't feel left out, celiacs – they've even got a bunch of gluten-free sweets.

ÉPICERIE BOULUD DELI, FRENCH $

Map p432 (☎212-595-9606; www.epicerieboulud.com; 1900 Broadway, at W 64th St; sandwiches $9.50-14.50; ⊙7am-10pm Mon, to 11pm Tue-Sat, 8am-10pm Sun; ✎; Ⓢ1 to 66th St-Lincoln Center) A deli from star chef Daniel Boulud is no ordinary deli. Forget ham on rye – here you can order suckling pig confit, *jambon de Paris* and Gruyère on pressed ciabatta, or paprika-spiced flank steak with caramelized onions and three-grain mustard. Other options at this fast-gourmet spot include salads, soups, roast vegetables, pastry, gelato, coffee…and in the evening, oysters and wine.

When the weather's good, park yourself at one of its sidewalk tables – or better yet, take it across the street and sit by Lincoln Center's central fountain.

PEACEFOOD CAFE VEGAN $

Map p432 (☎212-362-2266; www.peacefoodcafe.com; 460 Amsterdam Ave, at 82nd St; mains $12-18; ⊙10am-10pm; ✎; Ⓢ1 to 79th St) This bright and airy vegan haven dishes up a popular fried seitan panini (served on homemade focaccia and topped with cashew cheese, arugula, tomatoes and pesto), as well as pizzas, roasted-vegetable plates and an excellent quinoa salad. There are daily raw specials, energy-fueling juices and rich desserts. Healthy and good – for you, the animals and the environment.

JIN RAMEN JAPANESE $

Map p432 (☎646-657-0755; www.jinramen.com; 462 Amsterdam Ave, btwn 82nd & 83rd Sts; mains $13-17; ⊙lunch 11:30am-3:30pm, dinner 5-11pm Mon-Thu, to midnight Fri & Sat, to 10pm Sun; ✎; Ⓢ1 to 79th St) This buzzing little joint off Amsterdam Ave serves up delectable bowls of piping hot ramen. *Tonkotsu* (pork broth) ramen is a favorite, though vegetarians also have options. Don't neglect the appetizers: *shishito* peppers, pork buns and *hijiki* salad. The mix of rustic wood elements, exposed bulbs and red industrial fixtures gives the place a cozy vibe.

BIRDBATH BAKERY BAKERY $

Map p432 (☎646-722-6562; www.thecitybakery.com/birdbath-bakery; 274 Columbus Ave, at 73rd St; mains $10-15; ⊙8am-7pm; ✎; Ⓢ1/2/3, B, C to 72nd St) Aside from not having much seating inside, it's hard to find fault with this delightful cafe. The menu changes daily and features excellent sandwiches, vitamin-rich juices and salads (try the chicken kale corn salad). Bakery items are outstanding. Birdbath also has an ecofriendly ethos implemented through the use of green building materials, recycled wood and deliveries made on bicycle.

TUM & YUM THAI $

Map p432 (☎212-222-1998; 917 Columbus Ave, at 105th St; mains $10-20; ⊙11:30am-10:45pm; ⓈB, C to 103rd St) This small neighborhood Thai eatery whips up excellent curries, crispy roast duck and steaming bowls of rich Tom Yum shrimp soup, best washed down with fresh coconut juice or a sweet Thai iced coffee. The rustic, all-wooden interior makes for a cozy retreat when the weather sours.

WEST 79TH STREET BOAT BASIN CAFÉ CAFE $

Map p432 (☎212-496-5542; www.boatbasincafe.com; W 79th St, at Henry Hudson Parkway; mains $14; ⊙11am-11pm Apr-Oct, weather permitting; Ⓢ1 to 79th St) New ownership and an award-winning Culinary Institute of America chef are revitalizing this perennially popular waterside spot. The Robert Moses–era structure, with an elegant colonnade opening onto an outdoor rotunda, provides great marina and Hudson River views. Always deservedly popular for sunset drinks, the menu of salads, sandwiches, seafood and innovative NYC 'street food' is now another drawing card.

GRAY'S PAPAYA HOT DOGS $

Map p432 (☎212-799-0243; 2090 Broadway, at 72nd St, entrance on Amsterdam Ave; hot dogs $2.50; ⌚24hr; S1/2/3, B, C to 72nd St) It doesn't get more New York than bellying up to this classic stand-up joint – founded by a former partner of crosstown rival Papaya King (p219) – in the wake of a beer bender. The lights are bright, the color palette is 1970s and the hot dogs are unpretentiously good.

Granted, the papaya drink is a bit more 'drink' than papaya, but you can't go wrong with Gray's famous 'Recession Special': $5.95 for two grilled dogs and a beverage. Deal.

★CANDLE CAFE WEST VEGAN $$

Map p432 (☎212-769-8900; www.candlecafe.com; 2427 Broadway, btwn 89th & 90th Sts; mains $17-23; ⌚11:30am-10:30pm Mon-Sat, to 9:30pm Sun, closed 4-5pm; ✎; S1 to 86th St) The wide-ranging menu at this popular, candlelit restaurant is entirely vegan, entirely organic and entirely delicious: with options like spaghetti and 'wheatballs', seitan piccata, chimichuri-grilled portobello steak, summer-vegetable risotto and lasagna, you will not go hungry. It also has huge salads, fresh juices and smoothies and housemade ginger ale. Gluten-free options also available.

JACOB'S PICKLES AMERICAN $$

Map p432 (☎212-470-5566; www.jacobspickles.com; 509 Amsterdam Ave, btwn 84th & 85th Sts; mains $16-24; ⌚10am-2am Mon-Thu, to 4am Fri, 9am-4am Sat, to 2am Sun; S1 to 86th St) Jacob's elevates the humble pickle to exalted status at this inviting and warmly lit eatery. Aside from briny cukes and other preserves, you'll find heaping portions of upscale comfort food, such as catfish tacos, wine-braised turkey-leg dinner, and mushroom mac 'n' cheese. The biscuits are top-notch.

The two dozen or so craft beers on tap showcase unique brews from New York, Maine and beyond.

KEFI GREEK $$

Map p432 (☎212-873-0200; www.michaelpsilakis.com/kefi; 505 Columbus Ave, btwn 84th & 85th Sts; small sharing plates $8-17, mains $17-28; ⌚noon-3pm & 5-10pm Mon-Thu, noon-3pm & 5-11pm Fri, 11am-11pm Sat, to 10pm Sun; ✎ 👪; SB, C to 86th St) This homey, whitewashed eatery run by chef Michael Psilakis channels a sleek taverna vibe while dispensing excellent rustic Greek dishes. Expect favorites such as spicy lamb sausage, sheep-milk dumplings and creamy sun-dried-tomato hummus. You can also assemble a feast of meze (sharing plates), including crispy calamari, meatballs and tzatziki, and grilled octopus and bean salad.

BLOSSOM ON COLUMBUS VEGAN $$

Map p432 (☎212-875-2600; www.blossomnyc.com; 507 Columbus Ave, btwn 84th & 85th Sts; mains lunch $19-24, dinner $20-24; ⌚lunch 11:30am-4pm Mon-Fri, from 10:30am Sat & Sun, dinner 5-10pm Sun-Thu, to 11pm Fri & Sat; ✎; SB, C, 1 to 86th St) The elegantly modern surrounds at this upscale vegan restaurant elevate the plant-based menu to a higher realm. Opt for something veggie-forward like the beet carpaccio salad bowl, or else go for something a bit, um, meatier – pan-seared seitan cutlets in white wine and rosemary. Portions are generous; the food, divine. Pair dinner with an organic wine from an international list.

PIER I CAFÉ CAFE $$

Map p432 (☎212-362-4450; www.piericafe.com; at W 70th St & Riverside Blvd; mains $14-22; ⌚8am-midnight May–mid-Oct; S1/2/3 to 72nd St) A casual cafe along the Hudson River esplanade, Pier i Café is a perfect pit stop for hungry cyclists and runners, or anyone who wants to fuel up and catch some rays. Live music some nights, big juicy burgers, fries (with garlic if you like), lobster rolls, hot dogs, beer and wine, plus an early morning coffee bar, mean it's always packed.

BARNEY GREENGRASS DELI $$

Map p432 (☎212-724-4707; www.barneygreengrass.com; 541 Amsterdam Ave, at 86th St; mains $12-26; ⌚8:30am-4pm Tue-Fri, to 5pm Sat & Sun; S1 to 86th St) The self-proclaimed 'King of Sturgeon', Barney Greengrass serves up the same heaping dishes of eggs and salty lox, luxuriant caviar and melt-in-your-mouth chocolate babkas that first made it famous when it opened over a century ago. Pop in to fuel up in the morning or for a quick lunch (there are rickety tables set amid the crowded produce aisles).

BOULUD SUD MEDITERRANEAN $$$

Map p432 (☎212-595-1313; www.bouludsud.com; 20 W 64th St, btwn Broadway & Central Park W; 3-course prix fixe 5-7pm Mon-Sat $63, mains lunch $24-34, dinner $32-58; ⌚11:30am-2:30pm & 5-11pm Mon-Fri, 11am-3pm & 5-11pm Sat, 11am-3pm & 5-10pm Sun; S) Pear-wood paneling and a yellow-grey palette lend a 1960s *Mad Men* feel to Daniel Boulud's take on cuisines from around the entire Mediterranean region: Catalan lobster paella, Marseille-style *soupe de poisson* (fish soup), Moroccan spiced pumpkin soup, Lebanese braised lamb with smoked-eggplant tahini, Greek taramosalata with smoked cod roe and many more, with an emphasis on fish, vegetables and regional spices.

If you're attending a performance at Lincoln Center, go for their three-course pre-theatre dinner – a bargain at $63.

DOVETAIL MODERN AMERICAN **$$$**

Map p432 (212-362-3800; www.dovetailnyc.com; 103 W 77th St, cnr Columbus Ave; prix fixe $68-88, tasting menu $145; 5:30-10pm Mon-Thu, to 10:30pm Fri & Sat, 5-10pm Sun; ; S B, C to 81st St-Museum of Natural History; 1 to 79th St) This Michelin-starred restaurant showcases its Zen-like beauty in both its decor (exposed brick, bare tables) and its delectable, seasonal menus – think striped bass with sunchokes and burgundy truffle, and venison with bacon, golden beets and foraged greens. Each evening there are two seven-course tasting menus: one for omnivores ($145) and one for vegetarians ($125).

On Mondays chef John Fraser offers a four-course vegetarian tasting menu ($68) that is winning over carnivores with dishes such as plump hen of the woods mushrooms with d'Anjou pears and green peppercorns. An excellent wine list (from around $16 per glass) features top vintages from all over the world, with charming anecdotes about some of the vineyards.

BURKE & WILLS MODERN AUSTRALIAN **$$$**

Map p432 (646-823-9251; www.burkeandwillsny.com; 226 W 79th St, btwn Broadway & Amsterdam Ave; mains lunch $19-32, dinner $19-39; lunch noon-3pm Mon-Fri, dinner 5:30-11:30pm daily, brunch 11am-4pm Sat & Sun; S 1 to 79th St) This ruggedly attractive bistro and bar brings a touch of the outback to the Upper West Side. The menu leans toward Modern Australian pub grub: juicy kangaroo burgers with triple-fried chips, rack of Australian lamb, braised pork belly with bacon and duck confit, and seafood platters with oysters, clams and crab claws.

LAKESIDE RESTAURANT AT LOEB BOATHOUSE AMERICAN **$$$**

Map p432 (212-517-2233; www.thecentralparkboathouse.com; Central Park Lake, Central Park, near E 74th St; mains lunch $27-38, dinner $27-45; restaurant noon-4pm Mon-Fri, 9:30am-4pm Sat & Sun year-round, 5:30-9:30pm Mon-Fri, from 6pm Sat & Sun Apr-Nov; S B, C to 72nd St; 6 to 77th St) Perched on the northeastern tip of the Central Park Lake with views of the midtown skyline in the distance, the Loeb Boathouse provides one of New York's most idyllic spots for a meal. That said, you're paying for the setting. While the food is generally good (crab cakes are the standout), we've often found the service to be indifferent.

If you want to experience the location without having to lay out the bucks, a better bet is to hit the adjacent open-air bar, where you can enjoy cocktails on the lake.

DRINKING & NIGHTLIFE

As a noted family neighborhood, the Upper West Side isn't exactly the number-one destination for hard-core drinkers. But though it may not be party central, it has some beer halls, cocktail lounges and wine bars worth checking out.

★MANHATTAN CRICKET CLUB LOUNGE

Map p432 (646-823-9252; www.mccnewyork.com; 226 W 79th St, btwn Amsterdam Ave & Broadway; 6pm-late; S 1 to 79th St) Above an Australian bistro (p237) (ask its host for access), this elegant drinking lounge is modeled on the classy Anglo-Aussie cricket clubs of the early 1900s. Sepia-toned photos of batsmen adorn the gold brocaded walls, while mahogany bookshelves and Chesterfield sofas create a fine setting for quaffing well-made (but pricey) cocktails. It's a guaranteed date-pleaser.

BIRCH CAFE COFFEE

Map p432 (212-686-1444; www.birchcoffee.com; 750 Columbus Ave, btwn 96th & 97th Sts; 7am-8pm; S B, C, 1/2/3 to 96th St) An uber-hip cafe with dark wood and copper accents – check out the copper 'coffee rings' set into the tables – but its coffee's the real deal, manually roasted in small batches in Long Island City, Queens. There's no wi-fi, so you drink to the soothing buzz of conversation, not keyboards clicking. It even offers 'conversation starter cards' for the tongue-tied.

IRVING FARM ROASTERS COFFEE

Map p432 (212-874-7979; www.irvingfarm.com; 224 W 79th St, btwn Broadway & Amsterdam Ave;

BRADY TAYLOR / SHUTTERSTOCK ©

FRANCOIS-ROUX / GETTY IMAGES ©

SONGQUAN DENG / SHUTTERSTOCK ©

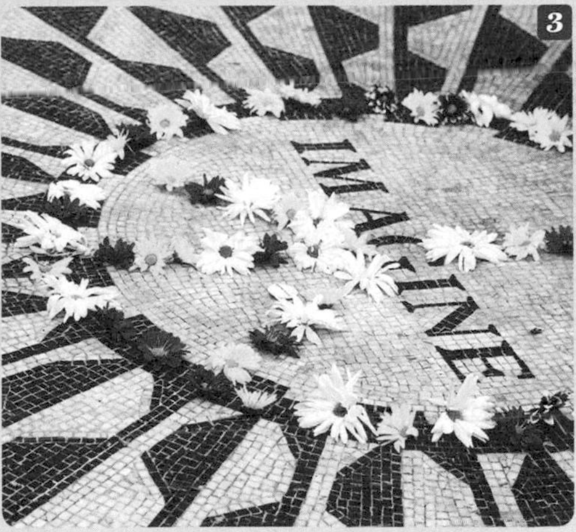

MIKI BRAMMER / LONELY PLANET ©

1. Metropolitan Opera (p232)
The Metropolitan Opera forms part of the Lincoln Center and features murals by Marc Chagall.

2. Central Park (p228)
It took 20 years and 20,000 laborers to transform pig farms and an African American village into a park.

3. Strawberry Fields (p229)
The memorial garden to John Lennon is in Central Park.

4. American Museum of Natural History (234)
The museum contains 30 million artifacts.

⌚7am-10pm Mon-Fri, 8am-10pm Sat & Sun; S1 to 79th St) Tucked into a little ground-floor shop, the Upper West Side branch of this popular local coffee chain is bigger on the inside – beyond the coffee counter the space opens up into a backroom with a sunny skylight. Enjoy a menu of light meals along with your fresh-pulled espresso. No wi-fi.

EARTH CAFÉ CAFE

Map p432 (☎646-964-5192; 2580 Broadway, at 97th St; ⌚7am-11pm Mon-Fri, from 8am Sat & Sun; 📶; S1/2/3 to 96th St) This charming neighborhood cafe beckons you inside with its cheery, sunny interior of whitewashed brick walls and the scent of fresh-roasted coffee beans lingering in the air. Order an expertly poured almond latte, take a seat at the street-facing counter behind large French windows and watch the city glide past.

DEAD POET BAR

Map p432 (☎212-595-5670; www.thedeadpoet.com; 450 Amsterdam Ave, btwn 81st & 82nd Sts; ⌚noon-4am; S1 to 79th St) This narrow, mahogany-paneled pub is a neighborhood favorite. It takes its Guinness pours seriously, and features cocktails named after deceased masters of verse, including a Walt Whitman Long Island Iced Tea ($13) and a Pablo Neruda spiced-rum sangria ($12). Feeling adventurous? Order the signature cocktail ($15), a secret recipe of seven alcohols – you even get to keep the glass.

MALACHY'S PUB

Map p432 (☎212-874-4268; www.malachysnyc.com; 103 W 72nd St, at Columbus Ave; ⌚noon-4am; SB/C, 1/2/3 to 72nd St) Giving new meaning to the word 'dive,' this crusty local holdout has a long wooden bar, classic rock on the speakers, a lineup of regulars and a bartender with a sense of humor. In other words: the perfect place for daytime drinking. There's also a cheap menu of classic bar food.

WEST END HALL BEER GARDEN

Map p432 (☎212-662-7200; www.westendhall.com; 2756 Broadway, btwn 105th & 106th Sts; ⌚3pm-midnight Mon & Tue, to 1am Wed & Thu, to 2am Fri, 11am-2am Sat, to midnight Sun; S1 to 103rd St) Beer drinkers of the Upper West Side have much to celebrate at this large beer hall that showcases craft brews from around Belgium, Germany, the US and beyond. There are about 20 drafts on rotation, along with another 30 bottle choices, most of which go nicely with the meaty menu of sausages, schnitzel, pork sliders and an excellent truffle burger.

The interior sports a mix of communal tables, exposed brick walls and a long wooden bar where you can watch the barkeeps in action (or sports if the game is on); it also has a collection of board games for guest use. Head to the backyard garden on warm nights.

☆ ENTERTAINMENT

Beyond Lincoln Center (p232), there are many other venues across the Upper West Side that cater to the cultured set.

NEW YORK CITY BALLET DANCE

Map p432 (☎212-496-0600; www.nycballet.com; Lincoln Center, Columbus Ave at W 63rd St; 👪; S1 to 66th St-Lincoln Center) This prestigious ballet company was first directed by renowned Russian-born choreographer George Balanchine back in the 1940s. Today, the company has 90 dancers and is the largest ballet organization in the US, performing 23 weeks a year at Lincoln Center's David H Koch Theater. During the holidays the troupe is best known for its annual production of *The Nutcracker*.

Depending on the ballet, ticket prices can range from $30 to $170; rush tickets for those under age 30 are available for $30. There are also select one-hour Family Saturday performances, appropriate for young audiences ($22 per ticket).

METROPOLITAN OPERA HOUSE OPERA

Map p432 (☎tickets 212-362-6000, tours 212-769-7028; www.metopera.org; Lincoln Center, Columbus Ave at W 64th St; S1 to 66th St-Lincoln Center) New York's premier opera company is the place to see classics such as *Carmen, Madame Butterfly* and *Macbeth,* not to mention Wagner's Ring Cycle. It also hosts premieres and revivals of more contemporary works, such as John Adams' *The Death of Klinghoffer*. The season runs from September to April.

Ticket prices start at $25 and can get close to $500. Note that the box seats can be a bargain, but unless you're in boxes right over the stage, the views are dreadful: seeing the stage requires sitting with your head cocked over a handrail – a literal pain in the neck.

For last-minute ticket-buyers there are other deals. You can get bargain-priced standing-room tickets ($20 to $30) from 10am on the day of the performance. (You won't see much, but you'll hear everything.) Monday through Friday at noon and Saturdays at 2pm, a number of rush tickets are put on sale for starving-artist types – just $25 for a seat; these are available online only. Matinee tickets go on sale four hours before curtain.

Don't miss the gift shop, which is full of operatic knickknacks, including Met curtain cufflinks and Rhinemaidens soap. (Seriously.)

For a behind-the-scenes look, guided tours ($30) are offered weekdays at 3pm and Sundays at 10:30am and 1:30pm during the performance season.

The 2016–17 season marked the 50th anniversary of the Met's home in Lincoln Center.

FILM SOCIETY OF LINCOLN CENTER CINEMA

Map p432 (☎212-875-5367; www.filmlinc.com; Lincoln Center; S1 to 66th St-Lincoln Center) The Film Society is one of New York's cinematic gems, providing an invaluable platform for a wide gamut of documentary, feature, independent, foreign and avant-garde art pictures. Films screen in one of two facilities at Lincoln Center: the **Elinor Bunin Munroe Film Center** (Map p432; ☎212-875-5232; 144 W 65th St, btwn Broadway & Amsterdam Ave), a more intimate, experimental venue, or the **Walter Reade Theater** (Map p432; ☎212-875-5601; 165 W 65th St, btwn Broadway & Amsterdam Ave), with wonderfully wide, screening-room style seats.

Every September both venues host the **New York Film Festival**, featuring plenty of New York and world premieres. In March you'll find the New Directors/New Films series on view. It's highly recommended for cinephiles.

NEW YORK PHILHARMONIC CLASSICAL MUSIC

Map p432 (☎212-875-5656; www.nyphil.org; Lincoln Center, Columbus Ave at W 65th St; ♿; S1 to 66 St-Lincoln Center) The oldest professional orchestra in the US (dating back to 1842) holds its season every year at David Geffen Hall (known as Avery Fisher until 2015); music director Jaap van Zweden took over from Alan Gilbert in 2017. The orchestra plays a mix of classics (Tchaikovsky, Mahler, Haydn) and contemporary works, as well as concerts geared toward children.

Tickets run in the $29 to $125 range. If you're on a budget, check out the open rehearsals held several times a month (starting at 9:45am) on the day of the concert for only $22. In addition, students with a valid school ID can pick up rush tickets for $18 up to 10 days before an event.

SYMPHONY SPACE LIVE PERFORMANCE

Map p432 (☎212-864-5400; www.symphonyspace.org; 2537 Broadway, at 95th St; S1/2/3 to 96th St) Symphony Space is a multidisciplinary gem supported by the local community. It often hosts three-day series that are dedicated to one musician, and also has an affinity for world music, theater, film, dance and literature (with appearances by acclaimed writers).

BEACON THEATRE LIVE MUSIC

Map p432 (☎212-465-6500; www.beacontheatre.com; 2124 Broadway, btwn 74th & 75th Sts; S1/2/3 to 72nd St) This historic 1929 theater is a perfect medium-size venue with 2829 seats (not a terrible one in the house) and a constant flow of popular acts from ZZ Top to Wilco (plus comedians like Jerry Seinfeld and Patton Oswalt). A 2009 restoration left the gilded interiors – a mix of Greek, Roman, Renaissance and rococo design elements – totally sparkling.

MERKIN CONCERT HALL CLASSICAL MUSIC

Map p432 (☎212-501-3330; www.kaufman-center.org/mch; 129 W 67th St, btwn Amsterdam Ave & Broadway; S1 to 66th St-Lincoln Center) Just north of Lincoln Center, this 450-seat hall, part of the Kaufman Center, is one of the city's more intimate venues for classical music, as well as jazz, world music and pop. The hall hosts Tuesday matinees (a deal at $20) that highlight emerging classical solo artists.

SMOKE JAZZ

Map p432 (☎212-864-6662; www.smokejazz.com; 2751 Broadway, btwn 105th & 106th Sts; ⊙5:30pm-3am Mon-Sat, 11am-3am Sun; S1 to 103rd St) This swank but laid-back lounge – with good stage views from plush sofas – brings out old-timers and local faves, such as George Coleman and Wynton Marsalis. Most nights there's a $10 cover (but it can go as high as $45), plus a $38 per person minimum spend on food and drink. On Sundays there's a soulful jazz brunch from

11am to 4pm. Purchase tickets online for weekend shows.

Late nights, you can stop by for free shows (no cover but $20 minimum applies) that kick off around 11:30pm.

CLEOPATRA'S NEEDLE JAZZ, BLUES

Map p432 (212-769-6969; www.cleopatrasneedleny.com; 2485 Broadway, btwn 92nd & 93rd Sts; 3:30pm-late; S 1/2/3 to 96th St) Named after an Egyptian obelisk that resides in Central Park, this slightly dated venue has live jazz and blues musicians playing every night of the week from 7pm or 8pm (from 4pm Sundays). No cover, but a $10 minimum spend. Come early to enjoy happy hour until 7pm daily (until 6pm Sunday), when select cocktails are half price.

Be prepared to stay up: Cleopatra's is famous for its late-night jam sessions that hit their peak after midnight.

SHOPPING

The stretch of Broadway that runs through the Upper West Side has been colonized by chain stores, so local flavor can be hard to find outside of some old-school food markets. That said, there are some unique shopping stops to be found, especially on and around Columbus Ave.

BOOK CULTURE BOOKS, GIFTS & SOUVENIRS

Map p432 (212-595-1962; www.bookculture.com; 450 Columbus Ave, btwn 81st & 82nd St; 9am-10pm Mon-Sat, to 8pm Sun; ; S B, C to 81st St-Museum of Natural History) The warm aesthetic and friendliness of this neighborhood bookstore belies its size and selection. It caters not just to literary types but to browsers looking for unique gifts, writers stocking up on Euro-style journals and parents desperate to occupy little ones in the large downstairs kids' space, which hosts regular story-time sessions in several languages (check the website for times).

It also stocks a great selection of design-oriented gifts and accessories, such as Japanese-print ceramics, imported soaps, scented candles, mod backpacks and NYC-themed items.

SHISHI FASHION & ACCESSORIES, CLOTHING

Map p432 (646-692-4510; www.shishiboutique.com; 2488 Broadway, btwn 92nd & 93rd Sts; 11am-8pm Mon-Sat, to 7pm Sun; S 1/2/3 to 96th St) A welcome addition to a fashion-challenged hood, Shishi is a delightful boutique stocking an ever-changing selection of stylish but affordable apparel: elegant sweaters, sleeveless shift dresses and eye-catching jewelry, among others. (All its clothes are wash-and-dry friendly too.) It's fun for browsing, and with the enthusiastic staff kitting you out, you'll feel like you have your own personal stylist.

MAGPIE ARTS & CRAFTS

Map p432 (212-579-3003; www.magpienewyork.com; 488 Amsterdam Ave, btwn 83rd & 84th Sts; 11am-7pm Mon-Sat, to 6pm Sun; S 1 to 86th St) This charming little outpost carries a wide range of ecofriendly objects: elegant stationery, beeswax candles, hand-painted mugs, organic-cotton scarves, recycled resin necklaces, hand-dyed felt journals and wooden earth puzzles are a few things that may catch your eye. Most products are fair-trade, made of sustainable materials or locally designed and made.

ICON STYLE VINTAGE, JEWELRY

Map p432 (212-799-0029; www.iconstyle.net; 104 W 70th St, near Columbus Ave; noon-8pm Tue-Fri, 11am-7pm Sat, noon-6pm Sun; S 1/2/3 to 72nd St) This tiny gem of a vintage shop, tucked away on a side street, specializes in carefully curated dresses, gloves, bags, hats and other accessories, as well as antique fine and costume jewelry. Half of the shop is covered in a strikingly restored apothecary's wall, with the goods displayed in open drawers. Stop by and indulge your inner Grace Kelly.

CENTURY 21 DEPARTMENT STORE

Map p432 (212-518-2121; www.c21stores.com; 1972 Broadway, at W 66th St; 10am-10pm Mon-Sat, 11am-8pm Sun; S 1 to 66th St-Lincoln Center) Exceedingly popular with fashionable locals and foreign travelers, the Century 21 chain is a bounty of season-old brand-name and designer labels, from Missoni to Marc Jacobs, sold at a steep discount.

ZABAR'S FOOD

Map p432 (212-787-2000; www.zabars.com; 2245 Broadway, at W 80th St; 8am-7:30pm Mon-Fri, to 8pm Sat, 9am-6pm Sun; S 1 to 79th St) A bastion of gourmet kosher foodie-ism, this sprawling local market has been a neighborhood fixture since the 1930s. And what a fixture it is! It features a heavenly array of cheeses, meats, olives, caviar, smoked fish, pickles, dried fruits, nuts and baked goods, including pillowy, fresh-out-of-the-oven knishes (Eastern European-style potato dumplings wrapped in dough).

T2 TEA

Map p432 (☎646-998-5010; www.t2tea.com; 188 Columbus Ave, btwn 68th & 69th Sts; ⊙10am-8pm Mon-Sat, 11am-7pm Sun; Ⓢ1 to 66th St-Lincoln Center; B, C to 72nd St) Aficionados of the brewed leaf will find more than 200 varieties at this outpost of an Australian tea company: oolong, green, black, yellow, herbals, you name it. But you don't just have to go by smell – the staff will brew samples of anything you care to try on the spot. It also carries a selection of tea-related gifts.

FLYING TIGER COPENHAGEN HOMEWARES

Map p432 (☎646-998-4755; www.flyingtiger.com; 424 Columbus Ave, btwn 80th & 81st Sts; ⊙10am-8pm Mon-Sun; 👪; ⓈB, C to 81st St-Museum of Natural History) In the market for well-designed, quirky and inexpensive doodads and tchotchkes? This Danish import will scratch that itch. Something of a miniature Ikea, with items grouped thematically (kitchen, kids, arts and crafts, etc) – you could never have imagined the things you didn't know you needed. Remove the price tag and friends will think you've spent too much on a gift.

With more than 600 stores in 29 countries, it's no surprise there are two other locations in the city: one on the Upper East Side (p224) and another in the Flatiron area.

WEST SIDE KIDS TOYS

Map p432 (☎212-496-7282; www.westsidekidsnyc.com; 498 Amsterdam Ave, at 84th St; ⊙10am-7pm Mon-Sat, 11am-6pm Sun; Ⓢ1 to 86th St) A great place to pick up a gift for that little someone special, no matter their age. In stock are lots of hands-on activities and fun educational games, as well as puzzles, mini musical instruments, science kits, magic sets, snap circuits, old-fashioned wooden trains and building kits.

WESTSIDER RECORDS MUSIC

Map p432 (☎212-874-1588; www.westsiderbooks.com/recordstore.html; 233 W 72nd St, btwn Broadway & West End Ave; ⊙11am-7pm Mon-Thu, 10am-9pm Fri & Sat, noon-6pm Sun; Ⓢ1/2/3 to 72nd St) Featuring more than 30,000 LPs, this shop has got you covered when it comes to everything from funk to jazz to classical, plus opera, musical theater, spoken word, film soundtracks and other curiosities. (Don't miss the $1 bins up front.) It's a good place to lose all track of time – as is its **bookstore** (Map p432; ☎212-362-0706; www.westsiderbooks.com; 2246 Broadway, btwn 80th & 81st Sts; ⊙10am-10pm; Ⓢ1 to 79th St) further uptown.

GRAND BAZAAR NYC MARKET

Map p432 (☎212-239-3025; www.grandbazaarnyc.org; 100 W 77th St, near Columbus Ave; ⊙10am-5:30pm Sun; ⓈB, C to 81st St-Museum of Natural History; 1 to 79th St) One of the oldest open-air shopping spots in the city, browsing this friendly, well-stocked flea market is a perfect activity for a lazy Upper West Side Sunday morning. You'll find a little bit of everything here, including vintage and contemporary furnishings, antique maps, custom eyewear, hand-woven scarves, handmade jewelry and so much more.

It moves inside during the cold and is also open on occasional Saturdays in warm months; call ahead or check the website.

SPORTS & ACTIVITIES

BIKE & ROLL CYCLING

Map p432 (☎212-260-0400; www.bikeandrollnyc.com; 451 Columbus Ave, btwn 81st & 82nd Sts; bike rentals per 2hr/4hr/day adult $28/39/44, child $16/20/25; ⊙9am-6pm; 👪; ⓈB, C to 81st St-Museum of Natural History; 1 to 79th St) Located just one block from Central Park, this friendly outfit rents out bicycles for adults and kids, with helmet, U-lock, handlebar bag, rear storage rack and a free cycling map all included. Baby seats are available too. Credit cards only.

CHARLES A DANA DISCOVERY CENTER FISHING

Map p432 (☎212-860-1370; www.centralparknyc.org; Central Park, at 110th St, btwn Fifth & Lenox Aves; ⊙10am-5pm; 👪; Ⓢ2/3 to Central Park North-110th St) FREE This visitor center was built in the early 1990s during the restoration of **Harlem Meer** (from the Dutch for 'lake'). It offers a variety of activities for families, including an exhibit about the geology and military history of the northern part of the park; a Discovery Kit with birding field guides, binoculars and art supplies; and a summertime performance festival

BELVEDERE CASTLE BIRDWATCHING

Map p432 (212-772-0288; www.centralparknyc.org; Central Park, at W 79th St; 10am-4pm; ; S1/2/3, B, C to 72nd St) FREE For a DIY birding expedition with kids, borrow a 'Discovery Kit' at Belvedere Castle in Central Park, which comes with binoculars, a bird book, colored pencils and paper – a perfect way to get the kids excited about birds. Picture ID required.

Belvedere Castle closed for renovations in February 2018. It is expected to reopen in 2019. Check the website for updates.

CENTRAL PARK TENNIS CENTER TENNIS

Map p432 (212-316-0800; www.centralparktenniscenter.com; Central Park, btwn W 94th & 96th Sts; 6:30am-dusk Apr-Nov; SB, C to 96th St) This daylight-hours-only facility has 26 clay courts for public use and four hard courts for lessons. You can buy single-play tickets ($15; cash only) here, and can reserve a court if you pick up a $15 permit at **Arsenal** (Map p432; gallery 212-360-8163; www.nycgovparks.org; Central Park, at Fifth Ave & E 64th St; 9am-5pm Mon-Fri; SN/R/W to 5th Ave-59th St) FREE. The least busy times are roughly from noon to 4pm weekdays. Closest park entrance is Central Park West and 96th St.

LOEB BOATHOUSE BOATING

Map p432 (212-517-2233; www.thecentralparkboathouse.com; Central Park, btwn 74th & 75th Sts; boating per hr $15; 10am-dusk Mar or Apr–mid-Nov; ; SB, C to 72nd St; 6 to 77th St) Central Park's boathouse has a fleet of 100 rowboats, as well as a Venetian-style gondola that you can reserve for up to six people if you'd rather someone else do the paddling ($45 for 30 minutes). Rentals include life jackets and require ID and a $20 deposit. Cash only.

WOLLMAN SKATING RINK SKATING

Map p432 (212-439-6900; www.wollmanskatingrink.com; Central Park, btwn E 62nd & 63rd Sts; adult Mon-Thu $12, Fri-Sun $19, child $6, skate rentals $9; 10am-2:30pm Mon & Tue, to 10pm Wed & Thu, to 11pm Fri & Sat, to 9pm Sun late Oct-early Apr; ; SF to 57 St; N/Q/R/W to 5th Ave-59th St) This rink is much larger than the Rockefeller Center skating rink (p186), and not only does it allow all-day skating, its position at the southeastern edge of Central Park offers magical views. There's locker rental for $5 and a spectator fee of $5. Cash only.

TOGA BIKE SHOP CYCLING

Map p432 (212-799-9625; www.togabikes.com; 110 West End Ave, btwn 64th & 65th Sts; rentals per 24hr hybrid/road bike $35/150; 11am-7pm Mon-Fri, 10am-6pm Sat, 11am-6pm Sun; S1 to 66th St-Lincoln Center) This friendly, longstanding bike shop is conveniently located right next to the Hudson River bike path (and only a few blocks from Central Park) and rents out both hybrid and road models (but no children's bikes). Rental prices include a helmet.

CHAMPION BICYCLES INC CYCLING

Map p432 (212-662-2690; www.championbicycles.com; 896 Amsterdam Ave, at 104th St; rentals per hr/day from $7/30; 10am-7pm Mon-Fri, to 6pm Sat & Sun; S1 to 103rd St) This place stocks a variety of bicycles for rent and has free copies of the helpful *NYC Cycling Map* (www.nyc.gov/bikes), which details several hundred miles of bike lanes around New York City.

Harlem & Upper Manhattan

MORNINGSIDE HEIGHTS | HARLEM | EAST HARLEM | HAMILTON HEIGHTS & SUGAR HILL | WASHINGTON HEIGHTS & INWOOD | WEST HARLEM

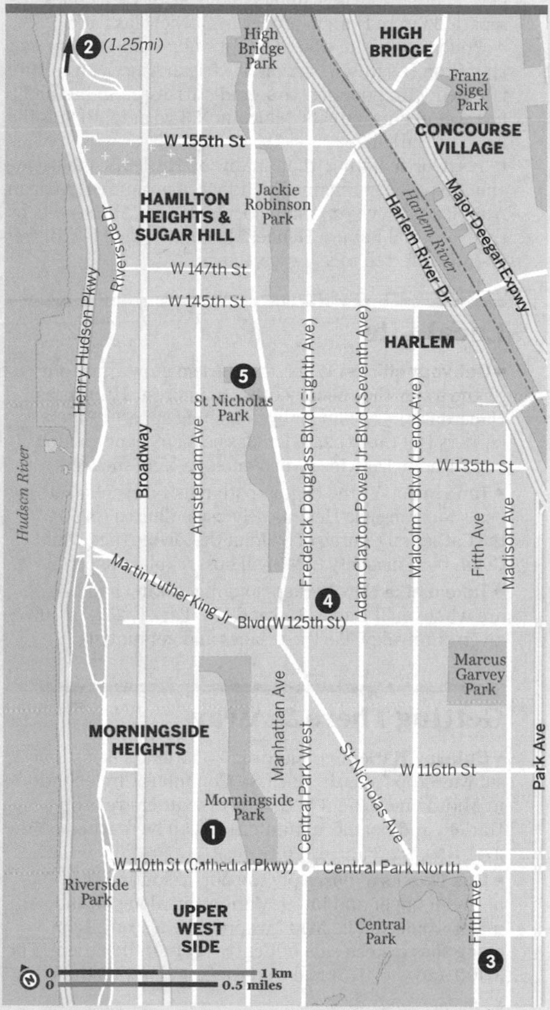

For more detail of this area see Map p434

Neighborhood Top Five

❶ **Cathedral Church of St John the Divine** (p247) Exploring the fine artistry and hidden treasures inside the gloriously epic yet still-unfinished St John the Divine, the largest house of worship in the US.

❷ **Cloisters Museum & Gardens** (p252) Taking a fantastical journey into the Middle Ages at this monastic reconstruction, replete with Flemish tapestries and other medieval masterpieces.

❸ **El Museo del Barrio** (p251) Catching cutting-edge exhibitions from the Latin American diaspora in East Harlem.

❹ **Apollo Theater** (p250) Joining the celebratory crowds at this venerable concert hall in the heart of Harlem.

❺ **Hamilton Grange** (p251) Visiting the Federal-style home of Alexander Hamilton, one of America's founding fathers – and everyone's favorite 19th-century New Yorker thanks to the musical *Hamilton*.

Lonely Planet's Top Tip

Manhattan's uptown communities tend to be locally minded, with bars, restaurants and shops catering to a neighborhood crowd. These establishments tend to be sleepiest on weekday mornings and liveliest in the evenings and on weekends.

To make the most of your visit, hit one of the museums or historic sights in the afternoon, then stick around for dinner when these areas come to life.

Best Places to Eat

- Red Rooster (p256)
- Seasoned Vegan (p254)
- Dinosaur Bar-B-Que (p253)
- Sylvia's (p254)
- BLVD Bistro (p256)

For reviews, see p253.

Best Places to Drink

- Silvana (p256)
- Shrine (p257)
- 67 Orange St (p257)
- Bier International (p257)
- Ginny's Supper Club (p257)

For reviews, see p256.

Best Places for Live Jazz

- Marjorie Eliot's Parlor Jazz (p257)
- Apollo Theater (p250)
- Ginny's Supper Club (p257)

For reviews, see p257.

Explore Harlem & Upper Manhattan

The top half of Manhattan is a lot of territory to cover, with numerous points of interest a distance away from one another and no subways to take you across town (the bus is an option). So pick a neighborhood (or, better yet, a couple of contiguous neighborhoods) and stick to it. If you like your cities to feel a little bit country, then head to Inwood, which has parks with Hudson River views and a spectacular museum (p252). Work your way down the West Side to the gargantuan Cathedral Church of St John the Divine (p247) and the environs of Columbia University (p249), where academics roam. The university's massive new Manhattanville campus, along with City College, is separated from Harlem proper by St Nicholas Park.

Prefer an urban vibe? Then it's all about Harlem and Hamilton Heights, a bastion of African American culture jammed with hopping bars, soul-stirring churches and a few architectural treats. Malcolm X Blvd at 125th St is the heart of Harlem.

It's worth noting that many of Harlem's major avenues have been renamed in honor of prominent African Americans; however, many locals still call the streets by their original names. Hence, Malcolm X Blvd is still frequently referred to as Lenox Ave.

Local Life

- **Get your chic on** When the Harlem crowd goes out on the town, they usually dress to impress. Hit Harlem Haberdashery (p259) for eye-catching apparel, Flamekeepers Hat Club (p259) for classic men's caps and hats, and Atmos (p259) for stylish one-of-a-kind sneakers.
- **Tune in** For off-the-beaten-path musical events, nothing beats Morningside Heights. Riverside Church (p250), the Cathedral Church of St John the Divine (p247) and Columbia University (p249) all host regular concerts.
- **Take a hike** New Yorkers jogging, hiking and biking are what you'll find at Inwood Hill Park (p252) on any given sunny day. Tie those laces and get moving.

Getting There & Away

- **Subway** Harlem's main drag – 125th St – is just one subway stop from the 59th St–Columbus Circle Station in Midtown on the A and D trains. Other areas of Harlem and northern Manhattan can be reached on the A/C, B/D, 1/2/3 and 4/5/6 trains.
- **Bus** Dozens of buses ply the north–south route between upper and lower Manhattan along all the major avenues. The M10 bus provides a scenic trip along the western side of Central Park into Harlem. The M100 and the M101 run east to west along 125th St.

OUTCAST85 / GETTY IMAGES ©

TOP SIGHT
CATHEDRAL CHURCH OF ST JOHN THE DIVINE

The largest place of worship in America has yet to be completed – and probably won't be anytime soon. But this glorious Episcopal cathedral nonetheless commands attention with its ornate Gothic-style facade, booming vintage organ and extravagantly scaled nave – twice as wide as London's Westminster Abbey.

An Unfinished History

The first cornerstone for the cathedral was laid on St John's Day in 1892, but construction was hardly smooth. Engineers had to dig 70ft in order to find bedrock to which they could anchor the building. Architects died or were fired, and in 1911, the initial Romanesque design was exchanged for a bigger, Gothic-inspired plan.

Depleted funds have seen construction regularly halted. The north tower remains unbuilt, and a 'temporary' domed roof, constructed out of terra-cotta tile in 1909, still rises above the epicenter of the church. A raging fire in 2001 caused significant damage, including to the north transept, which is yet to be rebuilt.

If it is ever completed, the 601ft-long cathedral will rank as the world's third-largest church, behind Rome's St Peter's Basilica and Côte d'Ivoire's Basilica of Our Lady of Peace at Yamoussoukro.

The Portal Sculptures

Framing the western entrance are two rows of sculptures carved in the 1980s and '90s by British artist Simon Verity. On the central pillar stands St John the Divine himself,

DON'T MISS

- Portal sculptures
- Great Rose Window
- Great Organ
- Keith Haring Triptych

PRACTICALITIES

- Map p434, B6
- ☎ tours 212-316-7540
- www.stjohndivine.org
- 1047 Amsterdam Ave, at W 112th St, Morningside Heights
- $10, Highlights Tour $14, Vertical Tour $20
- ⏱7:30am-6pm, Highlights Tour 11am & 2pm Mon, 11am & 1pm Tue-Sat, 1pm selected Sun, Vertical Tour 10am Mon, noon Wed & Fri, noon & 2pm Sat
- S B/C, 1 to 110th St-Cathedral Pkwy

TOP TIPS

Aside from the daily Highlights and Vertical Tours, the cathedral also hosts periodic Spotlight Tours. These delve into unique aspects of the cathedral's place in New York City, from architecture to sociopolitical topics. Be sure to call ahead to reserve a spot.

The cathedral hosts numerous events, from morning prayer and yoga to poetry readings, organ concerts and the occasional lecture on 14th-century Christian mystics. Aside from big productions (like the Winter Solstice Celebration), most activities are free.

The cathedral was involved in the civil rights movement as far back as the early 1950s and has regularly worked with members of the community on issues of inequity. It is also a long-running cultural outpost, hosting holiday concerts, lectures and exhibits, and it has been the site of memorial services for many famous New Yorkers, including trumpeter Louis Armstrong and artist Keith Haring.

author of the Book of Revelation. (Note the Four Horsemen of the Apocalypse under his feet.) Themes of devastation are rife, but most unnerving is the statue of Jeremiah (third on the right), which stands on a base that shows the New York City skyline – Twin Towers included – being destroyed.

The Nave

Illuminated by the Great Rose Window (America's largest stained-glass window), the nave is lined with two magisterial sets of 17th-century tapestries. The Barberini Tapestries depict scenes from Christ's life, while the Mortlake Tapestries, based on cartoons by Raphael, show the Acts of the Apostles.

Keith Haring Triptych

Behind the choir is the white-gold and bronze triptych *Life of Christ*, carved by '80s pop artist Keith Haring (1958–90). It's one of the last works of art he produced prior to succumbing to an AIDS-related illness aged 31.

Great Organ

One of the most powerful organs in the world, the Great Organ was originally installed in 1911, then enlarged and rebuilt in 1952. It contains 8500 pipes arranged in 141 ranks. A 2001 fire damaged the instrument, but a careful five-year restoration brought it back.

Visiting the Cathedral

One-hour Highlight Tours are offered at 11am and 2pm Monday, 11am and 1pm Tuesday to Saturday, and at 1pm on select Sundays. One-hour Vertical Tours, which take you on a steep climb to the top of the cathedral (bring your own flashlight), are at 10am on Monday, at noon Wednesday and Friday, and at noon and 2pm Saturday. Two services worth seeing are the Blessing of the Animals, a pilgrimage for pet owners held on the first Sunday of October, and the Blessing of the Bikes, held on a Saturday in mid- to late April, when local riders cruise in on everything from sleek 10-speeds to clunky cruisers.

SIGHTS

Latino culture is the focus of East Harlem's El Museo del Barrio, while Harlem's Studio Museum and Schomburg Center for Research in Black Culture fly the flag for African American expression. During the Harlem Renaissance, the northern edge of the neighborhood was dubbed 'Sugar Hill' as it was here that the Harlem elite lived the 'sweet life.' Columbia University and America's largest cathedral dominate Morningside Heights, while Washington Heights takes its name from America's first president, who set up a fort here during the Revolutionary War. Topping the lot is Inwood, home to the Metropolitan Museum of Art's medieval booty.

Morningside Heights

CATHEDRAL CHURCH OF ST JOHN THE DIVINE — CATHEDRAL

See p247.

COLUMBIA UNIVERSITY — UNIVERSITY

Map p434 (www.columbia.edu; Broadway, at W 116th St, Morningside Heights; **S**1 to 116th St-Columbia University) Founded in lower Manhattan in 1754 as King's College, the oldest university in New York is now one of the world's premier research institutions. In 1897 the Ivy League school moved to its current location (the site of a former asylum), where its gated campus now channels a New England vibe and offers plenty of cultural happenings.

The principal point of interest is the **main courtyard** (located on either side of College Walk, at 116th St), which is surrounded by various Italian Renaissance–style buildings. In the northern half, you'll find the statue of the open-armed *Alma Mater* seated before the Low Memorial Library. On the eastern end of College Walk, at the corner of Amsterdam Ave, is Hamilton Hall, a key site during the famous student uprising of 1968.

Your best bet for navigating the grounds is to download architectural historian Andrew Dolkart's self-guided audio tour

FULL PEWS: GOSPEL HARLEM CHURCH SERVICES

What started as an occasional pilgrimage has turned into a tourist-industry spectacle: entire busloads of travelers now make their way to Harlem every Sunday to attend a gospel service. The volume of visitors is so high that some churches turn away people due to space constraints. In some cases, tourists have been known to outnumber congregants.

Naturally, this has led to friction. Many locals are upset by visitors who chat during sermons, leave in the middle of services or show up in skimpy attire. Plus, for some, there's the uncomfortable sense that African American spirituality is something to be consumed like a Broadway show.

The churches, to their credit, remain welcoming spaces. But if you do decide to attend, be respectful: dress modestly (Sunday best!), don't take pictures and remain present for the duration of the service. Also, keep in mind that most churches will not allow large backpacks.

Sunday services generally start at 10am or 11am and can last for two or more hours. There are roughly five dozen participating churches. The superb Sunday gospel services at **Abyssinian Baptist Church** (Map p434; 212-862-7474; www.abyssinian.org; 132 Odell Clark Pl, btwn Adam Clayton Powell Jr & Malcolm X Blvds, Harlem; tourist gospel service 11:30am Sun early Sep-Jul; **S**2/3 to 135th St) are a raucous, soulful affair and the city's most famous. You'll need to arrive at least an hour before the service to queue up, and ensure you adhere to the strict entry rules: no tank tops, flip-flops, shorts, leggings or backpacks. Others include **Canaan Baptist Church** (Map p434; 212-866-0301; www.cbccnyc.org; 132 W 116th St, btwn Adam Clayton Powell Jr & Malcolm X Blvds, Harlem; service 10am Sun; **S**2/3 to 116th St), a neighborhood church founded in 1932, and **Convent Avenue Baptist Church** (Map p434; 212-234-6767; www.conventchurch.org; 420 W 145th St, at Convent Ave, Hamilton Heights; services 8am & 11am Sun; **S**A/C, B/D or 1 to 145th St), which has been conducting traditional baptist services since the 1940s.

If you're less interested in the preaching and more interested in the feel-good singing and celebration, a number of Harlem spots offer Sunday gospel brunches, including Sylvia's (p254) and Ginny's Supper Club (p257).

(www.columbia.edu/content/self-guided-walking-tour.html) from the Columbia University website.

GENERAL ULYSSES S GRANT NATIONAL MEMORIAL MEMORIAL

Map p434 (☎212-666-1640; www.nps.gov/gegr; Riverside Dr, at 122nd St, Morningside Heights; ⏲10am-5pm Wed-Sun; Ⓢ1 to 125th St) FREE Popularly known as Grant's Tomb ('Who's buried in Grant's Tomb?' 'Who?' 'Grant, stupid!' goes a classic joke), this landmark holds the remains of Civil War hero and 18th president Ulysses S Grant and his wife, Julia. Completed in 1897 – 12 years after his death – the imposing granite structure is the largest mausoleum in America. A gallery covers key events in Grant's life. Rangers lead guided tours at various times throughout the day and answer questions about the general and statesman.

Seventeen Gaudí-inspired mosaic benches, designed by Chilean artist Pedro Silva in the 1970s, surround the mausoleum. It's a downright hallucinatory installation – and a good spot to contemplate the musings of the late, great comedian George Carlin, who was known to light up here back in the day.

RIVERSIDE CHURCH CHURCH

Map p434 (☎212-870-6700; www.theriversidechurchny.org; 490 Riverside Dr, at 120th St, Morningside Heights; ⏲9am-5pm; Ⓢ1 to 116th St) This imposing neo-Gothic beauty was built by the Rockefeller family in 1930. While the sparseness of the interior evokes an Italian Gothic style, the stained-glass windows in the narthex are actually Flemish, dating back to the 16th century. The church rings its 74 carillon bells with an extraordinary 20-ton bass bell (the world's largest) at 10:30am, 12:30pm and 3pm on Sunday. Interdenominational services are held at 10:45am on Sunday, with free tours offered immediately after (at 12:30pm).

The church also hosts high-profile events, including concerts (see the website).

Harlem

MALCOLM SHABAZZ HARLEM MARKET MARKET

Map p434 (52 W 116th St, btwn Malcolm X Blvd & Fifth Ave, Harlem; ⏲9am-8pm; 👪; Ⓢ2/3 to 116th St) FREE This semi-enclosed market is a little slice of West Africa in Harlem. You'll

TOP SIGHT
APOLLO THEATER

More than simply historic, Harlem's Apollo Theater is a swinging testament to Harlem's astounding musical legacy. Originally a whites-only burlesque joint, the neoclassical venue reinvented itself in 1934 with 'Jazz à la Carte.' Soon after, virtually every major black artist was performing here, from Duke Ellington and Louis Armstrong to Count Basie and Billie Holiday.

The revamped Apollo also introduced the legendary Amateur Night, its long list of then-unknown competitors including Ella Fitzgerald, Gladys Knight, Jimi Hendrix, the Jackson 5 and Lauryn Hill. The event still kicks off every Wednesday night, its wild and ruthless crowd as fun to watch as tomorrow's next big things. Beyond Amateur Night is a thriving year-round program of music, dance, master classes and special events, with shows spanning Cuban salsa tributes to Afro-Latin jazz suites.

While guided tours of the interior are available only for groups of 20 or more with advance reservations, individuals are welcome to join group tours based on availability. Take the tour and expect to see a fragment of the Tree of Hope, a long-gone elm performers would rub for good luck before taking to the stage.

DON'T MISS

- Amateur Night
- The iconic theater marquee
- Guided tours
- Tree of Hope

PRACTICALITIES

- Map p434, C5
- ☎212-531-5300, tours 212-531-5337
- www.apollotheater.org
- 253 W 125th St, btwn Frederick Douglass & Adam Clayton Powell Jr Blvds, Harlem
- tickets from $16
- ⓈA/C, B/D to 125th St

THE REBIRTH OF A HARLEM ICON

In 2018, on the 50th anniversary of the **Studio Museum in Harlem** (Map p434; 212-864-4500; www.studiomuseum.org; 144 W 125th St, at Adam Clayton Powell Jr Blvd, Harlem; suggested donation $7, Sun free; noon-9pm Thu & Fri, 10am-6pm Sat, noon-6pm Sun; S 2/3 to 125th St), work began on a brand-new building on 125th St. Designed by the Ghanaian-British architect David Adjaye, the cutting-edge five-story structure will be over twice the size of the current museum, with a total exhibition space of some 17,000 sq ft. There will be an auditorium for concerts and special events, and a roof deck with sweeping views of the Harlem skyline. The previous museum closed in early 2018 as work commenced on the new building, which is scheduled to emerge on the same location in 2021.

find leather goods, wood carvings, textiles, woven baskets, oils, drums, clothing, sculptures and a stupendous array of assorted African everything. It's also an excellent spot to get your hair braided. The market is run by the Malcolm Shabazz Mosque, the former pulpit of slain Muslim orator Malcolm X.

SCHOMBURG CENTER FOR RESEARCH IN BLACK CULTURE CULTURAL CENTER

Map p434 (917-275-6975; www.nypl.org/locations/schomburg; 515 Malcolm X Blvd, at 135th St, Harlem; 10am-6pm Mon & Thu-Sat, to 8pm Tue & Wed; S 2/3 to 135th St) FREE The nation's largest collection of documents, rare books and photographs relating to the African American experience resides at this scholarly center run by the New York Public Library. It's named after Arthur Schomburg, a black Puerto Rican activist who amassed a singular collection of manuscripts, slave narratives and other important artifacts. Regular exhibitions, lectures and film screenings are held on-site.

East Harlem

EL MUSEO DEL BARRIO MUSEUM

Map p434 (212-831-7272; www.elmuseo.org; 1230 Fifth Ave, btwn 104th & 105th Sts, East Harlem; suggested donation adult/child $9/free; 11am-6pm Tue-Sat; S 6 to 103rd St) *Bienvenido* to one of New York's premier Latino cultural institutions, with thoughtful rotating exhibitions that span all media, from painting and photography to video and site-specific installations. The shows often highlight El Museo's strong permanent collection, which includes pre-Columbian artifacts, traditional folk works and a stellar array of postwar art made by a wide range of Latino artists.

The museum includes pieces by well-known historical figures like Chilean surrealist Roberto Matta and established contemporary artists such as Félix González-Torres and Pepón Osorio.

Hamilton Heights & Sugar Hill

HAMILTON GRANGE HISTORIC BUILDING

Map p434 (646-548-2310; www.nps.gov/hagr; St Nicholas Park, at 141st St; 9am-5pm Wed-Sun, guided tours 10am, 11am, 2pm & 4pm; S A/C, B/D to 145th St) FREE This Federal-style retreat belonged to Founding Father Alexander Hamilton, who owned a 32-acre country estate here in the early 1800s. Unfortunately, Hamilton was able to enjoy his abode for only two years before his life was cut short in a fatal duel with political rival Aaron Burr. Moved from Convent Ave to its present location in 2008, the building is one of several Hamilton-related sights seeing an increase in visitors – by some 75% – thanks to Lin-Manuel Miranda's musical, *Hamilton*.

HAMILTON HEIGHTS HISTORIC DISTRICT AREA

Map p434 (Convent Ave & Hamilton Tce, btwn 141st & 145th Sts, Hamilton Heights; S A/C, B/D to 145th St) Two parallel streets in Hamilton Heights – Convent Ave and Hamilton Tce – contain a landmark stretch of historic limestone and brownstone town houses from the period between 1866 and 1931. Wes Anderson fans may recognize the turreted building on the southeastern corner of Convent Ave and 144th St from the film *The Royal Tenenbaums*.

STRIVERS' ROW AREA

Map p434 (W 138th & 139th Sts, btwn Frederick Douglass & Adam Clayton Powell Jr Blvds, Harlem;

(S B, C to 135th St) Also known as the St Nicholas Historic District, these streets were the darling of Harlem's elite in the 1920s. The graceful row houses and apartments, many of which date back to the 1890s, were designed by three of the era's most celebrated architects: James Brown Lord, Bruce Price and Stanford White.

White's row of elegant Italianate creations along the northern side of W 139th St are arguably the most beautiful. Keep your eyes peeled for alleyway signs advising visitors to 'walk your horses.'

Washington Heights & Inwood

★CLOISTERS MUSEUM & GARDENS MUSEUM

(☎212-923-3700; www.metmuseum.org/cloisters; 99 Margaret Corbin Dr, Fort Tryon Park; 3-day pass adult/senior/child $25/$17/free, residents of New York State & students from Connecticut, New York or New Jersey free; ⏲10am-5:15pm; S A to 190th St) On a hilltop overlooking the Hudson River, the Cloisters is a curious architectural jigsaw, its many parts made up of various European monasteries and other historic buildings. Built in the 1930s to house the Metropolitan Museum's medieval treasures, its frescoes, tapestries and paintings are set in galleries that sit around a romantic courtyard, connected by grand archways and topped with Moorish terra-cotta roofs. Among its many rare treasures is the beguiling 16th-century tapestry series *The Hunt of the Unicorn*.

Also worth seeking out is the remarkably well-preserved 15th-century Annunciation Triptych (Merode Altarpiece). Then there's the stunning 12th-century Saint-Guilhem cloister and the Bonnefant cloister, the latter featuring plants used in medieval medicine, magic, ceremony and the arts.

Your ticket gives you three-day admission to the Cloisters as well as the Metropolitan Museum of Art (p214) and the Met Breuer (p218).

DYCKMAN FARMHOUSE MUSEUM MUSEUM

(☎212-304-9422; www.dyckmanfarmhouse.org; 4881 Broadway, at 204th St, Inwood; donation suggested; ⏲11am-4pm Thu-Sat, to 3pm Sun; S A to Inwood-207th St) FREE Built in 1784 on a 28-acre farm, the Dyckman House is Manhattan's lone surviving Dutch farmhouse. Excavations of the property have turned up valuable clues about colonial life, and the museum includes period rooms and furniture, decorative arts, a half acre of gardens, and an exhibition on the neighborhood's history. To get here, take the subway to the Inwood–207th St station (not Dyckman St) and walk one block south.

INWOOD HILL PARK PARK

(www.nycgovparks.org/parks/inwoodhillpark; Dyckman St, at the Hudson River; ⏲6am-1am; S A to Inwood-207th St) This 196-acre oasis contains the last natural forest and salt marsh in Manhattan. It's a cool escape in summer and a great place to explore anytime, as you'll find hilly paths for hiking and mellow, grassy patches and benches for quiet contemplation. It's so bucolic, in fact, that the treetops serve as frequent nesting sites for bald eagles.

Let your sporty side rip on basketball courts or soccer and football fields, or pack some produce and join locals who barbecue at designated grills on summer weekends.

MORRIS-JUMEL MANSION MUSEUM HISTORIC BUILDING

Map p434 (☎212-923-8008; www.morrisjumel.org; 65 Jumel Tce, at 160th St, Washington Heights; adult/child $10/free; ⏲10am-4pm Tue-Fri, to 5pm Sat & Sun; S C to 163rd St-Amsterdam Ave) Built in 1765 as a country retreat for Roger and Mary Morris, this columned mansion is the oldest house in Manhattan. It is also famous for having served as George Washington's headquarters after it was seized by the Continental Army in 1776. The mansion's beautifully appointed rooms contain many original furnishings, including a bed that reputedly belonged to Napoléon. Come on weekends (Saturday at noon, Sunday at 2pm) for a one-hour guided tour ($12).

HISPANIC SOCIETY OF AMERICA MUSEUM & LIBRARY MUSEUM

Map p434 (☎212-926-2234; www.hispanicsociety.org; Broadway, btwn 155th & 156th Sts, Washington Heights; ⏲10am-4:30pm Tue-Sun; S 1 to 157th St) FREE Housed in a beaux-arts structure that naturalist John James Audubon once called home, this treasure contains the largest collection of 19th-century Spanish art and manuscripts outside of Spain – as well as paintings by El Greco, Goya and Velázquez. While Anna Hyatt Huntington's majestic sculpture *El Cid* dominates the exterior courtyard, Goya's 1797 masterpiece *The Duchess of Alba* takes pride of place in-

LOCAL KNOWLEDGE

555 EDGECOMBE AVE

When completed in 1916, this brick beaux-arts **giant** (Map p434; 555 Edgecombe Ave, at 160th St, Washington Heights; S A/C to 163rd St-Amsterdam Ave; 1 to 157th St) was Washington Heights' first luxury apartment complex, with a concierge, a separate workers' entrance and no fewer than three elevators. It was initially available only to whites, but the neighborhood's transformation from predominantly Irish and Jewish to African American saw the building's residents become mostly black by the 1940s.

Its tenants would include some of New York's most prominent African Americans, among them boxer Joe Louis and music heavyweights Lena Horne, Count Basie, Duke Ellington and Billy Strayhorn. Today the building's cultural legacy lives on every Sunday afternoon, when veteran musician Marjorie Eliot (p257) throws open the doors to her apartment, inviting anyone and everyone into her living room for one of the city's most enchanting jazz jams.

doors. In 2017 the Hispanic Society closed for an extensive $15-million renovation. It's scheduled to reopen in late 2019.

SYLVAN TERRACE HISTORIC SITE

Map p434 (Sylvan Tce, Washington Heights; S C to 163rd St-Amsterdam Ave) The wooden houses on storybook Sylvan Terrace – resplendent with their high narrow stoops, dentiled canopies and boldly paneled wooden doors – constitute NYC's first attempt at building affordable abodes for workers. The street itself is graced by its original late-19th-century gas lamps, while its cobblestones are Belgian, not Dutch, as is the case in Lower Manhattan and Brooklyn.

EATING

Harlem remains justifiably famous for its soul food, both classic and reinvented, with a growing number of international options, including French. Long populated by the students and teachers of Columbia University, Morningside Heights offers cheap and late-night diners, mixed in with convivial bistro-style hangouts. Further north, Washington Heights is known for its traditional preponderance of Dominican joints, and further still, cozy cafes give Inwood's vaguely suburban blocks lovely depth of character.

Morningside Heights & West Harlem

PISTICCI ITALIAN $$

Map p434 (212-932-3500; www.pisticcinyc.com; 125 La Salle St, Morningside Heights; mains $15-24; noon-11pm Mon-Fri, from 11am Sat & Sun; ; S 1 to 125th St) When the weather is lousy, Pisticci makes a fine retreat, with its cozy two-room interior graced by low-lit chandeliers, vintage paintings and globe lights over the bar. Creative cocktails make a fine prelude to the excellent Italian fare and daily specials like baked tilapia. Many vegetables are grown at Pisticci's upstate farm (don't miss the flavor-packed grilled eggplant).

Brunch, with such offerings as spinach-and-goat-cheese omelets or lemon ricotta pancakes, is also a hit.

DINOSAUR BAR-B-QUE BARBECUE $$

Map p434 (212-694-1777; www.dinosaurbarbque.com; 700 W 125th St, at Twelfth Ave, Harlem; mains $13-32; 11:30am-11pm Mon-Thu, to midnight Fri & Sat, noon-10pm Sun; S 1 to 125th St) Jocks, hipsters, moms and pops: everyone dives into this honky-tonk rib bar for a rockin' feed. Get messy with dry-rubbed, slow-pit-smoked ribs, slabs of juicy steak and succulent burgers, or watch your waistline with the lightly seasoned grilled-chicken options. The (very) few vegetarian choices include a fantastic version of Creole-spiced deviled eggs.

COMMUNITY FOOD & JUICE AMERICAN $$

Map p434 (212-665-2800; www.communityrestaurant.com; 2893 Broadway, btwn 112th & 113th Sts, Morningside Heights; sandwiches $12-15, mains $14-32; 8am-9.30pm Mon-Thu, to 10pm Fri, 9am-10pm Sat, to 9:30pm Sun; ; S 1 to 110th St) The convivial, spacious Community is a brunch staple for frenzied families and hungover Columbia University students. Get here before 10:30am or be prepared to wait for your veggie scramble or sausage-and-egg biscuit sandwich. Better yet, skip the weekend brunch rush and stop in for a candlelit dinner. Both the fluffy blueberry pancakes and the veggie burger deserve an A.

Harlem

SEASONED VEGAN VEGAN $

Map p434 (☎212-222-0092; www.seasonedvegan.com; 55 St Nicholas Ave, at 113th St, Harlem; mains $11-17; ⏲5-10pm Tue-Thu, to 2am Fri, 11am-2am Sat, 11am-9pm Sun; ✎; Ⓢ2/3, 5 to 110th St) Run by a mother-and-son team, the Seasoned Vegan has earned a loyal following for its delicious twist on soul food. Everything here is organic and made entirely without animal products. You'll find creative takes on barbecued ribs (made with lotus root and fermented soy), po'boys (featuring yams) and mac 'n' cheese (made with cashew milk).

Go early, as waits can be long at prime time.

AMY RUTH'S RESTAURANT AMERICAN $$

Map p434 (☎212-280-8779; www.amyruths.com; 113 W 116th St, btwn Malcolm X & Adam Clayton Powell Jr Blvds, Harlem; waffles $11-18, mains $14-25; ⏲11am-11pm Mon, 8:30am-11pm Tue-Thu, to 5am Fri & Sat, to 11pm Sun; ⓈB, C, 2/3 to 116th St) Perennially crowded Amy Ruth's serves up classic Southern soul food, from fried catfish to mac 'n' cheese and fluffy biscuits. But it's the waffles that really merit a trip here – dished up 14 different ways, including with catfish. Our all-time favorite is the 'Rev Al Sharpton,' a plate of waffles topped with succulent fried chicken.

SYLVIA'S SOUTHERN US $$

Map p434 (☎212-996-0660; www.sylviasrestaurant.com; 328 Malcolm X Blvd, btwn 126th & 127th Sts, Harlem; mains $14-27; ⏲8am-10:30pm Mon-Sat, 11am-8pm Sun; Ⓢ2/3 to 125th St) Founded by Sylvia Woods back in 1962, this Harlem icon has been dazzling Harlemites and visitors (including a few presidents) with its lip-smackingly good down-home Southern cooking – fried chicken, baked mac 'n' cheese and cornmeal-dusted catfish, plus requisite sides like collard greens. Come on Sundays for the gospel brunch.

MAISON HARLEM FRENCH $$

Map p434 (☎212-222-9224; www.maisonharlem.com; 341 St Nicholas Ave, at 127th St, Harlem;

Local Life
Harlem Soul

Harlem: the neighborhood where Cab Calloway crooned: where Ralph Ellison penned *Invisible Man,* his epic novel on truth and intolerance; where acclaimed artist Romare Bearden pieced together his first collages. Simultaneously vibrant and effusive, brooding and melancholy, Harlem is the deepest recess of New York's soul.

❶ Tom's Restaurant

Rev your engine with a cuppa joe and a side of nostalgia at Greek-American **Tom's Restaurant** (Map p434; ☎212-864-6137; www.tomsrestaurant.net; 2880 Broadway, at 112th St; mains $8-13; ⏲6am-1:30am Sun-Thu, 24hr Fri & Sat; Ⓢ1 to 110th St). Distinguished by its red-neon marquee, the diner's exterior stood in for the fictional Monk's Café on the TV comedy *Seinfeld*. The place is also immortalized in Suzanne Vega's iconic song 'Tom's Diner.'

❷ Cathedral Church of St John the Divine

Vega's song includes the line 'I'm listening to the bells of the cathedral.' The cathedral in question is the Cathedral Church of St John the Divine (p247), its epic scale more Old World than New. A yet-to-be-completed blend of neo-Gothic and Romanesque styles, it's the largest place of worship in the US.

❸ Malcolm Shabazz Harlem Market

Trawl the low-key, semi-enclosed Malcolm Shabazz Harlem Market (p250), run by the Malcolm Shabazz Mosque, where slain Muslim orator Malcolm X once preached. Pick up African jewelry, textiles, drums, leather goods and oils, or get your hair braided.

❹ Flamekeepers Hat Club

Harlem's Gilded Age lives on at Flamekeepers Hat Club (p259), a friendly corner boutique lined with elegant hats and caps. If you simply can't decide, seek Marc Williamson's keen eye. The owner has quite a knack for picking the right piece for every face and shape. Just don't

RARRARORRO / SHUTTERSTOCK ©

Apollo Theater (p250)

be surprised if you end up lingering; Williamson is also a consummate conversationalist.

❺ Strivers' Row

On the blocks of 138th and 139th Sts, Strivers' Row (p251) is graced with 1890s town houses. Ever since ambitious African Americans first moved here in the 1920s and gave the area its nickname, these buildings have housed some of Harlem's greatest luminaries, among them songwriters Eubie Blake and Noble Sissle, blues veteran WC Handy and singer-dancer Bill 'Bojangles' Robinson.

❻ Red Rooster

Taste the 'new Harlem' at Red Rooster (p256), where Ethiopian-born, Swedish-raised chef Marcus Samuelsson gives comfort food a capable, respectful makeover. The cornbread (paired with honey butter) is reason enough to roll in, while basement Ginny's Supper Club keeps the drinks and tunes flowing till the wee small hours.

❼ Apollo Theater

One of the best places to catch a concert in Harlem is the Apollo Theater (p250), 'where stars are born and legends are made.' Ella Fitzgerald made her singing debut here in November 1934, at one of the theater's earliest Amateur Nights. Eight decades on, Amateur Night takes place every Wednesday, notorious crowds and all.

❽ Shrine

A mainstay on Harlem's nightlife circuit, Shrine (p257) hosts an incredible lineup of music every night of the week. Founded back in 2007 by musicians and lovers of the arts, the bar hosts several different bands a night, and you might be able to hear calypso, Afropunk, French electro, Latin jazz or straight-up soul at this feel-good music-forward spot.

mains $14-32; ⏲11am-midnight Mon-Thu, to 1am Fri-Sun; 📶; Ⓢ A/C, B/D to 125th St) Run by two French *amis,* this swinging little bar-bistro is like a second home for locals, who drop in at all hours to nibble on French toast, slurp onion soup, or loosen their belts over slow-cooked duck-leg confit. For the full effervescent effect, head here on weekends when DJs and wine-fueled merriment may just lead to dancing.

BLVD BISTRO AMERICAN $$

Map p434 (☎212-678-6200; www.boulevardbistrony.com; 239 Malcolm X Blvd, at 122nd St, Harlem; mains $16-28; ⏲11am-3:30pm & 5-11pm Tue-Fri, 9am-4pm & 6-11pm Sat, 10am-6pm Sun; Ⓢ 2/3 to 125th St) Tiny, bustling BLVD Bistro takes quality seasonal produce and turns it into subtly tweaked Southern soul food. Heading the kitchen is Mississippi-born Carlos Swepson, whose roots shine bright in dishes like blueberry-packed buttermilk pancakes, seven-cheese macaroni with pecan-wood-smoked bacon, and oh-so-fine biscuits and gravy. The popular Sunday brunch runs all day. Praise the Lord!

PIKINE SENEGALESE $$

Map p434 (☎646-922-7015; 243 W 116th St, Harlem; mains $12-17; ⏲noon-11pm; Ⓢ B, C to 116th St) Harlem's 116th St has become something of a Little Senegal in recent decades, with restaurants like Pikine serving up a taste of home to West African expats. Here you'll find all the classic Senegalese staples like *thiebou djeun* (a fish-and-cassava stew), *domoda* (tomato-based stew over vegetables) and excellent grilled lamb dishes.

Come at lunch for the widest variety. The dinner menu features mostly grilled items.

★RED ROOSTER MODERN AMERICAN $$$

Map p434 (☎212-792-9001; www.redroosterharlem.com; 310 Malcolm X Blvd, btwn W 125th & 126th Sts, Harlem; mains lunch $18-32, dinner $24-38; ⏲11:30am-10:30pm Mon-Thu, to 11:30pm Fri, 10am-11:30pm Sat, to 10pm Sun; Ⓢ 2/3 to 125th St) Transatlantic superchef Marcus Samuelsson laces upscale comfort food with a world of flavors at his effortlessly cool, vibrant brasserie. Like the work of the New York–based contemporary artists displayed on the walls, dishes are up to date: mac 'n' cheese joins forces with lobster, blackened catfish pairs with pickled mango, and spectacular Swedish meatballs salute Samuelsson's home country.

The prix-fixe lunch is a bargain at $25.

Hamilton Heights

HARLEM PUBLIC AMERICAN $

Map p434 (☎212-939-9404; www.facebook.com/harlempublic; 3612 Broadway, at 149th St, Hamilton Heights; mains $12-16; ⏲noon-2am Mon-Thu, 11am-3am Fri & Sat, to 2am Sun; Ⓢ 1, A/C, B/D to 145th St) Amiable hipsters at the bar, old-school funk on the speakers, and finger-licking bar grub: Harlem Public sets the scene for a night out. Celebrate neighborhood discoveries with mouthwatering feel-good food, whether it's a crab-cake burger with Cajun remoulade or a plate of poutine. The drinks menu showcases all things local, from Brooklyn craft beers to small-batch upstate New York liquors.

CHARLES' PAN-FRIED CHICKEN AMERICAN $

Map p434 (☎212-281-1800; 2461 Frederick Douglass Blvd, btwn 151st & 152nd Sts; fried chicken from $11; ⏲11am-11pm Mon-Sat, from 12:30pm Sun; Ⓢ B/D to 155th St) It's a hole-in-the-wall, but charismatic Charles Gabriel makes some of the best fried chicken in the city. Crisp and beautifully seasoned, it's served with sides including collard greens, yams, mac 'n' cheese and corn bread. Don't expect designer touches: just unadorned tables, food on trays, and proof that a book (or chicken joint) must never be judged by its cover.

Inwood

NEW LEAF MODERN AMERICAN $$

(☎212-568-5323; www.newleafrestaurant.com; 1 Margaret Corbin Dr, Inwood; mains $15-28; ⏲noon-9pm Mon-Thu, to 10pm Fri & Sat, 11am-9pm Sun; Ⓢ A to 190th St) Nestled in Fort Tryon Park, a short walk from the Cloisters (p252), this 1930s stone building feels like a country tavern. Settle in for market-fresh ingredients in bistro-style dishes such as salmon with seasonal vegetables or watermelon salad with feta cheese, kalamata olives and mint. If possible, grab a table on the all-weather patio for that garden-party vibe.

DRINKING & NIGHTLIFE

SILVANA BAR

Map p434 (www.silvana-nyc.com; 300 W 116th St; ⏲8am-4am; Ⓢ 2/3 to 116th St) This appealing Middle Eastern cafe and shop whips up tasty hummus and falafel plates; the real draw, though, is the hidden downstairs club, which draws a friendly, easygoing local crowd with good cocktails and live bands (kicking off around 6pm) followed by DJs. The lineup is eclectic, with jazz, Cuban *son*, reggae and Balkan gypsy punk all in the rotation.

SHRINE BAR

Map p434 (www.shrinenyc.com; 2271 Adam Clayton Powell Jr Blvd, btwn 133rd & 134th Sts, Harlem; ⌚4pm-4am; S2/3 to 135th St) To see what's happening on the global music scene, the friendly, unpretentious Shrine – run by the talented team behind Silvana – is a great place to start. Here you'll find live bands taking the small stage every day of the week. Blues, reggae, Afro-beat, funk, soca, Ethiopian grooves and indie rock are among the sounds you'll hear, with no cover charge.

GINNY'S SUPPER CLUB COCKTAIL BAR

Map p434 (☎212-421-3821; www.ginnyssupperclub.com; 310 Malcolm X Blvd, btwn W 125th & 126th Sts, Harlem; ⌚6pm-midnight Thu, to 3am Fri & Sat, brunch 10:30am-2pm Sun; S2/3 to 125th St) Looking straight out of the TV series *Boardwalk Empire,* this roaring basement supper club is rarely short of styled-up regulars sipping cocktails, nibbling on soul and global bites – from Red Rooster's kitchen upstairs – and grooving to live jazz from 7:30pm Thursday to Saturday and DJ-spun beats from 11pm Friday and Saturday. Don't miss the weekly Sunday gospel brunch (reservations recommended).

BIER INTERNATIONAL BEER HALL

Map p434 (☎212-280-0944; www.bierinternational.com; 2099 Frederick Douglass Blvd, at 113th St, Harlem; ⌚4pm-1am Mon-Wed, to 2am Thu & Fri, noon-2am Sat, noon-1am Sun; SB, C, 1 to 110th St-Cathedral Pkwy; 2/3 to 110th St-Central Park North) A fun, buzzing beer garden that peddles some 18 different drafts from Germany, Belgium and the UK, plus local brews from the Bronx Brewery and Brooklyn's Sixpoint. The extensive menu makes it worthwhile to stick around. Think catfish tacos, truffle fries with shaved Parmesan and Vienna-style schnitzel. Cash only.

67 ORANGE STREET COCKTAIL BAR

Map p434 (☎212-662-2030; www.67orangestreet.com; 2082 Frederick Douglass Blvd, btwn 112th & 113th Sts; ⌚6pm-midnight Sun-Tue, to 2am Wed & Thu, to 4am Fri & Sat; SB,C to 116th St) Named after the address where NYC's first black-owned bar stood (back in the 1840s!), 67 Orange Street serves up beautifully crafted cocktails in a cozy, speakeasy-like setting. Exposed brick, flickering candles and original artwork on the walls make a fine backdrop for sipping creative elixirs like the red rosemary gin, with its rooibos-infused gin and refreshing rosemary.

THE CHIPPED CUP CAFE

Map p434 (☎212-368-8881; www.chippedcupcoffee.com; 3610 Broadway, btwn 148th & 149th Sts, Hamilton Heights; ⌚7am-8pm Mon-Fri, 8am-8pm Sat & Sun; 📶; S1, A/C, B/D to 145th St) Hipsterdom gets all cozy at the Chipped Cup, where coffee-slurping scribes and students work away among dainty teacups, worn novels and quirky artwork. If the weather is behaving, order a latte and *pain au chocolat,* grab a copy of the *New York Times* and rediscover life's simpler pleasures in the leafy back garden.

☆ ENTERTAINMENT

★MARJORIE ELIOT'S PARLOR JAZZ JAZZ

Map p434 (☎212-781-6595; 555 Edgecombe Ave, Apartment 3F, at 160th St, Washington Heights; ⌚3:30pm Sun; SA/C to 163rd St-Amsterdam Ave; 1 to 157th St) Each Sunday the charming Ms Eliot provides one of New York's most magical experiences: free, intimate jazz jams in her own apartment. Dedicated to her two deceased sons, the informal concerts feature a revolving lineup of talented musicians, enchanting guests from all over the globe. Go early, as this event is popular (there's usually a line by 2:30pm).

MAYSLES DOCUMENTARY CENTER CINEMA

Map p434 (☎212-537-6843; www.maysles.org; 343 Malcolm X Blvd, btwn 127th & 128th Sts, Harlem; films from $10; S2/3 to 125th St) This small, not-for-profit cinema founded by the late director Albert Maysles (of *Grey Gardens* fame) shows documentary and other independent films – particularly some excellent works coming out of Africa. Check the website for details of upcoming screenings and events, which also include Q&A sessions with filmmakers, lectures and live performances.

WORTH A DETOUR

THE BRONX

The Bronx covers a relatively wide area, with numerous points of interest a distance away from each other. Your best bet is to focus on one specific area or a couple of adjacent neighborhoods. You could easily combine a visit to the Bronx Zoo or the New York Botanical Garden with an exploration of Arthur Ave in neighboring Belmont. Similarly, an early afternoon tour of Yankee Stadium is easily followed by a snoop around Bronx Museum. The B/D subway line makes travel a breeze between Bronx Museum and Edgar Allan Poe Cottage. From the latter, it's an easy 0.2-mile walk west to Kingsbridge Rd subway station, from where the 6 line heads north to nearby Woodlawn Cemetery.

A few highlights include the following:

➡ Listening to the roar of the crowds when the fabled 'Bronx Bombers' take to the field in one of America's most famous stadiums, **Yankee Stadium** (Map p434; ☎718-293-4300, tours 646-977-8687; www.mlb.com/yankees; E 161st St, at River Ave; tours $25; ⓢB/D, 4 to 161st St-Yankee Stadium).

➡ Spending the day exploring the 50 acres of beautifully landscaped **New York Botanical Garden** (☎718-817-8716; www.nybg.org; 2900 Southern Blvd; weekdays adult/child $23/10, weekends $28/12, Wed & 9-10am Sat grounds admission free; ⏲10am-6pm Tue-Sun; 👪; 🚆Metro-North to Botanical Garden), particularly stunning in springtime.

➡ Dabbling in a different kind of wild life at New York's historic **Bronx Zoo** (☎718-220-5100; www.bronxzoo.com; 2300 Southern Blvd; full experience tickets adult/child $37/27, suggested donation Wed; ⏲10am-5pm Mon-Fri, to 5:30pm Sat & Sun Apr-Oct, to 4:30pm Nov-Mar; ⓢ2, 5 to West Farms Sq-E Tremont Ave).

➡ Pushing your cultural boundaries at **Bronx Museum** (☎718-681-6000; www.bronxmuseum.org; 1040 Grand Concourse, at 165th St; ⏲11am-6pm Wed, Thu, Sat & Sun, to 8pm Fri; ⓢB/D to 167th St) FREE, an unexpectedly brilliant museum.

➡ Spending quiet time with Duke Ellington and Herman Melville in beautiful **Woodlawn Cemetery** (☎877-496-6352, 718-920-0500; www.thewoodlawncemetery.org; Webster Ave, at E 233rd St; ⏲8:30am-4:30pm; ⓢ4 to Woodlawn).

➡ Contemplating the haunting words of a great American writer at **Edgar Allan Poe Cottage** (☎718-881-8900; www.bronxhistoricalsociety.org/poe-cottage; 2640 Grand Concourse, at Kingsbridge Rd; adult/child $5/3; ⏲10am-3pm Thu & Fri, to 4pm Sat, 1-5pm Sun; ⓢB/D to Kingsbridge Rd).

When hunger strikes, head over to Arthur Ave in Belmont, a much-loved strip lined with nostalgic Italian restaurants and delis serving up delicacies from the Old World. A few hits include mozzarella and prosciutto sandwiches at **Casa della Mozzarella** (☎718-364-3867; www.facebook.com/casadellamozzarella; 604 E 187th St, at Arthur Ave; sandwiches $6-13; ⏲7:30am-6pm Mon-Sat, to 1pm Sun; ⓢB/D to Fordham Rd, 🚆Metro-North to Fordham), pizza at **Zero Otto Nove** (☎718-220-1027; www.089bronx.com; 2357 Arthur Ave, at 186th St; pizzas $12-18, dinner mains $18-29; ⏲noon-2:30pm & 4:30-10pm Tue-Thu, to 11pm Fri & Sat, 1-9pm Sun; 📶; ⓢB/D to Fordham Rd, 🚆Metro-North to Fordham) and cannoli from **Madonia Brothers Bakery** (☎718-295-5573; 2348 Arthur Ave, at 186th St; bakery items from $1.50; ⏲6am-7pm Mon-Sat, 7am-6pm Sun; ⓢB/D to Fordham Rd, 🚆Metro-North to Fordham).

Afterward, head over to the South Bronx for craft beers at the **Bronx Brewery** (☎718-402-1000; www.thebronxbrewery.com; 856 E 136th St, btwn Willow & Walnut Aves; ⏲3-7pm Mon-Wed, to 8pm Thu & Fri, noon-8pm Sat, noon-7pm Sun; ⓢ6 to Cypress Ave).

MINTON'S JAZZ

Map p434 (☎212-243-2222; www.mintonsharlem.com; 206 W 118th St, btwn St Nicholas Ave & Adam Clayton Powell Jr Blvd; $10-15; ⏲6-11pm Wed-Sat, noon-3pm & 6-10pm Sun; ⓢB/C, 2/3 to 116th St) Birthplace of bebop, this Harlem jazz-and-dinner club is a formal spot for catching live music. Everyone from Dizzy Gillespie to Louis Armstrong has jammed here, and dinner (mains $22 to $42) in its tinted-mirror-lined dining room is an experience to behold. Book ahead, dress to impress and savor Southern flavors while catching live, honey-sweet jazz.

SHOPPING

HARLEM HABERDASHERY FASHION & ACCESSORIES

Map p434 (212646-707-0070; www.harlemhaberdashery.com; 245 Malcolm X Blvd, btwn 122nd & 123rd Sts; noon-8pm Mon-Sat; S 2/3 to 125th St) Keep your wardrobe fresh at this uber-hip uptown boutique, which has covetable apparel in all shapes and sizes. Lovely T-shirts, high-end sneakers, dapper woven hats, bespoke denim jackets and perfectly fitting button-downs are among the ever-changing collections on display.

NILU GIFTS & SOUVENIRS

Map p434 (646-964-4926; www.shopnilu.com; 191 Malcolm X Blvd, btwn 119th & 120th Sts, Harlem; 11am-8pm Tue-Sun; S B/C, 2/3 to 116th St) A great little boutique to stop into while strolling through the neighborhood, NiLu (named after the owner's sons Nigel and Luke) has something for everyone. There's all manner of Harlem-themed merchandise, including T-shirts for kids (and grown-ups), canvas bags, mugs and artwork of neighborhood icons, plus finely crafted chocolates, grooming kits for men, scented candles, one-of-a-kind stationery sets and more.

REVOLUTION BOOKS BOOKS

Map p434 (212-691-3345; www.revolutionbooksnyc.org; 437 Malcolm X Blvd at 132nd St, Harlem; noon-9pm Tue-Sun; S 2/3 to 135th St) This fiercely independent bookstore stocks a range of titles related to social issues, politics, gender studies and human rights. There are author readings and discussions once a week or so. Check the website for upcoming events.

FLAMEKEEPERS HAT CLUB FASHION & ACCESSORIES

Map p434 (212-531-3542; 273 W 121st St, at St Nicholas Ave; noon-7pm Tue & Wed, to 8pm Thu-Sat, to 6pm Sun; S A/C, B/D to 125th St) Polish your look at this sassy little hat shop owned by affable Harlem local Marc Williamson. His carefully curated stock is a hat-lover's dream: soft Barbisio fedoras from Italy, Selentino top hats from the Czech Republic, and woolen patchwork caps from Ireland's Hanna Hats of Donegal. Prices range from $90 to $350, with optional customization for true individualists.

ATMOS SHOES

Map p434 (212-666-2242; www.atmosnyc.blogspot.com; 203 W 125th St, at Adam Clayton Powell Jr Blvd; 11am-8pm Mon-Sat, noon-7pm Sun; S A/C, B/D, 2/3 to 125th St) Sneaker fetishists both high and low sprint to Atmos to pimp their feet (Method Man from the Wu-Tang Clan has been seen here). A top spot for high-end kicks, limited-edition releases and rereleases, the Harlem store is well-known for its collaborations with partners including Nike, Puma and K-Swiss.

SPORTS & ACTIVITIES

TREAD CYCLING

(212-544-7055; www.treadbikeshop.com; 250 Dyckman St; per hr/day $8/30; 10am-7pm Mon-Sat, to 6pm Sun; ; S A to Dyckman St) Located in Inwood Hill Park, right off the New York Greenway Bike Trail, is this family-friendly rental shop – perfect for when you want to navigate the long and winding paths of Upper Manhattan on wheels.

RIVERBANK STATE PARK HEALTH & FITNESS

Map p434 (212-694-3600; www.nysparks.com/parks/93; entrance via 145th St at Riverside Dr, Hamilton Heights; pool adult/child $2/1, fitness room $5, ice skating adult/child $5/3, roller skating $1.50, skate rental $6; 6am-11pm; ; S 1 to 145th St) This 28-acre, five-building facility, perched atop a wastewater-treatment plant (not as crazy as it sounds), has an Olympic-size indoor pool, an outdoor lap pool, a fitness room, basketball and tennis courts, a running track around a soccer field, a playground and a roller-skating rink (with ice skating from November to March, weather permitting).

Brooklyn

BROOKLYN HEIGHTS, DOWNTOWN BROOKLYN & DUMBO | BOERUM HILL, COBBLE HILL, CARROLL GARDENS & RED HOOK | FORT GREENE, CLINTON HILL & BED-STUY | PARK SLOPE, GOWANUS & SUNSET PARK | PROSPECT HEIGHTS, CROWN HEIGHTS & FLATBUSH | WILLIAMSBURG, GREENPOINT & BUSHWICK | CONEY ISLAND & BRIGHTON BEACH

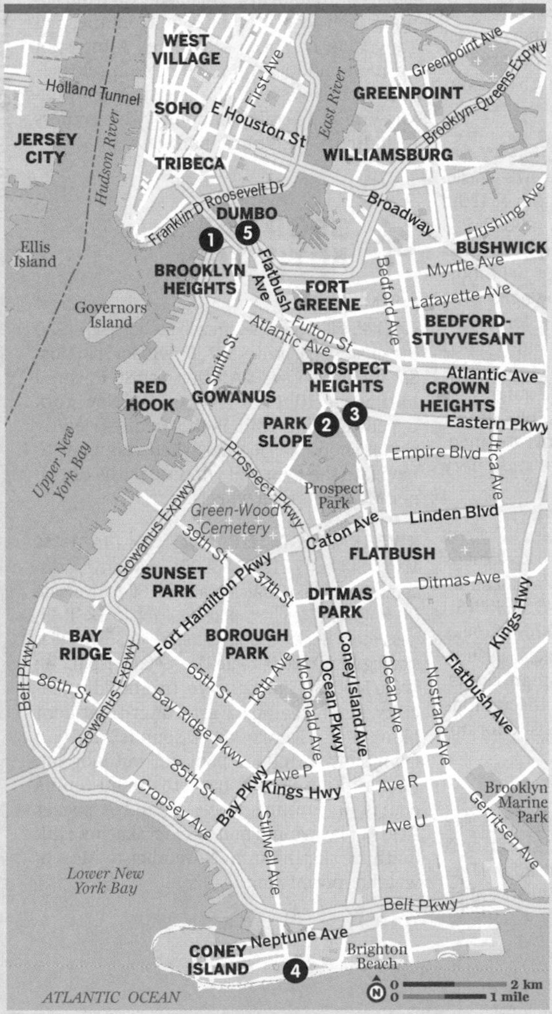

For more detail of this area see Map p436, p438, p440, p443 and p444

Neighborhood Top Five

❶ **Brooklyn Bridge Park** (p263) Running, cycling, lounging, skating, bouldering, watching the sun set – and more – at these 85 acres of multifarious parkland perfectly situated along the East River.

❷ **Prospect Park** (p264) Wandering through the nearly 600 acres of woodlands, meadows, lakes and more in the park that Central Park designers Vaux and Olmsted considered their crowning achievement.

❸ **Brooklyn Museum** (p265) Discovering the prodigious collections of Brooklyn's largest museum, from one of the nation's finest exhibits of ancient Egyptian art to groundbreaking feminist art from the 1970s.

❹ **Coney Island** (p275) Riding a wooden roller coaster, strolling the boardwalk and taking in colorful street art in murals in this fun-time, seaside district.

❺ **Brooklyn Flea** (p298) Browsing through dozens of tables of vintage clothes, old LPs, housewares and other interesting bric-a-brac at Brooklyn's favorite weekend market.

Explore Brooklyn

Home to more than 2.6 million people spread across 71 sq miles, Brooklyn is a universe unto its own. There's much to see here, from charming brownstone-lined neighborhoods and beautifully landscaped parks to cutting-edge art galleries and seaside amusement parks.

For day-trip purposes, it is best to pick a neighborhood and stick to it. South Brooklyn, especially Brooklyn Heights and neighboring Dumbo, offers lots of history and great Manhattan views. Prospect Park is just as magnificent a green space as Central Park (and only slightly smaller), and many of the residential neighborhoods surrounding it are great for architectural walks, window shopping and cafe-hopping. In the same area are two other big draws: the sprawling Brooklyn Museum and the Brooklyn Botanic Gardens.

Fans of vintage amusement parks and beachside strolls should head to Coney Island. For nightlife, north Brooklyn is the place to be. The trendy enclave of Williamsburg lies just a single subway stop from Manhattan and is loaded with bars and restaurants. Greenpoint and Bushwick have more indie cred, with atmospheric drinking dens and live-music spots.

Local Life

➡ **Rock and roll** Hit the hot music spots in Williamsburg and Bushwick to hear the latest indie sounds.

➡ **Park sloping** Join the stroller brigade for a lap or two around Prospect Park (p264). Or go window-shopping and cafe-hopping on Fifth Ave.

➡ **Farmers markets** Shop at the Saturday produce markets – Grand Army Plaza (p298), Fort Greene Park (p269), Borough Hall, McCarren Park (p274) – followed by a picnic at a park nearby.

➡ **Recreation** Riverside Brooklyn Bridge Park (p263) has ample amusement: pickup basketball, idle strolls or bike rides along the riverfront, or just lying on the grass and taking in the magnificent bridge and skyline views.

Getting There & Away

➡ **Subway** Seventeen lines travel to/from Brooklyn; all run through downtown. Key routes from Manhattan include the A/C, 2/3, 4/5, D/F, N/R/Q and L trains (p273). The G runs only between Queens and Brooklyn, from Long Island City to south of Prospect Park.

➡ **Bus** Take the B61 or B57 for Red Hook. The B62 runs from downtown to Williamsburg/Greenpoint.

➡ **Boat NYC Ferry** (Map p436; www.ferry.nyc; S 10th St, off Kent Ave, Williamsburg; 1-way trip $2.75; B32, Q59 to Kent Ave, S J/M/Z to Marcy Ave) runs from Manhattan's Wall St to E 34th St, with Brooklyn stops in Dumbo, Williamsburg, Greenpoint, Cobble Hill, Red Hook and Sunset Park.

Lonely Planet's Top Tip

If you want to get a sense of what old New York was like, be sure to wander around Brighton Beach. Under the elevated tracks on Brighton Beach Ave, the bustling Russian district known as 'Little Odessa' is packed with greengrocers and emporiums dispensing smoked fish and pierogi. On the street, you'll find a cross section of humanity – from grandmas to teens – chattering in dozens of different languages.

Best Places to Eat

➡ Olmsted (p284)
➡ Modern Love (p285)
➡ Miss Ada (p280)
➡ Smorgasburg (p285)
➡ Juliana's (p276)
➡ Zenkichi (p286)

For reviews, see p276. ➡

Best Places to Drink

➡ House of Yes (p290)
➡ Brooklyn Barge (p290)
➡ Radegast Hall & Biergarten (p291)
➡ Northern Territory (p291)
➡ Union Hall (p289)
➡ Maison Premiere (p290)

For reviews, see p288. ➡

Best Green Spaces

➡ Prospect Park (p264)
➡ Brooklyn Bridge Park (p263)
➡ Brooklyn Botanic Garden (p273)
➡ Fort Greene Park (p269)

For reviews, see p263. ➡

TTSTUDIO / SHUTTERSTOCK ©

TOP SIGHT
BROOKLYN BRIDGE

The Brooklyn Bridge, one of NYC's undisputed architectural masterpieces, opened in 1883. With a record-breaking span of 1596ft, it became the first land connection between Brooklyn and Manhattan, as well as the world's first steel suspension bridge. This magnificent example of urban design has inspired poets, writers and painters – and even today, the Brooklyn Bridge continues to dazzle.

DID YOU KNOW?

➡ In May 1884, circus impresario PT Barnum marched 21 elephants over the bridge to prove to skeptics that the structure was safe.

PRACTICALITIES

➡ S 4/5/6 to Brooklyn Bridge-City Hall; J/Z to Chambers St; R/W to City Hall

The Bridge's Heavy Toll

A German-born engineer named John Roebling designed the bridge, but due to an accident on the pier in Fulton Landing in June 1869, he contracted tetanus and died before construction of the bridge even began. His son, Washington Roebling, supervised construction of the bridge, which lasted 14 years, though a few years in he suffered a paralyzing injury from the bends while helping to excavate the riverbed for the western tower, and remained bedridden for much of the project. His wife, Emily Warren Roebling, studied higher mathematics and civil engineering and oversaw construction in his stead, also dealing with budget overruns and unhappy politicians. Not only the Roeblings suffered, though: some 20 to 30 workers (no official figure exists) died during the bridge's construction. There was one final tragedy to come in 1883, six days after the official opening: a massive crowd of pedestrians was bottlenecked at a stairway, causing a young woman to trip and fall down the stairs – the resulting shrieks set off a mad rush (people apparently thought the bridge was giving way), and 12 people were trampled to death in the ensuing stampede.

Crossing the Bridge

A stroll across the Brooklyn Bridge usually figures quite high on the 'must-do' list for NYC visitors. The pedestrian walkway affords a wonderful vista of Lower Manhattan; observation points under the support towers offer brass 'panorama' histories of the waterfront. It's about a mile across the bridge, which can take 20 to 40 minutes to walk, depending on how often you stop to admire the view.

TOP SIGHT
BROOKLYN BRIDGE PARK

This 85-acre, multi-use waterfront park is one of Brooklyn's most celebrated new sights. Wrapping around a bend on the East River, it runs for 1.3 miles from Jay St in Dumbo to the west end of Atlantic Ave in Cobble Hill. Its development has revitalized a once-barren stretch of shoreline, turning a series of abandoned piers into public parkland.

Empire Fulton Ferry

This section of the park, just east of the Brooklyn Bridge in the northern section of Dumbo, is a sweeping grassy lawn offering stunning views of the East River. At the northeastern point is Jane's Carousel (p266), a lovingly restored 1922 carousel set inside a glass pavilion designed by Pritzker Prize–winning architect Jean Nouvel. The park is bordered on one side by the Empire Stores & Tobacco Warehouse (p266), several Civil War–era structures that now house restaurants, shops and an acclaimed avant-garde theater.

Pier 1

A 9-acre pier just south of the Brooklyn Bridge is home to a stretch of park featuring a playground, walkways and the Harbor and Bridge View lawns, both of which overlook the river. Every Thursday from July through August, free films are screened alfresco against a stunning backdrop of Manhattan; other free open-air events (outdoor dance parties, group yoga classes, Shakespeare performances, history tours) happen throughout the summer; check the park's website for the event calendar. At the north end of the pier, you can catch the NYC Ferry (www.ferry.nyc) to Manhattan.

Pier 6

At the southern end of the park, off Atlantic Ave, Pier 6 has a fantastic playground and a small water-play area for tots. There's also a few seasonal concessions (May to October), including wood-fired pizza, beer and Italian treats at Fornino (p277), which has a rooftop deck that's perfect for sundowners. A free ferry runs on weekends from Pier 6 to Governors Island (p76).

Other Areas

The **Squibb Park Bridge** gives pedestrians a direct link up to Brooklyn Heights, leading from Columbia Heights between Middagh and Cranberry Sts directly down to Pier 1.

Pier 2 is all about sport and amusement, with a roller rink, an outdoor gym with free fitness equipment, and courts for bocce, handball, basketball and shuffleboard. **Pier 3** has more lawns and granite steps for sitting on to admire the views, while **Pier 4** has a small beach where you can dip your toes into the East River. **Pier 5** has walkways, sand volleyball courts, soccer fields and barbecue grills.

Main St Park, just south of the Manhattan Bridge, has a bouldering wall, a dog run, a nautical-themed playground and a pebble beach.

DON'T MISS

- Views of downtown Manhattan from Pier 1
- Empire Fulton Ferry at sunset
- A stroll across the Brooklyn Bridge

PRACTICALITIES

- Map p443, B1
- 718-222-9939
- www.brooklynbridgepark.org
- East River Waterfront, btwn Atlantic Ave & John St, Brooklyn Heights/Dumbo
- admission free
- 6am-1am, some sections to 11pm, playgrounds to dusk
- (pet-friendly)
- B63 to Pier 6/Brooklyn Bridge Park; B25 to Old Fulton St/Elizabeth Pl, East River or South Brooklyn routes to Dumbo/Pier 1, S A/C to High St; 2/3 to Clark St; F to York St

TOP SIGHT PROSPECT PARK

The designers of the 585-acre Prospect Park, Calvert Vaux and Frederick Olmsted, considered this an improvement on their other New York project, Central Park. Created in 1866, Prospect Park has many of the same features: a gorgeous meadow, a scenic lake, forested pathways and rambling hills that are straddled by leafy walkways.

DON'T MISS

- The peaceful view from the boathouse
- A stroll along Lullwater Creek
- A picnic and kite-flying on Long Meadow

PRACTICALITIES

- Map p440, E3
- ☎718-965-8951
- www.prospectpark.org
- Grand Army Plaza
- ⌚5am-1am
- Ⓢ2/3 to Grand Army Plaza; F to 15th St-Prospect Park; B, Q to Prospect Park

Grand Army Plaza

A large, landscaped **traffic circle** (Map p440; Flatbush Ave & Eastern Pkwy, Prospect Park; ⌚6am-midnight; Ⓢ2/3 to Grand Army Plaza; B, Q to 7th Ave) with a massive ceremonial arch marks the entrance to Prospect Park. The arch, which was built in the 1890s, is a memorial to Civil War Union soldiers.

A Greenmarket (p298) is held here Saturdays from 8am to 4pm year-round, while King David Tacos (p281) provides authentic, Austin-style breakfast tacos every morning.

Long Meadow

The 90-acre Long Meadow, which is bigger than Central Park's Great Lawn, lies to the south of the park's formal entrance at Grand Army Plaza. It's a super spot for strolling and lounging, filled with pickup ball games and families flying kites. On the south end is the **Picnic House**, with a snack stand and public bathrooms.

Children's Corner

The Children's Corner contains a terrific 1912 **carousel**, originally from Coney Island, and the **Prospect Park Zoo** (Map p440; ☎718-399-7339; www.prospectparkzoo.com; 450 Flatbush Ave; adult/child $8/5; ⌚10am-5pm Mon-Fri, to 5:30pm Sat & Sun Apr-Oct, to 4:30pm Nov-Mar; 👪), featuring sea lions, red pandas, wallabies and a small petting zoo. Eighteenth-century **Lefferts Historic House** (Map p440; ☎718-789-2822; www.prospectpark.org/lefferts; near Flatbush Ave & Empire Blvd; suggested donation $3; ⌚noon-5pm Thu-Sun Apr-Jun & Sep-Oct, to 6pm Jul-Aug, to 4pm Sat & Sun Nov-Dec, closed Jan-Mar; 👪) has plenty of old-fashioned toys to goof around with.

Audubon Center Boathouse

Sitting on a northern finger of Prospect Park Lake, the photogenic boathouse hosts a range of activities throughout the year: guided bird-watching sessions, free yoga classes, nature-themed art exhibitions, hands-on craft activities for kids and more. From here, there is a trailhead for 2.5 miles of woodsy **nature trails** (the route which takes you along Lullwater Creek is particularly scenic). Check the website for maps or ask at the boathouse for details.

Prospect Park Bandshell

This band shell southwest of the Long Meadow hosts free outdoor concerts during the summer. Performance calendars can be found online or at the Audubon Center Boathouse.

LeFrak Center at Lakeside

After several years of construction, Prospect Park's newest attraction continues to turn heads. This 26-acre **complex** (Map p440; ☎718-462-0010; www.lakesideprospectpark.com; 171 East Dr, near Ocean & Parkside Aves; skating $6-9, skate rentals $6-7, boat rentals per hr $15-35, bike rental per hr $8-35; ⌚hours vary by season; 👪; ⓈQ to Parkside Ave) features a pair of rinks for indoor and outdoor ice-skating in the winter plus indoor roller-skating in the summer (the outdoor rink becomes a watery splash area for small children), as well as a cafe, new walking trails and a small concert space. In the summer you can also hire paddleboats.

TOP SIGHT
BROOKLYN MUSEUM

This five-story, 560,000-sq-ft beaux-arts building was designed by McKim, Mead & White in the early 1890s and meant to be the largest single-site museum in the world – but the plan lost steam when Brooklyn was incorporated into NYC. Today, it houses more than 1.5 million objects, including ancient artifacts, 19th-century period rooms, and sculptures and paintings from across several centuries.

Egyptian Art

A particular highlight is the excellent collection of Egyptian art, which spans a period of 5000 years. Housed in the 3rd-floor galleries, it includes bas-reliefs and Roman-era portraits, some of which are drawn from the museum's ongoing excavations in Egypt. A mummy chamber holds sarcophagi and ritual objects. But the most incredible piece is the so-called 'Bird Lady,' a delicate terra-cotta figurine with an abstracted face and arms raised above her head, dating back to 3300–3650 BC. Look for her in a standalone vitrine.

American Art

The museum possesses one of the great collections of American art, including an iconic portrait of George Washington by Gilbert Stuart; Childe Hassam's celebrated 1900 urban landscape, *Late Afternoon, New York, Winter;* and dozens of paintings by late-19th-century portraitist John Singer Sargent. Don't miss a trip to the 5th floor to see them.

DON'T MISS

- Egyptian art
- *The Dinner Party*
- American art
- Visible Storage Center

PRACTICALITIES

- Map p440, F3
- 718-638-5000
- www.brooklynmuseum.org
- 200 Eastern Pkwy, Prospect Park
- suggested admission adult/child $16/free
- 11am-6pm Wed & Fri-Sun, to 10pm Thu, to 11pm 1st Sat of month Oct-Aug
-
- S 2/3 to Eastern Pkwy-Brooklyn Museum

A Room of Their Own

This is one of the few mainstream arts institutions to devote permanent space to showcasing the works of women artists. The 8300-sq-ft Elizabeth Sackler Center for Feminist Art on the 4th floor exhibits an engaging mix of one-person and historical shows that examine topics like women in video or pop art. At the gallery's core, you'll find Judy Chicago's seminal 1979 installation, *The Dinner Party.*

Other Highlights

There are other worthwhile galleries devoted to African sculpture, Latin American textiles, and contemporary art. For a peek behind the scenes, head to the Visible Storage and Study Center on the 5th floor to see glass cases stuffed with everything from vintage bicycles to a bulbous Gaston Lachaise sculpture.

On the first Saturday of every month except September, the museum stays open until 11pm and hosts a free evening of art, performances and live music (sometimes there's even a dance floor set up). It's a big draw for families.

SIGHTS

Brooklyn Heights, Downtown Brooklyn & Dumbo

When Brooklyn ferry services started in the early 1800s, well-to-do Manhattanites began building beautiful houses in Brooklyn Heights; it's still ultradesirable today for its tree-lined streets and stellar river views. Below, the shore-hugging Brooklyn Bridge Park has completely revitalized a formerly derelict waterfront. Meanwhile, Downtown is boom town. High-rise condos have transformed the skyline, as national retail chains have done to Fulton Mall.

The cobblestoned waterfront area of Dumbo was once strictly industrial, but today is home to luxury condos, shops, art galleries and upmarket restaurants; its tiny, easternmost residential enclave is called Vinegar Hill.

BROOKLYN BRIDGE BRIDGE

See p262.

BROOKLYN BRIDGE PARK PARK

See p263.

JANE'S CAROUSEL HISTORIC SITE

Map p443 (718-222-2502; www.janescarousel.com; Old Dock St, Brooklyn Bridge Park, Dumbo; tickets $2; 11am-7pm Wed-Mon mid-May–mid-Sep, to 6pm Thu-Sun mid-Sep–mid-May; ; S F to York St; A/C to High St) Behold the star attraction of the north end of Brooklyn Bridge Park (p263): a vintage carousel built by the Philadelphia Toboggan Company back in 1922. It was purchased by Dumbo artist Jane Walentas in 1984, who spent the next two decades faithfully restoring the vintage paint scheme on the ornate, carved-wood elements.

The carousel has 48 horses, two chariots and 1200 lights, and is the first of its kind to be placed on the National Register of Historic Places. This working treasure is housed in a clear acrylic pavilion designed by Pritzker Prize–winning architect Jean Nouvel.

BROOKLYN HISTORICAL SOCIETY MUSEUM

Map p443 (718-222-4111; www.brooklynhistory.org; 128 Pierrepont St, at Clinton St, Brooklyn Heights; suggested admission $10; noon-5pm Wed-Sun; S R to Court St; 2/3, 4/5 to Borough Hall) Housed in a majestic, landmarked 1881 building with striking terra-cotta details, this museum is devoted to all things Brooklyn. Its priceless collection contains a rare 1770 map of NYC and a signed copy of the Emancipation Proclamation, with regularly rotating exhibits on Brooklyn life. Don't miss peeking into the stunning 2nd-floor **Othmer Library**, with its original 19th-century balcony of black ash. The lobby **gift shop** (open noon to 5pm daily) is a fantastic resource for Brooklyn-themed books and upscale gifts.

The society also organizes regular exhibitions and neighborhood walks; check the website for details.

NEW YORK TRANSIT MUSEUM MUSEUM

Map p443 (718-694-1600; www.mta.info/mta/museum; Schermerhorn St, at Boerum Pl, Downtown Brooklyn; adult/child $10/5; 10am-4pm Tue-Fri, 11am-5pm Sat & Sun; ; S 2/3, 4/5 to Borough Hall; R to Court St) Occupying an old subway station built in 1936 (and out of service since 1946), this kid-friendly museum takes on 100-plus years of getting around town. The best part is the downstairs area, on the platform, where you can climb aboard 13 original subway and elevated train cars dating to 1904. Temporary exhibitions highlight the subway's fascinating history, including one dedicated to the recently inaugurated Second Ave line. The museum's gift shop sells popular subway-map gifts.

EMPIRE STORES & TOBACCO WAREHOUSE HISTORIC BUILDING

Map p443 (www.empirestoresdumbo.com; 53-83 Water St, near Main St, Dumbo; 8am-7:30pm; B25 to Water/Main Sts, S F to York St; A/C to High St) The Empire Stores and Tobacco Warehouse was a long-abandoned series of hollow, Civil War–era buildings that have been undergoing a long transformation into high-end retail shops, restaurants, offices and a food market. The cutting-edge theater St Ann's Warehouse (p294) opened in 2015; more recent openings have included furniture store West Elm, Detroit accessories store Shinola (p84) and a gallery-and-shop outpost of the Brooklyn Historical Society.

Boerum Hill, Cobble Hill, Carroll Gardens & Red Hook

Just south of Brooklyn Heights and Downtown Brooklyn, this cluster of family-oriented, tree-lined, brownstone-filled neighborhoods – Boerum Hill (east of Court

Neighborhood Walk
Brownstones & Bridges

START ST GEORGE HOTEL
END JANE'S CAROUSEL
LENGTH 2 MILES; TWO HOURS

Studded with historic structures, the area around Brooklyn Heights also has sublime views of Manhattan. Start at the corner of Clark and Henry Sts, at the base of the 30-story **1 St George Hotel**. Built between 1885 and 1930, it was once the city's largest hotel with 2632 rooms.

Two blocks to the north on Orange St is **2 Plymouth Church**. In the mid-19th century, Henry Ward Beecher gave abolitionist sermons here, and held 'mock auctions' to raise money to buy slaves their freedom.

Continue west on Orange and then south on Willow St. The yellow 11-bedroom mansion at 70 Willow served as **3 Truman Capote's house** while he was writing *Breakfast at Tiffany's*. Continue south, turning right on Pierrepont St, and follow as it bends to the left. The street turns into **4 Montague Tce**, a one-block lane lined with stately old brownstones. Thomas Wolfe penned *Of Time and the River* at No 5.

From here, follow Remsen St west to reach the **5 Brooklyn Heights Promenade**. This scenic walking park with staggering city views was built by planner Robert Moses in 1942, as a way of placating locals irritated by the construction of the roaring expressway underneath. Enjoy a stroll north along the promenade, then continue north along Columbia Heights, and take the pedestrian-only **6 Squibb Park Bridge** down into **7 Brooklyn Bridge Park** (p263). Once there, you can keep admiring the view while meandering across the park's grassy Pier 1.

Nearby is **8 Fulton Ferry Landing**. George Washington made an important hasty retreat here during the Battle of Long Island in 1776. From here, follow Water St under the **9 Brooklyn Bridge** (completed 1883), and past the Civil War–era brick structures of the **10 Empire Stores & Tobacco Warehouse** (p266), now a retail and office center (and a great place to grab a snack). The walk ends at Empire Fulton Ferry, a section of Brooklyn Bridge Park and home to the gleaming 1922 **11 Jane's Carousel** (p266).

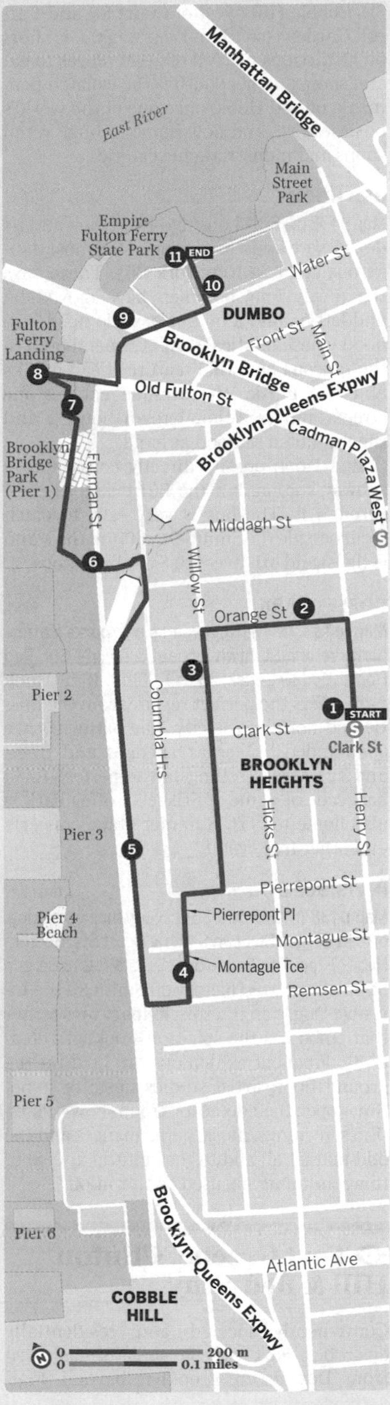

St), Cobble Hill (west of Court St) and Carroll Gardens (south of Degraw St) – is short on attractions but full of great places to eat and shop. Further south is the isolated peninsula of Red Hook, once one of the world's busiest ports and now home to huge retail shops and industrial-chic eateries.

RED HOOK AREA

Map p438 (B61) Long ago Red Hook and its docks were known as some of the most dangerous areas in New York City. These days the rowdy longshoremen have moved on and left behind a quaint bayside neighborhood whose nautical past is remembered in the raucous bars that feature cheap drinks and live music, the antique cobblestone streets and traditional town houses, and the top-notch seafood at hand.

Red Hook doesn't directly connect to a subway station, but the B61 bus goes right through it. The bus is very easy to catch right outside the Smith–9th Sts (on the F and G lines) and 4th Ave–9th St (R line) stops.

COFFEY PARK PARK

Map p438 (www.nycgovparks.org/parks/coffey-park; Verona St, btwn Richard & Dwight Sts, Red Hook; dawn-dusk) FREE This Red Hook park offers the perfect respite from the hustle and noise of the city. The pathways are surrounded by verdant hedges and trees, and cut across rolling lawns perfect for a barbecue or game of Frisbee. Coffey Park is also home to NYC Summer Stage concerts and other free events.

INVISIBLE DOG GALLERY

Map p438 (347-560-3641; www.theinvisibledog.org; 51 Bergen St, btwn Smith & Court Sts, Boerum Hill; 1-7pm Thu-Sat, to 5pm Sun; S F, G to Bergen St) In a converted factory off Smith St, the Invisible Dog is an interdisciplinary arts center that embodies the spirit of Brooklyn's creativity. Frequent exhibitions are held on the ground floor; artist studios upstairs sometimes open their doors for group shows. Plays, film screenings, music performances and the odd market all add to the cultural appeal of this community-focused organization.

Fort Greene, Clinton Hill & Bed-Stuy

Conveniently located and residentially desirable, Fort Greene spreads eastward from Downtown Brooklyn beyond Flatbush Ave; it's home to two local institutions: the Brooklyn Academy of Music and the 1927 Williamsburgh Savings Bank Tower, for decades Brooklyn's tallest building (now dwarfed by steel-and-glass condo skyscrapers). Gorgeously preserved (and appropriately unaffordable) 19th-century brownstones line Fort Greene's leafy side streets, as with its more remote neighbor, Clinton Hill, home to the Pratt Institute, a private art and design university. Washington and Clinton Aves in particular have some beautiful post–Civil War row houses.

MUSEUM OF CONTEMPORARY AFRICAN DIASPORAN ARTS MUSEUM

Map p438 (MoCADA; 718-230-0492; www.mocada.org; 80 Hanson Pl, at S Portland Ave, Fort Greene; adult/student/child $8/4/free; noon-7pm Wed, Fri & Sat, to 8pm Thu, to 6pm Sun; S C to Lafayette Ave; B/D, N/Q/R, 2/3, 4/5 to Atlantic Ave-Barclays Ctr) This small museum hosts a wide range of thought-provoking installations exploring social and political issues facing people of the African Diaspora in an attempt to rediscover cultural traditions lost during colonization and the transatlantic slave trade. A rotation of temporary exhibitions includes photography, sculpture, sound and multimedia works. The museum also hosts performance pieces, music nights, artist talks and discussions. Don't miss the on-site shop, with its range of one-of-a-kind art, jewelry, apparel and home decor by contemporary designers.

At the time of research, the museum was scheduled move to roomier digs (tripling its exhibition space) in BAM South, a massive new mixed-use complex across from the BAM Fisher Building (p294), a few short blocks away on Ashland Pl.

BRIC HOUSE CULTURAL CENTER

Map p438 (718-683-5600; www.bricartsmedia.org; 647 Fulton St, cnr Rockwell Pl, Fort Greene; gallery 10am-6pm Tue-Sun; S B, Q/R to DeKalb Ave; 2/3, 4/5 to Nevins St) This long-running Brooklyn arts organization (responsible for **free summer concerts** (near Prospect Park W & 11th St, Prospect Park Bandshell, Park Slope; Jun-Aug) in Prospect Park, among other things) is housed in an impressive 40,000-sq-ft space. The multidisciplinary arts complex stages art exhibitions, media events and a wide range of cultural fare – poetry slams, plays, concerts, dance performances – inside its 400-seat theater. There's also a branch of the **Hungry Ghost**

(Map p438; ☎718-797-3595; www.hungryghost brooklyn.com; 781 Fulton St, at S Oxford St, Fort Greene; sandwiches from $7, breakfasts from $3, coffees from $3; ⊙7am-8pm; S C to Lafayette Ave, G to Fulton St) cafe, and a glassworking facility (which also has exhibitions) next door.

FORT GREENE PARK PARK

Map p438 (www.fortgreenepark.org; btwn Myrtle & DeKalb Aves & Washington Park & St Edwards St, Fort Greene; ⊙6am-1am; ; S B, Q/R to DeKalb Ave; C to Lafayette St; G to Fulton St) This 30-acre park sits on land that housed military forts during the Revolutionary War. In 1847, the area was designated Brooklyn's first park (a measure supported by newspaper editor Walt Whitman); by 1896, Calvert Vaux and Frederick Olmsted – famed designers of Central Park (p228) and Prospect Park (p264) – were redesigning the place into the attractive hilltop landscape it is today. There are walkways, tennis courts, ball fields and a playground.

At the center of the park stands the **Prison Ship Martyrs' Monument**, at the time of its construction the world's tallest Doric column at 149ft. Designed by Stanford White (of prominent architectural firm McKim, Mead & White), it was built in 1905 to memorialize the 11,500 American prisoners of war who died in wretched conditions in British prison ships during the American Revolution. Some of their remains are interred in a crypt beneath its base.

If you're there on a Saturday don't miss the year-round Greenmarket (p280) featuring all kinds of fresh regional produce, held at the southeastern corner of the park. In autumn months (from September to mid-November) it's joined by an **artisan market** featured locally made artwork and crafts from independent artists.

KINGS COUNTY DISTILLERY DISTILLERY

(☎347-689-4211; www.kingscountydistillery.com; 299 Sands St, at Navy St, Brooklyn Navy Yard; tours $14; ⊙tours 3pm & 5pm Tue-Sun, every 30 min 1-4pm Sat, tasting room 10am-6pm Mon, to 10pm Tue-Fri, noon-10pm Sat, to 8pm Sun; B62, B67 to Sands/Navy Sts, S F to York St) Set in an 1899 brick building in the Brooklyn Navy Yard, this distillery uses New York grain and traditional equipment to create some mighty smooth craft spirits. Come on

GREEN-WOOD CEMETERY

If you really want to enjoy a slice of scenic Brooklyn in total peace and quiet, make for **Green-Wood Cemetery** (Map p440; www.green-wood.com; 500 25th St, at Fifth Ave, Greenwood Heights; ⊙7am-7pm Jun-Aug, from 7:45am May & Sep, to 6pm mid-Mar–Apr & Oct, to 5pm Nov–mid-Mar; S R to 25th St) FREE. This historic burial ground set on the borough's highest point covers almost 500 hilly acres with more than 7000 trees (many of which are over 150 years old); its myriad tombs, mausoleums, lakes and patches of forest are connected by a looping network of roads and footpaths, making this a perfect spot for some aimless rambling.

Founded in 1838, the cemetery is the final resting place of some 560,000 people, including many notable and historic personalities, such as inventors Samuel Morse and Elias Howe, abolitionist Henry Ward Beecher, designer Louis Comfort Tiffany and 1980s artist Jean-Michel Basquiat.

Don't miss **Battle Hill**, the cemetery's highest point, where the Continental Army fought off British troops during the 1776 Battle of Long Island. The event is commemorated by the 7ft statue of Minerva, the Roman goddess of wisdom, whose upright arm waves to the Statue of Liberty, facing back from a few miles across the harbor. The hill is located in the northeast sector of the cemetery, off Battle Ave. Musical legend Leonard Bernstein and Brooklyn Dodgers owner Charles Ebbets are both buried in the vicinity.

Admission is free and free maps are available at the entrance. On Wednesdays and Sundays at 1pm, you can take a two-hour trolley-bus tour (per person $20; advance booking recommended). Note the squawking green monk parakeets nesting within the nooks of the glorious Gothic entry gate – some allegedly broke free from an airport crate in the 1960s and started a colony that's lived here ever since.

Tip: pack mosquito repellent in the summer.

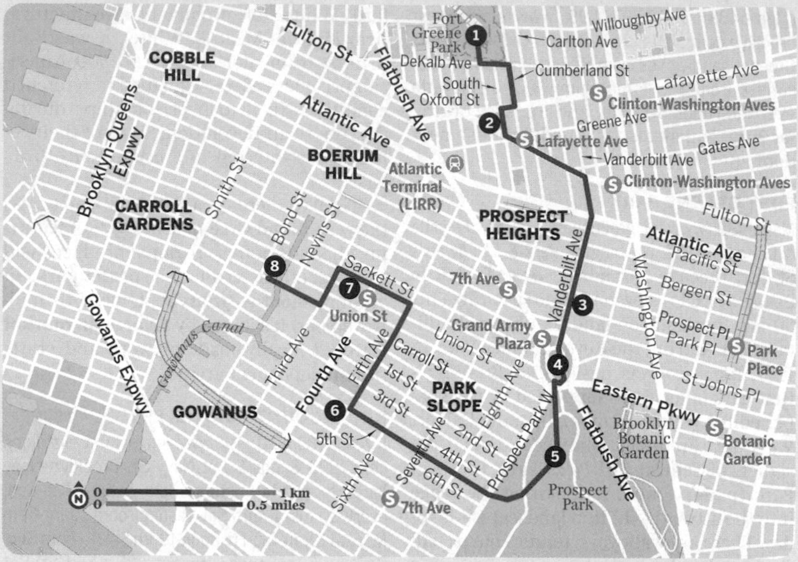

Local Life
South Brooklyn

This 4-mile walk takes in some of Brooklyn's most fascinating neighborhoods, where new eateries, bars and shops are rapidly changing the urban landscape. You'll stroll through leafy neighborhoods, down brownstone-lined streets and across two pretty parks. To hit the Greenmarkets mentioned here, do this walk on a Saturday.

❶ Fort Greene Park

A stroll across pleasant 30-acre Fort Greene Park (p269) is a leisurely way to kick off the day. Climb the hill to the Prison Ship Martyrs' Monument for views of Manhattan. On Saturday morning there's a Greenmarket at the southeast corner of the park. (The apple-cider doughnuts are delicious!)

❷ Coffee & Brownstones

The pleasant neighborhood surrounding the park is also called Fort Greene. Restaurant-lined DeKalb Ave is one of its main commercial strips, while the side streets have some of Brooklyn's loveliest residential architecture. Head to Fulton St and grab a coffee at Hungry Ghost (p268).

❸ Vanderbilt Avenue

Crossing Atlantic Ave will bring you to **Prospect Heights**, another charming Brooklyn 'hood. Vanderbilt Ave is the main drag, with shops, restaurants and cafes aplenty.

❹ Grand Army Plaza

Continue down to Grand Army Plaza (p264), a giant traffic circle crowned by a massive arch. Just south, at the Prospect Park entrance, is another popular Saturday Greenmarket with a rotating cast of food trucks.

❺ New York's Other Park

Prospect Park (p264), Brooklyn's version of Central Park, was created by the same designers and features many of the same landscape features – but with far fewer crowds. A grassy meadow (perfect for picnics and kite-flying), forested trails and a scenic lake are the big draws.

❻ Heroic Accessories

Strolling west out of the park, you'll enter the residential neighborhood of Park Slope, which features tree-lined streets and coveted historic brownstones in every direction. Seventh and Fifth Aves are the two main commercial streets; on Fifth is the

Brownstones in Brooklyn

curious shop Brooklyn Superhero Supply Co (p298), where you can buy capes, disguises and particle guns.

❼ Unique Finds

Have a dig through the racks at **No Relation** (Map p440; ☎718-858-4906; http://ltrainvintage.com; 654 Sackett St, near Fourth Ave, Gowanus; ⏲noon-8pm; Ⓢ R to Union St), a huge vintage shop on the western fringe of Park Slope. You might score an old sports jersey, a piece of vintage designer wear or an oversized, ugly-cool '90s sweater.

❽ Lavender Lake

Just west of Park Slope is Gowanus, a formerly industrial neighborhood currently undergoing a cultural and residential renaissance; it's named after the (polluted) canal flowing through it. Take the picturesque wood-plank bridge on Carroll St and have a waterside look before stopping at **Lavender Lake** (Map p440; ☎347-799-2154; www.lavenderlake.com; 383 Carroll St, btwn Bond Sts & Gowanus Canal, Gowanus; ⏲4pm-midnight Mon-Wed, to 1am Thu, to 2am Fri, noon-2am Sat, to midnight Sun; Ⓢ F, G to Carroll St; R to Union St), an enticing bar with a relaxing backyard open in the summer.

a 45-minute **guided tour** (advance booking recommended) for a look at the distilling process from grain to bottle, with a bit of a history thrown in to boot (the 19th-century Whiskey Wars, which erupted in nearby Vinegar Hill, devastated Brooklyn). At the end, you'll get to taste some of the product.

You can also stop in at the gatehouse **tasting room** to try some of the classic or experimental KCD cocktails, as well as whiskey flights (or just grab a bottle or two to take home). Kings County Distillery produces bourbon (aged in charred, American oak barrels), moonshine (made of 80% corn, and not nearly as undrinkable as the name might imply) and limited-edition seasonal varieties like pumpkin-spice whiskey. Some imbibers also enjoy KCD's chocolate whiskey, infused with cacao-bean husks from the neighboring Mast Brothers Chocolate factory.

BLDG 92 MUSEUM

(www.bldg92.org; 63 Flushing Ave, at Carlton Ave, Brooklyn Navy Yard; ⏲noon-6pm Wed-Sun; 🚌B57, B69 to Cumberland St/Flushing Ave, Ⓢ G to Fulton St; F to York St) FREE In the Brooklyn Navy Yard, this free museum gives an excellent overview of the key historical events that have played out on this plot of land over the past 200 years. The building of America's naval ships, of course, features front and center, but exhibits also tie into events happening on both the local and global stages.

Park Slope, Gowanus & Sunset Park

Known for leafy streets and classic brownstones, Park Slope is Brooklyn's answer to Manhattan's Upper West Side. This former working-class area is today filled with gay and straight couples with toddlers and designer dogs, plus great eateries and boutiques. To the east is Brooklyn's most important green space, the 585-acre Prospect Park. West is the Gowanus area, with new condominiums, shops and nightlife opening on and around formerly derelict Fourth Ave.

South lies the historically significant Green-Wood Cemetery (p269) and its immediate neighborhood, **Greenwood Heights**, and beyond, the demographically diverse neighborhood Sunset Park.

PROSPECT PARK PARK

See p264.

BUSH TERMINAL PIERS PARK PARK

(☎888-697-2757; Marginal St, Sunset Park; ⊙dawn-dusk, hours vary seasonally) FREE Bush Terminal Piers Park is located a short walk from the studios, shops and restaurants of Industry City and features some of the best views in Brooklyn. Inside the park are trails, basketball courts, and plenty of grassy knolls to sit and take in the stunning bay with Lower Manhattan in the distance. It's especially eye-catching at sunset.

You can enter the park from 43rd St.

SUNSET PARK PARK

Map p440 (www.nycgovparks.org/parks/sunset-park; 41st to 44th Sts, btwn Fifth & Seventh Aves, Sunset Park; ; B63 to 42nd or 44th St, S R to 45th St; D, N to 36th St) Sunset Park is a lovely hangout spot. On summer evenings, families keep cool in its Olympic-size outdoor swimming pool, and kids love its large, modern playground. It's small enough to walk easily, but large enough to spread out for picnics and relaxation. True to its name, it features incredible sunset views of New York Harbor and the Statue of Liberty.

Prospect Heights, Crown Heights & Flatbush

Just north of Prospect Park is the small, easygoing neighborhood Prospect Heights, filled with families and young professionals. Broad, tree-lined Eastern Pkwy runs off to the east through Crown Heights, a primarily Caribbean and African American neighborhood with a significant Hasidic Jewish community.

To the east and south are the sedate areas **Prospect Lefferts Gardens**, **Prospect Park South** and **Ditmas Park**, home to many beautiful 19th-century brownstones and houses. Beyond stretches the larger suburban area of Flatbush, one of the original towns founded by Dutch colonists in the mid-1600s.

BROOKLYN MUSEUM MUSEUM

See p265.

BROOKLYN BOTANIC GARDEN GARDENS

Map p440 (☎718-623-7200; www.bbg.org; 150 Eastern Pkwy, Prospect Park; adult/student/child $15/8/free, 10am-noon Fri free, Tue-Fri Dec-Feb free; ⊙8am-6pm Tue-Fri, from 10am Sat & Sun

WORTH A DETOUR

DITMAS PARK

A few subway stops south of Prospect Park, **Ditmas Park** (Map p440; around Cortelyou Rd, Flatbush; P; S Q to Cortelyou Rd or Newkirk Plaza; B to Newkirk Plaza), contained within the larger Flatbush area, is right on the subway line but feels like a completely different world – certainly not the big bad city. You'll find tranquil, tree-lined side streets boasting elegant freestanding houses built in the early 1900s in the Colonial Revival, arts-and-crafts, Victorian, Queen Anne and other architectural styles. Even commercial Cortelyou Rd is bustling but laid-back. Visit this area to experience another side of Brooklyn.

Two districts in particular have the most noteworthy houses. For the **Prospect Park South Historic District**, take the B or Q to Church Ave; walk west down Church and turn left onto Buckingham, the first of these beautiful blocks. When you get to Albemarle Rd, stroll up and down the two long blocks of the next three roads – Marlborough, Rugby and Argyle – between there and Cortelyou Rd to see these grand old structures. The **Ditmas Park Historic District** is just a couple of blocks to the southeast, bordered neatly by Dorchester Rd, Ocean Ave, Newkirk Ave and E 16th St.

When you've finished your perambulations, there are plenty of great bars and restaurants to discover in Ditmas Park, including the beloved **Mimi's Hummus** (Map p440; ☎718-284-4444; www.mimishummus.com; 1209 Cortelyou Rd, btwn Westminster & Argyle Rds, Ditmas Park; hummus $9, mains $8-17; ⊙9am-10:30pm Mon-Thu, to 11:30pm Fri, 11am-11pm Sat, to 10:30pm Sun; S Q to Cortelyou Rd) and quirky bourbon bar **Sycamore** (Map p440; www.sycamorebrooklyn.com; 1118 Cortelyou Rd, at Westminster Rd, Ditmas Park; ⊙2pm-2am Mon-Thu, to 4am Fri, noon-4am Sat, to 2am Sun), and local-fave cafe **Milk & Honey** (☎718-513-0441; www.milkandhoneycafeny.com; 1119 Newkirk Ave, at Westminster Rd, Ditmas Park; mains $8-14; ⊙7am-8pm; ; S B, Q to Newkirk Plaza). Both avenues have subway stops for the return trip.

Mar-Oct, 8am-4:30pm Tue-Fri, from 10am Sat & Sun Nov, 10am-4:30pm Tue-Sun Dec-Feb; ; 2/3 to Eastern Pkwy-Brooklyn Museum; B, Q to Prospect Park) One of Brooklyn's most picturesque attractions, this 52-acre garden is home to thousands of plants and trees, as well as a **Japanese garden** where river turtles swim alongside a Shinto shrine. The best time to visit is late April or early May, when the blooming cherry trees (a gift from Japan) are celebrated in **Sakura Matsuri**, the **Cherry Blossom Festival** (Apr or May).

A network of trails connects the Japanese garden to other popular sections devoted to native flora, bonsai trees, a wood covered in bluebells and a rose garden. The **Discovery Garden** is a hands-on, immersive space for kids, with regular family activities. There's also a good cafe on-site (with outdoor seating, of course).

There are three entrances; the most direct one to get to is immediately west of the Brooklyn Museum (p265). The Washington Ave entrance around the corner (at President St) leads to a striking and eco-designed **visitors center** with a 'living roof' covered in 40,000 plants.

WEEKSVILLE HERITAGE CENTER HISTORIC SITE

(718-756-5250; www.weeksvillesociety.org; 1698 Bergen St, btwn Rochester & Buffalo Aves, Crown Heights; tours adult/student $8/6; tours 3pm Tue-Fri; A/C to Ralph Ave) In 1838 a former enslaved man by the name of James Weeks purchased a tract of land on the fringes of Brooklyn's settled areas to build a free African American community of entrepreneurs, doctors, laborers and craftsmen. Over time, the village was absorbed into Brooklyn, but three of the historic wooden houses (known as the Hunterfly Road Houses) can be visited.

BROOKLYN CHILDREN'S MUSEUM MUSEUM

(718-735-4400; www.brooklynkids.org; 145 Brooklyn Ave, at St Marks Ave, Crown Heights; $11, 2-6pm Thu free; 10am-5pm Tue-Wed & Fri, to 6pm Thu, to 7pm Sat & Sun; ; C to Kingston-Throop Aves; 3 to Kingston Ave) A bright-yellow, L-shaped structure houses this hands-on kids' favorite, which was founded in 1899. The collection contains almost 30,000 cultural objects (musical instruments, masks and dolls) and natural-history specimens (rocks, minerals and a complete Asian elephant skeleton). But Brooklyn is very much in the house, with a re-created bodega, a pizza joint, and a Caribbean market that kids can play-act in. The museum is located next to Brower Park and is about a mile from the Grand Army Plaza.

L TRAIN SHUTDOWN!

In April 2019, NYC is planning to close the Canarsie Tunnel, which connects Manhattan with Williamsburg on the L train line for much-needed repairs. The upcoming closure, slated to last 15 months, has caused much anxiety in North Brooklyn. During its closure, there will be regular L eastward service from Bedford Ave to Canarsie, but no service across to Manhattan, or within Manhattan itself. If planning to visit Williamsburg from Manhattan, be sure to research your options ahead of time: taking an alternate subway line (J, M, Z or G) and walking or bussing it, cycling by Citi Bike over the Williamsburg Bridge, or going by NYC Ferry (p384).

Get the latest subway updates at http://web.mta.info.

WYCKOFF HOUSE MUSEUM HISTORIC BUILDING, MUSEUM

(718-629-5400; www.wyckoffmuseum.org; 5816 Clarendon Rd, at E 59th St, East Flatbush; suggested admission adult/child $5/3; grounds noon-4pm Fri & Sat, guided house tours every 30min 1-4pm Fri & Sat; ; B8 to Beverly Rd/E 59th St, B, Q to Newkirk Plaza then) Built in 1652, the Pieter Claesen Wyckoff House is New York City's oldest building and one of the oldest in the US. A working farm until 1901, this Dutch Colonial H-frame house has shingled walls and split doors; a guided tour explains the family's history and the successive additions made to the house in the 18th and 19th centuries. Reservations recommended for tours. It's located a ways out in East Flatbush; call or check the website for directions.

Williamsburg, Greenpoint & Bushwick

Once filled with full-sleeve tats and man buns, the Williamsburg scene has been transformed by young professionals and families pouring into new high-rise condominiums (a Whole Foods even opened

BUSHWICK STREET ART

Further cementing Bushwick's status as Brooklyn's coolest neighborhood is **Bushwick Collective** (www.instagram.com/thebushwickcollective; around Jefferson & Troutman Sts, Bushwick; S L to Jefferson St), an outdoor gallery of murals by some of the most talented street artists in NYC and beyond. The works change regularly, and can be found mainly along Jefferson and Troutman Sts between Cypress and Knickerbocker Aves, with others along Gardner Ave (north of Flushing Ave).

Other street art can be found around the Morgan Ave L stop, particularly on Siegel and Grattan Sts, which are conveniently near Roberta's (p287) and Pine Box Rock Shop (p293), great places to stop for a pizza or some drinks.

Though overall safe to visit, Bushwick still has occasional incidents of crime, so pay attention to your surroundings in this area, especially late at night and on weekends.

in 2016). But it's still a top-notch evening destination for food, drinks and entertainment. East of the Brooklyn–Queens Expwy (BQE) also has some cool spots, while south of Division Ave is an ultra-orthodox Jewish enclave that offers little for visitors. South of Myrtle Ave is mainly residential.

Traditionally Polish Greenpoint and mainly Latino Bushwick have recently seen an influx of young creatives seeking cheaper rents.

★CITY RELIQUARY — MUSEUM

Map p436 (718-782-4842; www.cityreliquary.org; 370 Metropolitan Ave, near Havemeyer St, Williamsburg; $7; noon-6pm Thu-Sun; S L to Lorimer St; G to Metropolitan Ave) A tiny, community-supported museum housed in a former bodega, the curiously fascinating City Reliquary is filled with New York–related ephemera from throughout the city's history. Cases and shelves are stuffed full of artifacts such as old shop signs, souvenir tchotchkes, vintage pencil sharpeners, subway tokens, seltzer bottles and artifacts from the old Yankee Stadium. Rotating exhibits offer a more focused look at particular facets of NYC life.

BROOKLYN ART LIBRARY — GALLERY, LIBRARY

Map p436 (718-388-7941; www.sketchbookproject.com; 28 Frost St, btwn Union Ave & Lorimer St, Williamsburg; 10am-6pm Wed-Sun; S L to Lorimer St) FREE Lining the walls of this intriguing space are more than 30,000 sketchbooks, which contain a wild mix of graphic design, collage, fine art, poetry, irreverent comics and personal essays. To browse the collection, sign up for a free library card, then do a search by subject matter, theme, artist name or even country (contributors from over 130 countries have added their sketchbooks to the library). Ask the friendly librarian for personal favorites.

If you feel inspired after paging through a few books, join in on the fun. You can buy a sketch book ($30 for the 5"x7" book that each artist must use) and fill it with whatever you like; let your imagination run wild or use one of the suggested yearly themes; once received by the library (you can mail it back from home) it will be added to the collection.

MCCARREN PARK — PARK

Map p436 (718-965-6580; www.nycgovparks.org/parks/mccarren-park; N 12th St, at Bedford Ave, Williamsburg; pool 11am-3pm & 4-7pm Memorial Day-Labor Day; S G to Nassau Ave; L to Bedford Ave) The grassy 35-acre McCarren Park makes a good picnic spot on warm days, though on sweltering days you might want to head to the free **swimming pool** – a huge, historic community spot that reopened in 2012 after being closed for almost three decades. Go early to avoid the worst of the crowds. Free movies and live-music nights are held on Wednesdays in July and August (see www.summerscreen.org for details).

EAST RIVER STATE PARK — PARK

Map p436 (718-782-2731; www.parks.ny.gov/parks/155; Kent Ave, btwn 8th & 9th Sts, Williamsburg; 9am-dusk; S L to Bedford Ave) The 7-acre waterfront East River State Park is a slice of greenery with sublime views of Manhattan. Its grassy lawn is home to a vast assortment of events and activities, including the odd summer concert. There is also summer-only ferry service to Governor's Island and year-round ferry service on the **NYC Ferry** (Map p436; www.ferry.nyc; N 6th

St, off Kent Ave, Williamsburg; 1-way trip $2.75; B32 to N 6th St, S L to Bedford Ave). No pets allowed.

BROOKLYN BREWERY BREWERY

Map p436 (718-486-7422; www.brooklynbrewery.com; 79 N 11th St, btwn Berry St & Wythe Ave, Williamsburg; tours Sat & Sun free, 5pm Mon-Thu $15; tours 5pm Mon-Thu, 1-5pm Sat, 1-4pm Sun; tasting room 6-11pm Fri, noon-8pm Sat, noon-6pm Sun; S L to Bedford Ave) Harking back to a time when this area of New York was a beer brewing center, the Brooklyn Brewery not only brews and serves tasty local suds, but also offers tours of its facilities.

Tours offered from Monday to Thursday include tastings of four beers, plus history and insight into the brewery; reserve a spot online. On weekends, tours are free (just show up) but don't include tastings. Instead, you can buy beer tokens ($5 each or five for $20) to sample the refreshing brews. Or you can skip the tour altogether and just while away a weekend afternoon in the bare-bones tasting room.

Interesting fact: the brewery's cursive logo was designed by none other than Milton Glazer, of 'I Heart New York' fame, who did the job in exchange for a share of the profits and free beer for life.

WILLIAMSBURG BRIDGE BRIDGE

Map p436 (www.nyc.gov/html/dot/html/infrastructure/williamsburg-bridge.shtml; S 5th St, Williamsburg; S J/M/Z to Marcy Ave) Built in 1903 to link Williamsburg and the Lower East Side (at Delancey St), this steel-frame suspension bridge helped transform the area into a teeming industrial center. Its foot and bike paths offer excellent views of Manhattan and the East River. While the Brooklyn Bridge is more attractive, it's capped by less-than-interesting government areas – whereas the Williamsburg Bridge connects two neighborhoods with plenty of bars and restaurants, offering the possibility of refreshments on both ends.

Coney Island & Brighton Beach

An hour by subway from midtown Manhattan, Coney Island was once New York's most popular beachside amusement area. After decades in the doldrums, revitalization has

TOP SIGHT
CONEY ISLAND

Coney Island – a name synonymous in American culture with seaside fun and frolicking in days of yore – achieved worldwide fame as a working-class amusement park and beach-resort area at the turn of the 20th century. After decades of seedy decline, its kitschy charms have experienced a 21st-century revival. Though it's no longer the booming, peninsula-wide attraction it once was, it still draws crowds of tourists and locals alike for roller-coaster rides, hot dogs and beer on the beachside boardwalk.

Luna Park (Map p444; 718-373-5862; www.lunaparknyc.com; Surf Ave, at 10th St, Coney Island; Apr-Oct) is one of Coney Island's most popular amusement parks and contains one of its most legendary rides: the Cyclone ($10), a wooden roller coaster that reaches speeds of 60mph and makes near-vertical drops. The pink-and-mint-green **Deno's Wonder Wheel** (Map p444; 718-372-2592; www.denoswonderwheel.com; 1025 Riegelmann Boardwalk, at W 12th St, Coney Island; rides $8; from noon Jul & Aug, from noon Sat & Sun Apr-Jun & Sep-Oct;), which has been delighting New Yorkers since 1920, is the best place to survey Coney Island from up high.

DON'T MISS

- Cyclone roller-coaster ride
- Cold beer at Ruby's
- Nathan's Famous hot dogs

PRACTICALITIES

- Map p444, C2
- www.coneyisland.com
- Surf Ave & Boardwalk, btwn W 15th & W 8th Sts
- S D/F, N/Q to Coney Island-Stillwell Ave

brought the summertime crowds back for hot dogs, roller coasters, minor-league baseball games and strolls down the boardwalk. Directly to the east along the boardwalk is Brighton Beach, dubbed 'Little Odessa' for its large population of Ukrainian and Russian families. Running under the elevated subway tracks, its bustling main street, Brighton Beach Ave, is lined with Slavic shops, restaurants and cafes.

CONEY ART WALLS PUBLIC ART

Map p444 (www.coneyartwalls.com; 3050 Stillwell Ave, off Surf Ave, Coney Island; noon-10pm Jun-Sep; D/F, N/Q to Coney Island-Stillwell Ave) FREE One of Coney Island's newest sights, this open-air public museum of street art features 36 freestanding walls transformed each season into colorful murals by both emerging and renowned graffiti artists (such as street-art pioneer Lee Quinones) from around the world. It's co-curated by art dealer and former museum director Jeffrey Deitch. On summer weekends, food trucks and live music make it one big Instagram-worthy street party.

EATING

Brooklyn's culinary identity, hard to pin down and argued over with the passion of Talmudic scholars, is nevertheless assured. Why else would Manhattanites trek out to the far reaches of Kings County for a meal these days? Credentialed, ambitious chefs have created their own subspecies of restaurant here – small, retro, bespoke and locavore. Williamsburg and Greenpoint have perhaps the greatest variety, followed by the nexus of Carroll Gardens, Cobble Hill and Park Slope; honorable mention goes to a few gems in the Fort Greene/Clinton Hill area. Concentrations of ethnic foodie wonderlands extend from Sunset Park to Brighton Beach.

Brooklyn Heights, Downtown Brooklyn & Dumbo

DEKALB MARKET HALL FOOD HALL $

Map p443 (www.dekalbmarkethall.com; City Point, 445 Albee Square W, at DeKalb Ave, Downtown Brooklyn; 7am-9pm Sun-Wed, to 10pm Thu-Sat; ; B, Q/R to DeKalb Ave; 2/3 to Hoyt St; A/C, G to Hoyt-Schermerhorn) One of Downtown Brooklyn's best options for a quick feed is this popular basement food hall in the City Point retail center. Choose from 40 different vendors with offerings across the culinary spectrum: pastrami sandwiches, arepas, tacos, pickles, pierogi, rice bowls, sushi, rotisserie chicken, crepes, you name it. Finish up with a cone of Ample Hills (p280) ice cream.

ARCHWAY CAFE AMERICAN $

Map p443 (718-522-4325; www.archwaycafe.com; 57b Pearl St, btwn Water & Front Sts, Dumbo; mains $11-14, sandwiches $10-12; 8am-9pm Mon-Fri, to 7pm Sat & Sun; ; A/C to High St; F to York St) One of the best places for a casual bite in Dumbo, Archway Cafe is a good anytime spot. Join the morning crowd over avocado toast, baked eggs with chorizo, or a smoked-salmon-and-egg breakfast sandwich, or stop in later for lunchtime sandwiches (BBQ pulled pork, portobello with ricotta) or salads. There's also excellent La Colombe espresso and fresh bakery items.

GOVINDA'S VEGETARIAN LUNCH INDIAN, VEGAN $

Map p443 (718-875-6127; www.radhagovindanyc.com; 305 Schermerhorn St, btwn Bond & Nevins Sts, Downtown Brooklyn; mains $7-12; noon-3:30pm Mon-Fri; ; 2/3, 4/5 to Nevins St; A/C, G to Hoyt-Schermerhorn) Located on the bottom floor of a Hare Krishna temple, Govinda's prepares five or six different vegan options for lunch each day (eggplant parmesan, vegetable curry, lentil soup, samosas and the like), plus rich desserts, all served cafeteria-style. There's not much ambience, but vegheads on a budget will love it. The menu is posted each day on the website.

★JULIANA'S PIZZA $$

Map p443 (718-596-6700; www.julianaspizza.com; 19 Old Fulton St, btwn Water & Front Sts, Brooklyn Heights; pizzas $18-32; 11:30am-10pm, closed 3:15-4pm; ; A/C to High St) Legendary pizza maestro Patsy Grimaldi has returned to Brooklyn, with delicious, thin-crust perfection in both classic and creative combos – like the No 1, with mozzarella, *scamorza affumicata* (an Italian smoked cow's cheese), pancetta, scallions and white truffles in olive oil. It's in Brooklyn Heights, close to the continually developing Brooklyn waterfront. (Note that

Juliana's closes for 45 minutes every afternoon to stoke the pizza oven.)

GANSO RAMEN RAMEN, JAPANESE **$$**

Map p443 (718-403-0900; www.gansonyc.com; 25 Bond St, btwn Fulton & Livingston Sts, Downtown Brooklyn; ramen $16-17; 11:30am-10pm Sun-Thu, to 11pm Fri & Sat; S 2/3 to Hoyt St; A/C, G to Hoyt-Schermerhorn) Tucked away in an unlikely corner of Brooklyn (just off Fulton Mall (p297)), Ganso is a cozy, wood-lined spot that serves up some of the best ramen in Brooklyn. Spicy miso with pork belly is a winner; there are also versions with beef, chicken and shrimp (as well as a vegetarian option).

ALMAR ITALIAN **$$**

Map p443 (718-855-5288; www.almardumbo.com; 111 Front St, btwn Adams & Washington Sts, Dumbo; mains lunch $11-16, dinner $19-36; 8am-10:30pm Mon-Thu, to 11pm Fri, 9am-11pm Sat, 10am-5pm Sun; ; S F to York St; A/C to High St) This welcoming Italian eatery serves breakfast, lunch and dinner in a homey, wood-lined space in Dumbo. Co-owner Alfredo's meatballs are top-notch, as is the rich and meaty lasagna Bolognese. But if you're into seafood, don't miss the simple and delicious cavatelli (small pasta shells) with mussels, clams, shrimp and cherry tomatoes – it doesn't skimp on the shellfish. Cash only.

SUPERFINE MODERN AMERICAN **$$**

Map p443 (718-243-9005; www.superfine.nyc; 126 Front St, at Pearl St, Dumbo; mains lunch $12-17, dinner $18-36; 11:30am-3pm & 6-11pm Tue-Sat, 11am-3pm & 6-10pm Sun; S F to York St) This casual hangout is known for its Sunday brunches, where Dumbo locals sip Bloody Marys while DJs spin lazy tunes. Windows line two sides, and the rumble of the subway on the Manhattan Bridge overhead puts a bumpy thrill into the meal. The menu features the likes of fish tacos for lunch and grass-fed steak au poivre for dinner.

FORNINO AT PIER 6 ITALIAN **$$**

Map p443 (718-422-1107; www.fornino.com; Pier 6, Brooklyn Bridge Park, Brooklyn Heights; pizzas $10-26; 10am-midnight Memorial Day-mid-Sep, weather permitting Apr, May & Oct; B63 to Brooklyn Bridge Park/Pier 6, S 2/3, 4/5 to Borough Hall; R to Court St) From the end of May through mid-September, Fornino dishes out excellent wood-fired pizza, sandwiches, beer and Italian treats right on Pier 6. The rooftop deck with picnic tables and spectacular views of Lower Manhattan makes a great spot for groups. (The restaurant also opens in April, May and October when the weather is fine, but is completely closed in winter.)

RIVER CAFE AMERICAN **$$$**

Map p443 (718-522-5200, 917-757-0693; www.rivercafe.com; 1 Water St, near Old Fulton St, Brooklyn Heights; fixed-price menus dinner 3/6 courses $130/160, lunch $47, brunch $60; dinner 5:30-11:30pm, lunch 11:30am-2pm Sat, brunch 11:30am-2pm Sun; S A/C to High St) Situated at the foot of the Brooklyn Bridge, this floating wonder offers unrivaled views of downtown Manhattan – not to mention solidly rendered Modern American cooking. Standouts include Wagyu steak tartare, roasted rabbit, crispy lavender-glazed duck breast and poached Nova Scotia lobster. The atmosphere is sedate (jackets required at dinner) but incurably romantic. Don't miss the chocolate Brooklyn Bridge for dessert.

VINEGAR HILL HOUSE AMERICAN **$$$**

Map p443 (718-522-1018; www.vinegarhillhouse.com; 72 Hudson Ave, btwn Water & Front Sts, Vinegar Hill; mains dinner $23-33, brunch $14-18; dinner 6-11pm Mon-Thu, to 11:30pm Fri & Sat, 5:30-11pm Sun, brunch 10:30am-3:30pm Sat & Sun; ; B62 to York Ave/Navy St, S F to York St) Tucked into out-of-the-way Vinegar Hill (east of Dumbo), this homey spot is decked out in a charming array of thrift-store bric-a-brac. Don't let the low-key decor fool you: chef Brian Leth cooks up an evolving menu that is bracingly fresh and unfussy, such as cast-iron chicken with potato, shallots and a sherry-vinegar jus or cavatelli with blistered tomato and garlic.

Boerum Hill, Cobble Hill, Carroll Gardens & Red Hook

MILE END DELI **$**

Map p438 (718-852-7510; www.mileenddeli.com; 97a Hoyt St, Boerum Hill; sandwiches $12-18; 8am-4pm & 5-10pm Mon-Fri, from 10am Sat & Sun; S A/C, G to Hoyt-Schermerhorn) You can almost taste the smoked meats as you enter this small Boerum Hill eatery, which has exposed-brick walls and a couple of communal tables. Try a smoked beef brisket on

THE BEST OF BROOKLYN PIZZA

New York is known for a lot of things: screeching subways, towering skyscrapers, bright lights. It is also known for its pizza, which comes in a variety of gooey, chewy, sauce-soaked varieties. These are some of the top places in Brooklyn to grab a slice or a whole pie:

Di Fara Pizza (☎718-258-1367; www.difarany.com; 1424 Ave J, cnr E 15th St, Midwood; pizza slices $5; ⊙noon-8pm Wed-Sat, from 1pm Sun; SQ to Ave J) In operation since 1964 in the Midwood section of Brooklyn, this old-school slice joint is still lovingly tended to by proprietor Dom DeMarco, who makes the pies himself. Expect long lines.

Totonno's (Map p444; ☎718-372-8606; www.totonnosconeyisland.com; 1524 Neptune Ave, near W 16th St, Coney Island; pizzas $18-21, toppings $2.50; ⊙noon-8pm Thu-Sun; ; SD/F, N/Q to Coney Island-Stillwell Ave) A classic, family-owned Coney Island pizzeria that makes pies till the dough runs out.

Grimaldi's (Map p443; ☎718-858-4300; www.grimaldis-pizza.com; 1 Front St, cnr of Old Fulton St, Brooklyn Heights; pizzas $14-18; ⊙11:30am-10:45pm Mon-Thu, to 11:45pm Fri, noon-11:45pm Sat, to 10:45pm Sun; SA/C to High St) Legendary pizzas (and legendary lines) abound at this tourist magnet in Brooklyn Heights.

Juliana's (p276) The home of pizza legend Patsy Grimaldi's celebrated return to the Brooklyn dining scene in 2013.

Lucali (p279) Neapolitan-style pies started as a hobby for this noted Carroll Gardens *pizzaiolo* (pizza maker).

Roberta's (p287) Divine pies with cheeky names like 'Beastmaster'; set in the artsy district at the confluence of Bushwick and East Williamsburg.

If you want to try several pizzas in one go, sign up for an outing with **Scott's Pizza Tours** (☎212-913-9903; www.scottspizzatours.com; tours incl pizza $45-65), which will take you to the most vaunted brick ovens around the city by foot or by bus.

rye with mustard ($15) – the bread is sticky soft and the meat will melt in your mouth.

FAIRWAY SUPERMARKET $

Map p438 (☎718-254-0923; www.fairwaymarket.com; 480-500 Van Brunt St, Red Hook; ⊙7am-10pm; ; B61 to Van Brunt & Coffee Sts, SF, G to Smith-9th Sts then) This sprawling supermarket offers an array of breads, cheeses, olives and smoked meats, as well as delicious prepared foods. An on-site cafe serves simple breakfasts and lunch, and offers excellent views of the Red Hook waterfront.

★POK POK THAI $$

Map p438 (☎718-923-9322; www.pokpokny.com; 117 Columbia St, at Kane St, Columbia St Waterfront District; sharing plates $15-20; ⊙5:30-10pm Mon-Fri, from noon Sat & Sun; SF to Bergen St) Andy Ricker's NYC outpost is a smashing success, wowing diners with a rich, complex menu inspired by northern Thailand street food. Fiery, fish-sauce-slathered chicken wings; spicy green-papaya salad with salted black crab; smoky grilled eggplant salad and sweet pork belly with ginger, turmeric and tamarind are among the many unique dishes. The setting is fun and ramshackle. Reserve ahead.

HOMETOWN BAR-B-QUE BARBECUE $$

Map p438 (☎347-294-4644; www.hometownbarbque.com; 454 Van Brunt St, Red Hook; meat per pound from $12, sides $4-8; ⊙noon-10pm Tue-Thu, to 11pm Fri & Sat, to 10pm Sun, closed Mon) Anyone who loves huge plates of juicy BBQ and intense craft cocktails will be well served at Hometown Bar-B-Que in Red Hook. The restaurant is in a large space that provides ample room for big parties and those with kids. In the main dining hall the meat and sides are order-by-the-pound, while the bar serves up drinks and live music.

RED HOOK LOBSTER POUND SEAFOOD $$

Map p438 (☎718-858-7650; www.redhooklobster.com; 284 Van Brunt St, Red Hook; Lobster rolls from $24, mains from $18; ⊙11:30am-9pm Sun-Thu, 11:30am-10pm Fri-Sat, closed Mon) You may have already seen its iconic food truck trawling the streets of New York, so why not stop by the flagship restaurant? It offers a menu bursting with northeast seafood favorites and fun twists on the theme, like lobster mac 'n' cheese. The Maine lobsters here are so fresh you can see them in the tank before you eat.

BUTTERMILK CHANNEL AMERICAN $$

Map p438 (718-852-8490; www.buttermilkchannelnyc.com; 524 Court St, at Huntington St, Carroll Gardens; mains lunch $11-27, brunch $12-24, dinner $16-32; lunch 11:30am-3pm Mon-Fri, brunch 10am-3pm Sat & Sun, dinner 5-10pm Sun-Thu, to 11:30pm Fri & Sat; S F, G to Smith-9th Sts) There's nothing quite like crispy, buttermilk-fried chicken or a savory plate of eggs with lox and green onions. Buttermilk Channel (named for the waterway between Brooklyn and Governors Island) offers a range of simple, perfectly executed dishes. A comprehensive list of specialty cocktails – the brunch Bloody Mary menu alone is worth the visit – round out this delicious dining experience.

BATTERSBY MODERN AMERICAN $$

Map p440 (718-852-8321; www.battersbybrooklyn.com; 255 Smith St, btwn Douglass & Degraw Sts, Carroll Gardens; mains $16-32, tasting menu $75; 5:30-11pm Tue-Sat; S F, G to Bergen St) A top choice in Brooklyn, Battersby serves magnificent seasonal dishes. The small menu changes regularly, but be on the lookout for chicken-liver mousse, vermilion snapper with peas and spinach, and the delightful lobster *stratiacella* (buffalo-milk cheese) with fava beans. The space is Brooklyn-style quaint (plank floors, brick walls, tin ceiling), but tiny and cramped.

LUCALI PIZZA $$

Map p438 (718-858-4086; www.lucali.com; 575 Henry St, at Carroll St, Carroll Gardens; pizzas $24, toppings $3; 5:45-10pm, closed Tue; B57 to Court & President Sts, S F, G to Carroll St) One of New York's tastiest pizzas comes from this unlikely little spot run by Mark Iacono. Pizzas are all one size, with chewy crusts, fresh tomato sauce and superfresh mozzarella. Toppings are limited, but the Brooklyn accent is for real. Cash only; beer or wine are BYOB.

FRANKIES 457 SPUNTINO ITALIAN $$

Map p438 (718-403-0033; www.frankies457.com; 457 Court St, btwn 4th Pl & Luquer St, Carroll Gardens; mains $14-22; 11am-11pm Sun-Thu, to midnight Fri & Sat; S F, G to Smith-9th Sts) Frankies is a neighborhood magnet, attracting local couples, families and plenty of Manhattanites with hearty pasta dishes like cavatelli with hot sausage and pappardelle with braised lamb. But as a *spuntino* (snack joint), this place is more about the small plates, with a seasonal menu that boasts excellent fresh salads, cheeses, cured meats and heavenly crostini. No reservations.

Fort Greene, Clinton Hill & Bed-Stuy

★DOUGH BAKERY $

(347-533-7544; www.doughdoughnuts.com; 448 Lafayette Ave, cnr Franklin Ave, Bedford-Stuyvesant; doughnuts around $3; 6am-9pm; S G to Classon Ave) Situated on the border of Clinton Hill and Bed-Stuy, this tiny, out-of-the-way spot is a bit of a trek, but worth it if you're a pastry fan. Puffy raised doughnuts are dipped in a changing array of glazes, including pistachio, blood orange and hibiscus. Doughnut divinity for the tongue.

67 BURGER BURGERS $

Map p438 (718-797-7150; www.67burger.com; 67 Lafayette Ave, at S Elliott Pl, Fort Greene; specialty burgers $8-11; 11:30am-9pm Tue-Thu & Sun, to 10pm Fri & Sat; S G to Fulton St; C to Lafayette Ave; B/D, N/Q/R, 2/3, 4/5 to Atlantic Ave-Barclays Ctr) If anyplace could give Shake Shack a run for its money, it's 67 Burger. Choose a specialty burger, such as the Parisian (sautéed onions and mushrooms with Dijonnaise) or the Oaxaca (avocado, cheddar cheese and homemade chipotle mayo), or create your own big, beautiful, messy burger from a choice of beef, chicken, turkey, veggie or tofu patties.

FORT GREENE GREENMARKET MARKET $

Map p438 (212-788-7476; www.grownyc.org; Fort Greene Park, cnr Cumberland St & DeKalb Ave, Fort Greene; 8am-3pm Sat; B38 to DeKalb Ave/Carlton St, S G to Fulton St; C to Lafayette Ave) This beloved neighborhood farmers market is held at the southeastern corner of Fort Greene Park (p269) every Saturday, year-round. Find regional produce that includes everything from heritage ducks, charcuterie and wild-caught fish to organic fruits, aged cheeses and small-batch baked goods – the apple-cider doughnuts are a particular treat.

GREEN GRAPE ANNEX AMERICAN $

Map p438 (www.greenegrape.com/annex; 753 Fulton St, at S Portland Ave, Fort Greene; mains $7-9; 7am-9pm Mon-Thu, 7am-10pm Fri, 8am-10pm Sat, 8am-9pm Sun; S G to Fulton Ave; C to Lafayette Ave) Looking for a quick coffee – quality roasts that are perfectly brewed – or a hearty meal? The Green Grape Annex is a well-appointed cafe in Fort Greene that offers a wide array of food and beverage options in a large, airy space where it's rare to fight for space. In addition to coffee bar it also serves beer and wine.

★**MISS ADA** MEDITERRANEAN, ISRAELI $$

Map p438 (917-909-1023; www.missadanyc.com; 184 DeKalb Ave, at Carlton Ave, Fort Greene; mains $16-28; 5:30-10:30pm Tue-Thu & Sun, to 11:30pm Fri & Sat, closed Mon; ; S G to Fulton St; B, Q/R to DeKalb Ave) One of the newest stars in Fort Greene's dining constellation is this cozy restaurant from chef-owner Tomer Blechman (formerly of Gramercy Tavern (p170)), presenting Mediterranean dishes from his native Israel given a new spin with Latvian influences (a nod to his parents' place of birth) and flavored with herbs grown in the large backyard, which features canopied dining in warmer months.

PEACHES SOUTHERN US $$

(718-942-4162; www.peachesbrooklyn.com; 393 Lewis Ave, at MacDonough St, Bedford-Stuyvesant; mains $17-21; 11am-10pm Mon-Thu, to 11pm Fri & Sat, 10am-10pm Sun, closed 4-5pm; S A/C to Utica Ave) The homey atmosphere and tasty Southern food make Peaches a Bed-Stuy favorite. Stone-ground grits with blackened catfish is popular at all hours, while the granola-crusted French toast with fresh berries is in demand at brunch. Black-kale salad, roasted-beet salad and sides like garlic-sautéed broccoli or gooey mac 'n' cheese are the best of the rather limited vegetarian options.

OLEA MEDITERRANEAN $$$

Map p438 (718-643-7003; www.oleabrooklyn.com; 171 Lafayette Ave, at Adelphi St, Fort Greene; mains brunch $13-19, dinner $20-32; 10am-11pm Mon-Thu, to midnight Fri & Sat; ; S C to Lafayette Ave; G to Clinton-Washington Aves) A bustling Mediterranean restaurant with charming interior design and world-class food. On the dinner menu Olea serves roasted whole branzino, creamy paellas and light, delicious vegetarian pastas; at brunch the kitchen specializes in Mediterranean spins on old standbys, such as lamb hash. A tapas menu offers tasty options for those looking for a less substantial meal.

ROMAN'S ITALIAN $$$

Map p438 (718-622-5300; www.romansnyc.com; 243 DeKalb Ave, btwn Clermont & Vanderbilt Aves, Fort Greene; mains $24-40; 5-11pm Sun-Thu, to midnight Fri & Sat; B38, B69 to Vanderbilt/DeKalb Aves, S G to Clinton-Washington Aves) In a small, buzzing space on restaurant-dotted DeKalb Ave, Roman's is a celebration of seasonal locavorism, with a focused menu that changes nightly. Dishes feature imaginative combinations (sourced from small, sustainable farms) and are beautifully executed: short-rib agnolotti (similar to ravioli), *sedani* pasta with broccoli rabe and sausage, and blackfish with butternut squash *brodetto* (stew).

Park Slope, Gowanus & Sunset Park

★**AMPLE HILLS CREAMERY** ICE CREAM $

Map p440 (347-725-4061; www.amplehills.com; 305 Nevins St, at Union St, Gowanus; cones $4-7; noon-11pm Sun-Thu, to midnight Fri & Sat, shorter hours in winter; S R to Union St; F, G to Carroll St) Ice-cream lovers: we found the mother ship. All of Ample Hills' magnificently creative flavors – snap mallow pop (a deconstructed Rice Krispies treat), Mexican hot chocolate, salted crack caramel – are whipped up right here in the creamery's Gowanus factory. Grab a cone and watch the goods being made through the kitchen's picture window.

FOUR & TWENTY BLACKBIRDS BAKERY $

Map p440 (718-499-2917; www.birdsblack.com; 439 Third Ave, cnr 8th St, Gowanus; pie slices $5.75; 8am-8pm Mon-Fri, from 9am Sat, 10am-7pm Sun; ; S R to 9th St) Sisters Emily and Melissa Elsen use flaky, buttery crusts and seasonal, regionally sourced fruits to create NYC's best pies, hands down. Any time is just right to drop in to their shop for a slice – the plum-strawberry streusel is *divine* – and a cup of Irving Farm coffee. Add a dollop of fresh whipped cream and you'll be in pie heaven.

WHOLE FOODS MARKET $

Map p440 (718-907-3622; www.wholefoodsmarket.com; 214 3rd St, btwn Third Ave & Gowanus Canal, Gowanus; 8am-11pm; ; R to Union; F, G to 4th Ave-9th St) Brooklyn's first Whole Foods is pretty impressive, with all the gourmet goodies you'd expect, plus a few surprises – including a 20,000-sq-ft greenhouse (where some of the produce is grown), an in-house coffee roaster and a sprawling prepared-foods area. After browsing the staggering selection, head upstairs to the small bar, with 16 craft beers on tap and a small food menu.

KING DAVID TACOS TACOS $

Map p440 (929-367-8226; www.kingdavidtacos.com; Grand Army Plaza, Prospect Park; tacos $4; 7-11am Mon-Fri, to 2pm Sat, 8am-1pm Sun; ; 2/3 to Grand Army Plaza) Native Texan Liz Solomon found NYC missing one thing: authentic, Austin-style breakfast tacos. So in 2016 she decided to make her own. Her outdoor stand at Grand Army Plaza offers three potato, egg and cheese tacos daily, made that morning and ready to go: the BPEC (with bacon added), the 'queen bean' (vegetarian refried beans) and the 'or'izo' (Mexican chorizo).

BAKED IN BROOKLYN BAKERY $

Map p440 (718-499-1818; www.bakedinbrooklynny.com; 755 Fifth Ave, btwn 25th and 26th Sts, Greenwood Heights; pastries from $2; 6:30am-7pm Mon-Sat, 7am-6pm Sun; R to 25th St) The flagship bakery for a popular local brand of baked goods is small, but filled to the brim with amazing treats: large, flaky cinnamon rolls, buttery croissants, crisp and savory pita chips, gooey cookies and more. Coffee is served as well, which makes it a perfect morning or afternoon treat, especially after a visit to Green-Wood Cemetery (p269) across the street.

LUKE'S LOBSTER SEAFOOD $$

Map p440 (347-457-6855; www.lukeslobster.com; 237 Fifth Ave, Park Slope; lobster roll $17, lobster bisque $7-11; 11am-10pm; R train to Union Ave.) Each location of Luke's Lobster prides itself on providing fresh, sustainable and mouthwatering seafood at reasonable prices. This is all true of the Park Slope location, which serves Luke's legendary menu in a small, well appointed restaurant complete with a charming backyard patio.

SIDECAR AMERICAN $$

Map p440 (718-369-0077; www.sidecarbrooklyn.com; 560 Fifth Ave, btwn 15th and 16th Sts, Park Slope; mains $14-27; 6pm-2am Mon-Wed, to 4am Thu, 3pm-4am Fri, 11am-4am Sat, to 2am Sun; R to Prospect Ave) Upscale classic American cuisine doesn't get much better than Sidecar. This atmospheric restaurant serves unfussy takes on classics that add a modern touch, such as fried chicken served with a savory root mash and sautéed kale with bacon on the side. Sidecar specializes in cocktails that you can pair with your meal, or enjoy on their own at the bar.

LOT 2 MODERN AMERICAN $$

Map p440 (718-499-5623; www.lot2restaurant.com; 687 Sixth Ave, btwn 19th & 20th Sts, Greenwood Heights; mains $18-32; 6-10pm Wed & Thu, to 10:30pm Fri & Sat, 5-9:30pm Sun; B63, B67, B69 to 18th St, R to Prospect Ave) This rustic, intimate spot serves locally sourced, high-end comfort food in Greenwood Heights, south of Park Slope. The menu is small but big on flavors. Try the grilled-cheese sandwich (with cheddar, provolone and Parmesan), shrimp and grits with chorizo and white cheddar, or a juicy grass-fed burger with thick-cut, duck-fat fries. The Sunday three-course special is a deal at $35.

Prospect Heights, Crown Heights & Flatbush

★AMPLE HILLS CREAMERY ICE CREAM $

Map p440 (347-240-3926; www.amplehills.com; 623 Vanderbilt Ave, at St Marks Ave, Prospect Heights; ice-cream cones $4-7; noon-11pm Sun-Thu, to midnight Fri & Sat; B, Q to 7th Ave; 2/3 to Grand Army Plaza) Named for a line in a Walt Whitman poem, Ample Hills makes singular ice cream that's an art form of its own: from ooey gooey butter cake in a creamy vanilla base or Nonna D's oatmeal lace (brown-sugar-and-cinnamon ice cream with oatmeal cookies) to 'the munchies' (pretzel-infused ice cream with potato chips, pretzels, Ritz crackers and mini M&Ms).

LOOK BY PLANT LOVE HOUSE THAI $

Map p440 (718-622-0026; http://plantlovehouse.wixsite.com/thai; 622 Washington Ave, btwn Pacific & Dean Sts, Prospect Heights; mains $10-20; noon-10pm Tue-Sun; ; 2/3 to Bergen St; C to Clinton-Washington Aves) Snug and adorable, this ultra-authentic Thai cafe serves modest portions of incendiary soups (*num tok*, enriched with pork blood, is a specialty) and home-style dishes such as

1

GUILLAUME GAUDET / LONELY PLANET ©

2

4

T PHOTOGRAPHY / SHUTTERSTOCK ©

YOUPRODUCTION / SHUTTERSTOCK ©

1. Coney Island (p275)
Coney Island is synonymous with seaside fun and frolicking.

2. Brooklyn Botanic Garden (p272)
This garden celebrates their cherry trees during the Cherry Blossom Festival.

3. Dumbo (p266)
This Brooklyn neighborhood earns its name from its location: Down Under the Manhattan Bridge Overpass.

4. Jane's Carousel (p266)
The 1922 carousel is the star attraction of Brooklyn Bridge Park (p263).

khao kha moo (braised pork knuckles) and 'old-school' shrimp pad Thai. (Many dishes can be made with tofu upon request.) A satisfying and transporting meal. Cash only.

CHUKO JAPANESE **$**

Map p440 (☎347-425-9570; www.chukobk.com; 565 Vanderbilt Ave, cnr Pacific St, Prospect Heights; ramen $15; ⊙noon-3pm & 5:30-11pm; ; S B/Q to 7th Ave; 2/3 to Bergen St) This contemporary, minimalist ramen shop brings a top-notch noodle game to Prospect Heights. Steaming bowls of al dente ramen are paired with one of several spectacularly silky broths, including an excellent roasted pork and a full-bodied vegetarian. The appetizers are *very* worthwhile, particularly the fragrant salt-and-pepper chicken wings.

LINCOLN STATION CAFE **$**

Map p440 (☎718-399-2211; www.stationfoods.com; 409 Lincoln Pl, near Washington Ave, Prospect Heights; sandwiches $10-12, dinner mains $8-16.50; ⊙7am-9pm Mon-Fri, from 8am Sat & Sun; ; S 2/3 to Eastern Pkwy-Brooklyn Museum) By day, join the laptop-toting hordes at the long center table of this neighborhood favorite for top-notch espresso drinks, or grab a draft beer ($6) in the evening, when candles set a romantic mood. Quality food is as much an emphasis: the after-5pm menu features a delicious rotisserie chicken ($16.50) and a veggie lasagna ($16) big enough for two.

Located on the Crown Heights side of Washington Ave, Lincoln Station makes for a great stop after visiting the Brooklyn Museum (p265) just a block away.

BERG'N FOOD HALL **$**

Map p440 (www.bergn.com; 899 Bergen St, btwn Classon & Franklin Aves, Crown Heights; mains $7-14, pizzas $19-28; ⊙food 9am-10pm Tue-Thu, 10am-11pm Fri & Sat, 10am-10pm Sun, bar 11am-11pm Tue-Thu & Sun, 11am-late Fri & Sat; ; S C, 2/3, 4/5 to Franklin Ave) From the same team behind Smorgasburg (p285), Berg'n is a large brick food hall with long wooden tables where you can feast on smoky brisket (Mighty Quinn's), fried chicken sandwiches and beef or veggie burgers (Land Haus), Filipino-inspired rice bowls (Lumpia Shack) and gourmet pizzas (Brooklyn Pizza Crew).

TOM'S RESTAURANT DINER **$**

Map p440 (☎718 636 9738; 782 Washington Ave, at Sterling Pl, Prospect Heights; mains $8-14; ⊙7am-4pm Mon-Sat, from 8am Sun; S 2/3 to Eastern Pkwy-Brooklyn Museum) Open since 1936, Tom's successfully traffics in old-school Brooklyn nostalgia and delivers good, greasy-spoon cooking just three blocks from the Brooklyn Museum (p265). Breakfast is served all day and it's a deal, with most items costing less than $15. Copious wall signs advertise specials – the blueberry-ricotta pancakes with lemon zest are unrivaled.

★OLMSTED MODERN AMERICAN **$$**

Map p440 (☎718-552-2610; www.olmstednyc.com; 659 Vanderbilt Ave, btwn Prospect & Park Pls, Prospect Heights; small plates $13-16, large plates $22-24; ⊙5-10:30pm; S B, Q to 7th Ave) Chef-owner Greg Baxtrom creates seasonally inspired dishes so skillfully done that even Manhattanites cross the river for this extremely popular restaurant. Olmsted's locavore credentials are evident: much of the menu comes from the restaurant's own backyard garden – which makes a lovely place for cocktails or dessert (try the DIY s'mores) while you wait. Reservations recommended (Mondays are walk-ins only).

CHERYL'S GLOBAL SOUL FUSION **$$**

Map p440 (☎347-529-2855; www.cherylsglobalsoul.com; 236 Underhill Ave, btwn Eastern Pkwy & St Johns Pl, Prospect Heights; sandwiches $8-14, dinner mains $14-21; ⊙8am-4pm Mon, to 10pm Tue-Thu & Sun, to 11pm Fri & Sat; ; S 2/3 to Eastern Pkwy-Brooklyn Museum) Around the corner from the Brooklyn Museum (p265) and the Brooklyn Botanic Garden (p273), this homey brick-and-wood favorite serves up fresh, unpretentious cooking that draws on a world of influences: from sake-glazed salmon with jasmine rice to exceptional homemade quiche to a long list of tasty sandwiches. There are veggie options and a separate kids' menu. Expect long waits for weekend brunch.

Williamsburg, Greenpoint & Bushwick

CRIF DOGS HOT DOGS **$**

Map p436 (☎718-302-3200; www.crifdogs.com; 555 Driggs Ave, at N 7th St, Williamsburg; hot dogs $3.50-6; ⊙noon-2am Sun-Thu, to 4am Fri & Sat; ; S L to Bedford Ave) Many a late-night Billyburg excursion has ended up at this laid-back hot-dog joint, which has both beef and veggie dogs done up any way you like, with two dozen toppings to choose from. Get a draft beer and a side of tater tots and keep the party going even longer.

DUN-WELL DOUGHNUTS VEGAN, BAKERY $

Map p436 (347-294-0871; www.dunwelldoughnuts.com; 222 Montrose Ave, at Bushwick Ave, East Williamsburg; doughnuts $2-2.75; 7am-7pm Mon-Fri, from 8am Sat & Sun; ; L to Montrose Ave) 'Brooklyn's finest artisanal vegan doughnuts' might sound like peak hipster, but here truth beats out the hype. Om-nom your way through delicious plant-powered treats, handmade daily with organic ingredients in myriad flavors, including French toast, eggnog, lemon poppy, PB&J, blueberry coconut, cinnamon sugar, vanilla chip, chocolate peanut and the Homer, an uncanny real-life version of a *Simpsons* doughnut.

PETER PAN DONUT & PASTRY SHOP BAKERY $

Map p436 (718-389-3676; www.peterpandonuts.com; 727 Manhattan Ave, btwn Norman & Meserole Aves, Greenpoint; snacks $1-3; 5:30am-8pm Mon-Sat, to 7pm Sun; G to Nassau Ave) On the main drag in Greenpoint, Peter Pan is a much-loved classic for its unfussy, well-made baked goods – doughnuts especially – and excellent breakfast sandwiches on house-baked rolls or bagels (try the bacon-egg-and-cheese on a toasted poppy-seed roll), all at rock-bottom prices. Have a seat at the wraparound counter, or take it away and munch in McCarren Park (p274).

CHAMPS DINER VEGAN, DINER $

Map p436 (718-599-2743; www.champsdiner.com; 197 Meserole St, btwn Humboldt St & Bushwick Ave, East Williamsburg; sandwiches & salads $11-13; 9am-midnight; ; L to Montrose Ave) This airy little diner whips up delicious plates of American comfort food, all entirely vegan. The reasonable prices and all-day breakfasts keep things busy (don't expect speedy service). Try the French toast slam (with tofu scramble and tempeh or seitan bacon), chocolate-chip-and-banana pancakes, mac 'n' cheese or a 'bacon cheeseburger' (a black-bean burger with tempeh bacon and vegan cheese).

MILK & PULL CAFE $

(347-627-8511; www.milkandpull.com; 181 Irving Ave, Bushwick; coffee $3-5; 7am-6pm Mon-Fri, 8am-5pm Sat & Sun; L train to DeKalb Ave) There is no substitute for a well-brewed cup of coffee or well-steamed cappuccino. The baristas at Milk & Pull in Bushwick are masters of the art, no matter how you take your cup. They also serve baked goods from bakeries around Brooklyn, such as huge, sticky Dough doughnuts, as well as more substantial dishes.

LOCAL KNOWLEDGE

SMORGASBURG!

The largest foodie **event** (www.smorgasburg.com; 11am-6pm Sat & Sun Apr-Oct) in Brooklyn brings together more than 100 vendors selling an incredible array of goodness: Italian street snacks, duck confit, Indian flatbread tacos, roasted-mushroom burgers, vegan Ethiopian comfort food, sea-salt caramel ice cream, passion-fruit doughnuts, craft beer and much more. Smorgasburg locations tend to change from season to season, so check the website for the latest.

Most recently the Smorg has been held in Williamsburg, on the waterfront (p274), on Saturdays and Prospect Park, near Lakeside (p264), on Sundays from April to October, in addition to a smaller location in SoHo (Manhattan) that stays open through the end of December.

★MODERN LOVE VEGAN, AMERICAN $$

Map p436 (929-298-0626; www.modernlovebrooklyn.com; 317 Union St, at S 1st St, East Williamsburg; mains brunch $16, dinner $19-24; 6-10:30pm Wed & Thu, to 11pm Fri, 5:30-11pm Sat, 11am-3pm & 5-10:30pm Sun, closed Mon & Tue; ; L to Lorimer St; G to Metropolitan Ave) This new restaurant from celebrated chef Isa Chandra Moskowitz serving 'swanky vegan comfort food' is a welcome addition to the scene, with delicious, plant-based versions of classics like mac 'n' shews (with creamy cashew cheese and pecan-cornmeal crusted tofu), Manhattan glam chowder, seitan Philly cheesesteak and truffle poutine. It's always buzzing, so bookings are a good idea (though not required).

★ZENKICHI JAPANESE $$

Map p436 (718-388-8985; www.zenkichi.com; 77 N 6th St, at Wythe Ave, Williamsburg; tasting menus vegetarian/regular $65/75; 6pm-midnight Mon-Sat, 5:30-11:30pm Sun; ; L to

Bedford Ave) A temple of refined Japanese cuisine, Zenkichi presents beautifully prepared dishes in an atmospheric setting that has wowed foodies from far and wide. The recommendation here is the *omakase*, a seasonal eight-course tasting menu featuring highlights like salmon marinated and cured with *shiso* and basil and topped with caviar, or roasted Hudson Valley duck breast with seasonal vegetables.

★ **FETTE SAU** BARBECUE **$$**

Map p436 (☎718-963-3404; www.fettesaubbq.com; 354 Metropolitan Ave, btwn Havemeyer & Roebling Sts, Williamsburg; meats per lb $23-29; ⊙5-11pm Mon, from noon Tue-Thu, noon-midnight Fri-Sun, to 11pm Sun; SL to Bedford Ave) BBQ-craving Brooklynites descend en masse on the 'Fat Pig,' a cement-floored, wood-beamed space (formerly an auto-body repair shop) dishing up ribs, brisket, pork belly and duck – all smoked in-house, accompanied by a range of sides. Try the burnt-end baked beans, which are peppery, not too sweet and chock-full of meaty bits. There's a good choice of bourbon, whiskey and beer.

FIVE LEAVES MODERN AMERICAN **$$**

Map p436 (☎718-383-5345; www.fiveleavesny.com; 18 Bedford Ave, at Lorimer St, Greenpoint; mains lunch $12-18, dinner $16-22; ⊙8am-1am; B48, B62 to Lorimer St, SG to Nassau Ave) An anchor of the Greenpoint scene, Five Leaves draws a wide mix of neighborhood regulars who create a lively buzz at both outdoor tables in front and in the vintage-filled interior. Stop by in the morning for ricotta pancakes, fresh pastries and great coffee (from Parlor Coffee), or at lunch for a Reuben toastie, truffle fries and chopped black-kale salads.

RABBITHOLE MODERN AMERICAN **$$**

Map p436 (☎718-782-0910; www.rabbitholerestaurant.com; 352 Bedford Ave, btwn S 3rd & S 4th Sts, Williamsburg; mains breakfast & lunch $12-19, dinner $16-24; ⊙9am-11pm; ; B62 to S 4th St, SJ/Z, M to Marcy Ave) A warm and inviting spot in South Williamsburg, the very charming Rabbithole is a fine spot to disappear into, particularly if you're craving breakfast (served till 5pm). There's casual cafe-seating up front for good coffee and even better housemade pastries. Head

BROOKLYN COOKBOOKS

Locally sourced products, ecological sustainability and large doses of culinary creativity are all hallmarks of Brooklyn's celebrated dining scene. To learn more about the magic behind the cuisine – and more importantly how to make the dishes at home – check out the following titles:

➡ *The New Brooklyn Cookbook* (2010) Recipes, stories and culinary insights from 31 of Brooklyn's top restaurants.

➡ *Pok Pok* (2013) Andy Ricker delves deeply into northern Thai cooking, with precise instructions on creating those complex and heady dishes.

➡ *Roberta's Cookbook* (2013) Diver scallops in plum juice, orecchiette with oxtail ragu and glorious pizza perfection.

➡ *Four & Twenty Blackbirds Pie Book* (2013) Take your pastry skills up a notch with these tantalizing recipes by the Elsen sisters.

➡ *Franny's: Simple, Seasonal, Italian* (2013) An essential reference for making memorable pizzas, pastas and gelato at home.

➡ *The Frankies Spuntino* (2010) Beautifully designed cookbook packed with recipes of reimagined Italian American comfort fare.

➡ *One Girl Cookie* (2012) Moist, tender whoopie pies and other sweet indulgences.

➡ *The Mile End Cookbook* (2012) Reinventing Jewish comfort food.

➡ *Brooklyn Brew Shop's Beer Making Book* (2011) Easy-to-follow guide for making refreshing brews at home.

➡ *Veganomicon: 10th Anniversary Edition* (2017) Celebrated Brooklyn chef Isa Chandra Moskowitz teaches you how to whip up delicious vegan fare like you'll find at her East Williamsburg restaurant.

For the latest on the borough's dining scene, seek out *Edible Brooklyn* magazine (www.ediblebrooklyn.com).

to the back or the relaxing rear garden for creamy eggs Benedict or fresh fruit and granola.

PAULIE GEE'S PIZZA, VEGAN **$$**

(☎347-987-3747; www.pauliegee.com; 60 Greenpoint Ave, btwn West & Franklin Sts, Greenpoint; pizzas $12-19; ⏰6-11pm Mon-Fri, from 5pm Sat, 5-10pm Sun; Ⓥ👪; ⓈG to Greenpoint Ave) Greenpoint's best pizza place has a cozy cabin-in-the-woods vibe, with flickering candles and old-school beats playing overhead. Diners huddle over chunky wooden tables while digging in to delicious, creatively topped thin-crust pizzas. For the full experience, add on craft brews, affordable wine selections, zesty salads and dessert decadence (flourless chocolate cake, Van Leeuwen ice cream).

OKONOMI & YUJI RAMEN JAPANESE **$$**

Map p436 (www.okonomibk.com; 150 Ainslie St, btwn Lorimer & Leonard Sts, Williamsburg; set menus $21-35, ramen $15-20; ⏰set menus 9am-3pm Mon-Tue & Thu-Fri, 10am-4pm Sat & Sun, ramen 6-11pm Mon-Fri; ⓈL to Lorimer St; G to Metropolitan Ave) For a dazzling breakfast that doesn't involve eggs or French toast, make a pilgrimage to this exquisite little wood-lined eatery in East Williamsburg, called Okonomi by day. Only set menus are served: a small vegetable dish, baked egg, seven-grain rice and tender fish (such as salt-roasted tuna or miso-marinaded mackerel), accompanied by a tasty green tea with barley – perfection.

ROBERTA'S PIZZA **$$**

Map p436 (☎718-417-1118; www.robertaspizza.com; 261 Moore St, near Bogart St, East Williamsburg; pizzas $12-19; ⏰11am-midnight Mon-Fri, from 10am Sat & Sun; Ⓥ; ⓈL to Morgan Ave) This hipster-saturated warehouse restaurant consistently produces some of the best pizza in NYC. Service can be lackadaisical and the waits long (lunch is best), but the brick-oven pies are the right combination of chewy and fresh. The classic margherita is sublimely simple; more adventurous palates can opt for the seasonal hits like 'speckenwolf' (mozzarella, *speck,* crimini and onion).

MONTANA'S TRAIL HOUSE MODERN AMERICAN **$$**

(☎917-966-1666; www.montanastrailhouse.com; 445 Troutman St, btwn Cypress & St Nicholas Aves, Bushwick; mains $14-24; ⏰5pm-midnight Mon-Thu, 3pm-4am Fri, from 11am Sat, 11am-midnight Sun; ⓈL to Jefferson Ave) A wild repurposing of a former gas station, Montana's is all reclaimed-plank walls, industrial light fixtures, taxidermy and bookshelves that hide a secret passageway to an outdoor patio. Order a cocktail (something with rye or mezcal) and dine on seasonal, creative comfort food like root-beer-braised brisket, sweet-tea-brined fried chicken and fried-green-tomato sliders.

MISS FAVELA BRAZILIAN **$$**

Map p436 (☎718-230-4040; www.missfavela.com; 57 S 5th St, cnr Wythe St, Williamsburg; mains $22-30, sandwiches $14; ⏰noon-midnight Sun-Thu, to 1am Fri & Sat; ⓈJ/Z, M to Marcy Ave; L to Bedford Ave) This ramshackle little spot near the Williamsburg Bridge serves hearty plates of Brazilian cooking like *moqueca* (a coconut-milk-flavored fish stew) and *picanha* (a juicy cut of prime steak), best preceded by *bolinhos de bacalhau* (codfish croquettes) and accompanied by a caipirinha. Or maybe three? There's live Latin music on Thursday nights and Saturday afternoons, and sidewalk seating on warm days.

MARLOW & SONS MODERN AMERICAN **$$$**

Map p436 (☎718-384-1441; www.marlowandsons.com; 81 Broadway, btwn Berry St & Wythe Ave, Williamsburg; mains lunch $16-18, dinner $34-36; ⏰8am-11pm Sun-Thu, to midnight Fri & Sat, closed 4-5:30pm; ⓈJ/Z, M to Marcy Ave; L to Bedford Ave) The dimly lit, wood-lined space feels like an old farmhouse cafe, and hosts a buzzing nighttime scene as diners and drinkers crowd in for oysters, tip-top cocktails and a changing daily menu of locavore specialties (miso-braised beef, crunchy-crust pizzas, fluffy Spanish-style tortillas). Brunch is also a big draw, so prepare for lines (tip: you can now book on the website).

Coney Island & Brighton Beach

NATHAN'S FAMOUS HOT DOGS **$**

Map p444 (☎718-333-2202; www.nathansfamous.com; 1310 Surf Ave, cnr Stillwell Ave, Coney Island; hot dogs from $4; ⏰10am-midnight; 📶; ⓈD/F to Coney Island-Stillwell Ave) The hot dog was invented in Coney Island in 1867, which means that eating a frankfurter is practically obligatory here. The top choice: Nathan's Famous, which has been around since 1916. The hot dogs are the real deal, but the menu runs the gamut from fried clams to fried chicken fingers – yep, the emphasis is on fried.

DRINKING & NIGHTLIFE

Brooklyn Heights, Downtown Brooklyn & Dumbo

FLOYD BAR

Map p443 (718-858-5810; www.floydny.com; 131 Atlantic Ave, btwn Henry & Clinton Sts, Brooklyn Heights; 5pm-4am Mon-Thu, from 4pm Fri, from noon Sat & Sun; B61, B63 to Atlantic Ave/Henry St, S 2/3, 4/5 to Borough Hall; R to Court St) This glass-front bar is home to young flirters who cuddle on tattered antique sofas while beer-swillers congregate around an indoor bocce court (games are free, first-come, first-served, outside of league nights). A good local hang.

Boerum Hill, Cobble Hill, Carroll Gardens & Red Hook

ROBERT BAR BAR

Map p438 (347-853-8687; www.robertbarbrooklyn.com; 104 Bond St, btwn Atlantic & Pacific Sts, Boerum Hill; 5pm-2am Mon-Thu, to 3am Fri & Sat, to 1am Sun; S A/C, G to Hoyt-Schermerhorn) With a side-room dartboard and jukebox full of 1970s and '80s hits, this place looks kinda like a dive bar, but the young, cool Brooklyn crowd listening to live DJs under a domino-tiled ceiling gives it away as something hipper. There are craft beers and a custom cocktail menu with drinks named after the jukebox songs.

CLOVER CLUB BAR

Map p438 (718-855-7939; www.cloverclubny.com; 210 Smith St, btwn Baltic & Butler Sts, Carroll Gardens; 4pm-2am Mon-Thu, to 4am Fri, 10:30am-4am Sat, to 1am Sun; B57 to Smith & Douglass Sts, S F, G to Bergen) This delightful cocktail parlor channels 19th-century elegance with a rich mahogany bar, vintage fixtures and vest-wearing barkeeps. Beautifully prepared cocktails draw in a mostly local crowd, here for lively conversation fueled by refined recipes such as the 'improved whiskey cocktail' (rye whiskey, maraschino, absinthe and bitters). Clover also serves big weekend brunches matched with excellent Bloody Marys and other libations.

61 LOCAL BAR

Map p438 (718-875-1150; www.61local.com; 61 Bergen St, btwn Smith St & Boerum Pl, Boerum Hill; 7am-midnight Mon-Thu, to 1am Fri, 9am-1am Sat, to midnight Sun; ; S F, G to Bergen) This roomy brick-and-wood hall in Boerum Hill manages to be both chic and warm, with large communal tables, a mellow vibe and a great selection of NYC-brewed and other regional craft beers. There's a simple menu of charcuterie, cheese boards and other snacks, including pulled-pork sliders, quiche and a Mediterranean platter of three dips with crostini and olives.

SUNNY'S BAR

Map p438 (718-625-8211; www.sunnysredhook.com; 253 Conover St, btwn Beard & Reed Sts, Red Hook; 6pm-2am Tue, 4pm-4am Wed-Fri, from 2pm Sat, 4-11pm Sun; B61 to Coffey & Conover Sts, S F, G to Carroll St) Surviving since the late 1800s in one form or another, this throw-back atmospheric bar way out in Red Hook is straight out of *On the Waterfront*. Of course, the longshoremen are long gone, replaced by loyal, passionate regulars and hipster newcomers looking for authenticity. Every Saturday at 10pm it hosts a foot-stomping bluegrass jam. Other banjo-pickin' and curious events happen throughout the week.

Hurricane Sandy dealt the bar a tough blow and it struggled to rebound from the damage. The bar's legendary owner Sunny Balzano passed away in 2016 and at the time of research its continuing existence was once more in doubt, this time by more ordinary real estate-related threats. *Sunny's Nights: Lost and Found at a Bar on the Edge of the World* by Tim Sultan (2016) is a loving portrait of the bar and its owner.

TRAVEL BAR BAR

Map p438 (718-858-2509; www.travelbarbrooklyn.com; 520 Court St, btwn Nelson & Huntington Sts, Carroll Gardens; 5pm-midnight Tue-Thu, 3:30pm-2am Fri, noon-2am Sat, to 9pm Sun; S F, G to Smith-9th Sts) When you want a bit of a break from your travels, drop into this chill local Carroll Gardens establishment and drink yourself around the world with a tasting flight of some of the bar's 200 international whiskeys. Or stay closer to home with NYC craft beers, including a strong IPA from Other Half Brewery, just four blocks away.

Fort Greene, Clinton Hill & Bed-Stuy

BLACK FOREST BROOKLYN BEER HALL

Map p438 (☎718-935-0300; www.blackforestbrooklyn.com; 733 Fulton St, btwn S Elliot Pl & S Portland Ave, Fort Greene; ⏰7am-midnight Sun-Thu, to 2am Fri & Sat; Ⓢ G to Fulton St; C to Lafayette Ave) Two German Brooklynites opened this hip take on a traditional beer hall, with dark ceiling timbers, exposed brick and handsome waiters in red-checked shirts serving up liters of imported Bavarian lagers, pilsners, wheat beers and more on draft. (Can't pick? Try the 13-beer flight.) A full menu of German food features numerous veggie options along with wursts and schnitzels.

Park Slope, Gowanus & Sunset Park

UNION HALL BAR

Map p440 (☎718-638-4400; www.unionhallny.com; 702 Union St, near Fifth Ave, Park Slope; drinks from $7; ⏰4pm-4am Mon-Fri, 1pm-4am Sat & Sun; Ⓢ R train to Union St) Anyone looking for an authentically Brooklyn night out should look no further than Union Hall. This bar and event space is located in a converted warehouse and boasts a double-sided fireplace, towering bookshelves, leather couches and two full-size indoor bocce courts. Head to the basement for live music and comedy.

SEA WITCH BAR

Map p440 (☎347-227-7166; www.seawitchnyc.com; 703 Fifth Ave, btwn 21st & 22nd Sts, Greenwood Heights; ⏰5pm-4am Mon-Thu, from 4pm Fri, from noon Sat & Sun, kitchen open to 12:30am Sun-Thu, to 1:30am Fri & Sat; 🚌B63 to 5th Ave/21st St, Ⓢ R to 25th St) Beyond the nautical whimsy – a shark's jawbone, mermaid mural, live tropical fish – Sea Witch offers top-notch seasonal cocktails, rotating craft beers on tap, occasional DJ music and a solid late-night menu of fish tacos, kielbasa sandwiches, fried whole-belly clam rolls and other comfort foods. The roomy patio out back is a perfect place to relax and unspool your sailors' yarns.

> **WHAT'S ON**
>
> Visit the websites of Free Williamsburg (www.freewilliamsburg.com), Brooklyn Based (www.brooklynbased.com), Greenpointers (www.greenpointers.com) and Bushwick Daily (www.bushwickdaily.com) to keep tabs on the latest music gigs, art openings and more.

EXCELSIOR GAY & LESBIAN

Map p440 (☎718-788-2710; www.excelsiorbrooklyn.com; 563 Fifth Ave, btwn 15th & 16th Sts, Park Slope; ⏰6pm-4am Mon-Fri, from 2pm Sat & Sun; Ⓢ R to Prospect Ave) This beloved neighborhood gay bar has reopened in a new location with a chic remodel that includes a back patio and upstairs event area that hosts dance parties, drag shows and karaoke. Excelsior tends to cater to an older crowd (although everyone is welcome, of course), and is known for its congenial atmosphere and hilarious bartenders.

ROYAL PALMS BAR

Map p440 (☎347-223-4410; www.royalpalmsshuffle.com; 514 Union St, btwn Third Ave & Nevins St, Gowanus; ⏰6pm-midnight Mon-Thu, to 2am Fri, noon-2am Sat, to 10pm Sun; Ⓢ R to Union St) If you're hankering for some sports but don't want to sweat or drift too far from the bar stool, Royal Palms is for you. Inside this 17,000-sq-ft space are 10 full shuffleboard courts ($40 per hour), plus board games (massive Jenga, oversize Connect Four), draft brews, cocktails and snacks provided by a food truck (a different rotation each week).

GREENWOOD PARK BEER GARDEN

Map p440 (☎718-499-7999; www.greenwoodparkbk.com; 555 Seventh Ave, btwn 19th & 20th Sts, Greenwood Heights; ⏰noon-2am Sun-Thu, to 3am Fri & Sat, shorter hours in winter; 📶👪; 🚌B67, B69 to 18th St, Ⓢ F, G to Prospect Park) Around the corner from the leafy Green-Wood Cemetery (p269), this 13,000-sq-ft indoor/outdoor beer hall in an open, industrial setting is a clever reconfiguration of a former gas station and mechanic's shop. (Look for the giant exterior wall made of old pallets.) You'll find more than two dozen beers on draft, plus panini, burgers, salads and other pub fare.

GINGER'S LESBIAN

Map p440 (☎718-788-0924; www.gingersbarbklyn.com; 363 Fifth Ave, at 5th St, Park Slope; ⏲5pm-4am Mon-Fri, from 2pm Sat & Sun; SF, G, R to 4th Ave-9th St) This bright blue-and-yellow lesbian watering hole comes complete with a friendly bartender, a jukebox, a pool table, a small back deck and lots of regulars. Happy hour goes to 8pm.

Prospect Heights, Crown Heights & Flatbush

★BUTTER & SCOTCH BAR

Map p440 (☎347-350-8899; www.butterandscotch.com; 818 Franklin Ave, btwn Eastern Pkwy & Union St, Crown Heights; ⏲5pm-midnight Mon, from 9am Tue-Thu, 9am-2am Fri, from 10am Sat, 10am-midnight Sun; S2/3 to Eastern Pkwy-Brooklyn Museum) Quick! What do you want – booze or cake? The ingenious women behind this bar-and-bakery think you shouldn't have to choose…unless it's whether to get a boozy milkshake or a vodka martini with key-lime pie. There are cakes, pies, ice cream and more, along with craft beers on tap and a dozen seasonal cocktails ($1 from each is donated to Planned Parenthood).

WEATHER UP COCKTAIL BAR

Map p440 (www.weatherupnyc.com; 589 Vanderbilt Ave, at Dean St, Prospect Heights; ⏲5:30pm-midnight Sun-Thu, to 2am Fri & Sat) Walk through the entrance curtain to find yourself in a dimly lit oasis of dark wood and subway tile. Have a seat at the bar to watch the bartenders expertly mix up your cocktail from the seasonal menu, or take refuge in the snug booth at the back. A back patio offers candlelit seclusion within leafy trellised walls. Cash only.

Williamsburg, Greenpoint & Bushwick

★HOUSE OF YES CLUB

(www.houseofyes.org; 2 Wyckoff Ave, at Jefferson St, Bushwick; tickets free-$40; ⏲hours vary by event, Tue-Sat; SL to Jefferson St) Anything goes at this highly regarded warehouse venue, with two stages, three bars and a covered outdoor area, which offers some of the most creative themed performance and dance nights in Brooklyn. You might see aerial-silk acrobats, punk bands, burlesque shows, drag queens or performance artists, with DJs spinning house and other deep beats for an artsy, inclusive crowd.

★MAISON PREMIERE COCKTAIL BAR

Map p436 (☎347-335-0446; www.maisonpremiere.com; 298 Bedford Ave, btwn S 1st & Grand Sts, Williamsburg; ⏲2pm-2am Mon-Wed, to 4am Thu & Fri, 11am-4am Sat, to 2am Sun; SL to Bedford Ave) We kept expecting to see Dorothy Parker stagger into this old-timey place, which features an elegant bar full of syrups and essences, suspender-wearing bartenders and a jazzy soundtrack to further channel the French Quarter New Orleans vibe. The cocktails are serious business: the epic list includes more than a dozen absinthe drinks, various juleps and an array of specialty cocktails.

BROOKLYN BARGE BEER GARDEN

(☎929-337-7212; www.thebrooklynbarge.com; 3 Milton St, off West St, Greenpoint; ⏲noon-2am Mon-Fri, from 11am Sat & Sun May-Oct; 🐾; SG to Greenpoint Ave) Greenpoint's newest summer drinking spot isn't just on the waterfront – it's on the *water*. A floating barge moored to land via a wooden bridge is home to an alfresco bar serving local beers on draft, summery bespoke cocktails and some wines and cider, as well as a menu of plates for sharing, nachos, tacos and sandwiches from the repurposed-shipping-container kitchen.

TOBY'S ESTATE COFFEE

Map p436 (☎347-457-6155; www.tobysestate.com; 125 N 6th St, btwn Bedford Ave & Berry St, Williamsburg; ⏲7am-7pm; 📶; SL to Bedford Ave) This small-batch roaster brings serious flavor to the streets of Billyburg with bold, aromatic pour-overs, creamy flat whites and smooth *cortados* (espresso with a dash of milk). There are a few couches and several communal tables generally crowded with MacBook users.

RADEGAST HALL & BIERGARTEN BEER HALL

Map p436 (☎718-963-3973; www.radegasthall.com; 113 N 3rd St, at Berry St, Williamsburg; ⏲noon-3am Mon-Fri, from 11am Sat & Sun; SL to Bedford Ave) An Austro-Hungarian beer hall in Williamsburg offers up a huge selection of Bavarian brews, and a kitchen full of munchable meats. You can hover in the dark, woody bar area or sit in the adjacent hall, which has a retractable roof and communal tables to feast at – perfect for pretzels, sausages and burgers. Live music every night; no cover.

SPUYTEN DUYVIL BAR

Map p436 (☎718-963-4140; www.spuytenduyvilnyc.com; 359 Metropolitan Ave, btwn Havemeyer & Roebling Sts, Williamsburg; ⏰5pm-2am Mon-Fri, noon-3am Sat, to 2am Sun; **S** L to Lorimer St; G to Metropolitan Ave) This low-key Williamsburg bar looks like it was pieced together from a rummage sale, with red-painted ceilings, vintage maps on the walls and what looks like thrift-store furniture. But the selection of beer and wine is staggering, the locals from various eras are chatty and there's a large backyard with leafy trees that's open in good weather.

NORTHERN TERRITORY ROOFTOP BAR

Map p436 (☎347-689-4065; www.northernterritorybk.com; 12 Franklin St, at Meserole Ave, Greenpoint; ⏰5pm-late Mon-Fri, from noon Sat & Sun summer, closed Mon & Tue winter; 🚌B32 to Franklin St/Meserole Ave, **S** G to Nassau Ave) The remoteness of this Australian rooftop bar, located on a little inlet along the edge of Greenpoint, seems fitting considering its namesake. But head upstairs to see the river and the Manhattan skyline laid out before you and you won't mind the extra few industrial blocks you had to walk. A sunset here with drink in hand is sublime.

ROCKA ROLLA BAR

Map p436 (486 Metropolitan Ave, at Rodney St, Williamsburg; ⏰noon-4am; **S** L to Lorimer St; G to Metropolitan Ave) This Midwestern-throwback rock-and-roll bar with cheap drinks and a hard-partying late-night crowd is located appropriately enough on a gritty stretch beneath the Brooklyn–Queens Expwy overpass. The owners, who also run **Skinny Dennis** (Map p436; www.skinnydennisbar.com; 152 Metropolitan Ave, at Berry St, Williamsburg; ⏰noon-4am; **S** L to Bedford Ave), look to the late '70s and early '80s for inspiration: think AC/DC on the jukebox, vintage light-up beer signs for decor and $3 goblets of Budweiser.

ROOKERY BAR

(www.therookerybar.com; 425 Troutman St, btwn St Nicholas & Wyckoff Aves, Bushwick; ⏰noon-4am Mon-Fri, from 11am Sat & Sun; **S** L to Jefferson St) A mainstay of the Bushwick scene is the industrial-esque Rookery on street-art-lined Troutman Ave. Come for cocktails, craft brews, fusion pub fare (curried-goat shepherd's pies, oxtail sloppy joes), obscure electro-pop and a relaxed vibe. High ceilings give the space an airy feel and the back patio is a great spot, afternoon or evening, in warm weather.

SPRITZENHAUS BEER HALL

Map p436 (☎347-987-4632; www.spritzenhaus33.com; 33 Nassau Ave, at Guernsey St, Greenpoint; ⏰4pm-1am Sun-Thu, noon-4am Sat & Sun; **S** G to Nassau Ave) Beer lovers shouldn't miss this place on the edge of McCarren Park, an open, somewhat industrial 6000-sq-ft beer hall with 20 or so beers on tap and dozens more by the bottle. German, Belgian and North American microbrews dominate, and there's lots of meaty pub grub (sausages mostly, but the Belgian fries with truffle oil are also a hit).

IDES BAR

Map p436 (☎718-460-8006; www.wythehotel.com/the-ides; 80 Wythe Ave, Wythe Hotel, at N 11th St, Williamsburg; cover after 6pm Sat & Sun $10; ⏰4pm-midnight Mon-Thu, from 2pm Fri, from noon Sat & Sun; **S** L to Bedford Ave) The rooftop bar of the Wythe Hotel (p344) offers magnificent views of Manhattan, with upscale bar snacks served until 10pm. No reservations, so come early to beat the crowds. There's a cover on Saturday and Sunday nights for nonguests of the hotel.

HOTEL DELMANO COCKTAIL BAR

Map p436 (☎718-387-1945; www.hoteldelmano.com; 82 Berry St, at N 9th St, Williamsburg; ⏰5pm-2am Mon-Thu, to 3am Fri, 1pm-3am Sat, to 2am Sun; **S** L to Bedford Ave) This low-lit cocktail bar aims for a speakeasy vibe, with old, smoky mirrors, unpolished floorboards and vintage chandeliers. Nestle into one of the nooks in back or have a seat at the curving, marble-topped bar and watch mustachioed barkeeps whip up a changing array of inventive cocktails (rye, gin and mescal are favored spirits).

BOSSA NOVA CIVIC CLUB CLUB

(☎718-443-1271; 1271 Myrtle Ave, at Hart St, Bushwick; ⏰5pm-4am Mon-Sat, to midnight Sun; **S** M to Central Ave) Yet another reason why you never need to leave Brooklyn, this smallish hole-in-the-wall club is a great place to get your groove on, with DJs spinning a wide mix of sounds in a (somewhat) tropical-themed interior. Great sound system, fairly priced drinks (at least as far as

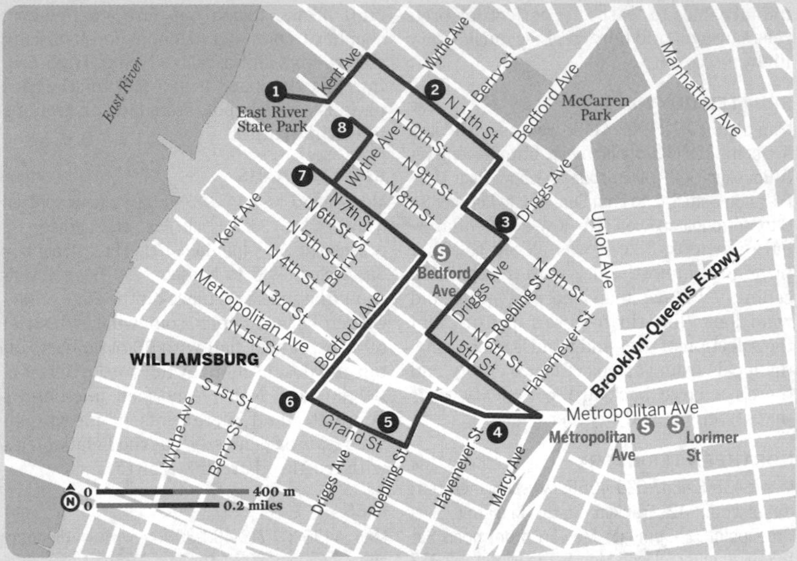

Local Life
Exploring Williamsburg

Once a bastion of Latino working-class life, Williamsburg is the dining and nightlife center of northern Brooklyn. This erstwhile bohemian magnet has seen the starving artists move to Bushwick for cheaper rents, leaving gleaming condos and refurbished brownstones to professionals and hip young families. There's lots to explore, from vintage-cocktail dens to shops selling one-of-a-kind creations from local craftspeople.

❶ Seeing Green

Offering fabulous, waterside Manhattan views, the East River State Park (p274) is an open green space that becomes a major draw in the summertime with picnicking and occasional concerts.

❷ Homegrown Hops

Once upon a time Williamsburg was the center of beer-brewing in New York. Continuing the tradition, the Brooklyn Brewery (p275) not only brews and serves tasty local suds, it also offers tours.

❸ Hipster Threads

If you want to expand your wardrobe to include some local flavor, stop in at **Buffalo Exchange** (Map p436; ☎718-384-6901; www.buffaloexchange.com; 504 Driggs Ave, at N 9th St; ⏰11am-8pm Mon-Sat, noon-7pm Sun; Ⓢ L to Bedford Ave), a much-loved resale shop, where you'll find lightly used, on-trend fashions for men and women.

❹ Bodega Ephemera

For a glimpse of curious old objects from the city's days of yore, visit City Reliquary (p274), a snug storefront museum packed with NYC relics, including exhibits on the 1939 World's Fair.

❺ Latin American Detour

A fun little shop for browsing, **Fuego 718** (Map p436; ☎718-302-2913; www.fuego718.com; 249 Grand St, btwn Roebling St & Driggs Ave; ⏰noon-8pm; Ⓢ L to Bedford Ave) transports you south of the border with Day of the Dead boxes, colorful frames and mirrors, and kitsch and crafts from Mexico, Peru and beyond.

JOSE OTERO / 500PX ©

Brooklyn Brewery (p275)

❻ More Brooklyn Booze
Crank that time machine back one more notch at retro Maison Premiere (p290), which features bespoke cocktails, oysters and other treats with a smart Southern vibe.

❼ Maker Multiverse
If it's a weekend, browse the aisles of Artists & Fleas (p299), a shopping warren of several dozen booths featuring locally crafted jewelry, accessories, artworks, cosmetics, housewares and vintage records and clothes.

❽ Vinyl Valhalla
Williamsburg is home to the lone American outpost of legendary UK record store **Rough Trade** (Map p436; ☎718-388-4111; www.roughtradenyc.com; 64 N 9th St, btwn Kent & Wythe Aves; ⊙11am-11pm Mon-Sat, to 9pm Sun; 📶; Ⓢ L to Bedford Ave), a warehouse-sized dream for music lovers and LP collectors that also hosts frequent in-store concerts of upcoming talents, with tickets usually not more than $15. You can finish up your neighborhood stroll with a fresh latte from the in-store cafe.

clubs are concerned) and snacks available when hunger strikes (empanadas, slow-cooked pork, arepas).

Draws a celebratory crowd that's ready to dance. It's free Monday to Thursday, $10 cover on Friday and Saturday.

PINE BOX ROCK SHOP BAR
Map p436 (☎718-366-6311; www.pineboxrockshop.com; 12 Grattan St, btwn Morgan Ave & Bogart St, East Williamsburg; ⊙4pm-2am Mon & Tue, to 4am Wed-Fri, 2pm-4am Sat, noon-2am Sun; Ⓢ L to Morgan Ave) The cavernous Pine Box Rock Shop – a former casket factory – has 17 drafts to choose from, as well as widely heralded, spicy, pint-sized Bloody Marys. It's run by a friendly vegan musician couple, so everything served here uses no animal products, including the empanadas and other bar snacks. Local artwork graces the walls, and a performance back room hosts regular gigs.

BLUE BOTTLE COFFEE COFFEE
Map p436 (☎718-387-4160; www.bluebottlecoffee.net; 160 Berry St, btwn N 4th & N 5th Sts, Williamsburg; coffees $3-5; ⊙6:30am-7pm Mon-Fri, 7am-7:30pm Sat & Sun; Ⓢ L to Bedford Ave) One for the coffee connoisseurs, this top-of-the-line cafe located in a former rope shop uses a vintage Probat roaster on its beans. All drinks are brewed to order, so be prepared to wait a bit for your Kyoto iced. A small selection of baked goods includes coffee cake made with a chocolate stout from Brooklyn Brewery (p275) – talk about locally sourced.

CLEM'S PUB
Map p436 (☎718-387-9617; www.clemsbrooklyn.com; 264 Grand St, at Roebling St, Williamsburg; ⊙2pm-4am Mon-Fri, from noon Sat & Sun; Ⓢ L to Lorimer St; G to Metropolitan Ave) This tidy Williamsburg pub keeps things chill. It has a long bar, friendly bartenders and a few outdoor tables that are perfect for summer people-watching. Stop by at happy hour (till 8pm) for a beer and a shot for only $6.

🍷 Coney Island & Brighton Beach

RUBY'S BAR & GRILL BAR
Map p444 (☎718-975-7829; www.rubysbar.com; 1213 Riegelmann Boardwalk, btwn Stillwell Ave & 12th St, Coney Island; ⊙11am-10pm Sun-Thu, to 1am Fri & Sat Apr-Sep, weekends only Oct; Ⓢ D/F, N/Q to Coney Island-Stillwell Ave)

The oldest and only dive bar on the Coney Island boardwalk is an institution: Ruby's has been around since 1934 and has been threatened with extinction by developers who want to upscale the boardwalk – yet it hangs on. Grab a stool, order a pint of Ruby's Ale and watch the waves (and salty locals) roll in. Avoid the food.

★ ENTERTAINMENT

★BROOKLYN ACADEMY OF MUSIC PERFORMING ARTS

Map p438 (BAM; ☎718-636-4100; www.bam.org; 30 Lafayette Ave, at Ashland Pl, Fort Greene; ; SB/D, N/Q/R, 2/3, 4/5 to Atlantic Ave-Barclays Ctr) Founded in 1861, BAM is the country's oldest performing-arts center. With several neighboring venues located in the Fort Greene area, the complex offers innovative and edgier works of opera, modern dance, music, cinema and theater – everything from Merce Cunningham retrospectives and multimedia shows by Laurie Anderson to avant-garde interpretations of Shakespeare and other classics.

The Italian Renaissance–style Peter J Sharp Building houses the **Howard Gilman Opera House** (Map p438), showing opera, dance, music and more; and the four-screen **Rose Cinemas** (Map p438), showing first-run, indie and foreign films; the on-site bar and restaurant, **BAMcafe** (Map p438; ☎dinner reservations 718-623-7811), stages free jazz, R&B and pop performances on weekends. A block away on Fulton St is the **Harvey Lichtenstein Theater** (Map p438; 651 Fulton St, near Rockwell Pl, Fort Greene; SB, Q/R to DeKalb Ave; 2/3, 4/5 to Nevins St), aka 'the Harvey', which stages cutting-edge, contemporary plays and sometimes radical interpretations of classics. Around the corner from the Sharp building is the **Fisher Building** (Map p438; ☎718-636-4100; www.bam.org/fisher; 321 Ashland Pl, near Lafayette Ave, Fort Greene), with its more intimate 250-seat theater.

From September through December, BAM hosts its acclaimed **Next Wave Festival** (tickets $20; Sep-Dec), which presents an array of international avant-garde theater and dance and artist talks. Buy tickets early.

★ST ANN'S WAREHOUSE THEATER

Map p443 (☎718-254-8779; www.stannswarehouse.org; 45 Water St, at Old Dock St, Dumbo; B25 to Water/Main Sts, SA/C to High St; F to York St) This avant-garde performance company hosts innovative theater, music and dance happenings – everything from genre-defying music by new composers to strange and wondrous puppet theater. In 2015, St Ann's moved from its old home several blocks away to this location in the historic Tobacco Warehouse (p266) in Brooklyn Bridge Park.

★BARBÈS LIVE MUSIC, JAZZ

Map p440 (☎718-965-9177; www.barbesbrooklyn.com; 376 9th St, at Sixth Ave, Park Slope; requested donation for live music $10; 5pm-2am Mon-Thu, 2pm-4am Fri & Sat, to 2am Sun; SF, G to 7th Ave; R to 4th Ave-9th St) This compact bar and performance space, named after a North African neighborhood in Paris, is owned by French musician (and longtime Brooklyn resident) Olivier Conan, who sometimes plays here with his Latin-themed band Las Rubias del Norte. There's live music all night, every night: the impressively eclectic lineup includes Afro-Peruvian grooves, West African funk and gypsy swing, among other sounds.

★NATIONAL SAWDUST LIVE PERFORMANCE

Map p436 (☎646-779-8455; www.nationalsawdust.org; 80 N 6th St, at Wythe Ave, Williamsburg; ; SL to Bedford Ave) Covered in wildly hued murals, this arts space dedicated to cutting-edge multidisciplinary programming opened to much fanfare in 2015. You can see daring works like contemporary opera with multimedia projections, electro-acoustic big-band jazz and concerts by experimental composers, along with more globally infused performances – Inuit throat singing, African tribal funk, and the singing of Icelandic sagas, among other things.

BROOKLYN BOWL LIVE MUSIC

Map p436 (☎718-963-3369; www.brooklynbowl.com; 61 Wythe Ave, btwn N 11th & N 12th Sts, Williamsburg; 6pm-midnight Mon-Wed, to 2am Thu & Fri, 11am-2am Sat, to midnight Sun; SL to Bedford Ave; G to Nassau Ave) A 23,000-sq-ft venue inside the former Hecla Iron Works Company combines bowling (p300), microbrews, food and top-notch music. In addition to the live bands (and occasional DJs) that regularly tear up the stage, there are NFL game days, karaoke and DJ nights. It's age 21 and up, except for 'family bowl' time on weekends (11am to 5pm Saturday, to 6pm Sunday).

BELL HOUSE LIVE PERFORMANCE

Map p440 (☎718-643-6510; www.thebellhouseny.com; 149 7th St, btwn Second & Third Aves, Gowanus; ⏰5pm-late; 📶; Ⓢ F, G, R to 4th Ave-9th St) A large, old venue in a mostly barren area of industrial Gowanus, the Bell House features high-profile live performances, indie rockers, DJ nights, comedy shows and burlesque parties. The handsomely converted warehouse has a spacious concert area, plus a friendly little bar in the front room with flickering candles, leather armchairs and 10 or so beers on tap.

JALOPY LIVE MUSIC

Map p438 (☎718-395-3214; www.jalopy.biz; 315 Columbia St, btwn Hamilton Ave & Woodhull St, Columbia St Waterfront District; ⏰4-9pm Mon, noon-midnight Tue-Sun; 👪; 🚌B61 to Columbia & Carroll Sts, Ⓢ F, G to Carroll St) This banjo shop and bar on the fringes of Carroll Gardens and Red Hook has a fun DIY space where it serves cold beer and stages bluegrass, country, klezmer and ukulele shows, including a no-cover feel-good Roots 'n' Ruckus show every Wednesday night at 9pm. Check the website for show schedules.

NITEHAWK CINEMA CINEMA

Map p436 (☎718-782-8370; www.nitehawkcinema.com; 136 Metropolitan Ave, btwn Berry & Wythe Sts, Williamsburg; tickets adult/child $12/9; 👪; Ⓢ L to Bedford Ave) This indie triplex has a fine lineup of first-run and repertory films, a good sound system and comfy seats…but the best part is that you can dine and drink all during the movie. Munch on hummus plates, sweet-potato risotto balls or short-rib empanadas, matched by a Blue Point toasted lager, a negroni or a movie-themed cocktail invention.

ALAMO DRAFTHOUSE CINEMA

Map p443 (☎718-513-2547; www.drafthouse.com; 445 Albee Square W, at DeKalb Ave, City Point, Downtown Brooklyn; tickets $15; Ⓢ B, Q/R to DeKalb Ave; 2/3 to Hoyt St; A/C, G to Hoyt-Schermerhorn) The NYC branch of this Texas-based movie-house phenomenon shows both first-run movies and special presentations in big-screen cinemas with wide, cushy seats and small tables; throughout the show, waiters bring your food and drink orders right to your seat. Treat yourself to an alcoholic ice-cream concoction – our fave is the black-and-white-cookie White Russian.

LITTLEFIELD LIVE PERFORMANCE

Map p440 (www.littlefieldnyc.com; 635 Sackett St, btwn Third & Fourth Aves, Gowanus; Ⓢ R to Union St) This performance and art space occupying a 6200-sq-ft former textile warehouse showcases a wide range of live music and other shows, including comedy, storytelling, theater, dance, film screenings and trivia nights. Wyatt Cenac hosts the popular *Night Train* comedy show on Mondays; other regular events include the

READING BROOKLYN

Brooklyn's literary roots run deep. The former Borough President Marty Markowitz described Brooklyn as 'New York's Left Bank,' and given the range of local talents who have shaped American literature, not to mention the countless authors living here today, he may not be far off the mark.

Here are a few quintessential reads from celebrated Brooklyn authors present and past:

➡ *Leaves of Grass* (1855) Walt Whitman's love letter to New York, 'Crossing Brooklyn Ferry,' is a particularly poignant part of his poetic celebration of life.

➡ *A Tree Grows in Brooklyn* (1943) Betty Smith's affecting coming-of-age story set in the squalid tenements of Williamsburg.

➡ *Sophie's Choice* (1979) William Styron's blockbuster centers on a boarding house in post-war Flatbush.

➡ *Motherless Brooklyn* (1999) Jonathan Lethem's brilliant and darkly comic tale of small-time hoods is set in Carroll Gardens and other parts of Brooklyn.

➡ *Literary Brooklyn* (2011) Evan Hughes provides an overview of great Brooklyn writers and their neighborhoods, from Henry Miller's Williamsburg to Truman Capote's Brooklyn Heights.

➡ *Manhattan Beach* (2017) Pulitzer Prize–winning author Jennifer Egan's novel follows a young woman working in the Brooklyn Navy Yard during WWII.

groan-inducing game show *Punderdome 3000* and embarrassing-story-telling night *Mortified*. No under-21s.

KINGS THEATRE THEATER

Map p440 (☎718-856-2220; www.kingstheatre.com; 1027 Flatbush Ave, at Tilden Ave, Flatbush; ⊙box office noon-5:30pm Mon-Sat; Ⓢ2, 5 or Q to Beverly Rd) Far from the crowds of Madison Square Garden (p206), this former movie palace is a gorgeous reminder of the past – and a top-notch concert venue to boot. Built in 1929, it was recently renovated to highlight its exceptional historic details. The lobby is grandiose in gold and red, while inside the 3000-seat theater are a breathtaking painted ceiling and plush chairs.

MCU PARK BASEBALL

Map p444 (☎718-372-5596; www.brooklyncyclones.com; 1904 Surf Ave, at 17th St, Coney Island; tickets $10-20, all tickets on Wed $10; ⓈD/F, N/Q to Coney Island-Stillwell Ave) The Minor League Baseball team **Brooklyn Cyclones**, part of the New York–Penn League, plays at this beachside park a few steps from the Coney Island boardwalk. Nearly every game has some sort of a fun theme like *Seinfeld* or 'princess and pirate' and on a warm summer evening it can feel quite magical, regardless of what's happening on the field.

THEATER FOR A NEW AUDIENCE PERFORMING ARTS

Map p438 (☎tickets 866-811-4111; www.tfana.org; 262 Ashland Pl, cnr Fulton St, Fort Greene; Ⓢ2/3, 4/5 to Nevins St; B, Q/R to Dekalb Ave) Part of the emerging cultural district surrounding BAM (p294), the Theater for a New Audience opened in late 2013, in a grand new building inspired by London's Cottesloe Theatre. The calendar features avant-garde productions of works by Shakespeare, Ibsen and Strindberg, as well as more recent works by playwrights like Richard Maxwell and his theater company the New York City Players.

PUPPETWORKS PUPPET THEATRE

Map p440 (☎718-965-3391; www.puppetworks.org; 338 Sixth Ave, at 4th St, Park Slope; adult/child $11/10; ⊙12:30pm & 2:30pm Sat & Sun; 👪; ⓈF, G to 7th Ave) In a tiny theater in Park Slope, this nonprofit outfit stages delightful marionette shows that earn rave reviews from pint-sized critics. Catch puppet adaptations of classics like *Beauty and the Beast*, *Goldilocks and the Three Bears* and (of course) *Pinocchio*. Most shows happen on Saturdays and Sundays at 12:30pm and 2:30pm. Check the website for schedules.

MUSIC HALL OF WILLIAMSBURG LIVE MUSIC

Map p436 (☎718-486-5400; www.musichallofwilliamsburg.com; 66 N 6th St, btwn Wythe & Kent Aves, Williamsburg; tickets $15-40; ⓈL to Bedford Ave) This popular Williamsburg music venue is *the* place to see indie bands in Brooklyn – everyone from They Might Be Giants to Kendrick Lamar has played here. (For many groups traveling through New York, this is their one and only spot.) It's got an intimate feel (capacity is 550) and the almost-nightly programming is solid.

WARSAW LIVE MUSIC

Map p436 (☎718-387-5252; www.warsawconcerts.com; 261 Driggs Ave, Polish National Home, at Eckford St, Greenpoint; 🚌B43 to Graham/Driggs Aves, ⓈG to Nassau Ave; L to Bedford Ave) A burgeoning Brooklyn classic, this stage is in the Polish National Home, with good views in the old ballroom for bands ranging from indie darlings the Dead Milkmen to funk legends like George Clinton. Polish ladies serve pierogi, kielbasa sandwiches and beers under the disco balls.

KNITTING FACTORY LIVE MUSIC

Map p436 (☎347-529-6696; http://bk.knittingfactory.com; 361 Metropolitan Ave, at Havemeyer St, Williamsburg; tickets $10-30; ⓈL to Lorimer St; G to Metropolitan Ave) A longtime outpost for folk, indie and experimental music in New York, Williamsburg's Knitting Factory is where to go to see everything from cosmic space jazz to rock. The stage is small and intimate. A separate barroom has a soundproof window with stage views.

BARGEMUSIC CLASSICAL MUSIC

Map p443 (☎718-624-4924; www.bargemusic.org; Fulton Ferry Landing, Brooklyn Heights; tickets adult/student $40/20; 👪; ⓈA/C to High St) The chamber-music concerts held on this 125-seat converted coffee barge (built c 1899) are a unique, intimate affair. For nearly 40 years, it has been a beloved venue, with beautiful views of the East River and Manhattan. There are free family concerts most Saturdays at 4pm.

BARCLAYS CENTER SPECTATOR SPORT, CONCERT VENUE

Map p440 (☎917-618-6100; www.barclayscenter.com; cnr Flatbush & Atlantic Aves, Prospect

Heights; ⓈB/D, N/Q/R, 2/3, 4/5 to Atlantic Ave-Barclays Ctr) The Dodgers still play baseball in Los Angeles, but the (currently woeful) **Brooklyn Nets** in the NBA (formerly the New Jersey Nets) now hold court at this high-tech stadium that opened in 2012. Basketball aside, Barclays also stages major concerts and big shows: Bruce Springsteen, Justin Bieber, Barbara Streisand, Cirque de Soleil, Disney on Ice…

SHOPPING

Brooklyn Heights, Downtown Brooklyn & Dumbo

POWERHOUSE @ THE ARCHWAY BOOKS

Map p443 (☎718-666-3049; www.powerhousebooks.com; 28 Adams St, cnr Water St, Dumbo; ⏰11am-7pm Mon-Fri, from 10am Sat, 11am-6pm Sun; Wi-Fi; ⓈA/C to High St; F to York St) An important part of Dumbo's cultural scene, Powerhouse Books hosts changing art exhibitions, book-launch parties and weird and creative events in its large, airy new digs just under the Manhattan Bridge. You'll also find intriguing books on urban art, photography and pop culture – all imprints of its namesake publishing house.

MODERN ANTHOLOGY CLOTHING

Map p443 (☎718 522 3020; www.modernanthology.com; 68 Jay St, btwn Water & Front Sts, Dumbo; ⏰11am-7pm Mon-Sat, noon-6pm Sun; ⓈF to York St; A/C to High St) For the rugged, city-dwelling man with money to spend, Modern Anthology has plenty of appeal. Among the finds: elegant but manly leather satchels, brassy bottle openers shaped like animal heads, woolly Pendleton blankets, leather boots, soft cotton button-downs and well-fitting dark-denim jeans.

FULTON MALL SHOPPING CENTER

Map p443 (Fulton St, from Boerum Pl to Flatbush Ave, Downtown Brooklyn; ⓈA/C, F, R to Jay St-Metrotech; B, Q/R to DeKalb Ave; 2/3, 4/5 to Nevins St) This outdoor shopping experience has been around for a long time, and features everything from big-name department stores such as Macy's to local favorites like Dr Jay's. The recent addition of stores such as H&M, Banana Republic and Nordstrom Rack make it a can't-miss for anyone looking to give their credit card a workout while in Brooklyn.

SAHADI'S FOOD

Map p443 (☎718-624-4550; www.sahadis.com; 187 Atlantic Ave, btwn Court & Clinton Sts, Brooklyn Heights; ⏰9am-7pm Mon-Sat; Ⓢ2/3, 4/5 to Borough Hall) The smell of fresh-roasted coffee and spices greets you as you enter this beloved Middle Eastern delicacies shop. The olive bar boasts two dozen kinds and there are loads of breads, cheeses, nuts and hummus. It's a great place to assemble a picnic before heading to Brooklyn Bridge Park (p263).

Boerum Hill, Cobble Hill, Carroll Gardens & Red Hook

BLACK GOLD RECORDS MUSIC

Map p438 (☎347-227-8227; www.blackgoldbrooklyn.com; 461 Court St, btwn 4th Pl & Luquer St, Carroll Gardens; ⏰7am-8pm Mon-Fri, 8am-9pm Sat, to 7pm Sun; ⓈF, G to Smith-9th Sts) Records, coffee, antiques and taxidermy await you in this tiny addition to the ever-expanding Court St scene in Carroll Gardens. Sample vintage vinyl – from John Coltrane to Ozzy Osbourne – on the turntable and enjoy a damn good cup of coffee, ground and brewed individually. Need a stuffed hyena from the Ozarks? Find it here.

TWISTED LILY PERFUME, COSMETICS

Map p438 (☎347-529-4681; www.twistedlily.com; 360 Atlantic Ave, btwn Bond & Hoyt Sts, Boerum Hill; ⏰noon-7pm Tue-Sun; ⓈF, G to Hoyt-Schermerhorn) Come out smelling like a rose from this boutique specializing in indie scents from around the world. Shop for perfumes and scented candles by fragrance notes (bergamot, clary sage, honeysuckle and many others); attentive staff will help you pick whatever your nose desires. The shop also carries niche skincare, hair and men's grooming products.

BROOKLYN STRATEGIST GAMES

Map p438 (☎718-576-3035; www.thebrooklynstrategist.com; 333 Court St, btwn Sackett & Union Sts, Carroll Gardens; ⏰11am-11pm; 👪; ⓈF, G to Carroll St) Whether you're into *Settlers of Catan* or checkers, this community games store has something for you. Besides the large selection of games for sale, $10 (per

BROOKLYN MARKETS

When the weekend arrives, Brooklynites are out and about, strolling the stoop sales and hitting the markets. Here are a few good places to unearth something unusual:

Brooklyn Flea (Map p443; www.brooklynflea.com; 80 Pearl St, Manhattan Bridge Archway, Anchorage Pl at Water St, Dumbo; ⏲10am-6pm Sun Apr-Oct; 🚻; 🚌B67 to York/Jay Sts, ⓈF to York St) On Sundays from April to November, about a hundred vendors sell their wares inside the massive archway beneath the Manhattan Bridge. You'll find antiques, records, vintage clothes, craft items, jewelry and more, and often some enticing food stalls with tasty treats to boot. (There's a smaller indoor flea market held both Saturday and Sunday, but in SoHo.)

Artists & Fleas (p299) In operation since 2003, this is a popular artists, designers and vintage market in Williamsburg, where you can find an excellent selection of crafty goodness.

Grand Army Plaza Greenmarket (Map p440; www.grownyc.org; Prospect Park W & Flatbush Ave, Grand Army Plaza, Prospect Park; ⏲8am-4pm Sat year-round; Ⓢ2/3 to Grand Army Plaza) Open on Saturdays year-round, this Greenmarket is a good spot to put together an impromptu picnic before heading into Prospect Park.

Neighborhood Greenmarkets You'll find other year-round Greenmarkets at **Brooklyn Borough Hall** (Downtown Brooklyn; Ⓢ2/3, 4/5 to Borough Hall) on Tuesdays; **Carroll Park** (Carroll Gardens; ⓈF, G to Carroll St) on Sundays; and **Fort Greene Park** (Fort Greene; ⓈB, Q/R to DeKalb Ave) on Saturdays. Check www.grownyc.org for other NYC Greenmarkets.

person) gets you four hours to play any of the several hundred games in its huge library. Tuesday nights there's open-play chess and board games; a small cafe keeps you fueled. Great rainy-day option.

Fort Greene, Clinton Hill & Bed-Stuy

GREENLIGHT BOOKSTORE BOOKS

Map p438 (☎718-246-0200; www.greenlightbookstore.com; 686 Fulton St, at S Portland Ave, Fort Greene; ⏲10am-10pm; ⓈC to Lafayette Ave; B/D, N/Q/R, 2/3, 4/5 to Atlantic Ave-Barclays Ctr) This independent bookstore has been a neighborhood mainstay for more than eight years. How does it stick around in the age of Amazon? Friendly, book-loving staff, a great selection of kids' books and works by local authors, and an event calendar full of interesting readings and talks. Great selection of Brooklyn- and NYC-themed books, too.

Park Slope, Gowanus & Sunset Park

BEACON'S CLOSET VINTAGE

Map p440 (☎718-230-1630; www.beaconscloset.com; 92 Fifth Ave, cnr Warren St, Park Slope; ⏲noon-9pm Mon-Fri, 11am-8pm Sat & Sun; Ⓢ2/3 to Bergen St; B, Q to 7th Ave) An excellent thrift shop stocked full of shoes, jewelry and bright vintage finds. There's a much bigger branch in Greenpoint (p299), and another one in Bushwick (p297).

BROOKLYN SUPERHERO SUPPLY CO GIFTS & SOUVENIRS

Map p440 (☎718-499-9884; www.superherosupplies.com; 372 Fifth Ave, btwn 5th & 6th Sts, Park Slope; ⏲11am-5pm; 🚻; ⓈF, G, R to 4th Ave-9th St) This fun-filled shop sells capes, masks, utility belts, invisibility goggles, buckets of antimatter and other essentials for budding superheroes. All sales provide support for 826NYC, a nonprofit that helps students improve their writing and literacy skills (the classroom area is concealed behind one of the shelves).

INDUSTRY CITY HOMEWARES, FOOD & DRINK

Map p440 (☎718-965-6450; www.industrycity.com; 220 36th St, btwn Second & Third Aves, Sunset Park; 📶; ⓈD, N/R to 36th St) In a few short years, Industry City has gone from a collection of warehouses to a bustling art, commerce and office hub. Come during the day to tour galleries, shop for accessories and furniture, or grab a bite at one of the restaurants or cafes. At night there are often events in the ultramodern courtyard covered in tasteful twinkle lights.

Williamsburg, Greenpoint & Bushwick

★ARTISTS & FLEAS MARKET

Map p436 (www.artistsandfleas.com; 70 N 7th St, btwn Wythe & Kent Aves, Williamsburg; 10am-7pm Sat & Sun; S L to Bedford Ave) In operation for over a decade, this popular Williamsburg flea market has an excellent selection of crafty goodness. Over a hundred artists, designers and vintage vendors sell their wares: clothing, records, paintings, photographs, hats, handmade jewelry, one-of-a-kind T-shirts, canvas bags and more. Two locations in Manhattan are smaller but open daily: one in SoHo, the other inside the Chelsea Market (p134).

QUIMBY'S BOOKSTORE NYC BOOKS

Map p436 (718-384-1215; www.quimbysnyc.com; 536 Metropolitan Ave, btwn Union Ave & Lorimer St, Williamsburg; S L to Lorimer St; G to Metropolitan Ave) This recent offshoot of the renowned indie bookstore in Chicago is a treasure chest of alternative publications on a range of interesting topics, such as punk music, cinema and the occult. It's also got hundreds of 'zines from all over the world (plus some taxidermied animals for sale). Weekly events include readings and photo exhibits.

CATBIRD JEWELRY

Map p436 (718-599-3457; www.catbirdnyc.com; 219 Bedford Ave, btwn N 4th & 5th Sts, Williamsburg; noon-8pm Mon-Fri, 11am-7pm Sat, noon-6pm Sun; S L to Bedford Ave) Still going strong in Williamsburg after 14 years, this jewelry shop stocks both its own pieces – made in a studio a few blocks away – and jewelry from independent makers around the world. Everything is either sterling silver or solid gold, and uses conflict-free, authentic gems. Catbird specializes in rings, especially stacking sets and engagement rings (hey, no pressure).

DESERT ISLAND COMICS BOOKS

Map p436 (www.desertislandbrooklyn.com; 540 Metropolitan Ave, btwn Union Ave & Lorimer St, Williamsburg; 2-7pm Mon, noon-9pm Tue-Sat, to 7pm Sun; S L to Lorimer St; G to Metropolitan Ave) Desert Island is an excellent indie comic-book shop located inside a former bakery in Williamsburg. Inside, you'll find hundreds of comics, graphic novels, local zines, prints and cards. Also on sale are original prints and lithographs by artists such as Adrian Tomine and Peter Bagge. Good tunes are provided by the turntable in back.

BEACON'S CLOSET VINTAGE

Map p436 (718-486-0816; www.beaconscloset.com; 74 Guernsey St, btwn Nassau & Norman Aves, Greenpoint; 11am-8pm; S L to Bedford Ave; G to Nassau Ave) Twenty-something groovers find this massive 5500-sq-ft warehouse of vintage clothing part goldmine, part grit. Lots of coats, polyester tops and '90s-era T-shirts are displayed by color, but the sheer mass can take time to conquer. You'll also find shoes of all sorts, flannels, hats, handbags, chunky jewelry and brightly hued sunglasses. There are other branches in **Bushwick** (Map p436; 718-417-5683; 23 Bogart St, btwn Varet & Cook Sts; 11am-8pm; S L to Morgan Ave) and Park Slope (p298).

A&G MERCH HOMEWARES

Map p436 (718-388-1779; www.aandgmerch.com; 111 N 6th St, btwn Berry & Wythe Sts, Williamsburg; 11am-7pm; S L to Bedford Ave) With its mix of whimsy and elegance, A&G Merch is a fun little shop to explore. Check out antique plates adorned with animal heads, rustic wicker baskets, cast-iron whale bookends, silver tree-branch-like candleholders, brassy industrial table lamps and other goods to give your nest that artfully rustic Brooklyn look.

SPOONBILL & SUGARTOWN BOOKS

Map p436 (718-387-7322; www.spoonbillbooks.com; 218 Bedford Ave, btwn N 5th & N 4th Sts, Williamsburg; 10am-10pm; S L to Bedford Ave) Williamsburg's favorite bookstore has an intriguing selection of art and coffee-table books, cultural journals, used and rare titles, and locally made works not found elsewhere. Check the website for upcoming readings and book-launch parties.

SPORTS & ACTIVITIES

BROOKLYN BOULDERS CLIMBING

Map p440 (347-834-9066; www.brooklynboulders.com; 575 Degraw St, at Third Ave, Gowanus; day pass $32, shoe & harness rental $12; 7am-midnight Mon-Fri, to 10pm Sat & Sun; S R to Union St) Brooklyn's biggest indoor climbing arena is housed in an airy and vibrant space on an industrial block in the Gowanus neighborhood. Ceilings top out at 30ft inside this 18,000-sq-ft facility, and its caves and freestanding 17ft boulder and climbing walls offer numerous routes for both beginners and experts. There are overhangs of 15, 30 and 45 degrees. Climbing classes are available.

BROOKLYN BRAINERY WALKING

Map p440 (☎347-292-7246; www.brooklynbrainery.com; 190 Underhill Ave, btwn Sterling & St Johns Pls, Prospect Heights; Ⓢ2/3 to Grand Army Plaza) This community educational resource hosts one-off evening talks and hands-on courses – on everything from the history of toilets to making your own lip balm – and also offers guided walking tours of off-the-beaten-track locations such as Green-Wood Cemetery (p269) or the Gowanus Canal, often touching on issues of local history, architecture or ecology.

RED HOOK BOATERS KAYAKING

Map p438 (www.redhookboaters.org; Louis Valentino Jr Park, cnr Coffey & Ferris Sts, Red Hook; ⏲1-4pm Sun Jun-Sep & 6-8pm Thu mid-Jun–mid-Aug; 🚌B61 to Coffey St, ⓈF, G to Smith-9th Sts then) FREE This boathouse, located in Red Hook, offers free kayaking in the small embayment off Louis Valentino Jr Park. Once in the water, you'll have beautiful views of Lower Manhattan and the Statue of Liberty. Check the website for the latest times before making the trip out.

BROOKLYN BOWL BOWLING

Map p436 (☎718-963-3369; www.brooklynbowl.com; 61 Wythe Ave, btwn N 11th & N 12th Sts, Williamsburg; lane rentals per 30min $25, shoe rentals $5; ⏲6pm-2am Mon-Fri, from 11am Sat & Sun; 👪; ⓈL to Bedford Ave; G to Nassau Ave) This incredible alley is housed in the 23,000-sq-ft former Hecla Iron Works Company, which provided ornamentation for several NYC landmarks at the turn of the 20th century. There are 16 lanes surrounded by cushy sofas and exposed brick walls. In addition to bowling, Brooklyn Bowl hosts concerts (p295) throughout the week, and there's always good food on hand.

Saturdays from 11am to 5pm and Sundays to 6pm are all-ages Family Bowl hours. (Nighttime bowling is for ages 21 and over only.)

AREA YOGA & SPA YOGA, SPA

Map p438 (☎718-797-3699; www.areayogabrooklyn.com; 389 Court St, btwn 1st & 2nd Pl, Carroll Gardens; classes $18, mat rentals $2; ⏲classes 7am-8:30pm Mon-Thu, to 7:30pm Fri, 8:30am-6pm Sat, 8am-6pm Sun; ⓈF, G to Carroll St) Area Yoga offers a wide range of classes and has locations in Cobble Hill, Brooklyn Heights and Park Slope. Some locations also offer deep-tissue massage and an infrared sauna.

ON THE MOVE CYCLING

Map p440 (☎718-768-4998; www.onthemovenyc.com; 219 9th St, btwn Third & Fourth Aves, Gowanus; bike rentals per day incl helmet $35; ⏲10am-6pm; ⓈF, G, R to 4th Ave-9th St) A little less than a mile due west of Brooklyn's Prospect Park (p264), On the Move rents and sells all manner of bikes and gear. The shop sometimes closes in inclement weather, so it's a good idea to call ahead.

Queens

LONG ISLAND CITY | ASTORIA | JACKSON HEIGHTS | FLUSHING & CORONA | ELMHURST | WOODSIDE

Neighborhood Top Five

❶ **MoMA PS1** (p303) Feeling inspired at the Museum of Modern Art's cross-river sibling. This cultural hub displays edgy, world-class artwork, not to mention lectures, performances and an electric summer party series.

❷ **Museum of the Moving Image** (p306) Reliving your favorite film and TV moments at Astoria's contemporary tribute to the small and silver screens.

❸ **Rockaways** (p307) Heading out to the seaside by subway (or better yet ferry) for surfing, rock-loving waterfront eateries and miles of shimmering beaches.

❹ **Roosevelt Avenue** (p313) Taking a snack crawl through Latin America, via food trucks along this melting-pot avenue.

❺ **Flushing** (p306) Immersing yourself in bustling Asian street life and feasting on chewy Chinese noodles, plump dumplings and plenty more.

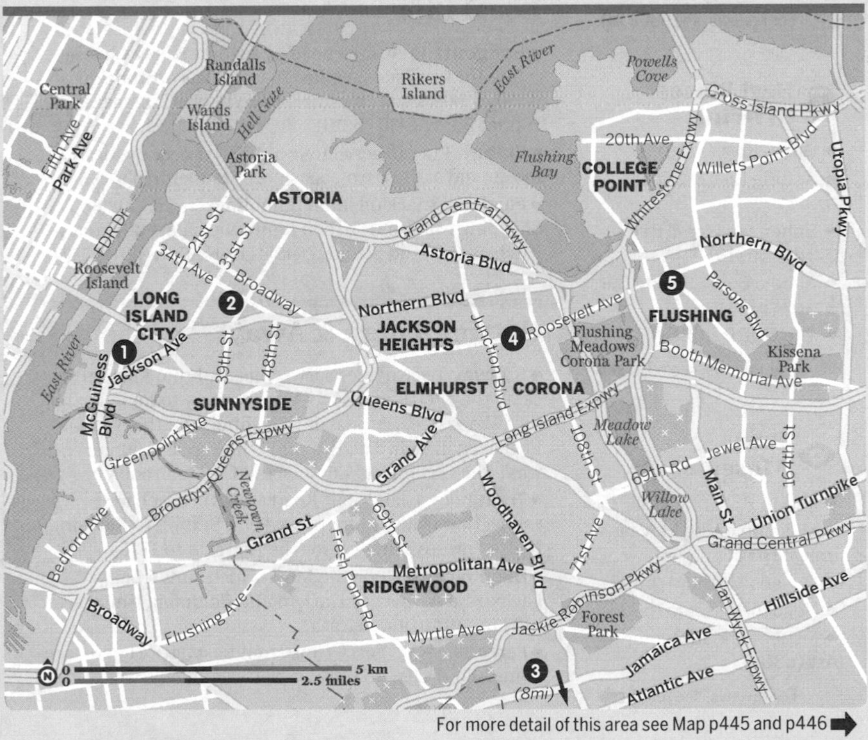

For more detail of this area see Map p445 and p446

Lonely Planet's Top Tip

Don't miss the Fisher Landau Center for Art (p305) for free modern art without the crowds. Occupying an old parachute-harness factory in Long Island City, the core of its stellar collection of painting, photography, sculpture and installations spans from the 1960s to today. The rotating exhibitions feature works from A-listers like Robert Rauschenberg, Cy Twombly and Jasper Johns.

Best Places to Eat

- Bahari (p312)
- Mombar (p312)
- Casa Enrique (p309)
- Taverna Kyclades (p312)
- Tortilleria Nixtamal (p314)

For reviews, see p308.

Best Places to Drink

- Dutch Kills (p316)
- Astoria Bier & Cheese (p316)
- Bohemian Hall & Beer Garden (p316)
- Anable Basin Sailing Bar & Grill (p316)
- The COOP (p316)

For reviews, see p316.

Best Museums

- MoMA PS1 (p303)
- Museum of the Moving Image (p306)
- Queens Museum (p307)
- Noguchi Museum (p305)
- Fisher Landau Center for Art (p305)

For reviews, see p303.

Explore Queens

Of the city's five boroughs, Queens is top dog in size and runner-up in head count. Anywhere else, it would be a major city in its own right. So where to begin?

Assuming it's not Tuesday or Wednesday (when many galleries are closed), start with a day in Long Island City, home to contemporary art hubs MoMA PS1 (p303), SculptureCenter (p305) and the Fisher Landau Center for Art (p305). Watch the sun set from Gantry Plaza State Park (p305), and sip-and-sup on neighborly Vernon Blvd.

Spend a day or two exploring Astoria, taste-testing a variety of eateries, sipping local brews, and checking out the Museum of the Moving Image (p306). If it's summer, catch an alfresco film at Socrates Sculpture Park (p305).

With its Hong Kong jumble of street foods, Asian groceries and kitschy malls, Flushing (home to NYC's biggest Chinatown) also merits a full-day adventure. Time poor? Spend the morning on Main St and Roosevelt Ave, then hit neighboring Corona for the Queens Museum (p307), Louis Armstrong House (p306) or New York Hall of Science (p308) for the kids.

If it's hot, tackle the surf at Rockaway Beach (p307), home to NYC's coolest beach scene. You can carry your board out there on the A train.

Local Life

- **Hangouts** Brew fans head to Astoria Bier & Cheese (p316) for local suds, while hipsters sans attitude quaff unfancy beers with mesmerizing views at Anable Basin Sailing Bar & Grill (p316).
- **Culture** Take an aerial tour of NYC without ever leaving the ground at the retro-cool Queens Museum (p307).
- **Flushing** Snack on lamb dumplings in the Golden Shopping Mall (p314), then ignite the palate at Hunan Kitchen of Grand Sichuan (p314) or Fu Run (p314).

Getting There & Away

- **Subway** Twelve lines serve Queens. From Manhattan, catch the N/Q/R and M to Astoria, the 7 to Long Island City, Woodside, Corona and Flushing, and the A to Rockaway Beach. The E, J and Z lines reach Jamaica, while the G connects Long Island City to Brooklyn.
- **Train** Long Island Rail Road (LIRR) has a handy connection from Manhattan's Penn Station to Flushing. It also runs to Jamaica, for the AirTrain to JFK airport.
- **Bus** Routes include the M60, which runs from LaGuardia Airport to Harlem and Columbia University in Manhattan, via Astoria.
- **Ferry** The NYC Ferry runs from East 34th St across to Long Island City, up to Roosevelt Island on to Astoria.

CY AUZE N / 500PX ©

TOP SIGHT
MOMA PS1

The smaller, hipper sibling of Manhattan's Museum of Modern Art, MoMA PS1 hunts down razor-sharp art and serves it up in an ex-school locale. Forget about lily ponds in gilded frames. Here you'll be peering at videos through floorboards and debating the meaning of nonstatic structures while staring through a hole in the wall. Nothing is predictable. Best of all, admission is free with your MoMA ticket.

Architecture

Built in the Renaissance Revival style and dating back to the early 1890s, the MoMA PS1 building housed the first school in Long Island City. Low attendance forced its closure in 1963. A three-year, award-winning restoration by LA-based architect Frederick Fisher in the mid-1990s saw the addition of the building's outdoor galleries and main staircase.

Roots, Radicals & PS1 Classics

PS1 first hit the scene in the 1970s. This was the age of Dia, Artists' Space and the New Museum – new-gen projects showcasing the city's thriving experimental, multimedia art scene. In 1976, Alanna Heiss – a supporter of art in alternative spaces – took possession of an abandoned school building in Queens and invited artists like Richard Serra, James Turrell and Keith Sonnier to create site-specific works. The end result was PS1's inaugural exhibition, *Rooms*. Surviving remnants include Richard Artschwager's oval-shaped wall 'blimps' and Alan Saret's light-channeling *The Hole at P.S.1, Fifth Solar Chthonic Wall Temple,* on the north wing's 3rd floor. These works are part of the gallery's

DON'T MISS

- Temporary and long-term exhibitions
- Summer 'Warm Up' parties
- Sunday Sessions

PRACTICALITIES

- Map p446, B5
- ☎718-784-2084
- www.momaps1.org
- 22-25 Jackson Ave, Long Island City
- suggested donation adult/child $10/free, free with MoMA ticket, Warm Up party online/at venue $18/22
- ⏲noon-6pm Thu-Mon, Warm Up parties noon-9pm Sat Jul-Aug
- [S] E, M to Court Sq-23rd St; G, 7 to Court Sq

TAKE A BREAK

M Wells Dinette (p308) gives regional ingredients a gutsy French-Canadian makeover. A few blocks from the museum, the LIC Market (p309) serves up creative American dishes.

Go online to see what exhibitions are on before heading out. Sometimes the museum has limited pieces on display, particularly between big shows.

long-term installations, which also include Pipilotti Rist's video *Selbstlos im Lavabad* (Selfless in the Bath of Lava) – viewable through the lobby floorboards – and Turrell's awe-inspiring *Meeting*, where the sky is the masterpiece.

Summer 'Warm Up' Parties

On Saturday afternoons from July to early September, rock on at one of New York's coolest weekly music/culture events, Warm Up. It's a hit with everyone from verified hipsters to plugged-in music geeks, who spill into the MoMA PS1 courtyard to eat, drink and catch a stellar lineup of top bands, experimental music and DJs. Featured artists have included acid-house deity DJ Pierre and techno pioneer Juan Atkins. It's like one big block party, albeit with better music and art than your usual neighborhood slap-up. Linked to it is the annual YAP (Young Architects Program) competition, in which one design team is selected to transform the museum courtyard with a large-scale structure that provides shade and creative party space.

Sunday Sessions

Another cultural treat is the Sunday Sessions, on Sundays from September to May. Spanning lectures, film screenings, music performances and even architectural projects, the lineup has included experimental comedy, postindustrial noise jams and Latin art-house dance. One week you might catch a symphony debut, the next an architectural performance from Madrid. Upcoming events are listed on the MoMA PS1 website.

Bookstore

Seek further enlightenment at Artbook (p318), the MoMA PS1 bookstore. Stock up on MoMA exhibition catalogs, coffee-table tomes, art-theory titles and out-of-print fodder. You'll also find contemporary culture, film and performance titles; art, architecture and design journals; magazines; CDs and new media. Scan the Artbook website for occasional readings and exhibition-based events.

SIGHTS

The Queens Tourism Council (www.itsinqueens.com) website offers information on attractions and events, while the Queens Council on the Arts (www.queenscouncilarts.org) promotes art in the borough. For a more personalized introduction, Hunter College urban-geography professor Jack Eichenbaum leads many unusual Walking Tours (p318) of Queens' ethnic neighborhoods, including a full-day walk/subway ride along the 7 train line.

Long Island City

Despite being only a 10-minute ride on the 7 train to Midtown, Long Island City remained undeveloped and undiscovered for decades. Now many years into its mini-boom, it remains on the edge of cool. Several cutting-edge art museums and repurposed industrial buildings lend it the prototypical vibe of a hip New York City neighborhood just past pioneering stage. There are great views to be had, particularly from Gantry Plaza State Par along the river.

To get there, take the G to 21st St or the New York City Ferry.

MOMA PS1 GALLERY

See p303.

★FISHER LANDAU CENTER FOR ART MUSEUM

Map p446 (www.flcart.org; 38-27 30th St, Long Island City; ⌚noon-5pm Thu-Mon; S N/Q to 39th Ave) FREE Surprisingly little visited, considering the caliber of the work shown, this private collection is a must for fans of modern and contemporary art. Whether it's Cy Twombly, Jenny Holzer, Agnes Martin or any other big name in art in the last 50 years, you'll see their work on display in this converted factory building.

Co-designed by late British architect Max Gordon (designer of London's Saatchi Gallery), the space also hosts the Columbia University School of Visual Arts MFA Thesis Exhibition each May – a highly respected showcase for talented up-and-coming artists.

NOGUCHI MUSEUM MUSEUM

Map p446 (www.noguchi.org; 9-01 33rd Rd, Long Island City; adult/child $10/free, by donation 1st Fri of the month; ⌚10am-5pm Wed-Fri, 11am-6pm Sat & Sun; S N/Q to Broadway) The art and the building here are the work of Japanese-American sculptor, furniture designer and landscape architect Isamu Noguchi, famous for iconic lamps and coffee tables, as well as elegant abstract stone sculptures. They are on display here, in serene concrete galleries and a minimalist rock garden – a complete aesthetic vision and an oasis of calm. To better understand Noguchi's work, start off in the upstairs gallery and watch the short film about his life.

The building itself was once a photo-engraving plant, located across the street from Noguchi's studio. Art aside, the space also hosts a small cafe and a gift shop, the latter stocking Noguchi-designed lamps and furniture, as well as a small range of other mid-20th-century design pieces.

SCULPTURECENTER GALLERY

Map p446 (☎718-361-1750; www.sculpture-center.org; 44-19 Purves St, Long Island City; suggested donation $5; ⌚11am-6pm Thu-Mon; S 7 to 45th Rd-Court House Sq; E, M to 23rd St-Ely Ave; G to Long Island City-Court Sq) Down a dead-end street, in a former trolley repair shop, SculptureCenter pages Berlin with its edgy art and industrial backdrop. Its hangar-like main gallery and cavernous underground space show both emerging and established artists. It's always a worthwhile add-on to a visit to nearby MoMA PS1 (p303).

SOCRATES SCULPTURE PARK PARK

Map p446 (www.socratessculpturepark.org; 32-01 Vernon Blvd, Long Island City; ⌚9am-dusk; S N/W to Broadway) FREE First carved out of an abandoned dump by sculptor Mark di Suvero, Socrates is now a city park on the river's edge with beautiful views and a rotating series of installations. Try to time a visit with free events – such as yoga on weekends from mid-May to late September, and Wednesday-night movies in July and August.

GANTRY PLAZA STATE PARK STATE PARK

Map p446 (☎718-786-6385; www.nysparks.com/parks/149; 4-09 47th Rd, Long Island City; S 7 to Vernon Blvd-Jackson Ave) This 12-acre riverside park directly across the water from the United Nations has gorgeous uninterrupted views of the Manhattan skyline. It's nicely designed, with public lounges for panoramic chilling, and attracts a good mix of Queens families. The restored gantries – in service until 1967 – are testament to the area's past as a loading dock for rail-car floats and barges.

Dating back to 1936, the giant Pepsi-Cola sign at the park's northern end is an icon of Long Island City. It once topped a nearby Pepsi bottling plant, which has been since demolished. This is also a handy spot for catching ferries across to E 34th St, or up to Roosevelt Island and Astoria.

THE KAUFMAN ARTS DISTRICT ARTS CENTER

Map p446 (www.kaufmanartsdistrict.com; 34-12 36th St; ⓢM or R train to Steinway St; N or Q train to 36th St) Anchored by the legendary Kaufman studios in Long Island City, this up-and-coming arts district is a place you'll want to check out – you can say you knew it before it becomes the new Chelsea. In addition to institutions like the Noguchi Museum, the Kaufman Arts District also puts on events and public art pieces around the area. There are plenty of restaurants and bars to pop into between gallery visits.

⊙ Astoria

Home to the largest Greek community in the world outside Greece, this is obviously the place to find amazing Greek bakeries, restaurants and gourmet shops, mainly along Broadway. An influx of Eastern European, Middle Eastern and Latino immigrants, not to mention young artsy types (especially aspiring actors), have created a rich and diverse mix. A reminder that movie-making started in Astoria in the 1920s; the Museum of the Moving Image exposes some of the mysteries of the craft with amazing exhibits and screenings in its ornate and renovated theater.

★MUSEUM OF THE MOVING IMAGE MUSEUM

Map p446 (☎718-777-6888; www.movingimage.us; 36-01 35th Ave, Astoria; adult/child $15/7, admission free 4-8pm Fri; ⊙10:30am-2pm Wed & Thu, to 8pm Fri, 11:30am-7pm Sat & Sun; ⓢM, R to Steinway St) This super-cool complex is one of the world's top film, television and video museums. Galleries show a collection of 130,000-plus artifacts, including Elizabeth Taylor's wig from *Cleopatra,* nearly everything related to *Seinfeld* and a whole room of vintage arcade games. Interactive displays – such as a DIY flipbook station – show the science behind the art.

You can also try your hand at film editing (including redubbing the 'We're not in Kansas anymore' scene from *The Wizard of Oz*), and get nostalgic over an impressive booty of vintage TVs and cameras. The museum's temporary exhibitions are usually fantastic, as are the regular film screenings – check the website for details.

GREATER ASTORIA HISTORICAL SOCIETY MUSEUM

Map p446 (☎718-278-0700; www.astorialic.org; 35-20 Broadway, 4th fl, Astoria; ⊙2-5pm Mon & Wed, noon-5pm Sat; ⓢN/Q to Broadway, M, R to Steinway) Get a glimpse of old-time Astoria at this labor-of-love community space. There's always some exhibit of neighborhood ephemera, and the group hosts lectures and films as well.

⊙ Jackson Heights

Spread out in a 50-block area from 70th to 90th Sts between Roosevelt and 34th is one of the nicest NYC neighborhoods that few New Yorkers know about. Roosevelt Ave is not to be missed. It's a veritable United Nations, best appreciated by chowing down at a restaurant or several. South Asians and Latinos from every community south of the border to the tip of Patagonia have significant presences.

To get here, take the 7 to 74th St-Broadway or E, F/M, R to Roosevelt Ave-Jackson Heights.

⊙ Flushing & Corona

The intersection of Main St and Roosevelt Ave, downtown Flushing, can feel like the Times Square of a city a world away from NYC. Immigrants from all over Asia, primarily Chinese and Korean, make up this neighborhood bursting at the seams with markets and restaurants filled with delicious and cheap delicacies.

To the southeast is Corona, most notable for the Flushing Meadows Corona Park (p308). Besides several worthwhile museums, the park (created to host the 1939 World's Fair) also contains the USTA Billie Jean King National Tennis Center (p317) where the US Open is held every August.

LOUIS ARMSTRONG HOUSE NOTABLE BUILDING

Map p445 (☎718-478-8274; www.louisarmstronghouse.org; 34-56 107th St, Corona; adult/child $10/7; ⊙10am-5pm Tue-Fri, noon-5pm Sat & Sun,

WORTH A DETOUR

ROCKAWAY BEACH

Immortalized by the Ramones' 1977 song 'Rockaway Beach,' America's largest urban beach – and one of the city's best – is just a $2.75 trip on the A train from Manhattan (or the same price on the ferry). Less crowded than Coney Island and with a wilder feel, Rockaway Beach is a long stretch with two social hubs.

On the west end, **Jacob Riis Park** (☎718-318-4300; www.nyharborparks.org/visit/jari.html; Gateway National Recreation Area, Rockaway Beach Blvd, Queens; ⏰9am-5pm Memorial Day-Labor Day; P 🚻; 🚌Q35 & Q22 to Jacob Riis Park, ⛴Sat, Sun and holidays from Pier 11 (Wall St) to Riis Landing (Rockaway)) FREE, part of the 26,000-acre Gateway National Recreation Area, mostly draws families. This area is also home to the cool green ruins of Fort Tilden, a decommissioned coastal artillery installation from WWI.

On the east end, starting around Beach 108th St, is a burgeoning scene of hipsters, artists and locavore food options, fronting the city's only designated surfing beaches (at Beach 92nd St and going east). On the boardwalk here, concrete concession booths peddle treats such as lobster rolls, ceviche and hipster pizza.

Extending from near JFK International Airport, the salty, marshy **Jamaica Bay Wildlife Refuge** covers the water north of the Rockaways' barrier island. As one of the most important migratory bird and wetland habitats along the eastern seaboard, it attracts more than 325 bird species in spring and fall, as they snap up all sorts of briny sea creatures like clams, turtles, shrimp and oysters. Each season brings different visitors. Spring features warblers and songbirds, and American woodcocks in late March. In mid-August shorebirds start to move south, landing here from Canada and fueling up for the trip to Mexico. Fall is when migrating hawks and raptors get mobile, along with ducks, geese, monarch butterflies and thousands and thousands of dragonflies. Birders and naturalists get the most action around the east pond, though casual visitors will enjoy the more scenic and better maintained west pond trail, which has a loop path of 2 miles. Just make sure to wear mud-resistant shoes, insect repellent and sunscreen, carry some water and watch out for poison ivy.

To get to the **visitor center** (☎718-318-4340; www.nyharborparks.org; Cross Bay Blvd, Broad Channel; ⏰trails sunrise-sunset, visitor center 9am-5pm; 🚌Q53 to Cross Bay Blvd/Wildlife Refuge, S A/S to Broad Channel) FREE, exit at Broad Channel station, walk west along Noel Rd to Cross Bay Blvd, turn right (north) and walk for 0.7 miles, and the center will be visible on the left side of the road.

When you're in need of sustenance, **Rippers** (☎718-634-3034; 8601 Shore Front Pkwy; cheeseburgers from $7.50; ⏰11am-8pm) is a favorite gathering spot on the boardwalk, with juicy burgers, frothy brews and a festive crowd, particularly on weekends, when there's usually live music.

A few blocks inland, the bohemian-loving **Rockaway Surf Club** (www.rockawaybeachsurfclub.com; 302 Beach 87th St; per tacos $3.50, cocktails $9; ⏰noon-11pm) serves up delicious tacos and tropical cocktails in a colorful courtyard and surfboard-studded bar.

last tour 4pm; S 7 to 103rd St-Corona Plaza) At the peak of his career and with worldwide fame at hand, legendary trumpeter Armstrong settled in this modest Queens home, and lived there until his death in 1971. The place has been immaculately preserved in groovy style, down to the dazzling turquoise kitchen fixtures. Guided tours (40 minutes) tell Armstrong's story through audio clips and insightful commentary on some of the objects connected to the great jazz man.

Satchmo shared the house with his fourth wife, Lucille Wilson, a dancer at the Cotton Club. Armstrong's den, of which he was most proud, features a portrait of the great painted by none other than Benedetto (aka Tony Bennett). During the summer, live concerts are held in the garden (tickets sell out well in advance).

QUEENS MUSEUM MUSEUM

Map p445 (QMA; ☎718-592-9700; www.queensmuseum.org; Flushing Meadows Corona Park, Queens; suggested donation adult/child $8/free; ⏰11am-5pm Wed-Sun; S 7 to 111th St or Mets-Willets Point) The Queens Museum is one of the city's most unexpected pleasures. Its most famous installation is the Panorama

WORTH A DETOUR

FARM LIFE

Frolic with cows, sheep and goats at **Queens County Farm Museum** (718-347-3276; www.queensfarm.org; 73-50 Little Neck Pkwy, Floral Park; 10am-5pm; ; Q46 to Little Neck Pkwy) FREE, the last patch of farmland within the city limits. It's a long way from Manhattan, but for anyone with an interest in urban agriculture – or kids who need a break from city energy – this is a tranquil destination. It hosts an annual powwow for tribes from all over America, plus many seasonal events (including a haunted house in late October).

of New York City, a gob-smacking 9335-sq-ft miniature New York City, with all buildings accounted for and a 15-minute dusk-to-dawn light simulation. The museum also hosts top exhibitions of global contemporary art, reflecting the diversity of Queens. A fascinating upcoming exhibit explores some of the most interesting and avant-garde NYC designs that never came to fruition, realized through drawings and 3D models.

The QM is housed in a historic building made for the 1939 World's Fair (and once home to the UN), and you'll find a retro-fabulous collection of memorabilia from both the '39 and '64 fairs on display (with reproductions in the gift shop).

FLUSHING MEADOWS CORONA PARK PARK
Map p445 (www.nycgovparks.org/parks/fmcp; Grand Central Pkwy, Corona; S 7 to Mets-Willets Point) FREE Central Queens' biggest attraction is this 1225-acre park, built for the 1939 World's Fair and dominated by Queens' most famous landmark, the stainless-steel Unisphere – it's the world's biggest globe, at 120ft high and weighing 380 tons. Facing it is the former New York City Building, now home to the fantastic Queens Museum (p307).

Just south are three weather-worn, Cold War–era New York State Pavilion Towers, part of the New York State Pavilion for the 1964 World's Fair. (You may recognize them as alien spaceships from the film *Men in Black*.) If entering the park from the north, via the 7 train, look for the 1964 World's Fair mosaics by Salvador Dalí and Andy Warhol. Also nearby is Citi Field (p318), and the USTA Billie Jean King National Tennis Center (p317). Head west over the Grand Central Pkwy to find a few more attractions, including the New York Hall of Science. The park has grounds, too, on its eastern and southern edges. The top-notch Astroturf soccer fields are popular for organized and pick-up soccer, and there's a pitch-and-putt golf course that's lit up for golfers at night.

NEW YORK HALL OF SCIENCE MUSEUM
Map p445 (718-699-0005; www.nysci.org; 47-01 111th St; adult/child $16/13, admission free 2-5pm Fri & 10-11am Sun; 9:30am-5pm Mon-Fri, 10am-6pm Sat & Sun; S 7 to 111th St) Occupying a weird 1965 building, rippling with stained glass, this science museum is unapologetically nerdy. An outdoor mini-golf course and playground don't require as much brain power.

UNISPHERE MONUMENT
Map p445 (Flushing Meadows Park; S 7 to 111th St or Mets-Willets Point) Designed for the 1964 World's Fair, this 12-story-high stainless-steel globe is the focal point of Flushing Meadows Park, and the de facto icon of Queens. (Nowadays, it's probably most recognizable as the backdrop for the Beastie Boys' *Licensed to Ill* album cover or scenes in the films *Men in Black* and *Iron Man 2*). In summer, it's ringed with fountains; at other times, it's crisscrossed by skateboarders.

EATING

Long Island City

M WELLS DINETTE CANADIAN $
Map p446 (718-786-1800; www.magasinwells.com; 22-25 Jackson Ave, Long Island City; mains $9-14; noon-6pm Thu-Mon; S E, M to 23rd St-Court Sq, G, 7 Court Sq) Like being back at school (but with better grub), this cultish nosh spot sits inside school-turned-museum MoMA PS1 (no need to pay museum admission). Desk-like tables face the open kitchen, where Quebecois head chef Hugue Dufour creates changing weekly menus that hopscotch around the globe: yakisoba omelet with plum sauce and bonito flakes, for instance.

CYCLO VIETNAMESE $
Map p446 (718-786-8309; www.cyclolic.com; 5-51 47th Ave, Long Island City; mains $9-12;

noon-10pm; ; 7 to Vernon Blvd-Jackson Ave) Set in a humdrum brick building just off Vernon Blvd, Cyclo has a cozy interior of wood-paneled walls and rustic tables – just right for noshing on those warm, perfectly crusted baguette sandwiches packed with flavorful ingredients.

Banh mi aside, there are also steaming bowls of oxtail broth pho, spicy papaya and shrimp salad, and rich clay-pot rice dishes.

SWEETLEAF CAFE $

Map p446 (917-832-6726; http://sweetleaf-coffee.com; 10-93 Jackson Ave, Long Island City; 7am-2am Mon-Fri, from 8am Sat & Sun; G train to 21st St-Van Alst, 7 train to Vernon Blvd-Jackson Ave) Looking for a place to curl up with a warm drink and a good book? Sweetleaf has a study-like atmosphere, with plush couches and chairs, making an enticing spot for a relaxing, low-key coffee shop experience. By evening, Sweetleaf transitions into a livelier drinking den with cocktails and other libations served up to a laid-back neighborhood crowd.

JOHN BROWN SMOKEHOUSE BARBECUE $

Map p446 (347-617-1120; www.jakessmokehousebbq.com; 10-43 44th Dr, Long Island City; mains $10-16; noon-10pm Mon-Thu, to 11pm Fri & Sat, to 9pm Sun; E, M to Court Sq-23rd St) Red-checked tablecloths, local craft beers on tap and the heavenly scent of beef brisket set the stage for a carnivorous feast at this Kansas City–style barbecue joint. It's an unfussy affair – order at the counter, then grab a seat there are also tables on a back terrace where bands play most nights (from 7pm to 9pm).

This place gets packed. Go early to beat the crowds.

LIC CORNER CAFE CAFE $

Map p446 (718-806-1432; 21-03 45th Rd; pastries from $3, coffee $3-5; 7am-6pm Mon-Fri, 9am-5pm Sat & Sun; E & M train to Court Sq/23rd St; 7 train to Court Sq; G train to Court Sq) As its name suggests, the Long Island City Corner Cafe is on an unassuming corner across the street from a park in Hunter's Point, Long Island City. The cafe's vibrant facade is the perfect introduction to what's inside: a cozy atmosphere, hearty pastries, housemade quiche, and luxe coffee and tea options.

CANNELLE PATISSERIE BAKERY $

Map p446 (718-937-8500; 5-11 47th Ave, Long Island City; pastries from $3; 6:30am-8pm Mon-Fri, from 7am Sat, 7am-5pm Sun; 7 to Vernon Blvd-Jackson Ave) A surprising source of flawless French pastry, this cafe sits on a slick block in new-build LIC – but one bite of a flaky croissant or a gem-like fruit tart will take you straight to Paris. This is a branch of the original business, set in an even more unlikely location: a dreary strip mall in Jackson Heights.

LIC MARKET CAFE $$

Map p446 (718-361-0013; www.licmarket.com; 21-52 44th Dr, Long Island City; mains lunch $11-14, dinner $18-28; 8am-3:30pm Mon, to 10pm Tue-Fri, 10am-10pm Sat, 10am-3:30pm Sun; ; E, M to 23rd St-Ely Ave, 7 to 45th Rd-Court House Sq) Local creatives and office workers mix at this cool little cafe, trimmed in local artwork and cooking pots. Breakfast winners include the 'sausage and onions' sandwich (fried eggs, breakfast sausage, cheddar and caramelized onion), while ever-changing lunch and dinner options can include scallops, soulful risottos and seasonal game.

CASA ENRIQUE MEXICAN $$

Map p446 (347-448-6040; www.henrinyc.com/casa-enrique.html; 5-48 49th Ave, Long Island City; mains $18-28; 5-11pm Mon-Fri, 11am-3:30pm & 5-11pm Sat & Sun; 7 to Vernon Blvd-Jackson Ave; G to 21st St/Van Alst) Don't let the unassuming facade of Casa Enrique fool you: this upscale eatery has a Michelin star and serves some of the best Mexican food in New York City. The menu is full of delicious high-end formulations of Mexican favorites, such as tequila-marinated *carne asada* (grilled skirt steak) and *mole de piaxtla* (Pueblan-style chicken and rice with a spicy chocolate sauce).

Seating is limited, so a reservation is recommended.

M WELLS STEAKHOUSE STEAK $$$

Map p446 (718-786-9060; www.magasinwells.com; 43-15 Crescent St, Long Island City; mains $24-65; 5-11pm Wed-Sat; E, M to 23rd St-Court Sq; G, 7 to Court Sq) Carnivores with a taste for decadence will appreciate Quebecois chef Hugue Dufour's satisfying take on steak. Try the showstopping New York strip, with its Korean-style maple rub, or opt for the perfectly tender Wagyu flank steak. There's also whole trout and a mussels dish for pescatarians, plus a side of poutine for homesick Canadians. Loud, exuberant ambience. Reserve on weekends.

There's no need to tip here; a 20% hospitality fee is added to all orders – with fair wages paid to all staff.

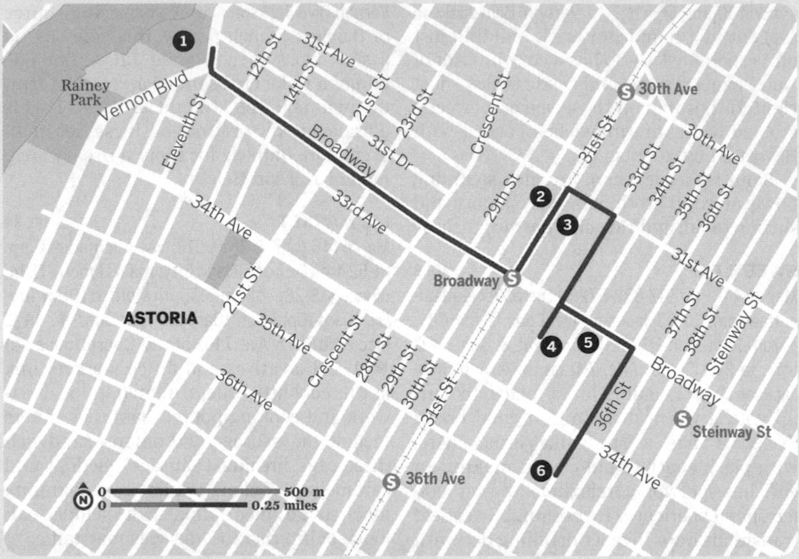

Local Life
A Stroll Through Astoria

A short hop from Midtown Manhattan, Astoria is a charmingly diverse neighborhood of restaurant-lined boulevards, tree-lined side streets and indie shops and cafes. Come with an appetite, as eating and drinking is an essential part of the Astoria experience. The best time to visit is on weekends, when the neighborhood is at its liveliest.

❶ Socrates Sculpture Park

Amid cutting-edge installations and wispy birch trees, this picturesque waterside park (p305) offers serene views across to Manhattan. It's hard to believe this abandoned landfill was once an illegal dump site. On summer weekends, there's often something afoot, including yoga and tai chi, markets and kayaking in Hallets Cove.

❷ King Souvlaki

Follow the plumes of smoke wafting along 31st St to this celebrated food truck (p311), one of the best in Astoria. Come for the pita sandwiches stuffed with mouthwatering morsels of pork, chicken or beef, along with a side of feta-topped Greek fries.

❸ Astoria Bookshop

This much-loved indie **bookstore** (Map p446; ☎718-278-2665; www.astoriabookshop.com; 31-29 31st St, Astoria; ⏱11am-7pm; S N, W to Broadway) has ample shelf space dedicated to local authors – pick up a title about the Queens dining scene or the borough's ethnic diversity. A bulwark of the community, Astoria also hosts author readings, discussion groups and even writing workshops where you can hone your narrative skills.

❹ Lockwood

You'll find loads of gift ideas in this whimsical **store** (Map p446; ☎718-626-3040; http://lockwoodshop.com; 32-15 33rd St, Astoria; ⏱11am-8pm; S N, W to Broadway), including plenty of intriguing Queens-related objects. Think vintage wall hangings, paper doll books of famous women, skull candles, scented candles, eye-catching flasks and so on. Lockwood also has a stationery store a few doors up.

Museum of the Moving Image (p306)

❺ Astoria Bier & Cheese

A neighborhood institution, this deli and drinkery (p316) serves up a wide variety of temptations, including gourmet grilled cheeses, mac and cheese plates, avocado toast and fancy sandwiches stuffed with prosciutto and other goodness. The rotating selection of craft brews is an even bigger draw. There's outdoor seating in back – ideal for warm days.

❻ George's

Set inside the Kaufman Astoria Studios, George's (p312) feels like a hidden spot with its side-door entrance, low-lit interior and vintage vibe. Step up to the bar and order one of the signature cocktails, while taking in a bit of live music and surveying the 1920s interior. There's also a full menu on hand of American classics with a modern twist.

Astoria

Spanakopita? *Khao man gai? Encebol de mariscos?* If it exists, you can devour it in Queens. Head to Long Island City for locavore eateries, and to Astoria for anything from Greek to bagels – hot spots here include 30th Ave, Broadway (between 31st and 35th Sts) and 31st Ave. Steinway Ave between Astoria Blvd and 30th Ave is Astoria's 'Little Cairo.' Further east, Elmhurst is home to a cluster of straight-outta-Bangkok Thai options, while Roosevelt Ave is perfect for a Latin food-truck crawl. At the end of the 7 subway line lies Flushing, New York's 'Chinatown without the tourists.'

★PYE BOAT NOODLE THAI $

Map p446 (☎718-685-2329; 35-13 Broadway, Astoria; noodles $10-13; ⏰11:30am-10:30pm, to 11pm Fri & Sat; ✍; ⓈN/W to Broadway; M, R to Steinway) Young Thai waitresses in matching fedoras greet you at this cute place decked out like an old-fashioned country house. The specialty is rich, star-anise-scented boat noodles, topped with crispy pork cracklings. There's also delicate seafood *yen ta fo* (mild seafood soup, tinted pink), a rarity in NYC – good with a side of papaya salad (off-menu request: add funky fermented crab).

KING SOUVLAKI FOOD TRUCK $

Map p446 (☎917-416-1189; www.facebook.com/KingSouvlaki; 31st St, near 31st Ave; mains $6-10; ⏰9am-11pm Mon-Wed, to 5am Thu-Sat, 11am-11pm Sun; ⓈN, W to Broadway) Follow the scent of char-grilled decadence (not to mention the plumes of smoke wafting along 31st St) to this celebrated food truck, one of the best in Astoria. Come for the pita sandwiches stuffed with mouthwatering morsels of pork, chicken or beef, along with a side of feta-topped Greek fries.

Cash only – though there's an ATM on the side of the truck!

JERUSALEM PITA HOUSE MIDDLE EASTERN $

Map p446 (☎718-932-8282; http://jerusalempitaastoriany.com; 25-13 30th Ave, Astoria; mains $5-11; ⏰noon-10pm; ⓈN/W train to 30th Ave) This small, family-owned restaurant makes you feel welcome the second you come in. They specialize in warm pitas stuffed with spicy, grilled meat or crispy falafel served to take away or eat quickly in the restaurant.

THE STRAND SMOKEHOUSE BARBECUE $

Map p446 (☎718-440-3231; www.thestrandsmokehouse.com; 25-27 Broadway, Astoria; BBQ per pound $16-20; ⊙4pm-midnight Mon-Thu, to 2am Fri, noon-4am Sat, noon-midnight Sun; SN or W train to Broadway) This good old-fashioned southern-style BBQ restaurant is usually one large party. There is live music on weekends and a full bar with local craft brews and moonshine cocktails. Of course, there are also hearty plates of ribs, brisket and pulled pork, plus delectable sides like homemade cornbread and spicy mac and cheese.

BROOKLYN BAGEL & COFFEE COMPANY BAKERY $

Map p446 (☎718-204-0141; www.brooklynbagelandcoffeecompany.com; 35-05 Broadway, Astoria; bagels $1.25; ⊙6am-4:30pm; SN/Q to Broadway; M, R to Steinway St) It may be in Queens, not Brooklyn, but there's little confusion about the caliber of the bagels here. With a good crust and chewy interior, they come in a number of fine variations, including sesame, onion, garlic, and wholewheat with oats and raisins. Mix and match with a dazzling repertoire of flavored cream cheese, including wasabi lox and baked apple.

★BAHARI GREEK $$

Map p446 (☎718-204-8968; 31-14 Broadway, Astoria; mains $14-29; ⊙noon-midnight; ; SN/Q to Broadway) Many of Astoria's Greek restaurants are standard grill joints. Bahari branches out with the full range of casseroles and stews: moussaka with crusty-creamy bechamel, velvety slow-cooked beans, spinach-flecked rice. A meal of these rich dishes is a bargain, especially in the elegant surroundings. (Note: fish is pricier.) Excellent staff and plenty of room, compared with most NYC restaurants.

KABAB CAFE EGYPTIAN $$

Map p446 (☎718-728-9858; 25-12 Steinway St, Astoria; mains $12-26; ⊙1-5pm & 6-10pm Tue-Sun; ; SN/Q to Astoria Blvd) Chef Ali is a larger-than-life personality and an anchor on the Steinway strip known as Little Egypt – though his creative, earthy food, often served straight from the frying pan to your plate, ranges much further than his Alexandrian roots. Start with mixed apps, for fluffy green Egyptian-style falafel, then pick any lamb dish.

Herbivores can opt for a vegetarian platter with its spread of baba ghanoush, hummus and falafel, perhaps followed by Egyptian moussaka (sautéed eggplant with zucchini, potato, tomato and spices).

MOMBAR EGYPTIAN $$

Map p446 (☎718-726-2356; 25-22 Steinway St, Astoria; mains $14-26; ⊙5-10pm Tue-Sun; ; SN/Q to Astoria Blvd) A legendary restaurant in the Steinway strip of Arab businesses, Mombar is worth a visit for the decor alone – its collage style of found objects was assembled over years as chef Mustafa saved money to open the place. It's a jewel-box setting for his refined Egyptian food; definitely get the signature *mombar*, a light, rice-stuffed sausage.

TAVERNA KYCLADES GREEK $$

Map p446 (☎718-545-8666; www.tavernakyclades.com; 33-07 Ditmars Blvd, Astoria; mains $18-32; ⊙noon-11pm Mon-Sat, to 10pm Sun; SN/Q to Ditmars Blvd) Kyclades is tops when it comes to Greek seafood – and repeat diner Bill Murray agrees. Simple classics include succulent grilled octopus and whole fish, backed up with *saganaki* (pan-fried cheese) and a hearty salad. Skip the overpriced Kyclades Specialty, and go early to beat the daunting line. (Ironically, the Manhattan location, in the East Village, is less crowded.)

GEORGE'S AT KAUFMAN ASTORIA STUDIOS AMERICAN $$

Map p446 (☎718-255-1947; www.georges.nyc; 35-11 35th Ave; mains $15-33; ⊙4-10pm Tue-Thu, to 11pm Fri & Sat, 11:30am-9pm Sun; SM, R to Steinway St) Secreted away inside the Kaufman Astoria Studios, this classy dining room and bar serves up high-end comfort fare (short ribs stroganoff, fried chicken with baby bok choy, crab cakes). If you're not up for a meal, however, it's worthwhile stopping by the bar to soak up the 1920s atmosphere, while lingering over a well-made cocktail.

There's live music, live comedy and other events plus everyday happy hour specials (from 4pm to 7pm). On warm days, the outdoor Landmark Cafe around the corner makes a fine spot for refreshment.

SEK'END SUN AMERICAN $$

Map p446 (☎917-832-6414; www.sekendsun.com; 32-11 Broadway, Queens; ⊙5pm-2am Mon-Thu, 5pm-4am Fri, 11am-4am Sat, 11am-2am Sun; ; SN/W train to Broadway) This Astoria bar and restaurant has a breezy rustic vibe that sets the mood for an impromptu happy hour or an offbeat dinner. Dig into some upscale pub grub like mac and cheese with aged cheddar and parmesan (perhaps topped with pulled pork), which make a fine accompaniment to SS's well-blended signature cocktails.

VESTA TRATTORIA & WINE BAR ITALIAN $$
Map p446 (☎718-545-5550; www.vestavino.com; 21-02 30th Ave, Astoria; pizzas $15-17, mains $19-26; ⊙11am-4pm & 5-10pm Mon-Thu, to 11pm Fri, 11am-3pm & 4:30-11pm Sat, 11am-3pm & 4-10pm Sun; S N/Q to 30th Ave) Vesta is one of those neighborhood secrets, with chatty regulars at the bar, local art on the walls and organic produce from a Brooklyn rooftop farm. The menu is simple and seasonal, with satisfying steamed mussels with garlic crostini, bubbling thin-crust pizzas and wide-ranging mains along the likes of spaghetti with calamari and anchovies, pan-seared *branzino* (sea bass), and wild boar lasagna.

Star of the popular weekend brunch is the Hangover Pizza, with spicy tomato sauce, potatoes, bacon, sausage and baked egg.

Woodside

SRIPRAPHAI THAI $$
Map p446 (☎718-899-9599; 64-13 39th Ave, Woodside; mains $12-24; ⊙11:30am-9:30pm Thu-Tue; S 7 to 69th St) The first restaurant in NYC to serve Thai food for Thai people, no punches pulled. In some ways it has been outpaced by newer, more single-minded restaurants (the menu here is epic, from all over the country), but it is still a legend and a satisfying place for a big dinner of everything from curries to heavenly fried soft shell crab. Cash only.

Jackson Heights

LITTLE TIBET TIBETAN $
Map p446 (☎718-505-8423; 72-19 Roosevelt Ave, Jackson Heights; mains $7-12; ⊙noon-10pm; S 7 to 74 St-Broadway; E, F/M, R to Roosevelt Ave-Jackson Heights) Little Tibet could be the nickname for all of Jackson Heights, where traditionally Indian shops and restaurants are slowly giving way to entrepreneurs from the Himalayas, both Tibet and Nepal. This little place has exceptional neighborhood loyalty and a cozy, wood-paneled atmosphere. Wash down the *momos* (dumplings) with a huge list of Queens microbrews.

Elmhurst

KHAO KANG THAI $
Map p446 (☎718-806-1807; 76-20 Woodside Ave, Elmhurst; meals $9-10; ⊙11am-9pm Tue-Sun;

ROOSEVELT AVENUE FOOD CRAWL

When it comes to sidewalk grazing, it's hard to beat Roosevelt Ave and its army of late-night Latino food trucks, carts and secret delis. Just one stroll from 90th St to 103rd St will have you sipping on *champurrados* (a warm, thick corn-based chocolate drink), nibbling on a *cemita* (Mexican sandwich) and making a little more room for some Ecuadoran fish stew. It's cheap, authentic and quintessentially Queens. Hungry? Then set off on a taste-testing mission of Roosevelt Ave's best.

On the south side or Roosevelt head for the intersection with Forley St. Here you'll find the celebrated food stall **Taco Veloz** (Map p446; 86-10 Roosevelt Ave, Jackson Heights; tacos from $2.50; ⊙noon-2am; S 7 to 90th St-Elmhurst), which whips up delicious tacos as well as first-rate *cemitas* ($7).

A short stroll further east along Roosevelt Ave lies the corner deli **La Esquina del Camarón** (Map p446; ☎347-885-2946; 80-02 Roosevelt Ave, Jackson Heights; shrimp cocktail $8-12; ⊙11am-2am; S 7 to 82nd St-Jackson Hts). Never mind the nondescript entrance; head to the back where you'll find a food counter where skilled staffers whip up some of the best shrimp cocktails on the planet. They come loaded with shrimp (and/or octopus) and are topped with sliced avocado – zingy, refreshing and mouthwateringly good.

Keep rolling along Roosevelt Ave to Warren St. A major Warren St star is **El Guayaquileño** (Warren St, btwn Roosevelt Ave & 40th Rd, Jackson Heights; dishes $5-11; ⊙8am-10:30pm Sun-Thu, to around 4am Fri & Sat; S 7 to Junction Blvd), famous for its Ecuadoran *encebollado* – a stew made of tuna, yuca, cilantro, onion, lemon, cumin and toasted corn kernels. It's flavorsome, wonderfully textured and a meal in itself. If you're more in the mood for something meaty, the food truck a few feet away serves up roast pig with crackling and all the fixings.

(S E, F/M, R to Roosevelt Ave-Jackson Heights; 7 to 74 St-Broadway) New-era Thai food at its best, where you can eat like a business-luncher in Bangkok, pointing at two or three hot dishes – creamy-hot pumpkin with eggs and basil, caramelized pork and more – to eat over rice. It's fast and inexpensive, but doesn't skimp on style. Desserts are a treat too.

Flushing & Corona

★TORTILLERIA NIXTAMAL MEXICAN $

Map p445 (☎718-699-2434; www.tortillerianixtamal.com; 104-05 47th Ave, Corona; tacos $3-4, mains $10-14; ⊙11am-9pm Thu & Sun, to 11pm Fri & Sat; S 7 to 103rd St-Corona Plaza) The red-and-yellow picnic benches at this lo-fi gem are never short of a roaming gastronome, here for super-authentic Mexican snacks. The secret weapon is the Rube Goldbergian machine, which transforms additive-free masa into super-tasty tacos and tamales.

The guys here are purists, their tacos adorned with a simple garnish of cilantro, onion and lime. Other must-tries include the pork-broth pozole soup, spiked with chopped onion, radish, oregano and crushed red peppers. Cool down with a *horchata fresca* (spiced rice-and-almond-milk drink) while cheering on El Tricolor.

FU RUN CHINESE $

Map p445 (☎718-321-1363; www.furunflushing.com; 40-09 Prince St, Flushing; mains $12-27; ⊙11:30am-11pm; S 7 to Flushing-Main St) Fu Run has a cult following for very good reason: its northeast Chinese cooking is extraordinary – rustic, sometimes subtle, always impeccably fried. Reconfigure your understanding of the country's flavors over sour cabbage–laced pork dumplings or the unforgettable Muslim lamb chop (deep-fried ribs dressed in dried chilies, cumin and sesame seeds).

NAN XIANG XIAO LONG BAO DUMPLINGS $

Map p445 (☎718-321-3838; 38-12 Prince St, Flushing; mains $6-10; ⊙8am-midnight; S 7 train to Main St) Juicy, savory soup dumplings; thick, sticky noodles; spicy wontons – everything you'd want from a dumpling house you'll find at Nan Xiang Xiao Long Bao. This place is a no-frills affair and is usually very busy, but tables tend to open up quickly and the dishes come out fast. Bring some friends and order in excess. Cash only.

GOLDEN SHOPPING MALL CHINESE $

Map p445 (41-36 Main St, Flushing; meals from $5; ⊙10am-10pm; S 7 to Flushing-Main St) A chaotic jumble of hanging ducks, airborne noodles and greasy Laminex tables, Golden Mall's basement food court dishes up fantastic hawker-style grub. Don't be intimidated by the lack of English menus: most stalls have at least one English speaker, and the regulars are usually happy to point out their personal favorites, whether it's Lanzhou hand-pulled noodles or spicy pig ears.

Don't miss the flavor-packed dumplings (try the pork with dill) from Tianjin Dumpling House. The unsigned entrance is easy to miss; the stairs are a few steps from 41st Rd.

NEW WORLD MALL FOOD HALL $

Map p445 (www.newworldmallny.com; Main St, btwn 41st & Roosevelt Aves, Flushing; mains from $4; ⊙10am-10pm; S 7 to Flushing-Main St) Head to the lower level for all manner of Eastern culinary wonders, from hand-pulled Lanzhou noodles to Korean-style barbecue – dumplings, sushi, bubble tea and Vietnamese pho is just the beginning. Come with an appetite. There's also a sprawling Asian supermarket in the mall. There's also an entrance on Roosevelt Ave.

HUNAN KITCHEN OF GRAND SICHUAN CHINESE $$

Map p445 (☎718-888-0553; www.hunankitchenofgrandsichuanny.com; 42-47 Main St, Flushing; mains $12-23; ⊙11am-9:30pm; S 7 to Flushing-Main St) Work up a sweat at this respectable Flushing restaurant, best known for its specialties from Hunan province. Standout dishes include a deliciously salty white-pepper smoked beef, tender chicken with hot red pepper, and lovely warming fish soup. If you're in a large group, order the house specialty: BBQ duck, Hunan-style.

ASIAN JEWELS DIM SUM $$

Map p445 (☎718-359-8600; 13330 39th Ave, Flushing; mains $14-24; ⊙11am-9:30pm; P; S 7 train to Main St station) Any food-savvy New Yorker will tell you that the city's best Chinese food is in Queens, and Asian Jewels has a solid reputation for its dim sum. This is a dim sum restaurant in the classic tradition. The restaurant is large, but very popular, so expect a wait. However, you won't be disappointed when the carts of dumplings and other intriguing delights begin to roll by.

Valet parking for customers of Asian Jewels is offered by the restaurant.

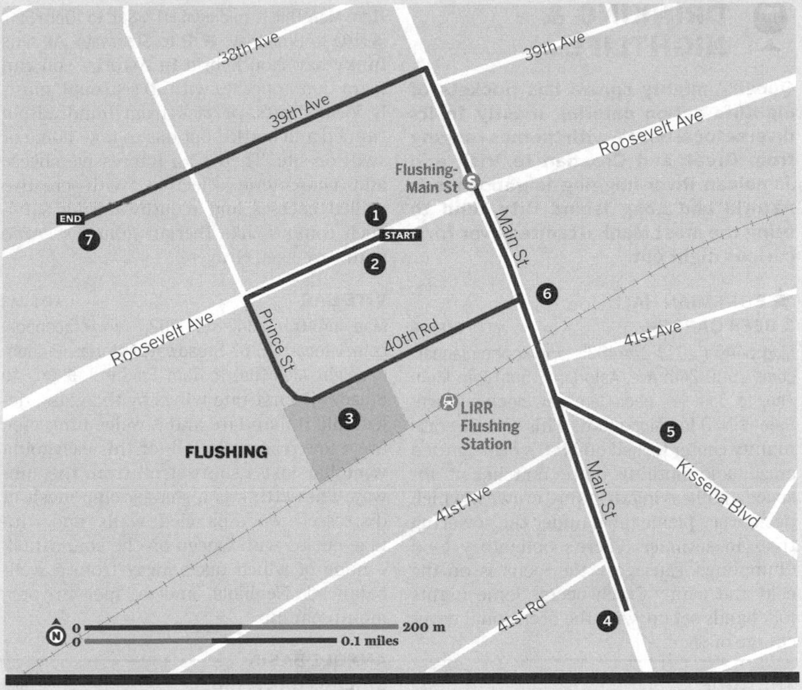

Neighborhood Walk
Chinatown in Flushing

START ROOSEVELT AVE
END 39TH AVE
LENGTH 1 MILE; 2½ HOURS

Bring an appetite before you start this food-loving stroll through Flushing, home to New York's biggest and most authentic Chinatown. Start off with a beautifully prepared oolong at **1 Fang Gourmet Tea** (p317). It's hidden in the back of a mini-mall and is a Zen-like retreat from the frenzy outside. Cross busy Roosevelt Ave and find **2 Soy Bean Chen Flower Shop**. Aside from pretty roses and fragrant peonies, this shop has a counter in front that serves up silky servings of tofu, with a side of ginger syrup for drizzling on top. Take your warm treat around the corner to **3 Bland Playground**, which has benches that provide a fine setting for relaxing.

Continue along 40 Rd and turn right onto people-packed Main St, Flushing's most vibrant thoroughfare. Just past 41st Rd, take the stairs leading down to the **4 Golden Shopping Mall** (p314). Here you'll find a chaotic jumble of food stalls serving up a variety of delicacies. Grab a seat at Tianjin Dumpling House for plump, perfectly prepared dumplings.

Once sated, walk back up Main St and turn right down Kissena Blvd. You'll shortly reach **5 Kung Fu Tea**, one of the best bubble tea purveyors in town. The choices are astonishing with dozens of varieties, including matcha red bean, taro milk green tea and mung bean – though there are also fruitier varieties like pineapple, peach and passion fruit. Drink in hand, head back to Main St and walk half a block up to the **6 New World Mall** (p314). This bustling shopping mall has a magnificent food court in the lower level. Aside from culinary goodness from China, you'll also find Korean, Thai and Vietnamese fare. Don't miss the hand-pulled noodles served up at Lan Zhou Noodles. Exiting the mall, continue up to 39th Ave and turn left. Two blocks on you'll reach the Hyatt Place Hotel. Head inside and take the elevator to the 10th floor where you'll find **7 Leaf Bar & Lounge**. High above the din below, you can nurse a cocktail while reflecting on the day's culinary adventures.

DRINKING & NIGHTLIFE

Queens' mighty sprawl has pockets of nightlife action catering mostly to its diverse local base – with themes ranging from Greek and Croatian to Irish and Jamaican. River-hugging neighborhoods Astoria and Long Island City tend to bring the most Manhattanites over for a curious night out.

★BOHEMIAN HALL & BEER GARDEN
BEER GARDEN

Map p446 (718-274-4925; www.bohemianhall.com; 29-19 24th Ave, Astoria; 5pm-1am Mon-Thu, to 3am Fri, noon-3am Sat, noon-midnight Sun; S N/Q to Astoria Blvd) This Czech community center kicked off NYC's beer-garden craze, and nothing quite matches it for space and heaving drinking crowds, which pack every picnic table under the towering trees in summer. There's obligatory food (dumplings, sausages); the focus is on the cold and foamy Czech beers. Some nights folk bands set up, with the occasional cover charge of $5.

THE COOP
BAR

Map p445 (718-358-9333; www.thecoopnyc.com; 133-42 39th Ave #103, Flushing; noon-2am Sun-Wed, noon-3am Thu-Sat; S 7 train to Main St) Crisp cocktail culture meets Korean fusion food at the COOP, located in the middle of Flushing's bustling main drag. Enjoy a full meal of Korean delicacies, or just order a round of small plates such as pork belly sliders or kimchi egg rolls (mains $12 to $25). The chic vibe makes it a perfect place to start a night out.

DUTCH KILLS
BAR

Map p446 (718-383-2724; www.dutchkillsbar.com; 27-24 Jackson Ave, Long Island City; 5pm-2am; S E, M or R train to Queens Plaza; G train to Court Sq) When you step into Dutch Kills – through an unassuming door on an old industrial building in Long Island City – you are stepping back in time. This speakeasy style bar is all about atmosphere and amazing craft cocktails. Its menu of specialty drinks is extensive, but if you're looking for an old standard, you can trust the expert bartenders to deliver.

ASTORIA BIER & CHEESE
BEER HALL

Map p446 (718-545-5588; www.astoriabierandcheese.com; 34-14 Broadway, Astoria; noon-11pm Mon-Thu, to midnight Fri & Sat, to 10pm Sun; S N/Q to Broadway; M, R to Steinway) At this funky bar-shop hybrid in Astoria, you can foam that upper lip with 10 seasonal, mostly local drafts, or pick from hundreds of canned and bottled options to take home or swill on-site. There's an impressive cheese and charcuterie selection, with creative grilled cheeses and mouthwatering sandwich combos (like Iberian *jamón serrano* with cave-aged Gruyère).

VITE BAR
WINE BAR

Map p446 (347-813-4702; www.facebook.com/vitebar; 25-07 Broadway, Astoria; noon-midnight Mon-Thu, to 1am Fri-Sun; S N/Q to Broadway) First-rate wines by the glass, delectable Italian fare and a welcoming vibe are a few reasons to fall for this easygoing wine bar just a short stroll from the subway. The setting is a shabby chic mesh of distressed wood-paneled walls and vintage curios with Queen on the soundtrack – none of which takes away from a well-balanced Nebbiola and a melt-in-your-mouth panini.

ANABLE BASIN SAILING BAR & GRILL
BAR

Map p446 (718-433-9269; www.anablebasin.com; 44th Dr & East River, Long Island City; 4:30pm-2am Mon-Fri, from 11:30am Sat & Sun; S E, M to Court Sq-23rd St) It feels like a bit of an adventure getting here, as you'll pass slumbering warehouses and industrial grit en route. Once you've arrived, however, you'll be rewarded with a mesmerizing view of Manhattan from this open-air waterside perch. Stake out a picnic table around sunset and watch the spires of Midtown light up while sipping bottles of Kona Longboard.

BIEROCRACY
BEER HALL

Map p446 (718-361-9333; www.bierocracy.com; 12-23 Jackson Ave, Long Island City; 4pm-midnight Mon-Wed, to 1am Thu, 4pm-2am Fri, 11am-2am Sat, 11am-midnight Sun; S 7 train to Vernon Blvd-Jackson Ave; G train to 21st St-Van Alst St) Anyone looking to grab a beer and watch the game will feel right at home in Bierocracy, located in Long Island City. This large beer hall is perfect for big groups and families, and comes equipped with large TVs all around the seating areas. There is an extensive beer list, as well as fish and chips, flatbread pizzas and big, doughy pretzels.

FANG GOURMET TEA TEAHOUSE

Map p445 (888-888-0216; www.fangtea.com; 135-25 Roosevelt Ave, Flushing; 10:30am-7:30pm; S 7 to Flushing-Main St) Despite the location near the heart of Flushing's Chinatown, this small tea parlor offers a peaceful retreat from the bustle beyond. Tucked in the back of a mini-mall, Fang Gourmet Tea has an astonishingly diverse selection of high-end teas, from subtle roasted oolongs to herbaceous greens as well as exotic varieties like silver needle white tea and Yunnan-style Pu'er tea.

Tastings start at $5 per person. You'll be seated at one of the small tables across from the tea maestro, who prepares perfect brews – and drinks the tea along with you!

STUDIO SQUARE BEER GARDEN

Map p446 (718-383-1001; www.studiosquare beergarden.com; 35-33 36th St, Astoria; 4pm-4am Mon-Thu, from 3pm Fri, noon-4am Sat & Sun; S M, R to 36th St; N/Q to 36th Ave) A next-generation beer garden, this place might not have big trees or old-world ambience, but it makes up for it with a massive beer menu, plenty of room to move and Queens-inspired diverse clientele. There's much going on here throughout the year, with sporting events shown on the big screen, movie nights, concerts and summertime barbecues.

ICON BAR GAY

Map p446 (917-832-6364; www.iconastoria.com; 31-84 33rd St, Astoria; 5pm-4am; S N/W train to Broadway station) New York's famous gay nightlife scene doesn't end once you leave Manhattan. Icon Bar brings strong drinks and flirtatious ambience to Astoria. It frequently hosts special DJ nights and drag shows, as well as a two-for-one happy hour on weekday evenings. All great reasons to head across the river.

THE REAL KTV KARAOKE

Map p445 (718-358-6886; 136-20 Roosevelt Ave, 3rd fl, Flushing; private rooms from $15; 1pm-4am daily; S 7 train to Main St) Few places do karaoke like Queens, and in Queens, few places do it like the Real KTV. The private rooms here are affordable, but don't skimp on the amenities – think luxurious standing mics – or atmosphere. The staff are attentive and there is a large selection of drinks, nibbly food and, most importantly, tunes to belt.

★ ENTERTAINMENT

★ TERRAZA 7 LIVE MUSIC

Map p446 (718-803-9602; http://terraza7.com; 40-19 Gleane St, Elmhurst; 4pm-4am; S 7 to 82nd St-Jackson Hts) Come to Queens for multicultural eats, then stay for equally diverse sounds at this cool bi-level performance space. It makes creative use of the tiny room, setting the live band in a loft above the bar. Latin jazz is the mainstay, but performers can hail from as far away as Morocco.

CREEK AND THE CAVE COMEDY

Map p446 (917-865-4575; www.creeklic.com; 10-93 Jackson Ave, Long Island City; 11am-2am Sun-Thu, to 4am Fri & Sat; S 7 to Vernon Blvd-Jackson Ave) The biggest and best known of a handful of fringy comedy clubs in the neighborhood, the Creek and the Cave has two stages, a Mexican restaurant, a chilled-out backyard and a bar with well-maintained pinball machines. With so much fun in one place, it's no surprise this venue is a kind of clubhouse for young comedy scenesters.

USTA BILLIE JEAN KING NATIONAL TENNIS CENTER SPECTATOR SPORT

Map p445 (718-760-6200; www.usta.com; Flushing Meadows Corona Park, Corona; 6am-midnight; S 7 to Mets-Willets Pt) The US Open, one of the city's premier sporting events, takes place in late August. As of 2016, the Arthur Ashe Stadium (capacity 23,771) now has a retractable roof, there's a new stadium (the Grandstand, which replaced the Old Grandstand), and outer courts have been renovated. Tickets usually go on sale at Ticketmaster in April or May, but are hard to get for marquee games. General admission to early rounds is easier.

The USTA has 12 indoor DecoTurf courts, 19 field courts, four climate-controlled clay bubbled courts, and three stadium courts that can be hired (hourly rates vary). Reservations can be made up to two days in advance.

CITI FIELD STADIUM

Map p445 (www.newyork.mets.mlb.com; 120-01 Roosevelt Ave, Flushing; S 7 to Mets Willets Point) The home of the New York Mets, the city's underdog baseball team, Citi Field opened in 2009, replacing the earlier Mets HQ, Shea Stadium. The exterior facade features a repeated arches pattern, somewhat old-fashioned compared to the very contemporary interior features – and the food offerings, about as far removed from old-timey hot dogs and peanuts as you can get, range the gamut from barbecued brisket to thin-crust pizza. It also houses a small Mets Hall of Fame and museum.

SHOPPING

LOVEDAY 31 — VINTAGE

Map p446 (☎718-728-4057; www.facebook.com/Loveday31nyc; 3306 31st Ave, Astoria; ⏰1-8pm Tue-Fri, from noon Sat, noon-7pm Sun; Ⓢ N, W to 30th Ave) Fashion-conscious Astorians have a certain fondness for this sweet little boutique, with its well-curated selection of dresses, blouses, tops, scarves, shoes, jewelry and sunglasses. Bonus points for the helpful staff. The prices are quite reasonable, and there's usually a discount rack in front.

MIMI & MO — FASHION & ACCESSORIES

Map p446 (☎718-440-8585; www.mimiandmonyc.com; 4545 Center Blvd, Long Island City; ⏰11am-7pm Mon-Sat, to 5pm Sun; Ⓢ7 to Vernon Blvd-Jackson Ave) Near the waterfront, this sunny boutique stocks a fine assortment of wares, including soft cotton graphic T-shirts, Herschel hats, Happy Socks, Nest candles and one-of-a-kind gift cards. There's gear for kids too: colored pencils, crafty games and clothing among other things.

ARTBOOK — BOOKS

Map p446 (☎718-433-1088; www.artbook.com/artbookps1.html; 22-25 Jackson Ave, Long Island City; ⏰noon-6pm Thu-Mon; Ⓢ E, M to 23rd St-Court Sq; G, 7 to Court Sq) The bookshop at MoMA PS1 is, appropriately, well stocked with beautiful tomes and eye-popping periodicals.

SPORTS & ACTIVITIES

WORLD'S FARE TOURS — WALKING

(www.chopsticksandmarrow.com; 2/3hr tours incl food $75/85) Dedicated Queens eater Joe DiStefano leads three different culinary tours around the borough's fantastic ethnic eateries. Tours focus on Flushing's vibrant Chinatown, the Himalayan dumpling eateries clustered in Jackson Heights or the Southeast Asian goodness of Elmhurst.

CLIFFS — CLIMBING

Map p446 (☎718-729-7625; www.thecliffsclimbing.com; 11-11 44th Dr, Long Island City; day pass $30, shoes/harness rental $6/5; ⏰6am-midnight Mon-Fri, 9am-10pm Sat & Sun; Ⓢ E, M to Court Sq-23rd St; 7 to Court Sq) New York's largest indoor climbing facility has more than 30,000 sq ft of climbing surface, with some 125 top-rope stations, 16ft top-out bouldering, a rappel tower and auto-belays for climbers without a partner. There's also a gym with cardiovascular machines and exercise equipment, plus group classes (yoga, core workouts).

NEW YORK SPA CASTLE — SPA

(☎718-939-6300; http://ny.spacastleusa.com; 131-10 11th Ave, College Point; weekday/weekend $40/50; ⏰8am-midnight; Ⓢ7 to Flushing-Main St) A slice of cutting-edge Korean bathhouse culture in an industrial corner of Queens, this 100,000-sq-ft spa complex is a bubbling dream of mineral and massage pools, saunas of dazzling variety, steam rooms and waterfalls. It also has a food court, beauty treatments and massages (30 minutes from $50). Avoid the place on weekends as it gets packed.

A free shuttle bus runs to/from the One Boutique Hotel near the corner of Northern Blvd and Union St, a few blocks north of the Flushing–Main St subway station. Shuttles generally depart every 10 and 40 minutes past the hour – but check the schedule online before making the trip out.

GEOGRAPHY OF NEW YORK CITY WITH JACK EICHENBAUM — WALKING

(☎718-961-8406; www.geognyc.com; 2hr/full-day tour $20/49) Urban geographer Jack Eichenbaum leads insightful walking (and sometimes subway) tours around Queens, focusing on the strange collisions between planning and reality, history and diverse modern use.

QUEENS HISTORICAL SOCIETY — WALKING

Map p445 (☎718-939-0647; www.queenshistoricalsociety.org; 143-35 37th Ave, Flushing; admission $5, tours from $20; ⏰2:30-4:30pm Tue, Sat & Sun; Ⓢ7 to Flushing-Main St) Set in the 18th-century Kingsland Homestead, this group has a small museum and offers walking tours through various neighborhoods in Queens. These include nearby sites associated with early religious-freedom movements and later Underground Railroad efforts.

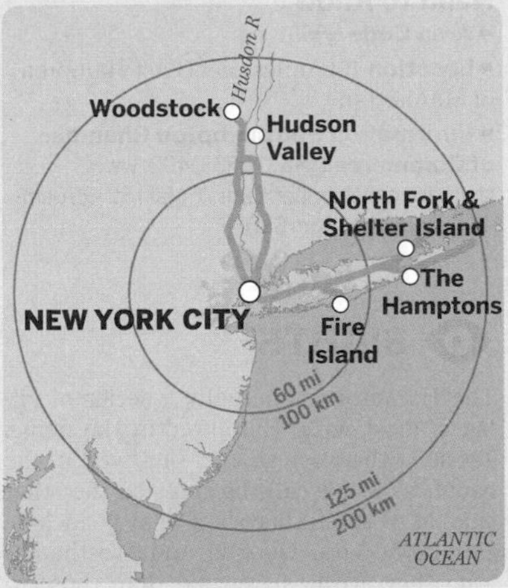

Day Trips from New York City

The Hamptons p320

New York's version of Malibu is a sweeping coastline studded with opulent mansions that host see-and-be-seen summer parties. Surprises include Native American sites, charming village main streets and wild state parks.

Fire Island p322

This car-free getaway ramps up in summer with tiny rental bungalows, chill beach bars and, at one end, a famous gay scene, roaring with drag queens and carefree clubs. The wild setting, with sand streets and miles of beaches, restores calm.

North Fork & Shelter Island p323

Wine tasting at Long Island's vineyards is a fun day's ramble, capped by main-street strolling and alfresco dining at waterside Greenport.

Hudson Valley p325

You could spend weeks exploring this region, with great hiking, open air sculpture, charming towns and historic homes of American greats (Irving, Roosevelt and Vanderbilt included).

Woodstock p327

Supplement your pilgrimage to hippiedom with a round of antiquing and quiet walks in protected parks.

The Hamptons

Explore

This string of villages is a summer escape for Manhattan's wealthiest, who zip to mansions by helicopter. Mere mortals take the Hampton Jitney bus and chip in on rowdy rental houses. Behind the glitz is a long cultural history, as noted artists and writers have lived here. Beneath the glamour, the gritty and life-risking tradition of fishing continues. The area is small, connected by often traffic-clogged Montauk Hwy.

The Best...

➡ **Sight** Pollock-Krasner House (p321)

➡ **Place to Eat** Clam Bar at Napeague (p321)

➡ **Place for a Beach Stroll** Montauk Point State Park (p321)

Top Tip

Those in search of summer solitude should plan a visit on a weekday, as the weekends are stuffed to the gills with refugees from the urban jungle.

Getting There & Away

➡ **Car** Take the Midtown Tunnel out of Manhattan onto I-495/Long Island Expwy.

➡ **Bus** The Hampton Jitney (www.hamptonjitney.com; one way $33) is a 'luxury' express bus. Its Montauk line departs from Manhattan's East Side, with stops on Lexington Ave between 77th and 76th Sts, then 69th St, 59th St and 40th St. It makes stops at villages along Rte 27 in the Hamptons.

➡ **Train** The Long Island Rail Road (LIRR; www.mta.info/lirr; furthest zone one way off-peak/peak $22/30) leaves from Penn Station in Manhattan, making stops in West Hampton, Southampton, Bridgehampton, East Hampton and Montauk.

Getting Around

The app-driven, cool turquoise converted school buses offered by Hampton Hopper (www.hamptonhopper.com) are an economical, hassle-free way around the towns and run into the bar hours.

Need to Know

➡ **Area Code** 631

➡ **Location** 100 miles east (East Hampton) of Manhattan

➡ **Information Southampton Chamber of Commerce** (631-283-0402; www.southamptonchamber.com; 76 Main St; 10am-4pm Mon-Fri, to 2pm Sat)

SIGHTS

The Hamptons is actually a series of villages, most with 'Hampton' in the name. Those at the western end – or 'west of the canal,' as locals call the spots on the other side of the Shinnecock Canal – include Hampton Bays, Quogue and Westhampton. They are less frenzied than those to the east, which start with the village of Southampton.

Southampton

Compared with some of its neighbors, Southampton is an old-money, rather conservative spot. It's home to sprawling old mansions, awe-inspiring churches, a main street with no 'beachwear' allowed, and some lovely beaches.

PARRISH ART MUSEUM MUSEUM

(631-283-2118; www.parrishart.org; 279 Montauk Hwy, Water Mill; adult/child $10/free, Wed free; 10am-5pm Mon, Wed, Thu, Sat & Sun, to 8pm Fri) In a sleek long barn designed by Herzog & de Meuron, this institution spotlights local artists such as Jackson Pollock, Willem de Kooning and Chuck Close.

For more Pollock, make reservations to see his nearby paint-drizzled studio and home.

SOUTHAMPTON HISTORICAL MUSEUM MUSEUM

(631-283-2494; www.southamptonhistoricalmuseum.org; 17 Meeting House Lane; adult/child $4/free; 11am-4pm Wed-Sat Mar-Dec) Before the Hamptons was the Hamptons, there was this clutch of buildings, now nicely maintained, and spread around Southampton. The main museum is Rogers Mansion, once owned by a whaling captain. Also visit a former dry-goods store, now occupied by a local jeweler, around the corner on Main St; and a 17th-century homestead, the Halsey House (Saturday only July to October).

Bridgehampton & Sag Harbor

To the east of Southampton, Bridgehampton is tiny but packed with trendy boutiques and restaurants. Turn north here and go 7 miles north to reach the old whaling town of Sag Harbor, on Peconic Bay, edged with historic homes. You can pick up a walking-tour map at the Sag Harbor Chamber of Commerce on Long Wharf at the end of Main St.

SAG HARBOR WHALING & HISTORICAL MUSEUM MUSEUM
(631-725-0770; www.sagharborwhalingmuseum.org; 200 Main St; adult/child $6/2; 10am-5pm Apr-Nov) The cool collection here includes actual artifacts from 19th-century whaling ships: sharp flensing knives, battered pots for rendering blubber, delicate scrimshaw and more. It's a bit surreal to see photos of the giant mammals in a village that's now a cute resort town.

East Hampton

Don't be fooled by the oh-so-casual-looking summer attire, heavy on pastels and sweaters tied around the neck – the sunglasses alone probably cost a month's rent. Some of the highest-profile celebrities have homes here.

EAST HAMPTON TOWN MARINE MUSEUM MUSEUM
(www.easthamptonhistory.org; 301 Bluff Rd, Amagansett; $4; 10am-5pm Sat, noon-5pm Sun Apr-Oct) One of your last outposts before you drive on to Montauk, this small museum dedicated to the fishing and whaling industries is as interesting as its counterpart in Sag Harbor, full of old harpoons, boats half the size of their prey, and a beautiful black-and-white photographic tribute to the local fishers and their families.

POLLOCK-KRASNER HOUSE ARTS CENTER
(631-324-4929; www.stonybrook.edu/pkhouse; 830 Springs Fireplace Rd; general admission $5, guided tours $10; 1-5pm Thu-Sat May-Oct) Tour the home of husband-and-wife art stars Jackson Pollock and Lee Krasner – worth it just to see the paint-spattered floor of Pollock's studio. Reservations required for the guided tour at noon.

Montauk

Once a sleepy and humble stepsister to the Hamptons, these days Montauk, at the far eastern end of Long Island, has developed a cool reputation for the surfing beach Ditch Plains. Now there are affluent hipsters and boho-chic hotels, but the area is still far more of a democratic scene than the Hamptons, with proudly blue-collar residents and casual seafood restaurants.

'The End,' as Montauk is affectionately called, is buffered from the Hamptons by the forested dunes of Hither Hills State Park, where camping, fishing and hiking are options. The road divides just before the park – go straight through, or meander along the beachfront on Old Montauk Hwy. The roads converge in town, then wind up at the far eastern tip of the island, in **Montauk Point State Park** (631-668-3781; www.parks.ny.gov; 2000 Montauk Hwy/Rte 27; per car $8; dawn-dusk), with **Montauk Point Lighthouse** (631-668-2544; www.montauklighthouse.com; 2000 Montauk Hwy; adult/child $11/4; 10:30am-5:30pm Sun-Fri, to 7pm Sat mid-Jun–Aug, reduced hours mid-Apr–mid-Jun & Sep-Nov) as a marker.

EATING

CANDY KITCHEN DINER $
(631-537-9885; 2391 Montauk Hwy, Bridgehampton; mains $5-12; 7am-9pm;) An antidote to glitz, this corner diner has been serving good soups, homemade ice cream and other staples since 1925. Its policy is similarly old-school – cash only, please.

★**CLAM BAR AT NAPEAGUE** SEAFOOD $$
(631-267-6348; www.clambarhamptons.com; 2025 Montauk Hwy, Amagansett; $15-30; 11:30am-6pm Apr-Oct, 11:30am-6pm Sat & Sun Nov & Dec) You won't get fresher seafood or a saltier waitstaff, and holy mackerel, those lobster rolls are good, even if you choke a bit on the price. Three decades in business – the public has spoken – with cash only, of course. Locals favor this one. Find it on the road between Amagansett and Montauk.

NICK & TONI'S MEDITERRANEAN $$$
(☎631-324-3550; www.nickandtonis.com; 136 N Main St, East Hampton; pizzas $17, mains $24-42; ⏲6-10pm Mon, Wed & Thu, to 11pm Fri & Sat, 11:30am-2:30pm & 6-10pm Sun) This Hamptons institution serves finely prepared Italian specialties using locally sourced ingredients; wood-fired pizzas are available on Monday, Thursday and Sunday. Despite attracting celebrity regulars, nonfamous names are treated well and can even get a table.

Fire Island

Explore

Fire Island is a skinny, 50-mile-long barrier island most notable for the absence of cars. Sand streets, concrete paths and boardwalks connect the dozen or so tiny residential communities, and the only traffic is fat-tire bikes and the little wagons regulars haul their belongings in. Several enclaves are famed getaways for the gay community, but there's something for everyone here, including families, couples and single travelers – gay and straight alike. The island is federally protected as the Fire Island National Seashore, and much of it is wild dunes and windswept forest. In summer, expect hamlets jam-packed with nightclubs next to neighboring stretches of sand where you'll find nothing but pitched tents and deer. Don't forget bug repellent: the mosquitoes are both fierce and abundant on Fire Island. While day trips are easy here, staying for a night or two is a real treat (even if hotel offerings aren't great), especially in the quieter spring and fall.

The Best...

- **Sight** Sunken Forest (p322)
- **Place to Eat** Sand Castle (p323)
- **Place to Drink** CJ's (p323)

Top Tip

On summer weekends, skip out before 3pm on Sunday or (better) spend the night and leave Monday – the line for the ferry on Sunday evenings is impossible.

Getting There & Away

- **Car** You can drive to Fire Island by taking the Long Island Expwy to Exit 53 (Bayshore), 59 (Sayville) or 63 (Patchogue).
- **Train** Take the LIRR to one of three stations with connections to the ferries: Patchogue, Bayshore or Sayville.
- **Ferry Fire Island Ferries** (☎631-665-3600; www.fireislandferries.com; 99 Maple Ave, Bay Shore; one-way adult/child $10/5, 1am ferry $19) run from near the Bay Shore LIRR station to Kismet, Ocean Beach and other western communities. Sayville Ferry Service goes from Sayville to Cherry Grove and Fire Island Pines. Davis Park Ferry goes to Davis Park and Watch Hill – the easternmost ferry-access point of the island.

Need to Know

- **Area Code** ☎631
- **Location** 60 miles east of Manhattan
- **Information** (www.fireisland.com)

SIGHTS

The gem-like parts of Fire Island are the car-free zones in the center (rather than the ends, reached by causeways). Davis Park, Fair Harbor, Kismet, Ocean Bay Park and Ocean Beach combine small summer homes with tiny clusters of basic grocery stores and restaurants. Of these communities, Ocean Beach ('OB' to locals) is the liveliest, with a miniature downtown by the ferry port and a little strip of bars. Perhaps the most infamous villages are those that have evolved into gay destinations: Cherry Grove and The Pines, in the center of Fire Island. Biking between towns isn't feasible, as streets turn into deep sand. For exploring further than you can walk, Fire Island Water Taxi runs a lateral ferry service along the bay side – but this shuts down in October, along with most other tourist-oriented businesses.

SUNKEN FOREST FOREST
(☎631-597-6183; www.nps.gov/fiis; Fire Island; ⏲visitor center mid-May–mid-Oct) FREE This 300-year-old forest, a surprisingly dense stretch of trees behind the dunes, is easily accessible via a 1.5-mile boardwalk trail

looping through it. It's pleasantly shady in summer, and vividly colored when the leaves change in fall. It's accessible by its own ferry stop (Sailors Haven, where there's also a visitor center), or a long walk in the winter season, after the ferry shuts down. Ranger-guided tours available.

The beach straight south of here is also an impressively wild, yet reasonably accessible, stretch of the island.

EATING & DRINKING

SAND CASTLE SEAFOOD **$$**
(☎631-597-4174; www.fireislandsandcastle.com; 106 Lewis Walk, Cherry Grove, Fire Island; mains $15-30; ⏲11am-11pm Mon, Tue & Thu-Sat, 9:30am-11pm Sun May-Sep) One of Fire Island's only oceanfront (rather than bayfront) options, Sand Castle serves up satisfying appetizers (fried calamari, portobello fries) and lots of seafood temptations (mussels, crab cakes, seared sea scallops). Nice cocktails and people-watching.

CJ'S AMERICAN **$$**
(☎631-583-9890; www.palmshotelfireisland.com; 479 Bay Ave, Ocean Beach, Fire Island; mains $12-18; ⏲11am-3am May-Sep) Open year-round, CJ's is raucous and fun and a great place to wait for your ferry. It's packed on summer weekend nights, so get here early. Renowned for its 'rocket fuel' frozen drink, it's owned by the nearby Palms Hotel.

WORTH A DETOUR

LONG BEACH

Beautiful Long Beach, one of the best stretches of sand in the area, is only a few miles outside New York City's limits. It's easily accessible by train and has clean beaches, a hoppin' main strip with ice-cream shops and eateries within walking distance of the ocean, a thriving surf scene and many city hipsters. The downside: a $15 day-use fee. Long Island Rail Road runs 'beach getaways,' which include discounted admission and round-trip train fare during the summer, with departures from both Penn Station and Atlantic Terminal in Brooklyn.

North Fork & Shelter Island

Explore

The North Fork of Long Island is known for its bucolic farmland and vineyards (though weekends can draw rowdy limoloads on winery crawls). Rte 25, the main road through the towns of **Jamesport**, **Cutchogue** and **Southold**, is pretty and edged with farm stands.

The largest town on the North Fork is **Greenport**, a laid-back place with working fishing boats, a history in whaling, and an old carousel in its Harbor Front Park. It's compact and easily walkable from the LIRR station.

Like a little pearl in Long Island's claw, Shelter Island rests between the North and South Forks. The island is a smaller, lower-key version of the Hamptons, with a touch of maritime New England. Parking is limited; long **Crescent Beach**, for instance, has spots only by permit. If you don't mind a few hills, it's a nice place to visit by bike.

The Best...

- ➡ **Sight** Mashomack Nature Preserve (p324)
- ➡ **Place to Eat** North Fork Table & Inn (p325)
- ➡ **Place to Drink** Pugliese Vineyards (p324)

Top Tip

The North Folk wineries are an easy DIY adventure. Consider taking the train out to Long Island and renting a car there (Riverhead is a good place to look). Prices are cheaper than in Manhattan and you'll save time, gas and frustration.

Getting There & Away

➡ **Bus** The Hampton Jitney bus picks up passengers on Manhattan's East Side on 96th, 83rd, 77th, 69th, 59th and 40th Sts. It makes stops in 10 North Fork villages.

➡ **Car** Take the Midtown Tunnel out of Manhattan, which will take you onto I-495/Long Island Expwy. Take this until

WORTH A DETOUR

JONES BEACH

Jones Beach State Park (☎516-785-1600; www.parks.ny.gov; 1 Ocean Pkwy, Wantagh; per car $10, lounge chairs $10, pools adult/child $3/1, mini-golf $5; ⏲hours vary by area) is 6.5 miles of clean sand covered with bodies. Its character differs depending on which 'field' you choose – for example, 2 is for the surfers and 6 is for families, and there's a gay beach way east – but it's a scene no matter where you spread your blanket.

The ocean gets quite warm by midsummer (up to about 70°F) and there are plenty of lifeguards. In between sunning and riding waves you might also hop into one of the two massive on-site pools for a swim; play shuffleboard or basketball on beachside courts; stroll the 2-mile boardwalk; visit the still waters of the bay beach; or, at Castles in the Sand, learn how master-builder Robert Moses transformed Long Island with the creation of Jones Beach in the 1940s.

Biking and running are allowed along a 4-mile path that stretches through the park, and there are places to rent bikes along the beach. When the sun goes down, you can grill at one of the many barbecues in the sand, grab burgers at the few local restaurants near the beach, or head to the **Jones Beach Theater** (Northwell Health at Jones Beach Theater; ☎866-558-8468, 516-785-1600; www.jonesbeach.com; 1000 Ocean Pkwy, Wantagh; ⏲concerts May-Sep), where alfresco concerts under the stars feature famous pop stars.

it ends at Riverhead and follow signs onto Rte 25 for all points east.

➡ **Train** The LIRR line is the Ronkonkoma Branch, with trips leaving from Penn Station and Brooklyn and running all the way out to Greenport.

Need to Know

➡ **Area Code** ☎631

➡ **Location** 100 miles east of Manhattan

➡ **Information** Long Island Wine Council (☎631-369-5887; www.liwines.com)

SIGHTS

MASHOMACK NATURE PRESERVE — NATURE RESERVE

(☎631-749-1001; www.shelter-island.org/mashomack.html; Rte 114, Shelter Island; donation adult/child $3/2; ⏲9am-5pm Mar-Sep, to 4pm Oct-Feb) The 2000 acres of this Shelter Island reserve, shot through with creeks and marshes, are great for kayaking, birding and hiking (no cycling allowed). Take precautions against ticks, an ever-present problem on the island.

ORIENT BEACH STATE PARK — BEACH

(☎631-323-2440; www.parks.ny.gov; 40000 Main Rd, Orient; per car $10, kayaks per hr $25; ⏲8am-dusk, swimming only Jul-Aug) A sandy slip of land at the end of the North Fork where you can swim in the calm ocean water (July and August) or rent kayaks to paddle in the small bay. True believers can view four different lighthouses, including the Orient Point Lighthouse, known to sailors as 'the coffee pot' for its stout bearing.

PUGLIESE VINEYARDS — WINERY

(☎631-734-4057; www.pugliesevineyards.com; 34515 Main Rd, Cutchogue; tastings from $12; ⏲11am-5pm Sun-Fri, to 6pm Sat) Producing wine since 1980, Pugliese does especially nice sparkling varieties. The winery is pleasantly family-run (with some vintages named after favorite aunts) and small scale, unlike some of its more corporate-feeling neighbors. Enjoy a sip next to the koi pond outside.

LENZ WINERY — WINERY

(☎631-734-6010; www.lenzwine.com; 38355 Main Rd, Peconic; ⏲10am-6pm Jun-Sep, to 5pm Oct-May) Established in 1978, this is one of the oldest North Fork wineries, and still one of the more eclectic, focusing on European-style wines. The sparkling wines and Gewürztraminer are especially good. Flights from $12.

VINTAGE TOURS — WINE

(☎631-765-4689; www.vintagetour1.com; tours incl lunch $99-112) Drink all you like – a driver takes care of the rest on this five- to six-hour tour of four wineries in the North Fork, with a behind-the-scenes peek at one of the operations. Pick-up is from your lodgings.

EATING

LOVE LANE KITCHEN MODERN AMERICAN $$

(☎631-298-8989; www.lovelanekitchen.com; 240 Love Lane, Mattituck; mains lunch $13-16, dinner $16-32; ⏲7am-4pm Tue & Wed, 8am-9:30pm Thu-Mon) At this popular place on a cute street, local meat and vegetables drive the global-diner menu: burgers, of course, plus spicy chickpeas and duck tagine.

NORTH FORK TABLE & INN AMERICAN $$$

(☎631-765-0177; www.nofoti.com; 57225 Main Rd, Southold; 3-course set menu $70; ⏲5:30-8pm Mon, Thu & Sun, to 10pm Fri & Sat) A favorite foodies' escape, this four-room inn (rooms from $250) has an excellent farm-to-table restaurant, run by alums of the esteemed Manhattan restaurant Gramercy Tavern. Dinner is served Thursday to Monday, but if you're hankering for a gourmand-to-go lunch ($11 to $15), the inn's food truck is parked outside on those days from 11:30am to 3:30pm.

CLAUDIO'S SEAFOOD $$$

(☎631-477-0627; www.claudios.com; 111 Main St, Greenport; mains $25-36; ⏲11:30am-9pm Sun-Thu, to 10pm Fri & Sat May-Oct) A Greenport legend, owned by the Portuguese Claudio family since 1870. For a casual meal, hit Claudio's Clam Bar, on the nearby pier.

Hudson Valley

Explore

Winding roads along the Hudson River take you by picturesque farms, Victorian cottages, apple orchards and old-money mansions built by New York's elite. Painters of the Hudson River School romanticized these landscapes – you can see their work at art museums in the area as well as in NYC. Autumn is a particularly beautiful time for a trip up this way. The eastern side of the river feels more populated – less so the further north you go – while the western side has a rural feel, with hills leading into the Catskills mountain region.

The Best...

- **Sight** Dia: Beacon (p326)
- **Place to Eat** Roundhouse Restaurant & Lounge (p327)
- **Place to Hike** Harriman State Park (p326)

Top Tip

Foodies should gravitate toward Rhinebeck or Beacon, which have some of the best restaurants in the area.

Getting There & Away

- **Car** From Manhattan, take the Henry Hudson Pkwy across the George Washington Bridge (I-95) to Palisades Pkwy. Head for the New York State Thruway to Rte 9W or Rte 9, the principal scenic river routes. You can also take the Taconic State Pkwy north from Ossining, a pretty road in autumn.
- **Bus** Short Line (www.coachusa.com) runs regular trips to Bear Mountain, Harriman, Hyde Park, Rhinebeck and other destinations.
- **Train** The Metro-North (www.mta.info/mnr) commuter train makes several stops on the Lower and Middle Hudson Valleys (take the Hudson Line). Amtrak runs to Hudson.

Need to Know

- **Area Code** ☎845
- **Location** 95 miles north (Hyde Park) of Manhattan
- **Information Dutchess Tourism** (☎800-445-3131; www.dutchesstourism.com; 3 Neptune Rd; ⏲8am-5pm Mon-Fri), **Hudson Valley Network** (www.hudsonvalleyvoyager.com)

SIGHTS

Lower Hudson Valley

Several magnificent homes can be found near Tarrytown and Sleepy Hollow, east of the Hudson. Further north, the village of Cold Spring offers good hiking on trails not far from the train station. For arts, the formerly industrial Beacon, also easily reached by train, has been revived as an outpost of the avant-garde. If you have a car, cross to the Hudson's west bank to explore Harriman State Park and adjacent Bear Mountain State Park, with views down to Manhattan from its 1303ft peak.

★DIA: BEACON GALLERY

(☎845-440-0100; www.diaart.org; 3 Beekman St; adult/child $15/free; ⏰11am-6pm Thu-Mon Apr-Oct, 11am-4pm Fri-Mon Nov-Mar) The 300,000 sq ft of a former Nabisco box printing factory beside the Hudson River is now a storehouse for a series of stunning monumental works by the likes of Richard Serra, Dan Flavin, Louise Bourgeois and Gerhard Richter. The permanent collection is complemented by temporary shows of large-scale sculptures and installations, making this a must-see for contemporary art fans.

HARRIMAN STATE PARK STATE PARK

(☎845-947-2444; www.parks.ny.gov; Seven Lakes Dr, Bear Mountain Circle, Ramapo; per car Apr-Oct $10; ⏰dawn-dusk) This park on the west side of the Hudson covers 72 sq miles and provides swimming, hiking, camping, 200 miles of walking trails, and a visitor center.

A seven-plus mile section of the **Appalachian Trail** (www.appalachiantrail.org) runs through here and it's not uncommon to see grizzled hikers with walking sticks, loaded down with packs, alongside the highway or peeking out from the forest like creatures from a secret world.

BEAR MOUNTAIN STATE PARK STATE PARK

(☎845-786-2701; www.parks.ny.gov; Palisades Pkwy/Rte 6, Bear Mountain; per car Apr-Oct $10; ⏰8am-dusk) The main draw here is views of the Manhattan skyline from the 1303ft peak (accessible by car), but there's also ice skating in winter and boating and swimming in summer. There are several scenic roads snaking their way past secluded lakes with gorgeous vistas.

STORM KING ART CENTER GALLERY

(☎845-534-3115; www.stormking.org; 1 Museum Rd, off Old Pleasant Hill Rd, New Windsor; adult/child $18/8; ⏰10am-5:30pm Wed-Sun Apr-Oct, to 4:30pm Nov) This 500-acre sculpture park, established in 1960, has works by the likes of Barbara Hepworth, Mark di Suvero, Andy Goldsworthy and Isamu Noguchi. All have been carefully sited across the grassy estate's natural breaks and curves.

There's also a visitor center, a cafe and some indoor galleries. Check the website for details of package bus tours from NYC.

SUNNYSIDE HISTORIC BUILDING

(☎914-591-8763, Mon-Fri 914-631-8200; www.hudsonvalley.org; 3 W Sunnyside Lane, Tarrytown; adult/child $12/6; ⏰tours 10:30am-3:30pm Wed-Sun May–mid-Nov) Washington Irving, famous for tales such as *The Legend of Sleepy Hollow,* built this imaginative home, which he said had more nooks and crannies than a cocked hat. Tour guides in 19th-century costume tell good stories, and the wisteria Irving planted a century ago still climbs the walls.

The closest train station to Sunnyside is Irvington, one stop before Tarrytown.

KYKUIT HISTORIC SITE

(☎914-366-6900; www.hudsonvalley.org; 200 Lake Rd, Pocantico Hills; tour from adult/child $25/23; ⏰tour hours vary Thu-Sun May-Sep, Wed-Mon Oct) Built by oil tycoon John D Rockefeller as his summer home and completed in 1913, this 40-room mansion is listed on the National Register and has lovely grounds landscaped by Frederick Law Olmsted. On display as sculptures around the estate and in an underground art gallery is a remarkable collection of modern art including works by Picasso, Chagall and Warhol.

Admission is only by tour, which depart from **Philipsburg Manor** (☎Mon-Fri 914-631-8200, Sat & Sun 914-631-3992; www.hudsonvalley.org; 381 N Broadway, Sleepy Hollow; adult/child $12/6; ⏰tours 10:30am-3:30pm Wed-Sun May–mid-Nov); a shuttle bus will take you out to the estate from here.

⊙ Poughkeepsie & Hyde Park

FRANKLIN D ROOSEVELT HOME HISTORIC BUILDING

(☎845-486-7770; www.nps.gov/hofr; 4097 Albany Post Rd; adult/child $18/free, museum only adult/child $9/free; ⏰9am-5pm) Rangers lead interesting hour-long tours around Springwood, the home of Franklin D Roosevelt (FDR) who won a record four presidential elections and led America from the Great Depression through WWII. Considering his family wealth, it's a modest abode, but can be unpleasantly crowded in summer. Intimate details have been preserved, including his desk – left as it was the day before he died

– and the hand-pulled elevator he used to hoist his polio-stricken body to the 2nd floor.

The home is part of a 1520-acre estate, formerly a working farm, which also includes walking trails and the **FDR Presidential Library and Museum** (☎845-486-7770; www.fdrlibrary.org; 4079 Albany Post Rd; adult/child $18/free; ⏲9am-6pm Apr-Oct, to 5pm Nov-Mar), which details important achievements in FDR's presidency. Admission tickets last two days and include the Springwood tour and the presidential library.

WALKWAY OVER THE HUDSON PARK

(☎845-834-2867; www.walkway.org; 61 Parker Ave; ⏲7am-sunset) This is the main eastern entrance (with parking) to what was once a railroad bridge crossing the Hudson. It's now the world's longest pedestrian bridge – 1.28 miles – and a state park. The span provides breathtaking views along the river.

If you have time, there's a 3.6-mile loop walking trail you can follow across this bridge and back along the Mid-Hudson Bridge to Poughkeepsie.

Rhinebeck & Hudson

★OLANA HISTORIC SITE

(☎518-828-0135; www.olana.org; 5720 Rte 9G; house tours adult/child $12/free; ⏲grounds 8am-sunset daily, house tours 10am-4pm Tue-Sun Jun-Oct, 11am-3pm Fri-Sun Nov-May) This is one of the finest of the Hudson Valley mansions, as its owner, celebrated landscape painter Frederic Church, designed every detail, inspired by his travels in the Middle East and his appreciation of the beautiful views across the Hudson to the Catskills. The 'Persian fantasy' house is extraordinary and it's well worth booking ahead for a tour of the interior, hung with many of Church's paintings.

Year-round it's also possible to take a self-guided tour of part of Olana's 250 acres of landscaped grounds ($5). In season, guided tours of the grounds on foot ($12) or by electric vehicle ($25) are offered.

EATING

★ROUNDHOUSE RESTAURANT & LOUNGE AMERICAN $$

(☎845-765-8369; www.roundhousebeacon.com; 2 E Main St; ramen $16-21, mains $26-36, tasting menus from $85; ⏲3-9pm Mon & Tue, 11:30am-9pm Wed & Thu, to 10pm Fri & Sat, 11am-8pm Sun; ✎) The Roundhouse restaurant pulls out all the culinary stops, with dishes celebrating the cream of Hudson Valley produce. There's a lot of nose-to-tail dining here, but also inventive vegetarian cooking, including a tasting course and a veg ramen. That said, it's the superbly rich duck-leg ramen, available from the more casual lounge menu, that's the business.

★BLUE HILL AT STONE BARNS AMERICAN $$$

(☎914-366-9600; www.bluehillfarm.com; 630 Bedford Rd, Pocantico Hills; set menu $258; ⏲5-10pm Wed-Sat, 1-7:30pm Sun) Go maximum locavore at chef Dan Barber's farm (it also supplies his Manhattan restaurant). Settle in for an eye-popping multicourse feast based on the day's harvest lasting at least three hours, where the service is as theatrical as the presentation. Be sure to book around two months in advance and note the dress code: jackets and ties preferred for gentlemen, shorts not permitted.

By day, visitors are welcome to tour **Stone Barn Center for Food & Agriculture** (☎914-366-6200; http://story.stonebarnscenter.org; 630 Bedford Rd, Pocantico Hills; adult/child $20/10; ⏲10am-5pm Wed-Sun), which has a basic takeout cafe.

FISH & GAME AMERICAN $$$

(☎518-822-1500; www.fishandgamehudson.com; 13 S 3rd St; mains $26-45; ⏲5:30-10pm Thu & Fri, noon-10pm Sat & Sun) This James Beard Award–winning restaurant and bar has New York gourmets going all light-headed over rustic yet elegant modern American dishes. Chef Zakary Pelaccio is often on hand to explain his creations using the best local produce to diners, and service is relaxed and friendly.

Woodstock

Explore

In the southern Catskills, the town of Woodstock symbolizes the tumultuous 1960s, when young people questioned authority, experimented with freedom and redefined popular culture.

WORTH A DETOUR

SAUGERTIES

Around 10 miles northeast of Woodstock, the town of Saugerties (www.discoversaugerties.com) dates back to the Dutch settling here in the mid-17th century. Today it's well worth making a day trip to a couple of local attractions. **Opus 40 Sculpture Park & Museum** (☎845-246-3400; www.opus40.org; 50 Fite Rd, Saugerties; adult/child $10/3; ⏰11am-5:30pm Thu-Sun May-Sep) is where artist Harvey Fite worked for nearly four decades to coax an abandoned quarry into an immense work of land art, all sinuous walls, canyons and pools. The picturesque 1869 **Saugerties Lighthouse** (☎845-247-0656; www.saugertieslighthouse.com; 168 Lighthouse Dr, Saugerties; tour suggested donation adult/child $5/3; ⏰trail dawn-dusk), on the point where Esopus Creek joins the Hudson, can be reached by a half-mile nature trail. Classic-rock-lovers may also want to search out **Big Pink** (www.bigpinkbasement.com; Parnassus Lane, West Saugerties; house $480; ❄📶), the house made famous by Bob Dylan and the Band, although note it's on a private road. It's possible to stay at both the Lighthouse and Big Pink, but you'll need to book well ahead.

Today, Woodstock still attracts an arty, music-loving crowd and cultivates the free spirit of that era, with rainbow tie-dye style and local grassroots everything, from radio to a respected indie film festival and a farmers market (fittingly billed as a farm festival).

The Best...

➡ **Sight** Bethel Woods Center for the Arts (p328)

➡ **Place to Eat** Garden Cafe (p329)

➡ **Place to Drink** Shindig (p329)

Top Tip

Bring an empty bag – you never know what you'll unearth in the many antique shops and markets (plus weekend yard sales!) found in the area.

Getting There & Away

➡ **Car** Take the New York State Thruway (via the Henry Hudson Pkwy north from Manhattan) or I-87 to Rte 375 for Woodstock, Rte 32 for Saugerties or Rte 28 for other points.

➡ **Bus** Frequent buses from NYC to Saugerties and Woodstock ($29, three hours) are operated by Trailways (www.trailwaysny.com).

Need to Know

➡ **Area Code** ☎845

➡ **Location** 110 miles north (Saugerties) of Manhattan

SIGHTS

BETHEL WOODS CENTER FOR THE ARTS ARTS CENTER

(☎866-781-2922; www.bethelwoodscenter.org; 200 Hurd Rd, Bethel; museum adult/child $15/6; ⏰museum 10am-7pm daily May-Sep, to 5pm Thu-Sun Oct-Apr) The site of the 1969 Woodstock Music & Art Fair, on Max Yasgur's farm outside Bethel, is 70 miles southwest from the town of Woodstock. It's now home to an outdoor amphitheater with great summer concerts and an evocative **museum** with exhibits that burst with the music and images that made Woodstock such a cultural force.

CENTER FOR PHOTOGRAPHY AT WOODSTOCK ARTS CENTER

(☎845-679-9957; www.cpw.org; 59 Tinker St; ⏰noon-5pm Thu-Sun) FREE Founded in 1977, this creative space gives classes, hosts lectures and mounts exhibitions that expand the strict definition of the art form, thanks to a lively artist-in-residence program.

This was formerly the Café Espresso, and Bob Dylan once had a writing studio above it – that's where he typed up the liner notes for *Another Side of Bob Dylan* in 1964 – and Janis Joplin was a regular performer.

KARMA TRIYANA DHARMACHAKRA BUDDHIST MONASTERY

(☎845-679-5906; www.kagyu.org; 335 Meads Mountain Rd; ⏰8:30am-5:30pm) Join stressed-out New Yorkers and others needing a spiritual break and get your karma and chakras checked at this blissful Buddhist monastery about 3 miles from Woodstock.

Soak up the serenity in the carefully tended grounds. Inside the shrine room is a giant golden Buddha statue; as long as you take off your shoes, you're welcome to sit down and meditate.

Check online for details of daily prayers and meditations, guided tours and retreats.

EATING

SHINDIG AMERICAN $

(845-684-7091; www.woodstockshindig.com; 1 Tinker St; mains $10-15; 10am-9pm Tue-Thu, 9am-10pm Fri & Sat, to 9pm Sun;) What's not to love about this cheery hipster cafe-bar? It serves breakfast until 3pm, there's a great range of craft beers and inventive cocktails, and the trout BLT puts a tasty new twist on the classic sandwich.

★GARDEN CAFE VEGAN $

(845-679-3600; www.thegardencafewoodstock.com; 6 Old Forge Rd; mains $9-20; 11:30am-9pm Mon & Wed-Fri, 10am-9pm Sat & Sun;) All the ingredients used at this relaxed, charming cafe are organic. The food served is appealing, tasty and fresh, and includes salads, sandwiches, rice bowls and veggie lasagna. It also serves freshly made juices, smoothies, organic wines, craft beers, and coffee with a variety of nondairy milks.

DRINKING & NIGHTLIFE

STATION BAR & CURIO BAR

(845-810-0203; www.stationbarandcurio.com; 101 Tinker St; 4pm-2am Mon-Thu, noon-2am Fri-Sun) The 1900 Ulster & Delaware Railroad Company station that this bar occupies was once located 10 miles south in Brown's Station, a village now lying beneath the Ashokan Reservoir. It offers eight local craft beers on tap, many more by the bottle, cocktails and wine.

Live jazz and blues is played here most weekends.

Sleeping

With over 60 million visitors descending upon the city every year, you can expect that hotel rooms fill up quickly. Accommodations options range from boxy cookie-cutter rooms in Midtown high-rises to stylish boutique options downtown. You'll also find a few B&Bs set in residential neighborhoods as well as penny-pinching hostels sprinkled about the metropolis.

Booking Accommodations

In New York City, the average room rate is well over $300. But don't let that scare you as there are great deals to be had – almost all of which can be found through savvy online snooping. To get the best deals, launch a two-pronged approach: if you don't have your heart set on a particular property, then check out the generic booking websites. If you do know where you want to stay – it might sound simple – but it's best to start at your desired hotel's website. These days it's not uncommon to find deals and package rates directly on the site of your accommodations of choice.

Room Rates

New York City doesn't have a 'high season' in the common way that beach destinations do. Sure, there are busier times of the year when it comes to tourist traffic, but with a constant flow of arrivals throughout the year, the Big Apple never needs to worry when it comes to filling up beds. As such, room rates fluctuate based on availability; in fact, most hotels have a booking algorithm in place that spits out a price quote relative to the number of rooms already booked on the same night, so the busier the evening the higher the price goes. If you're looking to find the best room rates, then flexibility is key – weekdays are often cheaper, and you'll generally find that accommodations in winter months have smaller price tags. If you are visiting over a weekend, try for a business hotel in the Financial District, which tends to empty out when the work week ends.

Hotels

With over 100,000 hotel rooms, NYC does not lack for options. You'll find brilliantly designed boutique beauties and bland cookie-cutter chains, plus lots of serviceable options that fall somewhere between the two. The better places offer loads of amenities, including rooftop bars, celebrated dining rooms or stylish bars that draw an A-list crowd. Even at the priciest lodgings, rooms may not be all that spacious but will generally have luxury furnishings and high-end details (oversize rain showers, quality bath products, uber-comfy beds).

Guesthouses & B&Bs

New York has a handful of smaller guesthouses and B&Bs. You'll find these throughout the leafier districts of the city, particularly in the West Village, Chelsea, Harlem and Brooklyn. Quality varies of course, but in general, you'll find more atmosphere and human interaction than in your average NYC hotel. Many B&B owners go out of their way to make their guests feel at home and can provide useful insight into the surrounding neighborhood.

Hostels

There are plenty of options for budget travelers to the city, with hostels sprinkled around Manhattan and Brooklyn. A new breed of budget digs has arrived in recent years, with festive outdoor spaces and cafe-bars attached to some spots.

Lonely Planet's Top Choices

Crosby Street Hotel (p334)

Bowery Hotel (p335)

NoMad Hotel (p340)

Gramercy Park Hotel (p338)

Best By Budget

$

Local NYC (p346)

Harlem Flophouse (p343)

Carlton Arms (p338)

Boro Hotel (p346)

$$

Citizen M (p339)

Wall Street Inn (p333)

$$$

Knickerbocker (p340)

Hôtel Americano (p337)

Best Boutique Digs

Chatwal New York (p340)

Wythe Hotel (p344)

Ace Hotel (p340)

Best For Families

Hotel Beacon (p343)

Bubba & Bean Lodges (p341)

Nu Hotel (p345)

Best For Honeymooners

Lafayette House (p334)

Andaz Fifth Avenue (p340)

Plaza (p341)

Best For Jetsetters

Hotel Gansevoort (p337)

Broome (p334)

McCarren Hotel & Pool (p345)

Best Views

Standard (p337)

Z Hotel (p346)

Four Seasons (p341)

Williamsburg Hotel (p344)

Best in Brooklyn

Henry Norman Hotel (p344)

Lefferts Manor Bed & Breakfast (p344)

Wythe Hotel (p344)

Akwaaba Mansion Inn (p345)

NEED TO KNOW

Prices

The following price ranges refer to the standard range in rates for a standard double room regardless of the time of year. Unless otherwise stated, breakfast is included in the price.

$	less than $200
$$	$200 to $350
$$$	more than $350

Reservations

Reservations are essential – walk-ins are practically impossible and rack rates are almost always unfavorable relative to online deals. Reserve your room as early as possible and make sure you understand your hotel's cancellation policy. Expect check-in to be in the middle of the afternoon and check-out to be late morning.

Websites

newyorkhotels.com (www.newyorkhotels.com) The self-proclaimed official website for hotels in NYC.

NYC (www.nycgo.com/hotels) Loads of listings from the NYC Official Guide.

Lonely Planet (www.lonelyplanet.com/usa/new-york-city/hotels) Accommodations reviews and online booking service.

Tipping

You must always tip the maid – leave $3 to $5 per night in an obvious location with a note. Porters should receive a dollar or two, and service staff bringing items to your room should be tipped accordingly as well.

Where to Stay

NEIGHBORHOOD	FOR	AGAINST
Financial District & Lower Manhattan	Convenient to Tribeca's nightlife and ferries. Cheap weekend rates at business hotels.	The southernmost areas can feel impersonal, though Tribeca has some great dining options.
SoHo & Chinatown	Shop to your heart's content right on your doorstep.	Crowds (mostly tourists) swarm the commercial streets of SoHo almost any time of day.
East Village & the Lower East Side	Funky and fun, the area feels the most quintessentially 'New York' to visitors and Manhattanites alike.	Options skew toward very pricey or bare-bones basic, with not much in the middle.
West Village, Chelsea & the Meatpacking District	Brilliantly close-to-everything feel in a thriving, picturesque part of town that has an almost European feel.	Prices soar for traditional hotels, but remain reasonable for B&Bs.
Union Square, the Flatiron District & Gramercy	Convenient subway access to anywhere in the city. You're also steps away from the Village and Midtown.	Prices are high and there's not much in the way of neighborhood flavor.
Midtown	In the heart of the postcard's version of NYC: skyscrapers, museums, shopping and Broadway shows.	One of the most expensive areas; expect small rooms. Can feel touristy and impersonal.
Upper East Side	You're a stone's throw from top-notch museums and the rolling hills of Central Park.	Fewer options and wallet-busting prices; not particularly central.
Upper West Side & Central Park	Convenient access to Central Park, Lincoln Center and the Museum of Natural History.	More family style than lively scene.
Harlem & Upper Manhattan	Great neighborhood vibe, better prices, close to Central Park.	Long subway rides (or pricey cab rides) to the action downtown and in Brooklyn.
Brooklyn	Better prices; great for exploring some of NYC's most creative neighborhoods.	It can be a long commute to Midtown and points north.
Queens	Cheaper, tourist-free and well-located for NYC's best ethnic restaurants. Long Island City is a short subway ride from Midtown.	Locations further out in Queens, particularly Flushing, can be a long haul on the subway.

Lower Manhattan & the Financial District

Most hotels in the Financial District are geared toward business travelers, which often means discounted rates on weekends. To the north, hipper Tribeca harbors a handful of trendy fashionables, among them Robert De Niro's Greenwich Hotel.

ROXY HOTEL TRIBECA HOTEL **$$**

(212-519-6600; www.roxyhotelnyc.com; 2 Sixth Ave, at White St; standard/superior/deluxe r from $235/255/335; ; S1 to Franklin St; A/C/E to Canal St) What's playing at the Roxy? We'll tell you – 201 guest rooms with bold brown-and-gold palettes and modern fittings, surrounding a spacious central atrium with multiple bars, a boutique **art-house cinema** (212-519-6820; www.roxycinematribeca.com; tickets $10) and subterranean jazz club. Pets can stay for free, but if Cody and Bella can't make the trip, a complimentary goldfish can be brought to your room for some company.

ANDAZ WALL ST BOUTIQUE HOTEL **$$**

Map p406 (212-590-1234; http://wallstreet.andaz.hyatt.com; 75 Wall St, at Water St; r from $215; ; S2/3 to Wall St) A favorite of hip downtown business types, the 253-room Andaz takes sleek and handsome and gives it a relaxed, new-school vibe. Guests are checked-in on iPads and treated to complimentary wi-fi, local calls and minibar soda and snacks. Rooms are spacious, contemporary and elegantly restrained, with 7ft-high windows, oak floors and sublimely comfortable beds with 300-thread-count cotton sheets.

Slurp craft brews at Andaz's seasonal Beer Garden or crafty cocktails at year-round Dina Rata, then work it all off at the spa or 24-hour fitness center. Weekend rates can drop well below $300 per night.

GILD HALL BOUTIQUE HOTEL **$$**

Map p406 (212-232-7700; www.thompsonhotels.com/hotels/gild-hall; 15 Gold St, at Platt St; r from $229; ; S2/3 to Fulton St) Boutique and brilliant, Gild Hall's entryway leads to a bilevel library and wine bar that exudes hunting-lodge chic. Rooms fuse Euro elegance and American comfort with high tin ceilings, glass-walled balconies, Sferra linens and well-stocked minibars. King-size beds sport leather headboards, which work perfectly in their warmly hued, minimalist surroundings.

Rates often drop on weekends.

WALL STREET INN HOTEL **$$**

Map p406 (212-747-1500; www.thewallstreetinn.com; 9 S William St; r $140-280; ; S2/3 to Wall St) The sedate stone exterior of this affordable, intimate inn belies its warm, colonial-style interior. Beds are big and plush, and rooms have glossy wood furnishings and long drapes. The bathrooms are full of appreciated touches, like Jacuzzis in the deluxe rooms and tubs in the others. Wi-fi and breakfast are included.

The building is a piece of history, too – the 'LB' tile in the hotel entrance dates from the previous tenants, the Lehman Brothers banking company.

★**GREENWICH HOTEL** BOUTIQUE HOTEL **$$$**

Map p406 (212-941-8900; www.thegreenwichhotel.com; 377 Greenwich St, btwn N Moore & Franklin Sts; r from $625; ; S1 to Franklin St; A/C/E to Canal St) From the plush drawing room (complete with crackling fire) to the lantern-lit pool inside a reconstructed Japanese farmhouse, nothing about Robert De Niro's Greenwich Hotel is generic. Each of the 88 individually designed rooms feature aged-wood floors and bathrooms with opulent Carrara marble or Moroccan tiling. French windows open onto a Tuscan-inspired inner courtyard in some of the rooms.

SMYTH TRIBECA BOUTIQUE HOTEL **$$$**

Map p406 (212-587-7000; www.thompsonhotels.com/hotels/nyc/smyth; 85 W Broadway, btwn Warren & Chambers Sts; r from $415; ; SA/C, 1/2/3 to Chambers St) Revamped by Gachot Studios, the Smyth delivers the same combo of luxury and laid-back hipness you'll find at sister hotels Gild Hall and the Beekman. Modernist furniture, rugs and book-lined shelves give the lobby a snug, chic, Scandinavian vibe, while the 100 soundproofed rooms are a soothing combo of charcoal carpets, walnut paneling and slinky bathrooms with irresistible rain showers.

Extra in-house perks include a fine-dining, season-driven restaurant from A-list restaurateur Andrew Carmellini, a complimentary town-car service; and twice-daily housekeeping service.

CONRAD NEW YORK LUXURY HOTEL **$$$**

(212-945-0100; www.conradnewyork.com; 102 North End Ave, at Vesey St; d $300-700; ;

A/C to Chambers St) In Battery Park City, this well-heeled all-suites hotel (part of the Hilton group) is a top choice for business travelers. Despite its Financial District cred (or perhaps because of it?), there's a trove of artwork around the hotel, including a massive mural by Sol LeWitt in the 16-story atrium. The rooms are handsomely designed, featuring earthy tones with high-end furnishings.

Suites can also be set up for meetings. A frosted sliding glass door separates the lounge area from the bedroom. The most coveted rooms deliver sparkling views of the Hudson River.

SoHo & Chinatown

Style fiends hyperventilate over SoHo's fashion-conscious streets and hoteliers have taken note. There's no shortage of coveted accommodation options to choose from along these star-studded lanes, but they come at quite a cost. Is it worth it? Totally. You'll have some of the world's best shopping, drinking and dining at your doorstep, and you're a short subway hop or taxi ride from some of Manhattan's other great neighborhoods. Slightly cheaper digs await in the borderlands of Chinatown and Nolita. For true budget options, however, you'll need to leave the neighborhood and go further afield.

BOWERY HOUSE HOSTEL $

Map p408 (212-837-2373; www.thebowery house.com; 220 Bowery, btwn Prince & Spring Sts, Nolita; s/d with shared bath from $80/130; R/W to Prince St) Across the street from the New Museum, this former 1920s-era flophouse has been resurrected as an upmarket hostel, its rooms decked out with Bowery-themed film posters and custom-made mattresses (ie shorter and narrower), while communal bathrooms feature rain showers and heated floors. There's also a stylish lounge area with chesterfield sofas and chandeliers, a buzzing bar and a roof terrace.

Light sleepers may wish to avoid this place, which attracts a nightlife-loving crowd; earplugs come standard with every room.

LEON HOTEL HOTEL $$

Map p411 (212-390-8833; www.leonhotelnyc.com; 125 Canal St, btwn Bowery & Chrystie St, Chinatown; d $170-300; B/D to Grand St) At the entrance to the Manhattan Bridge and surrounded by hectic streets, this boxy space offers clean, no-frills accommodation that is decent value in wallet-draining NYC. Rooms are comfortable, if minimally furnished, and some have fetching views of Lower Manhattan and the taller-than-thou One World Trade Center. The staff are friendly and the location is super-handy for exploring Chinatown, Nolita and the Lower East Side.

★CROSBY STREET HOTEL BOUTIQUE HOTEL $$$

Map p408 (212-226-6400; www.firmdalehotels.com; 79 Crosby St, btwn Spring & Prince Sts, SoHo; r from $695; 6 to Spring St; N/R to Prince St) Step into Crosby Street for afternoon tea and you'll never want to leave. It's not just the scones and clotted cream that will grab you, but the eccentric, loft-like lobby, buzzing bar, film screening room and one-of-a-kind rooms. Some are starkly black and white while others are as floral as an English garden, but all are plush, refined and subtly playful.

BROOME BOUTIQUE HOTEL $$$

Map p408 (212-431-2929; www.thebroomenyc.com; 431 Broome St, at Crosby St, SoHo; r from $460; N/R to Prince S; 6 to Spring St) Occupying a handsomely restored, 19th-century building, the Broome opened in 2014. Spread across five stories, its 14 rooms are the epitome of simple, muted elegance, each with locally sourced fittings, including furnishings by Mitchell Gold + Bob Williams and oversized mirrors from BDDW. Topping it off are beautiful, personable service and a soothing, tranquil vibe that offers respite from SoHo's relentless energy.

LAFAYETTE HOUSE GUESTHOUSE $$$

Map p408 (646-306-5010; http://lafayettehousenyc.com; 38 E 4th St, btwn Fourth Ave & Lafayette St, NoHo; r $367; 6 to Bleecker St; B/D/F/M to Broadway-Lafayette St) A former town house, this Victorian beauty offers eight homely rooms with big beds, thick drapes, marble fireplaces and old-fashioned armoires. Two rooms feature their own private garden, while another two come with private terrace or balcony. Light sleepers beware: rooms facing the street can feel a bit noisy.

East Village & the Lower East Side

Statement-making structures have been cropping up in these once grittier neighborhoods, giving the area a fun, world-in-one feel that still remains distinctly New York in style. Visitors seeking that true city feel will be perfectly happy taking up residence along these low-numbered streets, especially if you've got the dime for a room at the Bowery or Cooper Square hotels. Stay west if subway convenience is a primary concern – underground transport thins as you head east, especially beyond First Ave.

ST MARK'S HOTEL HOTEL **$**

Map p412 (212-674-0100; www.stmarkshotel.net; 2 St Marks Pl, at Third Ave, East Village; d from $130; ; S 6 to Astor Pl) This East Village budget option draws a young, nightlife-loving crowd, who enjoy having one of the city's liveliest concentrations of bars and restaurants right outside the front door. With such low prices, it's best to lower your expectations as the rooms are quite small and dated. Street noise is an issue for light sleepers and there's no lift.

EAST VILLAGE HOTEL HOTEL **$$**

Map p412 (646-429-9184; www.eastvillagehotel.com; 147 First Ave, at 9th St, East Village; d from $312; ; S 6 to Astor Pl) In a vibrant location in the East Village, this place has clean, simple rooms with exposed brick walls (a little larger than most in NYC), comfy mattresses, wall-mounted flat-screen TVs and small kitchenettes. Street noise is an issue (beware, light sleepers), and it's in an old building, so you'll have to walk your luggage up a few flights.

There's no lobby or other common areas. Guests receive an access code to the door to come and go as they please, so there's little interaction with other guests.

LUDLOW HOTEL **$$**

Map p414 (212-432-1818; www.ludlowhotel.com; 180 Ludlow St, btwn Houston & Stanton Sts, Lower East Side; d from $355, loft from $465; ; S F to 2nd Ave) Nearly a decade in the making, this 184-room boutique hotel finally opened its doors in 2014 to much fanfare. Rooms are beautifully designed with unique features (some have tree-trunk nightstands made of petrified wood), mosaic-tiled bathrooms and small balconies. On the downside, the least expensive rooms are tiny and extremely cramped.

There's a gorgeous lobby bar and outdoor patio, plus a stylish French bistro.

SAGO HOTEL BOUTIQUE HOTEL **$$**

Map p414 (212-951-1112; www.sagohotel.com; 120 Allen St, btwn Rivington & Delancey Sts, Lower East Side; r from $250, studio from $320; ; S F to Delancey; J/M/Z to Essex) No matter the weather in NYC it always appears to be cool in the Sago Hotel. It's located in the bustling center of the Lower East Side and the rooms all bear the markings of the current vibe of the neighborhood: clean lines, gray brick and unfussy contemporary furniture. There are terraces on the upper floors that provide stunning city views.

Rooms range from tiny 200-sq-ft mini-suites to multistory penthouses. Head upstairs in the evenings for a nightly wine and cheese social.

BLUE MOON BOUTIQUE HOTEL HOTEL **$$**

Map p414 (347-294-4552; www.bluemoon-nyc.com; 100 Orchard St, btwn Broome & Delancey Sts, Lower East Side; dm/d from $60/229; ; S F to Delancey St; J/M to Essex St) You'd never guess that this welcoming brick guesthouse – full of festive yellows, blues and greens – was once a foul tenement back in the day (the day being 1879). With touches including original wood shutters and wrought-iron bed frames, Blue Moon's small, spare rooms are vintage-inspired and comfortable. The best rooms are bright, with balconies that offer fine views.

The hotel also has two dorm rooms with four single beds each (no bunk beds) – one mixed room, one for females only.

BOWERY HOTEL BOUTIQUE HOTEL **$$$**

Map p412 (212-505-9100; www.thebowery hotel.com; 335 Bowery, btwn 2nd & 3rd Sts, East Village; r $295-535; @; S F/V to Lower East Side-2nd Ave; 6 to Bleecker St) Pick up your old-fashioned gold room key with its red tassel in the dark, hushed lobby filled with antique velvet chairs and faded Persian rugs. Then follow the mosaic-tiled floors to your room with huge factory windows and elegant four-poster beds. Settle in to watch a movie on your 42in plasma TV, or raid the luxury bathroom goodies.

The Bowery's zinc-topped bar, outside garden patio and rustic Italian eatery, Gemma, are always packed.

STANDARD EAST VILLAGE HOTEL $$$
Map p412 (212-475-5700; www.standardhotels.com; 25 Cooper Sq (Third Ave), btwn 5th & 6th Sts, East Village; s from $349, d $499; ; R/W to 8th St-NYU; 4/6 to Bleecker St; 4/6 to Astor Pl) Rising above the East Village like an unfurled sail, Cooper Square's gleaming white structure looms strikingly out of place in low-rise East Village – even with the ersatz graffiti wall its designers placed at the entrance. For a more authentic glimpse of the old East Village, head to the outdoor patio bars.

Rooms are well equipped with comfy beds, big windows (most are floor-to-ceiling), Bluetooth audio speakers and high-end bath amenities.

West Village, Chelsea & the Meatpacking District

Real estate in the desirable West Village is the highest in the city, as evidenced by hotel rates. Staying here, however, is well worth the extra dough: you'll be treated to a wonderful neighborhood vibe at some of the more memorable properties in town. The Meatpacking District is known for towering boutique hotels, while just a few blocks up in Chelsea, you'll find a spike in new development with a horde of swanky properties promising cutting-edge spaces befitting the pages of a Scandinavian design magazine. Nights in Chelsea will ensure convenient, walkable access to boutique shopping, eating and drinking downtown.

JANE HOTEL HOTEL $
Map p416 (212-924-6700; www.thejanenyc.com; 113 Jane St, btwn Washington St & West Side Hwy, West Village; r with shared/private bath from $115/295; P ; A/C/E, L to 8th Ave-14th St; 1 to Christopher St-Sheridan Sq) The claustrophobic will want to avoid the Jane's tiny 50-sq-ft rooms, but if you want to live like a luxury sailor, check into this renovated red-brick gem, which was built for mariners in the early 20th century (*Titanic* survivors also stayed here in 1912). The gorgeous ballroom/bar looks like it belongs in a five-star hotel. More expensive captain's quarters come with private commodes.

CHELSEA INTERNATIONAL HOSTEL HOSTEL $
Map p420 (212-647-0010; www.chelseahostel.com; 251 W 20th St, btwn Seventh & Eighth Aves, Chelsea; dm $55, s $68-107, d from $127; ; 1, C/E to 23rd St; 1 to 18th St) Occupying some serious real estate in the desirable Chelsea neighborhood, this old bastion of backpackerdom is a good pick if location ranks at the top of your list. Capitalizing on its convenience with somewhat steep prices, considering the bare-bones furnishings, but it's kept clean and there's access to common rooms and kitchens where budget travelers meet and hang.

INCENTRA VILLAGE HOUSE B&B $$
Map p416 (212-206-0007; www.incentravillage.com; 32 Eighth Ave, btwn 12th & Jane Sts, West Village; r from $239; ; A/C/E, L to 8th Ave-14th St) Boasting a great location in the West Village, these two red-brick, landmark town houses were built in 1841 and later became the city's first gay inn. Today, the 11 rooms get booked way in advance by many queer travelers; call early to get in on its gorgeous Victorian parlor and antique-filled, serious-Americana rooms.

The Garden Suite is especially picturesque as it has access to a small garden out back. The hotel advertises wi-fi that reaches all the rooms, but it's not always reliable. It does have a computer in the parlor that is free for guests to use.

CHELSEA PINES INN B&B $$
Map p416 (888-546-2700, 212-929-1023; www.chelseapinesinn.com; 317 W 14th St, btwn Eighth & Ninth Aves, Chelsea; s/d from $229/269; ; A/C/E, L to 8th Ave-14th St) With its five walk-up floors coded to the rainbow flag, the 26-room Chelsea Pines is serious gay-and-lesbian central, but guests of all stripes are welcome. It helps to be up on your Hitchcock beauties, as vintage movie posters not only plaster the walls but rooms are named for starlets, such as Kim Novak, Doris Day and Ann-Margret.

There's a sink in the walk-in closet of standard rooms, with clean bathrooms down the hall. The small lounge downstairs opens to a tiny courtyard out back, and breakfast is included in the rates.

COLONIAL HOUSE INN B&B $$
Map p420 (800-689-3779, 212-243-9669; www.colonialhouseinn.com; 318 W 22nd St, btwn Eighth & Ninth Aves, Chelsea; r $130-350; ; 1, C/E to 23rd St) Friendly and simple, this 20-room gay inn is tidy but a bit worn and small. Most rooms have small walk-in closets (with a small TV and refrigerator) and

sinks. When the weather is nice, the rooftop deck sees some nude sunbathing. The smaller rooms have shared baths, while the deluxe suite has a private bath and private access to the back garden.

A continental breakfast and a regular coffee and tea service in the lobby are included in the price. The hotel's lobby and common spaces also serve as a gallery for the artworks of hotel founder and Chelsea icon Mel Cheren.

TOWNHOUSE INN OF CHELSEA B&B **$$**

Map p420 (212-414-2323; www.townhouseinnchelsea.com; 131 W 23rd St, btwn Sixth & Seventh Aves, Chelsea; d $150-300; ; S1, F/M to 23rd St) Housed in a lone 19th-century, five-story town house with exposed brick and wood floors, this 14-room B&B on busy 23rd St is a Chelsea gem. Bought in 1998 and extensively renovated (with an elevator installed), the rooms are big and welcoming, with fanciful fabrics on big brass or poster beds and TVs held in huge armoires.

There's an honor-system bar and an ol' piano for you to play boogie-woogie on in the lounge, and a 2nd-floor, all-Victorian library that doubles as a breakfast room.

GEM HOTEL **$$**

Map p420 (212-675-1911; www.thegemhotel.com; 300 W 22nd St, btwn Eight & Ninth Aves, Chelsea; r from $210; P; S1, C/E to 23rd St) With an incredible location in the heart of Chelsea, clean rooms, friendly staff and a rooftop bar to boot, the GEM is one of the better reasonably priced options available in lower Manhattan. That said, some of the furniture in the lobby is a bit dingy and the open-concept bathrooms in some of the rooms may be undesirable for those traveling together.

STANDARD BOUTIQUE HOTEL **$$$**

Map p416 (212-645-4646; www.standardhotels.com; 848 Washington St, at 13th St, Meatpacking District; d from $509; ; SA/C/E, L to 8th Ave-14th St) Hipster hotelier André Balazs has built a wide, boxy, glass tower that straddles the High Line. Every room has sweeping Meatpacking District views and is filled with cascading sunlight, which makes the Standard's glossy, wood-framed beds and marbled bathrooms glow in a particularly homey way. There's also a hyper-modern Standard in the East Village.

The amenities are first-rate, with a buzzing German beer garden and a brasserie at street level (and ice rink in winter), and a plush nightclub on the top floor. The location is unbeatable, with the best of NYC right outside your door.

MARITIME HOTEL BOUTIQUE HOTEL **$$$**

Map p420 (212-242-4300; www.themaritimehotel.com; 363 W 16th St, btwn Eighth & Ninth Aves, Chelsea; r from $403; ; SA/C/E, L to 8th Ave-14th St) This white tower dotted with portholes has been transformed into a marine-themed luxury inn by a hip team of architects. It feels like a luxury *Love Boat* inside, as its 135 rooms, each with their own round window, are compact and teak-paneled, with gravy in the form of 20in flat-screen TVs and DVD players.

The most expensive quarters feature outdoor showers, a private garden and sweeping Hudson views. The building was originally the site of the National Maritime Union headquarters (and then a shelter for homeless teens).

HÔTEL AMERICANO HOTEL **$$$**

Map p420 (212-216-0000; www.hotel-americano.com; 518 W 27th St, btwn Tenth & Eleventh Aves, Chelsea; r from $245; ; S1, C/E to 23rd St) Design geeks will go giddy when they walk into one of Hôtel Americano's perfectly polished rooms. It's like sleeping in a bento box, but the food's been replaced by a carefully curated selection of minimalist and muted furniture. Oh, and that thing hanging from the ceiling that looks like a robot's head? It's a suspended fireplace, of course.

HOTEL GANSEVOORT LUXURY HOTEL **$$$**

Map p416 (212-206-6700; www.hotelgansevoort.com; 18 Ninth Ave, at 13th St, Meatpacking District; r from $475; ; SA/C/E, L to 8th Ave-14th St) Coated in zinc-colored panels the 14-floor Gansevoort has been a swank swashbuckler of the Meatpacking District since it opened in 2004. Rooms are luscious and airy, with chocolate-colored suede headboards, plasma-screen TVs and illuminated bathroom doors. Rooftop bar Plunge attracts long lines and guests swim in the skinny pool overlooking the Hudson River.

There's also a street-level restaurant and a very swanky cocktail lounge/nightclub called Provacateur, as well as a full-service spa called exhale.

HIGH LINE HOTEL HOTEL **$$$**

Map p420 (212-929-3888; www.thehighlinehotel.com; 180 Tenth Ave, btwn 20th & 21st Sts, Chelsea; d from $470; S1, C/E to 23rd St)

Serenity is assured during a stay inside this neo-Gothic building that was once part of the General Theological Seminary (still functioning in a building around the corner). The 60-room hotel has attractive guest rooms that blend contemporary and antique furnishings. The location is perfect for taking in the galleries of Chelsea or strolling the leafy High Line.

The courtyard in front of the building is a lovely place to unwind, particularly with a coffee in hand (Intelligentsia serves coffee from the antique Citroën H-Van parked inside the gates). You can also enjoy a beer, wine or cocktail by night at the bar hidden inside, or on the back patio. Guests can borrow an elegant Shinola bicycle for a spin around town.

Union Square, the Flatiron District & Gramercy

Countless visitors lay their weary heads under the blinding lights of Times Square for convenience, but consider for a second that Union Sq and its neighbors are just as handy. A quick glance at the subway map will show a handful of lines that crisscross in this busy downtown hub – you're a straight shot to Lower Manhattan and the museums on the Upper East Side, with the adorable nooks of the Village at your doorstep. The area's slumber options are varied and eclectic, ranging from the high-priced chic-boutique to a few shared-bathroom, penny-saving options.

CARLTON ARMS — HOTEL $

Map p422 (212-679-0680; www.carltonarms.com; 160 E 25th St, at Third Ave, Gramercy; d with shared/private bath $120/150; S 6 to 23rd St or 28th St) The Carlton Arms channels the downtown edgy art-world scene of yesteryear with the works of artists from all over the world adorning nearly every inch of the interiors. Murals follow the walls up five flights of stairs, and into each of the tiny guest rooms and shared bathrooms (there is a small sink in each guest room).

Not surprisingly, it draws an eclectic mix of bohemian travelers, who don't mind the rustic accommodations in exchange for big savings. Prepare to work those legs: there's no lift.

The Carlton Arms has gone through many incarnations during its 100 years as a hotel, from nights of subterfuge (the lobby was a speakeasy during Prohibition) to days of dereliction (as a refuge for addicts and prostitutes in the 1960s).

MARCEL AT GRAMERCY — BOUTIQUE HOTEL $$

Map p422 (212-696-3800; www.themarcelatgramercy.com; 201 E 24th St, at Third Ave, Gramercy; d from $300; @; S 6 to 23rd St) The minimalist, 97-room Marcel is a poor-man's chic boutique, and that's not a bad thing. Rooms are simple yet modern (standard ones are walk-in closet size), their gray-and-beige color scheme shaken up by bold, canary-yellow chesterfield bedheads. Bathrooms are uninspired but clean, while rooms on the avenue have decent views. Downstairs, the sleek lounge makes for a nifty place to unwind.

The 10th-floor business lounge has free wi-fi; otherwise, there's a $10 per day surcharge for in-room access.

HOTEL HENRI — HOTEL $$

Map p422 (212-243-0800; www.wyndham.com; 37 W 24th St, btwn Fifth & Sixth Aves, Flatiron District; r from $247; S F/M, N/R to 23rd St) Nearly equidistant from Chelsea and Union Sq is the Hotel Henri, part of the Wyndham chain. What was once a serviceable but dull hotel in a great location now boasts a chic interior design (slate gray walls, 1960s-inspired furniture) in addition to the great service and amenities.

★GRAMERCY PARK HOTEL — BOUTIQUE HOTEL $$$

Map p422 (212-920-3300; www.gramercyparkhotel.com; 2 Lexington Ave, at 21st St, Gramercy; r from $600, s from $800; S 6, R/W to 23rd St) Formerly a grand old dame, the Gramercy's major face-lift has it looking young and sexy. Dark wood paneling and red suede rugs and chairs greet you in the lobby, while the rooms – overlooking nearby Gramercy Park – deliver customized oak furnishings, 400-count Italian linens and big, feather-stuffed mattresses on sprawling beds. Colors are rich and alluring, fit for a Spanish grandee.

The largest rooms – sprawling suites with French doors dividing living and sleeping areas – start at $800. Add zest to your life with drinks at the celebrity-studded Rose and Jade bars, and dinner at Maialino (p169), Danny Meyer's rustic Italian eatery.

HOTEL GIRAFFE BOUTIQUE HOTEL $$$

Map p422 (212-685-7700; www.hotelgiraffe.com; 365 Park Ave S, at 26th St, Gramercy; r from $368; R/W, 6 to 23rd St) It mightn't be particularly cool or cutting-edge, but the affable, 12-floor Giraffe earns its stripes – or dots – with clean, plush rooms, complimentary breakfast, and free wine and cheese between 5pm and 8pm. Most of the 72 rooms have small balconies and all come with flat-screen TVs and DVD players, and granite work desk. Corner suites add a living room with pull-out sofa.

Midtown

If you want to be in the heart of the action, consider Midtown East, which encompasses the area around Grand Central Terminal and the UN. It's not as crazy and eclectic as Midtown West, but options are endless, from a design-conscious 'budget' option with shared bathrooms to thousand-dollar suites with private terraces overlooking Gotham's blinking lights. Light sleepers beware – Midtown West is a 24-hour kind of place, though it's especially convenient for Broadway fans.

MURRAY HILL EAST SUITES HOTEL $

Map p424 (212-661-2100; http://murrayhillsuites.com; 149 E 39th St, btwn Lexington & Third Aves, Midtown East; r from $163; 4/5/6, 7 to Grand Central) The dated brick facade is a suitable introduction to the rooms, where uninspiring furniture and carpet page the eras of flares and shoulder pads. If you can overlook the design shortcomings, you'll enjoy remarkably spacious quarters, with separate sitting areas and kitchenettes. A plethora of great eating and drinking options are nearby. The catch: a minimum 30-day stay.

PARK SAVOY HOTEL $

Map p428 (212-245-5755; www.parksavoyny.com; 158 W 58th St, btwn Sixth & Seventh Aves; d from $145; N/Q/R to 57th St-7th Ave) The best thing about the Park Savoy is the low price and nifty location near the lovely gateway of Central Park. Naturally, there's a trade-off and that's the rooms: worn carpets, cheap bedspreads and showers with low water pressure, to say nothing of the unhelpful staff and an online reservation system that's often nonfunctioning.

★YOTEL HOTEL $$

Map p428 (646-449-7700; www.yotel.com; 570 Tenth Ave, at 41st St, Midtown West; r from $250; A/C/E to 42nd St-Port Authority Bus Terminal; 1/2/3, N/Q/R, S, 7 to Times Sq-42nd St) Part futuristic spaceport, part *Austin Powers* set, this uber-cool 669-room option bases its rooms on airplane classes: premium cabin (economy), first cabins (business) and VIP suites (first); some first cabins and VIP suites include a private terrace with hot tub. Small but cleverly configured, premium cabins include automated adjustable beds, while all cabins feature floor-to-ceiling windows with killer views, slick bathrooms and iPod connectivity.

Perks include free morning muffins, a gym and the city's largest outdoor hotel terrace, complete with a stunning skyscraper backdrop (naturally).

POD 39 HOTEL $$

Map p424 (212-865-5700; https://thepodhotel.com/pod-39; 145 E 39th St, btwn Lexington & Third Aves, Midtown East; r from $240; S, 4/5/6, 7 to Grand Central-42nd St) It's a case of good things coming in very small packages at funky Pod 39. The sibling of budget-luxe Pod 51 (p339), its 367 rooms offer hip-n-functional design, private bathroom and city views in Pod's trademark tiny dimensions. Cranking up the Millennial cred is a Technicolor taqueria, eclectic lobby lounge, light-strung rooftop bar and games room (complete with oh-so-retro Ping-Pong table).

POD 51 HOTEL $$

Map p424 (212-355-0300; www.thepodhotel.com; 230 E 51st St, btwn Second & Third Aves, Midtown East; r with shared/private bathroom from $165/210; 6 to 51st St; E/M to Lexington Ave-53rd St) A dream come true for folks who would like to live inside a cocoon – this affordable hot spot has a range of room types, most barely big enough for the bed. 'Pods' have bright bedding, tight workspaces, flat-screen TVs, iPod docking stations and 'raindrop' showerheads. In the warmer months, sip a drink on the perky rooftop deck.

CITIZEN M HOTEL $$

Map p428 (212-461-3638; www.citizenm.com; 218 W 50th St, btwn Broadway & Eighth Ave, Midtown West; r from $270; 1, C/E to 50th St) A few steps from Times Square, Citizen M is a true millennial. Speedy self-service counters provide lightning-fast check-in and check-out, communal areas are upbeat, contemporary and buzzing, and rooms are smart and compact. A tablet in each controls lighting, blinds and room temperature, and the plush mattresses, free movies and soothing rain showers keep guests purring. On-site perks include gym, rooftop bar and 24-hour canteen.

★NOMAD HOTEL BOUTIQUE HOTEL **$$$**

Map p428 (☎212-796-1500; www.thenomadhotel.com; 1170 Broadway, at 28th St, Midtown West; r from $479; ❄📶; ⓈN/R to 28th St) Crowned by a copper cupola and featuring interiors designed by Frenchman Jacques Garcia, this beaux-arts dream is one of the city's hottest addresses. Rooms channel a nostalgic NYC-meets-Paris aesthetic, in which recycled hardwood floors, leather-steam-trunk minibars and clawfoot tubs mix it with flat-screen TVs and high-tech LED lighting. Wi-fi is free, while in-house restaurant/bar NoMad (p198) is one of the neighborhood's most coveted hangouts.

★ANDAZ FIFTH AVENUE BOUTIQUE HOTEL **$$$**

Map p424 (☎212-601-1234; https://newyork5thavenue.andaz.hyatt.com; 485 Fifth Ave, at 41st St, Midtown East; r from $465; ❄📶; ⓈS, 4/5/6 to Grand Central-42nd St; 7 to 5th Ave; B/D/F/M to 42nd St-Bryant Park) Youthful, chic Andaz ditches stuffy reception desks for hip, mobile staff who check you in on laptops in the art-laced lobby. The hotel's 184 rooms are svelte and contemporary, with NYC-inspired details like 'Fashion District' rolling racks and subway-inspired lamps. We especially love the sexy, spacious bathrooms, complete with rain showers, black porcelain foot baths and Beekman 1802 amenities.

It also has a 'secret' basement bar serving limited-edition spirits and locavore-focused dishes, and regular talks by guest artists and curators. Check the website for special deals.

★QUIN HOTEL **$$$**

Map p428 (☎212-245-7846; www.thequinhotel.com; 101 W 57th St, at Sixth Ave, Midtown West; d from $492; ❄📶; ⓈF to 57th St; N/W to 5th at 57th St) Opened to much acclaim in late 2013, the Quin delivers opulence with a dash of new-school verve. Its beautiful, slinky common areas are anything but 'common' – the hotel lounge comes complete with 15ft video wall for showcasing art installations. Rooms are quiet, exceedingly comfortable and elegantly restrained, with custom-made, king-sized Duxiana beds, svelte marble bathrooms with glass-enclosed shower, and Nespresso machines.

★KNICKERBOCKER BOUTIQUE HOTEL **$$$**

Map p428 (☎212-204-4980; http://theknickerbocker.com; 6 Times Sq, at 42nd St; d $654; ❄📶; ⓈA/C/E, N/Q/R/W, S, 1/2/3, 7 to Times Sq-42nd St) Originally opened in 1906 by John Jacob Astor, the 330-room Knickerbocker exudes a restrained, monochromatic elegance (unlike its Times Square location!). Rooms are dashingly chic, hushed and modern, decked out with adjustable 55in flat-screen TV, bedside tablet and USB charging ports. Carrara-marble bathrooms come with a spacious shower, with some offering stand-alone tub.

Hotel facilities include a sophisticated lounge, cocktail bar and Modern American bites, as well as a fabulous rooftop bar, complete with bookable private nooks, cigars and occasional DJs.

ACE HOTEL BOUTIQUE HOTEL **$$$**

Map p424 (☎212-679-2222; www.acehotel.com/newyork; 20 W 29th St, btwn Broadway & Fifth Ave, Midtown West; r from $454; ❄📶; ⓈN/R to 28th St) A hit with cashed-up creatives, the Ace's standard and deluxe rooms recall upscale bachelor pads – plaid bedspreads, quirky wall stencils, leather furnishings and fridges. Some even have Gibson guitars and turntables. All have free wi-fi. For cool kids with more 'cred' than 'coins,' there are 'mini' and 'bunk' rooms (with bunk beds), both of which can slip under $200 in winter.

The Ace vibe is upbeat and fun, with a hipster-packed lobby serving up live bands and DJs, superlative espresso bar Stumptown Coffee Roasters (p199) and two of the area's top nosh spots – turf-centric **Breslin Bar & Dining Room** (Map p424; ☎212-679-1939; www.thebreslin.com; 16 West 29th St, btwn Broadway & Fifth Ave; lunch mains $17-27, dinner mains $27-39; ⏰7am-midnight) and surf-centric **John Dory Oyster Bar** (Map p424; ☎212-792-9000; www.thejohndory.com; 1196 Broadway, at 29th St; plates $11-55; ⏰noon-midnight).

CHATWAL NEW YORK LUXURY HOTEL **$$$**

Map p428 (☎212-764-6200; www.thechatwalny.com; 130 W 44th St, btwn Sixth Ave & Broadway, Midtown West; r from $695; ❄📶🏊; ⓈN/Q/R, S, 1/2/3, 7 to Times Sq-42nd St) A restored art-deco jewel in the heart of the Theater

District, the Chatwal is as atmospheric as it is historic; the likes of Fred Astaire and Irving Berlin once supped, sipped and sung in its Lambs Club restaurant/bar. Vintage Broadway posters adorn the uber-luxe guest rooms, inspired by steamer cabin trunks and featuring suede-lined walls, 400-thread Frette linen counts and cocktail sets for an in-room tipple.

Additional perks include complimentary butler service, valet parking, and use of laptops and preprogrammed iPods, while the in-house luxury spa spells easy-access pampering. The beaux-arts building itself is the work of Stanton White, creator of the Washington Square Arch.

FOUR SEASONS LUXURY HOTEL **$$$**
Map p424 (212-758-5700; www.fourseasons.com/newyork; 57 E 57th St, btwn Madison & Park Aves, Midtown East; r from $825; S N/W/R to 5th Ave-59th St; 4/5 to Lexington Ave & 59th St) Housed in a 52-floor tower designed by IM Pei, the five-star Four Seasons delivers seamless luxury. Even the smallest of the neutrally hued rooms are generously sized, with spacious closets and HD TVs in the Tuscan-marble bathrooms. The views over Central Park from the 'Park View' rooms are practically unfair, with *oohs* and *aahs* also induced by the hotel's esteemed spa.

PLAZA LUXURY HOTEL **$$$**
Map p424 (888-240-7775, 212-759-3000; www.theplazany.com; 768 5th Ave, at Central Park S; r $995; S N/R to Fifth Ave-59th St) Set in a landmark French Renaissance–style building, the iconic Plaza's 282 guest rooms are a regal affair, with sumptuous Louis XV–style furniture and 24-carat gold-plated bathroom faucets. On-site drawcards include the Guerlain Spa and fabled Palm Court, the latter famed for its stained-glass ceiling and afternoon tea. Less enticing is the hotel's $14.95 wi-fi surcharge, less if booked online.

INK48 BOUTIQUE HOTEL **$$$**
Map p428 (212-757-0088; www.ink48.com; 653 Eleventh Ave, at 48th St, Midtown West; r $459; S C/E to 50th St) The Kimpton hotel group has braved Midtown's wild far west with Ink48, perched on the subway-starved edge of Manhattan. Occupying a converted printing house, the compensation is sweet: stellar skyline and Hudson River views, chic contemporary rooms, a boutique spa and restaurant, and a stunning rooftop bar. Topping it off is easy walking access to Hell's Kitchen's thriving restaurant scene.

Dog owners will appreciate the free bowl of kibble and water that's just outside the lobby. Wi-fi is free only if one joins the Kimpton loyalty program; otherwise, it's a hefty $13.95 per day.

Upper East Side

The Upper East Side contains some of the wealthiest zip codes in the country, so accommodations here aren't cheap (though there are occasionally deals to be found). But that's the price you pay for being walking distance from some of New York's grandest cultural attractions.

BUBBA & BEAN LODGES B&B **$**
Map p430 (917-345-7914; www.bblodges.com; 1598 Lexington Ave, btwn E 101st & 102nd Sts; d $110-190, tr $120-230, q $130-260; S 6 to 103rd St) Owners Jonathan and Clement have turned a charming Manhattan town house into an excellent home-away-from-home. The five guest rooms are simply furnished, with crisp, white walls, hardwood floors and navy linens, providing the place with a modern, youthful feel. All units in this three-floor walk-up have private baths as well as equipped kitchenettes.

1871 HOUSE INN **$$**
Map p430 (212-756-8823; www.1871house.com; 130 E 62nd St, btwn Park & Lexington Aves; half-floor ste $220-345, full-floor $365-645; S N/Q/R to Lexington Ave-59th St) Named for the year it was built, this historic home now serves as a quaint inn. Its seven individually designed suites are like mini-apartments, with kitchenette, private baths, queen beds and period-style furnishings (those occupying a full floor have multiple bedrooms and can sleep up to five). All the rooms are light-filled, with airy 12ft ceilings.

This is a good-value place for the neighborhood, but note that this is a characterful, vintage structure: there is no elevator, the floors are a bit creaky and, in winter, heat is provided by steam radiators. A choice of self-catering gourmet breakfast hampers are available at extra cost.

FRANKLIN HOTEL **$$**
Map p430 (212-369-1000; www.franklinhotel.com; 164 E 87th St, btwn Lexington & Third Aves;

d from $299; ❄📶; S 4/5/6, Q to 86th St) Fronted by a classic gold awning, this longtime, 50-room hotel channels a 1930s feel – starting with the vintage elevator. As with many old-timey New York buildings, the rooms and their bathrooms are tiny. But the decor is modern, the staff congenial and the location couldn't be more ideal – walking distance from Central Park and many museums.

In addition, wine and cheese are served in the evenings – very civilized. Rooms facing the back are quieter.

MARK HOTEL **$$$**
Map p430 (☎212-744-4300; www.themarkhotel.com; 25 E 77th St, cnr Madison Ave; d from $750, ste from $1300; ❄📶; S 6 to 77th St) French designer Jacques Grange left his artful mark on the Mark, with bold geometric shapes and rich, playful forms that greet visitors in the lobby (the zebra-striped marble floor is pure eye candy). Upstairs, lavishly renovated rooms and multibedroom suites boast a more subdued aesthetic, though one equally embracing of high style.

Light and airy rooms are set with coffered ceilings, fine Italian linens and elegant custom-made furnishings. Touch-screen panels control temperature, the lighting scheme and audio speakers from Bang & Olufsen. Marble bathrooms feature double sinks, a separate shower and soaking tub – and even a flat-screen TV embedded in the mirror. On the downside, the least expensive rooms can feel small, and service can sometimes be a little hipper-than-thou.

Upper West Side & Central Park

If you're after arts and culture, the Upper West Side has obvious appeal, with numerous celebrated theaters, cinemas and concert halls (particularly Lincoln Center) at your doorstep. Proximity to the lush oases of bustling Central Park (p228) and peaceful Riverside Park (p233) adds to the allure. Sleeping options here run the gamut from budget-minded hostels to pricey luxury hotels.

JAZZ ON THE PARK HOSTEL HOSTEL **$**
Map p432 (☎212-932-1600; www.jazzhostels.com; 36 W 106th St, btwn Central Park West & Manhattan Ave; dm $48-70, d $165-200; ❄@📶; S B, C to 103rd St) This flophouse-turned-hostel right off Central Park is generally a good bet, with clean dorms sporting four to 12 bunks in co-ed and single-sex configurations. It's a social place, with free nightly activities (comedy and movie nights, pub crawls, summer barbecues). The rather dark downstairs lounge, aka 'the dungeon', has a pool table, couches and big-screen TV.

There's also an area for eating, an accessible rooftop and several small terraces.

HOTEL NEWTON HOTEL **$**
Map p432 (☎212-678-6500; www.thehotelnewton.com; 2528 Broadway, btwn 94th & 95th Sts; d $100-300; ❄📶; S 1/2/3 to 96th St) The nine-story Newton isn't going to win any interior-design awards, but it's clean and well managed, making it a solid budget option. The 108 guest rooms are small but come stocked with TVs, minirefrigerators, coffeemakers and microwaves. Bathrooms are all well-maintained. Larger 'suites' are roomier and feature a sitting area. Wi-fi costs $6 per day extra.

NYLO HOTEL BOUTIQUE HOTEL **$$**
Map p432 (☎212-362-1100; www.nylo-nyc.com; 2178 Broadway, at 77th St; r from $299; ❄📶; S 1 to 77th St) This modern boutique hotel has 285 casually stylish rooms with warm earth tones. Niceties include plush bedding, wood floors, elegant lighting, roomy (for New York) bathrooms, coffeemakers and flat-screen TVs. 'NYLO Panoramic' rooms have furnished private terraces and extravagant Manhattan views.

The handsomely designed lounge and bar areas on the ground floor are great places to decamp after a day spent exploring. Friendly service and a great location.

LUCERNE HOTEL **$$**
Map p432 (☎212-875-1000; www.thelucernehotel.com; 201 W 79th St, cnr Amsterdam Ave; d from $300; ❄📶; S B, C to 81st St) This unusual 1903 structure breaks away from beaux arts in favor of the baroque with an ornately carved, terra-cotta-colored facade. Inside is a stately 200-room hotel, ideal for couples and families with children (Central Park and the American Museum of Natural History are a stone's throw away). Nine types of guest rooms evoke a contemporary Victorian look.

Think: flowered bedspreads, scrolled headboards and plush pillows with fringe.

Service is courteous and Nice Matin, a nice French-Mediterranean restaurant, is on-site.

HOTEL BEACON HOTEL $$

Map p432 (212-787-1100, reservations 800-572-4969; www.beaconhotel.com; 2130 Broadway, btwn 74th & 75th Sts; d $175-350; ; S1/2/3 to 72nd St) Adjacent to the Beacon Theatre, this family favorite offers a winning mix of attentive service, comfortable rooms and convenient location. The Beacon has 260 rooms (some multibedroom suites) decorated in muted shades of Pottery Barn green. The units are well-maintained and quite roomy; all come with coffeemakers and kitchenettes. Amenities include a gym and a self-service laundry room.

Upper stories have views of Central Park in the distance. It's a good deal, and steep discounts can be found off-season.

EMPIRE HOTEL HOTEL $$$

Map p432 (212-265-7400; www.empirehotelnyc.com; 44 W 63rd St, at Broadway; r from $370; ; S1 to 66th St-Lincoln Center) The bones are all that remain of the original Empire, just across the street from Lincoln Center, with wholesale renovations dressing them in earthy tones and contemporary stylings complete with canopied pool deck, sexy rooftop bar and a dimly lit lobby lounge studded with zebra-print settees. Its 400-plus rooms come in various configurations, and feature brightly hued walls with plush dark leather furnishings.

Harlem & Upper Manhattan

HARLEM FLOPHOUSE GUESTHOUSE $

Map p434 (347-632-1960; www.harlemflophouse.com; 242 W 123rd St, btwn Adam Clayton Powell Jr & Frederick Douglass Blvds, Harlem; d with shared bath $99-150; ; SA/B/C/D, 2/3 to 125th St) Rekindle Harlem's Jazz Age in this atmospheric 1890s town house, its nostalgic rooms decked out with brass beds and vintage radios (set to a local jazz station). It feels like a delicious step back in time, which also means shared bathrooms, no air-con and no TVs. The owner is a great source of local information.

Last but not least is friendly house cat Phoebe, who completes the homely, welcoming vibe.

LA MAISON D'ART GUESTHOUSE $

Map p434 (718-593-4108; www.lamaisondartny.com; 259 W 132nd St, btwn Adam Clayton Powell Jr & Frederick Douglass Blvds, Harlem; r from $183; ; S2/3 to 135th St) Situated above an art gallery, this welcoming Harlem abode harbors five comfy rooms bursting with character. Each has unique features, from antiques and a four-poster bed to an oversize Jacuzzi (the lilac-painted walls and gold curtains in the Victorian room may not be everyone's cup of tea). An added delight is the garden out back, perfect for some low-key R&R.

It's in a classic Harlem brownstone, with decent eating and drinking options in the area. It's also an easy subway ride to Midtown and other Manhattan neighborhoods.

MOUNT MORRIS HOUSE B&B GUESTHOUSE $$

Map p434 (917-478-6213; www.mountmorrishousebandb.com; 12 Mt Morris Park W, btwn 121st & 122nd Sts, Harlem; ste/apt from $175/235; ; S2/3 to 125th St) Set inside a stunning Gilded Age town house from 1888, this cozy inn offers three extravagantly spacious slumber options: a one- and a two-bedroom suite and a studio apartment with a fully equipped kitchen. Each one impresses with lovely original details and period furnishings, including Persian-style rugs and brocaded settees, not to mention fireplaces and vintage bathtubs.

Breakfast isn't offered, though complimentary coffee, tea and cakes are available all day. The property is an easy walk to 125th St. Cash preferred.

ALOFT HARLEM HOTEL $$

Map p434 (212-749-4000; www.aloftharlem.com; 2296 Frederick Douglass Blvd, btwn 123rd & 124th Sts, Harlem; d from $227; ; SA/C, B/D, 2/3 to 125th St) Designed for younger travelers, Aloft channels a luxury vibe but at accessible prices. Guest rooms are snug (285 sq ft) but chic, with crisp white linens, fluffy comforters and colorful striped bolsters. The modern bathrooms are small (no tubs) but highly functional and feature amenities courtesy of Bliss, the upscale spa chain.

A basement lounge with pool tables can get boisterous, but it'll be stumbling distance to your room. All around, Aloft is convenient (the Apollo Theater and the bustling 125th St commercial district are nearby) and a good deal.

Brooklyn

LEFFERTS MANOR BED & BREAKFAST B&B $

Map p440 (347-351-9065; www.leffertsmanorbedandbreakfast.com; 80 Rutland Rd, btwn Flatbush & Bedford Aves, Prospect Lefferts Gardens; r with shared bath $109-139, with private bath $149; ; B, Q to Prospect Park) Six sunny rooms in this classic Brooklyn brownstone feature tiled closed fireplaces, subtle color palettes and historically styled decor. Five rooms upstairs share two gleaming-white bathrooms, while the Parlor Suite has a private toilet and a clawfoot tub in a curtained niche. Downtown Manhattan is only 30 minutes away by subway. Optional continental breakfast is available; three-night minimum stay.

The owners also have rooms available in two similar properties nearby, as well as two apartments with full kitchens in Fort Greene.

SERENITY AT HOME B&B $

Map p440 (646-479-5138; www.serenityah.com; 57 Rutland Rd, btwn Bedford & Flatbush Aves, Prospect Lefferts Gardens; tw/r with shared bath from $75/130, r with private bath $165; ; B, Q to Prospect Park) A short stroll from Prospect Park in Brooklyn, this charming guesthouse is set in a lovely pre-war row house. Each of four guest rooms has wooden floors, attractive furnishings and high-quality mattresses and bedding. Note that three rooms share bathrooms, while one spacious room has its own private bathroom (boasting a clawfoot tub, no less).

Zenobia, the owner, makes guests feel right at home, and has loads of useful advice for exploring the neighborhood and the city beyond. Note that shoes are not worn inside the house (it's recommended that you bring slippers). Minimum three-night stay.

EVEN HOTEL BOUTIQUE HOTEL $

Map p443 (718-552-3800; www.evenhotels.com; 46 Nevins St, at Schermerhorn St, Downtown Brooklyn; r from $149; ; 2/3, 4/5 to Nevins St; A/C, G to Hoyt-Schermerhorn) This wellness-concept hotel has everything a fitness-minded traveler could want: an in-room 'workout zone' (with personal yoga mat, foam roller, yoga block and stability ball), a 24-hour gym, organic food and a fresh-squeezed OJ machine in the cafe, and free laundry service for your workout clothes. Its central location in Downtown Brooklyn is super convenient for subway stops, too.

LORALEI BED & BREAKFAST B&B $

(646-228-4656; www.loraleinyc.com; 667 Argyle Rd, off Foster Ave, Ditmas Park; r $145-195; ; B, Q to Newkirk Plaza) A freestanding 1904 house with wraparound porch, the Loralei feels like a small New England B&B. Two 2nd-floor suites offer queen beds, Victorian furnishings, sitting areas and private baths; the sitting room of 'the Sutton' can also be used for an additional single occupancy. Continental breakfast is included; two-night minimum stay. Downtown Manhattan is about 45 minutes away by subway.

WYTHE HOTEL BOUTIQUE HOTEL $$

Map p436 (718-460-8000; www.wythehotel.com; 80 Wythe Ave, at N 11th St, Williamsburg; d from $265; ; L to Bedford Ave; G to Nassau Ave) Set in a converted 1901 factory, the red-brick Wythe Hotel brings a serious dash of high design to Williamsburg. The industrial-chic rooms have beds made from reclaimed lumber, custom-made wallpaper (from Brooklyn's own Flavor Paper), exposed brick, polished concrete floors and original 13ft timber ceilings.

On the ground floor, Reynard dishes up brasserie classics in a lovely setting of tile floors, brick walls, soaring wood ceilings and vintage fixtures. The top-floor Ides Bar is a great spot for sunset cocktails, craft brews and memorable skyline views of Manhattan.

WILLIAMSBURG HOTEL BOUTIQUE HOTEL $$

Map p436 (718-362-8100; www.thewilliamsburghotel.com; 96 Wythe Ave, at N 10th St, Williamsburg; d from $250; ; L to Bedford Ave) Williamsburg's newest boutique hotel, just two blocks from the water, has 110 guest rooms with spectacular river and Manhattan views; it's worth paying extra for one of the 'terrace' rooms on the north side, which give you an unbroken view of the Empire State Building, Chrysler Building and Upper East Side from your artificial-grass-carpeted balcony (some have swing chairs).

The rooms aren't huge, but floor-to-ceiling windows and glassed-in showers with bright subway tiles make them feel more open. Minibars, safes and essential-oil amenities by local maker Apotheke all come standard. A rooftop bar (in the shape of a classic NYC water tower) and a swimming pool are planned to open by mid-2018.

HENRY NORMAN HOTEL BOUTIQUE HOTEL **$$**

(☎646-604-9366; www.henrynormanhotel.com; 251 N Henry St, btwn Norman & Meserole Aves, Greenpoint; lofts from $299; ; B48 to Nassau Ave/Monitor St, S G to Nassau Ave) Set in a former 19th-century warehouse, this striking brick building (once home to artists' lofts) offers bohemian chic in its high-ceilinged rooms, with hardwood floors, muted color schemes (decorated in white and gray), artwork on the walls and iPod docking stations. Pricier rooms have terraces (some with city views) and better-equipped kitchenettes. Discounted rates can be found on the website.

It's on an industrial stretch of roadway, but the hip bars, shops and cafes of Greenpoint are about a 15-minute walk away. Or take the complimentary shuttle service to avoid the bleak cityscape. The same owners also run the **Box House Hotel** (☎646-582-0172; www.theboxhousehotel.com; 77 Box St, at McGuinness Blvd, Greenpoint; r/loft/1-bedroom ste/2-bedroom ste from $170/249/379/699; ; B43 to Box St/Manhattan Ave, S 7 to Vernon Blvd-Jackson Ave; G to Greenpoint Ave), found further north in Greenpoint.

AKWAABA MANSION INN B&B **$$**

(☎718-455-5958, 866-466-3855; www.akwaaba.com; 347 MacDonough St, btwn Lewis & Stuyvesant Aves, Bedford-Stuyvesant; r $195-225; ; S A/C to Utica Ave) Sitting on a tree-lined block of tidy, century-old town houses in Bedford-Stuyvesant, this graceful B&B is tucked into a sprawling Italianate mansion built by a local beer baron back in 1860. Period design flourishes include brass beds, marble fireplaces, the original parquet floors and a screened-in wraparound porch – the perfect spot to settle in with a good book.

African textiles and vintage photographs add a personal touch. The mansion has four roomy suites, each with private bathroom (three of which have Jacuzzi tubs for two).

MCCARREN HOTEL & POOL BOUTIQUE HOTEL **$$**

Map p436 (☎718-218-7500; www.mccarrenhotel.com; 160 N 12th St, btwn Bedford Ave & Berry St, Williamsburg; d from $300; ; S L to Bedford; G to Nassau) This hip hotel just across from McCarren Park is almost insufferably chic, offering 63 minimalist rooms with bamboo flooring and marble-filled bathrooms. Pricier rooms have balconies and rain showers. The upper-level bar with retractable rooftop offers jaw-dropping views of Manhattan, while the large saltwater swimming pool is a great spot on sunny days. A gym is available for guest use.

NU HOTEL HOTEL **$$**

Map p438 (☎718-852-8585; www.nuhotelbrooklyn.com; 85 Smith St, at Atlantic Ave, Boerum Hill; d from $220; @; S F, G to Bergen St) The 93 stripped-down rooms in this hotel on the border of Boerum Hill and Downtown Brooklyn feature lots of crisp whiteness – sheets, walls, duvets – with recycled-teak furnishings and cork floors. Groups can consider the 'Bunkbed' suite with a queen and twin bunks, or for something more daring, book a 'NU Perspectives' room, adorned with colorful murals by Brooklyn artists.

There is a small lobby lounge and bikes are available. Ask for a room away from busy Atlantic Ave if you're a light sleeper.

HOTEL LE BLEU HOTEL **$$**

Map p440 (☎718-625-1500; www.hotellebleu.com; 370 Fourth Ave, at 5th St, Gowanus; d from $220; P; S F, G, R to 4th Ave-9th St) Situated on a busy avenue in Gowanus, this hotel manages to pull off 48 attractive units in a sleek palette of brown, white and blue. (It's not 'Le Bleu' for nothing.) Rooms are chock-full of amenities, including bathrobes and coffeemakers, and the rate includes a light breakfast. During off-peak periods, the low prices make this a deal.

While Fourth Ave isn't pretty, the location is excellent – it's walking distance to restaurants and bars in the heart of Park Slope and the music venues of Gowanus. Whole Foods (p280), around the corner, is a great resource for quick meals.

Queens

This sprawling borough still lags behind Manhattan and Brooklyn in terms of boutique and B&B charmers, but a rash of new hotels in Long Island City offer jaw-dropping views of Manhattan and easy access to Midtown. They are mostly chains, with a few independents, and all can offer some excellent deals.

BORO HOTEL DESIGN HOTEL **$**

Map p446 (☎718-433-1375; www.borohotel.com; 38-28 27th St, Long Island City; r from $189; P; S N/Q to 39th Ave) The Boro offers minimalist city luxe (Frette linens, plush robes, soaking tubs) for far less than you'd pay in Manhattan – with the benefit of glittering skyline views from the floor-to-ceiling windows. The hyper-minimalist, wood-floor rooms have high ceilings; many have expansive balconies. Continental breakfast is better than average, with flaky croissants and Greek yogurt.

LOCAL NYC HOSTEL **$**

Map p446 (☎347-738-5251; www.thelocalny.com; 13-02 44th Ave, Long Island City; dm/d from $60/169; ❄📶; ⓈE, M to Court Sq-23rd St) This hostel has clean and small, simply designed rooms, with comfy mattresses and plenty of natural light. Guests have access to a fully stocked kitchen and the airy cafe-bar is a fine place to meet other travelers, with good coffee by day, and wine and beer by night. Throughout the week, there's a regular lineup of events (movie nights, live music, pub quizzes).

Friendly staff are helpful in highlighting some of NYC's lesser-known gems. Don't miss the view from the rooftop.

PAPER FACTORY HOTEL HOTEL **$**

Map p446 (☎718-392-7200; www.thepaperfactoryhotel.com; 37-06 36th St, Long Island City, Queens; d $120-309; ❄📶; ⓈM, R to 36th St) In the semi-industrial neighborhood of Long Island City, you'll find this whimsical gem set in a former paper factory and warehouse. Unlike nearby chain motels, there's a level of sophistication in the industrial chic rooms, and unlike Manhattan hotels, they feel gargantuan by comparison. Reclaimed lumber and polished concrete (with vintage maps embedded in the floors) feature prominently in the lobby.

The rooms themselves continue the vintage aesthetic, albeit with comfy modern beds, good showers and big-city views. The 12ft ceilings and large windows add to the spacious feel, and locally created artwork and old-fashioned furniture make each room feel unique. The graffiti-stained rooftop has entrancing views of Manhattan, and the in-house restaurant, Mundo, serves eclectic global fare.

Z HOTEL BOUTIQUE HOTEL **$$**

Map p446 (☎877-256-5556, 212-319-7000; www.zhotelny.com; 11-01 43rd Ave, Long Island City; r from $230; ❄📶; ⓈF to 21st-Queensbridge; E, M to Court Sq-23rd St) Its location screams 'industrial wasteland,' but this design-savvy tower delivers jaw-dropping views of Manhattan. The 100 rooms are snug but stylish, in dark, contemporary shades, and the heated bathroom floors and oversized shower heads are nice extras. More astounding views await at the rooftop bar.

Freebies include wi-fi, local and international calls, and bike rental. Bargain room rates may be available online.

RAVEL BOUTIQUE HOTEL **$$**

Map p446 (☎718-289-6101; www.ravelhotel.com; 8-08 Queens Plaza S, Long Island City; r from $210; Ⓟ❄📶; ⓈF to 21st St-Queensbridge) The location may feel a little desolate, but this Long Island City option is two short subway stops from Midtown. Rooms are not as boutique-luxe as the hotel claims, but they are reasonably smart and contemporary, with vibrant accents, plush bedding and bathrooms featuring rainforest showers (the superior rooms have soaking tubs). The sleek rooftop restaurant/bar offers fine Manhattan views.

Understand New York City

NEW YORK CITY TODAY **348**
Grappling with inequality and fixing the city's aging infrastructure are among New York's biggest challenges.

HISTORY **350**
Epic triumphs, shady transactions, roaring populations and devastating storms; the story of old New York reads better than a Dickens novel.

THE NYC TABLE **359**
Fast-food favorites, a Slow Food revolution, and a rising tide of elegant cocktails, microbrews and coffee: feast the NYC way.

THE ARTS **363**
America's capital of cultural production pumps out a kaleidoscope of artistic endeavors, from the bright lights of Broadway to back-alley jazz lounges.

ARCHITECTURE **367**
Colonial abodes, Gothic Revival churches, Gotham skyscrapers and starchitect statements: NYC is a wondrous architectural drawing board.

QUEER CITY: FROM STONEWALL TO MARRIAGE EQUALITY **372**
Out and proud, New York has long led the fight for rights. It hasn't always been smooth sailing, but it's always been one heck of a ride.

NYC ON SCREEN **375**
The setting of more movies than anywhere else on earth, NYC is a seasoned star of the silver screen.

New York City Today

New York remains an economic dynamo with record-low unemployment, overflowing city coffers and a building boom that stretches across the five boroughs. Beneath the veneer, however, there are plenty of challenges, including an aging transit system, rising homelessness and the ongoing threat of terrorism. This is a city, however, that takes everything in its stride. As former president Barack Obama wrote on Twitter in 2017, 'New Yorkers are as tough as they come.'

Best on Film

Breakfast at Tiffany's (1961) New York in all its glamour and idiosyncrasy is on full display.

Taxi Driver (1976) Martin Scorsese's story of a troubled Vietnam vet turned taxi driver.

Do the Right Thing (1989) Spike Lee's critically acclaimed comedy-drama probes the racial turmoil lurking just beneath the surface.

Requiem for a Dream (2000) An unusual tale of a Brooklyn junkie and his doting Jewish mother.

Margaret (2015) Kenneth Lonergan's second film explores the devastating effects of an accident on a Manhattan teen.

Best in Print

The Amazing Adventures of Kavalier & Clay (Michael Chabon; 2000) Touches upon Brooklyn, escapism and the nuclear family.

Down These Mean Streets (Piri Thomas; 1967) Memoirs of tough times growing up in Spanish Harlem.

Invisible Man (Ralph Ellison; 1952) Poignant exploration of the situation of African Americans in the early 20th century.

Vanishing New York (Jeremiah Moss; 2017) Delves into gentrification and how NYC has changed in the 21st century.

A Progressive Mayor

Mayor Bill de Blasio came into office in 2014 aiming to address the egregious inequalities in New York. One of his big early successes was the creation of free universal prekindergarten for all New Yorkers. By September 2015, some 68,000 four-year-olds were enrolled in a free one-year head start on their educational path. In 2015 and 2016, under de Blasio, the city also instituted a rent-freeze, which benefited more than two million people living in rent-controlled apartments.

Creating affordable housing was another central goal of his agenda – envisioning the creation or preservation of 200,000 units of affordable housing by 2024. By the end of his first term in 2017, the mayor trumpeted the creation of 77,000 affordable housing units.

In the realm of wages, he gave all 50,000 city workers a raise, increasing the minimum wage to $15 an hour, which would go into effect by the end of 2018. Under the mayor, unemployment also reached record lows – 4.3% its lowest in nearly 40 years – with the private sector adding 100,000 new jobs a year during his first term. The city has also seen record-low crime rates under de Blasio.

Given his many successes, Bill de Blasio coasted to victory during his bid for reelection, winning handily his second term as the head of America's largest city in 2017.

Subway Blues

One of the big challenges New York faces is maintaining its transit system. The century-old subway has been much afflicted lately, with a host of problems. Severely overcrowded trains and the increasing frequency of train breakdowns have led to much public resentment toward the Metropolitan Transit Authority (better known as the MTA). During rush hour, some carriages are so crowded that commuters must wait for one or two trains to pass by before they can jam themselves inside. Part of the problem stems from the 1930s-era signal system that the subway still uses. According to MTA officials, updating the system would take decades and cost billions of dollars.

Adding to many New Yorkers' woes is the planned shutdown of the L train for much-needed repairs. During Hurricane Sandy in 2012, the Canarsie Tunnel, which runs under the East River, was flooded with millions of gallons of seawater, causing serious damages. This key Manhattan–Brooklyn provides service for some 400,000 riders daily. They'll have to find alternate means of transport when the L train is shut down (for a scheduled 15 months) starting in April 2019.

Tale of Two Cities

In many ways, New York is becoming ever more divided between the haves and the have-nots. Staggering development projects and high-priced apartments litter the landscape, from the $4.5-billion Hudson Yards to 432 Park, the Rafael Viñoly–designed superslim tower complete with a penthouse that recently listed for $82 million. For the wealthy, New York is the playground par excellence. One Upper East Side property, selling for $85 million, also came with a $1 million yacht and two Rolls Royce Phantoms.

Meanwhile, as developers race toward building ever taller and more luxurious condos across the city, the ranks of the homeless continue to grow. Today, there are more than 63,000 homeless in the city, over twice as many as there were in 2002. Stagnant wages and skyrocketing rents have helped fuel the crisis. From 2000 to 2014, the median NYC rent increased by nearly 20% while incomes rose by just 5%.

Most New Yorkers live between the two extremes, though the lack of affordable housing has placed a huge strain on residents. As more neighborhoods undergo gentrification, prices go up and landlords chip away at rent-stabilized apartments to command ever higher returns. This leaves many New Yorkers paying unsustainably high rents – on average residents pay nearly 60% of their income on rent. It's no wonder that of the families living in NYC's homeless shelters, one-third of the adults in these families have a job.

population per sq mile

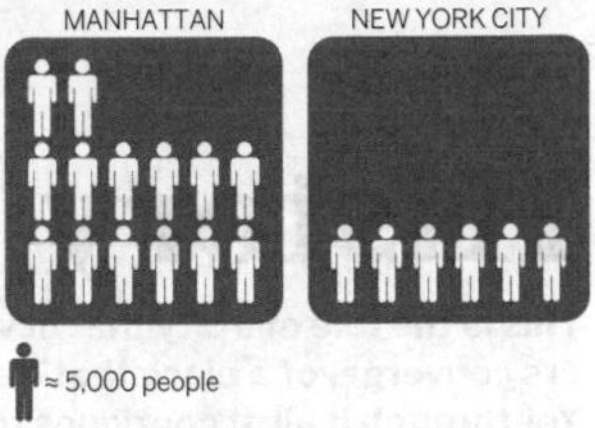

housing
(% of population)

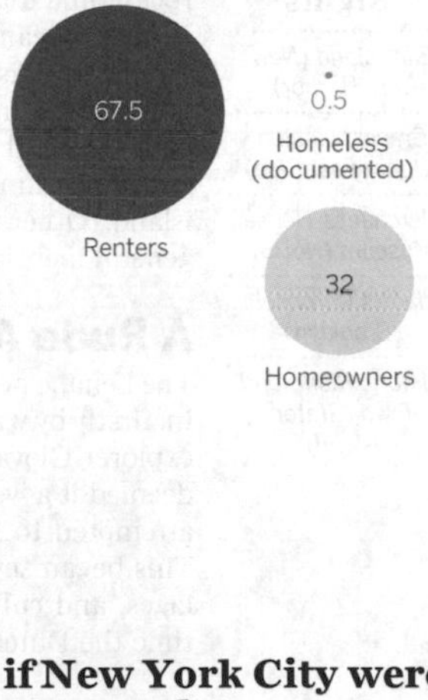

if New York City were 100 people

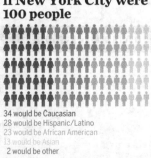

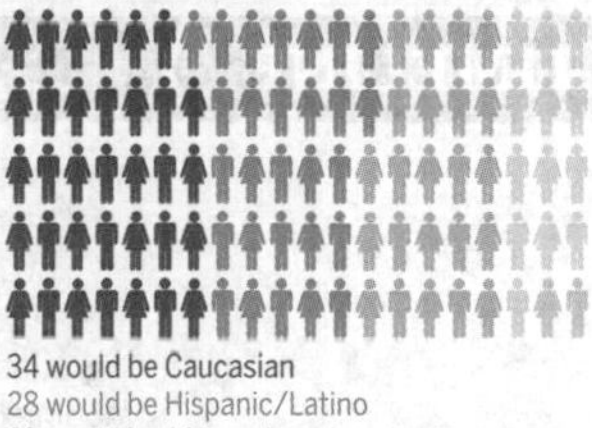

History

This is the tale of a city that never sleeps, of a kingdom where tycoons and world leaders converge, of a place that's seen the highest highs and the most devastating lows. Yet through it all, it continues to reach for the sky (both figuratively and literally). And to think it all started with $24 and a pile of beads...

Living off the Land

Long before the days of European conquest, the swath that would eventually become NYC belonged to Native Americans known as the Lenape (Original People), who resided in a series of seasonal campsites. They lived up and down the eastern seaboard, along the signature shoreline, and on hills and in valleys sculpted by glaciers after the Ice Age left New York with glacial debris now called Hamilton Heights and Bay Ridge. Glaciers scoured off soft rock, leaving behind Manhattan's stark rock foundations of gneiss and schist. Around 11,000 years before the first Europeans sailed through the Narrows, the Lenape people foraged, hunted and fished the regional bounty here. Spear points, arrowheads, bone heaps and shell mounds testify to their presence. Some of their pathways still lie beneath streets such as Broadway. In the Lenape language of Munsee, the term *Manhattan* may have translated as 'hilly island.' Others trace the meaning to a more colorful phrase: 'place of general inebriation.'

NYC's Top Historical Sights

- *Ellis Island (New York Harbor)*
- *Gracie Mansion (Upper East Side)*
- *Merchant's House Museum (NoHo)*
- *Jane's Carousel (Brooklyn)*
- *Historic Richmond Town (Staten Island)*

A Rude Awakening

The Lenape people lived undisturbed until European explorers muscled in, firstly by way of the French vessel *La Dauphine,* piloted by Florentine explorer Giovanni da Verrazano. He explored the Upper Bay in 1524, deemed it a 'very beautiful lake,' and, while anchored at Staten Island, attempted to kidnap some of the Native Americans he encountered. This began several decades of European explorers raiding Lenape villages, and cultivated the Lenape's deep mistrust of outsiders. By the time the Dutch West India Company employee Henry Hudson arrived

TIMELINE

c AD 1500

About 15,000 Native Americans live in 80 sites around the island. The groups include the feuding Iroquois and Algonquins.

1625–26

As the population of New Amsterdam reaches 200, the Dutch West India Company imports slaves from Africa to work in the fur trade and construction.

1646

The Dutch found the village of Breuckelen on the East River shore of Long Island, naming it after Breukelen in the Netherlands; it will remain an independent city until 1898.

in 1609, encounters with Native Americans were often dichotomized into two crude stories that alternated between 'delightful primitives' and 'brutal savages.'

Buying Manhattan

The Dutch West India Company sent 110 settlers to begin a trading post here in 1624. They settled in Lower Manhattan and called their colony New Amsterdam, touching off bloody battles with the unshakable Lenape. It all came to a head in 1626, when the colony's first governor, Peter Minuit, became the city's first – but certainly not the last – unscrupulous real-estate agent, by purchasing Manhattan's 14,000 acres from the Lenape for 60 guilders ($24) and some glass beads.

Peg Leg, Iron Fist

Following the purchase of Manhattan in 1626, the colony quickly fell into disrepair under the governance of Willem Kieft. Then Peter Stuyvesant stepped in and busily set about fixing the demoralized settlement, making peace with the Lenape, establishing markets and a night watch, repairing the fort, digging a canal (under the current Canal St) and authorizing a municipal wharf. His vision of an orderly and prosperous trading port was partially derived from his previous experience as governor of Curaçao. The burgeoning sugar economy in the Caribbean inspired an investment in slave trading that soon boosted New Amsterdam's slave workforce to 20% of the population. After long service, some were partially freed and given 'Negroe Lots' near today's Greenwich Village, the Lower East Side and City Hall. The Dutch West India Company encouraged the fruitful connection to plantation economies on the islands, and issued advertisements and offered privileges to attract merchants to the growing port. Although these 'liberties' did not at first extend to the Jews who fled the Spanish Inquisition, the Dutch West India Company turned Stuyvesant's intolerance around. By the 1650s, warehouses, workshops and gabled houses were spreading back from the dense establishments at the river's edge on Pearl St.

By 1664, the English showed up in battleships, ready for a fight. Stuyvesant was tired, though, and avoided bloodshed by surrendering without a shot. King Charles II promptly renamed the colony after his brother, the Duke of York. New York became a prosperous British port with a population of 11,000 by the mid-1700s. The city grew in prominence as the change point for the exchange of slaves and goods between worlds. The honeymoon, however, was short lived.

NYC Names & Their Dutch Origins

Gramercy: Kromme Zee ('crooked lake')

Coney Island: Konijneneiland ('rabbits island')

Yonkers: Jonker ('squire')

Bowery: bouwerij (old-fashioned word for 'farm')

Bronx: named for Jonas Bronck

1754

The first institution of higher learning, King's College, is founded by royal charter from George II. After the American Revolution, it's reborn as Columbia University.

1776

American colonies sign the *Declaration of Independence* on July 4. Figures who helped create this document include John Hancock, Samuel Adams and Benjamin Franklin.

1784

Alexander Hamilton founds the Bank of New York, with holdings of $500,000. Almost a decade later, it will become the first corporate stock to be traded on the NYSE.

1789

Following a seven-day procession from his home in Mount Vernon, George Washington is inaugurated at Federal Hall as the country's first president.

Freedom of the Press & the Great Negro Plot

New York City was the first capital of the United States – George Washington took his first presidential oath at Federal Hall in 1789.

Rising tensions were evident in the colonial press, as John Peter Zenger's *New York Weekly Journal* flayed the king and royal governor so regularly that the authorities tried to convict Zenger for seditious libel in 1733. He was acquitted and that was the beginning of what we know today as 'freedom of the press.'

In 1741, a spate of fires occurred across the city, including one at Fort George, then home of Lieutenant Governor George Clarke. The blazes were widely blamed on African-American slaves, and rumors quickly spread of a planned rebellion by blacks and poorer white settlers to burn down New York City. Despite contradictory accounts and a lack of solid evidence, the so-called Great Negro Plot led to the arrest and execution of numerous slaves and their alleged conspirators.

Revolution & War

Patriots clashed in public spaces with Tories, who were loyal to the king, while Lieutenant Colonel Alexander Hamilton, an intellectual, became a fierce anti-British organizer. Citizens fled the city, sensing the oncoming war, and revolutionary battle began in August of 1776, when General George Washington's army lost about a quarter of its men in just a couple of days. He retreated, and fire encompassed much of the colony. But soon the British left and Washington's army reclaimed their city. After a series of celebrations, banquets and fireworks at Bowling Green, General Washington bade farewell to his officers at what is now the Fraunces Tavern Museum and retired as commander in chief.

However, in 1789, to his surprise, the retired general found himself addressing crowds at Federal Hall, gathered to witness his presidential inauguration. Alexander Hamilton, meanwhile, began rebuilding New York and became Washington's secretary of the treasury, working to establish the New York Stock Exchange. But people distrusted a capitol located adjacent to the financial power of Wall St merchants, and New Yorkers lost the seat of the presidency to Philadelphia shortly thereafter.

On December 16, 1835, a gas line broke in a dry-goods store near Hanover Square, causing a massive fire to quickly spread south down Stone St and northeast toward Wall St. Raging for over a day, it destroyed much of what remained of the original Dutch and British colonial city.

Population Bust, Infrastructure Boom

The 19th century brought with it plenty of setbacks: the bloody Draft Riots of 1863, massive cholera epidemics, rising tensions among 'old' and new immigrants, and the serious poverty and crime of Five Points, the city's first slum, located where Chinatown now lies. Eventually, though, the city was prosperous and found resources to build mighty public works. A great aqueduct system brought Croton Water to city

1811

Manhattan's grid plan is developed by Mayor DeWitt Clinton, which leads to reshaping the city by leveling hills, filling in swamps and laying out plans for future streets.

1825

The Erie Canal, considered one of the greatest engineering feats of the era, is ceremoniously completed, greatly influencing trade and commerce in New York.

1853

The State Legislature authorizes the allotment of public lands, which removes 17,000 potential building sites from the real-estate market for what will later become Central Park.

1863

The Civil War Draft Riots erupt in New York, lasting for three days and ending only when President Lincoln dispatches combat troops from the Federal Army to restore order.

dwellers, relieving thirst and stamping out the cholera that was sweeping the town. Irish immigrants helped dig a 363-mile 'ditch' – the Erie Canal – linking the Hudson River with Lake Erie. The canal's chief backer, Mayor DeWitt Clinton, celebrated the waterway by ceremonially pouring a barrel of Erie water into the sea. Clinton was also the mastermind behind the modern-day grid system of Manhattan's street layout – a plan created by his commission to organize the city in the face of an oncoming population explosion.

And there was yet another grand project afoot – one to boost the health of the people crammed into tiny tenement apartments – in the form of an 843-acre public park. Begun in 1855 in an area so far uptown that some immigrants kept pigs, sheep and goats there, Central Park was both a vision of green reform and a boon to real-estate speculation.

Another vision was realized by German-born engineer John Roebling, who sought a solution to a series of winter freezes that had shut down the ferry system connecting downtown Manhattan to Brooklyn, then an independent city. He designed a soaring symphony of spun wire and Gothic arches to span the East River, and his Brooklyn Bridge accelerated the fusion of the neighboring cities.

By the turn of the 20th century, elevated trains carried one million people a day in and out of the city. Rapid transit opened up areas of the Bronx and Upper Manhattan, spurring mini building booms in areas near the lines. At this point, the city was simply overflowing with the masses of immigrants arriving from southern Italy and Eastern Europe, who had boosted the metropolis's population to around three million. The journey from immigrant landing stations at Castle Garden and Ellis Island led straight to the Lower East Side. There, streets reflected these myriad origins with shop signs in Yiddish, Italian, German and Chinese.

New York's Brooklyn Bridge opened with suitable fanfare on May 24, 1883. After New York mayor Franklin Edison and Brooklyn mayor Seth Low led President Chester Arthur and Governor Grover Cleveland across the structure, more than 150,000 members of the public followed suit, each paying a penny for the honor.

Class Lessons

All sorts of folks were living in squalor by the late 19th century, when the immigration processing center at Ellis Island opened, welcoming one million newcomers in just its first year. They crammed into packed tenements, shivered in soup lines and shoveled snow for nickels.

Meanwhile, newly wealthy folks – boosted by an economy jump-started by financier JP Morgan, who bailed out sinking railroads and led to the city becoming the headquarters of Standard Oil and US Steel – began to build increasingly splendid mansions on Fifth Ave. Modeled on European chateaux, palaces such as the Vanderbilt home, on the corner of 52nd St and Fifth Ave, reached for new summits of opulence. Tapestries adorned marble halls, mirrored ballrooms reflected

1882

Thomas Edison switches on the city's first electric lights at the JP Morgan bank at 23 Wall St. On the same November day, electricity is delivered to 85 Manhattan addresses.

1883

The Brooklyn Bridge, which was built at a cost of $15.5 million (and 27 lives) opens; 150,000 people walk across its span at the inaugural celebration.

1886

The Statue of Liberty's pedestal is completed, allowing the large lady to be presented to New York at a dedication ceremony that takes place before thousands of citizens.

1898

The *Charter of New York* is ratified and the five boroughs of Brooklyn, Staten Island, Queens, the Bronx and Manhattan unite to become the largest city in America.

bejeweled revelers, and liveried footmen guided grand ladies from their gilded carriages in a society where Astors, Fricks and Carnegies ruled. Reporter and photographer Jacob Riis illuminated the widening gap between the classes by writing about it in the *New York Tribune* and in his now-classic 1890 book, *How the Other Half Lives,* eventually forcing the city to pass much-needed housing reforms.

New York City has around 660 miles of subway tracks used for passenger services. Counting railyards and other nonpassenger-service tracks, the figure exceeds 840 miles.

Factory Tragedy, Women's Rights

Wretched factory conditions – low pay, long hours, abusive employers – in the early 20th century were highlighted by a tragic event in 1911. The infamous Triangle Shirtwaist Company fire saw rapidly spreading flames catch onto the factory's piles of fabrics, killing 146 of 500 female workers who were trapped behind locked doors. The event led to sweeping labor reforms after 20,000 female garment workers marched to City Hall. At the same time, suffragists held street-corner rallies to obtain the vote for women. Nurse and midwife Margaret Sanger opened the first birth-control clinic in Brooklyn, where 'purity police' promptly arrested her. After her release from jail in 1921 she formed the American Birth Control League (now Planned Parenthood), which provided services for young women and researched methods of safe birth control.

The Jazz Age

The 1920s saw the dawning of the Jazz Age, when Prohibition outlawed the sale of alcohol, encouraging bootlegging and speakeasies, as well as organized crime. Congenial mayor James Walker was elected in 1925, Babe Ruth reigned at Yankee Stadium and the Great Migration from the South led to the Harlem Renaissance, when the neighborhood became a center of African American culture and society. It produced poetry, music, painting and an innovative attitude that continues to influence and inspire. Harlem's daring nightlife in the 1920s and '30s attracted the flappers and gin-soaked revelers who marked the complete failure of Prohibition, and provided a foretaste of the liberated nightlife New Yorkers enjoy today. But the fun could not last forever – economic collapse was looming.

Forgotten-NY.com is Queens native Kevin Walsh's compendium of historical NYC, with not-found-elsewhere tales about everything from old subway stations to cemeteries.

Hard Times

The stock market crashed in 1929, beginning the Great Depression of the 1930s, which the city dealt with through a combination of grit, endurance, rent parties, militancy and a slew of public-works projects. The once-grand Central Park blossomed with shacks, derisively called Hoovervilles, after the president who refused to help the needy.

1904

Luna Park in Coney Island opens, followed by Dreamland amusement park. Meanwhile, the IRT subway carries 150,000 passengers on its very first day of operation.

1919

The Yankees acquire slugger Babe Ruth from Boston, leading to their first championship.

1931

The Empire State Building (1454ft tall) supersedes the Chrysler Building as the world's tallest skyscraper; the World Trade Center's north tower steals the crown in 1970.

1939

The World's Fair opens in Queens. With the future as its theme, the exposition invites visitors to take a look at 'the world of tomorrow.'

But Mayor Fiorello La Guardia found a friend in President Franklin Roosevelt, and worked his Washington connections to great effect to bring relief money – and subsequent prosperity – home.

WWII brought troops galore to the city, ready to party down to their last dollar in Times Square, before being shipped off to Europe. Converted to war industries, the local factories hummed, staffed by women and African American workers who had rarely before had access to good, unionized jobs. The explosion of wartime activity led to a huge housing crunch, which brought New York its much-imitated, tenant-protecting Rent Control Law.

There were few evident controls on business, as Midtown bulked up with skyscrapers after the war. The financial center marched north, while banker David Rockefeller and his brother, Governor Nelson Rockefeller, dreamed up the Twin Towers to revitalize downtown.

Enter Robert Moses

Working with Mayor La Guardia to usher the city into the modern age was Robert Moses, an urban planner who would influence the physical shape of the city more than anyone else in the 20th century – either wonderfully or tragically, depending on whom you ask. He was the mastermind behind the Triborough Bridge (now the Robert F Kennedy Bridge), Jones Beach State Park, the Verrazano-Narrows Bridge, the West Side Hwy and the Long Island parkway system – not to mention endless highways, tunnels and bridges. His vision was one of doing away with intimate neighborhoods of brownstones and town houses, and of creating sweeping parks and soaring towers. The approach got preservationists fired up and their efforts to stop him from bulldozing neighborhoods led to the Landmarks Preservation Commission being formed in 1965.

NYC's Tallest Buildings

Woolworth Building (792ft; 1913–1930)

Chrysler Building (1046ft; 1930–31)

Empire State Building (1454ft; 1931–1972 & 2001–2012)

World Trade Center (1368ft; 1972–2001)

One World Trade Center (1776ft; 2012–present)

Move to the Beats

The 1960s ushered in an era of legendary creativity and anti-establishment expression, with many of its creators centered right downtown in Greenwich Village. One movement was abstract expressionism, a large-scale outbreak of American painters – Mark Rothko, Jackson Pollock, Lee Krasner, Helen Frankenthaler and Willem de Kooning among them – who offended and intrigued with incomprehensible squiggles and blotches and exuberant energy. Then there were the writers, such as Beat poets Allen Ginsberg and Jack Kerouac and novelist/playwright Jane Bowles. They gathered in Village coffeehouses to exchange ideas and find inspiration, which was often found in the form of folk music from burgeoning big names, such as Bob Dylan.

1941

Duke Ellington's band leader Billy Strayhorn, inspired by the subway line that leads to Harlem, composes 'Take the A Train,' which becomes the band's signature song.

1945

The United Nations, headquartered on Manhattan's east side, is established after representatives of 50 countries meet in San Francisco to agree on a charter.

1963

The original Penn Station is demolished to build Madison Square Garden; outcry leads to the foundation of the Landmarks Preservation Commission.

1969

On June 28, eight police officers raid the gay-friendly Stonewall Inn. Patrons revolt, sparking days of rioting and the birth of the modern gay-rights movement.

THREE WOMEN WHO CHANGED NEW YORK

Margaret Sanger (1879–1966) A nurse, midwife and activist, Margaret Sanger opened the first birth-control clinic in the country in NYC in 1916. She eventually founded the American Birth Control League, which would later become Planned Parenthood.

Jane Jacobs (1917–2006) Sprung into action against Robert Moses' plan to clear a huge tract of her neighborhood for public housing, Jane Jacobs defended preservation and inspired the creation of the Landmarks Preservation Commission (the first such US group).

Christine Quinn (b 1966) In 2006 Christine Quinn became the first woman and open lesbian to become City Council Speaker, breaking gender and sexuality boundaries as the second-most-powerful official (after the mayor) in NYC.

'Drop Dead'

By the early 1970s, deficits had created a serious fiscal crisis, effectively demoting the elected mayor Abraham Beame to a figurehead, turning over the city's real financial power to Governor Carey and his appointees. President Ford's refusal to lend federal aid – summed up nicely by the *Daily News* headline 'Ford to City, Drop Dead!' – marked the nadir of relationships between the US and the city it loved to hate. As massive layoffs decimated the city's working class, untended bridges, roads and parks reeked of hard times.

The traumatic '70s – which reached a low point in 1977 with a citywide blackout and terrorizing serial killer David Berkowitz – saw rents fall, which helped nourish an exciting alternative culture that staged performances in abandoned schools, opened galleries in unused storefronts and breathed new life into the hair-dye industry with the advent of the punk-rock aesthetic. The fees from shooting the movie *Fame* at PS 122 at 9th St and First Ave, for example, helped pay for the renovation of the still-popular performance space. Ramones-loving punks turned former warehouses into pulsing meccas of nightlife, transforming the former industrial precincts of SoHo and Tribeca. Immortalized in Nan Goldin's famous photographic performance piece *The Ballad of Sexual Dependency,* this renaissance challenged gender roles and turned the East Village into America's center of tattooing and independent filmmaking.

History on the Pages

The Historical Atlas of New York City (Eric Homberger; 1998)

Gotham (Edwin G Burrows and Mike Wallace; 2003)

The Restless City (Joanne Reitano; 2006)

Taxi! (Graham Russell Gao Hodges; 2007)

New York: The Novel (Edward Rutherfurd; 2010)

Out of the Ashes

During the 1970s a wave of arson attacks reduced blocks of apartment houses in the South Bronx to cinders. Amid the smoke, an influential

1977

Following a lightning strike at a power substation, a summer blackout leaves New Yorkers in the dark for 24 sweltering hours, which leads to rioting around the city.

1988

Squatters, who had turned the East Village's Tompkins Square Park into a massive homeless encampment, riot when cops attempt to remove them from their de facto home.

1993

On February 26, terrorists detonate a bomb below the North Tower of the World Trade Center. The explosion kills six people and injures more than 1000.

2001

On September 11, terrorist hijackers fly two planes into the Twin Towers, destroying the World Trade Center and killing nearly 3000 people.

hip-hop culture was born, fueled by the percussive rhythms of Puerto Rican salsa. Rock Steady Crew, led by 'Crazy Legs' Richie Colón, pioneered athletic, competitive break dancing. Kool DJ Herc spun vinyl for break beat all-night dance parties. Afrika Bambaataa, another founding hip-hop DJ, formed Zulu Nation, bringing DJs, break dancers and graffiti writers together to end violence.

Daring examples of graffiti dazzled the public with train-long graphics. The best-known 'masterpiece' belied the graf writers' reputation as vandals: Lee 163, with the Fab 5 crew, painted a whole car of trains with the message 'Merry Christmas, New York.' Some of these maestros of the spray can infiltrated the art world, most notably Jean-Michel Basquiat, once known by his tag 'Samo.'

Some of the money snagged in the booming stock markets of the 1980s was spent on art, but even more was blown up the noses of young traders. While Manhattan neighborhoods struggled with the spread of crack cocaine, the city reeled from the impact of addiction, citywide crime and an AIDS epidemic that cut through communities.

David Berkowitz (nicknamed Son of Sam) terrified New York from 1976 to 1977 with a spate of shootings that killed six and wounded seven. The attacks were ruthless and unexpected, with several victims shot while sitting in their cars. When caught in August 1977, Berkowitz quipped, 'What took you so long?'.

Dot-Com Days

A *Time* magazine cover in 1990 sported a feature story on 'New York: The Rotting Apple.' Still convalescing from the real-estate crash at the end of the 1980s, the city faced crumbling bridges and roads, jobs leaking south and Fortune 500 companies hopping the rivers to suburbia. And then the dot-com market roared in, turning geeks into millionaires and the New York Stock Exchange into a speculator's fun park. Buoyed by tax receipts from IPO (initial public offering) profits, the city launched a frenzy of building, boutique-ing and partying unparalleled since the 1920s.

With pro-business, law-and-order-loving Rudy Giuliani as mayor, the dingy and destitute were swept from Manhattan's yuppified streets to the outer boroughs, leaving room for Generation X to score digs and live the high life. Mayor Giuliani grabbed headlines with his campaign to stamp out crime, even kicking the sex shops off notoriously seedy 42nd St. The energetic mayor succeeded in making New York America's safest big city, by targeting high-crime areas and using statistics to focus police presence. Crime dropped, restaurants boomed, real-estate prices sizzled, and *Sex & the City* beamed a vision of sophisticated singles in Manolos around the world.

Still, things were faltering in New York at the dawn of the new millennium, and, when that fateful day came in 2001, it forever changed the perspective of both the city and the world.

2002

Gambino crime-family boss John Gotti (the Dapper Don) dies of cancer in prison while serving a sentence for murder, racketeering, tax evasion and other charges.

2008–9

The stock market crashes due to mismanagement by major American financial institutions. The Global Financial Crisis spreads worldwide.

2009

On January 15, US Airways Flight 1549 plunges in the Hudson River after losing engine power. All 150 passengers and five crew members are successfully evacuated.

2011

The second phase of the High Line opens, effectively doubling its size. A third portion, opened in September 2014, revamps industrial land in the West 30s.

September 11

On September 11, 2001, terrorists flew two hijacked planes into the World Trade Center's Twin Towers, turning the whole complex to dust and rubble and killing nearly 3000 people. Downtown Manhattan took months to recover from the ghastly fumes wafting from the ruins as forlorn missing-person posters grew ragged on brick walls. While the city mourned its dead and recovery crews coughed their way through the debris, residents braved constant terrorist alerts and an anthrax scare. Shock and grief drew people together, uniting the oft-fractious citizenry in a determined effort not to succumb to despair.

The September 11 terrorist attacks caused an estimated $60 billion in damages to the World Trade Center site, including damage to infrastructure, the subway system and surrounding buildings. It took 3.1 million hours of labor to clean up 1.8 million tons of debris, at a cost of $750 million.

Protests, Storms & Political Change

The decade after September 11 was a period of rebuilding – both physically and emotionally. In 2002, then-mayor Michael Bloomberg began the unenviable task of picking up the pieces of a shattered city that had thrust all of its support behind his predecessor, Mayor Giuliani, whose popularity rose in the wake of September 11.

Much to Bloomberg's pleasure, New York saw much renovation and reconstruction, especially after the city hit its stride with spiking tourist numbers in 2005. In 2008, however, the economy buckled under its own weight, in what has largely become known as the Global Financial Crisis. Anger toward the perceived recklessness of America's financial institutions saw thousands take to the Financial District's Zuccotti Park on September 17, 2011, in a stand against the nation's unfair division of personal wealth. Known as Occupy Wall Street, the protest subsequently spread to hundreds of other cities across the world.

Fury of the meteorological kind hit New York in 2012, in the form of superstorm Hurricane Sandy. While a prestorm surge on October 28 turned parts of Brooklyn and New Jersey into a New World Venice, Sandy saved her ultimate blow for the following day. Cyclonic winds and drenching rain pounded the city, causing severe flooding and property damage, including to the NYC subway system, Hugh L Carey Tunnel and World Trade Center site. A major power blackout plunged much of Lower Manhattan into surreal darkness, while trading at the New York Stock Exchange was suspended for two days in its first weather-related closure since 1888.

The winds of political change swept through the city in November 2013, when Bill de Blasio became the city's first Democrat mayor since 1989. The 52-year-old self-proclaimed 'progressive' also became the first white mayor of NYC with an African American spouse.

2012
Superstorm Sandy hits NYC in October, causing major flooding and property damage, cutting power and shutting down the New York Stock Exchange for two days.

2013
Bill de Blasio wins the NYC mayoral election, defeating opponent Joseph J Lhota and becoming the city's first Democratic mayor in almost 20 years.

2014
The World Trade Center redevelopment nears completion with the opening of the National September 11 Memorial Museum and One World Trade Center.

2017
After many successes in the realms of creating universal pre-K, lowering unemployment and raising the minimum wage, Bill de Blasio wins a second term as mayor.

The NYC Table

Unlike California or the South, New York doesn't have one defining cuisine. Ask for some 'New York food' and you'll wind up with anything from brick-oven pizza to vegan soul food in Harlem. Cuisine in the multicultural city is global by definition, a testament to the immigrants who have unpacked their bags and recipes on its streets. And just like the city itself, it's a scene that's constantly evolving, driven by insatiable ambition.

Urban Farm to Table

Whether it's upstate triple-cream Kunik at Bedford Cheese Shop (p174) or Montauk Pearls oysters at fine-dining Craft (p170), New York City's passion for all things local and artisanal continues unabated. The city itself has become an unlikely food bowl, with an ever-growing number of rooftops, backyards and community gardens finding new purpose as urban farms.

While you can expect to find anything from organic tomatoes atop Upper East Side delis to beehives on East Village tenement rooftops, the current queen of the crop is Brooklyn Grange (www.brooklyngrangefarm.com), an organic farm covering two rooftops in Long Island City and the Brooklyn Navy Yards. At 2.5 acres, it's purportedly the world's biggest rooftop farm, producing over 50,000lb of organically cultivated goodness annually, from eggs to carrots, chard and heirloom tomatoes. The project is the brainchild of young farmer Ben Flanner. Obsessed with farm-to-table eating, this former E*Trade marketing manager kick-started NYC's rooftop revolution in 2009 with the opening of its first rooftop soil farm – Eagle Street Rooftop Farm – in nearby Greenpoint. Flanner's collaborators include some of the city's top eateries, among them Marlow & Sons (p287) and Roberta's (p287) in Brooklyn, and Dutch (p97) in Manhattan.

Bargain-savvy gastronomes love the biannual NYC Restaurant Week. Taking place in January to February and July to August, it sees many of the city's restaurants, including some of its very best, serve up three-course lunches for $29, or three-course dinners for $42. Check www.nycgo.com/restaurantweek for details and reservations.

Food Specialties

While the concept of 'New York cuisine' is inherently ambiguous, this town is not without its edible icons. It's the bites with the longest histories that folks usually have in mind when they refer to NYC specialties. Among these are bagels and pizza, introduced by Eastern European Jews and Italians, among the earliest wave of immigrants. Have one! Have three! But leave room for the cheesecake, egg creams and dogs.

Bagels

Bagels may have been invented in Europe, but they were perfected around the turn of the 19th century in NYC – and once you've had one here, you'll have a hard time enjoying one anywhere else. It's a straightforward masterpiece: a ring of plain-yeast dough that's first boiled and then baked, either left plain or topped with various finishing touches, from sesame seeds to chocolate chips. 'Bagels' made in other parts of the country are often just baked and not boiled, which makes them nothing more than a roll with a hole. And even if they do get boiled elsewhere, bagel-makers here claim that it's the New York water that adds an elusive sweetness never to be found anywhere else. Which baker creates the 'best' bagel in New York is a matter of (hotly contested) opinion, but most agree that Manhattan's Ess-a-Bagel (p194) and Queens' Brooklyn Bagel & Coffee Company (p312) rank pretty high. The most traditionally New York way to order one is by asking for a 'bagel and a schmear,' which will yield you said bagel with a small but thick swipe of cream cheese. Or splurge and add some lox – thinly sliced smoked salmon – as was originally sold from pushcarts on the Lower East Side by Jewish immigrants back in the early 1900s.

Pizza

Pizza is certainly not indigenous to Gotham. But New York–style pizza is a very particular item, and the first pizzeria in America was **Lombardi's** (Map p408; ☎212-941-7994; www.firstpizza.com; 32 Spring St, btwn Mulberry & Mott Sts, Nolita; small/large pizza from $21.50/24.50; ⏰11:30am-11pm Sun-Thu, to midnight Fri & Sat; Ⓢ6 to Spring St; J/Z to Bowery) in Manhattan's Little Italy, which opened in 1905.

While Chicago–style pizza is 'deep dish' and Californian tends to be light and doughy, New York prides itself on pizza with a thin crust, an even thinner layer of sauce and triangular slices (unless they're Sicilian-style, in which case they're rectangular). Pizza made its way over to New York in the 1900s through Italian immigrants and its regional style soon developed, the thin crust allowing for faster cooking time in a city where everyone is always in a hurry.

Today there are pizza parlors about every 10 blocks, especially in Manhattan and most of Brooklyn, where you'll find standard slices for $3. The style at each place varies slightly – some places touting cracker-thin crust, others offering slightly thicker and chewier versions, and plenty of nouveau styles throwing everything from shrimp to cherries on top. The city's booming locavore movement has also made its mark, with hipster pizzerias like Roberta's (p287) in Brooklyn peddling wood-fired pies topped with sustainable, local produce.

City Harvest (www.cityharvest.org) is a nonprofit organization that distributes unused food to around 1.4 million struggling New Yorkers each year. A whopping 150,000lb of food is rescued daily from city restaurants, bakeries and catering companies. Individuals wanting to make a monetary donation can do so via the City Harvest website.

Hot Dogs

The hot dog made its way to New York via various European butchers in the 1800s. One, Charles Feltman of Germany, was apparently the first to sell them from pushcarts along the Coney Island seashore. But Nathan Handwerker, originally an employee of Feltman's, opened his own shop across the street, offering hot dogs at half the price of those at Feltman's and put his former employer out of business. Today, the original and legendary Nathan's still stands in Coney Island, while its empire has expanded on an international scale. There is barely a New York neighborhood that does not have at least a few hot-dog vendors on its street corners, although some locals would never touch one of those 'dirty-water dogs,' preferring the new wave of chichi hot-dog shops that can be found all over town. Enjoy yours, wherever it's from, with 'the works': smothered with spicy brown mustard, relish, sauerkraut and onions.

Egg Creams

Now don't go expecting eggs or cream in this frothy, old-school beverage – just milk, seltzer water and plenty of chocolate syrup (preferably the classic Fox's U-Bet brand, made in Brooklyn). When Louis Auster of Brooklyn, who owned soda fountains on the Lower East Side, invented the treat back in 1890, the syrup he used was indeed made with eggs and he added cream to thicken the concoction. The name stuck, even though the ingredients were modified, and soon they were a staple of every soda fountain in New York. While Mr Auster sold them for 3¢ apiece, today they'll cost you anywhere from $2.50 to $5, depending on where you find one – which could be from old-school institutions such as Katz's Delicatessen (p119) in the Lower East Side or Tom's Restaurant (p284) in Brooklyn.

New York–Style Cheesecake

In one form or another, cheesecake has been around for quite a while. Look back 2400 years and you'll notice that Greek historian Thucydides and his posse were already kneading honey into fresh feta and baking it over hot coals for a sweet treat. Centuries later, the Romans adopted it, tweaking the concept by incorporating spelt flour for a more 'cake-like' form. This would be followed by countless more tweaks across the continent and centuries.

It would, however, take the error of a 19th-century New York farmer to create the key ingredient in New York–style cheesecake: cream cheese. A botched attempt at making French Neufchâtel cheese resulted in a curious product with the texture of polyethylene plastic. Enter James Kraft, founder of Kraft Foods, who picked it up in 1912, reformulated it, wrapped it in foil and introduced the country to the wonder of cream cheese.

Classic New York cheesecake would be immortalized by Lindy's restaurant in Midtown. Opened by Leo Lindemann in 1921, the particular type of confection served there – made of cream cheese, heavy cream, a dash of vanilla and a cookie crust – became wildly popular in the '40s. Today, this calorific local masterpiece is a staple on countless dessert menus, whether you're at a Greek diner or haute-cuisine hot spot. The most famous (and arguably best) cheesecake in town is that from Brooklyn stalwart Junior's (www.juniorscheesecake.com), whose well-known fans include Barack Obama.

There's a plethora of books about NYC's culinary history. Top reads include William Grimes' *Appetite City: A Culinary History of New York*, Arthur Schwartz's *New York City Food: An Opinionated History and More Than 100 Legendary Recipes*, and *Gastropolis: Food & New York City*, edited by Annie Hauck-Lawson and Jonathan Deutsch.

Drink Specialties

Cocktails

New York City is a master of mixed libations. After all, this is the home of Manhattans, legendary speakeasies and cosmo-clutching columnists with a passion for fashion. Legend has it that the city's namesake drink, the Manhattan – a blend of whiskey, sweet vermouth and bitters – began life on the southeastern corner of 26th St and Madison Ave, at the long-gone Manhattan Club. The occasion was a party in 1874, allegedly thrown by Jennie Churchill (mother of British prime minister Winston) to celebrate Samuel J Tilden's victory in the New York gubernatorial election. One of the barmen decided to create a drink to mark the occasion, naming it in honor of the bar.

Another New York classic was born that very year – the summer-centric Tom Collins. A mix of dry gin, sugar, lemon juice and club soda, the long drink's name stems from an elaborate hoax in which hundreds of locals were informed that a certain Tom Collins had been sullying their good names. While many set out to track him down, clued-in bartenders relished the joke by making the drink and naming it for the fictitious troublemaker. When the aggrieved stormed into the bars looking for a Tom Collins, they were served the drink to cool their tempers.

These days, NYC's kicking cocktail scene is big on rediscovered recipes, historical anecdotes and vintage speakeasy style. Once, obscure bartenders such as Harry Johnson and Jerry Thomas are now born-again legends, their vintage concoctions revived by a new generation of braces-clad mixologists. Historic ingredients such as Crème de Violette, Old Tom gin and Batavia Arrack are back in vogue. In the Financial District, cocktail bar Dead Rabbit (p81) has gone one further, reintroducing the 17th-century practice of pop-inns, drinks that fuse ale, liqueurs, spices and botanicals.

Then there are the city's revered single-spirit establishments, among them whiskey-versed **Ward III** (Map p406; ☎212-240-9194; www.ward3tribeca.com; 111 Reade St, btwn Church St & W Broadway; ⏰4pm-4am Mon-Fri, 5pm-4am Sat, to 2am Sun; 📶; Ⓢ A/C, 1/2/3 to Chambers St) in Tribeca, and the self-explanatory Brandy Library (p81) and Rum House (p202), in Tribeca and Midtown respectively. There's even a drinking den devoted to Moonshine – Wayland (p120) – in the East Village.

Borough Brews

Beer brewing was once a thriving industry in the city – by the 1870s, Brooklyn boasted a belly-swelling 48 breweries. Most of these were based in Williamsburg, Bushwick and Greenpoint, neighborhoods packed with German immigrants with extensive brewing know-how. By the eve of Prohibition in 1919, the borough was one of the country's leading beer peddlers, as famous for kids carrying growlers (beer jugs) as for its bridges. By the end of Prohibition in 1933, most breweries had shut shop. And while the industry rose from the ashes in WWII, local flavor gave in to big-gun Midwestern brands.

The first public brewery in America was established by colonial governor Peter Minuit (1580–1638) at the Market (Marckvelt) field in what is now known as the Financial District in Lower Manhattan. Minuit is credited with 'purchasing' Manhattan from the native Lenape people in May 1626.

Fast-forward to today and Brooklyn is once more a catchword for a decent brewski as a handful of craft breweries put integrity back on tap. Head of the pack is Brooklyn Brewery (p275), its seasonal offerings include a nutmeg-spiked Post Road Pumpkin Ale (available August to November) and a luscious Black Chocolate Stout (a take on Imperial Stout, available October to March). The brewery's comrades-in-craft include SixPoint Craft Ales (www.sixpoint.com), Threes Brewing (www.threesbrewing.com) and Other Half Brewing Co (www.otherhalfbrewing.com). Justifiably famed for its piney, hoppy Imperial IPA Green Diamonds, Other Half Brewing Co gathers its hops and malts from local farms.

Up-and-coming Queens is home to nanobrewery Transmitter Brewing (www.transmitterbrewing.com) and beach-born Rockaway Brewing Company (www.rockawaybrewco.com). The borough's dominant player remains SingleCut Beersmiths (www.singlecutbeer.com); its launch in 2012 saw Queens welcome its first brewery since Prohibition. Its offerings include unusual takes on lager, among them the Jan White Lagrrr, brewed with coriander, chamomile flowers, oranges, matzo and Sichuan peppercorns. Further north, the Bronx lays claim to Bronx Brewery (p258) and Gun Hill Brewing Co (http://gunhillbrewing.com), the latter making waves with its Void of Light, a jet-black, roastalicious stout.

The Arts

The spectacles of Broadway, the gleaming white-box galleries of Chelsea, joints playing jazz, music halls blaring moody indie rock and opera houses that bellow melodramatic tales – for more than a century, New York City has been America's capital of cultural production. And while gentrification has pushed many artists out to the city's fringes and beyond, New York nonetheless remains a nerve center for the visual arts, music, theater, dance and literature.

Dynamo of the Arts

That New York claims some of the world's mightiest art museums attests to its enviable artistic pedigree. From Pollock and Rothko to Warhol and Rauschenberg, the city has nourished many of America's greatest artists and artistic movements.

On any given week, New York is home to countless art exhibits, installations and performances. Get a comprehensive listing of happenings at www.nyartbeat.com.

The Birth of an Arts Hub

In almost all facets of the arts, New York really got its sea legs in the early 20th century, when the city attracted and retained a critical mass of thinkers, artists, writers and poets. It was at this time that the homegrown art scene began to take shape. In 1905, photographer (and husband of Georgia O'Keeffe) Alfred Stieglitz opened 'Gallery 291,' a Fifth Ave space that provided a vital platform for American artists and helped establish photography as a credible art form.

In the 1940s, an influx of cultural figures fleeing the carnage of WWII saturated the city with fresh ideas – and New York became an important cultural hub. Peggy Guggenheim established the Art of this Century gallery on 57th St, a space that helped launch the careers of painters such as Jackson Pollock, Willem de Kooning and Robert Motherwell. These Manhattan-based artists came to form the core of the abstract-expressionist movement (also known as the New York School), creating an explosive and rugged form of painting that changed the course of modern art as we know it.

An American Avant-Garde

The abstract expressionists helped establish New York as a global arts center. Another generation of artists then carried the ball. In the 1950s and '60s, Robert Rauschenberg, Jasper Johns and Lee Bontecou turned paintings into off-the-wall sculptural constructions that included everything from welded steel to taxidermy goats. By the mid-1960s, pop art – a movement that utilized the imagery and production techniques of popular culture – had taken hold, with Andy Warhol at the helm.

By the '60s and '70s, when New York's economy was in the dumps and much of SoHo lay in a state of decay, the city became a hotbed of conceptual and performance art. Gordon Matta-Clark sliced up abandoned buildings with chainsaws and the artists of Fluxus staged happenings on downtown streets. Carolee Schneemann organized performances that utilized the human body. At one famous 1964 event, she had a crew of nude dancers roll around in an unappetizing mix of paint, sausages and dead fish in the theater of a Greenwich Village church.

Art Now

Today, the arts scene is mixed and wide-ranging. The major institutions – the Metropolitan Museum of Art (p214), the Museum of Modern Art (p182), the Whitney Museum (p139), the Guggenheim Museum (p213), the Met Breuer (p218) and the Brooklyn Museum (p265) – deliver major retrospectives covering everything from Renaissance portraiture to contemporary installation. The New Museum (p110), on the Lower East Side, is more daring, while countless smaller institutions, among them the excellent Bronx Museum (p258), El Museo del Barrio (p251) and the Studio Museum (p251) in Harlem, focus on narrower slices of art history.

New York remains the world's gallery capital, with more than 800 spaces showcasing all kinds of art all over the city. The blue-chip dealers can be found clustered in Chelsea and the Upper East Side. Galleries that showcase emerging and midcareer artists dot the Lower East Side, while prohibitive rents have pushed the city's more emerging and experimental scenes further out, with current hot spots including Harlem and the Brooklyn neighborhoods of Bushwick, Greenpoint, Clinton Hill and Bedford-Stuyvesant (Bed-Stuy).

In January 2018, the Metropolitan Museum of Art (p214) announced that it would begin charging admission to out-of-state visitors for the first time since 1970. The decision was a controversial one: while many recognized the museum's financial bind – only 8% of its income comes from government funds – others mourned the loss of the open-door policy that allowed universal access to a world-class art collection.

Graffiti & Street Art

Contemporary graffiti as we know it was cultivated in NYC. In the 1970s, the graffiti-covered subway train became a potent symbol of the city and work by figures such as Dondi, Blade and Lady Pink became known around the world. In addition, fine artists such as Jean-Michel Basquiat and Keith Haring began incorporating elements of graffiti into their work.

The movement received new life in the late 1990s when a new generation of artists – many with art-school pedigrees – began using materials such as cut paper and sculptural elements. Well-known New York City artists working in this vein include John Fekner, Stephen 'Espo' Powers, Swoon and the twin-brother duo Skewville.

Less celebratory was the 2013 closure of iconic 5Pointz, a cluster of Long Island City warehouses dripping with Technicolor graffiti. Not even a plea from legendary British artist Banksy could save the veritable gallery, condemned to demolition. These days, spray-can and stencil hot spots include the Brooklyn side of the Williamsburg Bridge and the corner of Troutman St and St Nicholas Ave in Bushwick, also in Brooklyn. In Astoria, Queens, explore the Technicolor artworks around Welling Ct and 30th Ave.

A Musical Metropolis

This is the city where jazz players such as Ornette Coleman and Miles Davis pushed the limits of improvisation in the '50s. It's where various Latin sounds – from cha-cha-cha to rumba to mambo – came together to form the hybrid we now call salsa, where folks singers such as Bob Dylan and Joan Baez crooned protest songs in coffeehouses, and where bands such as the New York Dolls and the Ramones tore up the stage in Manhattan's gritty downtown. It was the ground zero of disco. And it was the cultural crucible where hip-hop was nurtured and grew – then exploded.

The city remains a magnet for musicians to this day. The local indie-rock scene is especially vibrant: groups including the Yeah Yeah Yeahs, LCD Soundsystem and Animal Collective all emerged out of NYC. Williamsburg is at the heart of the action, packed with clubs and bars, as well as indie record labels and internet radio stations. The best venues for rock include the Music Hall of Williamsburg (p296) and the Brooklyn Bowl (p294), as well as Manhattan's Bowery Ballroom (p128).

Brooklyn has a hopping indie-music scene, with local bands performing regularly in Williamsburg and Bushwick. To hear the latest sounds, log on to www.newtownradio.com.

All That Jazz

Jazz remains a juggernaut – from the traditional to the experimental. The best bets for jazz are the Village Vanguard (p158) in the West

A NEW YORK HIP-HOP PLAYLIST

New York is the cradle of hip-hop. Rap to the following classics from the city's finest:

'Rapper's Delight', Sugarhill Gang (1979) – The single that launched the commercial birth of hip-hop, from a New York–New Jersey trio.

'White Lines,' Grandmaster Flash and the Furious Five (1983) – The ultimate '80s party song from the Bronx.

'It's Like That,' Run DMC (1983) – That's just the way it is from the legendary Queens trio.

'Fat Boys,' Fat Boys (1984) – Brooklyn's ultimate beat-boxers.

'No Sleep Till Brooklyn,' Beastie Boys (1986) – The NYC trio who fought for their right to party.

'Ain't No Half Steppin',' Big Daddy Kane (1988) – Mellifluous rhymes from a Brooklyn master.

'Fight the Power,' Public Enemy (1989) – A politically charged tour de force from Long Island's hip-hop royals.

'C.R.E.A.M.,' Wu-Tang Clan (1993) – The rules of street capitalism rapped out by Staten Island's finest crew.

'N.Y. State of Mind,' NAS (1994) – From from the debut album of a Brooklyn-born, Queens-raised rap deity.

'99 Problems,' Jay-Z (2004) – This Bed-Stuy, Brooklyn boy is now a music mogul.

Village and the Jazz Standard (p203) near Madison Square Park. For more highbrow programming, there's Midtown's Jazz at Lincoln Center (p205), which is run by trumpeter Wynton Marsalis and features a wide array of solo outings by important musicians, as well as tribute concerts to figures such as Dizzy Gillespie and Thelonious Monk.

Classical & Opera

The classics are alive and well at Lincoln Center (p232). Here, the Metropolitan Opera (p240) delivers a wide array of celebrated operas, from Verdi's *Aida* to Mozart's *Don Giovanni*. The New York Philharmonic (p241) (the symphony that was once directed by one of the 20th-century's great maestros, Leonard Bernstein) is also based here out of the newly refurbished David Geffen Hall. Carnegie Hall (p205), the Merkin Concert Hall (p241) and the Frick Collection (p224) also offer wonderful – and more intimate – spaces to enjoy great classical music.

For more avant-garde fare, try the Center for Contemporary Opera (http://centerforcontemporaryopera.org) and the Brooklyn Academy of Music (BAM) (p294) – the latter is one of the city's vital opera and classical-music hubs. Another excellent venue, featuring highly experimental work, is St Ann's Warehouse (p294) in Brooklyn. If you like your performance *outré,* keep an eye on its calendar.

On Broadway & Beyond

In the early 20th century, clusters of theaters settled into the area around Times Square and began producing popular plays and suggestive comedies – a movement that had its roots in early vaudeville. By the 1920s, these messy works had evolved into on-stage spectacles like *Show Boat,* an all-out Oscar Hammerstein production about the lives of performers on a Mississippi steamboat. In 1943, Broadway had its first runaway hit – *Oklahoma!* – that remained on stage for a record 2212 performances.

Today, Broadway musicals are shown in one of 40 official Broadway theaters, lavish early 20th-century jewels that surround Times Square, and are a major component of cultural life in New York. If you're on a budget, look for off-Broadway productions. These tend to be more intimate, inexpensive and often just as good.

NYC bursts with theatrical offerings beyond Broadway, from Shakespeare to David Mamet to rising experimental playwrights including Young Jean Lee. In addition to Midtown staples such as Playwrights Horizons (p205) and Second Stage Theatre (p205), the Lincoln Center theaters (p232) and smaller companies like Soho Rep (p83) are important hubs for works by modern and contemporary playwrights.

For comprehensive theater listings, news and reviews (both glowing and scathing), visit www.nytimes.com/section/theater. You'll also find listings, synopses and industry news at www.playbill.com.

Across the East River, Brooklyn Academy of Music (BAM; p294), PS 122 (p126) and St Ann's Warehouse (p294) all offer edgy programming. Numerous festivals, such as **FringeNYC** (www.fringenyc.org; ⏲Oct), BAM's epic Next Wave Festival (p294) and the biennial **Performa** (www.performa-arts.org; ⏲Nov) offer brilliant opportunities to catch new work.

Bust a Move: Dance & the City

For nearly 100 years, New York City has been at the center of American dance. It is here that the American Ballet Theatre (ABT) – led by the fabled George Balanchine – was founded in 1949. The company promoted the idea of cultivating American talent, hiring native-born dancers and putting on works by choreographers such as Jerome Robbins, Twyla Tharp and Alvin Ailey. The company continues to perform in New York and around the world.

But NYC is perhaps best known for nurturing a generation of modern-dance choreographers – figures such as Martha Graham, who challenged traditional notions of dance with boxy, industrial movements on bare, almost abstract sets. The boundaries were pushed ever further by Merce Cunningham, who disassociated dance from music. Today, companies such as STREB (http://streb.org) are pushing dance to its limits.

Lincoln Center (p232) and Brooklyn Academy of Music (p294) host regular performances, while up-and-coming acts feature at spaces including Chelsea's Kitchen (p159), Joyce Theater (p159) and New York Live Arts (p158), as well as Midtown's Baryshnikov Arts Center (http://bacnyc.org).

New York in Letters

The city that is home to the country's biggest publishing houses has also been home to some of its best-known writers. In the 19th century, Herman Melville (*Moby Dick*), Edith Wharton (*The House of Mirth*) and Walt Whitman (*Leaves of Grass*) all congregated here. But things really got cooking in the early part of the 20th century. There were the liquor-fueled literary salons of poet-communist John Reed in the 1910s, the acerbic wisecracks of the Algonquin Round Table in the 1920s and the thinly veiled novels of Dawn Powell in the '40s, a figure whose work often critiqued New York's media establishment.

The 1950s and '60s saw the rise of writers who questioned the status quo. Poet Langston Hughes examined the condition of African Americans in Harlem and Beat poets such as Allen Ginsberg rejected traditional rhyme in favor of free-flowing musings. The last few decades of the 20th century offered a wide gamut to choose from, including Jay McInerney, chronicler of the greed and coke-fueled '80s, to new voices from under-represented corners of the city such as Piri Thomas and Audre Lorde.

NYC scribes continue to cover a vast array of realities in their work, from the immigrant experience (Imbolo Mbue) and the Manhattan music business (Jennifer Egan), to the crazy impossibility that is New York in Michael Chabon's Pulitzer-winning *The Amazing Adventures of Kavalier & Clay*. Among the latest crop of Gotham-based talent is award-winning Ben Lerner, whose metafiction novel *10:04* is as much about the city's visceral intensity as it is about its neurotic, heart-troubled protagonist.

PAUL PELLEGRINO / SHUTTERSTOCK ©

Architecture

New York's architectural history is a layer cake of ideas and styles – one that is literally written on the city's streets. Humble colonial farmhouses and graceful Federal-style buildings can be found alongside ornate beaux-arts palaces from the early 20th century. There are the revivals (Greek, Gothic, Romanesque and Renaissance) and the unadorned forms of the International style. And, in recent years, there has been the addition of the torqued forms of deconstructivist architects. For the architecture buff, it's a bricks-and-mortar bonanza.

Colonial Foundations

New York's architectural roots are modest. Early Dutch-colonial farmhouses were all about function: clapboard-wood homes with shingled, gambrel roofs were positioned to take advantage of daylight and retain heat in winter. A number of these have somehow survived to the present. The most remarkable is the Pieter Claesen Wyckoff House (p273)

Above Chrysler Building (p187)

in East Flatbush, Brooklyn. Originally built in 1652 (with additions made over the years), it is the oldest house in the entire city.

After the Dutch colony of New Amsterdam became the British colony of New York in 1664, architectural styles moved to Georgian. Boxy, brick and stone structures with hipped roofs began to materialize. In the northern Manhattan district of Inwood, the Morris-Jumel Mansion (p252) from 1765 is an altered example of this: the home was built in the Georgian style by Roger Morris, then purchased by Stephen Jumel, who added a neoclassical facade in the 19th century. Another British-colonial building of interest is the Fraunces Tavern (p72), where George Washington bid an emotional farewell to the officers who had accompanied him throughout the American Revolution. Today the structure contains a museum and restaurant.

On the ceremonial end is St Paul's Chapel (p73), south of City Hall Park. Built in the 1760s, it is the oldest surviving church in the city. Its design was inspired by the much bigger St Martin-in-the-Fields church in London.

Architecture in the New Republic

Must-See Buildings

- *Chrysler Building (Midtown)*
- *Grand Central Terminal (Midtown)*
- *Morris-Jumel Mansion (Washington Heights)*
- *Empire State Building (Midtown)*
- *Temple Emanu-El (Upper East Side)*
- *New Museum of Contemporary Art (Lower East Side)*

In the early 1800s, architecture grew lighter and more refined. The so-called Federal style employed classical touches – slim, columned entrances, triangular pediments at the roofline and rounded fanlights over doors and windows. Some of the best surviving examples are tied to municipal government. **City Hall** (Map p406; guided tours 212-788-2656; Park Row, City Hall Park; guided tours noon Wed; S 4/5/6 to Brooklyn Bridge-City Hall; R/W to City Hall; J/Z to Chambers St) FREE, built in 1812, owes its French form to émigré architect Joseph François Mangin and its Federal detailing to American-born John McComb Jr. The interior contains an airy rotunda and curved cantilevered stairway.

Uptown, on the Upper East Side, 1799 Gracie Mansion (p219), the official residence of New York City's mayor since 1942, is a fine example of a Federal residence, with its broad, river-view porch and leaded glass sidelights. This stretch of riverfront was once lined with buildings of the sort – a sight that impressed Alexis de Tocqueville during his tour of the United States in the early 19th century.

Other Federal-style specimens include the 1793 James Watson House at 7 State St right across from Battery Park, and the 1832 Merchant's House Museum (p91), in NoHo. The latter still contains its intact interiors.

Greek, Gothic & Romanesque: the Revivals

Following the publication of an important treatise on Greek architecture in the late 1700s, architects began to show a renewed interest in pure, classical forms. In the US, a big instigator of this trend was Minard Lafever, a New Jersey–born carpenter-turned-architect-turned-author-of-pattern-books. By the 1830s, becolumned Greek Revival structures were going up all over New York.

Manhattan contains a bevy of these buildings, including the gray granite St Peter's Church (1838) and the white-marble Federal Hall (1842; p73) – both of which are located in the Financial District. In Greenwich Village, a row of colonnaded homes built on the north side of Washington Square (Numbers 1–13; p138) in the 1820s are fine residential interpretations of this style.

Starting in the late 1830s, the simple Georgian and Federalist styles started to give way to more ornate structures that employed Gothic and Romanesque elements. This was particularly prominent in church construction. An early example was the Church of the Ascension (1841) in Greenwich Village – an imposing brownstone structure studded with

Grand Central Terminal (p184)

pointed arches and a crenelated tower. The same architect – Richard Upjohn – also designed downtown Manhattan's Trinity Church (1846; p72) in the same style.

By the 1860s, these places of worship were growing in size and scale. Among the most resplendent are St Patrick's Cathedral (1858–1879; p193), which took over an entire city block at Fifth Ave and 51st St, and the perpetually under construction Cathedral Church of St John the Divine (since 1911; p247), in Morningside Heights. Indeed, the style was so popular that one of the city's most important icons – the Brooklyn Bridge (1870–83) – was built à la Gothic Revival.

Romanesque elements (such as curved arches) can be spotted on structures all over the city. Some of the most famous include the Joseph Papp Public Theater (formerly the Astor Library) in Greenwich Village, built between 1853 and 1881, and the breathtaking Temple Emanu-El (1929; p219) on Fifth Ave on the Upper East Side.

AIA Guide to New York (5th edition) is a comprehensive guide to the most significant buildings in the city.

Beaux-Arts Blockbusters

At the turn of the 20th century, New York entered a gilded age. Robber barons such as JP Morgan, Henry Clay Frick and John D Rockefeller – awash in steel and oil money – built themselves lavish manses. Public buildings grew ever more extravagant in scale and ornamentation. Architects, many of whom trained in France, came back with European design ideals. Gleaming white limestone began to replace all the brownstone, first stories were elevated to allow for dramatic staircase entrances, and buildings were adorned with sculptured keystones and Corinthian columns.

McKim Mead & White's Villard Houses, from 1884 (now the Palace Hotel), show the movement's early roots. Loosely based on Rome's Palazzo

Woolworth Building (p77)

della Cancelleria, they channeled the symmetry and elegance of the Italian Renaissance. Other classics include the central branch of the New York Public Library (1911; p191), designed by Carrère and Hastings; the 1902 extension of the Metropolitan Museum of Art (p214), by Richard Morris Hunt; and Warren and Wetmore's stunning Grand Central Terminal (1913; p184), which is capped by a statue of Mercury, the god of commerce.

Reaching Skyward

By the time New York settled into the 20th century, elevators and steel-frame engineering had allowed the city to grow up – literally. This period saw a building boom of skyscrapers, starting with Cass Gilbert's neo-Gothic 57-story Woolworth Building (1913; p77). To this day it remains one of the 50 tallest buildings in the United States.

Others soon followed. In 1930, the Chrysler Building (p187), the 77-storey art deco masterpiece designed by William Van Alen, became the world's tallest structure. The following year, the record was broken by the Empire State Building (p180), a clean-lined moderne monolith crafted from Indiana limestone. Its spire was meant to be used as mooring mast for dirigibles (airships) – an idea that made for good publicity, but which proved to be impractical and unfeasible.

The influx of displaced European architects and other thinkers who had resettled in New York by the end of WWII fostered a lively dialogue between American and European architects. This was a period when urban planner Robert Moses furiously rebuilt vast swaths of New York – to the detriment of many neighborhoods – and designers and artists became obsessed with the clean, unadorned lines of the International style.

One of the earliest projects in this vein were the UN buildings (1948–52; p190), the combined effort of a committee of architects, including the Swiss-born Le Corbusier, Brazil's Oscar Niemeyer and America's Wallace K Harrison. The Secretariat employed New York's first glass curtain wall – which looms over the ski-slope curve of the General Assembly. Other significant modernist structures from this period include Gordon Bunshaft's Lever House (p192), a floating, glassy structure on Park Ave and 54th St, and Ludwig Mies van der Rohe's austere, 38-story Seagram Building (p192), located just two blocks to the south.

The New Guard

By the late 20th century, numerous architects began to rebel against the hard-edged, unornamented nature of modernist design. Among them was Philip Johnson. His pink granite AT&T Building (now Sony Tower; 1984) – topped by a scrolled, neo-Georgian pediment – has become a postmodern icon of the Midtown skyline.

Esteemed New York architecture critic Ada Louise Huxtable gathers some of her most important essays in the book *On Architecture: Collected Reflections on a Century of Change.*

What never became an icon was Daniel Libeskind's twisting, angular design for the One World Trade Center (2013) tower, replaced by a boxier architecture-by-committee glass obelisk. On the same site, budget blowouts led to tweaks of Santiago Calatrava's luminous design for the World Trade Center Transportation Hub (2016). According to critics, what should have looked like a dove in flight now resembles a winged dinosaur. The latest WTC site controversy involves Two World Trade Center, its original Sir Norman Foster design recently scrapped for one by Danish firm Bjarke Ingels Group (BIG). According to the chief operating officer of 21st Century Fox, James Murdoch, Foster's design was too conventional for what will become the media company's new base. BIG responded with its trademark unconventionalism: a tower of giant, differently sized boxes, soaring playfully into the sky.

Not that Sir Foster is a hack at cutting-edge style. The British architect's Hearst Tower (p192) – a glass skyscraper zigzagging its way out of a 1920s sandstone structure – remains a Midtown trailblazer. The building is one of numerous daring 21st-century additions to the city's architectural portfolio, among them Brooklyn's sci-fi arena Barclays Center (2012; p296), Thom Mayne's folded-and-slashed 2009 **41 Cooper Square** (Map p412; www.cooper.edu/about/history/41-cooper-square; 41 Cooper Sq, btwn 6th & 7th Sts; S 6 to Astor Pl) in the East Village, and Frank Gehry's rippling, 76-storey apartment tower New York by Gehry (2011) in the Financial District.

Starchitects on the Line

Frank Gehry's IAC Building (2007) – a billowing, white-glass structure often compared to a wedding cake – is one of a growing number of starchitect creations appearing around railway-turned-urban-park, the High Line. The most prolific of these is Renzo Piano's new Whitney Museum (2015; p139). Dramatically asymmetrical and clad in blue-gray steel, the building has received significant praise for melding seamlessly with the elevated park. Turning heads eight blocks to the north is 100 Eleventh Ave (2010), a 23-story luxury condominium by French architect Jean Nouvel. Its exuberant arrangement of angled windows is nothing short of mesmerizing, both cutting-edge in its construction and sensitive to the area's heritage. That the facade's patterning evokes West Chelsea's industrial masonry is not coincidental.

Public Art: New York by Jean Parker Phifer, with photos by Francis Dzikowski, is an informative guide to the city's public monuments.

The area's newest darling is Zaha Hadid's apartment complex at 520 West 28th St. Rising 11 stories, the luxury structure is the Iraqi-British architect's first residential project in the city, its voluptuous, sci-fi curves to be complimented by a 2500-sq-ft sculpture deck showcasing art presented by Friends of the High Line. Sadly the Pritzker Prize–winning architect wasn't able to see its completion; Zaha Hadid died in 2016.

Queer City: From Stonewall to Marriage Equality

New York City is out and damn proud. It was here that the Stonewall Riots took place, that the modern gay rights movement bloomed and that America's first Pride march hit the streets. Yet even before the days of 'Gay Lib,' the city had a knack for all things queer and fabulous, from Bowery sex saloons and Village Sapphic poetry to drag balls in Harlem. It hasn't always been smooth sailing, but it's always been one hell of a ride.

Before Stonewall

Subversion in the Villages

By the 1890s, New York City's rough-and-ready Lower East Side had established quite a reputation for scandalous 'resorts' – dancing halls, saloons and brothels – frequented by the city's 'inverts' and 'fairies.' From Paresis Hall at 5th St and Bowery to Slide at 157 Bleecker St, these venues offered everything from cross-dressing spectaculars and dancing to back rooms for same-sex shenanigans. For closeted middle-class men, these dens were a secret thrill – places reached undercover on trains for a fix of camaraderie, understanding and uninhibited fun. For curious middle-class straights, they were just as enticing – salacious destinations on voyeuristic 'slumming tours.'

America's first gay-rights rally was held in New York City in 1964. Organized by the Homosexual League of New York and the League for Sexual Freedom, the picket took place outside the Army Induction Center on Whitehall St, where protestors demanded an end to the military's anti-gay policies.

As New York strode into the 20th century, writers and bohemians began stepping into Greenwich Village, lured by the area's cheap rents and romantically crooked streets. The unconventionality and free thinking the area became known for turned the Village into an Emerald City for gays and lesbians, a place with no shortage of bachelor pads, more tolerant attitudes and – with the arrival of Prohibition – an anything-goes speakeasy scene. A number of gay-owned businesses lined MacDougal St, among them the legendary Eve's Hangout at number 129. A tearoom run by Polish Jewish immigrant Eva Kotchever (Eve Addams), it was famous for two things: poetry readings and a sign on the door that read 'Men allowed but not welcome.' There would have been little chance of welcome drinks when police raided the place in June 1926, charging Eve with 'obscenity' for penning her Lesbian Love anthology, and deporting her back to Europe. Three years later, Eve was honored by a Greenwich Village theater group, who staged a theatrical version of her book at Play Mart, a basement performance space on Christopher St.

Divas, Drag & Harlem

While Times Square had developed a reputation for attracting gay men (many of them working in the district's theaters, restaurants and speakeasy bars), the hottest gay scene in the 1920s was found further north, in Harlem. The neighborhood's flourishing music scene included numerous gay and lesbian performers, among them Gladys Bentley and Ethel

Waters. Bentley – who was as famous for her tuxedos and girlfriends as she was for her singing – had moved her way up from one-off performances at cellar clubs and tenement parties to headlining a revue at the famous Ubangi Club on 133rd St, where her supporting acts included a chorus line of female impersonators.

Even more famous were Harlem's drag balls, which became a hit with both gay and straight New Yorkers in the roaring twenties. The biggest of the lot was the Hamilton Lodge Ball, organized by Lodge #710 of the Grand United Order of Odd Fellows and held annually at the swank Rockland Palace on 155th St. Commonly dubbed the Faggot's Ball, it was a chance for both gay men and women to (legally) cross-dress and steal a same-sex dance, and for fashionable 'normals' to indulge in a little voyeuristic titillation. The evening's star attraction was the beauty pageant, which saw the drag-clad competitors vie for the title of 'Queen of the Ball.' Langston Hughes proclaimed it the 'spectacles of color' and the gay writer was one of many members of New York's literati to attend the ball. It was also attended by everyone from prostitutes to high-society families, including the Astors and the Vanderbilts. Even the papers covered the extravaganza, its outrageous frocks the talk of the town.

The Stonewall Revolution

The relative transgression of the early 20th century was replaced with a new conservatism in the following decades, as the Great Depression, WWII and the Cold War took their toll. Conservatism was helped along by Senator Joseph 'Joe' McCarthy, who declared that homosexuals in the State Department threatened America's security and children. Tougher policing aimed to eradicate queer visibility in the public sphere, forcing the scene further underground in the 1940s and '50s. Although crack downs on gay venues had always occurred, they became increasingly common.

Yet on June 28, 1969, when eight police officers raided the Stonewall Inn – a gay-friendly watering hole in Greenwich Village – patrons did the unthinkable: they revolted. Fed up with both the harassment and corrupt officers receiving payoffs from the bars' owners (who were mostly organized-crime figures), they began bombarding the officers with coins, bottles, bricks and chants of 'gay power' and 'we shall overcome.' They were also met by a line of high-kicking drag queens and their now-legendary chant, 'We are the Stonewall girls, we wear our hair in curls, we wear no underwear, we show our pubic hair, we wear our dungarees, above our nelly knees...'.

Their collective anger and solidarity was a turning point, igniting intense and passionate debate about discrimination and forming the catalyst for the modern gay rights movement, not just in New York, but across the US and in countries from the Netherlands to Australia.

LGBT HISTORY

1927

New York State amends a public-obscenity code to include a ban on the appearance or discussion of gay people on stage in reaction to the increasing visibility of gays on Broadway.

1966

On April 21, gay rights organization Mattachine Society stages a 'Sip-In' at NYC's oldest gay drinking hole, Julius Bar, challenging a ban on serving alcohol to LGBT people.

1969

Police officers raid the Stonewall Inn in Greenwich Village on June 28, sparking a riot that lasts several days and gives birth to the modern gay rights movement.

1987

ACT UP is founded to challenge the US government's slow response in dealing with AIDS. The activist group stages its first major demonstration on March 24 on Wall St.

2011

New York's Marriage Equality Act comes into effect at 12.01am on July 24. A lesbian couple from Buffalo take their vows just seconds after midnight in Niagara Falls.

2016

President Barack Obama declares a swath of the West Village, including the iconic Christopher Park, a US National Monument, the first such designation honoring the LGBT civil rights movement.

In the Shadow of AIDS

LGBT activism intensified as HIV and AIDS hit world headlines in the early 1980s. Faced with ignorance, fear and the moral indignation of those who saw AIDS as a 'gay cancer,' activists such as writer Larry Kramer set about tackling what was quickly becoming an epidemic. Out of his efforts was born ACT UP (AIDS Coalition to Unleash Power) in 1987, an advocacy group set up to fight the perceived homophobia and indifference of then-president Ronald Reagan, as well as to end the price gouging of AIDS drugs by pharmaceutical companies. One of its boldest protests took place on September 14, 1989, when seven ACT UP protesters chained themselves to the VIP balcony of the New York Stock Exchange, demanding pharmaceutical company Burroughs Wellcome lower the price of AIDS drug AZT from a prohibitive $10,000 per patient per annum. Within days, the price was slashed to $6400 per patient.

The epidemic itself had a significant impact on New York's artistic community. Among its most high-profile victims were artist Keith Haring, photographer Robert Mapplethorpe and fashion designer Halston. Yet out of this loss grew a tide of powerful AIDS-related plays and musicals that would not only win broad international acclaim, but would become part of America's mainstream cultural canon. Among these are Tony Kushner's political epic *Angels in America* and Jonathan Larson's rock musical *Rent*. Both works would win Tony Awards and the Pulitzer Prize.

Queer Screen Classics

- *Torch Song Trilogy (1988)*
- *The Boys in the Band (1970)*
- *Paris Is Burning (1990)*
- *Angels in America (2003)*
- *Jeffrey (1995)*

Marriage & the New Millennium

The LGBT fight for complete equality took two massive steps forward in 2011. On September 20, a federal law banning LGBT military personnel from serving openly – the so-called 'Don't Ask, Don't Tell' policy – was repealed after years of intense lobbying. Three months earlier persistence had led to an even greater victory – the right to marry. On June 15, by a margin of 80 to 63, the New York State Assembly passed the Marriage Equality Act. On June 24, the very eve of New York City Gay Pride, it was announced that the Act would be considered as the final bill of the legislative session. Considered and amended, the bill was approved by a margin of 33 to 29 and signed into law at 11.55pm by New York Governor Andrew Cuomo. State victory became a national one on June 26, 2015, when the US Supreme Court ruled that same-sex marriage is a legal right across the country, striking down the remaining marriage bans in 13 US states.

In the same year, organizers of New York City's St Patrick's Parade lifted their long-standing ban on LGBT groups, allowing Out@NBCUniversal – a group consisting of gay, lesbian, bisexual and transgender people working for NBCUniversal – to join the parade. The lifting of the ban no doubt met the approval of New York City mayor Bill de Blasio, who had famously boycotted the event in protest.

Despite these significant triumphs, New York City is not immune to intolerance and prejudice. In 2013, New Yorkers reeled when a Brooklyn man, Mark Carson, was fatally shot in Greenwich Village, one of Manhattan's most historically tolerant neighborhoods. Carson and a friend had been walking along 8th St in the early hours of May 18 when, after a short altercation with a group of men hurling homophobic abuse, the 32-year-old was shot at point-blank range. The attack prompted a midnight vigil in Carson's memory, as well as a sobering reminder that even in liberal New York City, not everyone is happy to live and let live.

LGBT Reads

- *Dancer from the Dance (Andrew Holleran)*
- *Last Exit to Brooklyn (Hubert Selby)*
- *Another Country (James Baldwin)*
- *City Boy (Edmund White)*

NYC on Screen

New York City has a long and storied life on screen. It was on these streets that a bumbling Woody Allen fell for Diane Keaton in *Annie Hall,* that Meg Ryan faked her orgasm in *When Harry Met Sally,* and that Sarah Jessica Parker philosophized about the finer points of dating and Jimmy Choos in *Sex & the City*. To fans, traversing the city can feel like one big déjà vu of memorable scenes, characters and one-liners.

Hollywood Roots & Rivals

Believe it or not, America's film industry is an East Coast native. Fox, Universal, Metro, Selznick and Goldwyn all originated here in the early 20th century, and long before Westerns were shot in California and Colorado, they were filmed in the (now former) wilds of New Jersey. Even after Hollywood's year-round sunshine lured the bulk of the business west by the 1920s, 'Lights, Camera, Action' remained a common call in Gotham.

The Kaufman Astoria Legacy

The heart of the local scene was Queens' still-kicking Kaufman Astoria Studios. Founded by Jesse Lasky and Adolph Zukor in 1920 as a one-stop-shop for their Famous Players–Lasky Corporation, the complex would produce a string of silent-era hits, among them *The Sheik* (1921) and *Monsieur Beaucaire* (1924), both starring Italian-born heartthrob Rudolph Valentino, and *Manhandled* (1924), starring early silver-screen diva Gloria Swanson. Renamed Paramount Pictures in 1927, the studios became known for turning Broadway stars into big-screen icons, among them the Marx Brothers, Fred Astaire and Ginger Rogers, the latter making her feature-film debut as a flapper in *Young Man of Manhattan* (1930).

Despite Paramount moving all of its feature film shoots to Hollywood in 1932, the complex – renamed Eastern Services Studio – remained the home of Paramount's newsreel division. Throughout the 1930s, it was also known for its 'shorts,' which launched the careers of homegrown talents including George Burns, Bob Hope and Danny Kaye. After a stint making propaganda and training films for the US Army between WWII and 1970, what had become known as the US Signal Corps Photographic Center was renamed the Kaufman Astoria Studios by George S Kaufman (the real-estate agent, not the playwright) in 1983. Modernized and expanded, the studio has gone on to make a

FILM LOCATIONS

Central Park Countless cameos, including in Woody Allen's *Annie Hall*, *Manhattan* and *Hannah & Her Sisters*.

64 Perry St Carrie Bradshaw's apartment exterior in *Sex & the City*.

Katz's Delicatessen Where Meg Ryan faux climaxes in *When Harry Met Sally*.

Tom's Restaurant Stand-in for Monk's Café in *Seinfeld*.

Tiffany & Co Where Audrey Hepburn daydreams in *Breakfast at Tiffany's*.

string of flicks, including *All that Jazz* (1979), *Brighton Beach Memoirs* (1986), *The Stepford Wives* (2004) and *Men in Black III* (2012). It was here that the Huxtables lived out their middle-class Brooklyn lives in the '80s TV sitcom *The Cosby Show,* and it's still here that small-screen favorites *Sesame Street* and *Orange is the New Black* are taped.

Metro Goldwyn Mayer's famous 'Leo the Lion' logo was designed by Howard Dietz. His inspiration was the mascot of New York's Columbia University, where the publicist had studied journalism. Leo's famous roar was first added to films in 1928.

Beyond Astoria

Slap-bang in the historic Brooklyn Navy Yard, the 26-acre Steiner Studios is the largest studio complex east of LA. Its film credits to date include *The Producers* (2005), *Revolutionary Road* (2008), *Sex & the City* 1 and 2 (2008, 2010), and *The Wolf of Wall Street* (2013). The studios have also been used for numerous TV shows, among them Martin Scorsese's critically acclaimed gangster drama *Boardwalk Empire* and fellow HBO series *Vinyl,* a rock drama by Scorsese, Mick Jagger and Terence Winter.

Back in Queens you'll find the city's other big gun, Silvercup Studios. Its list of features include NYC classics such as Francis Ford Coppola's *The Godfather: Part III* (1990) and Woody Allen's *Broadway Danny Rose* (1984) and *The Purple Rose of Cairo* (1985), plus TV gems such as mafia drama *The Sopranos* and the equally lauded comedy *30 Rock,* the latter starring Tina Fey as a TV sketch writer and Alec Baldwin as a network executive at the Rockefeller Center.

In reality, the Rockefeller Center is home to the NBC TV network, its long-running variety show *Saturday Night Live* the real inspiration behind Fey's *30 Rock* project. Other media networks dotted across Manhattan include the Food and Oxygen Networks, both housed in the Chelsea Market, as well as Robert De Niro's Tribeca Productions, based in the Tribeca Film Center.

Beyond the studios and headquarters are some of the top film schools: New York University's Tisch Film School, the New York Film Academy, the School of Visual Arts, Columbia University and The New School. But you don't have to be a student to learn, with both the Museum of the Moving Image (p306) in Astoria, Queens, and the Paley Center for Media (p193) in Midtown Manhattan acting as major showcases for screenings and seminars about productions both past and present.

Landmarks on Screen

Downtown Drama to Midtown Romance

The infamous subway grill scene in *The Seven Year Itch* (1955) – in which Marilyn Monroe enjoys a dress-lifting breeze – was shot at 586 Lexington Ave, outside the since-demolished Trans-Lux 52nd Street Theatre.

It's not surprising that NYC feels strangely familiar to many first-time visitors – the city itself has racked up more screen time than most Hollywood divas put together and many of its landmarks are as much a part of American screen culture as its red-carpet celebrities. Take the Staten Island Ferry (p384), which takes bullied secretary Melanie Griffith from suburbia to Wall St in *Working Girl* (1988); Battery Park (p74), where Madonna bewitches Aidan Quinn and Rosanna Arquette in *Desperately Seeking Susan* (1985); or the New York County Courthouse, where villains get their just deserts in *Wall Street* (1987) and *Goodfellas* (1990), as well as in small-screen classics such as *Cagney & Lacey*, *NYPD Blue* and *Law & Order*.

Few landmarks can claim as much screen time as the Empire State Building (p180), famed for its spire-clinging ape in *King Kong* (1933, 2005), as well as for the countless romantic encounters on its observation decks. One of its most famous scenes is Meg Ryan and Tom Hanks' after-hours encounter in *Sleepless in Seattle* (1993). The sequence – which uses the real lobby but a studio-replica deck – is a tribute of sorts to *An Affair to Remember* (1957), which sees Cary Grant and Deborah Kerr make a pact to meet and (hopefully) seal their love atop the skyscraper.

Sarah Jessica Parker is less lucky in *Sex & the City* (2008), when a nervous Chris Noth jilts her and her Vivienne Westwood wedding dress

CELLULOID SHORTLIST

It would take volumes to cover all the films tied to Gotham, so fire up your imagination with the following celluloid hits:

Taxi Driver (Martin Scorsese, 1976) Starring Robert De Niro, Cybill Shepherd and Jodie Foster. De Niro is a mentally unstable Vietnam War vet whose violent urges are heightened by the city's tensions. It's a funny, depressing, brilliant classic that's a potent reminder of how much grittier this place used to be.

Manhattan (Woody Allen, 1979) Starring Woody Allen, Diane Keaton and Mariel Hemingway. A divorced New Yorker dating a high-school student (the baby-voiced Hemingway) falls for his best friend's mistress in what is essentially a love letter to NYC. Catch romantic views of the Queensboro Bridge and the Upper East Side.

Desperately Seeking Susan (Susan Seidelman, 1985) Starring Madonna, Rosanna Arquette and Aidan Quinn. A case of mistaken identity leads a bored New Jersey housewife on a wild adventure through Manhattan's subcultural wonderland. Relive mid-80s East Village and long-gone nightclub Danceteria.

Summer of Sam (Spike Lee, 1999) Starring John Leguizamo, Mira Sorvino and Jennifer Esposito. Spike Lee puts NYC's summer of 1977 in historical context by weaving together the Son of Sam murders, the blackout, racial tensions and the misadventures of one disco-dancing Brooklyn couple, including scenes at CBGB and Studio 54.

Angels in America (Mike Nichols, 2003) Starring Al Pacino, Meryl Streep and Jeffrey Wright. This movie version of Tony Kushner's Broadway play recalls 1985 Manhattan: crumbling relationships, AIDS out of control and a closeted Roy Cohn – advisor to President Ronald Reagan – doing nothing about it except falling ill himself. Follow characters from Brooklyn to Lower Manhattan to Central Park.

Precious (Lee Daniels, 2009) Starring Gabourey Sidibe and based on the novel *Push* by Sapphire. This unflinching tale of an obese, illiterate teenager who is abused by her parents takes place in Harlem, offering plenty of streetscapes and New York–ghetto 'tude.

Birdman (Alejandro G Iñárritu, 2014) Oscar-winning black-comedy/drama starring Michael Keaton and featuring Zach Galifianakis, Edward Norton, Andrea Riseborough, Amy Ryan, Emma Stone and Naomi Watts. *Birdman* documents the struggles of a has-been Hollywood actor trying to mount a Broadway show.

Ghostbusters (Paul Feig, 2016) The reboot of the original 1984 film stars four female ghost hunters (comedy stars Melissa McCarthy, Kristen Wiig, Kate McKinnon and Leslie Jones) who light up NYC during their encounters with ghoulish creatures. Though receiving mixed reviews, the film broke new ground with its all-female leads.

at the New York Public Library (p191). Perhaps he'd seen *Ghostbusters* (1984) a few too many times, its opening scenes featuring the haunted library's iconic marble lions and Rose Main Reading Room. The library's foyer sneakily stands in for the Metropolitan Museum of Art in *The Thomas Crown Affair* (1999), in which thieving playboy Pierce Brosnan meets his match in sultry detective Rene Russo. It's at the fountain in adjacent Bryant Park (p193) that DIY sleuth Diane Keaton debriefs husband Woody Allen about their supposedly bloodthirsty elderly neighbor in *Manhattan Murder Mystery* (1993). True to form, Allen uses the film to showcase a slew of New York locales, among them the National Arts Club (p167) in Gramercy Park and one of his own former hangouts, Elaine's at 1703 Second Ave. It's here, at this since-closed Upper East Side restaurant, that Keaton explains her crime theory to Allen and dinner companions Alan Alda and Ron Rifkin. The restaurant was a regular in Allen's films, also appearing in *Manhattan* (1979) and *Celebrity* (1998).

Across Central Park (p228) – whose own countless scenes include Barbra Streisand and Robert Redford rowing on its lake in clutch-a-Kleenex

The Way We Were (1973) – stands the Dakota Building (p229), used in the classic thriller *Rosemary's Baby* (1968). The Upper West Side is also home to Tom's Restaurant (p254), the facade of which was used regularly in *Seinfeld*. Another neighborhood star is the elegant Lincoln Center (p232), where Natalie Portman slowly loses her mind in the psychological thriller *Black Swan* (2010), and where love-struck Brooklynites Cher and Nicolas Cage meet for a date in *Moonstruck* (1987). The Center sits on what had previously been a run-down district of tenements, captured in Oscar-winning gangland musical *West Side Story* (1961).

The more recent Oscar-winner *Birdman* (2014) shines the spotlight on Midtown's glittering Theater District, in which a long-suffering Michael Keaton tries to stage a Broadway adaptation at the St James Theatre on W44th St. Locked out of the building, a mortified Keaton fronts Times Square in nothing but his underwear. A few blocks further east, he spars over his play with Lindsay Duncan at historic drinking den Rum House (p202).

Dancing in the Street

Knives make way for leotards in the cult musical *Fame* (1980), in which New York High School of Performing Arts students do little for the city's traffic woes by dancing on Midtown's streets. The film's graphic content was too much for the city's Board of Education, who banned shooting at the real High School of Performing Arts, then located at 120 W 46th St. Consequently, filmmakers used the doorway of a disused church on the opposite side of the street for the school's entrance, and Haaren Hall (Tenth Ave and 59th St) for interior scenes.

Fame is not alone in turning Gotham into a pop-up dance floor. In *On the Town* (1949), starstruck sailors Frank Sinatra, Gene Kelly and Jules Munshin look straight off a Pride float as they skip, hop and sing their way across this 'wonderful town,' from the base of Lady Liberty (p64) to Rockefeller Plaza (p186) and the Brooklyn Bridge (p262). Another wave of campness hits the bridge when Diana Ross and Michael Jackson cross it in *The Wiz* (1978), a bizarre take on *The Wizard of Oz*, complete with munchkins in Flushing Meadows Corona Park (p308) and an Emerald City at the base of the WTC Twin Towers. The previous year, the bridge provided a rite of passage for a bell-bottomed John Travolta in *Saturday Night Fever* (1977), who leaves the comforts of his adolescent Brooklyn for the bigger, brighter mirror balls of Manhattan. Topping them all, however, is the closing scene in Terry Gilliam's *The Fisher King* (1991), which sees Grand Central Terminal's Main Concourse (p184) turned into a ballroom of waltzing commuters.

Film Festivals

Dance on Camera (January/February)

New York International Children's Film Festival (February/March)

Tribeca Film Festival (April)

Human Rights Watch International Film Festival (June)

NewFest: LGBT Film Festival (October)

New York Film Festival (September/October)

NYC TV Shows

Over 70 TV shows are filmed in NYC, from hit series such as *Law & Order: Special Victims Unit* and *The Good Fight* and quirky comedies like *Broad City*, to long-standing classics including *The Tonight Show Starring Jimmy Fallon* and *Saturday Night Live*. Combined, the city's TV and film industries spend over $8 billion on production annually and support 104,000 jobs. Over a third of professional actors in the US are based here.

Location Tours

Movie- and TV-location guided tours such as On Location Tours (p385) are a good way to visit some of the spots where your screen favorites were shot, including *The Devil Wears Prada, Spider-Man, How I Met Your Mother* and more. Alternatively, you can do it yourself after visiting the wonderfully comprehensive On the Set of New York website (www.onthesetofnewyork.com), which offers free downloadable location maps covering much of Manhattan.

Survival Guide

TRANSPORTATION . . 380

ARRIVING IN NEW YORK CITY 380

John F Kennedy International Airport 380

LaGuardia Airport 381

Newark Liberty International Airport 381

Port Authority Bus Terminal 381

Bus Stations 382

Penn Station 382

GETTING AROUND 382

Subway 382

Taxi 383

Ferry 384

Bus 384

Bicycle 384

Train 384

TOURS 384

DIRECTORY A–Z 386

Customs Regulations . . . 386

Discount Cards 386

Electricity 386

Emergency & Important Numbers 387

Internet Access 387

Legal Matters 387

Medical Services 387

Money 388

Opening Hours 389

Post 389

Public Holidays 389

Safe Travel 389

Taxes & Refunds 389

Telephone 389

Time 389

Toilets 389

Tourist Information 390

Travelers with Disabilities 390

Visas 390

Volunteering 390

Transportation

ARRIVING IN NEW YORK CITY

With its three bustling airports, two main train stations and a monolithic bus terminal, New York City rolls out the welcome mat for millions of visitors who come to take a bite out of the Big Apple each year.

Direct flights are possible from most major American and international cities. Figure six hours from Los Angeles, seven hours from London and Amsterdam, and 14 hours from Tokyo. Consider getting here by train instead of car or plane to enjoy a mix of bucolic and urban scenery en route, without unnecessary traffic hassles, security checks and excess carbon emissions.

Flights, tours and rail tickets can be booked online at www.lonelyplanet.com/bookings.

John F Kennedy International Airport

John F Kennedy International Airport (JFK; ☎718-244-4444; www.kennedyairport.com), 15 miles from Midtown in southeastern Queens, has six working terminals, serves nearly 50 million passengers annually and hosts flights coming and going from all corners of the globe. You can use the AirTrain (free within the airport) to move from one terminal to another.

The timeline is uncertain, but a massive $10-billion overhaul of the airport was recently approved. Architectural and structural changes are the focus, but plans also call for a substantial upgrade of amenities and transportation alternatives.

Taxi

A yellow taxi from Manhattan to the airport will use the meter; prices (often about $60) depend on traffic. Expect the ride to take 45 to 60 minutes. From JFK, taxis charge a flat rate of $52 to any destination in Manhattan (not including tolls or tip); it can take 45 to 60 minutes for most destinations in Manhattan. To/from a destination in Brooklyn, the metered fare should be about $45 (Coney Island) to $62 (downtown Brooklyn). Note that the Williamsburg, Manhattan, Brooklyn and Queensboro–59th St Bridges have no toll either way, while the Queens–Midtown Tunnel and the Hugh L Carey Tunnel (aka the Brooklyn–Battery Tunnel) cost $8.50 going into Manhattan.

Fares for ride-sharing apps like Lyft and Uber change depending on the time of day.

Shuttles & Car Service

Shared vans, like those offered by **Super Shuttle Manhattan** (www.supershuttle.com), cost around $20 to $26 per person, depending on the destination. If traveling to the airport from NYC, car services have set fares from $45.

Express Bus

The **NYC Airporter** (www.nycairporter.com) runs to Grand Central Terminal, Penn Station or the Port Authority Bus Terminal from JFK. The one-way fare is $18.

Subway

The subway is the cheapest but slowest way of reaching Manhattan. From the airport, hop on the AirTrain ($5, payable as you exit) to Sutphin Blvd-Archer Ave (Jamaica Station) to reach the E, J or Z line (or the Long Island Rail Road). To take the A line instead, ride the AirTrain to Howard Beach station. The E train to Midtown has the fewest stops. Expect the journey to take a little over an hour to Midtown.

Long Island Rail Road (LIRR)

This is by far the most relaxing way to arrive in the city. From the airport, take the AirTrain ($5, as you exit) to Jamaica Station. From there, LIRR trains go frequently to Penn Station in Manhattan or to Atlantic Terminal in Brooklyn (near Fort Greene, Boerum Hill and the Barclay Center). It's about a 20-minute journey from station to station. One-way fares to either Penn Station or Atlantic Terminal cost $10.25 ($7.50 at off-peak times).

LaGuardia Airport

Used mainly for domestic flights, **LaGuardia** (LGA; ☎718-533-3400; www.panynj.gov) is smaller than JFK but only 8 miles from midtown Manhattan; it sees nearly 30 million passengers per year.

Much maligned by politicians and ordinary travelers alike, the airport is set to receive a much-needed $4-billion overhaul of its terminal facilities. Scheduled in phases, from 2018 to 2021, plans call for a single, unified terminal to replace the four existing stand-alone ones, as well as an upgrade in amenities and transportation alternatives.

Taxi

A taxi to/from Manhattan costs about $42 for the approximately half-hour ride; it's metered, no set fare. Fares for ride-hailing apps like Lyft and Uber vary.

Car Service

A car service to LaGuardia costs around $35.

Express Bus

The **NYC Airporter** (www.nycairporter.com) costs $15 and goes to/from Grand Central, Penn Station and the Port Authority Bus Terminal.

Subway & Bus

It's less convenient to get to LaGuardia by public transportation than the other airports. The best subway link is the 74 St-Broadway station (7 line, or the E, F, M and R lines at the connecting Jackson Heights-Roosevelt Ave station) in Queens, where you can pick up the Q70 Express Bus to the airport (about 10 minutes to the airport). Or you can catch the M60 bus from several subway stops in upper Manhattan and Harlem or the N/Q stop at Hoyt Ave-32st St.

Newark Liberty International Airport

Don't write off New Jersey when looking for airfares to New York. About the same distance from Midtown as JFK (16 miles), **Newark** (EWR; ☎973-961-6000; www.panynj.gov) brings many New Yorkers out for flights (there's some 40 million passengers annually). It's a hub for United Airlines and offers the only nonstop flight to Havana, Cuba, in the area. A $2.4-billion redevelopment of Terminal A is scheduled to be completed in 2022.

Car Service

A car service runs about $50 to $70 for the 45-minute ride from Midtown; a taxi is roughly the same. You'll have to pay a whopping $15 to get into NYC through the Lincoln (at 42nd St) and Holland (at Canal St) Tunnels and, further north, the George Washington Bridge, though there's no charge going back through to NJ. There are a couple of cheap tolls on New Jersey highways too, unless you ask your driver to take Hwy 1 or 9.

Subway & Train

NJ Transit (www.njtransit.com) runs a rail service (with a $5.50 AirTrain connection) between Newark airport (EWR) and New York's Penn Station for $13 each way. The trip takes 25 minutes and runs every 20 or 30 minutes from 4:20am to about 1:40am. Hold onto your ticket, which you must show upon exiting at the airport.

Express Bus

The **Newark Liberty Airport Express** (www.newarkairportexpress.com) has a bus service between the airport and Port Authority Bus Terminal, Bryant Park and Grand Central Terminal in Midtown ($16 one way). The 45-minute ride goes every 15 minutes from 6:45am to 11:15pm and every half hour from 4:45am to 6:45am and 11:15pm to 1:15am.

Port Authority Bus Terminal

For long-distance bus trips, you'll arrive and depart from the world's busiest bus station, the **Port Authority Bus Terminal** (Map p428;

CLIMATE CHANGE & TRAVEL

Every form of transport that relies on carbon-based fuel generates CO_2, the main cause of human-induced climate change. Modern travel is dependent on airplanes, which might use less fuel per mile per person than most cars but travel much greater distances. The altitude at which aircraft emit gases (including CO_2) and particles also contributes to their climate change impact. Many websites offer 'carbon calculators' that allow people to estimate the carbon emissions generated by their journey and, for those who wish to do so, to offset the impact of the greenhouse gases emitted with contributions to portfolios of climate-friendly initiatives throughout the world. Lonely Planet offsets the carbon footprint of all staff and author travel.

☎212-502-2200; www.panynj.gov; 625 Eighth Ave, at W 42nd St; Ⓢ A/C/E to 42nd St-Port Authority Bus Terminal), which sees more than 65 million passengers each year. Efforts to replace the aging and less-than-salubrious station are always on the agenda. Bus companies leaving from here include the following:

Greyhound (www.greyhound.com) Connects New York with major cities across the country.

Peter Pan Trailways (www.peterpanbus.com) Daily express services to Boston, Washington, DC, and Philadelphia.

Short Line Bus (www.shortlinebus.com) Serves northern New Jersey and upstate New York, focusing on college towns such as Ithaca and New Paltz; part of Coach USA.

Trailways (www.trailwaysny.com) Bus service to upstate New York, including Albany, Ithaca and Syracuse, as well as Montreal, Canada.

Bus Stations

A number of budget bus lines operate from locations on the west side of Midtown:

BoltBus (Map p428; ☎877-265-8287; www.boltbus.com; W 33rd St, btwn Eleventh & Twelfth Aves; 📶) Services from New York to Philadelphia, Boston, Baltimore and Washington, DC. The earlier you purchase tickets, the better the deal. Notable for its free wi-fi, which occasionally actually works.

Megabus (Map p428; https://us.megabus.com; 34th St, btwn 11th & 12th Aves; 📶; Ⓢ 7 to 34th St-Hudson Yards) Travels from New York to Boston, Washington, DC, and Toronto, among other destinations. Free (sometimes functioning) wi-fi. Departures leave from 34th St near the Jacob K Javits Convention Center and arrivals come to 27th and 7th.

Vamoose (Map p428; ☎212-695-6766; www.vamoosebus.com; cnr Seventh Ave & 30th St; from $30; Ⓢ 1 to 28th St; A/C/E, 1/2/3 to 34th St-Penn Station) Buses head to Arlington, Virginia and Bethesda, Maryland, both not far outside Washington, DC.

Penn Station

Penn Station (W 33rd St, btwn Seventh & Eighth Aves; Ⓢ 1/2/3, A/C/E to 34th St-Penn Station) The oft-maligned departure point for all Amtrak (www.amtrak.com) trains, including the Acela Express services to Princeton, NJ, and Washington, DC (note that this express service costs twice as much as a normal fare). All fares vary, based on the day of the week and the time you want to travel. There's no baggage-storage facility at Penn Station. Derailments and maintenance issues plagued Amtrak lines out of Penn Station in the spring of 2017; repairs mean compromised service, with no certainty of when the issues will be resolved.

Long Island Rail Road (www.mta.info/lirr) Serves more than 300,000 commuters each day, with services from Penn Station to points in Brooklyn and Queens, and on Long Island. Prices are broken down by zones. A peak-hour ride from Penn Station to Jamaica Station (en route to JFK via AirTrain) costs $10.25 if you buy it at the station (or a whopping $16 onboard!).

NJ Transit (www.njtransit.com) Also operates trains from Penn Station, with services to the suburbs and the Jersey Shore.

New Jersey PATH (www.panynj.gov/path) An option for getting into NJ's northern points, such as Hoboken and Newark. Trains ($2.75) run from Penn Station along the length of Sixth Ave, with stops at 33rd, 23rd, 14th, 9th and Christopher Sts, as well as at the reopened World Trade Center site.

Metro-North Railroad (www.mta.info/mnr) The last line departing from the magnificent Grand Central Terminal, the Metro-North Railroad serves Connecticut, Westchester County and the Hudson Valley.

GETTING AROUND

Once you've arrived in NYC, getting around is fairly easy. The 660-mile subway system is cheap and (reasonably) efficient and can whisk you to nearly every corner of the city. There are also buses, ferries, trains, pedicabs and those ubiquitous yellow taxis (though don't expect to see many available when it's raining) for zipping around and out of town when the subway simply doesn't cut it.

The sidewalks of New York, however, are the real stars in the transportation scheme – this city is made for walking. Increasingly, it's also made for bicycles, with the addition of hundreds of miles of new bike lanes and greenways over the last few years.

Subway

The New York subway system, run by the Metropolitan Transportation Authority (www.mta.info), is iconic, cheap ($2.75 per ride, regardless of the distance traveled), round-the-clock and often the fastest and most reliable way to get around the city. It's also safer and (a bit) cleaner than it used to be. Free wi-fi is available in all underground stations.

It's a good idea to grab a free map from a station attendant. If you have a smartphone, download a useful app (like the free Citymapper), with subway map and alerts of service outages.

SUBWAY CHEAT SHEET

A few tips for understanding the madness of the New York subway:

Numbers, letters, colors Color-coded subway lines are named by a letter or number, and most carry a collection of two to four trains on their tracks.

Express & local lines A common mistake is accidentally boarding an 'express train' and passing by a local stop you want. Know that each color-coded line is shared by local trains and express trains; the latter make only select stops in Manhattan (indicated by a white circle on subway maps). For example, on the red line, the 2 and 3 are express, while the slower 1 makes local stops. If you're covering a greater distance – say from the Upper West Side to Wall St – you're better off transferring to the express train (usually just across the platform from the local) to save time.

Getting in the right station Some stations – such as SoHo's Spring St station on the 6 line – have separate entrances for downtown or uptown lines (read the sign carefully). If you swipe in at the wrong one – as even locals do on occasion – you'll either need to ride the subway to a station where you can transfer for free, or just lose the $2.75 and re-enter the station (usually across the street). Also look for the green and red lamps above the stairs at each station entrance; green means that it's always open, while red means that particular entrance will be closed at certain hours, usually late at night.

Weekends All the rules switch on weekends, when some lines combine with others, some get suspended, some stations get passed, others get reached. Locals and tourists alike stand on platforms confused, sometimes irate. Check www.mta.info for weekend schedules. Sometimes posted signs aren't visible until after you reach the platform.

When in doubt, ask someone who looks like they know what they're doing. They may not, but subway confusion (and frustration) is the great unifier in this diverse city. And if you're new to the underground, never wear headphones when you're riding, as you might miss an important announcement about track changes or skipped stops.

Taxi

Hailing and riding in a cab, once rites of passage in New York, are being replaced by the ubiquity of ride-hailing app services like Lyft and Uber. In fact, those two alone have over 50,000 cars operating in the five boroughs compared to the 13,580 yellow cabs. Still, most taxis in NYC are clean and, compared to those in many international cities, pretty cheap. When you get a driver who's a neurotic speed demon, which is often, don't forget to buckle up.

Taxi & Limousine Commission (TLC; www.nyc.gov/html/tlc/html/home/home.shtml) The taxis' governing body has set fares for rides (which can be paid with credit or debit card). It's $2.50 for the initial charge (first one-fifth of a mile), 50¢ for each additional one-fifth mile as well as per 60 seconds of being stopped in traffic, $1 peak surcharge (weekdays 4pm to 8pm), and a 50¢ night surcharge (8pm to 6am), plus a MTA State surcharge of 50¢ per ride. Tips are expected to be 10% to 15%, but give less if you feel in any way mistreated; be sure to ask for a receipt and use it to note the driver's license number.

Passenger rights The TLC keeps a Passenger's Bill of Rights, which gives you the right to tell the driver which route you'd like to take, or ask your driver to turn off an annoying radio station. Also, the driver does not have the right to refuse you a ride based on where you are going. Tip: get in first, then say where you're going.

Private car These services are a common taxi alternative in the outer boroughs. Fares differ depending on the neighborhood and length of ride, and must be determined beforehand, as they have no meters. These 'black cars' are quite common in Brooklyn and Queens, but it's illegal if a driver simply stops to offer you a ride – no matter what borough you're in. A couple of car services in Brooklyn include **Northside** (www.northsideservice.com; ☎718-387-2222) in Williamsburg and **Arecibo** (☎718-783-6465) in Park Slope.

Boro Taxis Green Boro Taxis operate in the outer boroughs and Upper Manhattan. These allow folks to hail a taxi on the street in neighborhoods where yellow taxis rarely roam. They have the same fares and features as yellow cabs, and are a good way to get around the outer boroughs (from, say, Astoria to Williamsburg, or Park Slope to Red Hook). Drivers are reluctant (but legally obligated) to take passengers into Manhattan as they aren't legally allowed to take fares going out of Manhattan south of 96th St.

Ride-sharing App-based car-hailing services have taken over the streets of the five boroughs. Now, with nearly five times as many cars as yellow cabs and growing, they're both convenient, indispensable for some, and of course adding to the already terrible traffic problem. Tipping is highly encouraged; drivers may give you a low rating if you stiff them.

Ferry

NYC Ferry (www.ferry.nyc; one-way $2.75) Operating in the East River only since May 2017 (it replaced the former East River Ferry service), these boats link Manhattan, Brooklyn, Queens and the Bronx. At only $2.75 a ride ($1 more to bring a bicycle on board) and with charging stations and mini convenience stores on board, it's an altogether more pleasurable commute than being stuck underground on the subway. It is rapidly becoming a popular and scenic way to reach beach spots in Rockaway, Queens.

NY Water Taxi (www.nywatertaxi.com) Has a fleet of zippy yellow boats that provide hop-on, hop-off services with a few stops around Manhattan (Pier 79 at W 39th St; World Financial Center and Pier 11 near Wall St) and Brooklyn (Pier 1 in Dumbo), plus a **ferry service** (Ikea Express; Map p438; ☎212-742-1969; www.nywatertaxi.com/ikea; 500 Van Brunt St, behind Fairway, Red Hook; adult/child $5/free, Sat & Sun free) between Pier 11 and the Ikea store in Red Hook, Brooklyn. At $35 for an all-day pass, though, it's priced more like a sightseeing cruise than practical transport.

Staten Island Ferry (Map p406; www.siferry.com; Whitehall Terminal, 4 South St, at Whitehall St; 24hr; S 1 to South Ferry; R/W to Whitehall St; 4/5 to Bowling Green) FREE Bright orange and large, this free commuter-oriented ferry to Staten Island makes constant journeys across New York Harbor. Even if you simply turn around to reboard in Staten Island, the views of lower Manhattan and the Statue of Liberty make this a great sightseeing experience and one of the cheapest romantic dates in the city.

Bus

Part of the Metropolitan Transportation Authority (www.mta.info), buses can be a handy way to cross town or to cover short distances when you don't want to bother going underground. Rides cost the same as subway ($2.75 per ride), and you can use your metrocard or pay in cash (exact change required) when entering the bus. If you pay with a metrocard, you get one free transfer from bus to subway, bus to bus, or subway to bus. If you pay in cash, ask for a transfer (good only for a bus-to-bus transfer) from the bus driver when paying.

You'll find the route indicated on the small display box mounted on the pole of the bus stop.

Bicycle

Hundreds of miles of designated bike lanes have been added over the past decade. Add to this the excellent bike-sharing network Citi Bike (www.citibikenyc.com), and you have the makings for a surprisingly bike-friendly city. Hundreds of Citi Bike kiosks in Manhattan and parts of Brooklyn house the iconic bright blue and very sturdy bicycles, which have reasonable rates for short-term users. Nearly 14 million City Bike 'trips' were taken in 2016 and there are there are an estimated 12,000 bikes in the system.

To use a Citi Bike, purchase a 24-hour or three-day access pass (around $12 or $24 including tax) at any Citi Bike kiosk. You will then be given a five-digit code to unlock a bike. Return the bike to any station within 30 minutes to avoid incurring extra fees. Reinsert your credit card (you won't be charged) and follow the prompts to check out a bike again. You can make an unlimited number of 30-minute checkouts during those 24 hours or three days.

Helmets aren't required by law, but strongly recommended. You'll need to bring your own. City parks like Central Park, the Brooklyn Waterfront Greenway and Prospect Park in Brooklyn are good places to test out your comfort level on wheels in less stressful environments than the chaotic city streets. And most importantly, for your safety and that of others, obey traffic laws.

You'll find routes and bike lanes for every borough on NYC Bike Maps (www.nycbikemaps.com). For downloadable maps and point-to-point route generator, visit NYC DOT (www.nyc.gov/html/dot/html/bicyclists/bikemaps.shtml). Free bike maps are also available at most bike shops.

Train

Long Island Rail Road (www.mta.info/lirr), NJ Transit (www.njtransit.com), New Jersey PATH (www.panynj.gov/path) and Metro-North Railroad (www.mta.info/mnr) all offer useful services for getting around NYC and surrounds.

TOURS

When it comes to guided tours, there are loads of options in NYC. You can take a historical walking tour, taste your way around ethnically rich neighborhoods, or do something more active on a bicycling, kayaking or bird-watching tour.

Big Apple Greeter (☎212-669-8159; www.bigapplegreeter.org) For an inside take on the NYC experience, book a walking tour in the neighborhood of your choice led by a local volunteer who just can't wait to show off their city to you. You'll be matched with a guide who suits your needs, whether that means speaking Spanish or American Sign Language, or knowing just where to find the best wheelchair-accessible spots in the city. Reserve four weeks in advance.

Big Onion Walking Tours (☎888-606-9255; www.bigonion.com; tours $25) Choose from nearly 30 tours, including Brooklyn Bridge and Brooklyn Heights, the 'Official' Gangs of New York Tour, a Gay and Lesbian History Tour – Before Stonewall, and Chelsea and the High Line.

Bike the Big Apple (☎347-878-9809; www.bikethebigapple.com; tours incl bike & helmet $99) Biking tours let you cover more ground than walking tours and give you a healthy dose of exercise to boot. Bike the Big Apple, recommended by NYC & Company (the official tourism authority of New York City and operators of www.nycgo.com), offers 10 set tours.

Circle Line Boat Tours (Map p428; ☎212-563-3200; www.circleline42.com; Pier 83, W 42nd St at Twelfth Ave; cruises from adult/child $30/25; 🚌westbound M42 or M50 to 12th Ave, ⓈA/C/E to 42nd St-Port Authority) The classic Circle Line guides you through all the big sights from the safe distance of a boat. Options include a 2½-hour full-island cruise, a shorter (90-minute) 'semi-circle' journey and a two-hour evening cruise. From May to October, the outfit also operates adrenaline-fueled cruises aboard the high-speed *Beast*.

New York City Audubon (Map p422; ☎212-691-7483; www.nycaudubon.org; 71 W 23rd St, Suite 1523, at Sixth Ave, Flatiron District; tours & classes free-$170; ⓈF/M to 23rd St) Throughout the year, the New York City Audubon Society runs bird-watching field trips (including seal- and waterbird-spotting on New York Harbor and eagle-watching in the Hudson Valley), lectures and beginners' birding classes.

Foods of New York (☎855-223-8684; www.foodsofny.com; tours from $54) The official foodie tour of NYC & Company offers various three-hour tours that help you eat your way through gourmet shops and eateries in either the West Village, Chelsea, Chinatown or Nolita. Prepare yourself for a moving feast of French bread, fresh Italian pasta, sushi, global cheeses, real New York pizza, local fish and freshly baked pastries.

Nosh Walks (www.noshwalks; tours from $60) Deeply knowledgeable foodie Myra Alperson leads food-themed walks all over the NYC area, with special attention given to the ethnically rich hoods of Queens and Brooklyn.

New York Gallery Tours (Map p420; ☎212-946-1548; www.nygallerytours.com; 526 W 26th St, at Tenth Ave, Chelsea; scheduled/private per person $25/$300 minimum; ⏱scheduled tours Sat, private tours 10am-6pm Tue-Sun; Ⓢ1, C/E to 23rd St) You know you're supposed to check out the array of amazing modern-art galleries in Chelsea. But where to begin? This excellent guided tour takes you to a slew of galleries and provides helpful commentary along the way. It also runs gay and lesbian tours that focus on a 'queer aesthetic.' Scheduled tours arranged around different themes happen every Saturday at different times and locations.

Museum Hack (☎347-282-5001; https://museumhack.com; 2hr tour from $59) For a fascinating, alternative perspective of the Met, sign up for a tour with Museum Hack. Knowledgeable but delightfully irreverent guides take on topics like 'Badass Witches' (a look at the dark arts in Egypt and the Middle Ages), paradigm-shifting feminist artists and an 'Unhighlights Tour' that will take you to corners of the museum few visitors known about. Museum Hack also runs tours in the Museum of Natural History, including a family-friendly option that delves into the science behind some extraordinary animals and the captivating stories of adventurers who collected the specimens.

On Location Tours (☎212-683-2027; www.onlocationtours.com; tours $49) Face it: you want to sit on Carrie Bradshaw's apartment stoop and check out the bar Michael Keaton frequents in *Birdman*. This company offers various tours – covering *Gossip Girl*, *Sex and the City*, *The Sopranos*, the *Real Housewives of NYC*, general TV and movie locations, and movie locations in Central Park – that let you live out your entertainment-obsessed fantasies. A couple of the tours are also available in French or German.

Wildman Steve Brill (☎914-835-2153; www.wildmanstevebrill.com; suggested donation $20) New York's best known naturalist – betcha didn't know there were any! – has been leading folks on foraging expeditions through city parks for more than 30 years. He'll trek with you through Central Park, Prospect Park, Inwood Park and many more, teaching you to identify natural riches including sassafras, chickweed, ginkgo nuts, garlic and wild mushrooms along the way.

Directory A-Z

Customs Regulations

US Customs allows each person over the age of 21 to bring 1L of liquor and 200 cigarettes into the US duty free. Agricultural items including meat, fruits, vegetables, plants and soil are prohibited. US citizens are allowed to import, duty free, up to $800 worth of gifts from abroad, while non-US citizens are allowed to import $100 worth. If you're carrying more than $10,000 in US and foreign cash, traveler's checks or money orders, you need to declare the excess amount. There is no legal restriction on the amount that may be imported, but undeclared sums in excess of $10,000 will probably be subject to investigation. If you're bringing prescription drugs, make sure they're in clearly marked containers. Obviously, leave the illegal narcotics at home. For updates, check www.cbp.gov.

Discount Cards

If you plan on blitzing the major sights, consider buying one of the numerous multi-attraction passes (see www.nycgo.com/attraction-passes). Getting one of these discount cards will save you a wad of cash. Go online for more details, and to purchase these passes.

New York CityPASS (www.citypass.com) Buys you admission to six major attractions (including the Empire State Building) for $122, saving around 40% if purchased separately.

The New York Pass (www.newyorkpass.com) This pass gives you one-day access to some 90 different sites for $119. Multiday passes also available (from two to 10 days).

Downtown Culture Pass (www.downtownculturepass.org) Purchase this $25 three-day pass for free admission (and shop discounts) at a handful of sites in Lower Manhattan, including the Museum of American Finance and the Museum of Jewish Heritage, both locations where you can purchase the pass in person.

Explorer Pass (www.smartdestinations.com) A pass that lets you choose between three and 10 attractions for discounted admission. You pick the sites from among 63 options, including the MoMA, the Intrepid Museum, Sightseeing cruises and the Top of the Rock. Prices start at $84 for three sites, up to $199 for 10 sites.

Electricity

The US electric current is 110V to 115V, 60Hz AC. Outlets are made for flat two-prong plugs (which often have a third, rounded prong for grounding). If your appliance is made for another electrical system (eg 220V), you'll need a step-down converter, which can be bought at hardware stores and drugstores. Most electronic devices (laptops, camera-battery chargers etc) are built for dual-voltage use, however, and will only need a plug adapter.

Type B
120V/60Hz

Emergency & Important Numbers

Local directory	☎411
Municipal offices & information	☎311
National directory information	☎212-555-1212
Operator	☎0
Fire, police & ambulance	☎911

Internet Access

Most public parks in the city now offer free wi-fi. Some prominent ones include the High Line, Bryant Park, Battery Park, Central Park, City Hall Park, Madison Square Park, Tompkins Square Park and Union Square Park (Brooklyn and Queens are also well covered). For other locations, check out www.nycgovparks.org/facilities/wifi.

Even underground subway stations now offer free wi-fi, offering a way to pass time or get work done while waiting for signal problems or other delays to be resolved. LinkNYC (www.link.nyc) rolled out in 2016 to replace anachronistic pay phones (once iconic symbols of the city and where Superman changed into his suit) with free internet-connected kiosks, replete with charging stations and wi-fi access. The network aims to install some 7500 of these structures throughout the five boroughs.

It's rare to find accommodations in New York City that don't offer wi-fi, though it isn't always free. Most cafes offer wi-fi for customers, as do the ubiquitous Starbucks around town.

Legal Matters

If you're arrested, you have the right to remain silent. There is no legal reason to speak to a police officer if you don't wish to – especially since anything you say 'can and will be used against you' – but never walk away from an officer until given permission. All persons who are arrested have the legal right to make one phone call. If you don't have a lawyer or family member to help you, call your consulate. The police will give you the number upon request.

Medical Services

Before traveling, contact your health-insurance provider to find out what types of medical care will be covered outside your hometown (or home country). Overseas visitors should acquire travel insurance that covers medical situations in the US, as nonemergency care for uninsured patients can be very expensive. For nonemergency appointments at hospitals, you'll need proof of insurance or cash. Even with insurance, you'll most likely have to pay up front for nonemergency care and then wrangle with your insurance company afterward in order to get your money reimbursed.

Travel MD (☎212-737-1212; www.travelmd.com) offers 24-hour medical advice for visitors to NYC, and appointments for hotel visits can be made.

Emergency Rooms & Hospitals

Emergency services can be stress-inducing and slow; a visit should be avoided if other medical services can be provided to mitigate the situation.

New York-Presbyterian Hospital (☎212-305-2500; www.nyp.org/locations/newyork-presbyterian-columbia-university-medical-center; 630 W 168th St, at Ft Washington Ave; Ⓢ A/C, 1 to 168th St) Reputable hospital.

Bellevue Hospital Center (☎212-562-4141; www.nychealthandhospitals.org/bellevue; 462 First Ave, at 27th St, Midtown East; Ⓢ 6 to 28th St) Major public hospital with emergency room and trauma center.

New York County Medical Society (☎212-684-4670; www.nycms.org) Provides doctor referrals over the phone, based on type of problem and language spoken.

Tisch Hospital (New York University Langone Medical Center; ☎212-263-5800; www.nyulangone.org/locations/tisch-hospital; 550 First Ave; ⏲24hr) Large, state-of-the-art facility with highly regarded departments in every critical care specialty.

Callen-Lorde Community Health Center (☎212-271-7200; www.callen-lorde.org; 356 W 18th St, btwn Eighth & Ninth Aves; ⏲8:15am-8:15pm Mon-Thu, to 4:45pm Fri, 8:30am-3:15pm Sat; Ⓢ A/C/E, L to 8th Ave-14th St) This medical center, dedicated to the LGBT community and people living with HIV/AIDS, serves people regardless of their ability to pay.

PRACTICALITIES

Newspapers & Magazines

New York Post (www.nypost.com) The *Post* is known for screaming headlines, conservative political views and its popular Page Six gossip column.

New York Times (www.nytimes.com) 'The gray lady' is far from staid, with hard-hitting political coverage, and sections on technology, arts and dining out.

Wall Street Journal (www.wallstreetjournal.com) This intellectual daily focuses on finance, though media mogul Rupert Murdoch has ratcheted up the general coverage.

New York Magazine (www.nymag.com) A biweekly magazine with feature stories and great listings about anything and everything in NYC, plus an indispensable website.

New Yorker (www.newyorker.com) This highbrow weekly covers politics and culture through its famously lengthy works of reportage; it also publishes fiction and poetry.

Time Out New York (www.timeout.com/newyork) A weekly magazine with event listings and restaurant and nightlife roundups.

Radio

NYC has some excellent radio options beyond commercial pop-music stations. An excellent programming guide can be found in the *New York Times* Entertainment section on Sunday. Our top pick is WNYC (820AM and 93.9FM; www.wnyc.org), NYC's public radio station that is the local NPR (National Public Radio) affiliate and offers a blend of national and local talk and interview shows, with a switch to classical music in the day on the FM station.

Die-hard sports fans tune in to call-in shows on WFAN (660AM and 101FM) throughout the day. Yankees and Mets fanatics tend to be the most obsessive callers, usually unwilling to give any credit to their rivals.

Smoking

Smoking is strictly forbidden in any location that's considered a public place, including subway stations, restaurants, bars, taxis and parks. A few hotels have smoking rooms, but the majority are entirely smoke-free.

Lenox Hill Hospital (☎212-434-2000; www.northwell.edu/find-care/locations/lenox-hill-hospital; 100 E 77th St, at Lexington Ave; ⊙24hr; Ⓢ6 to 77th St) A good hospital with a 24-hour emergency room and multilingual translators in the Upper East Side.

Mount Sinai Hospital (☎212-241-6500; www.mountsinai.org/locations/mount-sinai; 1468 Madison Ave, at E 101st St; ⊙24hr; Ⓢ6 to 103rd St) An excellent hospital in the Upper East Side.

Planned Parenthood (Margaret Sanger Center; ☎212-965-7000; www.plannedparenthood.org; 26 Bleecker St, btwn Mott & Elizabeth Sts, NoHo; ⊙8am-6:30pm Mon, Tue, Thu & Fri, to 8:30pm Wed, to 4:30pm Sat; ⓈB/D/F/V to Broadway-Lafayette St; 6 to Bleecker St) Provides birth control, STD screenings and gynecological care.

Pharmacies

New York is bursting with 24-hour 'pharmacies,' which are handy stores where you can buy over-the-counter medications; the pharmaceutical prescription counters have more limited hours. Major pharmacy chains include CVS, Duane Reade, Rite Aid and Walgreens.

Money

ATMs

ATMs are on practically every corner. You can either use your card at banks – usually in a 24-hour-access lobby, filled with up to a dozen monitors at major branches – or you can opt for the lone wolves, which sit in delis, restaurants, bars and grocery stores, charging fierce service fees that average $3 but can go as high as $5.

Most New York banks are linked by the New York Cash Exchange (NYCE) system, and you can use local bank cards interchangeably at ATMs – for a fee if you're banking outside your system.

Changing Money

Banks and money changers, found all over New York City (including all three major airports), will give you US currency based on the current exchange rate. **Travelex** (☎212-265-6063; www.travelex.com; 1578 Broadway, btwn 47th & 48th Sts, Midtown West; ⊙9am-10pm Mon-Sat, to 7pm Sun; ⓈN/Q/R to 49th St) has a branch in Times Square.

Credit Cards

Major credit cards are accepted at most hotels, restaurants and shops throughout New York City. In fact, you'll find it difficult to perform certain transactions, such as purchasing tickets to performances and renting a car, without one.

Stack your deck with a Visa, MasterCard or American Express, as these are the cards of choice here. Places that accept Visa and MasterCard also accept debit cards. Be sure to check with your bank to confirm that your debit card will be accepted in other states or countries – debit cards from large commercial banks can often be used worldwide.

If your cards are lost or stolen, contact the company immediately.

Opening Hours

Standard business hours are as follows:

Banks 9am–6pm Monday–Friday, some also 9am–noon Saturday

Bars 5pm–4am

Businesses 9am–5pm Monday–Friday

Clubs 10pm–4am

Restaurants Breakfast 6am–11am, lunch 11am–around 3pm, and dinner 5pm–11pm. Weekend brunch 11am–4pm.

Shops 10am–around 7pm weekdays, 11am–around 8pm Saturday, and Sunday can be variable – some stores stay closed while others keep weekday hours. Stores tend to stay open later in the neighborhoods downtown.

Post

Visit the US Postal Service (www.usps.com) website for up-to-date information about postage prices and branch locations throughout the city.

Public Holidays

Major NYC holidays and special events may force the closure of many businesses or attract crowds, making dining and accommodations reservations difficult.

New Year's Day January 1

Martin Luther King Day Third Monday in January

Presidents' Day Third Monday in February

Easter March/April

Memorial Day Late May

Gay Pride Last Sunday in June

Independence Day July 4

Labor Day Early September

Rosh Hashanah and Yom Kippur Mid-September to mid-October

Halloween October 31

Thanksgiving Fourth Thursday in November

Christmas Day December 25

New Year's Eve December 31

Safe Travel

New York City is one of the safest cities in the USA – in 2017 homicides fell to a record low of fewer than 300 and overall violent-crime statistics declined for the 27th straight year. Still, it's best to take a common-sense approach to the city.

➡ Don't walk around alone at night in unfamiliar, sparsely populated areas.

➡ Carry your daily walking-around money somewhere inside your clothing or in a front pocket rather than in a handbag or a back pocket.

➡ Be aware of pickpockets, particularly in mobbed areas like Times Square or Penn Station at rush hour.

➡ While it's generally safe to ride the subway after midnight, you may want to skip going underground and take a taxi instead, especially if traveling alone.

Taxes & Refunds

Restaurants and retailers never include the sales tax – 8.875% – in their prices, so beware of ordering the $4.99 lunch special when you only have $5 to your name. Several categories of so-called luxury items, including rental cars and dry cleaning, carry an additional city surcharge of 5%, so you wind up paying an extra 13.875% in total for these services. Clothing and footwear purchases under $110 are tax free; anything over that has a sales tax. Hotel rooms in New York City are subject to a 14.75% tax, plus a flat $3.50 occupancy tax per night. Since the US has no nationwide value-added tax (VAT), there is no opportunity for foreign visitors to make 'tax-free' purchases.

Telephone

Phone numbers within the US consist of a three-digit area code followed by a seven-digit local number. In NYC, you will always dial ten numbers: 1 + the three-digit area code + the seven-digit number. To make an international call (except to Canada), call ☎011 + country code + area code + number.

Time

New York City is in the Eastern Standard Time (EST) zone – five hours behind Greenwich Mean Time (London) and three hours ahead of Pacific Standard Time (California). Almost all of the USA observes daylight-saving time: clocks go forward one hour on the second Sunday in March and are turned back one hour on the first Sunday in November.

Toilets

Considering the number of pedestrians, there's a noticeable lack of public restrooms around the city. You'll find spots to relieve yourself in Grand Central Terminal, Penn Station and Port Authority Bus Terminal, and in parks, including Madison Square Park, Battery Park, Tompkins Square Park, Washington Square Park and Columbus Park in Chinatown, plus several places scattered around Central Park. The good bet, though, is to pop into a Starbucks (there's one about every three blocks), a department store (Macy's, Century 21, Bloomingdale's) or a neighborhood park like Tompkins Square in the East Village or Bleecker Playground (at W 11th and Hudson) in the West Village.

Tourist Information

In this web-based world you'll find infinite online resources to get up-to-the-minute information about New York. In person, try one of the official branches of **NYC Information Center** (☎212-484-1222; www.nycgo.com) at Times Square (Map p428; Broadway Plaza, btwn W 43rd & 44th Sts; ⏲9am-6pm Dec-Apr, 8am-8pm May-Nov; Ⓢ N/Q/R/W, S, 1/2/3, 7, A/C/E to Times Sq-42nd St), Macy's Herald Square (Map p428; Macy's, 151 W 34th St, at Broadway; ⏲10am-10pm Mon-Sat, to 9pm Sun; Ⓢ B/D/F/M, N/Q/R/W to 34th St-Herald Sq), City Hall (Map p406; City Hall Park, at Broadway; ⏲9am-6pm Mon-Sun; Ⓢ 4/5/6 to Brooklyn Bridge-City Hall; R/W to City Hall; J/Z to Chambers St) and South Street Seaport.

Explore Brooklyn (www.explorebk.com) has up-to-date event listings and lots of of other info on this borough.

Travelers with Disabilities

Much of the city is accessible with curb cuts for wheelchair users. All the major sites (the Met museum, the Guggenheim, and Lincoln Center) are also accessible. Some, but not all, Broadway theaters are accessible.

Unfortunately, only about 100 of New York's 468 subway stations are fully wheelchair accessible. In general, the bigger stations have access, such as West 4th St, 14th St-Union Sq, 34th St-Penn Station, 42nd St-Port Authority Terminal, 59th St-Columbus Circle, and 66th St-Lincoln Center. For a complete list of accessible subway stations, visit http://web.mta.info/accessibility/stations.htm. Also visit www.nycgo.com/accessibility.

On the plus side, all of NYC's MTA buses are wheelchair accessible, and are often a better option than cramped subway stations.

The city also provides paratransit buses for getting around town for the same price as a subway fare, though these aren't very practical as you must order them 24 hours in advance. Call **Access-a-Ride** (☎877-337-2017) to request transport.

More practical is simply ordering an accessible taxi through **Accessible Dispatch** (☎646-599-9999; http://accessibledispatch.org); there's also an app that allows you to request the nearest available service.

Another excellent resource is the **Big Apple Greeter** (☎212-669-8198; www.bigapplegreeter.org) FREE program, which has more than 50 volunteers on staff with physical disabilities who are happy to show off their corner of the city.

Download Lonely Planet's free Accessible Travel guide from http://lptravel.to/AccessibleTravel.

Visas

Visa Waiver Program

The US Visa Waiver Program (VWP) allows nationals from 38 countries to enter the US without a visa, provided you are carrying a machine-readable passport. For the up-to-date list of countries included in the program and current requirements, see the US Department of State (https://travel.state.gov) website.

Citizens of VWP countries need to register with the US Department of Homeland Security and fill out an ESTA application (Electronic System for Travel Authorization; www.cbp.gov/travel/international-visitors/esta) before your visit. There is a $14 fee for registration; when approved, the registration is valid for two years or until your passport expires, whichever comes first.

Visas Required

You must obtain a visa from a US embassy or consulate in your home country if:

- You do not currently hold a passport from a VWP country.
- You are from a VWP country, but don't have a machine-readable passport.
- You are planning to stay longer than 90 days.
- You are planning to work or study in the US.

Volunteering

There are numerous volunteer opportunities in NYC. You can help mentor struggling students, assist in cleaning up the parks, play Bingo with seniors or lend a hand serving food in a soup kitchen (a place where homeless or low-income residents can get a free meal). A few places where you can sign up to help include the following organizations:

New York Cares (www.newyorkcares.org)

NYC Service (www.nycservice.org)

Street Project (www.streetproject.org)

Behind the Scenes

SEND US YOUR FEEDBACK

We love to hear from travelers – your comments keep us on our toes and help make our books better. Our well-traveled team reads every word on what you loved or loathed about this book. Although we cannot reply individually to your submissions, we always guarantee that your feedback goes straight to the appropriate authors, in time for the next edition. Each person who sends us information is thanked in the next edition – the most useful submissions are rewarded with a selection of digital PDF chapters.

Visit **lonelyplanet.com/contact** to submit your updates and suggestions or to ask for help. Our award-winning website also features inspirational travel stories, news and discussions.

Note: We may edit, reproduce and incorporate your comments in Lonely Planet products such as guidebooks, websites and digital products, so let us know if you don't want your comments reproduced or your name acknowledged. For a copy of our privacy policy visit lonelyplanet.com/privacy.

WRITER THANKS

Regis St Louis

Many thanks to David Fung and Kristie Blase for their warm hospitality, to Jayson Mallic and Glen Brown for their friendship, and Ali and the felines for hosting me in Williamsburg. Special thanks to the staff at Mount Sinai Queens Hospital ER room for help after the late-night bike accident. As always, thanks to Cassandra and our daughters, Magdalena and Genevieve, for their support.

Robert Balkovich

Thank you to my mother, who first introduced me to Lonely Planet. To Jenny who is my forever MVP. To Lina for never believing my self doubt. To Adrian for always having a work around. To Celeste for the gallery tours. And most of all to Trisha for the opportunity.

Ray Bartlett

Thanks first and always to my family for making all this possible and for putting up with me. Thanks to Trisha P, editor extraordinaire, for giving this the green light, and to my coauthors for the help and camaraderie. Hugs and deepest gratitude to everyone who went out of their way to show me around their amazing city: Belinda, Jennifer, May-anne, Chang, Rebecca, Alex B, Clay, Danniel and Rachelle, Madoon, to name a few. And a shout out to all the other incredible NYC denizens who made researching this book such an awesome voyage. Can't wait to be back.

Ali Lemer

Many thanks to Will Coley, Nicole Marsella, Adam Michaels, Regis St Louis and Trisha Ping, and to Professor Kenneth Jackson, who taught me more about NYC history than anyone. My work is dedicated to the memory of my father, Albert Lemer, a 1st-generation New Yorker who inspired my enthusiasm for international travel as much as he kindled my love of our shared hometown – the greatest city in the world.

ACKNOWLEDGEMENTS

Illustrations p230–1 by Javier Zarracina.

Cover photograph: Brooklyn Bridge, Alan Copson/AWL ©

THIS BOOK

This 11th edition of Lonely Planet's *New York City* guidebook was researched and written by Regis St. Louis, Robert Balkovich, Ray Bartlett, Michael Grosberg, Brian Kluepfel and Ali Lemer. The previous edition was also written by Regis, along with Cristian Bonetto and Zora O'Neill. Regis and Cristian also worked on the 9th edition. This guidebook was produced by the following:

Destination Editor Trisha Ping

Product Editors Kathryn Rowan, Kate Mathews

Senior Cartographer Alison Lyall

Book Designer Meri Blazevski

Assisting Editors Melanie Dankel, Jennifer Hattam, Alison Morris, Anne Mulvaney, Kristin Odijk, Charlotte Orr, Susan Paterson, Christopher Pitts, Benjamin Spier

Assisting Book Designer Clara Monitto

Cover Researcher Naomi Parker

Thanks to Carolyn Boicos, Mikki Brammer, Kate Chapman, Nicholas Colicchia, Shona Gray, Donna Harshman, Bettina Kienzi, Virginia Moreno, Kirsten Rawlings, Remmelt van der Wal, Tony Wheeler

Index

See also separate subindexes for:

EATING P397

DRINKING & NIGHTLIFE P399

ENTERTAINMENT P400

SHOPPING P401

SPORTS & ACTIVITIES P402

SLEEPING P402

6th & B Garden 117
41 Cooper Square 371
432 Park Avenue 192
555 Edgecombe Ave 253

A

Abingdon Square 140
Abyssinian Baptist Church 249
accommodations 19, 330-46, *see also* Sleeping *subindex, individual neighborhoods*
activities 53-5, *see also* Sports & Activities *subindex, individual neighborhoods*
African Burial Ground National Monument 77
Alice Austen House 75
Alice in Wonderland 229
Alice Tully Hall 232
All People's Garden 117
American Folk Art Museum 234
American Museum of Natural History 234, **238**
Anastasia Photo 115
Apollo Theater 250, **255**
architecture 192, 367-71
Artists Space 74
arts 363-6
Asia Society & Museum 219
Astor Place 112
Astoria 306, 310-13, **446**
ATMs 388
Audubon Center Boathouse 264

B

bagels 359
Bank of America Tower 192
Barbara Gladstone Gallery 148
baseball 53
Basilica of St Patrick's Old Cathedral 91-2
basketball 53
bathrooms 389-90
Battery Park 74, 76
Battery Park City 74, 76
Battle Hill 269
Bear Mountain State Park (Hudson Valley) 326
Bed-Stuy 268-9, 271, 279-80
beer 362
Bethel Woods Center for the Arts (Woodstock) 328
Bethesda Fountain 228
Bethesda Terrace 228
bicycling 23, 244
BLDG 92 271
Blockhouse 229
boat travel 384
Boerum Hill 266, 268, 277-9, 288-9, 297, **438**
books 286, 295, 348
Bowery 114
Bowling Green 74
BRIC House 268-9
Bridgehampton 321
Brighton Beach 275-6, **444**
Brill Building 178
Brisas del Caribe 117
Broadway 7, 179, 204, 365-6
Broken Kilometer 91
Bronx, the 258
Bronx Museum 258
Bronx Zoo 258
Brooklyn 10, 61, 260-300, **260**, **436-44**, **11**, **282-3**
  accommodations 344-5
  drinking & nightlife 261, 288-91, 293-4
  entertainment 289, 294-7
  food 261, 276-88
  highlights 260, 262-5
  shopping 297-9
  sights 262-6, 268-9, 271-6
  sports & activities 299-300
  transportation 261, 273
  walks 267, 270-1, 292-3, **267**, **270-1**, **292-3**
Brooklyn Art Library 274
Brooklyn Botanic Garden 272-3, **282-3**
Brooklyn Brewery 275, **293**
Brooklyn Bridge 12, 262, **13**, **262**
Brooklyn Bridge Park 263
Brooklyn Children's Museum 273
Brooklyn Heights 276-7, 288, 297, **443**
Brooklyn Historical Society 266
Brooklyn Museum 265
Bryant Park 193, **37**
bus travel 382, 384
Bush Terminal Piers Park 272
Bushwick 273-5, 284-7, 290-3, 299
Bushwick Collective 274
business hours 389

C

Canaan Baptist Church 249
Capote, Truman 267
Carroll Gardens 266, 277-9, 288-9, 297-8, **438**
Castle Clinton 74
Cathedral Church of St John the Divine 247-8, **247**
cell phones 18
cemeteries 269
Center for Photography at Woodstock (Woodstock) 328
Central Park 61, 226-44, **226**, **432-3**
  accommodations 342-3
  drinking & nightlife 227, 237-40
  entertainment 227, 240-2
  food 227, 234-7
  highlights 226, 228-9
  sights 228-34
  sports & activities 243-4
  transportation 227
  travel tips 227
Central Park 9, 228-31, **8**, **33**, **35**, **228**, **238-9**
Central Park Zoo 228-9
Chanin Building 188
cheesecake 361
Cheim & Read 142
Chelsea 61, 132-63, **132**, **420-1**, **149**
  accommodations 336-8
  drinking & nightlife 133, 154-5
  entertainment 155, 158-60
  food 133, 147, 149-50
  highlights 132, 134-8
  shopping 162-3
  sights 134-42
  sports & activities 163
  transportation 133
  walks 148-9, **148**
Chelsea Hotel 141
Chelsea Market 134-5, **134**
Cherry Blossom Festival 30
children, travel with 33-4
Children's Corner 264
Children's Museum of the Arts 90
Chinatown 61, 86-106, **86**, **411**
  accommodations 334
  drinking & nightlife 87, 100-1, 103
  entertainment 103-4
  food 87, 99-100
  highlights 86, 88-9
  shopping 87, 104-6
  sights 88-9, 92-3
  sports & activities 106
  transportation 87
  walks 98, **98**
Chinatown 88-9, **88**
Chrysler Building 187-8, 201, **187**, **200**, **367**

Sights 000
Map Pages **000**
Photo Pages **000**

Church of the Transfiguration 93
Citi Bike 23
Citigroup Center 192
City Hall 368
City Reliquary 274
Clinton Hill 268-9, 271, 279-80
Cloisters Museum & Gardens 252
Cobble Hill 266, 277-9, 288-9, **438**
cocktails 361-2
Coffey Park 268
Columbia University 249-50
Columbus Park 93
Coney Art Walls 276
Coney Island 275-6, 287-8, 293-4, **444**, **282**
Conservatory Garden 229
Conservatory Water 229
Convent Avenue Baptist Church 249
Cooper-Hewitt National Design Museum 218
Cooper Union 112, **112**
Corona 306-8, 314-15
costs 18, 40, 44, 331, 386, 389
credit cards 389
Crown Heights 281-4, 290
culture 363-6
currency 18
currency exchange 388
customs regulations 386

D

dance 47, 366
David Geffen Hall 232
David H Koch Theater 232
David Rubenstein Atrium 232
David Zwirner 149
Delacorte Theater 229
Deno's Wonder Wheel 275
Dia: Beacon (Hudson Valley) 326
disabilities, travelers with 390
Ditmas Park 272
Ditmas Park Historic District 272
Donald Judd Home Studio 90-1
Drawing Center 90
drinking 43-5, 361-2, *see also* Drinking & Nightlife *subindex, individual neighborhoods*
Dumbo 266, 276-7, 297, **443**
Dyckman Farmhouse Museum 252

E

East Hampton 321
East Hampton Town Marine Museum (East Hampton) 321
East River Park 114
East River State Park 274-5
East River Waterfront 76
East Village 61, 107-31, **107**, **412**
  accommodations 335-6
  drinking & nightlife 108, 120, 122-3
  entertainment 126-8
  food 108, 115-18
  highlights 107, 112-13
  shopping 108, 128-9
  sights 112-14
  sports & activities 131
  transportation 108
  walks 121, **121**
Edgar Allan Poe Cottage 258
El Museo del Barrio 251
electricity 386
Elizabeth Sackler Center for Feminist Art 265
Ellis Island 7, 66-7, **78**
Elmhurst 313-14
emergencies 387
Empire State Building 12, 180-1, **12**, **180**
Empire Stores & Tobacco Warehouse 266
entertainment 46-9, *see also* Entertainment *subindex, individual neighborhoods*
etiquette 21
events 29

F

FDR Presidential Library and Museum (Hudson Valley) 327
Federal Hall 73-4
Federal Reserve Bank of New York 73
ferries 15, 17, 384
festivals 29
Fifth Avenue 191-3, 194, 196, 199, 202, 203, 208, 208-9, **424-5**
film 348, 375-8
Financial District 61, 62-85, **62**, **406-7**, **78-9**
  accommodations 333-4
  drinking & nightlife 63, 81, 83
  entertainment 83-4
  food 63, 77, 80-1
  highlights 62, 64-71
  shopping 84-5
  sights 64-74
  sports & activities 85
  transportation 63
Fire Island 322-3
Fisher Landau Center for Art 305
Flatbush 281-4
Flatiron Building 167, **21**
Flatiron District 61, 164-74, **164**, **422-3**
  accommodations 338-9
  drinking & nightlife 165, 170-2
  entertainment 172
  food 165, 168-70
  highlights 164, 166
  shopping 172, 174
  sights 166-8
  sports & activities 174
  transportation 165
  walks 173, **173**
Flushing 306-8, 314-15, **315**, **445**
Flushing Meadows Corona Park 308
food 11, 17, 39-42, 278, 359-62, *see also* Eating *subindex, individual neighborhoods*
football 53
Fort Greene 268-69, 271, 279-80, 289, 298, **438**
Fort Greene Park 269
Franklin D Roosevelt Four Freedoms Park 190-1
Franklin D Roosevelt Home (Hudson Valley) 326-7
Fraunces Tavern Museum 72
free attractions 27, 37-8
Freeman Alley 114
Frick Collection 218

G

Gagosian 141-2, 156, **156**
galleries 114, 148, **148**, *see also individual galleries*
Gantry Plaza State Park 305
gay travellers 56-7, 122
General Theological Seminary 141
General Ulysses S Grant National Memorial 250
gospel services 249
Governors Island 76
Gowanus 280-1
Grace Church 139
Gracie Mansion 219
Gramercy 61, 164-74, **164**, **422-3**
  accommodations 338-9
  drinking & nightlife 165, 170-2
  entertainment 172
  food 165, 168-70
  highlights 164, 166
  shopping 172, 174
  sights 166-8
  sports & activities 174
  transportation 165
  walks 173, **173**
Gramercy Park 168
Grand Army Plaza 264
Grand Central Terminal 184-5, **184**, **369**
Great Lawn 229
Greenpoint 273-5, 284-7, 290-1, 293, 299
Green-Wood Cemetery 269
Guggenheim Museum 213

H

Hamilton Grange 251
Hamilton Heights 251-2, 256
Hamilton Heights Historic District 251
Hamptons, the 320-2
Harlem 61, 245-59, **245**, **434-5**
  accommodations 343
  drinking & nightlife 246, 256-7
  entertainment 257-9
  food 246, 253-4, 256
  highlights 245, 247-8
  shopping 259
  sights 247-51
  sports & activities 259
  transportation 246
  walks 254-5, **255**
Harriman State Park (Hudson Valley) 326
Hearst Tower 192
Hell's Kitchen 202
Herald Square 194
High Line 9, 136-7, **9**, **136**, **157**
Hispanic Society of America Museum & Library 252-3

Sights 000
Map Pages **000**
Photo Pages **000**

Historic Richmond Town 75
history 350-8
hockey 53
Hole 114
holidays 389
hospitals 387-8
Hudson River Park 140
Hudson Valley 325-7
Hyde Park 326-7

I

Independence Day 31
insurance 387
International Center of Photography 90
internet access 387
Intrepid Sea, Air & Space Museum 194
Invisible Dog 268
Inwood 252-3, 256
Inwood Hill Park 252
itineraries 24-5

J

Jackson Heights 306, 313
Jacob Riis Park 307
Jacqueline Kennedy Onassis Reservoir 229
Jamaica Bay Wildlife Refuge 307
Jane's Carousel 266, 267, **282**
Japan Society 190
jazz 158
Jewish Museum 218
John F Kennedy International Airport 380
Jones Beach State Park 324

K

Karma Triyana Dharmachakra (Woodstock) 328-9
Kaufman Arts District 306
Kaufman Astoria Studios 375
Kehila Kedosha Janina Synagogue & Museum 115
Kings County Distillery 269, 271
Koreatown 196
Kykuit (Hudson Valley) 326

L

La Plaza Cultural 117
LaGuardia Airport 381
language 18
Le Carrousel 193
Le Petit Versailles 117
LeFrak Center 264
legal matters 387
Lehmann Maupin 114
Lenz Winery (North Fork & Shelter Island) 324
lesbian travellers 56-7
Lesley Heller 114
Leslie-Lohman Museum of Gay & Lesbian Art 90
Lever House 192
LGBTIQ travellers 56-7, 122, 372-4
Lincoln Center 232, **239**
Literary Walk 228
literature 366
Little Italy 92-3, 99-100, **411**
Little Italy 92
local life 35-6
Long Beach 323
Long Island City 305-6, 308-9
Long Meadow 264
Louis Armstrong House 306-7
Lower East Side 61, 107-31, **107**, **414-15**
- accommodations 335-6
- drinking & nightlife 108, 123, 126
- entertainment 126-8
- food 108, 118-20
- highlights 107, 109-13
- shopping 108, 129-31
- sights 109-11, 114-15
- sports & activities 131
- transportation 108

Lower East Side Tenement Museum 109
Lower Manhattan 61, 62-85, 79, **62**, **406-7**, **78**
- accommodations 333-4
- drinking & nightlife 63, 81, 83
- entertainment 83-4
- food 63, 77-85
- highlights 62, 64-71
- shopping 84-5
- sights 64-77
- sports & activities 85
- transportation 63
- walks 82, **82**

L train line 273
Luna Park 275
Lunar (Chinese) New Year Festival 29, **31**

M

Madison Square Park 167
Mahayana Temple 88, **94**
Main St Park 263
Malcolm Shabazz Harlem Market 250-1
markets
- Brooklyn 298, **50**
- Chelsea 134-5, **134**
- Fort Greene 279
- Harlem 250-1
- Lower East Side 129
- Meatpacking District 142
- Midtown 185, 209
- Union Square 172

marriage equality 374
Mary Boone Gallery 148
Mashomack Nature Preserve (North Fork & Shelter Island) 324
Matthew Marks 148
McCarren Park 274
Meatpacking District 61, 132-163, **132**, **416**
- accommodations 336-8
- drinking & nightlife 133, 150-4
- entertainment 155-60
- food 133, 142-3, 145-7
- highlights 132, 136-7
- shopping 160-2
- sights 136-7, 139-41
- sports & activities 163
- transportation 133

medical services 387
Merchant's House Museum 91
Mesler/Feuer 114
Met Breuer 17, 218
Metropolitan Life Tower 168
Metropolitan Museum of Art 9, 214-17, **8**, **214**
Metropolitan Opera 232
Midtown 61, 175-210, **175**, **424-8**
- accommodations 339-41
- drinking & nightlife 176, 199, 202-3
- entertainment 203-8
- food 176, 194-9
- highlights 175, 177-89
- shopping 208-10
- sights 177-94
- sports & activities 210
- transportation 176
- walks 195, **195**

mobile phones 18
MoMA 12, 17, 182-3, **13**, **182**
MoMA PS1 303-4, **303**
money 18, 331, 386, 388-9
Montauk 321
Montauk Point Lighthouse (Montauk) 321
Montauk Point State Park (Montauk) 321
Morgan Library & Museum 190
Morningside Heights 249-50, 253-4
Morris-Jumel Mansion Museum 252
Mulberry Street 92-3
Museum at Eldridge Street Synagogue 115
Museum at FIT 194
Museum of American Finance 73
Museum of Arts & Design 194
Museum of Contemporary African Diasporan Arts 268
Museum of Jewish Heritage 74
Museum of Modern Art (MoMA) 12, 17, 182-3, **13**, **182**
Museum of Sex 190
Museum of the City of New York 219
Museum of the Moving Image 306, **311**
museums 26
music 47, 48, 158
musical theatre 364-5

N

National Arts Club 167-8
National Museum of the American Indian 72
National September 11 Memorial Museum 16, 68-9, **16**, **68**
Neue Galerie 218
Newark Liberty International Airport 381
New Museum of Contemporary Art 110-11, **110**
New York Botanical Garden 258
New York City Fire Museum 90
New York Earth Room 91
New York Hall of Science 308
New York Public Library 191
New York Transit Museum 266
New York University 140-1
Newark Liberty International Airport 381
New-York Historical Society 233

Nicholas Roerich Museum 234
nightlife 10, 28, 43-5, *see also* Drinking & Nightlife *subindex, individual neighborhoods*
Noguchi Museum 305
NoHo 90-2, 93, 96-7, **408**
Nolita 90-2, 93, 96-7, **408**
North Fork & Shelter Island 323-5
NYC Pride 30, **31**

O

Olana (Hudson Valley) 327
One World Observatory 14, 71, **14**
One World Trade Center 70-1, **70**
opening hours 389
Opus 40 Sculpture Park & Museum (Saugerties) 328
Orient Beach State Park (North Fork & Shelter Island) 324

P

Pace Gallery 148
Paley Center for Media 193
parks 28
Park Slope 270, 271-2, 280-1, 298, **440**
Parrish Art Museum (Southampton) 320
Paula 149
Penn Station 382
pharmacies 388
Philipsburg Manor (Hudson Valley) 326
Picnic House 264
Pier 2 263
Pier 3 263
Pier 4 263
Pier 5 263
Pier 45 139
pizza 278, 360
planning
  budgeting 18, 37-8, 386
  children, travel with 33-4
  costs 18, 40, 44, 331, 386, 389
  festivals & events 29
  itineraries 24-5
  local life 35-6
  new visitors 20-1
  basics 18-19
  neighborhoods 60-1
  repeat visitors 17
  travel seasons 19
  websites 18
police 387
politics 348
Pollock-Krasner House (East Hampton) 321
population 349
Port Authority Bus Terminal 381
postal services 389
Poughkeepsie 326-7
Prospect Heights 281-4, 290
Prospect Park 264, **440**
Prospect Park Bandshell 264
Prospect Park South Historic District 272
public holidays 389
Pugliese Vineyards (North Fork & Shelter Island) 324

Q

Queens 61, 301-18, **301**, **445-7**
  accommodations 345-6
  drinking & nightlife 302, 316-17
  entertainment 317-18
  food 302, 308-9, 311-14
  highlights 301, 303-4
  shopping 318
  sights 303-8
  sports & activities 318
  transportation 302
  walks 310-11, 315, **310**, **315**
Queens County Farm Museum 308
Queens Museum 307-8
queer rights 372-4

R

Radio City Music Hall 193-4, 201, **201**
Ramble 229
Red Hook 266, 268, 277-9, 288-9, **438**
Revson Fountain 232
Rhinebeck 327
Riverside Church 250
Riverside Park 233-4
Rockaway Beach 307
Rockefeller Center 186
roller derby 53
Roosevelt Ave 313
Roosevelt Island 189
Rubin Museum of Art 141

S

safety 389
Sag Harbor 321
Sag Harbor Whaling & Historical Museum (Sag Harbor) 321
Salmagundi Club 139
Sara D Roosevelt Park 115
Saugerties 328
Saugerties Lighthouse (Saugerties) 328
Schomburg Center for Research in Black Culture 251
SculptureCenter 305
Seagram Building 192
September 11 358
Sheridan Square 141
shopping 16, 50-2, *see also* Shopping *subindex, individual neighborhoods*
Skyscraper Museum 76
skyscrapers 192
Smorgasburg 285
Snug Harbor Cultural Center & Botanical Garden 75
Socrates Sculpture Park 305
SoHo 61, 86-106, **86**, **408-9**, **95**
  accommodations 334-5
  drinking & nightlife 87, 100-1, 103
  entertainment 103-4
  food 87, 93-9
  highlights 86
  shopping 87, 104-6
  sights 90-2
  sports & activities 106
  transportation 87
  walks 102-3, **102**
South Street Seaport 77
South Street Seaport Museum 76
Southampton 320-1
Southampton Historical Museum (Southampton) 320-1
Southpoint Park 191
Sperone Westwater 114
sports & activities 53-5, *see also* Sports & Activities *subindex, individual neighborhoods*
Squibb Park Bridge 263
St Mark's in the Bowery 114
St Marks Place 112-13, **125**
St Patrick's Cathedral 193
St Paul's Chapel 73
Staten Island 75
Statue of Liberty 7, 64-5, **6**, **64**, **79**
Steiner Studios 376
Stonewall 373
Stonewall National Monument 17, 139
Storm King Art Center (Hudson Valley) 326
Straus Park 233
Strawberry Fields 229, **239**
street art 274, 276
Strivers' Row 251-2
subway 382-3
Sugar Hill 251-2
SummerStage 30
Sunken Forest (Fire Island) 322
Sunnyside (Hudson Valley) 326
Sunset Park 280-1, 298-9
Sunset Park 272
Sylvan Terrace 253

T

taxes 21, 389
taxi 383-4
telephone services 389
television shows 378
Temple Emanu-El 219
theater 178-9
Theodore Roosevelt Birthplace 167
Tibet House 168
time 18, 389
Times Square 7, 177-9, **6-7**, **177**, **201**
tipping 21
toilets 389-90
Tompkins Square Park 113
Top of the Rock 191
tours 384-5
tourist information 18, 390
train travel 382
transportation 380-5
travel to NYC 19, 380-2
travel within NYC 19, 22-3, 382-4
Tribeca Film Festival 30
Trinity Church 72-3
TV tapings 207

U

Union Square 61, 164-74, **164**, **422-3**
  accommodations 338-9

Sights 000
Map Pages **000**
Photo Pages **000**

drinking & nightlife 165, 170-2
entertainment 172
food 165, 168-70
highlights 164, 166
shopping 172, 174
sights 166-8
sports & activities 174
transportation 165
walks 173, **173**
Union Square 166
Unisphere 308
United Nations 190
Upper East Side 61, 211-225, **211**, **430**
accommodations 341-2
children, travel with 225
drinking & nightlife 212, 221, 223
entertainment 223-4
food 212, 219-21
highlights 211, 213-17
shopping 212, 224-5
sights 213-19
sports & activities 225
transportation 212
walks 222, **222**
Upper Manhattan 61, 245-59, **245**, **434-5**
accommodations 343
drinking & nightlife 246, 256-7
entertainment 257-9
food 246, 253-4, 256
highlights 245, 247-8
shopping 259
sights 247-53
sports & activities 259
transportation 246
walks 254-5, **255**
Upper West Side 61, 226-44, **226**, **432**
accommodations 342-3
drinking & nightlife 227, 237, 240
entertainment 227, 240-2
food 227, 234-7
highlights 226, 228-32
shopping 242-3
sights 228-34
sports & activities 243-4
transportation 227
urban farming 359
USCGC Lilac 74

V

vacations 389
views 26
Village Halloween Parade 32
Vintage Tours (North Fork & Shelter Island) 324
visas 18, 390
volunteering 390

W

walks
Brooklyn 267, 270-1, 292-3, **267**, **270**, **292**
Chelsea 148-9, **148**
Chinatown 98, **98**
East Village 121, **121**
Flatiron District 173, **173**
Gramercy 173, **173**
Harlem 254-5, **255**
Lower Manhattan 82, **82**
Midtown 195, **195**
SoHo 102-3, **102**
Union Square 173, **173**
Upper East Side 222, **222**
West Village 144, **144**
Walkway Over the Hudson (Hudson Valley) 327
Wall Street 72-4
Washington Heights 252-3
Washington Square Park 138, **156**
websites 18, 331
Weeksville Heritage Center 273
West Village 61, 132-63, **132**, **416-17**
accommodations 336-8
drinking & nightlife 133, 150-4
entertainment 155, 158-60
food 133, 142-3, 145-7
highlights 132, 138
shopping 133, 160-2
sights 134-41
sports & activities 163
transportation 133
walks 144, **144**
Whitney Museum of American Art 139
Williamsburg 273-5, 284-7, 290-3, 299, **292**, **436-7**, **11**
Williamsburg Bridge 275
Woodlawn Cemetery 258
Woodside 313
Woodstock 327-9
Woolworth Building 77, **370**
Wyckoff House Museum 273

Y

Yankee Stadium 258

EATING

67 Burger 279

A

ABC Kitchen 170
AlMar 277
Alta 146
Amazing 66 100
Ample Hills Creamery 280, 281
Amy Ruth's Restaurant 254
Amy's Bread 137
An Choi 118
Arcade Bakery 77
Archway Cafe 276
Artichoke Basille's Pizza 116
Asian Jewels 314
August Gatherings 99

B

Babu Ji 145
Bahari 312
Bait & Hook 116
Baked in Brooklyn 281
Bánh Mì Saigon Bakery 99
Barbuto 145
Barney Greengrass 236
Bâtard 80
Battersby 279
Baz Bagels 99
Bengal Tiger 197
Berg'n 284
Beyoglu 220
Big Daddy's 169
Birdbath Bakery 235
Bistro Les Amis 97
Blossom 149
Blossom on Columbus 236
Blue Hill 147
Blue Hill at Stone Barns (Hudson Valley) 327
BLVD Bistro 256
Boqueria 221
Boqueria Flatiron 169
Boulud Sud 236-7
Brookfield Place 80
Brooklyn Bagel & Coffee Company 312
Bryant Park Grill 193
Buddha Bodai 100
Burger Joint 197
Burke & Wills 237
Butcher's Daughter 96-7
Buttermilk Channel 279

C

Cafe 2 183
Café Boulud 221
Café Cluny 146
Café Gitane 96
Cafe Lalo 235
Cafe Mogador 117
Café Sabarsky 220
Candle Cafe 220
Candle Cafe West 236
Candy Kitchen (The Hamptons) 321
Cannelle Patisserie 309
Cannibal Beer & Butcher 196
Casa della Mozzarella 258
Casa Enrique 309
Champs Diner 285
Charles' Pan-Fried Chicken 256
Chefs Club 17, 97
Chelsea Market 147
Chelsea Square Diner 147
Cherche Midi 97
Cheryl's Global Soul 284
Chuko 284
Chumley's 147
CJ's (Fire Island) 323
Clam Bar at Napeague (The Hamptons) 321
Claudio's (North Fork & Shelter Island) 325
Clinton Street Baking Company 119
Clocktower 170
Community Food & Juice 253-4
Cookshop 149-50
Corner Bistro 143
Cosme 170
Cotenna 143
Craft 170
Crif Dogs 284-5
Cyclo 308-9

D

Da Mikele 80
Danji 198
Dean & DeLuca 103, **103**
Degustation 118
Deluxe Green Bo 99
Dhaba 196
Di Fara Pizza 278
Di Palo 99
Dimes 119
Dinosaur Bar-B-Que 253
Doma Na Rohu 146
Dominique Ansel Kitchen 143
Dominique Bistro 145
Don Antonio 198

Dough 279
Dovetail 237
Dun-Well Doughnuts 285
Dutch 97

E

Earl's Beer & Cheese 220
Eataly 169
Eisenberg's Sandwich Shop 169
El Aguila 220
El Guayaquileño 313
El Luchador 80
El Parador Cafe 196
Eleven Madison Park 169
Enoteca Maria 75
Épicerie Boulud 235
Esperanto 115
Ess-a-Bagel 194
Everything Goes Book Café & Neighborhood Stage 75

F

Fairway 278
Fat Radish 119
Ferrara Cafe & Bakery 100
Fette Sau 286
Fifty 147
FIKA 197
Fish & Game (Hudson Valley) 327
Five Leaves 286
Foragers Table 150
Fornino at Pier 6 277
Fort Greene Greenmarket 279
Four & Twenty Blackbirds 280
Frankies 457 Spuntino 279
Freemans 120
Fu Run 314
Fuku+ 197

G

Gansevoort Market 142, **39-42**
Ganso Ramen 277
Garden Cafe (Woodstock) 329
George's at Kaufman Astoria Studios 312
Golden Shopping Mall 314
Golden Steamer 100
Govinda's Vegetarian Lunch 276
Gramercy Tavern 170
Grand Banks 80
Grand Central Oyster Bar & Restaurant 196-7
Gray's Papaya 235-6
Green Grape Annex 280
Grey Dog 96
Grimaldi's 278

H

Hangawi 196
Harlem Public 256
Hearth 118
Heath 149
Hometown Bar-B-Que 278
Hunan Kitchen of Grand Sichuan 314

I

Il Buco Alimentari & Vineria 97
Ippudo NY 118

J

Jacob's Pickles 236
Jeffrey's Grocery 146
Jerusalem Pita House 311
Jin Ramen 235
John Brown Smokehouse 309
Juliana's 276-7, 278
Jun-Men 149

K

Kabab Cafe 312
Katz's Delicatessen 119, **124**
Kefi 236
King David Tacos 281
King Souvlaki 311
Kuma Inn 118

L

La Esquina 97
La Esquina del Camarón 313
La Esquina Taquería 219-20
Lakeside Restaurant at Loeb Boathouse 237
Lakruwana 75
Lan Larb 96
Larb Ubol 197
Lavagna 117
Le Bernardin 198
Le District 81
Le Grainne 150
LIC Corner Cafe 309
LIC Market 309
Lincoln Station 284
Locanda Verde 80
LOOK by Plant Love House 281-4
Lot 2 281
Love Lane Kitchen (North Fork & Shelter Island) 325
Lovely Day 96
Lucali 278, 279
Luke's Lobster 281
Luzzo's 117

M

M Wells Steakhouse 309
Mad Sq Eats 169
Madonia Brothers Bakery 258
Mah Ze Dahr 142
Maialino 169
Maison Harlem 254, 256
Malaparte 146
Mamoun's 115, 142
Marché Maman 96
Margon 197
Marlow & Sons 287
Meatball Shop 119
Mermaid Oyster Bar 145
Mighty Quinn's 116
Mikey Likes It 116
Milk & Pull 285
Mimi's Hummus 272
Minetta Tavern 147
Miss Ada 280
Miss Favela 287
Modern 198
Modern Love 285
Mombar 312
Momofuku Noodle Bar 116
Montana's Trail House 287
Morandi 146
Moustache 143
MUD 116

N

Nan Xiang Xiao Long Bao 314
Nathan's Famous 287-8
New Leaf 256
New World Mall 314
Nick & Toni's (The Hamptons) 322
Nix 145
Nom Wah Tea Parlor 99
NoMad 198-9
North End Grill 81
North Fork Table & Inn (North Fork & Shelter Island) 325
Nyonya 100

O

Okonomi & Yuji Ramen 287
Olea 280
Olmsted 284
O-ya 196

P

Papaya King 219
Paulie Gee's 287
Peacefood 145
Peacefood Cafe 235
Peaches 280
Peking Duck House 100
Peter Pan Donut & Pastry Shop 285
Pier i Café 236
Pikine 256
Pisticci 253
Pok Pok 278
Prince Street Pizza 93
Prune 118
P.S. Burgers 142
Pye Boat Noodle 311

R

Rabbithole 286
Rai Rai Ken 116
Red Bamboo 142
Red Hook Lobster Pound 278
Red Rooster 256
RedFarm 147
Republic 169
River Cafe 277
Roberta's 278, 287, **11**
Rockaway Surf Club 307
Roman's 280
Rosemary's 145
Roundhouse Restaurant & Lounge (Hudson Valley) 327
Ruby's 93
Russ & Daughters Cafe 119

S

Saigon Shack 143
Sand Castle (Fire Island) 323
Schaller & Weber 219
Seasoned Vegan 254
Sek'end Sun 312-13
Shake Shack 77, 80
Shindig (Woodstock) 329

Sights 000
Map Pages **000**
Photo Pages **000**

Sidecar 281
Siggi's 97
Smith 196
Snack Taverna 146
Souvlaki GR 198
Spaghetti Incident 118
Sripraphai 313
Superfine 277
Sweetleaf 309
Sylvia's 254

T
Taboon 199
Taco Veloz 313
Tacombi Café El Presidente 168
Tacombi Fonda Nolita 96
Taïm 143
Tanoshi 220
Taverna Kyclades 312
Terrace Five 183
The Strand Smokehouse 312
Tom's Restaurant 254, 284
Tortilleria Nixtamal 314
Totonno's 278
Totto Ramen 197
Trattoria Il Mulino 170
Tuck Shop 134
Tum & Yum 235
Two Boots 219
Two Boots Pizza 142
Two Hands 80, 93

U
Umami 143
Uncle Boons 96
Up Thai 220
Upstate 116
Urban Vegan Kitchen 146

V
Vanessa's Dumpling House 119
Veselka 116
Vesta Trattoria & Wine Bar 313
Via Quadronno 221
ViceVersa 198
Village Natural 143, 145
Vinegar Hill House 277

W
West 79th Street Boat Basin Café 235
Westville East 117-18
Whole Foods 198, 280

X
Xi'an Famous Foods 99

Z
Zenkichi 285-6
Zero Otto Nove 258

DRINKING & NIGHTLIFE
11th St Cafe 153
61 Local 288
67 Orange Street 257
71 Irving Place 171
124 Old Rabbit Club 151

A
ABC Beer Co 123
Anable Basin Sailing Bar & Grill 316
Angel's Share 120
Apothéke 101
Aria 151
Art Bar 151
Astoria Bier & Cheese 316
Attaboy 126
Auction House 223

B
Bar Centrale 202
Bar Goto 123
Bar SixtyFive 202
Barrage 203
Barrio Chino 126
Bathtub Gin 154
Beauty & Essex 126
Beauty Bar 171-2
Bell Book & Candle 150
Bemelmans Bar 221
Berlin 120
Bier International 257
Bierocracy 316
Birch Cafe 237
Birreria 171
Black Forest Brooklyn 289
Blue Bottle 153
Blue Bottle Coffee 293
Bluestone Lane 81
Bohemian Hall & Beer Garden 316
Boots and Saddle 153
Bossa Nova Civic Club 291, 293
Boxers NYC 172
Brandy Library 81
Brass Monkey 152
Bronx Brewery 258
Brooklyn Barge 290
Bryant Park Café 193
Butter & Scotch 290
Buvette 150

C
Café Integral 102
Caledonia 221
Cantor Roof Garden Bar 215
Cielo 152
Clem's 293
Clover Club 288
Cock 123
Cowgirl SeaHorse 81
Crocodile Lounge 122
Cubbyhole 153

D
Daisy 223
Dead Poet 240
Dead Rabbit 81
Death & Co 122
Drunken Munkey 223
Dutch Kills 316

E
Eagle NYC 155
Earth Café 240
Employees Only 150
Ethyl's Alcohol & Food 221
Excelsior 289

F
Fanelli's Cafe 101
Fang Gourmet Tea 317
Fat Cat 152
Flagship Brewing Company 75
Flaming Saddles 203
Flatiron Lounge 171
Flatiron Room 171
Floyd 288

G
Gallow Green 154
Genuine Liquorette 100-1
Ghost Donkey 100
Ginger's 290
Ginny's Supper Club 257
Greenwood Park 289
Gym Sportsbar 155

H
Happiest Hour 150
Henrietta Hudson 154
Hotel Delmano 291
House of Yes 290

I
Icon Bar 317
Ides 291
Immigrant 122
Industry 203
Irving Farm Roasters 223, 237-40

J
Jadis 123
Jimmy 101
Jimmy's Corner 202
Jimmy's No 43 120
Joe the Art of Coffee 153
Julius Bar 153-4

K
Kaffe 1668 South 83
Kettle of Fish 151
Kung Fu Tea 315

L
La Colombe 83, 103
La Compagnie des Vins Surnaturels 101
Lantern's Keep 202
Lavender Lake 271
Le Bain 152
Leaf Bar & Lounge 315
Lillie's Victorian Establishment 171
Little Branch 151
Little Collins 199
Lucy's 122

M
Macao Trading Co 83
Maison Premiere 290
Malachy's 240
Manhattan Cricket Club 237
Marie's Crisis 152
Matcha Bar 153
McSorley's Old Ale House 123, **125**
Middle Branch 199
Milk & Honey 272
Monster 154
Mulberry Project 101
Mulberry Street Bar 101, 103

N
Northern Territory 291
Nowhere 122

O
Old Town Bar & Restaurant 171
Oslo Coffee Roasters 223

P
PDT 123
Pegu Club 101
Peter McManus Tavern 154-5
Pete's Tavern 172
Phoenix 122
Pier 66 Maritime 154
Pier A Harbor House 83
Pine Box Rock Shop 293
Pouring Ribbons 122
Proletariat 122

R
Radegast Hall & Biergarten 290, **43**
Raines Law Room 171
Randolph 103
Robert 199
Robert Bar 288
Rocka Rolla 291
Rookery 291
Round K 126
Royal Palms 289
Ruby's Bar & Grill (Coney Island) 293-4
Rudy's Bar & Grill 203 (Midtown)
Rue B 120
Rum House 202

S
Sant Ambroeus 223
Sea Witch 289
Seamstress 221-2
Shrine 257
Silvana 256-7
Smith & Mills 83
Spring Lounge 101
Spritzenhaus 291
Spuyten Duyvil 291
Standard 152
Standard Biergarten 152
Station Bar & Curio (Woodstock) 329
Stonewall Inn 154
Studio Square 317
Stumptown Coffee Roasters 153, 199
Sunny's 288
Sycamore 272

T
Ten Bells 123
Ten Degrees Bar 122
Terroir Tribeca 81, 83
The Campbell 199
The Chipped Cup 257
The COOP 316
The Real KTV 317
Therapy 203
Three Seat Espresso & Barber 123
Toby's Estate 172, 290
Top of the Strand 202
Travel Bar 288-9
Troy Liquor Bar 151-2
Ty's 154

U
Uncommons 17, 151
Union Hall 289
Uva 223

V
Vin Sur Vingt 151
Vite Bar 316
Vol de Nuit 152

W
Wayland 120
Waylon 199
Weather Up 83, 290
Webster Hall 123
West End Hall 240

☆ ENTERTAINMENT

55 Bar 155
92nd Street Y 223-4

A
Abrons Arts Center 127
Al Hirschfeld Theatre 204-5
Aladdin 178
Alamo Drafthouse 295
Ambassador Theatre 206
AMC Empire 25 206
American Ballet Theatre 47
Amore Opera 48
Angelika Film Center 159-60
Anthology Film Archives 127
Atlantic Theater Company 158

B
Bar Next Door 155
Barbès 294
Barclays Center 296
Bargemusic 296
Barrow Street Theater 158
Beacon Theatre 241
Bell House 295
Birdland 206
Blue Note 158
Book of Mormon 204
Bowery Ballroom 128
Brooklyn Academy of Music 294
Brooklyn Bowl 294

C
Café Carlyle 224
Carnegie Hall 205
Caroline's on Broadway 206
Cherry Lane Theater 158-9
Chicago 206
Cinépolis Chelsea 159
Citi Field 317-18
City Vineyard 84
Cleopatra's Needle 242
Comedy Cellar 159
Comic Strip Live 224
Cornelia Street Café 155
County Bank Ballpark 75
Creek and the Cave 317

D
Don't Tell Mama 206
Duplex 159

E
Eugene O'Neill Theatre 204

F
Film Forum 103-4
Film Society of Lincoln Center 241
Flea Theater 83
Frick Collection Concerts 224
Full Frontal with Samantha Bee 207

G
Gershwin Theatre 207-8
Gotham Comedy Club 159
Gotham Girls Roller Derby 53

H
Hamilton 204

I
IFC Center 159
Irish Repertory Theatre 158
Irving Plaza 172

J
Jalopy 295
Jazz at Lincoln Center 205
Jazz Standard 203
Joe's Pub 103
Jones Beach Theater 324
Joyce Theater 159

K
Kings Theatre 296
Kinky Boots 204-5
Kitchen 159
Knitting Factory 296

L
La MaMa ETC 127
Last Week Tonight with John Oliver 207
Le Poisson Rouge 155
LGBT Community Center 160
Lincoln Center Out of Doors 232
Littlefield 295-6
LoftOpera 48
Lyceum Theatre 179

M
Madison Square Garden 206-7
Magnet Theater 206
Marjorie Eliot's Parlor Jazz 257
Maysles Documentary Center 257
MCU Park 296
Mercury Lounge 127
Merkin Concert Hall 241
MetLife Stadium 53
Metrograph 126
Metropolitan Opera House 240-1
Mezzrow 158
Midsummer Night Swing 232
Minskoff Theatre 207
Minton's 258
MoMA 183

Sights 000
Map Pages **000**
Photo Pages **000**

Music Hall of Williamsburg 296

N
National Sawdust 294
New Amsterdam Theatre 178
New Victory 178
New York City Ballet 240, **46**
New York City Center 206
New York Live Arts 158
New York Philharmonic 241
New York Theatre Workshop 127
Nitehawk Cinema 295
Nuyorican Poets Café 127

O
Opera on Tap 48

P
Peoples Improv Theater 172
Performance Space New York 126
Pianos 127
Playwrights Horizons 205
Public Theater 104
Puppetworks 296

R
Richard Rodgers Theatre 204, **48**
Rockwood Music Hall 126-7

S
Saturday Night Live 207
Second Stage Theatre 205-6
Shakespeare in the Park 233
Shubert Theatre 205
Sidewalk Café 128
Signature Theatre 205
Sleep No More 155
Slipper Room 126
Smalls 158
Smoke 241-2
Soho Rep 83
St Ann's Warehouse 294
Stone 127
Story 162
SummerStage 233
Symphony Space 241

T
Terraza 7 317
Theater for a New Audience 296
The Daily Show with Trevor Noah 207
The Late Show with Stephen Colbert 207
The Lion King 207
TKTS Booth 179

U
Upright Citizens Brigade Theatre 203
USTA Billie Jean King National Tennis Center 317

V
Village Vanguard 158

W
Warsaw 296
Wicked 207-8

SHOPPING
3x1 102
192 Books 163

A
A-1 Records 129
ABC Carpet & Home 172
Abracadabra 174
Adidas Flagship Store 105
Aedes de Venustas 162
A&G Merch 299
Aji Ichiban 106
Argosy 208
Artbook 318
Artists & Fleas 299
Assembly 130
Astoria Bookshop 310
Atmos 259

B
B&H Photo Video 209
Barneys (Midtown) 208
Barneys (Upper West Side) 208
Beacon's Closet 160, 298, 299
Bedford Cheese Shop 174
Bergdorf Goodman 208
Best Made Company 84
Black Gold Records 297
Bloomingdale's 208
Bluestockings 131
Book Culture 242
Books of Wonder 174
Bowne Stationers & Co 85
Brooklyn Flea 298, **50**
Brooklyn Strategist 297-8
Brooklyn Superhero Supply Co 298
Buffalo Exchange 292
By Robert James 130

C
Catbird 299
Century 21 84, 242
CityStore 85
CO Bigelow Chemists 162

D
De Vera 104-5
Desert Island Comics 299
Dinosaur Hill 129
Diptyque 224
Drama Book Shop 209
DSW 172, 174
Dylan's Candy Bar 208

E
Economy Candy 130
Edith Machinist 130
Encore 225
Evolution Nature Store 106

F
Fishs Eddy 174
Fjällräven 106
Flamekeepers Hat Club 259
Flight 001 161
Flying Tiger Copenhagen 224
Flying Tiger Copenhagen (Upper West Side) 243
Forbidden Planet 161
Fuego 718 292
Fulton Mall 297

G
Grand Army Plaza Greenmarket 298
Grand Bazaar NYC 243
Grand Central Market 185
Greenlight Bookstore 298
Greenmarkets 298
Greenwich Letterpress 161

H
Harlem Haberdashery 259
Hell's Kitchen Flea Market 209
Housing Works Bookstore 106
Housing Works Thrift Shop 162

I
Icon Style 242
Idlewild Books 160-1
INA Men 105
INA Women 105
Industry City 298

J
Jacadi 225
Joe's Jeans 105
John Derian Company 129
John Varvatos 128

L
Lockwood 310
Lodge 129
LoveDay 31 318

M
Macy's 209, **16**
Magpie 242
Mary Arnold Toys 224
Mask Bar 162
McNally Jackson 105
McNulty's Tea & Coffee Co, Inc 161
Michael's 225
Mimi & Mo 318
MiN New York 104
Modern Anthology 297
MoMA Design & Book Store 209
MoMA Design Store 102
Moo Shoes 130
Murray's Cheese 162

N
Nasty Pig 163
Nepenthes New York 209
New Kam Man 106
NiLu 259
No Relation 271
No Relation Vintage 129

O
Obscura Antiques 128
Odin 105, 160
Opening Ceremony 104

P
Pasanella & Son 84-5
Pearl River Mart 84
Personnel of New York 161

Philip Williams Posters 84
Powerhouse @ the Archway 297
Printed Matter 162
Purl Soho 106

Q

Quimby's Bookstore NYC 299

R

Rag & Bone 104
Reformation 130
Rent the Runway 174
Resurrection 105-6
Revolution Books 259
Ricky's NYC 224
Rough Trade 293
Rudy's Music 105
Russ & Daughters 131

S

Sahadi's 297
Saturdays 104, 161
Screaming Mimi's 162
Shakespeare & Co 225
Shinola 84
Shishi 242
Soy Bean Chen Flower Shop 315
Spoonbill & Sugartown 299
Steven Alan 85
Still House 128
Strand Book Store 160

T

T2 243
Three Lives & Company 161
Tictail Market 129
Tiffany & Co 208
Time Warner Center 209-10
Tokio 7 129
Top Hat 130
Trash & Vaudeville 129
Trina Turk 160
Twisted Lily 297

U

Union Square Greenmarket 172
Uniqlo 105, 209

Sights 000
Map Pages **000**
Photo Pages **000**

V

Verameat 128

W

West Side Kids 243
Westsider Records 243

Y

Yoya 161-2
Yumi Kim 130

Z

Zabar's 242

SPORTS & ACTIVITIES

24 Hour Fitness 210
Area Yoga & Spa 300
Art Farm in the City 225
Belvedere Castle 244
Bike & Roll 243
Brooklyn Boulders 299
Brooklyn Bowl 300
Brooklyn Brainery 300
Central Park Bike Tours 210
Central Park Tennis Center 244
Champion Bicycles Inc 244
Charles A Dana Discovery Center 243
Chelsea Piers Complex 163
Circle Line Boat Tours 210
Cliffs 318
Downtown Boathouse 85
Geography of New York City with Jack Eichenbaum 318
Grand Central Partnership 210
Great Jones Spa 106
Institute of Culinary Education 85
Jivamukti 174
Jump into the Light VR 131
Loeb Boathouse 244
Lucky Strike 210
Manhattan Community Boathouse 210
MNDFL 163
Municipal Art Society 185
NBC Studio Tours 210
New York Spa Castle 318
New York Trapeze School 163
On the Move 300
Pioneer 85
Queens Historical Society 318
Red Hook Boaters 300
Rink at Rockefeller Center 186
Riverbank State Park 259
Russian & Turkish Baths 131
Schooner Adirondack 163
Soul Cycle 174
Staten Island Ferry 85, 79, **15, 78**
Toga Bike Shop 244
Tread 259
West 4th Street Basketball Courts 163
Wollman Skating Rink 244, **35**
World's Fare Tours 318

SLEEPING

1871 House 341
Ace Hotel 340
Akwaaba Mansion Inn 345
Aloft Harlem 343
Andaz Fifth Avenue 340
Andaz Wall St 333
Big Pink (Saugerties) 328
Blue Moon Boutique Hotel 335
Boro Hotel 345-6
Bowery Hotel 335
Bowery House 334
Broome 334
Bubba & Bean Lodges 341
Carlton Arms 338
Chambers 197
Chatwal New York 340-1
Chelsea Pines Inn 336
Citizen M 339
Colonial House Inn 336
Conrad New York 333-4
Crosby Street Hotel 334
East Village Hotel 335
Empire Hotel 343
EVEN Hotel 344
Four Seasons 341
Franklin 341-2
GEM 337
Gild Hall 333
Gramercy Park Hotel 338
Greenwich Hotel 333
Harlem Flophouse 343
Henry Norman Hotel 345
High Line Hotel 337-8
Hôtel Americano 337
Hotel Beacon 343
Hotel Gansevoort 337
Hotel Giraffe 339
Hotel Henri 338
Hotel Le Bleu 345
Hotel Newton 342
Incentra Village House 336
Ink48 341, **10**
Iroquois Hotel 202
Jane Hotel 336
Jazz on the Park Hostel 342
Knickerbocker 340
La Maison d'Art 343
Lafayette House 334
Lefferts Manor Bed & Breakfast 344
Leon Hote 334
Local NYC 346
Loralei Bed & Breakfast 344
Lucerne 342
Ludlow 335
Marcel at Gramercy 338
Maritime Hotel 337
Mark 342
McCarren Hotel & Pool 345
Mount Morris House B&B 343
Murray Hill East Suites 339
NoMad Hotel 340
Nu Hotel 345
NYLO Hotel 342
Paper Factory Hotel 346
Park Savoy 339
Plaza 341
Pod 39 339
Pod 51 339
Quin 340
Ravel 346
Roxy Hotel Tribeca 333
Sago Hotel 335
Serenity at Home 344
Smyth Tribeca 333
St Mark's Hotel 335
Standard 337
Standard East Village 336
Townhouse Inn of Chelsea 337
Wall Street Inn 333
Williamsburg Hotel 344
Wythe Hotel 344
Yotel 339
Z Hotel 346

New York City Maps

Sights
- Beach
- Bird Sanctuary
- Buddhist
- Castle/Palace
- Christian
- Confucian
- Hindu
- Islamic
- Jain
- Jewish
- Monument
- Museum/Gallery/Historic Building
- Ruin
- Shinto
- Sikh
- Taoist
- Winery/Vineyard
- Zoo/Wildlife Sanctuary
- Other Sight

Activities, Courses & Tours
- Bodysurfing
- Diving
- Canoeing/Kayaking
- Course/Tour
- Sento Hot Baths/Onsen
- Skiing
- Snorkeling
- Surfing
- Swimming/Pool
- Walking
- Windsurfing
- Other Activity

Sleeping
- Sleeping
- Camping

Eating
- Eating

Drinking & Nightlife
- Drinking & Nightlife
- Cafe

Entertainment
- Entertainment

Shopping
- Shopping

Information
- Bank
- Embassy/Consulate
- Hospital/Medical
- Internet
- Police
- Post Office
- Telephone
- Toilet
- Tourist Information
- Other Information

Geographic
- Beach
- Gate
- Hut/Shelter
- Lighthouse
- Lookout
- Mountain/Volcano
- Oasis
- Park
- Pass
- Picnic Area
- Waterfall

Population
- Capital (National)
- Capital (State/Province)
- City/Large Town
- Town/Village

Transport
- Airport
- BART station
- Border crossing
- Boston T station
- Bus
- Cable car/Funicular
- Cycling
- Ferry
- Metro/Muni station
- Monorail
- Parking
- Petrol station
- Subway/SkyTrain station
- Taxi
- Train station/Railway
- Tram
- Underground station
- Other Transport

Note: Not all symbols displayed above appear on the maps in this book

Routes
- Tollway
- Freeway
- Primary
- Secondary
- Tertiary
- Lane
- Unsealed road
- Road under construction
- Plaza/Mall
- Steps
- Tunnel
- Pedestrian overpass
- Walking Tour
- Walking Tour detour
- Path/Walking Trail

Boundaries
- International
- State/Province
- Disputed
- Regional/Suburb
- Marine Park
- Cliff
- Wall

Hydrography
- River, Creek
- Intermittent River
- Canal
- Water
- Dry/Salt/Intermittent Lake
- Reef

Areas
- Airport/Runway
- Beach/Desert
- Cemetery (Christian)
- Cemetery (Other)
- Glacier
- Mudflat
- Park/Forest
- Sight (Building)
- Sportsground
- Swamp/Mangrove

MAP INDEX

1 Lower Manhattan & the Financial District (p406)
2 SoHo, NoHo & Nolita (p408)
3 Chinatown & Little Italy (p411)
4 East Village (p412)
5 Lower East Side (p414)
6 West Village & the Meatpacking District (p416)
7 Chelsea (p420)
8 Union Square, the Flatiron District & Gramercy Park (p422)
9 Midtown East & Fifth Avenue (p424)
10 Midtown West & Times Square (p428)
11 Upper East Side (p430)
12 Upper West Side & Central Park (p432)
13 Harlem & Upper Manhattan (p434)
14 Williamsburg (p436)
15 Boerum Hill, Carroll Gardens, Cobble Hill, Fort Greene & Red Hook (p438)
16 Park Slope & Prospect Park (p440)
17 Brooklyn Heights, Downtown Brooklyn & Dumbo (p443)
18 Coney Island & Brighton Beach (p444)
19 Flushing (p445)
20 Astoria (p446)

LOWER MANHATTAN & THE FINANCIAL DISTRICT *Map on p406*

Top Sights (p64)
1 Ellis Island ... B8
2 National September 11 Memorial & Museum ... C5
3 One World Trade Center ... B4
4 Statue of Liberty ... C8

Sights (p72)
5 African Burial Ground National Monument ... D3
6 Artists Space ... D2
7 Battery Park ... C7
8 Bowling Green ... C7
9 Castle Clinton ... C7
10 City Hall ... D4
11 Federal Hall ... D6
12 Federal Reserve Bank of New York ... D5
13 Fraunces Tavern Museum ... D7
14 Museum of American Finance ... D6
15 Museum of Jewish Heritage ... B7
16 National Museum of the American Indian ... D7
17 New York Stock Exchange ... D6
One World Observatory ... (see 3)
18 Pier 15 ... F6
19 Skyscraper Museum ... C7
20 South Street Seaport Museum ... E5
21 St Paul's Chapel ... C4
22 Trinity Church ... C6
23 USCGC Lilac ... A2
24 Woolworth Building ... C4

Eating (p77)
25 Arcade Bakery ... C3
26 Bâtard ... C2
27 Brookfield Place ... B5
28 Da Mikele ... C2
29 El Luchador ... E5
30 Grand Banks ... A3
Hudson Eats ... (see 27)
Le District ... (see 27)
31 Locanda Verde ... B2
32 North End Grill ... B4
33 Shake Shack ... B4
34 Two Hands ... C2

Drinking & Nightlife (p81)
35 Bluestone Lane ... D6
36 Brandy Library ... C2
37 Cowgirl SeaHorse ... F4
38 Dead Rabbit ... D7
39 Kaffe 1668 South ... B4
40 La Colombe ... C1
41 Macao Trading Co ... C1
42 Pier A Harbor House ... C7
Smile Newstand ... (see 58)
43 Smith & Mills ... B2
44 Terroir Tribeca ... B2
45 Ward III ... C3
46 Weather Up ... C3

Entertainment (p83)
47 City Vineyard ... A2
48 Flea Theater ... C3
49 Roxy Tribeca Cinema ... C2
50 Soho Rep ... C1

Shopping (p84)
51 Best Made Company ... C2
52 Bowne Stationers & Co ... E5
53 Century 21 ... C5
54 CityStore ... D3
55 Pasanella & Son ... F5
56 Pearl River Mart ... D2
57 Philip Williams Posters ... C3
58 Shinola ... B2
59 Steven Alan ... C2

Sports & Activities (p85)
60 Downtown Boathouse ... A2
61 Institute of Culinary Education ... B5
62 Pioneer ... E5
63 Staten Island Ferry ... D8

Sleeping (p333)
64 Andaz Wall St ... E6
65 Conrad New York ... A4
66 Gild Hall ... D5
Greenwich Hotel ... (see 31)
Roxy Hotel Tribeca ... (see 49)
67 Smyth Tribeca ... C3
68 Wall Street Inn ... D6

LOWER MANHATTAN & THE FINANCIAL DISTRICT

Key on p405

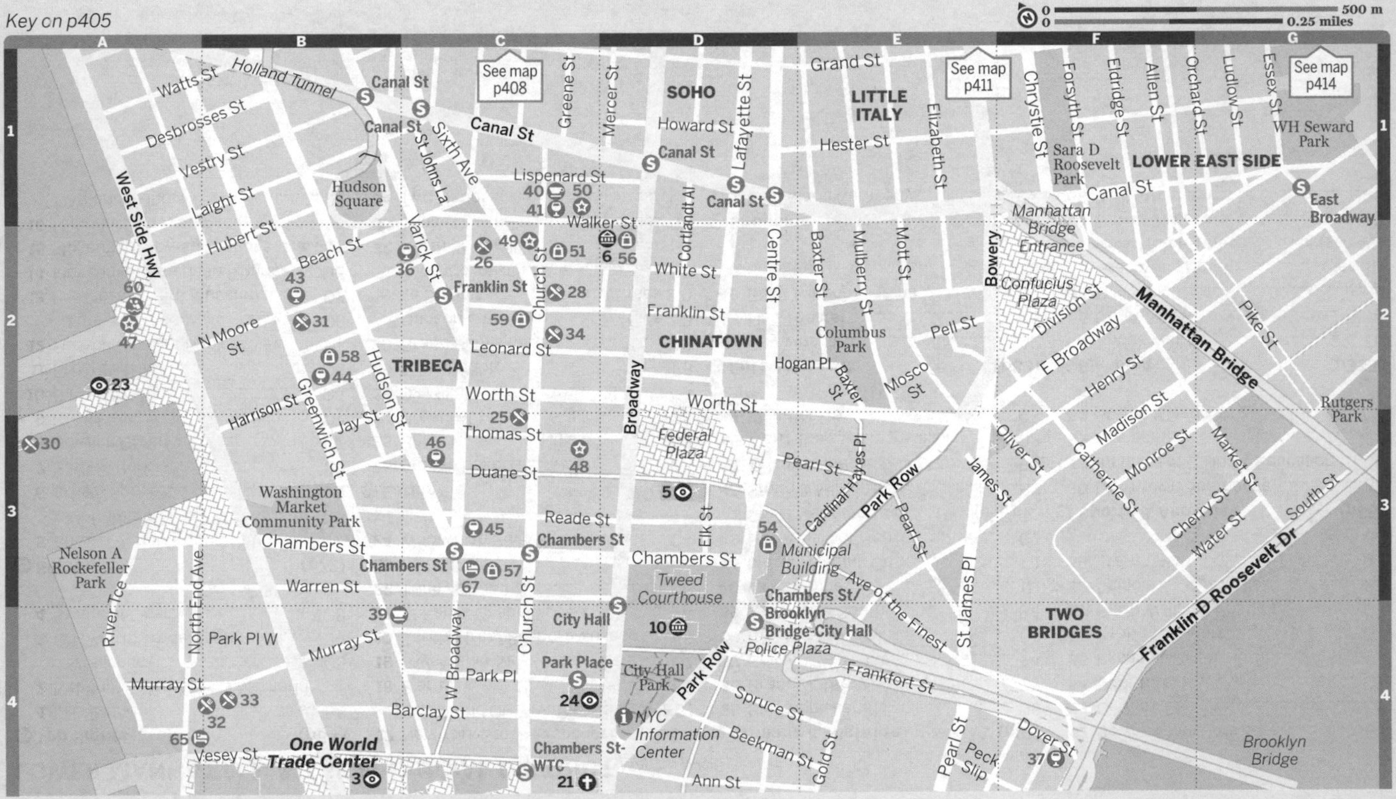

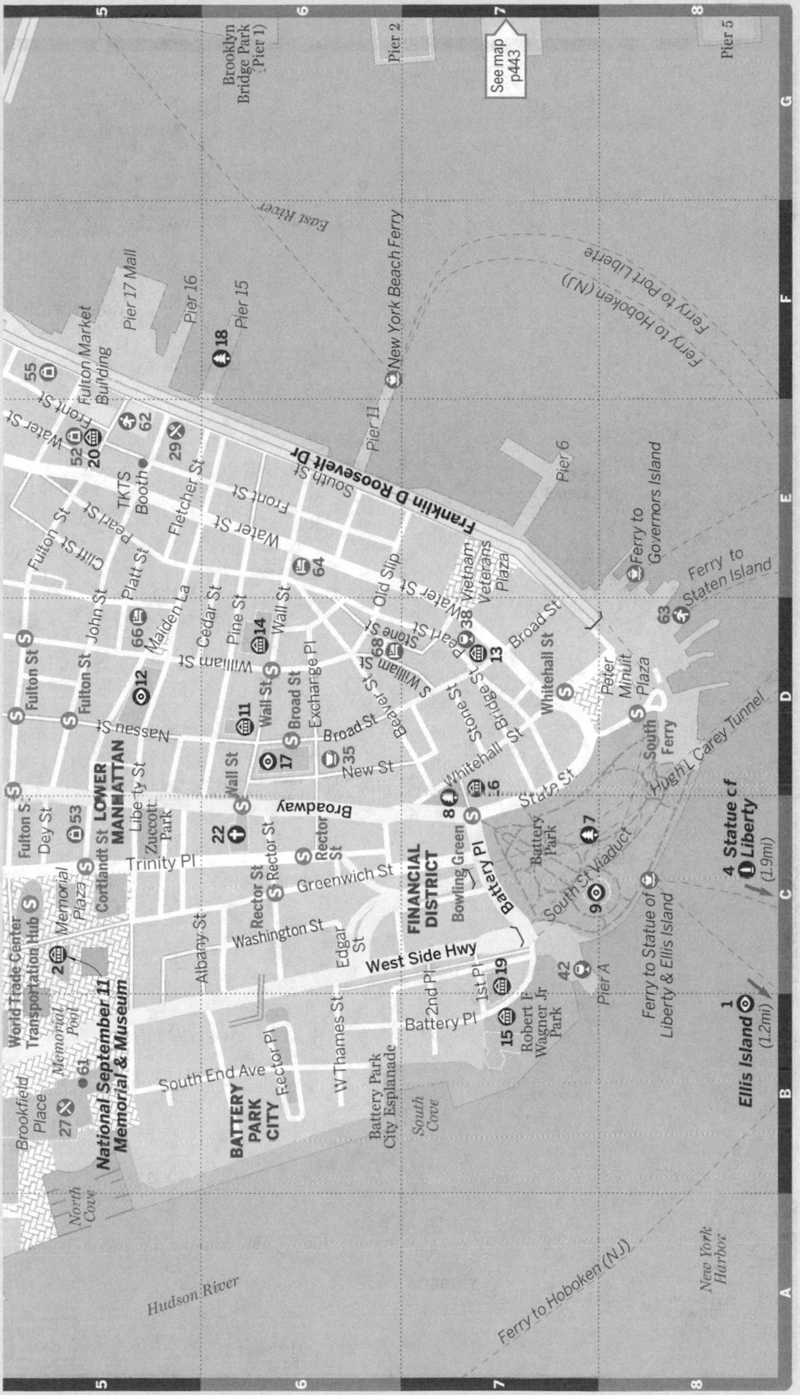

See map p443
Brooklyn Bridge Park (Pier 1)
Pier 2
Pier 5
East River
New York Beach Ferry
Ferry to Port Liberte
Ferry to Hoboken (NJ)
Pier 17 Mall
Pier 16
Pier 15
Fulton Market Building
Pier 11
Franklin D Roosevelt Dr
Pier 6
Ferry to Governors Island
Ferry to Staten Island
Vietnam Veterans Plaza
Peter Minuit Plaza
South Ferry
Hugh L Carey Tunnel
Statue of Liberty (1.9mi)
Ellis Island (1.2mi)
Ferry to Statue of Liberty & Ellis Island
Pier A
Robert F Wagner Jr Park
Battery Park
South St Viaduct
FINANCIAL DISTRICT
LOWER MANHATTAN
BATTERY PARK CITY
Battery Park City Esplanade
South Cove
North Cove
Brookfield Place
National September 11 Memorial & Museum
World Trade Center Transportation Hub
Memorial Pool
Memorial Plaza
Zuccotti Park
Bowling Green
Hudson River
New York Harbor
Ferry to Hoboken (NJ)
Broadway
West Side Hwy
Wall St
Water St
Front St
South St
Pearl St
Fulton St
John St
Maiden La
Cedar St
Pine St
William St
Nassau St
Broad St
New St
Exchange Pl
Beaver St
Stone St
Old Slip
Whitehall St
State St
Bridge St
Battery Pl
Greenwich St
Washington St
Trinity Pl
Rector St
Albany St
Cortlandt St
Dey St
Liberty St
Cliff St
Platt St
Fletcher St
Edgar St
W Thames St
South End Ave
Rector Pl
2nd Pl
1st Pl
S William St
TKTS Booth

Key on p410

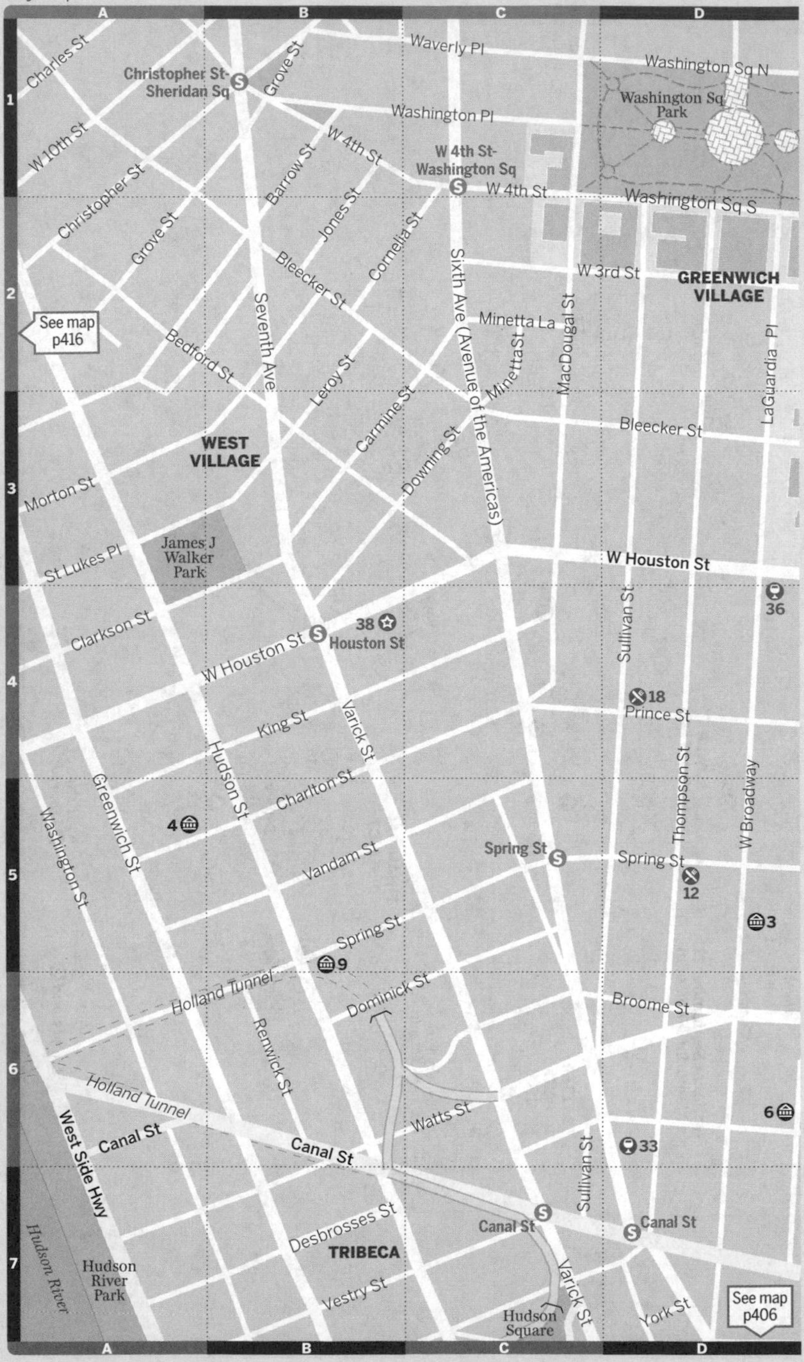
Charles St
Christopher St-Sheridan Sq
Grove St
Waverly Pl
Washington Sq N
Washington Sq Park
Washington Pl
W 4th St
W 4th St-Washington Sq
W 10th St
Christopher St
Barrow St
Jones St
Cornelia St
Washington Sq S
Grove St
Bleecker St
Seventh Ave
Sixth Ave (Avenue of the Americas)
W 3rd St
GREENWICH VILLAGE
MacDougal St
Minetta La
Minetta St
LaGuardia Pl
See map p416
Bedford St
Leroy St
Carmine St
Downing St
Bleecker St
WEST VILLAGE
Morton St
James J Walker Park
St Lukes Pl
W Houston St
Clarkson St
38
Houston St
W Houston St
Sullivan St
36
18
Prince St
King St
Varick St
Hudson St
Greenwich St
Washington St
Charlton St
Thompson St
W Broadway
4
Spring St
Spring St
Vandam St
12
3
Spring St
9
Holland Tunnel
Dominick St
Broome St
Renwick St
Holland Tunnel
West Side Hwy
Watts St
6
Canal St
Canal St
33
Sullivan St
Canal St
Canal St
Desbrosses St
TRIBECA
Hudson River
Hudson River Park
Vestry St
Varick St
Hudson Square
York St
See map p406

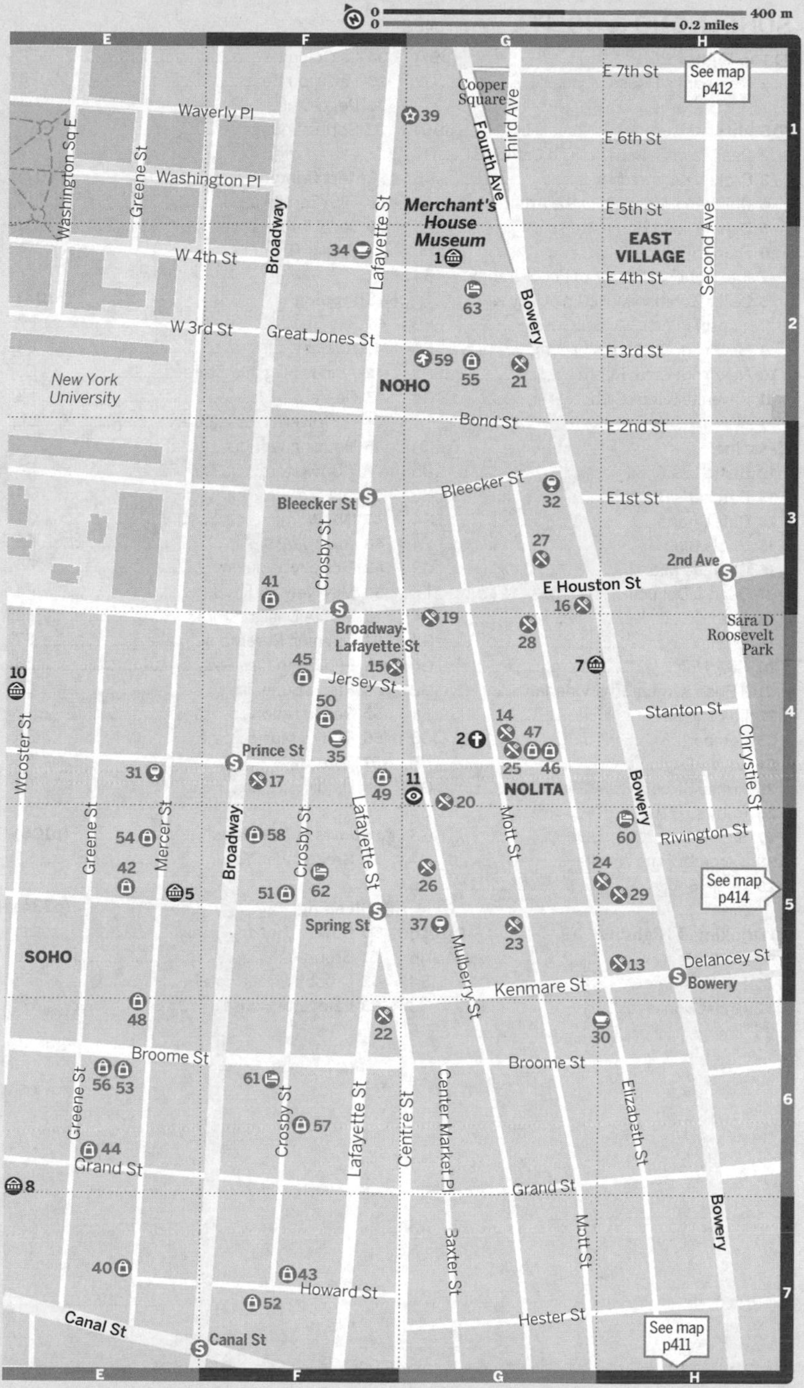
0 400 m
0 0.2 miles
E
F
G
H
1
2
3
4
5
6
7
See map p412
See map p414
See map p411
E 7th St
Cooper Square
Third Ave
Fourth Ave
Waverly Pl
Washington Sq E
Greene St
Washington Pl
E 6th St
E 5th St
Merchant's House Museum
EAST VILLAGE
W 4th St
Broadway
Lafayette St
E 4th St
Second Ave
Bowery
W 3rd St
Great Jones St
E 3rd St
NOHO
New York University
Bond St
E 2nd St
Bleecker St
E 1st St
Crosby St
2nd Ave
E Houston St
Broadway-Lafayette St
Sara D Roosevelt Park
Jersey St
Stanton St
Wooster St
Prince St
Chrystie St
NOLITA
Mercer St
Mott St
Rivington St
Spring St
Mulberry St
SOHO
Delancey St
Kenmare St
Bowery
Broome St
Centre St
Center Market Pl
Elizabeth St
Grand St
Baxter St
Howard St
Hester St
Canal St
1
2
5
7
8
10
11
13
14
15
16
17
19
20
21
22
23
24
25
26
27
28
29
30
31
32
34
35
37
39
40
41
42
43
44
45
46
47
48
49
50
51
52
53
54
55
56
57
58
59
60
61
62
63

SOHO, NOHO & NOLITA *Map on p408*

Top Sights (p91)

1 Merchant's House Museum G2

Sights (p90)

2 Basilica of St Patrick's Old Cathedral G4
3 Broken Kilometer D5
4 Children's Museum of the Arts A5
5 Donald Judd Home Studio E5
6 Drawing Center D6
7 International Center of Photography G4
8 Leslie-Lohman Museum of Gay & Lesbian Art E6
9 New York City Fire Museum B5
10 New York Earth Room E4
11 Ravenite Social Club G4

Eating (p93)

12 Bistro Les Amis D5
13 Butcher's Daughter H5
14 Café Gitane G4
15 Chefs Club F4
16 Cherche Midi G3
17 Dean & DeLuca F4
18 Dutch D4
19 Estela G4
20 Grey Dog G4
21 Il Buco Alimentari & Vineria G2
22 La Esquina F6
23 Lombardi's G5
24 Lovely Day H5
25 Prince Street Pizza G4
26 Ruby's G5
27 Siggi's G3
28 Tacombi Fonda Nolita G4
29 Uncle Boons H5

Drinking & Nightlife (p100)

30 Café Integral H6
31 Fanelli's Cafe E4
32 Ghost Donkey G3
33 Jimmy D6
34 La Colombe F2
35 La Colombe F4
36 Pegu Club D4
37 Spring Lounge G5

Entertainment (p103)

38 Film Forum B4
39 Joe's Pub G1
Public Theater .... (see 39)

Shopping (p104)

40 3x1 .... E7
41 Adidas F3
42 Adidas Flagship Store E5
43 De Vera F7
44 Fjällräven E6
45 Housing Works Bookstore F4
46 INA Men G4
47 INA Women G4
48 Joe's Jeans E6
49 McNally Jackson F4
50 MiN New York F4
51 MoMA Design Store F5
52 Opening Ceremony F7
53 Purl Soho E6
54 Rag & Bone E5
55 Resurrection G2
56 Rudy's Music E6
57 Saturdays F6
58 Uniqlo F5

Sports & Activities (p106)

59 Great Jones Spa G2

Sleeping (p334)

60 Bowery House H5
61 Broome F6
62 Crosby Street Hotel F5
63 Lafayette House G2

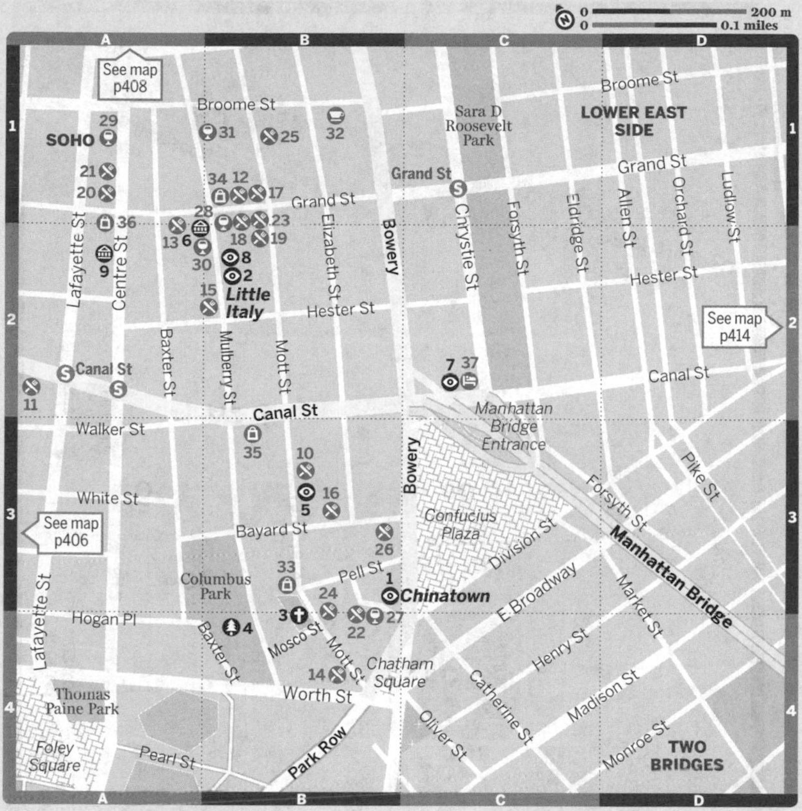

Top Sights (p86)
1 Chinatown........B3
2 Little Italy........B2

Sights (p92)
3 Church of the Transfiguration........B4
4 Columbus Park........B4
5 Eastern States Buddhist Temple........B3
6 Italian American Museum........A2
7 Mahayana Temple........C2
8 Mulberry Street........B2
9 Museum of Chinese in America........A2

Eating (p99)
10 Amazing 66........B3
11 August Gatherings........A2
12 Bánh Mì Saigon Bakery........B1
13 Baz Bagels........A2
14 Buddha Bodai........B4
15 Da Gennaro........B2
16 Deluxe Green Bo........B3
17 Di Palo........B1
18 Ferrara Cafe & Bakery........B1
19 Golden Steamer........B2
20 Lan Larb........A1
21 Marché Maman........A1
22 Nom Wah Tea Parlor........B4
23 Nyonya........B1
24 Peking Duck House........B3
25 Two Hands........B1
26 Xi'an Famous Foods........B3

Drinking & Nightlife (p100)
27 Apothéke........B4
28 Genuine Liquorette........B1
29 La Compagnie des Vins Surnaturels........A1
30 Mulberry Project........A2
31 Mulberry Street Bar........B1
32 Randolph........B1

Shopping (p104)
33 Aji Ichiban........B3
34 Alleva........B1
35 New Kam Man........B3
36 Odin........A1

Sleeping (p334)
37 Leon Hotel........C2

EAST VILLAGE

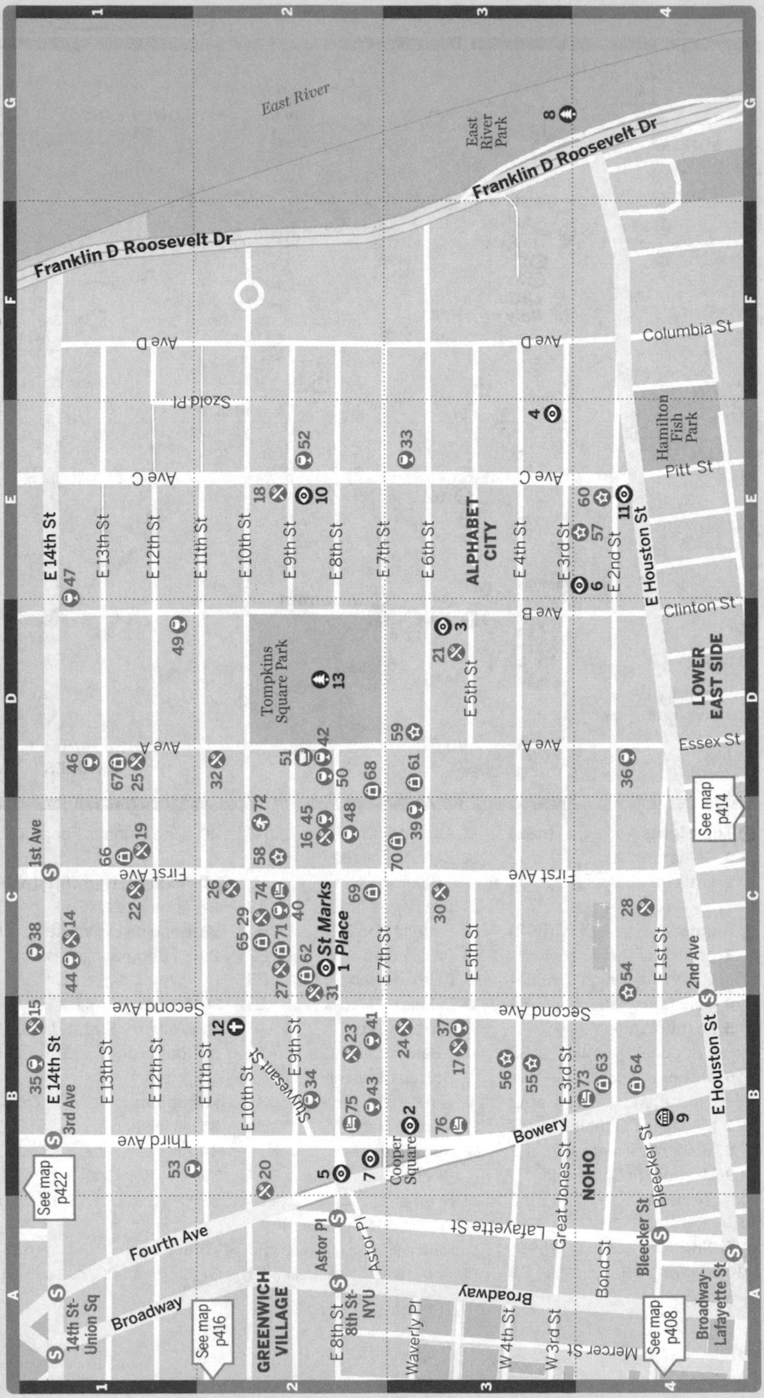

EAST VILLAGE

Top Sights (p112)
1 St Marks Place ... C2

Sights (p114)
2 41 Cooper Square ... B3
3 6th & B Garden ... D3
4 All People's Garden ... E3
5 Astor Place ... B2
6 Brisas del Caribe ... E4
7 Cooper Union Building ... B2
8 East River Park ... G3
9 Hole ... B4
10 La Plaza Cultural ... E2
11 Le Petit Versailles ... E4
12 St Mark's in the Bowery ... B2
13 Tompkins Square Park ... D2

Eating (p115)
14 Artichoke Basille's Pizza ... C1
15 Bait & Hook ... B1
16 Cafe Mogador ... C2
17 Degustation ... B3
18 Esperanto ... E2
19 Hearth ... C1
20 Ippudo NY ... B2
21 Lavagna ... D3
22 Luzzo's ... C1
23 Mamoun's ... B2
24 Mighty Quinn's ... B3
25 Mikey Likes It ... D1
26 Momofuku Noodle Bar ... C2
27 MUD ... C2
28 Prune ... C4
29 Rai Rai Ken ... C2
30 Upstate ... C3
31 Veselka ... C2
32 Westville East ... D2

Drinking & Nightlife (p120)
33 ABC Beer Co ... E3
34 Angel's Share ... B2
35 Beauty Bar ... B1
36 Berlin ... D4
37 Cock ... B3
38 Crocodile Lounge ... C1
39 Death & Co ... C3
40 Immigrant ... C2
41 Jimmy's No 43 ... B2
42 Lucy's ... D2
43 McSorley's Old Ale House ... B2
44 Nowhere ... C1
45 PDT ... C2
46 Phoenix ... D1
47 Pouring Ribbons ... E1
48 Proletariat ... C2
49 Rue B ... D1
50 Ten Degrees Bar ... D2
51 Three Seat Espresso & Barber ... D2
52 Wayland ... E2
53 Webster Hall ... B1

Entertainment (p126)
54 Anthology Film Archives ... C4
55 La MaMa ETC ... B3
56 New York Theatre Workshop ... B3
57 Nuyorican Poets Café ... E4
58 Performance Space New York ... C2
59 Sidewalk Café ... D3
60 Stone ... E4

Shopping (p128)
61 A-1 Records ... D3
62 Dinosaur Hill ... C2
63 John Derian Company ... B4
64 John Varvatos ... B4
65 Lodge ... C2
66 No Relation Vintage ... C1
67 Obscura Antiques ... D1
68 Still House ... D2
69 Tokio 7 ... C2
70 Trash & Vaudeville ... C3
71 Verameat ... C2

Sports & Activities (p131)
72 Russian & Turkish Baths ... C2

Sleeping (p335)
73 Bowery Hotel ... B4
74 East Village Hotel ... C2
75 St Mark's Hotel ... B2
76 Standard East Village ... B3

LOWER EAST SIDE

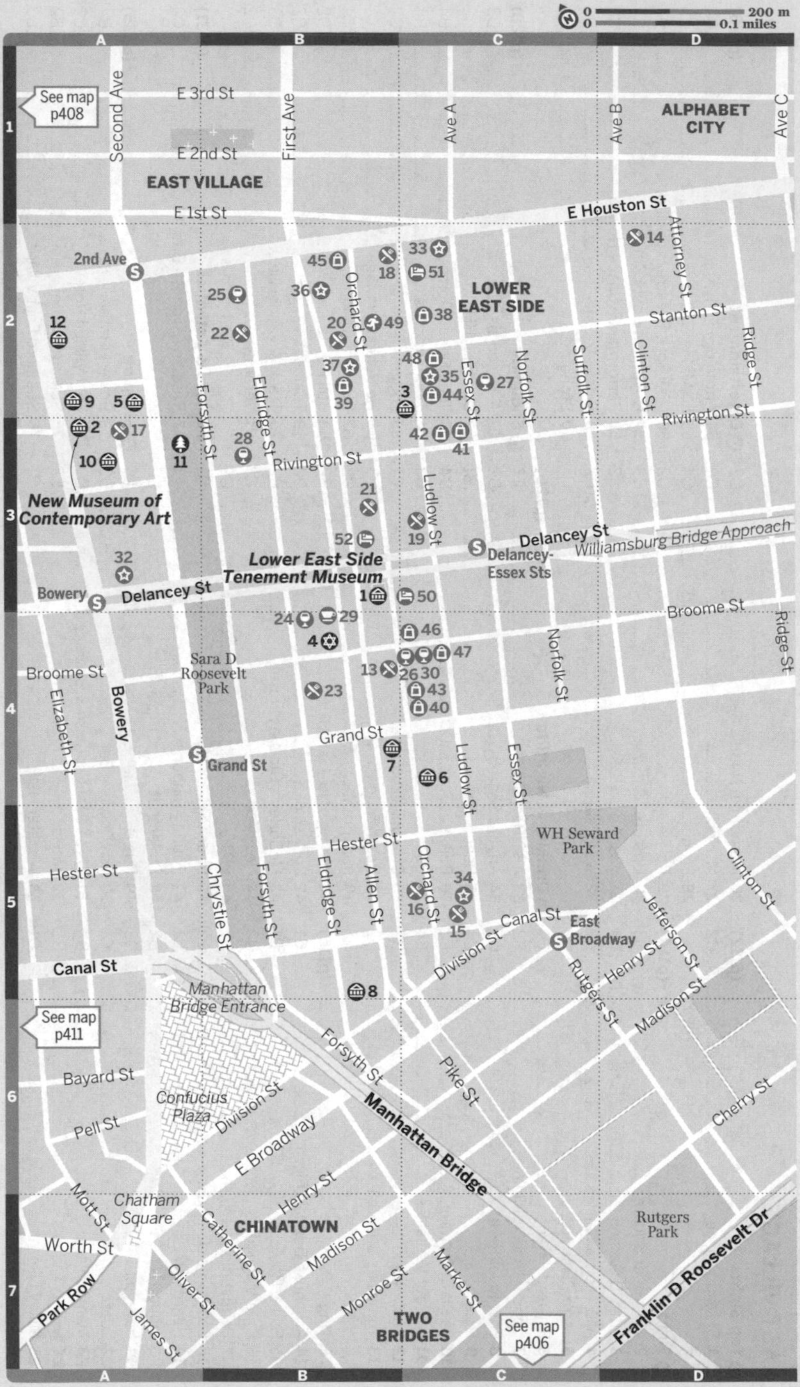

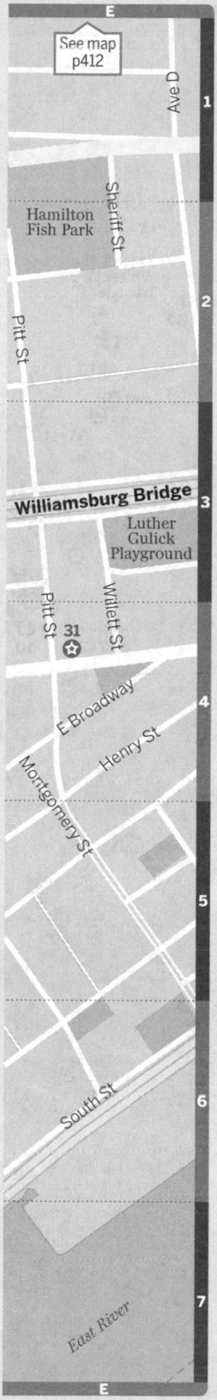

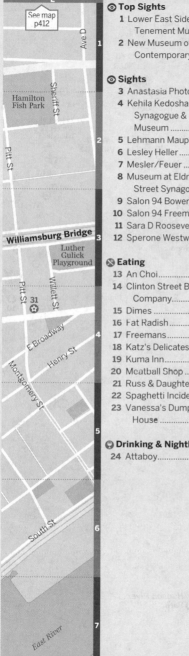

Top Sights (p109)
1 Lower East Side Tenement Museum B3
2 New Museum of Contemporary Art A3

Sights (p114)
3 Anastasia Photo C2
4 Kehila Kedosha Janina Synagogue & Museum B4
5 Lehmann Maupin A2
6 Lesley Heller C4
7 Mesler/Feuer B4
8 Museum at Eldridge Street Synagogue B5
9 Salon 94 Bowery A2
10 Salon 94 Freemans A3
11 Sara D Roosevelt Park A3
12 Sperone Westwater A2

Eating (p118)
13 An Choi B4
14 Clinton Street Baking Company D2
15 Dimes C5
16 Fat Radish C5
17 Freemans A3
18 Katz's Delicatessen B2
19 Kuma Inn C3
20 Meatball Shop B2
21 Russ & Daughters Cafe B3
22 Spaghetti Incident B2
23 Vanessa's Dumpling House B4

Drinking & Nightlife (p123)
24 Attaboy B4
25 Bar Goto B2
26 Barrio Chino C4
27 Beauty & Essex C2
28 Jadis B3
29 Round K B4
30 Ten Bells C4

Entertainment (p126)
31 Abrons Arts Center E4
32 Bowery Ballroom A3
33 Mercury Lounge C2
34 Metrograph C5
35 Pianos C2
36 Rockwood Music Hall B2
37 Slipper Room B2

Shopping (p129)
38 Assembly C2
39 Bluestockings B2
40 By Robert James C4
41 Economy Candy C3
42 Edith Machinist C3
43 Moo Shoes C4
44 Reformation C2
45 Russ & Daughters B2
46 Tictail Market C4
47 Top Hat C4
48 Yumi Kim C2

Sports & Activities (p131)
49 Jump into the Light VR B2

Sleeping (p335)
50 Blue Moon Boutique Hotel C3
51 Ludlow C2
52 Sago Hotel B3

Key on p418

A
B
C
D
1
2
3
4
5
6
7
See map p420
CHELSEA
MEATPACKING DISTRICT
WEST VILLAGE
W 15th St
W 14th St
W 13th St
W 12th St
W 11th St
W 10th St
W 4th St
W Houston St
Tenth Ave
Ninth Ave
Eighth Ave
Seventh Ave
Washington St
Gansevoort St
Horatio St
Jane St
Greenwich St
Greenwich Ave
Bethune St
Bank St
Perry St
Charles St
Christopher St
Barrow St
Morton St
St Lukes Pl
Leroy St
Clarkson St
King St
Charlton St
Hudson St
Bleecker St
Bedford St
Commerce St
Waverly Pl
West Side Hwy
8th Ave-14th St
14th St
Christopher St-Sheridan Sq
Jackson Sq
Corporal John A Seravalli Playground
Abingdon Sq
Bleecker Playground
St Vincent's Triangle
James J Walker Park
High Line
Hudson River Park
Hudson River
Pier 40
1
2
4
7
10
11
14
16
17
18
20
21
24
27
31
32
37
40
41
42
46
48
49
51
52
53
54
55
56
57
59
61
62
63
64
65
67
70
71
73
77
79
82
85
86
87
88
93
96
98
100
102
103
106
107
109
110
112
113
114
115

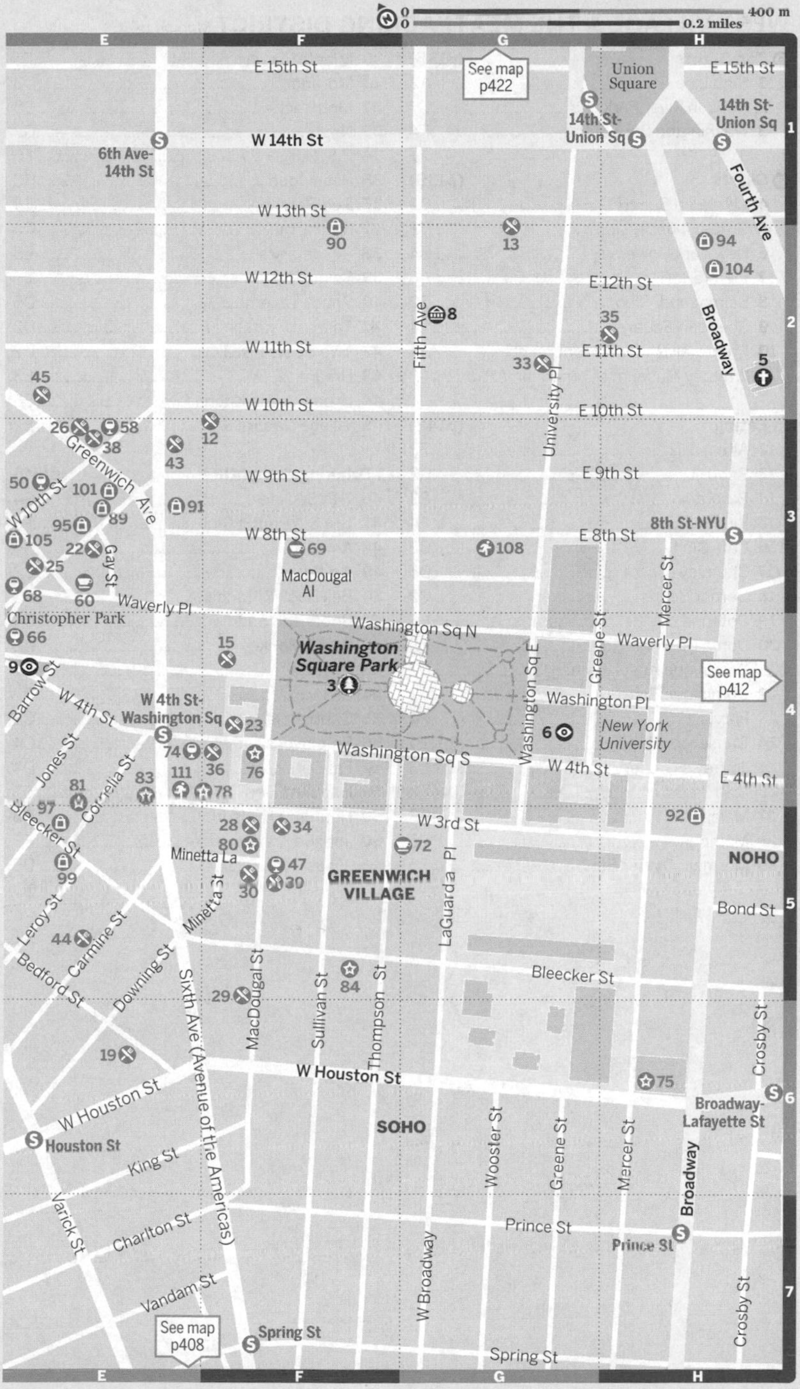

0 400 m
0 0.2 miles
E F G H
1 2 3 4 5 6 7
See map p422
See map p412
See map p408
Union Square
14th St-Union Sq
6th Ave-14th St
8th St-NYU
W 4th St-Washington Sq
Houston St
Broadway-Lafayette St
Prince St
Spring St
E 15th St
W 14th St
W 13th St
W 12th St
E 12th St
W 11th St
E 11th St
W 10th St
E 10th St
W 9th St
E 9th St
W 8th St
E 8th St
Fourth Ave
Broadway
Fifth Ave
University Pl
Greenwich Ave
W 10th St
Gay St
Waverly Pl
Christopher Park
MacDougal Al
Washington Sq N
Washington Square Park
Washington Sq E
Washington Sq S
Washington Pl
New York University
W 4th St
E 4th St
Greene St
Mercer St
Barrow St
Jones St
Cornelia St
Bleecker St
Leroy St
Carmine St
Bedford St
Downing St
Minetta La
Minetta St
MacDougal St
Sullivan St
Thompson St
LaGuardia Pl
W 3rd St
GREENWICH VILLAGE
NOHO
Bond St
Bleecker St
Crosby St
Sixth Ave (Avenue of the Americas)
W Houston St
SOHO
King St
Charlton St
Varick St
Vandam St
Wooster St
W Broadway
Prince St
Spring St
3 5 6 8 9 12 13 15 19 22 23 25 26 28 29 30 33 34 35 36 38 43 44 45 47 50 58 60 66 68 69 72 74 75 76 78 80 81 83 84 89 90 91 92 94 95 97 99 101 104 105 108 111

WEST VILLAGE & THE MEATPACKING DISTRICT *Map on p416*

Top Sights (p136)
1 High Line A2
2 Hudson River Park C7
3 Washington Square Park F4

Sights (p139)
4 Abingdon Square C3
5 Grace Church H2
6 New York University G4
7 Pier 45 A6
8 Salmagundi Club G2
9 Sheridan Square E4
10 Stonewall National Monument D4
11 Whitney Museum of American Art A2

Eating (p142)
12 Alta F3
13 Babu Ji G2
14 Barbuto B3
15 Blue Hill F4
16 Café Cluny C2
17 Chumley's D5
18 Corner Bistro C2
19 Cotenna E6
20 Doma Na Rohu D5
21 Dominique Ansel Kitchen D3
22 Dominique Bistro E3
23 Fifty F4
24 Gansevoort Market B1
25 Jeffrey's Grocery E3
26 Mah Ze Dahr E3
27 Malaparte B3
28 Mamoun's F5
29 Mermaid Oyster Bar F5
30 Minetta Tavern F5
31 Morandi D3
32 Moustache D5
33 Nix G2
34 P.S. Burgers F5
35 Peacefood H2
36 Red Bamboo F4
37 RedFarm C4
38 Rosemary's E3
39 Saigon Shack F5
40 Snack Taverna D5
41 Taïm D2
42 Two Boots Pizza D2
43 Umami E3
44 Urban Vegan Kitchen E5
45 Village Natural E2

Drinking & Nightlife (p150)
46 11th St Cafe B4
47 124 Old Rabbit Club F5
48 Aria C4
49 Art Bar C2
50 Bell Book & Candle E3
51 Boots and Saddle D4
52 Brass Monkey A2
53 Buvette D4
54 Cielo B2
55 Cubbyhole C2
56 Employees Only C4
57 Fat Cat D4
58 Happiest Hour E3
59 Henrietta Hudson D5
60 Joe the Art of Coffee E3
61 Julius Bar D3

62 Kettle of Fish D3
Le Bain (see 67)
63 Little Branch D6
64 Marie's Crisis D4
65 Matcha Bar C1
66 Monster E4
Standard (see 67)
67 Standard Biergarten A2
68 Stonewall Inn E3
69 Stumptown Coffee Roasters F3
Top of the Standard (see 67)
70 Troy Liquor Bar B1
71 Ty's D4
72 Uncommons G5
73 Vin Sur Vingt D2
74 Vol de Nuit E4

Entertainment (p155)
55 Bar (see 68)
75 Angelika Film Center H6
76 Bar Next Door F4
77 Barrow Street Theater D4
78 Blue Note F4
79 Cherry Lane Theater D5
80 Comedy Cellar F5
81 Cornelia Street Café E4
82 Duplex D3
83 IFC Center E4
84 Le Poisson Rouge F5
85 LGBT Community Center D1
86 Mezzrow D3
87 Smalls D3
88 Village Vanguard D2

Shopping (p160)
89 Aedes de Venustas E3
90 Beacon's Closet F2
91 CO Bigelow Chemists E3
92 Evolution Nature Store H5
93 Flight 001 D2
94 Forbidden Planet H2
95 Greenwich Letterpress E3
96 Idlewild Books D3
97 Mask Bar E5
98 McNulty's Tea & Coffee Co, Inc D4
99 Murray's Cheese E5
100 Odin D2
101 Personnel of New York E3
102 Saturdays D3
103 Screaming Mimi's C1
104 Strand Book Store H2
105 Three Lives & Company E3
106 Trina Turk B2
107 Yoya C3

Sports & Activities (p163)
108 MNDFL G3
109 New York Trapeze School B7
110 Waterfront Bicycle Shop B5
111 West 4th Street Basketball Courts E4

Sleeping (p336)
112 Chelsea Pines Inn C1
113 Hotel Gansevoort B2
114 Incentra Village House C2
115 Jane Hotel A3
Standard (see 67)

CHELSEA

0 0.2 miles
0 400 m
KOREA TOWN
See map p424
See map p422
See map p428
Sixth Ave (Avenue of the Americas)
Seventh Ave
Eighth Ave
Ninth Ave
Tenth Ave
Eleventh Ave
Eleventh Ave (West Side Hwy)
Twelfth Ave (West Side Hwy)
High Line
W 29th St
W 28th St
W 27th St
W 26th St
W 25th St
W 24th St
W 23rd St
W 22nd St
W 21st St
W 20th St
W 19th St
W 18th St
W 17th St
W 16th St
28th St
23rd St
18th St
CHELSEA
Chelsea Park
London Terrace
Chelsea Waterside Park
Hudson River Park
Chelsea Piers
Pier 66
Pier 62
Pier 61
Pier 60
Pier 59
Hudson River

Top Sights (p134)

1 Chelsea Market D5

Sights (p141)

2 Barbara Gladstone Gallery C2
3 Cheim & Read B2
4 Chelsea Hotel F3
5 David Zwirner C3
6 Gagosian B2
7 General Theological Seminary D3
8 Mary Boone Gallery C2
9 Matthew Marks Gallery C3
10 Pace Gallery C2
11 Paula Cooper Gallery C3
12 Rubin Museum of Art G4

Eating (p147)

Amy's Bread .... (see 1)
13 Blossom D3
Chelsea Market .... (see 1)
14 Chelsea Square Diner D3
15 Cookshop C3
16 Foragers Table E3
17 Heath C1
18 Jun-Men D2
19 Le Grainne D3
20 Tía Pol C3
Tuck Shop .... (see 1)

Drinking & Nightlife (p154)

21 Bathtub Gin D4
22 Blue Bottle D5
23 Eagle NYC C1
Gallow Green .... (see 34)
24 Gym Sportsbar E4
25 Peter McManus Tavern F4
26 Pier 66 Maritime A2

Entertainment (p155)

27 Atlantic Theater Company E3
28 Cinépolis Chelsea F3
29 Gotham Comedy Club F3
30 Irish Repertory Theatre G3
31 Joyce Theater E4
32 Kitchen C4
33 New York Live Arts F4
34 Sleep No More C1

Shopping (p162)

35 192 Books C3
36 Housing Works Thrift Shop G4
37 Nasty Pig E4
38 Printed Matter B2
39 Story C4

Sports & Activities (p163)

40 Chelsea Piers Complex B3
41 New York Gallery Tours C2
42 Schooner Adirondack B3

Sleeping (p336)

43 Chelsea International Hostel F3
44 Colonial House Inn E3
45 GEM D3
46 High Line Hotel C3
47 Hôtel Americano C1
48 Maritime Hotel E4
49 Townhouse Inn of Chelsea G2

UNION SQUARE, THE FLATIRON DISTRICT & GRAMERCY PARK

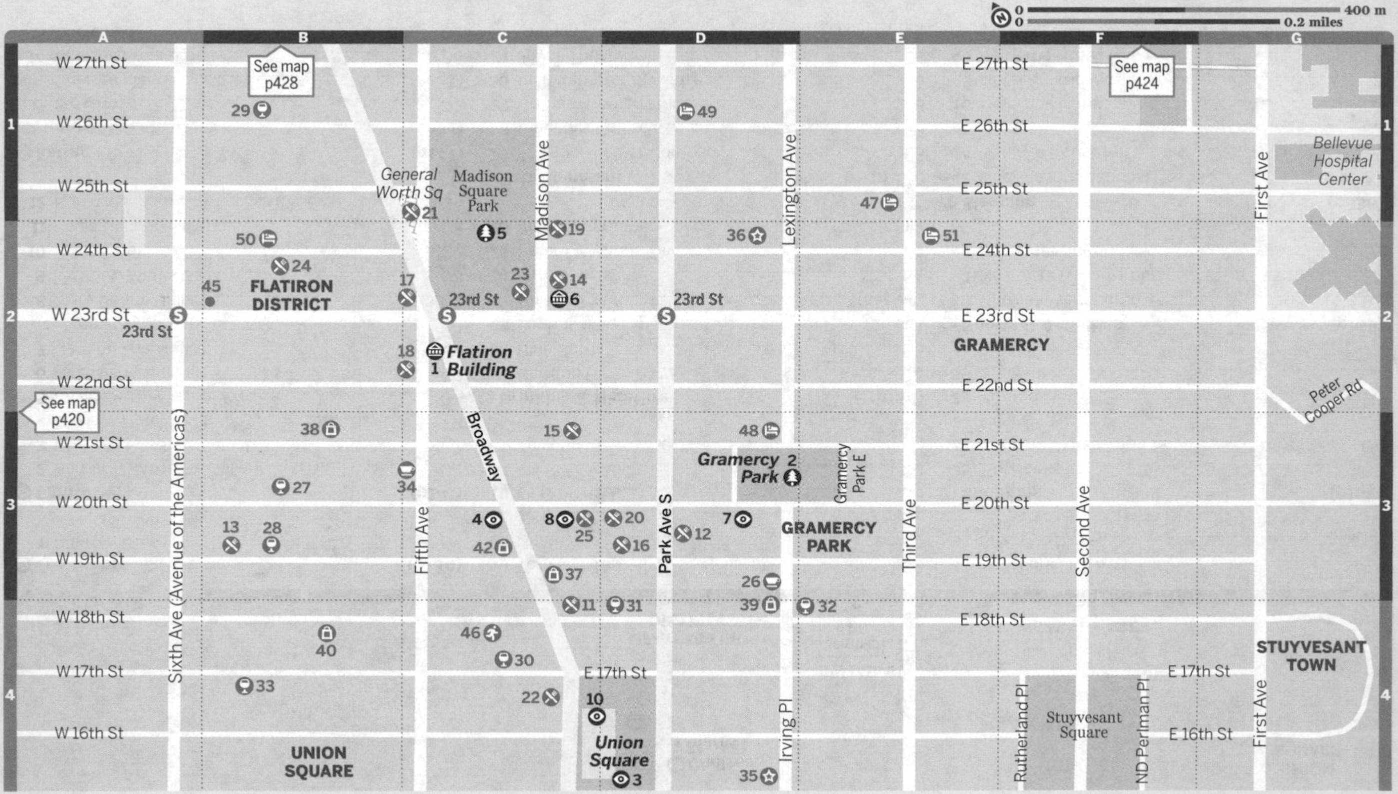

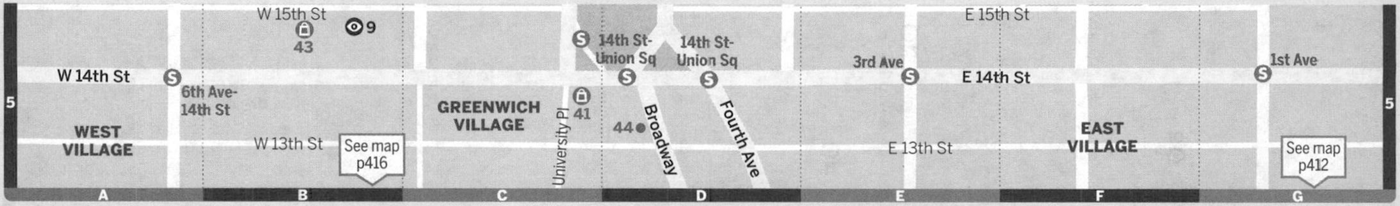

Top Sights (p166)
1 Flatiron Building C2
2 Gramercy Park D3
3 Union Square D4

Sights (p167)
4 Lord & Taylor Building C3
5 Madison Square Park C2
6 Metropolitan Life Tower C2
7 National Arts Club D3
8 Theodore Roosevelt Birthplace C3
9 Tibet House B5
10 Union Square Greenmarket C4

Eating (p168)
11 ABC Kitchen C4
12 Big Daddy's D3
13 Boqueria Flatiron B3
14 Clocktower C2
15 Cosme C3
16 Craft D3
17 Eataly C2
18 Eisenberg's Sandwich Shop C2
19 Eleven Madison Park C2
20 Gramercy Tavern D3
21 Mad Sq Eats C1
Maialino (see 48)
22 Republic C4
23 Shake Shack C2
24 Tacombi Café El Presidente B2
25 Trattoria Il Mulino C3

Drinking & Nightlife (p170)
26 71 Irving Place D3
Birreria (see 17)
27 Boxers NYC B3
28 Flatiron Lounge B3
29 Flatiron Room B1
30 Lillie's Victorian Establishment C4
31 Old Town Bar & Restaurant D4
32 Pete's Tavern E4
33 Raines Law Room B4
34 Toby's Estate C3

Entertainment (p172)
35 Irving Plaza D4
36 Peoples Improv Theater D2

Shopping (p172)
37 ABC Carpet & Home C3
38 Abracadabra B3
39 Bedford Cheese Shop D4
40 Books of Wonder B4
41 DSW C5
42 Fishs Eddy C3
43 Rent the Runway B5
Union Square Greenmarket (see 10)

Sports & Activities (p174)
44 Jivamukti D5
45 New York City Audubon B2
46 Soul Cycle C4

Sleeping (p338)
47 Carlton Arms E1
48 Gramercy Park Hotel D3
49 Hotel Giraffe D1
50 Hotel Henri B2
51 Marcel at Gramercy E2

MIDTOWN EAST & FIFTH AVENUE

Key on p426

MIDTOWN EAST & FIFTH AVENUE

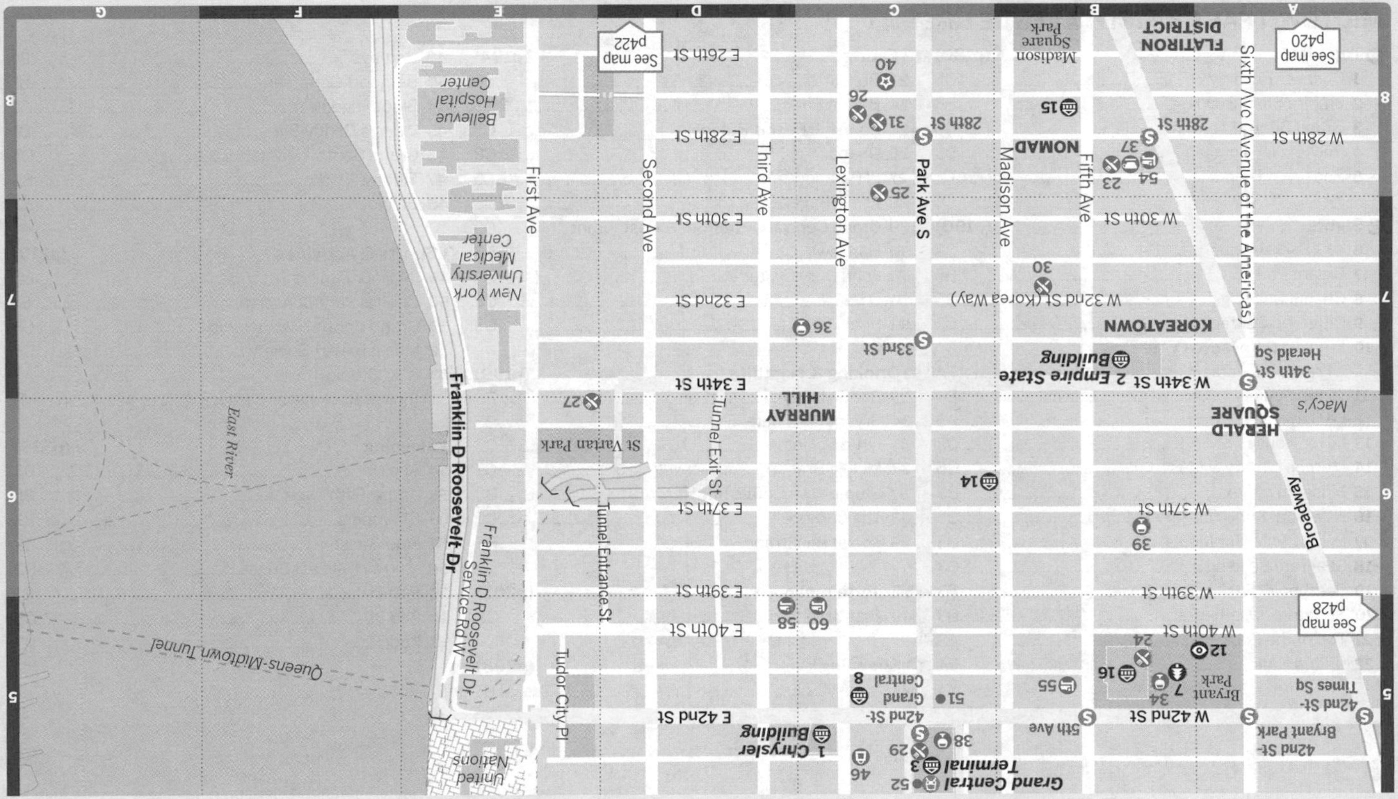

MIDTOWN EAST & FIFTH AVENUE *Map on p424*

Top Sights (p180)

1 Chrysler Building ... C5
2 Empire State Building ... B7
3 Grand Central Terminal ... C5
4 Rockefeller Center ... B3
5 Roosevelt Island ... G1

Sights (p190)

6 432 Park Avenue ... C2
7 Bryant Park ... B5
8 Chanin Building ... C5
9 Citigroup Center ... C2
10 Franklin D Roosevelt Four Freedoms Park ... F4
11 Japan Society ... E4
12 Le Carrousel ... A5
13 Lever House ... C2
14 Morgan Library & Museum ... C6
15 Museum of Sex ... B8
16 New York Public Library ... B5
17 Paley Center for Media ... B3
18 Seagram Building ... C3
19 Southpoint Park ... F3
20 St Patrick's Cathedral ... B3
21 Top of the Rock ... A3
22 United Nations ... E4

Eating (p194)

23 Breslin ... B8
24 Bryant Park Grill ... B5
25 Cannibal Beer & Butcher ... C8
26 Dhaba ... C8
27 El Parador Cafe ... E6
28 Ess-a-Bagel ... D3
29 Grand Central Oyster Bar & Restaurant ... C5
30 Hangawi ... B7
John Dory Oyster Bar ... (see 54)
31 O-ya ... C8
32 Smith ... D3

Drinking & Nightlife (p199)

33 Bar SixtyFive ... B3
34 Bryant Park Cafe ... B5
35 Little Collins ... C2
36 Middle Branch ... C7
37 Stumptown Coffee Roasters ... B8
38 The Campbell ... C5
39 Top of the Strand ... B6

Entertainment (p203)

40 Jazz Standard ... C8

Shopping (p208)

41 Argosy ... C1
42 Barneys ... B1
43 Bergdorf Goodman ... B1
44 Bloomingdale's ... C1
45 Dylan's Candy Bar ... D1
46 Grand Central Market ... C5
47 Tiffany & Co ... B2
48 Uniqlo ... B3

Sports & Activities (p210)

49 24 Hour Fitness ... C2
50 Central Park Conservancy ... B1
51 Grand Central Partnership ... C5
52 Municipal Art Society ... C5
53 NBC Studio Tours ... A3
Rink at Rockefeller Center ... (see 4)

Sleeping (p339)

54 Ace Hotel ... B8
55 Andaz Fifth Avenue ... B5
56 Chambers ... B2
57 Four Seasons ... C2
58 Murray Hill East Suites ... D5
59 Plaza ... B1
60 Pod 39 ... C5
61 Pod 51 ... D3

MIDTOWN WEST & TIMES SQUARE *Map on p428*

Top Sights (p177)
1 Museum of Modern Art...G2
2 Radio City Music Hall...F3
3 Times Square...E5

Sights (p193)
4 Bank of America Tower...F5
5 Brill Building...E3
6 Diamond District...G4
7 Hearst Tower...E2
8 Herald Square...F6
9 Intrepid Sea, Air & Space Museum...A4
10 Museum at FIT...E8
11 Museum of Arts & Design...E1

Eating (p197)
12 Bengal Tiger...F2
13 Burger Joint...F2
Cafe 2...(see 1)
14 Danji...D3
15 Don Antonio...D3
16 FIKA...C2
17 Fuku+...G2
18 Larb Ubol...D6
19 Le Bernardin...F3
20 Margon...F4
Modern...(see 1)
21 NoMad...G8
22 Souvlaki GR...E2
23 Taboon...C3
Terrace Five...(see 1)
24 Totto Ramen...D3
25 ViceVersa...D3
26 Whole Foods...D1

Drinking & Nightlife (p202)
27 Bar Centrale...D4
28 Barrage...D4
29 Flaming Saddles...D2
30 Industry...D3
31 Jimmy's Corner...F4
32 Lantern's Keep...G4
Robert...(see 11)
33 Rudy's Bar & Grill...D4
34 Rum House...E4
35 Therapy...D3
36 Waylon...C3

Entertainment (p204)
37 Al Hirschfeld Theatre...D4
38 Ambassador Theatre...E3
39 AMC Empire 25...E5
40 Birdland...D4
41 Carnegie Hall...E2
42 Caroline's on Broadway...E3
43 CBS Broadcast Center...C2
44 Don't Tell Mama...D4
45 Ed Sullivan Theater...E2
46 Eugene O'Neill Theatre...E3
47 Gershwin Theatre...E3
48 Harold and Miriam Steinberg Center for Theatre...F4
Jazz at Lincoln Center...(see 68)
49 Lyceum Theatre...E4
50 Madison Square Garden...E7
51 Magnet Theater...E8
52 Minskoff Theatre...E4
Museum of Modern Art...(see 1)
53 New Amsterdam Theatre...E5
54 New Victory Theater...E5
55 New York City Center...F2
56 Playwrights Horizons...D5
57 Richard Rodgers Theatre...E4
Roundabout Theatre Company...(see 48)
58 Second Stage Theatre...D5
59 Shubert Theatre...E4
60 Signature Theatre...C5
61 The Daily Show with Trevor Noah...B3
62 Upright Citizens Brigade Theatre...B5

Shopping (p209)
63 B&H Photo Video...D7
64 Drama Book Shop...E5
65 Hell's Kitchen Flea Market...D6
66 Macy's...F7
MoMA Design & Book Store...(see 1)
67 Nepenthes New York...D6
68 Time Warner Center...D1

Sports & Activities (p210)
69 Central Park Bike Tours...E1
70 Circle Line Boat Tours...A5
71 Lucky Strike...B5
72 Manhattan Community Boathouse...A2
73 Simple Studios...F8

Sleeping (p339)
74 Chatwal New York...F4
75 Citizen M...E3
76 Ink48...B4
Iroquois...(see 32)
77 Knickerbocker...F5
NoMad Hotel...(see 21)
78 Park Savoy...F1
79 Quin...F1
80 Yotel...C5

MIDTOWN WEST & TIMES SQUARE

Key on p427

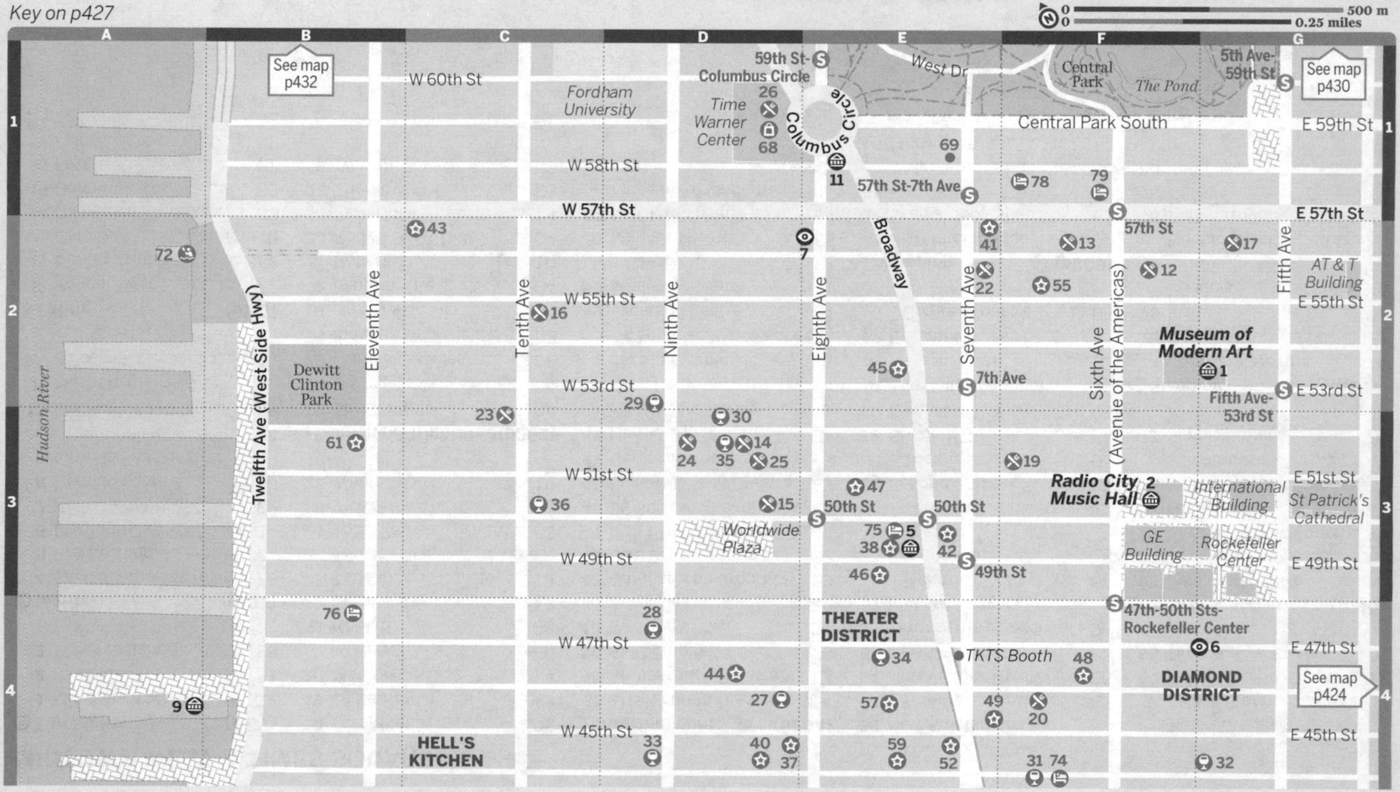

MIDTOWN WEST & TIMES SQUARE

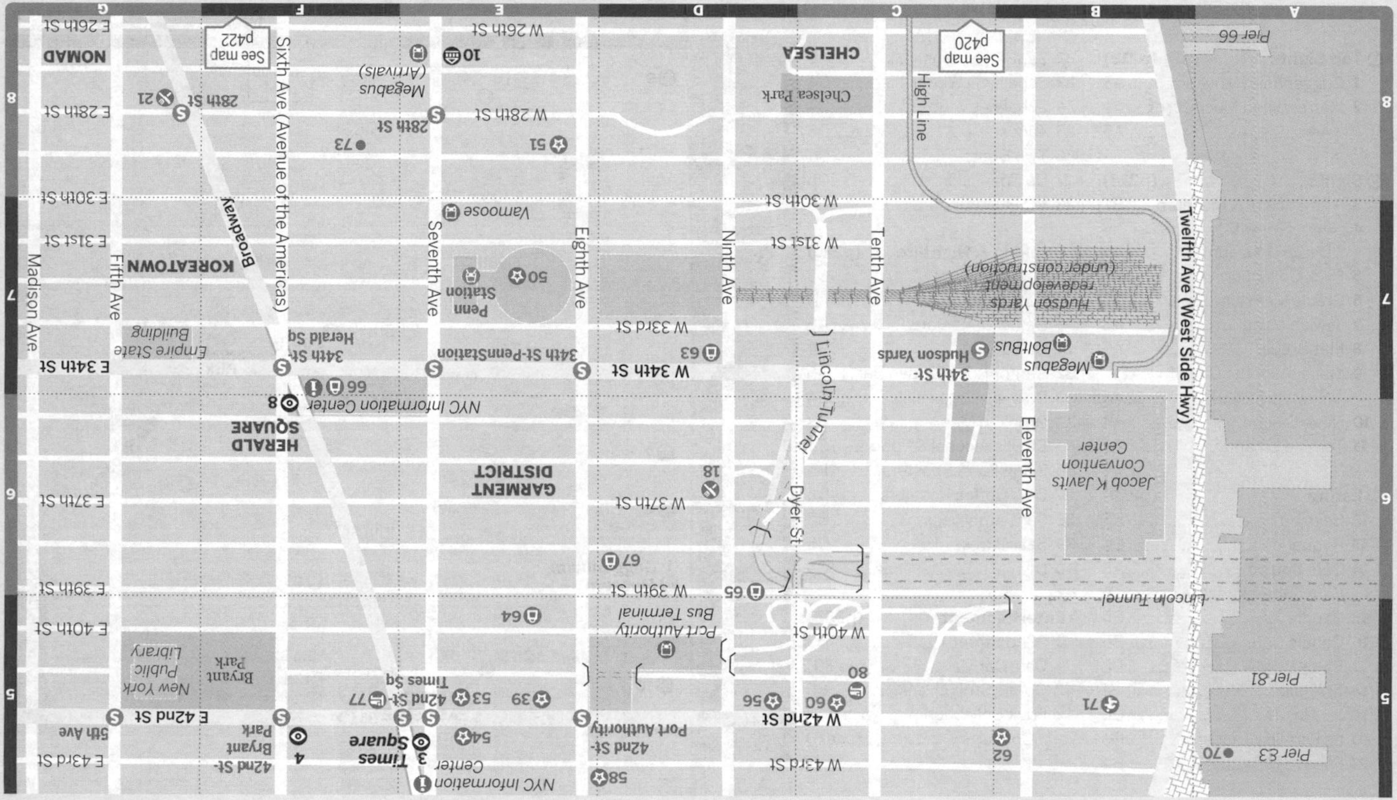

UPPER EAST SIDE

Top Sights (p213)

1 Guggenheim Museum A3
2 Metropolitan Museum of Art A5

Sights (p218)

3 Asia Society & Museum B7
4 Cooper-Hewitt National Design Museum A3
5 Frick Collection A7
6 Gracie Mansion D3
7 Jewish Museum A3
8 Met Breuer A6
9 Museum of the City of New York A1
10 Neue Galerie A4
11 Temple Emanu-El A7

Eating (p219)

12 Beyoglu B5
13 Boqueria C6
14 Café Boulud A6
Café Sabarsky .... (see 10)
15 Candle 79 .... B5
16 Candle Cafe B6
17 Earl's Beer & Cheese B2
18 El Aguila B1
19 JG Melon B6
20 La Esquina Taquería C6
21 Papaya King B4
22 Sant Ambroeus A5
23 Schaller & Weber C4
24 Schaller's Stube C4
25 Tanoshi D6
26 Two Boots C4
27 Up Thai C6
28 Via Quadronno A6

Drinking & Nightlife (p221)

29 Auction House C3
Bar Pleiades .... (see 14)
30 Bemelmans Bar A6
31 Caledonia C4
32 Cantor Roof Garden Bar A5
33 Daisy C4
34 Drunken Munkey C3
35 Ethyl's Alcohol & Food C4
36 Irving Farm Roasters B5
37 Oslo Coffee Roasters D6
38 Sant Ambroeus B8
39 Seamstress C6
40 Uva C5

Entertainment (p223)

41 92nd Street Y B3
Café Carlyle .... (see 30)
42 Comic Strip Live C5
Frick Collection Concerts .... (see 5)

Shopping (p224)

43 Diptyque A6
44 Encore A4
45 Flying Tiger Copenhagen B6
46 Jacadi B6
47 Mary Arnold Toys B5
48 Michael's A5
49 Ricky's NYC C6
50 Shakespeare & Co B7

Sports & Activities (p225)

51 Art Farm in the City D3

Sleeping (p341)

52 1871 House B8
53 Bubba & Bean Lodges B1
54 Franklin B4
55 Mark A5

UPPER WEST SIDE & CENTRAL PARK

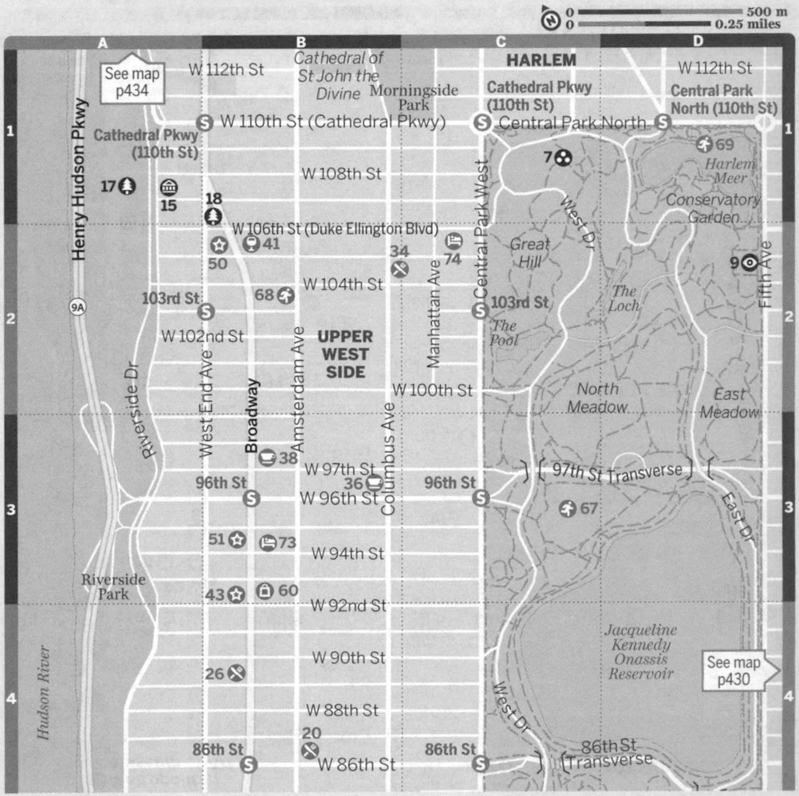

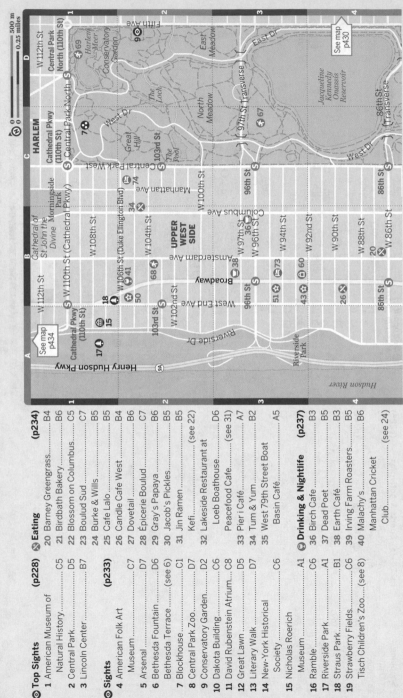

Top Sights (p228)

1 American Museum of Natural History....C5
2 Central Park....D5
3 Lincoln Center....B7

Sights (p233)

4 American Folk Art Museum....C7
5 Arsenal....D7
6 Bethesda Fountain....D6
Bethesda Terrace....(see 6)
7 Blockhouse....C1
8 Central Park Zoo....D7
9 Conservatory Garden....D2
10 Dakota Building....C6
11 David Rubenstein Atrium....C8
12 Great Lawn....D5
13 Literary Walk....D7
14 New-York Historical Society....C6
15 Nicholas Roerich Museum....A1
16 Ramble....C6
17 Riverside Park....A1
18 Straus Park....B1
19 Strawberry Fields....C6
Tisch Children's Zoo....(see 8)

Eating (p234)

20 Barney Greengrass....B4
21 Birdbath Bakery....B6
22 Blossom on Columbus....C5
23 Boulud Sud....C7
24 Burke & Wills....B5
25 Cafe Lalo....B5
26 Candle Cafe West....B4
27 Dovetail....B6
28 Épicerie Boulud....C7
29 Gray's Papaya....B6
30 Jacob's Pickles....B5
31 Jin Ramen....B5
Kefi....(see 22)
32 Lakeside Restaurant at Loeb Boathouse....D6
Peacefood Cafe....(see 31)
33 Pier i Café....A7
34 Tum & Yum....B2
35 West 79th Street Boat Basin Café....A5

Drinking & Nightlife (p237)

36 Birch Cafe....B3
37 Dead Poet....B5
38 Earth Café....B3
39 Irving Farm Roasters....B5
40 Malachy's....B6
Manhattan Cricket Club....(see 24)

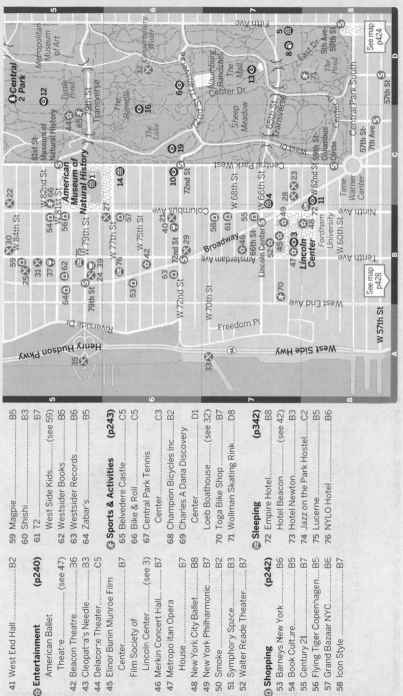

41 West End Hall B2

Entertainment (p240)

American Ballet Theatre .... (see 47)
42 Beacon Theatre B6
43 Cleopatra's Needle B3
44 Delacorte Theater C5
45 Elinor Bunin Munroe Film Center B7
Film Society of Lincoln Center .... (see 3)
46 Merkin Concert Hall B7
47 Metropolitan Opera House B7
48 New York City Ballet B8
49 New York Philharmonic B7
50 Smoke B2
51 Symphony Space B3
52 Walter Reade Theater B7

Shopping (p242)

53 Barneys New York B6
54 Book Culture B5
55 Century 21 .... B7
56 Flying Tiger Copenhagen B5
57 Grand Bazaar NYC B6
58 Icon Style B7
59 Magpie B5
60 Shishi B3
61 T2 .... B7
West Side Kids .... (see 59)
62 Westsider Books B5
63 Westsider Records B6
64 Zabar's B5

Sports & Activities (p243)

65 Belvedere Castle C5
66 Bike & Roll C5
67 Central Park Tennis Center C3
68 Champion Bicycles Inc B2
69 Charles A Dana Discovery Center D1
Loeb Boathouse .... (see 32)
70 Toga Bike Shop B7
71 Wollman Skating Rink D8

Sleeping (p342)

72 Empire Hotel B8
Hotel Beacon .... (see 42)
73 Hotel Newton B3
74 Jazz on the Park Hostel C2
75 Lucerne B5
76 NYLO Hotel B6

HARLEM & UPPER MANHATTAN

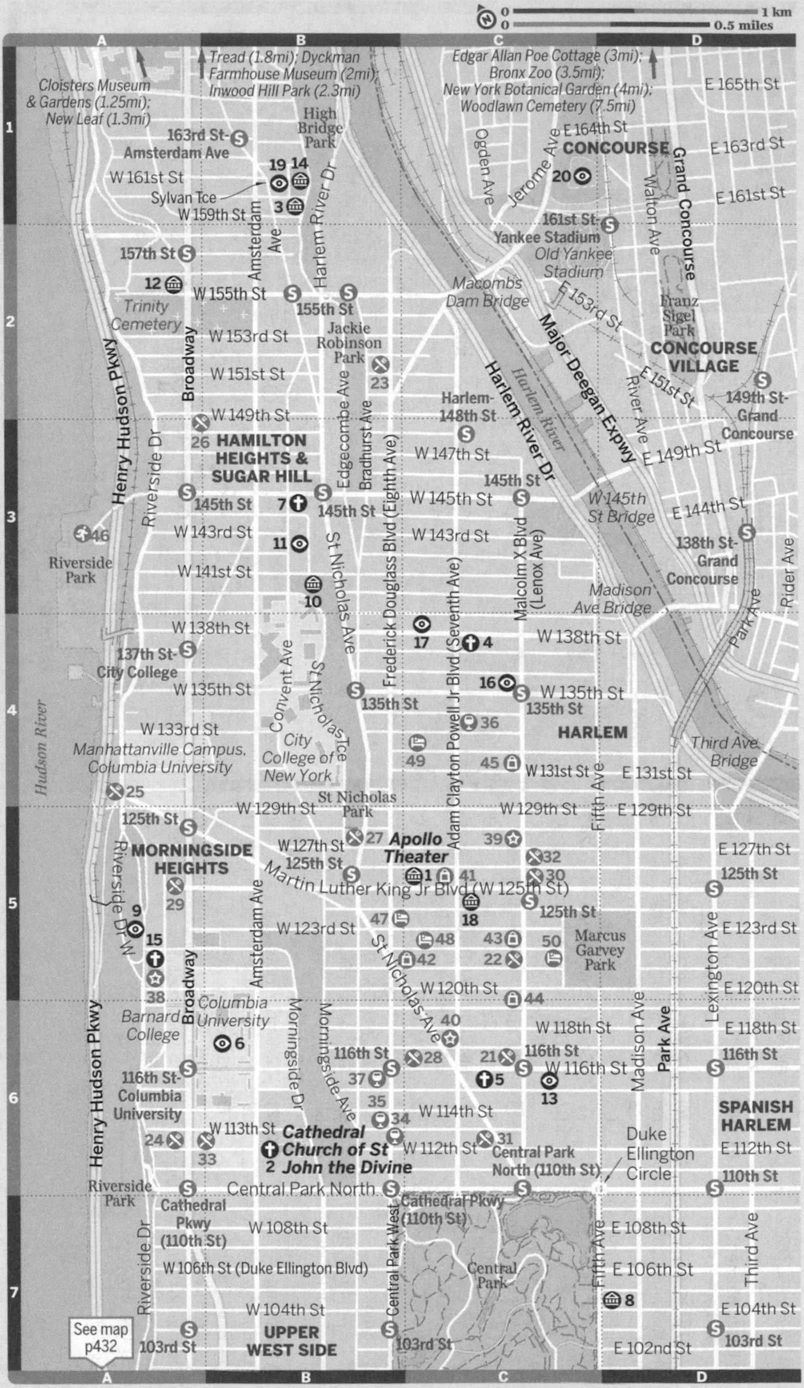

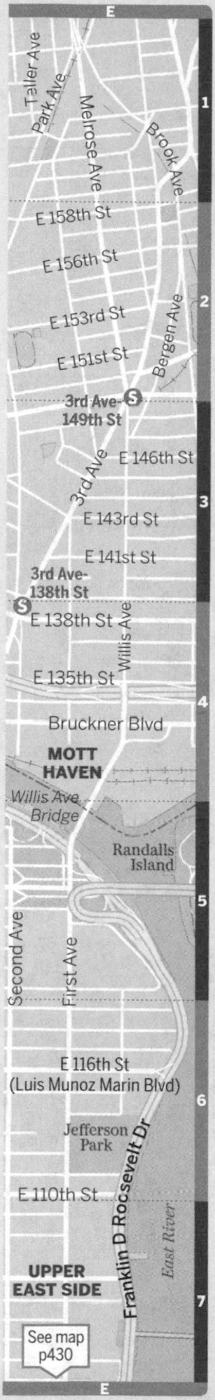

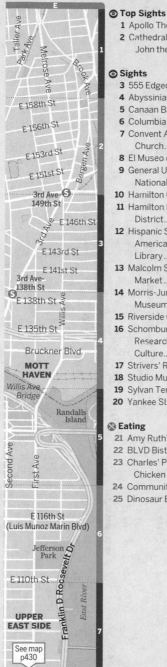

Top Sights (p247)

1 Apollo Theater........................C5
2 Cathedral Church of St John the Divine.................. B6

Sights (p249)

3 555 Edgecombe Ave B1
4 Abyssinian Baptist Church. C4
5 Canaan Baptist Church....... C6
6 Columbia University............ B6
7 Convent Avenue Baptist Church...............................B3
8 El Museo del Barrio...............D7
9 General Ulysses S Grant National Memorial A5
10 Hamilton Grange...................B3
11 Hamilton Heights Historic District...............................B3
12 Hispanic Society of America Museum & Library A2
13 Malcolm Shabazz Harlem Market C6
14 Morris-Jumel Mansion Museum B1
15 Riverside Church A5
16 Schomburg Center for Research in Black Culture.............................. C4
17 Strivers' Row C4
18 Studio Museum in Harlem...C5
19 Sylvan Terrace B1
20 Yankee Stadium.................... C1

Eating (p253)

21 Amy Ruth's Restaurant....... C6
22 BLVD Bistro..........................C5
23 Charles' Pan-Fried Chicken B2
24 Community Food & Juice A6
25 Dinosaur Bar-B-Que A4
26 Harlem Public.......................A3
27 Maison Harlem......................B5
28 Pikine....................................C6
29 Pisticci...................................A5
30 Red Rooster...........................C5
31 Seasoned Vegan...................C6
32 Sylvia's C5
33 Tom's Restaurant.................B6

Drinking & Nightlife (p256)

34 67 Orange Street..................B6
35 Bier International..................B6
Ginny's Supper Club ..(see 30)
36 Shrine C4
37 Silvana...................................B6
The Chipped Cup........(see 26)

Entertainment (p257)

38 Amore Opera.........................A5
Marjorie Eliot's Parlor Jazz........................... (see 3)
39 Maysles Documentary Center C5
40 Minton's C6

Shopping (p259)

41 Atmos.....................................C5
42 Flamekeepers Hat Club.......C5
43 Harlem Haberdashery C5
44 NiLu C5
45 Revolution Books..................C4

Sports & Activities (p259)

46 Riverbank State Park...........A3

Sleeping (p343)

47 Aloft Harlem..........................B5
48 Harlem Flophouse C5
49 La Maison d'Art.....................C4
50 Mount Morris House B&B ...C5

WILLIAMSBURG

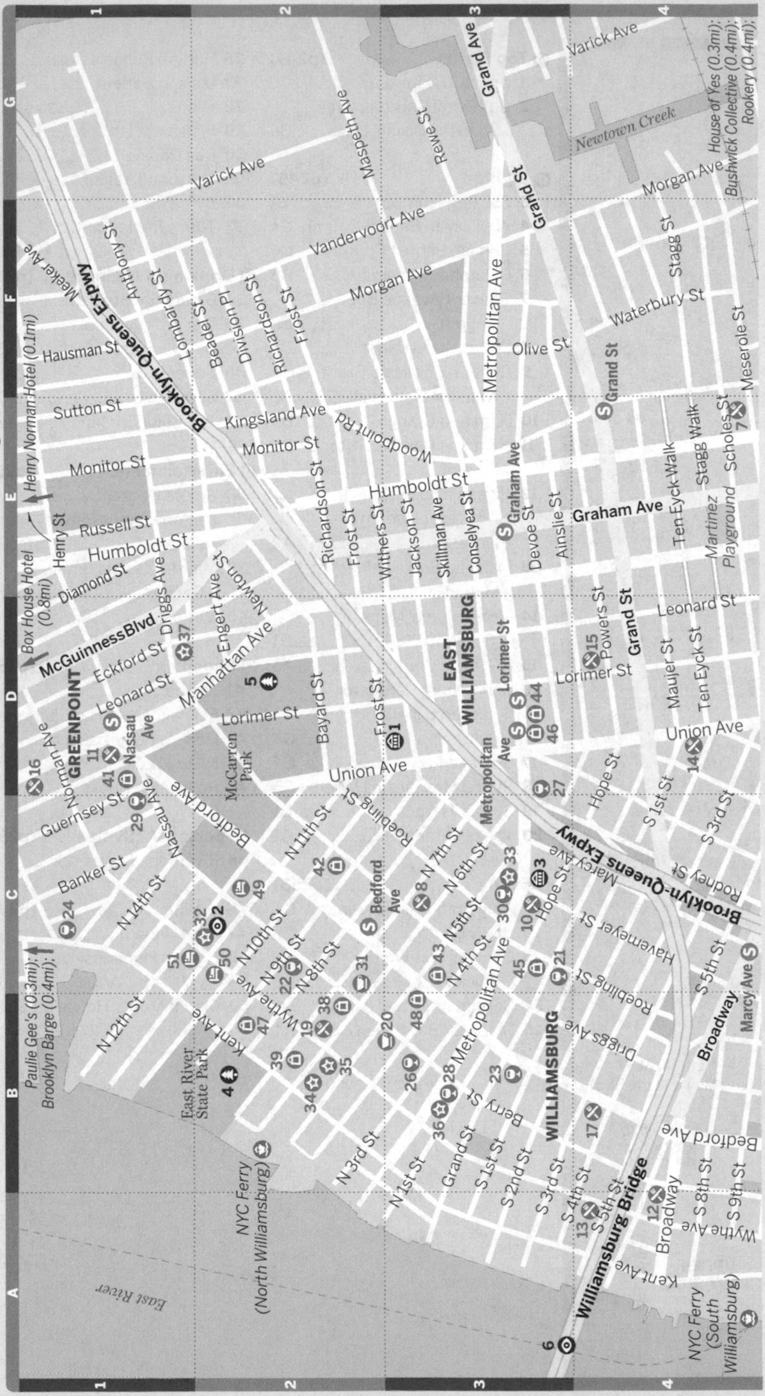

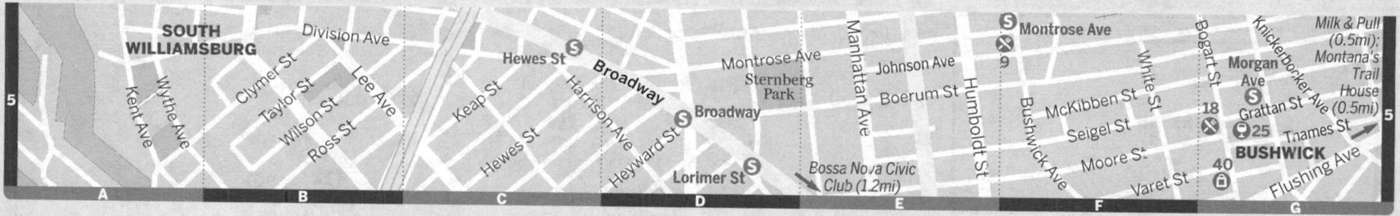

Sights (p273)

1 Brooklyn Art Library ... D3
2 Brooklyn Brewery ... C2
3 City Reliquary ... C3
4 East River State Park ... B2
5 McCarren Park ... D2
6 Williamsburg Bridge ... A3

Eating (p284)

7 Champs Diner ... E4
8 Crif Dogs ... C3
9 Dun-Well Doughnuts ... F5
10 Fette Sau ... C3
11 Five Leaves ... D1
12 Marlow & Sons ... A4
13 Miss Favela ... A4
14 Modern Love ... D4
15 Okonomi & Yuji Ramen ... D4
16 Peter Pan Donut & Pastry Shop ... D1
17 Rabbithole ... B4
18 Roberta's ... G5
19 Zenkichi ... B2

Drinking & Nightlife (p290)

20 Blue Bottle Coffee ... B3
21 Clem's ... C3
22 Hotel Delmano ... C2
Ides ... (see 51)
23 Maison Premiere ... B3
24 Northern Territory ... C1
25 Pine Box Rock Shop ... G5
26 Radegast Hall & Biergarten ... B3
27 Rocka Rolla ... D3
28 Skinny Dennis ... B3
29 Spritzenhaus ... C1
30 Spuyten Duyvil ... C3
31 Toby's Estate ... C2

Entertainment (p294)

32 Brooklyn Bowl ... C2
33 Knitting Factory ... C3
34 Music Hall of Williamsburg ... B2
35 National Sawdust ... B2
36 Nitehawk Cinema ... B3
37 Warsaw ... D1

Shopping (p299)

38 A&G Merch ... B2
39 Artists & Fleas ... B2
40 Beacon's Closet ... G5
41 Beacon's Closet ... D1
42 Buffalo Exchange ... C2
43 Catbird ... C3
44 Desert Island Comics ... D3
45 Fuego 718 ... C3
46 Quimby's Bookstore NYC ... D3
47 Rough Trade ... B2
48 Spoonbill & Sugartown ... B3

Sports & Activities (p299)

Brooklyn Bowl ... (see 32)

Sleeping (p344)

49 McCarren Hotel & Pool ... C2
50 Williamsburg Hotel ... C2
51 Wythe Hotel ... C1

BOERUM HILL, CARROLL GARDENS, COBBLE HILL, FORT GREENE & RED HOOK

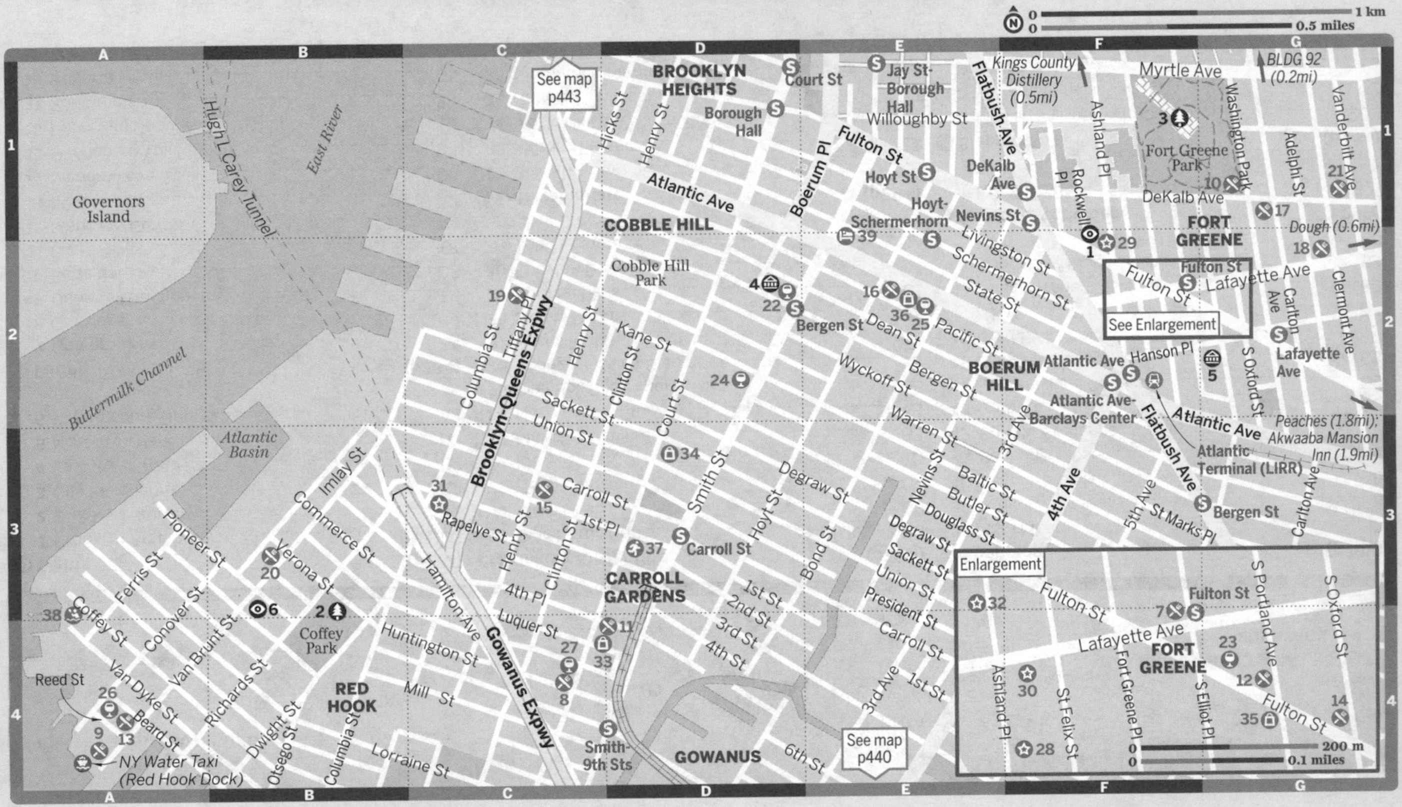

BOERUM HILL, CARROLL GARDENS, COBBLE HILL, FORT GREENE & RED HOOK

Sights (p266)

1 BRIC House ... F2
2 Coffey Park ... B3
3 Fort Greene Park ... F1
4 Invisible Dog ... D2
5 Museum of Contemporary African Diasporan Arts ... G2
6 Red Hook ... B3

Eating (p277)

7 67 Burger ... F4
8 Buttermilk Channel ... C4
9 Fairway ... A4
10 Fort Greene Greenmarket ... G1
11 Frankies 457 Spuntino ... D4
12 Green Grape Annex ... G4
13 Hometown Bar-B-Que ... A4
14 Hungry Ghost ... G4
15 Lucali ... C3
16 Mile End ... E2
17 Miss Ada ... G1
18 Olea ... G2
19 Pok Pok ... C2
20 Red Hook Lobster Pound ... B3
21 Roman's ... G1

Drinking & Nightlife (p288)

22 61 Local ... D2
23 Black Forest Brooklyn ... G4
24 Clover Club ... D2
25 Robert Bar ... E2
26 Sunny's ... A4
27 Travel Bar ... C4

Entertainment (p294)

28 BAM Fisher Building ... F4
29 BAM Harvey Theater ... F2
BAM Howard Gilman Opera House ... (see 30)
BAM Rose Cinemas ... (see 30)
30 BAMcafe ... F4
Brooklyn Academy of Music ... (see 30)
31 Jalopy ... C3
32 Theater for a New Audience ... E3

Shopping (p297)

33 Black Gold Records ... C4
34 Brooklyn Strategist ... D3
35 Greenlight Bookstore ... G4
36 Twisted Lily ... E2

Sports & Activities (p299)

37 Area Yoga & Spa ... D3
38 Red Hook Boaters ... A3

Sleeping (p344)

39 Nu Hotel ... E2

PARK SLOPE & PROSPECT PARK

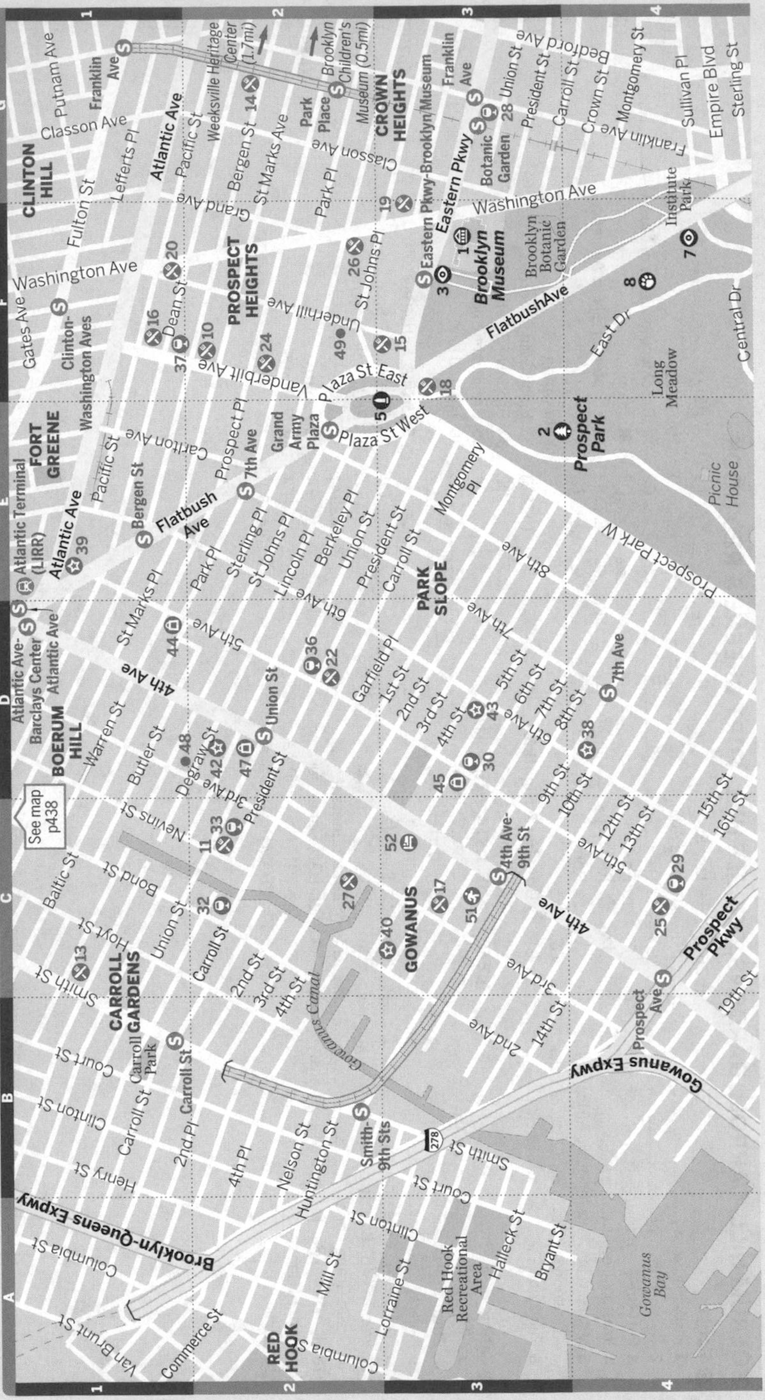

PARK SLOPE & PROSPECT PARK

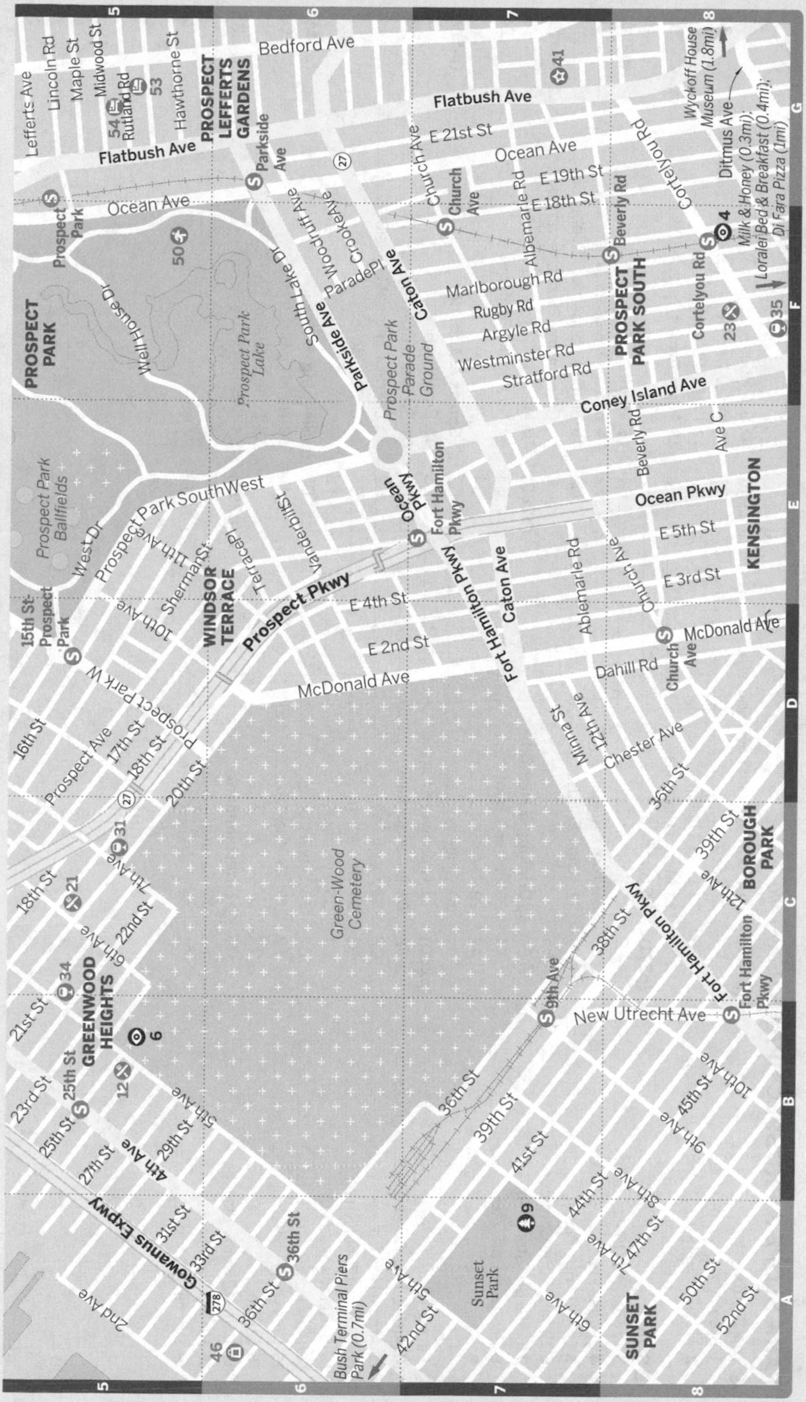

PARK SLOPE & PROSPECT PARK *Map on p440*

Top Sights (p264)
1 Brooklyn Museum F3
2 Prospect Park E3

Sights (p271)
3 Brooklyn Botanic Garden F3
4 Ditmas Park F8
5 Grand Army Plaza E3
6 Green-Wood Cemetery B5
7 Lefferts Historic House F4
8 Prospect Park Zoo F4
9 Sunset Park A7

Eating (p280)
10 Ample Hills Creamery F2
11 Ample Hills Creamery C2
12 Baked in Brooklyn B5
13 Battersby C1
14 Berg'n G2
15 Cheryl's Global Soul F3
16 Chuko F1
17 Four & Twenty Blackbirds C3
18 King David Tacos F3
19 Lincoln Station F3
20 LOOK by Plant Love House F1
21 Lot 2 C5
22 Luke's Lobster D2
23 Mimi's Hummus F8
24 Olmsted F2
25 Sidecar C4
26 Tom's Restaurant F2
27 Whole Foods C2

Drinking & Nightlife (p289)
28 Butter & Scotch G3
29 Excelsior C4
30 Ginger's D3
31 Greenwood Park C5
32 Lavender Lake C2
33 Royal Palms C2
34 Sea Witch C5
35 Sycamore F8
36 Union Hall D2
37 Weather Up F1

Entertainment (p294)
38 Barbès D4
39 Barclays Center E1
40 Bell House C3
41 Kings Theatre G7
42 Littlefield D2
43 Puppetworks D3

Shopping (p298)
44 Beacon's Closet D1
45 Brooklyn Superhero Supply Co. D3
Grand Army Plaza Greenmarket (see 18)
46 Industry City A6
47 No Relation Vintage D2

Sports & Activities (p299)
48 Brooklyn Boulders D1
49 Brooklyn Brainery F2
50 LeFrak Center at Lakeside F5
51 On the Move C3

Sleeping (p344)
52 Hotel Le Bleu C3
53 Lefferts Manor Bed & Breakfast G5
54 Serenity at Home G5

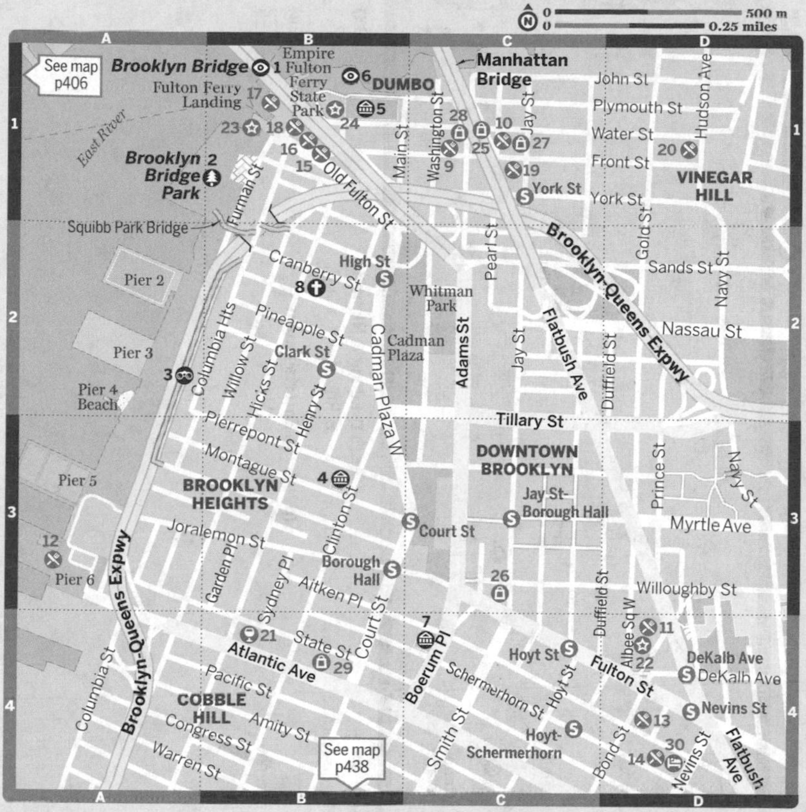

Top Sights (p262)

1 Brooklyn Bridge B1
2 Brooklyn Bridge Park B1

Sights (p266)

3 Brooklyn Heights Promenade A2
4 Brooklyn Historical Society B3
5 Empire Stores & Tobacco Warehouse B1
6 Jane's Carousel B1
7 New York Transit Museum C4
8 Plymouth Church B2

Eating (p276)

9 AlMar C1
10 Archway Cafe C1
11 DeKalb Market Hall D4
12 Fornino at Pier 6 .... A3
13 Ganso Ramen D4
14 Govinda's Vegetarian Lunch D4
15 Grimaldi's B1
16 Juliana's B1
17 River Cafe B1
18 Shake Shack B1
19 Superfine C1
20 Vinegar Hill House D1

Drinking & Nightlife (p288)

21 Floyd B4

Entertainment (p294)

22 Alamo Drafthouse D4
23 Bargemusic B1
24 St Ann's Warehouse B1

Shopping (p297)

25 Brooklyn Flea C1
26 Fulton Mall C3
27 Modern Anthology C1
28 Powerhouse @ the Archway C1
29 Sahadi's B4

Sleeping (p344)

30 EVEN Hotel D4

CONEY ISLAND & BRIGHTON BEACH

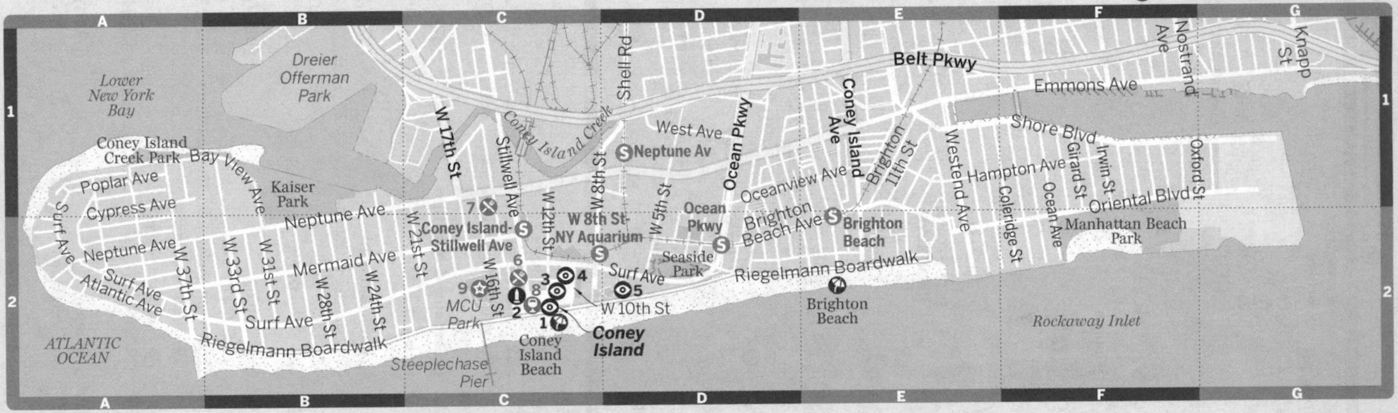

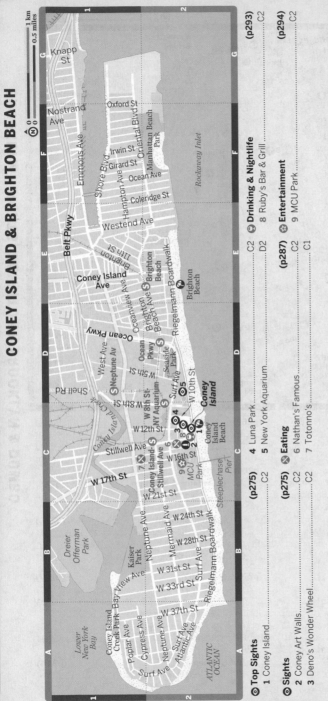

Top Sights (p275)

1 Coney Island C2

Sights (p275)

2 Coney Art Walls C2
3 Deno's Wonder Wheel C2
4 Luna Park C2
5 New York Aquarium D2

Eating (p287)

6 Nathan's Famous C2
7 Totonno's C1

Drinking & Nightlife (p293)

8 Ruby's Bar & Grill C2

Entertainment (p294)

9 MCU Park C2

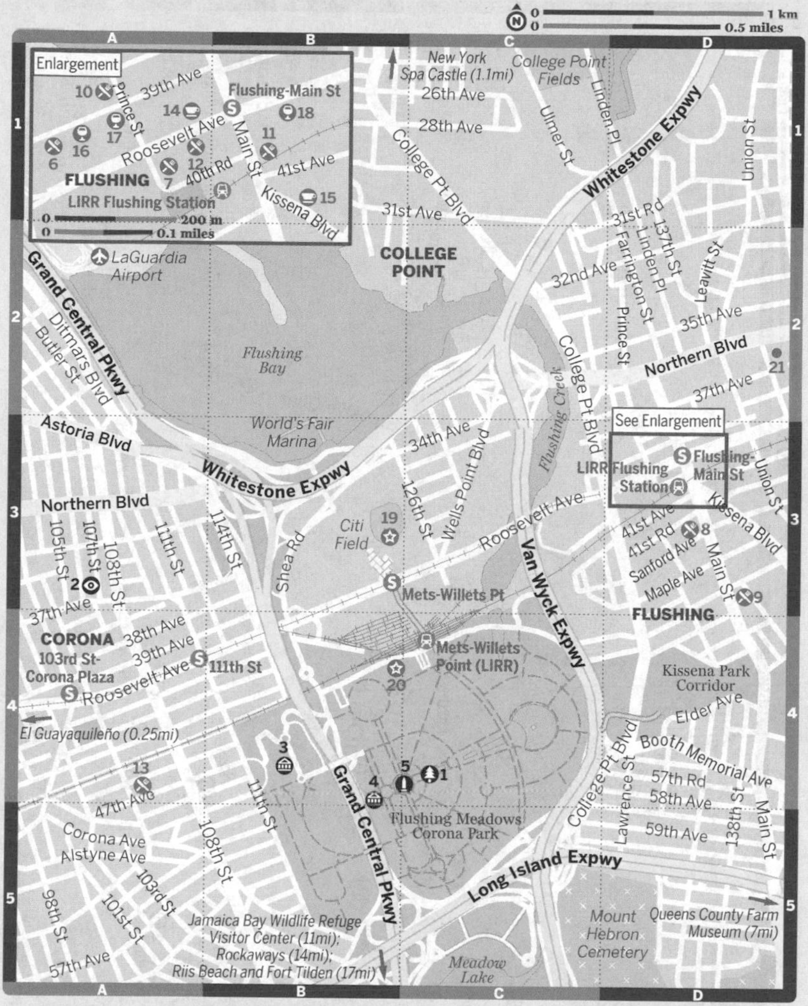

Sights (p306)

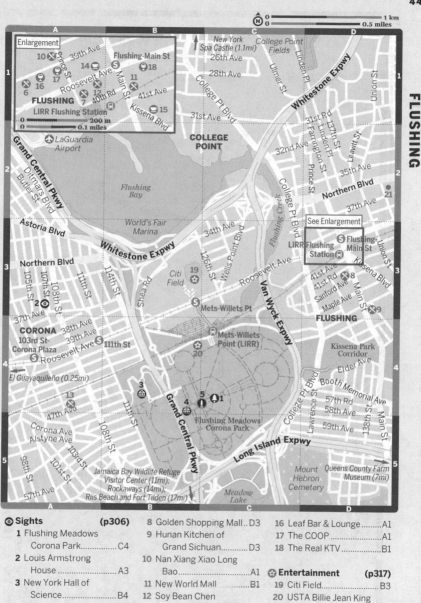

1 Flushing Meadows Corona Park C4
2 Louis Armstrong House A3
3 New York Hall of Science B4
4 Queens Museum B4
5 Unisphere C4

Eating (p314)

6 Asian Jewels A1
7 Fu Run A1
8 Golden Shopping Mall D3
9 Hunan Kitchen of Grand Sichuan D3
10 Nan Xiang Xiao Long Bao A1
11 New World Mall B1
12 Soy Bean Chen Flower Shop A1
13 Tortilleria Nixtamal A4

Drinking & Nightlife (p316)

14 Fang Gourmet Tea A1
15 Kung Fu Tea B1
16 Leaf Bar & Lounge A1
17 The COOP A1
18 The Real KTV B1

Entertainment (p317)

19 Citi Field B3
20 USTA Billie Jean King National Tennis Center B4

Sports & Activities (p318)

21 Queens Historical Society D2

ASTORIA

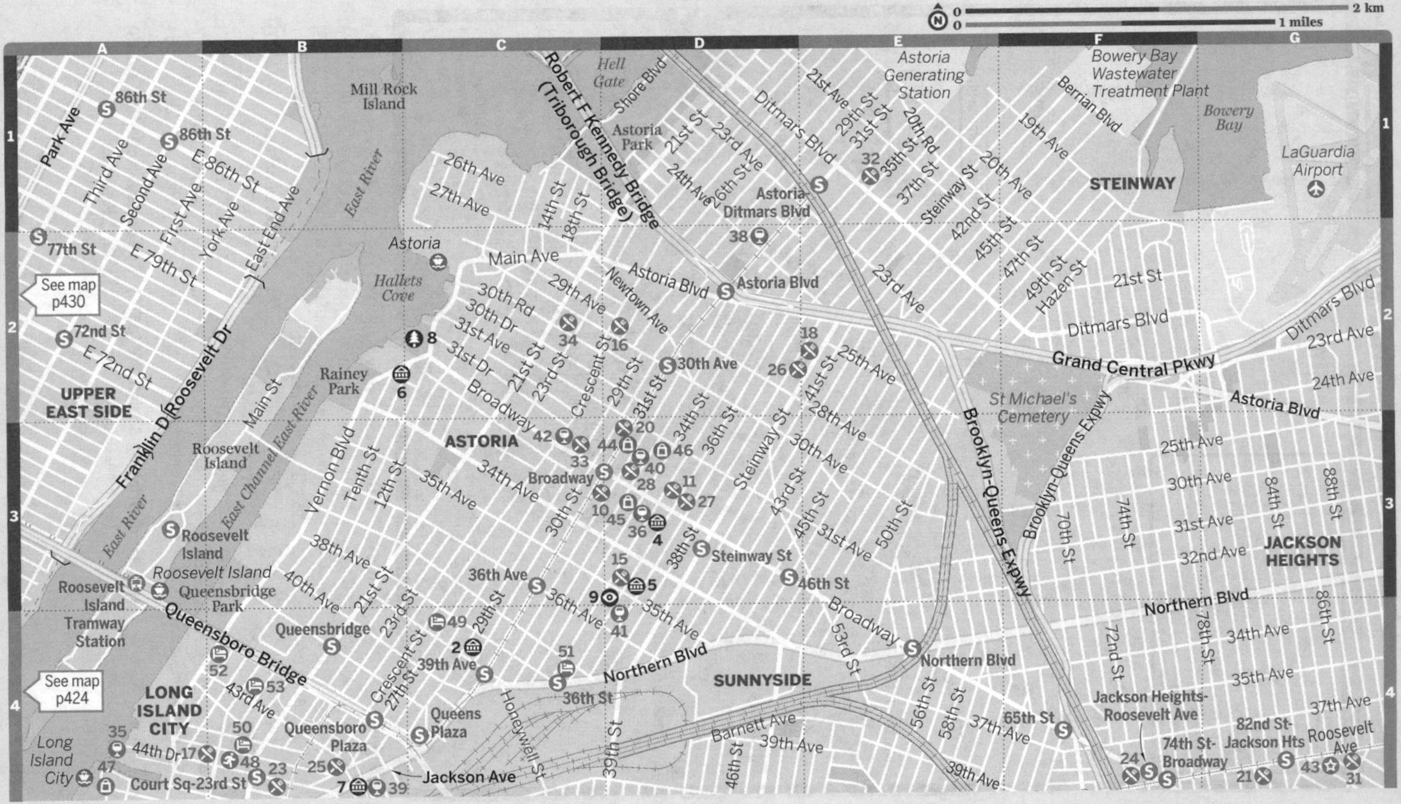
0 2 km
0 1 miles
A
B
C
D
E
F
G
1
2
3
4
Park Ave
86th St
86th St
Third Ave
Second Ave
E 86th St
First Ave
York Ave
East End Ave
77th St
E 79th St
See map p430
72nd St
E 72nd St
UPPER EAST SIDE
Franklin D Roosevelt Dr
Main St
East River
East Channel East River
Mill Rock Island
Astoria
Hallets Cove
Rainey Park
8
6
Roosevelt Island
Roosevelt Island
Roosevelt Island
Roosevelt Island Tramway Station
Queensbridge Park
Queensboro Bridge
Queensbridge
See map p424
LONG ISLAND CITY
Long Island City
35
47
44th Dr
17
50
48
23
52
53
43rd Ave
Court Sq-23rd St
Queensboro Plaza
25
Queens Plaza
7
39
Jackson Ave
Honeywell St
Robert F Kennedy Bridge (Triborough Bridge)
Hell Gate
Shore Blvd
Astoria Park
26th Ave
27th Ave
14th St
18th St
Main Ave
30th Rd
30th Dr
31st Ave
31st Dr
Broadway
21st St
23rd St
29th Ave
34
Newtown Ave
Crescent St
16
29th St
31st St
30th Ave
ASTORIA
42
33
44
20
46
34th St
36th St
Broadway
40
28
11
27
10
45
36
4
30th St
34th Ave
35th Ave
Vernon Blvd
Tenth St
12th St
38th Ave
40th Ave
21st St
23rd St
29th St
49
2
Crescent St
27th St
39th Ave
36th Ave
36th Ave
15
5
9
41
35th Ave
38th St
Steinway St
46th St
51
Northern Blvd
36th St
39th St
SUNNYSIDE
Barnett Ave
39th Ave
46th St
53rd St
Broadway
Northern Blvd
56th St
58th St
37th Ave
65th St
39th Ave
21st Ave
24th Ave
26th St
23rd Ave
21st St
Astoria-Ditmars Blvd
38
Astoria Blvd
Astoria Blvd
Ditmars Blvd
29th St
31st St
35th St
20th Rd
37th St
32
Astoria Generating Station
Steinway St
42nd St
45th St
47th St
49th St
Hazen St
20th Ave
19th Ave
23rd Ave
18
26
25th Ave
41st St
28th Ave
30th Ave
Steinway St
43rd St
45th St
31st Ave
50th St
Brooklyn-Queens Expwy
Brooklyn-Queens Expwy
St Michael's Cemetery
Grand Central Pkwy
Ditmars Blvd
21st St
Berrian Blvd
Bowery Bay Wastewater Treatment Plant
Bowery Bay
STEINWAY
LaGuardia Airport
Ditmars Blvd
23rd Ave
24th Ave
Astoria Blvd
25th Ave
30th Ave
31st Ave
32nd Ave
70th St
74th St
84th St
88th St
JACKSON HEIGHTS
Northern Blvd
72nd St
78th St
86th St
34th Ave
35th Ave
37th Ave
Jackson Heights-Roosevelt Ave
24
74th St-Broadway
82nd St-Jackson Hts
21
43
31
Roosevelt Ave

Top Sights (p301)

1 MoMA PS1 ... B5

Sights (p305)

2 Fisher Landau Center for Art ... C4
3 Gantry Plaza State Park ... A5
4 Greater Astoria Historical Society ... D3
5 Museum of the Moving Image ... D3
6 Noguchi Museum ... B2
7 SculptureCenter ... B4
8 Socrates Sculpture Park ... C2
9 The Kaufman Arts District ... D3

Eating (p308)

10 Bahari ... C3
11 Brooklyn Bagel & Coffee Company ... D3
12 Cannelle Patisserie ... A5
13 Casa Enrique ... A5
14 Cyclo ... A5
15 George's at Kaufman Astoria Studios ... D3
16 Jerusalem Pita House ... D2
17 John Brown Smokehouse ... A4
18 Kabab Cafe ... E2
19 Khao Kang ... G5
20 King Souvlaki ... D3
21 La Esquina del Camarón ... G4
22 LIC Corner Cafe ... B5
23 LIC Market ... B4
24 Little Tibet ... F4
M Wells Dinette ... (see 1)
25 M Wells Steakhouse ... B4
26 Mombar ... D2
27 Pye Boat Noodle ... D3
28 Sek'end Sun ... D3
29 Sripraphai ... F5
30 Sweetleaf ... A5
31 Taco Veloz ... G4
32 Taverna Kyclades ... E1
33 The Strand Smokehouse ... C3
34 Vesta Trattoria & Wine Bar ... C2

Drinking & Nightlife (p316)

35 Anable Basin Sailing Bar & Grill ... A4
36 Astoria Bier & Cheese ... D3
37 Bierocracy ... A5
38 Bohemian Hall & Beer Garden ... D2
39 Dutch Kills ... B4
40 Icon Bar ... D3
41 Studio Square ... D4
42 Vite Bar ... C3

Entertainment (p317)

Creek and the Cave ... (see 30)
43 Terraza 7 ... G4

Shopping (p318)

Artbook ... (see 1)
44 Astoria Bookshop ... D3
45 Lockwood ... D3
46 LoveDay 31 ... D3
47 Mimi & Mo ... A4

Sports & Activities (p318)

48 Cliffs ... B4

Sleeping (p345)

49 Boro Hotel ... C4
50 Local NYC ... B4
51 Paper Factory Hotel ... C4
52 Ravel ... B4
53 Z Hotel ... B4

Our Story

A beat-up old car, a few dollars in the pocket and a sense of adventure. In 1972 that's all Tony and Maureen Wheeler needed for the trip of a lifetime – across Europe and Asia overland to Australia. It took several months, and at the end – broke but inspired – they sat at their kitchen table writing and stapling together their first travel guide, *Across Asia on the Cheap*. Within a week they'd sold 1500 copies. Lonely Planet was born.

Today, Lonely Planet has offices in Franklin, London, Melbourne, Oakland, Dublin, Beijing and Delhi, with more than 600 staff and writers. We share Tony's belief that 'a great guidebook should do three things: inform, educate and amuse'.

Our Writers

Regis St Louis

Regis grew up in a small town in the American Midwest – the kind of place that fuels big dreams of travel – and he developed an early fascination with foreign dialects and world cultures. He spent his formative years learning Russian and a handful of Romance languages, which served him well on journeys across much of the globe. Regis has contributed to more than 50 Lonely Planet titles, covering destinations across six continents. His travels have taken him from the mountains of Kamchatka to remote island villages in Melanesia, and to many grand urban landscapes. When not on the road, he lives in New Orleans. Follow him on www.instagram.com/regisstlouis.

Robert Balkovich

Robert was born and raised in Oregon, but has called New York City home for almost a decade. When he was a child and other families were going to theme parks and grandma's house he went to Mexico City and toured Eastern Europe by train. He's now a writer and travel enthusiast seeking experiences that are ever so slightly out of the ordinary to report back on. Follow him on Instagram: oh_balky.

Ray Bartlett

Ray is a travel writer specializing in Japan, Korea, Mexico, and the United States. He has worked on many different Lonely Planet titles, starting with *Japan* in 2004 and going through the present.

Ali Lemer

Ali has been a Lonely Planet writer and editor since 2007, and has authored guidebooks and travel articles on Russia, NYC, Los Angeles, Melbourne, Bali, Hawaii, Japan and Scotland. A native New Yorker and naturalized Melburnian, Ali has also lived in Chicago, Prague and the UK, and has traveled extensively around Europe and North America.

Contributing Writers Michael Grosberg, Brian Kluepfel

Published by Lonely Planet Global Limited
CRN 554153
11th edition – August 2018
ISBN 978 1 78657 067 3

10 9 8 7 6 5 4 3 2 1
Printed in China